This latest instalment of Tom Lennie of Scottish revival, *Scotland Ablaze,* the ongoing revivals that endured into thrilling accounts of local awakenings, the leaders instrumental in them, and the effects they produced. Almost every district of Scotland is covered and one is left to wonder at the clear testimony given to the sovereign grace of God who brought revival to overlooked districts and to major cities by unknown leaders and international evangelists. Sometimes the revival was mixed with dangerous excess, and Lennie does not hide the messiness of these seasons. Nevertheless, great care has been taken to highlight places where deep and lasting works of grace occurred, providing much needed support for the validity of revival as a genuine movement of God. As Lennie makes clear, early reports of revival in Canada and Ulster were among the means God used to stir renewed longing for revival in Scotland in the 1850s. As we read what God did in our past, I pray this book will do the same for a new generation, and stir us to cry to God to do a similar mighty work again. May Scotland be set ablaze for His glory once more!

DAVID STRAIN
Senior pastor, First Presbyterian Church, Jackson, Mississippi

Reading about God's Spirit in action is always an encouragement. Tom Lennie delves into Scotland's rich history and assesses the numerous accounts of revival that set people on fire for the gospel in the second half of the 19th century. These stories embolden us to live out our faith with the assurance that the same God is at work today. Read and be inspired!

R. T. KENDALL
Former Minister of Westminster Chapel, London
Author and conference speaker

Scotland was deeply affected by revival during the two decades following 1858. Many people turned from nominal Christianity or even outright scoffing to deep personal faith. In this carefully documented book, Tom Lennie shows that the revival movement of 1859–61 broke out in every Scottish county and that the Americans Dwight L. Moody and Ira D. Sankey roused Edinburgh and Glasgow to a high pitch of spiritual enthusiasm. Scotland was far more ablaze than we have previously known.

DAVID BEBBINGTON
Professor of History, University of Stirling, Scotland

The phrase 'page turner' is often used of compelling and dramatic fiction. You will find that this is a book you will be reluctant to put down. In an age of 'fake news' it is refreshing to read such a detailed account of Scottish revivals leaning heavily on primary eye-witness accounts. Wherever you live in Scotland you will read of how God moved in your area and you will be moved to pray and work for another visit of the Holy Spirit. If you don't live in Scotland you will get a greater understanding of the spiritual legacy in a nation which is now, sadly, one of the most secular in Western Europe. As one who has a passion for the spread of the gospel in contemporary Scotland I will be recommending this book to the new generation of church planters and revitalisers, because we have access to the same spiritual power today. Tom Lennie's latest book is candid about the difficulties and controversies which arise in revival but the overall effect is to challenge us to pray for the valley of dry bones to come alive again as a great army.

DAVID C. MEREDITH
Mission Director, Free Church of Scotland

Lennie's historical grasp of the national and local context of the mid-Victorian era provides an insightful and scholarly grasp on what God was achieving during those years. In covering areas as geographically and culturally diverse as rural Aberdeenshire, industrial Lanarkshire, the borders and the north of Scotland Lennie has provided not only a scholar's understanding of the times, but he also describes the significance and importance of: passionate prayer, the role of the local church, itinerant preachers, and the impact of the Spirit on entire communities. Lennie's writing, however, should come with a 'health warning'; it is difficult to put it down once you begin to flick through its pages.

RICHARD GIBBONS
Senior pastor, First Presbyterian Church, Greenville, South Carolina

Once again Tom Lennie has put the Church in Scotland in his debt for the way in which he has so thoroughly searched out available written resources, this time to bring together a comprehensive chronicle of the movement of God's Spirit in almost every corner of Scotland in the period 1858-79. His particular focus on the '1859 Revival' shows that this revival was much more widespread than has yet been recognised by the academic community. On reading this book on the back of his two earlier volumes, I am left with a deep impression of the overwhelming vastness of the grace, mercy and favour of God towards our land in times past; but also with a deep sense of sadness at the way in which, as a nation and as churches within it, we have squandered and neglected these abundant mercies. Lord, have mercy upon us!

HECTOR MORRISON
Principal, Highland Theological College, Scotland

In the Bible we read of the Lamb's Book of Life being opened (Rev. 20:12), but there are several other lesser-known books mentioned in Scripture, including the book of truth (Dan. 10:21), the book of remembrance (Mal. 3:16), and the Register of the Peoples (Ps. 87:6). One of the greatest privileges a Christian can enjoy is to record the mighty works of God among the sons of men. Tom

Lennie has blessed the Body of Christ by lovingly and meticulously compiling *Scotland Ablaze*. My hope and prayer is that it will be read by many people not only in Scotland but around the world, and thousands will be encouraged by its record of the faithfulness of the Lord Jesus Christ and His power to save. The Living God is not done with revealing His revival glory to those who walk in repentance and faith, so it is also my prayer that this extraordinary book will not be read merely as an historical document, but that it will set hearts on fire for God and invigorate the people of God to seek Him once again for showers of blessing on a dry and thirsty land.

PAUL HATTAWAY
Founder and Director of Asia Harvest
Author of *Operation China*, *Project Pearl* and *The China Chronicles* series

I want to commend Tom Lennie's new book, *Scotland Ablaze*, to you. The very title is enough to make me tingle with anticipation for the feast contained within it. I have Tom's two previous books – *Land of Many Revivals* and *Glory in the Glen* – on my bookshelves and love to keep dipping in to them. What I love about Tom's writing is the scholarly research that he puts into them, and yet he has an ability to relay that material so that it becomes a story that you want to read … and keep reading. How today we, as the Church, need an outpouring of revival. Tom Lennie describes what happened in Scotland between 1858 and 1879, when God found people waiting to receive His revival power. My prayer is that through reading this book, many will say 'I am waiting and longing for Scotland to be Ablaze again with revival fires'!

GORDON PETTIE
CEO Revelation TV
Author of *Do It Again, Lord*, *Hey Howie* and *Not If, But When*

They say that history is boring – but what makes it interesting is when you get to the details. If that's the case then Tom Lennie's *Scotland Ablaze* must be one of the most interesting books on Scotland ever written. It is packed full of well-researched and evidenced detail. This is a book that will be used for decades to come as a source on the state of Christianity in Scotland in the 19th Century. You can dip in and out of it, but most of all it reminds us of a glorious time in Scottish history. *Scotland Ablaze* leads us to cry 'Lord, do it again!'

David Robertson
Minister, St Peter's Free Church of Scotland, Dundee & Associate Director of SOLAS, Centre for Public Christianity

Scotland Ablaze

**The Twenty-Year Fire of Revival
That Swept Scotland 1858-79**

TOM LENNIE

CHRISTIAN
FOCUS

Copyright © Tom Lennie 2018

paperback ISBN 978-1-5271-0267-5
epub ISBN 978-1-5271-0321-4
mobi ISBN 978-1-5271-0322-1

First published in 2018
By
Christian Focus Publications Ltd,
Geanies House, Fearn, Ross–shire
IV20 1TW, Scotland

www.christianfocus.com

CIP catalogue record for this book is available from the British Library.

Cover design by Daniel Van Straaten
Cover photo: Sea stacks at Mangersta, Isle of Lewis (fstopphotography)
Other than vintage photographs, landscape photos throughout
the book are courtesy of the author

Printed by Bell & Bain, Glasgow

CONTENTS

ABBREVIATIONS

BHMS – Baptist Home Missionary Society

BoT – Banner of Truth Magazine

DSCHT – Dictionary of Scottish Church History & Theology (Ed. Nigel M. de S. Cameron)

FC – Free Church

FCSRSRM – Free Church of Scotland Report on the State of Religion and Morals

GSS – Gaelic School Society

IA – Inverness Advertiser

NIDPCM – The New International Dictionary of Pentecostal and Charismatic Movements

OH – Orkney Herald

PFCSH&I – Proceedings of the Free Church of Scotland for the Highlands and Islands

PFCSHMC – Proceedings of the Free Church of Scotland Home Mission Committee

PGAFCS – Proceedings of the General Assembly of the Free Church of Scotland

RSCHS – Records of the Scottish Church History Society

SCM – Scottish Congregational Magazine

SG – The Scottish Guardian

SPGH – Society for Propagating the Gospel at Home

TB – Times of Blessing

TR – The Revival

UPC – United Presbyterian Church

WJ – Wynd Journal

DEDICATION

I wish to dedicate this book to the memory of five remarkable Christians of past generations – from very diverse traditions – whose lives have been a source of immense personal inspiration over many years.

Robert Murray McCheyne (1813–43) – Dundee Presbyterian pastor and preacher; renowned for his life of piety and prayer.

Rees Howells (1879–1950) – Intercessory prayer leader; Founder and first Director of the Bible College of Wales.

Francesco Forgione [Padre Pio] (1887–1968) – Italian priest, famed for his intense spirituality, supernatural insights and life of deep intercession.

Basilea Schlink (1904–2001) – Intercessory prayer leader; co-founder of the Evangelical Sisterhood of Mary, Darmstadt, Germany.

Leonard Ravenhill (1907–94) – International evangelist; man of prevailing prayer; author of *Why Revival Tarries*.

TOM LENNIE
October 2018

www.Truerevival.net
Author contact – blueyonder04@gmail.com

All Because Of You

When I, mine eyes lift to the heavens,
View myriad stars in midnight skies;
Survey the peaks of mountain splendour,
Above all earthly kingdoms rise.

When I through wooded glens do wander,
Soft verdant canopies above;
Or stroll the paths of rocky shoreline,
Watch mighty ocean waves unfurl.

BRIDGE
Upon such themes I often ponder,
My mind these glorious scenes review;
Yet deep within my heart I know,
Whence such blessings truly flow,
And it's all because of You.

CHORUS
It's all because of You, Lord,
It's all because of You,
That I'm overcome with wonder,
And my soul's refreshed anew.

Before Your throne I gladly bow down,
All my fleshly pride subdue;
You in glory who doth reign,
I exalt Your Holy Name,
For it's all because of You.

When I behold the King of Glory
Enthroned in majesty and might;
I feel His pow'r to shake the nations,
Send ten thousand men to flight.

Yet stepping low He draws beside them,
Who choose to walk His humble way;
Bestows rich grace on all who love Him,
Gives hope and strength for each new day.

BRIDGE AND CHORUS

Words and Music: TML

Introduction

Context

This is the third in a series of in-depth studies chronicling the history of the phenomenon known as 'religious revivals' in Scotland. My previous study, *Land of Many Revivals*, documented the remarkable succession of spiritual awakenings that occurred throughout the length and breadth of the country from the very beginnings of its revival heritage – the introduction of Protestantism to the land in the early 1500s, through three and a half centuries of church history, right up to the mid-1800s. *Glory in the Glen*, first published in 2009, continues Scotland's phenomenal revival journey, detailing a surprising sequence of revival activity across the land from 1880 up to 1940.

The present study seeks to bridge the gap between these two books. The 'gap-period' in question in fact constitutes a mere twenty-two years. But such was the prevalence and intensity of revival activity throughout Scotland during these two decades that an entire book is indeed required to record it. The truly major revival movement within this period was of course the revival of 1859–61.[1] This is by far the most extensive movement to have occurred in Scotland's religious history. It extended to every county in the land, and in some districts,

---

1. While sometimes termed 'The Laymen's Revival' because of the prominence of lay evangelists, this movement is generally referred to simply as 'The 1859 Revival', or 'The '59' for short. Sadly, it has never been accorded a more salubrious title. Some writers suggest the revival began in 1858, and others that it continued until 1862. The main period of revival activity almost everywhere in Scotland was between the years 1859 and 1861. Thus, in general, references in this study are to the revival of 1859–61. There were indeed a number of significant preparatory revival movements occurring in 1858 – these are considered separately (Chapter 3). Movements commencing in 1862 are also regarded as distinct, and are examined in the section, 'Revival Reverberations' (Chapter 17).

to almost every town and parish. The Free Church moderator in 1860, Robert Buchanan, observed how, 'from East Lothian to the Outer Hebrides: from the shores of the Moray Firth to those of the Solway, and all through the central mining and manufacturing districts of the Kingdom, we heard of scenes which carried us back to the days of the Lord, at Shotts and Stewarton and Cambuslang. Unless we greatly deceive ourselves, no former revival of religion which our church and country have witnessed has ever spread over so wide a field.'[2] Yet another account states that 'the years that followed the great revival of '59 and the sixties were the most fruitful in the annals of Christianity in this country of any since the Reformation'.[3]

Another writer referred to this revival as 'the most stupendous movement that the country had seen since the days of the Covenanters. Scotland has been said to be pre-eminently a land of revivals, but it may be doubted if ever even Scotland had a revival of greater depth, or one that shook the country more from its centre to its circumference than the revival of 1859 and the sixties did'.[4] More recently, Kenneth Jeffrey, who researched the 1859 awakening for his doctoral study, said: 'It began with the reawakening of Christians to a renewed spirit of prayer, and led not only to remarkable church growth, but also to the revitalisation of congregations in Scotland, and indeed across the world.' He concluded: 'The 1859 revival was not preceded and has not been succeeded by a similar movement that stretched so far across the country. Unparalleled, it remains the largest, most widespread revival in Scotland's history, and thus it is worthy of examination.'[5]

---

2. W. J. Couper, *Scottish Revivals*, Dundee, 1918, p. 130.

3. T. T. Matthews (Ed.), *Reminiscences of the Revival of Fifty-Nine and the Sixties*, Aberdeen, 1910, p. 16. *The Revival* periodical termed the 1859 revival, 'a very blessed season, perhaps the most extensive in its operation that we have ever known among us' (*TR*, 19/01/1865, quoted in James Edwin Orr, *The Second Evangelical Awakening*, London, 1949, p. 77).

4. Matthews, p. xi.

5. Kenneth S. Jeffrey, *When the Lord Walked the Land: The 1858-62 Revival in the North East of Scotland*, Carlisle 2002, p. 1, 38. More recently also, the Rev. Maurice Roberts remarked that during this widespread awakening, 'the entire land was brought by the extraordinary power of God into a condition of unusual susceptibility to spiritual impressions' (Maurice Roberts, 'Remembering the 1859 Revival in Scotland', *BoT*, vol. 252, January 1993, p. 4).

The 1859–61 revival was truly an international movement. Simultaneous with its outworking in Scotland, dramatic revival also spread through Wales during these fruitful years, Humphrey Jones and David Morgan being the main instruments.[6] To a lesser degree, parts of England were also affected.[7] But just as the revival did not begin in Britain (see Chapter 2), so it did not end there. The awakening later took on a more global aspect with its spread, on news of events in America and Great Britain, to Australia, the Pacific islands of Tonga, Fiji and Hawaii, South Africa (in which Worcester parish Andrew Murray served as pastor), Shanghai (among the missionaries), Beirut, Iran (among Nestorian Christians) and parts of India, especially among the indigenous people of Tamilnadu.[8]

J. Edwin Orr viewed the evangelical awakening beginning in 1858/9 not as a movement lasting two or three years, but as a 'distinct and definite period of the expansion of the Christian Church' continuing for decades. He saw the Moody and Sankey campaigns of the 1870s and '80s as part of this wider movement.[9] Harry Sprange, too, in pondering when the 1859 revival ended, believed that no clear answer could be given, 'but its effects clearly continued right up until the first visit to Scotland of Moody, and it released a flood of evangelistic activity that continued into the present (20th) century'.[10]

---

6. The revival in Wales was said to have been even more extensive, though not more powerful, than the more famed Welsh revival of 1904 (D. Geraint Jones, *Favoured With Frequent Revivals: Revivals in Wales 1762-1862*, Cardiff, 2001, p. 44). One analyst, however, errs in stating: 'Wales regularly received evangelical revival during the 18th and 19th century in a way that had, in the 19th century at least eluded the other British nations' (Daniel Boucher, 'The 1904-5 Welsh Revival and Social and Political Action: A Centenary Perspective' in Dyfed Wyn Roberts (Ed.), *Revival, Renewal and the Holy Spirit*, Milton Keynes, 2009, p. 243).

7. Orr, 1949, pp. 95-171; R. E. Davies, *I Will Pour Out My Spirit: A History and Theology of Revivals and Evangelical Awakenings*, Tunbridge Wells, 1992, pp. 157-60.

8. J. Edwin Orr, *The Fervent Prayer: The Worldwide Impact of the Great Awakening of 1858*, Chicago, 1974; Davies, pp. 160-3.

9. Orr, 1949, pp. 162-3. Orr quotes the daughter of evangelist Dr H. Grattan Guinness, and daughter-in-law of Dr Hudson Taylor, who clearly saw the revival within a wider context: 'Christian people do not seem to realise the importance of that wonderful Revival of 1859', she said. 'It lasted fifty years. … Fifty years!'

10. Sprange, p. 293. Janice Holmes views things in a different light. Regarding the 1859 revival as 'the last manifestation of traditional folk religion, with its spontaneity and emotionalism', she nevertheless believed that 'rather than fading into history,

Aim of Study

The main aim of this book is to show the extent to which religious revivals – in their multifarious forms – were prevalent in Scotland during the two decades from the late 1850s to the late 1870s. I have not been concerned with simply listing places where 'revival meetings' were held. On the contrary, I have sifted through a wide range of documents pertaining to the revivals of these years, and sought to include, in the main, essential information only on those that appeared to be of a deep, authentic nature.

It is important to recognise, however, that it is not always easy to distinguish – particularly after more than a century's time-lapse – between reports of a spontaneous revival and those of organised revival meetings which may have deeply impacted many people. Such distinction is even harder to make when documentation pertaining to the movement is sparse, and where no details are provided as to its lasting effects. Certainly, in some places there was more evidence of revivalism – i.e., man's attempts to reproduce revival scenes and its beneficiary results – than of genuine, spontaneous revival. Revival and revivalism – or, as some would see it, the work of God and the work of man – can and often do occur simultaneously. It is inevitable, therefore, that some elements of the latter as well as (many more instances of) the former would find their way into the narratives that follow, with elements of both sometimes even occurring in an individual setting.[11]

This is essentially a historical work. I seek to report the facts pertaining to events. While in the main narrative I endeavour to refrain from sharing my personal opinions, I realise it is impossible to avoid bias entirely. In any case, I do include a number of short evaluations throughout the study, usually at the end of a section, as well as, occasionally, in the copious footnotes. In particular, there are two whole chapters devoted to the appraisal of a) the 1859–61 revival (Chapter 16) and b) the Moody revival of 1873–5 (Chapter 22).

---

the revival became part of the regular cycle of church growth and decline' (*Religious Revivals in Britain and Ireland 1859–1905*, Dublin, 2000, pp. xvii., 47).

11. For more on the distinction between revival and revivalism, see Tom Lennie, *Glory in the Glen: A History of Evangelical Revivals in Scotland 1880–1940*, Fearn, 2009.

This isn't a purist study, reporting only events and outcomes favourable to revival movements. I seek to share the good, the bad and even, occasionally, the ugly. Where guided and overseen by experienced and discerning leaders, revivals have generally been guarded against falling into reproach. Occasionally, I home in – without commentary – on the more unusual, sensationalist, or intensely emotional displays of human behaviour that sometimes arise in the midst of uncontrolled revivalism – partly to add variety and colour to the narrative, but also to show just how obscure, outrageous and at times injurious were the agencies at work during the progress of an unchecked religious revival in a given location.

My research is extensive, but clearly not exhaustive. One can only guess the degree to which further study would show up a great many more revival seasons of spiritual awakening across the country during the twenty-two-year period covered in this book. It is impossible, also, to assess just how many local revivals occurred in different places during these years of which no written chronicle was ever made, or where the records have literally become lost in history.

Overview of Contents

This study is divided into four main sections. Parts One and Two devote themselves to a historical survey of the 1859–61 revival as it spread across Scotland. Given the widespread nature of this most significant of spiritual movements, their coverage takes up around two-thirds of the entire book. The first chapter provides an introductory overview of the main academic studies relating to the Scottish awakening that have appeared during the past seventy years, showing how, notwithstanding their helpful analysis, collectively, these failed to fully recognise the magnitude of the movement. The ensuing chapter sets the Scottish awakening in the context of its international origins – in Canada's Atlantic Provinces.

Chapter Three examines several interesting preludes to the Scottish revival of '59, such as the appearance of a number of 'Gentlemen' preachers who ministered throughout the country in the 1850s, and a clear rising tide of revival blessing in Aberdeen from as early as the autumn of 1858, which continued throughout most of the following year and beyond.

The focus of Chapter Four is the south-west of the country, which, being closest geographically to Ulster, constituted the earliest dissemination of the revival from across the Irish Sea in the summer of 1859. While it is impossible to ascertain with precision where the revival first made itself felt, I purposely choose Glasgow as my starting point. In this most populous of Scottish cities, one of the earliest works of revival activity centred on the Wynd Church. Its spirited diffusion across the metropolis over the ensuing two years is outlined chronologically.

The fervent revivalist scenes that sprang up in the Clyde-side ports of Greenock and Port Glasgow, accompanied by extraordinary displays of emotional distress, are vividly captured in Chapter Five, which also examines the outbreak of the revival elsewhere in Renfrewshire as well as in the neighbouring counties of Dunbartonshire and Lanarkshire.

The remaining eight chapters of Part One follow the course of this most penetrative of religious awakenings as it dispensed across the country. The chronicle progresses in an approximate anti-clockwise direction, with separate chapters detailing the advance of the revival in Ayrshire (it being especially pronounced in the north of the county), across the vast Borders country (the historic shires of Peebles, Selkirk, Roxburgh and Berwick), and through Dumfriesshire (much of which was not powerfully affected until 1861), Kirkcudbrightshire and Wigtownshire.

The revival's progress is closely monitored as it weaves its way through Edinburgh and the Lothians, and into the north-central regions of Stirlingshire, Clackmannanshire, Fife and Perth and Kinross. The revival's expression in Dundee and Forfarshire is next in line for study, its trail being followed northwards through the Mearns, and into the vast rural region that comprises Aberdeenshire. Here the revival was prominent in virtually all the major districts, not least Strathbogie, Garioch, Old and New Deer and Skene, as well as the string of fishing communities dotted along the county's coast. Taken together, Chapters Twelve and Thirteen necessarily comprise one of the lengthiest sections in Part One, providing as they do full scope to the rapid dissemination of revival along the Banffshire and Moray coast, forcefully affecting almost every town and village in its path, as well as impacting many inland localities.

Notably variant in its expression, revival across the rugged, sparsely populated terrain of Argyll and the Western Highlands and Islands is explored in Part Two, comparatively few of the islands that line the shores of the Western mainland shunning the influences of the movement. The Far North of Scotland is the final region to be studied, some explanation being sought for the revival's relative sparseness in Ross-shire and Sutherland, in contrast to its prominence in many Caithness townships, as well as Orkney, particularly the latter's northern islands. Part One closes with an evaluation of the revival movement, and considers such factors as denominational results, methods used for ascertaining the number of converts, extent and influence of the revival, and not least, its lasting impact.

Part Three examines the little-known waves of revival that coursed through the land in the aftermath of the 1859 revival. There appears to have been three distinct streams, and these are examined in turn. First are the revival reverberations which flowed copiously in the immediate wake of the '59, particularly affecting localities completely overlooked by the earlier movement (notably many Shetland districts, along with Peterhead), as well as other districts that were previously only partially moved.

Just a few years later, a further, more substantial resurgence of revival swept through many Scottish villages, towns, cities and rural districts. This occurred within the wider context of a more general, but almost completely unrecognised, movement to quicken the United Kingdom in these years – for notable revival influences were also felt in England, Wales and Ireland. Communities were affected from as far north as Shetland and Orkney to southern Wigtownshire and along the Scotland-England border in Roxburghshire. The movement was general in Fife, South Lanarkshire and other parts of central Scotland, being particularly prominent in the town of Kilsyth, renowned in Scotland revival history.

Yet another wave of religious revival was apparent in the early seventies, being most distinct in a number of north-east fishing communities, as had indeed the two previous tides of sixties' revival blessing – notably Portgordon – and in rural Aberdeenshire, where there arose a notable wave of blessing among the Brethren between 1870 and 1872.

The 'Moody Revival', so-called, is the theme of Part Four, being a thorough study of Dwight Moody and Ira Sankey's evangelistic campaign in Scotland beginning in November 1873. The mission centred on Edinburgh and Glasgow, but took the duo all over the country, indeed as far north as John o'Groats. Simultaneous with, and subsequent to, the Americans' Scottish sojourns, was the blossoming of a host of localised revival movements the length and breadth of the nation. The Strathbogie district of inland Aberdeenshire was particularly affected, as too was the island of Tiree, along with, yet again, various coastal Banffshire communities, notably Buckie and Portgordon. An evaluation of the Moody campaign is presented, suggesting reasons for the Americans' success, considering the various objections to the mission on grounds of its perceived anti-intellectualism, methodologies employed, and the use of hymns, and seeking to evaluate the results and lasting impact of the campaign.

The closing chapter – the shortest in the book – looks at a number of localised and independent seasons of spiritual quickening that arose in the remaining years of the 1870s, with little or no apparent connection to the Moody mission that had preceded them by several years. Such mini-revivals cropped up in places as geographically diverse as Croy, Kilmarnock, Unst and Coll.

Please note, I have in general sought to adopt the county names in current usage during the time-period of this study. Thus, I refer to Forfarshire rather than Angus, and I distinguish between the adjacent shires of Moray and Banff, which are both now united under the name, Moray. I have not been totally rigid in defining county borders, however. For example, whereas the historic county of Ross and Cromarty included the Hebridean island of Lewis, I have felt it appropriate to give consideration to revivals in Lewis separately.

PART 1

The Big One –
The 1859–61 Revival

CHAPTER 1

Academic Analyses

J. Edwin Orr

The first published work to document and analyse the 1859 revival in Britain was J. Edwin Orr's *The Second Evangelical Awakening in Britain* (1949).[1] Orr makes no attempt to conceal his deep esteem for 'this remarkable religious movement which profoundly influenced British life in the middle of the nineteenth century', and he has no hesitation in viewing it as 'a major development of English-speaking Christianity, comparable to its forerunner, the Evangelical Revival of the days of Wesley and Whitefield'.[2] His study holds much noteworthy

---

1. Orr only later realised his rather embarrassing miscalculation in denoting this movement the 'Second Evangelical Awakening in Britain'. Two religious movements have generally been recognised as having occurred prior to 1859; the 'Great Awakening' of the eighteenth century and the 'Second Evangelical Awakening' running from *c.* 1790 to 1830, making the 1859 movement the *third* general awakening in Britain. The extensive research of Orr (much of it as yet unpublished) on revival movements worldwide is quite staggering, especially given that it was undertaken prior to the electronic age. Richard Owen Roberts, one of the world's most eminent revival historians, said of Orr that 'his world-wide fame as a man of revival most certainly exceeds that of any other twentieth century figure' (Foreword to Orr, 1989, pp. vii-viii). F. F. Bruce wrote: 'Some men read history, some write it, and others make it. So far as the history of religious revivals is concerned, J. Edwin Orr belongs to all three categories' (www.jedwinorr.com). For more on Orr, see the two written accounts of his life: Newman Watts, *Edwin Orr: The Ubiquitous Ulsterman*, Croydon, 1947; A. J. Appasamy, *Write the Vision: A Biography of J. Edwin Orr*, London, 1964.

2. Orr, 1949, pp. 5-6, 9. Later in his book, Orr re-emphasises his earlier claim, stating that the 1859 revival 'was of the same magnitude as well as the same order as the eighteenth-century Evangelical Revival' (p. 263). These statements are contradicted

information, and continues to be oft-quoted by revival enthusiasts. But while it claims to present a 'carefully documented and authentic account' of the mid-century movement with 'attempt to analyse the results of the Awakening',[3] it is an almost totally uncritical work, the first two-thirds of which do little other than chronicle a series of historical facts concerning the proliferation of prayer meetings and high attendance at evangelistic events, without much attempt at assessing which of those occasions constitute real revival.[4] Perhaps the reasons for his scantiness of analysis lie in his confession that he held to 'an evangelical background of thought', and thus believed that 'any explanation of the Revival other than that of an outpouring of the Spirit is considered inadequate'.[5]

Just two years before Orr's book appeared, Oscar Bussey submitted a Ph.D. thesis to Edinburgh University covering the same movement, the same period of time and the same localities as Orr's work. Bussey's unpublished thesis follows a very similar format to that of Orr's. He is similarly uncritical in his analysis, and enthusiastically accepts the notion of a general religious revival throughout Britain during the period under examination.[6] In the two decades following the publication of Orr's work, several historical analyses rejected his theological interpretation of revivals in favour of explanations which

by R. E. Davies's contention that Orr felt the 1859 movement 'ought to be seen as the same kind of revival as the eighteenth-century one, not as being equal to it in significance' (Davies, p. 168).

3. ibid., pp. 5-6.

4. This is particularly true regarding Orr's three chapters, 'The Awakening in Southern England', 'East Anglia and the Midlands' and 'Northern England'. What is required is further research in attempt to discover whether genuine revival accompanied the many well-attended meetings, reports of which fill Orr's narratives. The observation of English Methodist minister and historian, John Kent, is that there was no general awakening in England at this time (Kent, *Holding the Fort: Studies in Victorian Revivalism*, London, 1978, pp. 71-132).

5. Orr, 1949, p. 8. It is still common today for evangelical writers to look at religious awakenings in a purely theological light, requiring no additional explanation (e.g., Iain H. Murray in *Pentecost Today? The Biblical Basis for Understanding Revival*, Edinburgh, 1998).

6. Oscar Bussey, *The Religious Awakening of 1858–60 in Great Britain and Ireland*, Ph.D. thesis, University of Edinburgh, 1947.

relied more on external factors such as economic depression, political instability and social transformation.[7]

Richard Carwardine and D. W. Bebbington

But it was not until the late seventies that the first serious doubts were cast – inadvertently – on the authenticity and extent of the 1859–61 revival in regard to Scotland.[8] Richard Carwardine's magisterial study, *Transatlantic Revivalism*, published in America in 1978, seeks to highlight the interconnectedness between revivalism in America and that in Britain.[9]

In his introduction, Carwardine states that 'in 1859 a remarkable wave of revivals spread over Ulster, Wales, much of Scotland, and part of England'. In detailing the progress of these movements, he provides an entire, lengthy section to the work in America, and whole paragraphs to the outworking of the revival in Ireland and Wales (acknowledging that in Ulster one of the most extraordinary revivals of the nineteenth century reached its peak in the summer of 1859). Yet he devotes only one sentence to the progress of the revival in Scotland (using a single reference source), stating that in the west of the country, 'geographically and religiously proximate to Ulster Presbyterianism, a wave of prayer meeting revivals, conversions and even some physical prostrations reached a crescendo in the second half of 1859', with the movement continuing in this region 'and in eastern and Highland Scotland into the following year'. It might be inferred from this that little in the way of genuine revival occurred anywhere in Scotland other than these particular locations, concerning which no specifics are

---

7. The best-known of these is E. P. Thomson's *The Making of the English Working Class*, London, 1963. See also R. B. Walker, 'The Growth of Wesleyan Methodism in Victorian England and Wales', in *The Journal of Ecclesiastical History*, vol. 24 (1973), pp. 267-84.

8. Also published in 1978, John Kent's *Holding the Fort* is a scathing attack on revivalism in Victorian England. He includes a chapter entitled '1858: The Failure of English Revivalism' (pp. 71-133). Kent, however, makes only incidental references to Scotland.

9. In regard to the 1858–9 awakening, however, the author surely overstates the case in suggesting that 'once the American revival had burst into flame a British conflagration was assured' (Richard J. Carwardine, *Transatlantic Revivalism: Popular Evangelicalism in Britain and America, 1790–1865*, Westport: Conn., 1978, p. 159).

provided. Carwardine's overall conclusion regarding mainland UK is that 'from a twentieth-century perspective ... this movement appears much less than an "awakening"'.[10]

A decade later, in 1989, David Bebbington published his masterly, *Evangelicalism in Modern Britain*, widely regarded as a standard text on the subject.[11] In his relatively brief section on 'Revivalism', the author downplays the magnitude of the 1859 revival in Scotland, suggesting that no nationwide revival took place at this time. He criticises Orr's failure to discriminate between 'spontaneous popular revival, deeply rooted in the community', and 'meetings carefully designed to promote the work of the gospel'. Setting aside Orr's findings, but using instead one of the Irish writer's main sources, *The Revival* periodical, Dr

10. ibid., pp. 171-3, 159. Carwardine is using the term 'awakening' here in the larger sense defined by William McLoughlin, in *Revivals, Awakenings, and Reform*. McLoughlin sees revivals in America (on which his research is focused) as times of 'revitalization ... reactions by religious conservatives to significant changes in societal structure'. They are periods of 'fundamental social and intellectual reorientation of the ... belief-value system, behaviour patterns, and institutional structure ... the results of critical disjunctions in our self-understanding ... profound cultural transformations affecting all Americans and extending over a generation or more'. McLoughlin believed further that 'Awakenings begin in periods of cultural distortion and grave personal stress, when we lose faith in the legitimacy of our norms, the viability of our institutions, and the authority of our leaders in church and state. They eventuate in basic restructurings of our institutions and redefinitions of our social goals .... They restore our cultural verve and our self-confidence, helping us to maintain faith in ourselves, our ideals, and our "covenant with God" even while they compel us to reinterpret that covenant in the light of new experience'. (William G. McLoughlin, *Revivals, Awakenings and Reform: An Essay on Religion and Social Change in America, 1607-1977*, Chicago, 1978, pp. 7-11). Thus McLoughlin saw the 1857–8 revival in America and Moody's urban campaigns in the same nation later in the century neither as awakenings nor as revitalisation movements. This is because 'in neither of these brief spans of time was there any major shift in the prevailing ideological consensus or any major reorientation in the belief-value system that had emerged after the Second Great Awakening (1800-30). In fact, both movements confirmed and sustained that consensus. They were extensions or reaffirmations of it. One might point to some "new measures" or techniques for saving souls in these movements, but new evangelistic methods did not change the terms of salvation or Americans' understanding of their relationship to God's will and laws' (p. 141).

11. In particular, the book is famed for introducing a simple fourfold definition of evangelicalism – i.e., comprising the qualities of conversionism, biblicism, crucicentrism, and activism.

Bebbington argues that the range of the mid-nineteenth century revival in Britain was 'severely limited'. Only 'parts of Scotland were affected' – he specifies Lewis, Greenock and the fishing ports along the north-east coast between Inverness and Aberdeen.[12] He is clear that 'community revivals were virtually confined to the periphery'. Bebbington concludes by stating that 'revival of the spontaneous variety was becoming marginal in Britain'.[13]

Janice Holmes

In the last thirty years, academic research on revivals has continued to downplay the extent of the 1859–61 awakening in Scotland. David Hempton and Myrtle Hill, in their thorough study of evangelical Protestantism in Ulster, include an illuminating chapter on the 1859 revival in that province. In reference to the reaction from the rest of the UK, the authors state that 'the English response was muted, but the west of Scotland, closest to Ulster in religion and culture, also witnessed some revival excitement'. They add that such awakenings took place 'on the Celtic fringes of the British Isles'.[14]

Kathryn Long's commendable analysis of the 1857–8 revival in the United States makes only passing reference to the subsequent movement in the UK. Seemingly influenced by Carwardine's work, which she

---

12. In a later study Bebbington appears to abandon the 'only parts of Scotland' assumption. With good reason he still claims, though, that Orr's denotation of the 1858–61 revival in Britain as the 'Second Evangelical Awakening' is 'exaggerated' since the revival occurred 'hardly at all in England' (D. W. Bebbington, *The Dominance of Evangelicalism: The Age of Spurgeon and Moody*, Leicester, 2005, pp. 100-1).

13. D. W. Bebbington, *Evangelicalism in Modern Britain: A History From the 1730s to the 1980s*, London, 1989, pp. 116-17. Meanwhile, Stuart Piggin also refers to the marginalisation of evangelical movements in twentieth century Scotland when he claims that 'revivals ... have been found only at the geographic peripheral; in ... . Moray, Firth (*sic*) and the Hebrides' (Stuart Piggin, *Firestorm of the Lord*, Carlisle, 2000, p. 114). However, earlier in his otherwise excellent study, Piggin enthuses about the 1905 revival in the very heart of Scotland's capital city! (p. 22).

14. David Hempton and Myrtle Hill, *Evangelical Protestantism in Ulster Society, 1740-1890*, London, 1992, p. 150. On the basis of this flawed thinking, Hempton and Hill suggest that one reason the revival translated so easily from America to Ulster, 'but not so readily to other parts of the Britain', was because (only) America and Ulster were undergoing a Roman Catholic resurgence (p. 159).

quotes, Long writes that 'most notable among the British revivals was an explosive popular movement in Ulster during 1859 that spread to the west of Scotland'.[15]

Janice Holmes's book, *Religious Revivals in Britain and Ireland 1859–1905*, based on a Ph.D. thesis, was published in 2000. The first part of Section One is an examination of 'The Ulster revival of 1859', while the second part considers 'The British response of 1859'. In this latter chapter, Holmes concentrates her efforts on attitudes within England and Scotland, believing that there appears to be little causal connection between the revival in Ireland and the Welsh revival of the same period.[16] In her introduction to the chapter, the author makes the unsupported claim that 'as a spontaneous outpouring, the 1859 revival failed to take root in all but a few areas (of England and Scotland), such as the isolated region of Cornwall and the western lowlands of Scotland'.[17] She believes that despite enormous interest in the Ulster awakening, British efforts to instigate a national revival went unchecked throughout the latter part of 1859.[18] British evangelicals had visited Ulster, held public lectures, established regular prayer meetings, brought in visiting speakers and imported Irish converts. They had made resolutions, published papers and even started a periodical devoted entirely to revival news. According to the revival formula, all this enthusiasm, prayer and hard work should have triggered a 'shower of the Holy Spirit' as it had in Ireland. But as 1859 wore on into 1860 it became increasingly obvious that a 'spontaneous religious awakening

---

15. Kathryn Long, *The Revival of 1857–58: Interpreting an American Awakening*, New York, 1998, pp. 154-5.

16. The prevalence of Wales's national language made the spread of revival news from Ulster to that nation difficult, as did poor communication links between the two regions. The revival in Wales, which occurred concurrently with that in Ireland, can be traced rather more directly to the influence of the American awakening of 1857–8. Only a tiny number of clergymen from Wales went to witness the Irish movement. By distinction, most of the many hundreds of English Christians who made the journey did so by travelling through North Wales to embark at Holyhead, generally being unaware that as profound a revival was stirring the villages and towns in the very Celtic land through which they were passing.

17. J. Holmes, p. 19. She mentions again 'the outbreak of revival in certain parts of western Scotland' on page 34.

18. ibid., p. 30.

was not going to occur'.[19] Holmes's opinion is that by November 1859 British popular interest in the revival began to decline, leaving evangelicals with 'several unpleasant realities. They recognised that the revival was over in Ireland and that it was unlikely to spread to England or Scotland. Throughout the closing months of 1859, they had waited in eager anticipation, proposing a variety of explanations for the revival's delay. After another year had elapsed, most of them realised it was never coming.'[20]

In her research Holmes in fact makes use of a number of general revival publications that testify to more widespread awakening in Scotland than she personally gives credit for, including Orr's 1949 study and William Reid's *Authentic Records of Revival*. She also makes reference to a number of biographies, such as that of James Turner, Duncan Matheson and Hay Macdowall Grant, each of which provides exhilarating accounts of revival in various parts of Scotland during 1859–61. Yet she fails to take their cumulative evidence seriously. The claims of Holmes and her predecessors have been broadly accepted by other historians,[21] although in his formative study of Scottish Brethrenism, Neil Dickson does concede that 'there were traditional spontaneous revivals in *some* areas of Scotland' during these critical years (emphasis mine).[22]

Clifford Marrs

The most hard-hitting refutation of widespread revival in Scotland during the years 1858–61 comes from Clifford Marrs in his unpublished Ph.D. thesis, *The 1859 Religious Revival in Scotland*, submitted to Glasgow University in 1995. Marrs draws attention to comments made by Dr Julius Wood at the Free Church General Assembly of 1861 in which the minister concluded: 'The revival with which God

---

19. ibid., p. 36.

20. ibid., p. 47.

21. For example, secular historian T. M. Devine acknowledges the occurrence of 'emotional religious revivals in several working-class communities … in the south-west and parts of the north-east (of Scotland) in 1859-62' (*The Scottish Nation*, London, 1999, p. 378).

22. Neil T. R. Dickson, *Brethren in Scotland 1838-2000: A Social Study of an Evangelical*, Carlisle, 2002, pp. 59-60.

has been pleased to bless us, extends over the length and breadth of the land.' Just three sentences on, however, Wood says: 'We trust that (the revival) … will yet prevail over the whole of Scotland.'[23] Marrs notes how keen most revival commentators have been to quote Wood's former remark, while they have unanimously avoided mention of his latter. A few weeks after this meeting of the General Assembly, Moody Stuart spoke on behalf of the Free Church deputation at the Irish Presbyterian Church General Assembly. There he confirmed that while the revival affected many locations in his native land, 'the whole of Scotland was still not moved'.[24] Marrs believes that enthusiastic revival protagonists exaggerated the magnitude and geographic pervasiveness of the revival,[25] which, in reality, he feels, had only minimal impact on the nation's populace.

Marrs strongly believes that although it affected only a relatively small number of congregations and a minority of the populace, the movement's leading protagonists were high profile, respected figures with access to publicity via the press, particularly *The Scottish Guardian*, *The Wynd Journal* and *The Revival*. 'The enthusiasm and inflated claims of these prominent individuals', he wrote, 'coupled with the coverage devoted to the movement by the aforementioned papers, created a mythical account of the revival which gave it considerably more significance than it merited. The exaggerated statements of pro-revival contemporaries were then seized upon and promoted by passionate scholars resulting in the continued distortion of its actual impact and importance and hence the perpetuation of the revival myth.'[26]

Marrs's overall conclusion is that the revival did not have the impact perceived and previously claimed. 'Panoramic observations, generalisations and exaggerated statements by prominent pro-revivalists

---

23. C. J. Marrs, *The 1859 Religious Revival in Scotland: A Review and Critique of the Movement with Particular Reference to the City of Glasgow*, Unpublished Ph.D. thesis, University of Glasgow, 1995, p. 188.

24. ibid.

25. One such example, seemingly overlooked by Marrs, is that of Henry Johnson, who, writing at the beginning of the twentieth century, claimed that 'by the end of 1860 there were not many places in Scotland unblessed by this new baptism of the Spirit of God' (Johnson, *Stories of Great Revivals*, London, 1906, p. 225).

26. ibid., pp. 205-06.

caught up in the midst of the movement, together with passionate, uncritical scholarship' combined to create and perpetuate the myth that Victorian Scotland was deeply stirred by the 1859 movement. He believes that the evidence shows that such views grossly exaggerate the reality and that Britain's churches, parishes, towns and cities were not enveloped by rampant revival, nor did the movement develop into a great catalyst for social action. 'The revival myth has been exposed. The movement was not the major influential, spiritual and social event of the Victorian era to which it has been popularly elevated.'[27]

Kenneth Jeffrey

It was not until 2002 that an academic publication fully acknowledging the pervasiveness of the 1859 revival in Scotland appeared. Kenneth Jeffrey, in his doctoral thesis, *When the Lord Walked the Land* (written under the academic supervision and guidance of Professor D. W. Bebbington), states that the 1859 revival has neither a precedent nor a successor as a revival movement of such national proportions. Jeffrey felt the movement had been 'largely ignored and inadmissibly overlooked for a considerable time', and thus he sought to provide a thorough modern understanding of the awakening, though he restricts his field of scope to the north-east of Scotland. Jeffrey's pioneering work is a fascinating examination of the varying ways in which the revival affected differing community types within that region. Jeffrey found that the revival had a potent influence on the city of Aberdeen, in virtually all the fishing communities spread along the north-east coast, and in a large number of the small towns, villages and parishes that constitute the vast rural hinterland of the region. (See Chapter 16 for a discussion of the various revival traditions that were apparent across the north-east and throughout the country during these years.)

---

27. ibid., pp. 342-3.

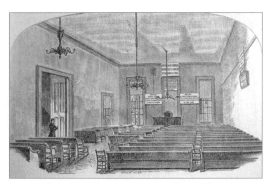

Fulton Street prayer meeting, New York 1857

*Sculpture of Jeremiah Lanphier,
leader of the Fulton Street
prayer meetings*

*Connor Presbyterian Church, one of the
first to experience revival in 1859*

*James McQuilkin of Kells, one of the central
figures of the revival in Ireland*

Old Schoolhouse, Kells, regarded as the birth-place of the Ulster revival

Chapter 2

Genesis of the Revival

International Origins

To conduct an examination of this significant revival movement, we have to first consider its international origins. The revival's beginnings lay in a growing movement which first appeared in both of Canada's Atlantic Provinces (Maritimes and Newfoundland) from 1856, and in Ontario, Canada in the autumn of 1857, as well as in a growing number of simultaneous, but unconnected interdenominational prayer meetings in cities and towns across America. One such meeting, held daily at 4 p.m. in Bethel, Connecticut, was attended by 'farmers, mechanics, and storekeepers' and claimed four hundred conversions.[1]

The burgeoning prayer movement that centred on Fulton Street, New York was thus only one of many series for intercession in the States throughout the autumn and early winter of 1857–8, yet it was these meetings that have become most strongly associated with the beginnings of the revival in America. Further, it has become almost universally accepted among both academic and popular revival historians[2] that the New York banking crash in October 1857 was the clear, initial cause of the revival in both Canada and America: the acceptance of mass revivalism by urban businessmen seeking God's help in a time of trouble. Orr goes to lengths, however, to stress that this movement

---

1. J. Edwin Orr, *The Event of the Century: The 1857–1858 Awakening*, Wheaton, 1989, p. 25. This study, a revision and reprint of Orr's 1943 thesis, remained the most thorough study of this widespread yet largely neglected movement until the appearance of Kathryn Long's academic thesis in 1998.

2. Not least William McLoughlin (*Revivals, Awakenings and Reform*, Chicago, 1980, pp. 141-2).

21

was well underway in Canada *before* the bank panic of October 1857.[3]
He also suggests that by the early winter of 1857 revival was so rapidly
extending through America that the movement was already being called
The Great Revival.[4] There seems little doubt, however, that the economic
meltdown – the severest in American history, and extending throughout
most of 1858 – *did* provide strong impetus to the revival movement,
allowing workers (thousands of whom had instantly found themselves
unemployed) both the time and the motivation to participate in prayer
meetings. As a result, significant and extensive revival spread throughout
the United States, being especially prominent in the north.

Just as eighteenth-century itinerant preachers such as George
Whitefield found themselves able to transcend international boundaries
and enjoy dramatic revival on both sides of the Atlantic, this practice
became further popularised in the following century by successful
evangelists like Lorenzo Dow, James Caughey and Charles Finney.
Yet this hardly makes it inevitable, as has been suggested, that the 1857
revival should be 'followed by spectacular revivals in Ulster, Wales, and
many parts of Britain'.[5] Of more significance, news of the American
awakening was quickly and widely reported in Ulster and two deputies
from Ireland's Presbyterian Church made the journey to the United
States to witness the revival for themselves, bringing back glowing
reports. Once again, this resulted in an increase in prayer effort, and
it was in connection with a prayer meeting in the mid-Antrim village
of Kells in the autumn/winter of 1858, and related gospel-meetings in
nearby Ahoghill early the following year, that revival began. At the
March Communion in Ahoghill, revival burst into flame, and almost
instantaneously spread to a score of places round about, with some four
to five thousand people reportedly being converted in this one district
in just six weeks. The revival spread rapidly across the Province,[6] which

3. Orr, 1989, p. 23.

4. ibid., p. 57.

5. Richard Carwardine, 'The Second Great Awakening in Comparative Perspective',
in Edith L. Blumhofer and Randall Balmer, *Modern Christian Revivals*, Illinois,
1993, p. 88.

6. Attention has been drawn to the part played by Scottish evangelist Brownlow
North, 'who contributed immeasurably to the revival movement' in Ulster. North
spent two months in Ireland, from the end of June to the end of August 1859, during

saw 'cyclone after cyclone of the outpouring of the Holy Spirit of God',[7] resulting in an immediate and intense impact upon many communities. Considerable attention was given to the movement, especially in regard to the sensational and oft-reported accounts of dramatic physical manifestations that accompanied its progress.[8]

Contributors to the Scottish Movement

General and Economic Environment

Just as stirring reports of spiritual quickening in America led to dramatic outbreak of revival across the Atlantic Ocean in Ulster, so first-hand accounts of revival in that Province played a significant part in both the genesis and furtherance of the deep spiritual movement that was to spread through many parts of mainland Britain in subsequent months. It is certainly extremely difficult to otherwise account for the striking impact and sweeping extent of the ensuing revival in Scotland, of which, in its

---

which time he spoke on around fifty occasions to crowds that often numbered in the thousands – such as the memorable open-air on Dunmull Hill near Portrush, where between 7,000 and 8,000 gathered to hear North speak (Nicholas M. Railton, *Revival On the Causeway Coast: The 1859 Revival In And Around Coleraine*, Fearn, 2009, p. 45).

7. The Rev. Ian R. K. Paisley, then First Minister of Northern Ireland, in Stanley Barnes, A *Pictorial History of the 1859 Revival and Related Awakenings in Ulster*, Belfast, 2009, p. 10. In speaking of this revival, Paisley states that 'of the many important happenings in the history of our country, nothing ever excelled the days when our Province rocked as in the days of the Great Awakening' (ibid.).

8. A plethora of books and pamphlets were quickly composed, enthusiastically out-lining the marked events that occurred in specific localities all across Ulster. These include: Rev. William J. Patton, *The Revival at Dromara in 1859*; Rev. Andrew Wilson, *The Revival at Dungannon in 1859*; Rev. William Richey, *Connor and Coleraine, or Scenes and Sketches of the Last Ulster Awakening*. Many more histories and analytical commentaries were published within a couple of years of the movement; some providing personal reports of the revival, others assessing its results and legacy; and a number offering rigorous defence of, or attack on the more controversial aspects of the movement. Over the following century and a half, many fresh assessments have been published. See, for example, Orr, 1949, pp. 38-57; Alfred Russell Scott, *The Ulster Revival of 1859*, Ballymena, 1994; John T. Carson, *God's River in Spate: The Story of the Religious Awakening of Ulster in 1859*, Belfast, 1958; Ian R. Paisley, *The 59 Revival: An Authentic History of the Great Ulster Awakening of 1859*, Belfast, 1958. More recently, the Rev. Stanley Barnes has drawn together dozens of primary documents to form the unique and comprehensive seven-volume *A History of the 1859 Ulster Revival*, Banbridge, 2008.

international setting, *The Scottish Guardian* wrote: 'We know not that in
any other country where the work has appeared there can be traced the
same systematic progress as may be noticed in the Revival of Scotland.'[9]

General economic recession in the early 1850s is unlikely to have
been a factor in the genesis and furtherance of the deep spiritual movement that was to spread through many parts of Scotland from the
close of the decade. By 1859 trade and price indices were well on the
upturn.[10] Marrs provides evidence which clearly suggests that there was
no external military threat to national security. Moreover, internally,
the country was experiencing relative political calm, and enjoying
sustained growth in industry and agriculture, with capital and labour
alike deemed to be flourishing. Further, while diseases such as small
pox were prevalent, in general the welfare data seems to suggest that the
population of the country was enjoying good health free from major
epidemics.[11] Marrs believed that the only disruption to the seemingly
universal and relentless national progress was in respect of shipping,
which was recognised as suffering a depression. Even here, however, the
forecast was optimistic. He concluded that 1859 was a stable, prosperous
year in Scotland, with 'no indication of anything to unsettle it'.[12] This
state of general stability did not always hold true in every localised
situation, however. For example, local economic issues such as the
disastrous fishing season of 1859 and the storms which devastated crops
in the north-east in 1860 and 1861 may well have been conducive to
the revival which occurred in these particular areas.[13]

---

9. *SG*, 21/03/1860.

10. Callum Brown, *The Social History of Religion in Scotland since 1730*, London,
1987, p. 147; Richard Carwardine, *Transatlantic Revivalism: Popular Evangelicalism in
Britain and America 1790-1865*, Westport, 1978, p. 170. Jeffrey's analysis reveals that
at the time of the revival Aberdeen had recovered from its industrial depression and
had entered another period of considerable prosperity (Jeffrey, p. 51). Dickson refers
to the possible relevance of the 'more general social change which continued unabated
throughout Scotland in rural and urban communities' (Dickson, 2002, p. 60).

11. Marrs, pp. 118, 111.

12. ibid., pp. 117-19.

13. Jeffrey, pp. 186-7, 115; William Nixon, A*n Account of the Work of God at Ferryden*, London, 1860, p. 10. The summer herring season in 1859 had been unusually
bad, the catch amounting to just three-quarters of its normal level. Furthermore,

Spiritual Influences

Nor was the Church in general in a depressed state prior to the revival. Marrs's research has revealed that the years prior to the 1859 revival were ones of church growth and increased membership, and thus he discounts any idea of the Church being in a depressed, sunken or backslidden state.[14] More significant as stimuli for the revival which followed were developing trends in religion. These included the novel emergence of a number of charismatic itinerant lay-preachers in the years immediately prior to the revival (see next chapter). A more longstanding factor was an increased focus on aggressive evangelism in Scottish towns and cities in the 1850s. The church extension programme, initiated by Thomas Chalmers prior to the Disruption, was continued by the Free Church in the 1840s and '50s, and a considerable number of new 'territorial churches' were planted in all Scotland's cities and many provincial towns. By May 1859, Dr Roxburgh said he could name twenty-six of these stations, 'which within a few years had risen into congregations, some of them most vigorous and flourishing, some of them shining as centres of light in the midst of the darkest and neediest districts'.[15]

Influence of American and Irish Revivals

But all was not well. In a great many churches there existed a ready acknowledgement throughout the 1850s of a steadily worsening moral depravity in society as a whole. Ministers greatly bemoaned such reality in countless sermons. The Rev. Rae of New Deer, writing fifty years after the event, remarked that the spiritual life of Scotland prior to the revival was 'so dull and dead that the godly in all the churches were filled with deep concern and alarm about the cause

---

by December, stormy weather was interfering with the ability of the boats to get out to sea.

14. Marrs, pp. 130-1. Bussey's reflection on the religious situation in Scotland prior to the revival is more equivocal, concluding that 'light and darkness intermingled' (Bussey, p. 25).

15. Bussey, p. 36. In Edinburgh, some of the city's poorest districts were carefully targeted. At West Port a preaching centre was begun in a tan-loft and in time a church was built. The Free Church at Fountainbridge, under Rev. Wilson, soon overflowed and gave off a separate congregation for Barclay Church; which itself became the means of starting the nearby Viewforth Church. Similar work was done in Dundee and Glasgow, particularly in the Wynds district of the latter city.

of religion in their midst'.[16] Another commentator argued that while there was fairly widespread religious knowledge in Scotland in the pre-revival period, there was a notable lack of spiritual life, and the prevalence of two particularly lamentable sins, 'those of drunkenness and immorality'.[17]

Concern about continuing social ills, and an awareness that spiritual conditions within their localities could be significantly better, led to a growing desire among believers for the Almighty to stretch forth his arm in awakening power. Then came the dissemination of news of spiritual outpourings in first, America, and then Ireland. This had the effect of deepening the longing for revival, such desire in turn leading to heightened expectation of an imminent move of God's Spirit in the nation. Thus, it would appear that the two most common factors which acted as stimuli for the appearance of revival in communities all across Scotland were spiritual longing coupled with growing expectancy.[18]

---

16. Matthews, p. 2.

17. Kenneth Moody Stuart, *Brownlow North: Records and Recollections*, London, 1878, pp. 83-4. Drunkenness and other vices, of course, remained a problem in many Scottish communities immediately after, and even during the revival in question.

18. In regard to revival in the north-east, Jeffrey states unequivocally: 'It was desired and expected in every community that felt its influence ... [Desire and expectancy] were the foundation stones upon which this awakening was built' (pp. 252-3). Not that great expectation in itself always leads to the inevitability of revival. Nicholas Railton has poignantly demonstrated this by comparing the effects of revival in America upon Ulster in the early 1830s to that in 1858 (pp. 7-8). When it met in Coleraine in 1830, the General Synod of Ulster became much stirred by a letter from the General Assembly of the Presbyterian Church in America, relating news of a deep revival in various parts of that distant country. When news of that awakening became more generally known throughout Ireland over the next few years, meetings were begun in attempt to help promote a similar revival within its own bounds. In Belfast a meeting of clergymen was arranged, whereby it was agreed to hold a united day of prayer and fasting with American believers on the other side of the Atlantic. This was set for 7 January 1833, and was used to implore the Lord for 'an outpouring of the Holy Spirit for the extension of religion throughout the world'. A number of meetings were subsequently held in Belfast, each one attracting a large number of people. Little more is known of this initiative, but it is clear that no revival occurred in Belfast or elsewhere in Ulster as a consequence of these methods, as it did so markedly in a similarly expectant and prayerful environment a quarter of a century later.

Accounts of overseas movements were widely reported in numerous religious publications in Britain throughout 1858, stimulating a marked increase in prayer meetings in many places (especially from the second half of 1858) among earnest believers desperate for a similar outpouring in their own congregations and communities. Paramount here was the appearance of *The British Messenger*, a monthly Christian journal which played a fundamental role in disseminating news of the American and Ulster revivals in Scotland.[19]

Fuelling this spirit of expectancy, the Free Church of Scotland arranged for Dr Maclean, an American minister, to come and speak of the ongoing revival in his country at their General Assembly in 1858. Maclean described the movement underway in his home nation as 'the most decided and extraordinary the world ever saw since the days of the apostles'. A year later, in October 1859, the Rev. Well of New York gave a similar address to the Free Church Presbytery of Glasgow. Numerous ministers and laymen from Ireland also spoke about the Ulster awakening at meetings throughout Scotland.[20] For example, the Rev. Alfred Canning of Coleraine, as a deputy of the Irish Presbyterian Church, addressed a meeting at Glasgow's City Hall as early as 11 August 1859. More significantly, the Rev. Thomas Toye, minister of Great George's Street Presbyterian Church in Belfast, and the central, though rather eccentric figure of the 1859 revival in that city, spoke at meetings in Glasgow in both 1860 and 1861 (in the latter year he was accompanied by the Rev. Melhurst of Coleraine Baptist Church).

In fact, there was a particularly strong connection between Scotland and the revival among Toye's congregation. Toye became

---

19. By 1857, *The British Messenger* had a circulation of 110,000.

20. Not every Scottish minister spoke favourably of goings-on in Ireland, however. Rev. George Gilfillan, Secession minister in Dundee and acclaimed author and poet, dogmatically pronounced that the revival *was* 'a work of the devil' (*The Daily Argus*, quoted in Rev. Samuel J. Moore, *The Great Revival in Ireland 1859*, reprinted Lisburn, n.d., pp. 53-4). It was said that his rationale for being so strongly opposed to a movement he hadn't personally observed was that he had witnessed a similar movement in Dundee some years previously, which had not been to his approval. Given that Gilfillan had moved to Dundee as early as 1836, one wonders if the revival in question was that which began in Murray McCheyne's St Peter's Church in 1839, a movement that was almost universally accredited to the work of the Spirit of God.

tenderly attached to some of the many Scots who visited his church when revival was in progress (as he did also to converts of his ministry during his Scottish visits of 1860 and 1861). One became a very special friend; this was a man from Glasgow, who, though already a believer, was greatly strengthened in faith through what he witnessed in Toye's Great George's Street Church in 1859 and went on to become a shining Christian witness. Another was a man from Port Glasgow on holiday in Ireland during the revival. Here he spent time going from meeting to meeting and was about to return home without finding the peace he so desired, when he was turned back because the boat was full. On the boat he had heard folk engage in lively discussion about the revival in progress and was led to attend a meeting in Toye's church. The preacher that night was himself a Scot – the Rev. Nelson of Renfrew – but at the end of the service, Toye characteristically moved from pew to pew, seeking out the anxious. He came to the Port Glasgow man, spoke with him, and then both men knelt to pray. For around twenty minutes the man groaned on his knees in agony of sin, but eventually rose with joy and thanksgiving to his new-found Saviour. Soon after, this man became manager of a busy and important business as well as a zealous evangelist, all his Sabbaths and evenings being spent in love for his Lord. He also became a lasting friend of Toye, despite some differences of belief.[21] Other Scottish ministers also preached in Toye's church during the revival, such as the Rev. Johnston of Belhelvie, Aberdeenshire, in July 1860.

Ulster Pilgrimage
Perhaps most significantly of all, a remarkably high number of ministers, as well as a considerable number of laymen and several women,[22] travelled from all over Scotland – as well as from England – between June and October 1859 to witness the Irish revival first-hand. These included

---

21. Jane Toye, *Brief Memorials of the Late Rev. Thomas Toye, Belfast*, Belfast, 1873, p. 97.

22. A number of 'delicate ladies, who had never before ventured from home, braved the winter sea passage from the north of Scotland to be convinced of the genuineness of the revival in Belfast' (*The Helensburgh and Gareloch Times*, quoted in Various, *Sketches of Churches and Clergy*, Helensburgh, 1889, p. 40.)

deputations from several large Church bodies in Scotland[23] as well as individual ministers on private pilgrimages. Of the lay visitors, the great majority were believers, but some were anxious inquirers hoping to find spiritual truth and light through the Irish revival. These clerical and lay visitors were so numerous that they became a prominent feature of the Ulster revival. Indeed, on occasion they threatened to outnumber locals! Dr James Begg of Newington Free Church, Edinburgh said that on his visit he had seen many instances of 'the power of God's Spirit in melting the hardest of hearts and in bringing infidels and Romanists to abandon their errors at once'.[24]

Janice Holmes conducted a survey of 123 clergymen from all over Britain who made the journey to Ulster. Out of the total, 40 per cent of visitors came from Scotland, and denominationally, Free Church of Scotland ministers were the most numerous.[25] One Irish newspaper that sought to make a log of all clerical visitors from outside the Province listed as many as 230 ministers who came from Scotland to see the revival in the town of Coleraine alone during July and August 1859, being just a fraction of the total number of visitors that came to Ulster during these two months. Many other pilgrims, who continued to arrive in Coleraine during September, by which time the revival was beginning to wane, are not included in the above figures. Of these

---

23. In a 16-page report on the Irish movement published in December 1859, the Edinburgh Presbytery of the United Presbyterian Church, a delegation from which denomination had travelled to witness the Irish movement, gave an overall favourable viewpoint on it, and pinpointed five lessons for the Church in Scotland: 1) The power and grace of the Holy Spirit; 2) Profound dissatisfaction with our own spiritual condition; 3) The power of prayer; 4) The suitability and sufficiency of the gospel of Christ; and 5) The power for good possessed by the private members of the Church – i.e., lay converts witnessing to family and neighbours. (*Address on Revival of Religion to the Congregations under their Inspection: With Especial Reference to the Revival in Ireland*, Edinburgh, 1859.)

24. R. J. Beggs, *Rev. Thomas Toye: God's Instrument in the 1859 Revival*, Belfast, 2009, p. 67.

25. Just over 50 per cent came from England, while the remainder came from Wales, North America and other parts of Ireland. After Free Church of Scotland ministers, the most numerous denominational visitors were pastors from the Church of England, Methodist, Baptist, Independent and English Presbyterian Churches respectively, together with ten clergymen whose denominational affiliations were unknown (J. Holmes, p. 22).

230 men, at least two dozen came from Glasgow and a slightly lesser number from Edinburgh. While these visitors came primarily simply to witness the movement in progress, many found themselves personally caught up in the work, either by addressing meetings, doing open-air work, or getting involved in the united prayer meetings held in the town. Records kept by the *Coleraine Chronicle* – the editor and proprietor of which, John McCombie, was a native of Ross-shire, and a member of the Free Church of Scotland – show that localities from which at least two or three such workers came include Edinburgh, Glasgow, Dundee, Stirling, Paisley, Inverness, Aberdeenshire, Perthshire, Ayrshire, Inverclyde, Fife, The Borders, Lanarkshire, East Lothian, West Lothian, Dunbartonshire, Forfarshire, Easter Ross, Dumfriesshire, Western Highlands, Isle of Bute and Wick. Indeed, virtually the only counties not represented are the north isles of Orkney and Shetland and the Western Isles! And these impressive details only apply to the town of Coleraine! Hundreds of other mainland ministers visited Belfast, Ballymena and other principal centres of the revival work in Ireland. All in all, it is clear that a very significant number of Scottish ministers, elders and laymen went to witness the Ulster revival in person, and many of these took home with them deep impressions of that remarkable movement, and in some cases the very flames of revival itself, to share with and impart unto their own congregations.

Arndilly House, Speyside

Brownlow North

Hay Macdowall Grant

William Hay Aitken   Alexander Moody Stuart   Reginald Radcliffe

Dallas, Moray

Rothesay, Isle of Bute

CHAPTER 3

Paving the Way for the '59

'Gentlemen' Preachers (1856–8)

Introduction

In regard to previous seasons of spiritual awakening in Scotland, there have often occurred one or more initiatory movements prior to the main outbreak of spiritual power.[1] This was true also of the 1859 awakening. In the present chapter we turn our attention to several streams of revival blessing which appeared to occur independently of the Canadian / American / Irish movements, and which arose in the months that led up to the major outbreak of revival in the summer of 1859.

The dramatic conversions of a number of members of the aristocracy who subsequently became itinerant preachers, led to the rapid spread of the gospel message in the north-east of Scotland and elsewhere from the mid-1850s. As well as Brownlow North and Hay Macdowall Grant, short accounts of whose efforts in the awakening are given below, 'Gentlemen' preachers of the north-east included John Gordon of Parkhill, a cousin of Brownlow North, and described as 'a good man, shy, reticent, slow of speech, but with a message of love to men which he delivered in his own quiet way'.[2] Gordon took a very deep interest in the movement, and erected a hall as an extension to his large manor in which to hold evangelistic services, and in which much blessing was subsequently received. Then there was the Earl of Kintore, and

---

1. Tom Lennie, *Land of Many Revivals; Scotland's Extraordinary Legacy of Christian Revivals over Four Centuries, 1527-1857*, Fearn, 2014.

2. Matthews, Chapter 1; see also M. Gordon, *John Gordon of Pitlurg and Parkhill, or, Memories of a Standard-Bearer*, London, 1885.

Lord Haddo, afterwards Earl of Aberdeen.[3] In addition, converted deist Gordon Forlong, a former lawyer, established a number of meetings for prayer and exhortation in and around Aberdeenshire in 1856–7, where, he wrote, 'the work of grace goes on hopefully'.[4]

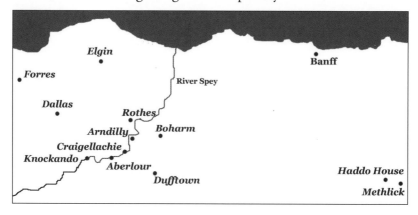

Hay Macdowall Grant

Converted in November 1854, Hay Macdowall Grant began his evangelistic career in the early spring of 1856, through the influence of his brother-in-law, the Rev. Robert Aitken, incumbent of Pendeen, Cornwall. Aitken was keen to evangelise while staying with Grant at his stately Arndilly home in Moray, and meetings were arranged. For example, Grant records in his diary for 27 April 1856: 'Mr A. preached in West Gauldwell Barn (Craigellachie) in the morning to about 800 people, and in the evening to more, for they had remained in the neighbourhood all day waiting for the second service, and more had come, though the day was wet and stormy. The sermons made a deep impression on the people.'[5] Grant was reluctantly persuaded to carry on meetings begun by Aitken in Rothes and neighbourhood after the latter's departure.

Throughout the remaining eight months of 1856, Grant laboured in the five neighbouring parishes of Boharm, Aberlour, Rothes, Dufftown and Knockando. During that time, he noted that he spoke privately with 212 people about their souls' concerns. Of these, sixty-two professed

---

3. For more information on Lord Haddo see Alexander Duff, *The True Nobility: Sketches of the Life and Character of Lord Haddo, Fifth Earl of Aberdeen*, London, 1868.

4. Jeffrey, p. 53.

5. Mrs Gordon, *Hay Macdowall Grant of Arndilly: His Life, Labours and Teaching*, London, 1876, p. 51.

to find peace, while over thirty were under a deep conviction.[6] Above all, Rothes and Boharm were upon Grant's heart, and one 'remarkable meeting in the mill of Tomnabrach', and another at Belnagarrow, were vividly remembered. One recalled how Grant 'visited from house to house, holding meetings at night, after walking through heathery and swampy moors the whole day'. Another writes how, on one occasion, 'his bodily needs had been so completely forgotten, both by himself and those whom he visited, that he actually fell on the road, a little above where we lived, through sheer exhaustion'. Grant said of his first twenty months itinerating around the north of Scotland: 'The work of the Lord ... has gone on increasing in an extraordinary manner',[7] as indeed it continued to do in subsequent years.

Brownlow North

But it was Brownlow North – son of a prebendary, grandson of a bishop and grand-nephew of Lord North, a former Prime Minister – whose name was most prominent in regard to lay evangelism in the years immediately prior to the 1859 revival. North's biographer, Kenneth Moody Stuart, states that the evangelist's work in Scotland during the years 1856–59 'prepared the way for the general wave of revival which in 1860 burst upon our land. Indeed, the springtide of blessing under his ministry ... reached its highest point in 1858 and 1859, and was therefore independent of the revivals in Ireland and America.'[8]

Like Macdowall Grant, though independently of him, North, too, experienced a dramatic conversion in November 1854, after a reckless youth spent as a 'gay and careless man about town'.[9] He reluctantly agreed to accept a preaching engagement in his former Moray home

---

6. ibid., p. 68.

7. ibid., p. 72; Gordon, p. 89.

8. K. Moody Stuart, *Brownlow North: His Life and Work*, London, 1878 (reprinted 1961), p. 280. Moody Stuart overstates the case, however, by saying that the subsequent revival, for which North's ministry acted as a providential preparation, 'in all human likelihood might otherwise have had as slight and partial effect upon Scotland as it had upon England and the Scottish Highlands; for in neither of these parts of the island had there been such deep ploughing of the soil of men's hearts which in the Scottish Lowlands had been stirred to its depths with the ploughshare of conviction under this Baptist-like preacher of Repentance' (ibid.).

9. Moody Stuart, 1878, p. 106.

village, Dallas, in May 1856, when its Free Church minister, the Rev.
Davidson, was called away from home. It was in Dallas that North had
been so dramatically awakened and converted just eighteen months
previously, and naturally he was apprehensive of preaching before
people who knew his former life so well. Interest was deepened by
a tragedy in the village while North was there, the drowning of two
children during a flood in the nearby river.

Such was the impression made by North's preaching that when
Davidson returned home he constrained the young evangelist to again
address the people. 'The church was crowded, people flocking from
a distance to hear the new preacher and his rousing message.' News
of North's popularity travelled quickly, and soon 'the tidings of this
work of awakening' were carried to nearby Forres, where North again
reluctantly agreed to speak. On 'the first night he had a large and
earnest audience; the next night the church was full, after which
passages, staircases, and doorways were thronged with eager and
anxious listeners'. It was said that 'permanent good was effected at
that time, and that the fruits of that, as of other revival movements,
were still to be traced two decades later'.[10]

The Rev. John Whyte, minister of Moyness parish, near Nairn, wrote
to North in December 1856, shortly after the evangelist had visited his
church. 'So far as I can ascertain', he remarked, 'the movement among
some of the young folks here is very cheering and hopeful, affording
cause of gratitude and praise. Your labours have evidently been blessed of
God, and I should be very wishful to widen and extend the movement.'
With that view Whyte proceeded to address the young people of his
congregation, urging 'the importance and necessity of the new birth'.[11]

Whole households came under the influence of North's dynamic
preaching. One gentleman wrote of the effect produced within his
own residence:

> The two nurses, I am happy to see, continue to evince much earnestness,
> the other two maids are also evidently enquiring, and the men-servants
> have become greatly sobered down and subdued. On Sabbath, instead
> of their wonted frolicsome and light habits, they are now found reading

10. ibid., pp. 39-40.
11. ibid., pp. 85-6.

the Bible and religious books. This in a 'bothy' is a step certainly in the right direction. We are making a very feeble effort to foster these sympathies by having a very interesting little prayer-meeting in our house.[12]

Lady Gordon, the widow of the Earl of Aberdeen, spoke most warmly of North's visit to Haddo House a few years later. The Balfours had asked North to pray for their eldest son, 'who had just come of age'. At a meeting in Methlick Free Church later that month, noted Gordon, North preached 'with great earnestness and power, and at the close, when all left the church, those who wished for special prayer on their behalf, that they might then decide for God, were invited to return. You may suppose how anxiously we waited, and with what joy we saw our sons come back into the church.'[13] The young men's consciences had been previously touched when their cousin, Walter Scott (later Lord Polwarth) had spoken to them of eternal matters, 'and this evening seemed to be the turning point', continued Lady Gordon. 'The following morning we all met in Mr North's sitting-room, when he read Isaiah 4, and spoke in a very affecting, solemn manner, and then he and each of them prayed in turn. There was at that time a great interest in religious subjects, a sort of "revival" throughout the whole household; but whether the impression was permanent in any case except our own family, I cannot say'.[14]

---

12. ibid., p. 85.

13. ibid., p. 316.

14. ibid.; it was not only with Brownlow North that 'household revivals' of this type occurred in this period. An unassuming localised awakening occurred in the summer of 1850 when David Sandeman, a young aristocrat-evangelist from Perthshire, came to stay for a short time at Westfield Farm, near Haddington. Through his well-seasoned personal communications and his private and public 'weepings of faith' – along with a day of fasting – for the unsaved around him, a number were 'awakened on the spot'. For several souls he 'travailed in birth till Christ was formed in them', at times feeling 'well nigh sunk under the oppressive burden of souls now laid upon him'. Those brought to saving faith included Sandeman's carriage-driver, a ploughman and a housemaid who, though she had previously taught a Sabbath class, felt for the first time that she was a sinner (Andrew Bonar, *Memoir of the Life and Brief Ministry of the Rev. David Sandeman, Missionary to China*, London, 1861, pp. 94-7. A few years later Sandeman journeyed to China to serve as a missionary, where he died in the midst of a cholera epidemic at the tender age of thirty-two. As he lay dying, a friend asked how he was. He answered, in all honesty of conscience, 'I am head-to-foot righteousness').

Free St Luke's, Edinburgh (1855–8)

Further south, Alexander Moody Stuart recalled a greatly deepened spiritual interest among his Free St Luke's congregation in Edinburgh from 1855–6. This church had also experienced revival fifteen years previously, when William Chalmers Burns reaped a substantial harvest here. More recently, there had arisen very earnest meetings for prayer, not only in the Session but among the people, and during one particular winter week the hall had been nearly filled each morning at 7.30 for prayer, while popular afternoon meetings took place in the church. Over thirty people brought certificates from ten different denominations outside the Free Church. A half-year later, on returning from the country, Stuart noted that in six weeks he had conversed with more than fifty enquirers: 'The convictions of some had been very deep, and the joy of deliverance … very great.' Stuart said that he felt like the friend of the Bridegroom rejoicing greatly because of the Bridegroom's voice.[15]

The first of numerous visits to St Luke's from Brownlow North in March 1857 resulted in 'dense crowds that filled passages and pulpit stairs', and in numbers being awakened to anxiety and brought to newness of life.[16] Also blessed were Macdowall Grant's plain and earnest appeals in this same church the following year, furthering the 'showers of blessing that were now descending'.[17] Indeed it was felt that Grant's plain and earnest exhibition of the gospel was even more largely blessed among the families of St Luke's than the fervid appeals of North. During this period Moody Stuart paid two visits to Ireland, where he assisted overpressed ministers in the midst of the remarkable awakening that was then sweeping across that land. Accounts of what he there witnessed, as well as the changes it affected in his own life, greatly encouraged his Edinburgh congregation.

'Winter on winter' for a number of years after his first visit to St Luke's, North preached in the 1,500-seater church to sizeable

---

15. K. Moody Stuart, *Alexander Moody Stuart: A Memoir*, London, 1899, p. 135.

16. ibid., pp. 136-7. North also created a great impression in several other Edinburgh churches during this first visit as an evangelist to the city. A journalist wrote of 'Edinburgh … flocking in thousands to his gatherings in the Tabernacle and elsewhere to see the strange sight of a godless man of sport and fashion transformed into a fiery, weeping messenger of the Cross' (Moody Stuart, 1878, p. 107).

17. Moody Stuart, 1899, p. 137.

congregations.[18] It was said that the fact that so many godly believers within the congregation gave themselves to wrestling in prayer for a spiritual blessing on North's preaching helped explain 'the abundant blessing which descended upon this place of worship'. During one visit in 1863, for example, no fewer than seventy anxious enquirers called to converse with North after his message in the Edinburgh church the previous evening, when something he had said about 'grace and peace' melted the congregation's hearts.[19] Meanwhile, a notable work was accomplished in Gorbals Free Church, Glasgow, following a visit from North in early 1858. The Rev. Alexander Cumming wrote that several young communicants at both the April and October sacraments of that year, all of whom had been satisfactorily examined by Cumming and his elders, had ascribed their conversion to North's labours.[20]

Rothesay (1858)

Brownlow North visited Rothesay on the Isle of Bute in February 1858.[21] The Rev. Robert Elder spoke of seeing more to encourage him in the two succeeding months than he had ever seen in his ministry before. About thirty came to converse with him 'under less or more concern. ... The best of them, after a good deal of emotion and warm feeling, were led after a time to far deeper views of sin and helplessness and a lost condition than they had at first', and many held back from joining the church at the following Communion. 'But on the next occasion', recalled Elder, 'in January following, I had, I think, the largest number of young communicants I have ever had here, and many of these I admitted with the greatest comfort. In June of the following year also I had the same experience.'[22] A number of new inquirers were added to the ranks of a fellowship

---

18. One who came under her first serious spiritual impressions when North preached here in 1859 was sixteen-year-old Jessie McFarlane. Within a year of her conversion, McFarlane had become a popular itinerant evangelist in the Scottish Lowlands (H. I. G., *Jessie McFarlane A Tribute of Affection*, London, 1872, pp. 4-5).

19. Moody Stuart, 1878, pp. 319-20.

20. ibid., p. 121.

21. His ministry there, Orr tells us, 'was followed up by another gentleman preacher whose open-air work attracted audiences increasing from 100 to 1,000' (Orr, 1949, pp. 62-3).

22. Moody Stuart, 1878, p. 305.

meeting, already in existence, which had been organised by several young female mill-workers, while other fellowship and prayer meetings were also kept up for a considerable time. While conversions were most numerous in Elder's church, other congregations also shared in the blessing, most of which were again touched by a further wave of awakening power that spread through the island the following year (see pp. 322-3).

Elder said he kept short notes regarding sixty-two people who came to converse with him during 1858–9 under some degree of soul concern. Many of these he was unable to trace at the time of writing twenty years later (1878), and some, he knew, had gone back from their impressions, or even 'lapsed into open wickedness'. But a large proportion, he was sure, had turned out well, giving hopeful evidence of saving change. He spoke of attending a few on their deathbeds, being cheered by the hope that they had gone to be with Christ. A good many had moved away from the area, but many others were still on the island and were 'earnest and consistent' members of his congregation, some of them being 'active and earnest workers on the Lord's side'.[23]

Thurso (1858)

North was invited by Sir George Sinclair to visit Thurso during the herring-fishing season, when thousands gathered in the place. Accompanied by 'Gentleman' preacher, Hay Macdowall Grant, North journeyed to the northern town in the autumn of 1858. After Grant's departure, as many as six thousand gathered to hear North one Sunday afternoon, many from 'the educated classes'. The Rev. W. R. Taylor, minister of Thurso's First Free Church, wrote to North in December:

> Since you left, my time has been chiefly occupied with individuals on the state of their souls. Of these, many were impressed or brought to a knowledge of the truth when you and Mr Grant were here. I am thankful to say that the interest in spiritual things is not abating. ... At our communion in the end of October, which was but four months after the preceding one, there were 25 new communicants, of whom about half received the truth when you and Mr Grant were among us. Besides these, several young people who received the truth at the same time did not apply for admission; but I have almost the whole of them, in company with a good many others, under instruction at a Bible-

23. ibid.

class, and I am thankful to see them holding fast, and, so far as I can learn, walking in the truth. A very pleasing change has taken place in a class that used to be rather a careless one here, that of female house-servants. It is interesting to hear these girls tell in their own way the particular manner in which an impression was first made on them.[24]

W. J. Couper spoke of this as a 'minor revival movement'[25] – it certainly acted as a potent precursor to the revival which broke out so quickly on Grant's second visit to Thurso the following year (see pp. 361-2). North also preached in numerous other districts in Caithness during his 1858 visit, including the Free Church of Canisbay, near John o'Groats, served by the Rev. Roderick MacGreggor. Here, around thirty-five names were added to the church roll as a result of the subsequent awakening that moved the parish.[26]

Independent Movement in Shetland (1858)

Of the abundance of revival movements that sprang up all over Scotland during the period 1858–61, one of the few that appears to have arisen independently of the Canada / North America / Ireland stream in 1857–8 is that which showed itself in Dunrossness Baptist chapel, in the south of Shetland in the spring of 1858. The movement came, according to pastor of the church, the Rev. Sinclair Thomson, after four years of 'comparatively few additions to our church'.[27] There began to appear 'some refreshing from his presence' by means of 'symptoms of life among the formerly careless' and 'the appearance of increasing piety and zeal'.[28] Four people were baptised in May 1858, eight in December, ten in January 1859, and another eight in March, making in all thirty, sixteen males and fourteen females.[29]

Thomson provides some interesting details of the awakening: 'We had three backsliders restored also, making 33. None of the number are

24. ibid., p. 300.

25. Couper, p. 131.

26. FCRSM, 1884, p. 18; J. M. Baikie, *Revivals in the Far North*, Wick, n.d., pp. 57-8.

27. Under the faithful ministry of Thomson, the church had previously been recipient of several remarkable seasons of divine blessing, however (see Lennie, 2014, pp. 234-6).

28. BHMS Report, 1858, p. 13.

29. ibid., 1859, pp. 10-11.

fully fifty years of age; the greater number are from twenty to twenty-one. ... We have had a Sabbath-school for the last forty-seven years, the number upon the roll being generally an average of sixty. In the course of three months back it has increased to over 120. Our place of worship is now overcrowded upon the Lord's day, and in fine weather many who come cannot find room. We recognise the present movement here, more immediately as being of God, as we have not resorted to any means which we have not practised for many years. Nor is there the least room left us for human boasting.'[30]

In this latter regard, Thomson spoke of how humbling it was, when conversing with those applying for church membership, to find how few, comparatively, had been brought under spiritual convictions by preaching. Some were struck by hearing some of those recently converted engaging in prayer in a common prayer meeting. Some by a few pithy remarks made by someone during a prayer meeting. Some, again, by the ardent exhortations of a young convert while travelling on the road together; and some by reading the Scriptures, when 'the threatenings of God in his book went to their hearts like daggers'.[31]

By the late spring of 1859 another twenty baptisms had taken place, making an addition of fifty to the church roll within twelve months. Thomson continues: 'This success in one Baptist Church in Shetland is unprecedented. ... The Lord is still doing wonders of mercy in this corner; so we expect soon to have another occasion for baptism. I cannot say the exact number, but they will not be under eight, and the most of them are young men from twenty-two to twenty-seven years of age.'[32] Thomson noted, too, the lack of excitement in the parish, 'with the exception of all the preachers belonging to other places of worship in it holding forth from their pulpits against us, Sabbath after Sabbath in rotation, and some of them repeatedly'.[33] The revival probably died down later in 1859 or during the next year. Certainly it had expired by 1862, for in that year Thomson was 'sorry to say the Lord's work does not appear to be progressing in any corner of this country at present to

---

30. ibid.

31. ibid.

32. ibid., 1860, p. 9.

33. ibid., 1863, p. 11.

any noticeable extent', although 'a few persons occasionally discover the truth which saves, and come forward …'[34] Fascinatingly, another deep and extensive movement was to spread through parts of Shetland just months after Thomson made these remarks (see pp. 417-8).

Aberdeen (1858–59)

Several churches in Aberdeen had initiated additional prayer meetings to their normal weekly routine from 1856 to 1857. Within these meetings a growing desire and expectancy for a move of God's Spirit was fostered. Meanwhile, two daily united prayer gatherings – attracting up to six hundred – met from September 1858.[35] The following month, at the time of the October Communion, 'deep and widespread impressions' resulted from the sermons of the Rev. H. Grattan Guinness, a young evangelist from Dublin, who had been invited to the city by the newly conceived Y.M.C.A.[36] But more than anything, it was the ongoing news stories that appeared in several Christian publications of the spiritual awakening underway in America that helped stimulate Aberdeen believers to pray and believe for a similar outpouring on their own town.

Revival Tide Rises

A definite 'rising tide of blessing' was evident from the very outset of the arrival in the city of evangelist Reginald Radcliffe – a lawyer from Liverpool – in November 1858,[37] coinciding with the start of a two-

---

34. ibid., 1862, p. 11.

35. ibid., p. 56.

36. Matthews, pp. 53, 43-4, 125. The significance of Guinness's labours in Aberdeen at this time was recalled by several witnesses in later years. The editor of the *Glasgow Examiner* wrote: 'Mr Guinness owes not a little to his appearance. He is thin and tall, in the freshness of youth, with a pleasant and expressive countenance … his power consists in great measure in the scripturalness of his preaching. He frequently expounds a chapter or Psalm, and the beautiful words of Scripture, pronounced by his admirable voice, have in themselves a power and fascination which no other words possess' (Introduction to Henry Grattan Guinness, *Preaching for the Million*, London, 1859, p. xxi).

37. Mrs Radcliffe, *Recollections of Reginald Radcliffe*, London, n.d., pp. 36-44; Orr, 1949, p. 59. Although a highly popular preacher, Radcliffe was described as having 'no outward display, not even eloquence', nor 'the intellectual robustness of some of his coadjutors' (W. G. Blaikie, *David Brown: Professor and Principal of the Free Church College*, London, 1898, p. 154).

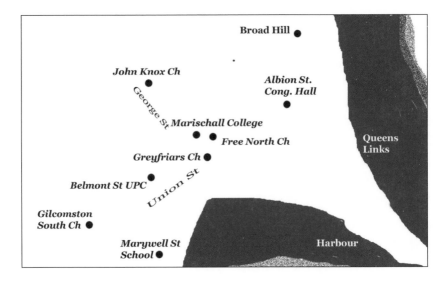

week visit from Brownlow North. 'In the town of his former wickedness, which was most outrageous', North got overcrowded meetings every night; one church being so densely packed that it took the evangelist some five minutes to squeeze his way through the crowd to the pulpit.[38] As for Radcliffe, he had come on a visit of ten days, but ended up staying five months! He spoke initially in a small Congregational hall in Albion Street, where he led services for children.[39] The interest of adults in the awakening was first aroused by the positive changes they observed in their young ones.[40] Thereafter, regular children's meetings were held in Marywell Street School each Monday and Saturday by

---

38. Radcliffe, pp. 38-9.

39. Albion Street Congregational Church had a number of Sunday school classes, and as many as sixty teachers. Pastor of the church, since July 1858, was the Rev. John Duncan. Duncan quickly developed a heavy schedule, preaching thrice on Sabbath, and holding other meetings every night of the week; all this apart from his pastoral work. He also held open-airs on King Street, which drew large crowds. Attendance at church meetings grew in the first few years of his ministry to the extent that the building was enlarged to seat an extra 300 people (James B. Allan, *Rev. John Duncan, D.D., Trinity Congregational Church, Aberdeen: A Memoir and a Tribute*, London, 1909, pp. 58-62). Strangely, Duncan's biographer, while listing a number of preachers who visited his church during his nine-year ministry at Albion Street, makes not a single reference to Radcliffe. Even more remarkably, no direct reference is made to the revival which so affected the city from 1858 to 1860, and which had its beginnings among his own congregation.

40. Radcliffe, p. 60.

Radcliffe, attracting in particular large crowds of boys. Among these a remarkable work was begun, converts being counted by the score. Boys' and girls' prayer meetings sprang up throughout the town, and one man remarked that 'within five minutes' walk from our place of residence, there are no fewer than six different meetings, composed of boys, whose ages vary from ten to fifteen years'. Some groups attracted between twenty and thirty youths and one as many as fifty or sixty.[41] Many of the boys afterwards went into the ministry; some became missionaries, while others became businessmen, and were known for their philanthropic labour.

Before the year end the work had become wider and deeper, and over the next few months dramatic scenes were witnessed, as people came to meetings in droves, especially to Greyfriars Parish Church, around which the revival had now become centred. Minister here was the Rev. James Smith, and great controversy ensued when he threw open his building to Radcliffe, a mere lay preacher. Many church leaders from both within and outwith Aberdeen railed against Smith for such unorthodox practice. Such controversy, of course, only served to increase attendances further.[42] At the height of the movement, as well as holding evening meetings each weeknight, Smith had to hold seven services each Sunday. 'Whenever a congregation dispersed, the waiting multitude without at once poured in and again filled the place.'[43]

This church almost doubled its membership within two years, from 103 in 1857 to 194 in 1859, and Smith, who testified that during these months of revival he 'preached as he had never preached before',[44] also claimed that he had seen more fruits of his ministry in one five or six

---

41. *Times of Refreshing*, quoted in Sprange, p. 169.

42. The opposition, often from evangelical ministers in both the Established and Free Churches, was itself productive of good in that it led to testimonies being printed authenticating the good done through the services of Radcliffe and others. James Smith also spoke before the Church of Scotland Synod, pointing out that Radcliffe 'did not wish to usurp the ministerial office, but simply to address the people on the things belonging to their salvation' (Roberts, 1993, p. 6). These factors, and increasing awareness that the revival was God-breathed, led to the gradual ebbing away of disapproval.

43. John Shearer, *Old Time Revivals: How the Fire of God Spread in Days Now Past and Gone*, Glasgow, 1930, p. 100.

44. M. Gordon, p. 55.

week stretch than in the previous twenty years.[45] He even compared the effects of the revival to those described in connection with the labours of Wesley and Whitefield. Radcliffe recalled one Sabbath at Greyfriars where he spoke to 'three thousand fully, counting about five hundred children'.[46] The gruelling discipline that such incessant activity necessitated, however, led to a breakdown in the Liverpudlian's health in the spring of 1859, which may have been one reason for a waning of revival intensity at that time.

Another church very much at the centre of activity in Aberdeen was the Free North Church, where 'membership increased until the accommodation was quite insufficient'.[47] It was said of the North Church that people were terrified to go to it in case they might get converted. The much-revered pastor here was the Rev. George Campbell, 'a rosy, genial, happy, gracious soul' who 'lived in the joy and in the enlargement of the Gospel'. It is fascinating to note the report from this church exactly forty years later which showed that the effects of the revival were still being felt at that time and that much of the prosperity of the congregation was said to have been due to it.[48]

Prayer and its Effects

In February 1859 Hay Macdowall Grant spoke at a prayer meeting held solely for converts of the awakening, at which about eight hundred were present. Dr David Brown estimated that by May, the converts must have numbered well over one thousand. Duncan Matheson spoke of the widespread nature of the work: 'I never during my life saw more deep

---

45. *The Revivalist*, May 1859, p. 113. It was believed that, during the revival, Smith was probably the first Established Church minister since the Disruption to give an address from a Free Church pulpit.

46. Radcliffe, p. 49. Though there was little trace of the impetus of the revival in the records of Gilcomston Parish Church, 'a day of thanksgiving for the late abundant harvest' was held there on 12 November 1859. Willie Still records that, though not one of the leaders of the revival, the Rev. Dr Macgilvary 'encouraged it as he could'. And the church benefitted, for the Huntly Street building was soon too small for the attendees. James Reid, then assistant minister at Gilcomston, and later minister at Banchory, was well to the fore in the revival and must be given much of the credit for the increase (Francis Lyall and William Still, *History of Gilcomston South Church, Aberdeen, 1868-1968*, Aberdeen, 1968, pp. 13-14).

47. Jeffrey, p. 81.

48. Matthews, Chap 1; FCSRSRM, 1899, p. 17.

concern for souls than I have seen here. … Groups of the young are to be found here and there throughout the whole city, meeting for prayer.'[49]

Prayer, indeed, seems to have been at the heart of the Aberdeen movement. It was in 1859 also that John Gordon, sensing the need for outreach to the upper classes, began a midday prayer meeting in the Mechanics Institute for such a group. These became highly popular, necessitating a move to the larger concert-room of the County Buildings. Meetings followed the pattern of those in New York's Fulton Street, and received a hearty boost with the arrival of two men from the States; one of whom was a Scot who had lived in America for twenty-five years and who saw his church being revived during the 1857–8 revival. In New York he attended the Fulton Street prayer meetings, where he announced his imminent departure for Aberdeen and requested prayer that revival blessing would be poured out on that far-away centre. He was now in the Granite City to witness those prayers being answered.[50]

The revival in Aberdeen was said to have been specially marked in the case of assistants in banks and solicitors' offices, in the numerous drapery and other establishments, and among engineers, joiners, painters, masons, plumbers, boat-builders, shipwrights and coach-builders. 'Scarcely a shop could be found in the whole length of Union Street without at least one young man who had come under the influence of the revival.'[51]

Throughout the summer of 1859 an enormous effort was adopted in order to keep the city movement alive. It was arranged for a series of open-air rallies to be conducted by teams of young preachers all over the city, on street corners, in open squares and parks, and at other strategic positions. These proved most successful, often attracting crowds that numbered many hundreds. George Campbell remarked that 'it was quite uncommon to have less than a thousand people who could be gathered in the thoroughfares listening to the preachers'.[52] Crowds estimated at

---

49. FCSRSRM, 1859, p. 297; John MacPherson, *The Life and Labours of Duncan Matheson: The Scottish Evangelist*, London, 1871, p. 114.

50. Apart from a break of around eighteen months, the daily prayer meeting originated by Gordon was said to be still in operation as late as the mid-1880s. Meanwhile, a week of universal prayer in the first week of every year soon came to be observed in Aberdeen, continuing till at least the end of the century (Blaikie, p. 158).

51. Matthews, p. 48.

52. Jeffrey, pp. 58, 60-1.

over ten thousand also gathered regularly to listen to evangelists on the Broad Hill, representing more than an eighth of the city's population of 75,800 people. Open-air meetings, indeed, were also held regularly at the pierhead, at the Gallowgate and at other locations.

Academic Participation

A number of leading academics in the city took great interest in the awakening, especially the work among students, among whom there was a considerable movement. Principal William Martin, Professor of Moral Philosophy at Marischal College, the Rev. Dr David Brown, Professor of Theology and Principal of Aberdeen Free Church College, and Dr Davidson – described as 'one of the greatest evangelical preachers in Scotland' – all engaged in the work.[53] Large numbers of students went to Greyfriars Church, which was situated at the entrance to Marischal College, to hear Radcliffe speak. Two prayer meetings were held weekly at King's College, while similar meetings were held in Marischal College. One prayer meeting held here was attended by seventy or eighty students. Under Martin's leadership and inspiration, a prayer union was established which in due time strongly influenced other seats of learning. In January 1859 those students who had personal experience of the revival issued letters to scholars of other universities, urging them to live fully for Christ.[54] Many students were also used to spread the movement throughout rural Aberdeenshire. One convert recorded that when the interest spread from the city to the country districts, they began to

---

53. Matthews, pp. 20, 49. W. Robertson Nicoll said that Brown 'was never so happy, never so much at home, as at a revival meeting. ... His conception of Christianity was that of a revival Christianity, and this conception dominated his life' (W. Robertson Nicoll, *Princes of the Church*, London, 1921, pp. 106-7). Brown underwent considerable criticism for his support of lay preachers in the city. Yet he, too, had concerns with the apparent fact that young converts found ordinary church services formal and cold, and deficient in 'social' qualities. He was likewise concerned that 'under the warm play of the emotions at a revival time, there was danger of forgetting the need of accurate knowledge; religion might become a mere matter of feeling instead of the product of a mind and heart united' (John Nicholls, 'The Revival of 1859 in Scotland', *BoT*, Apr. 1985, vol. 259, p. 5).

54. Among the students who were much used in the movement in Aberdeen in these days were Stewart Salmond (later Principal Salmond), George Cassie (later Rev. Cassie of Hopeman UFC), Alexander Whyte (later minister of Free St George's, Edinburgh and a prolific writer) and John Hunter (later minister of Trinity Church, Glasgow).

receive requests to hold services in various places, not least along the main line of the railway to the North. 'Every Saturday afternoon found several of us young men setting out for one of the Northern parishes to address meetings in schoolrooms, workshops, even barns.'[55]

Dr Reith, a student in Aberdeen at that time, reminisced about a fellow-student:

> [He was] detested by the whole class. He had hardly a redeeming feature. He had not a single friend among us, so he parted from us at the end of the session, but not so did he return at the beginning of the following. And the extraordinary rumour soon ran round the class that he was converted; so it really was in God's abounding mercy to him, and the evidences were not far to seek. They were seen in his very gestures and demeanour. They were seen in his face. I could hardly believe it, and felt inclined to agree with the sceptics, who didn't need a revival, that he was acting the part of a hypocrite for a change; but there was no hypocrisy in his prayer at the first students' weekly meeting I attended that session. What a prayer! Mount Sinai shaken to pieces, and pouring forth supplications with strong crying and tears; that was his prayer. And there was no hypocrisy in his subsequent life.[56]

A number of laymen in the city also took an active part in the movement, and opened their houses to young converts, encouraging them to pray, and giving advice and biblical instructions. Two such figures were William Smith, tea-merchant, and R. B. Tytler, retired tea-planter. More popular still was Alexander Brand, a chartered accountant from Dee Street. Frequently, inquirers would walk nearly a mile from where Radcliffe was preaching to Brand's house. Sometimes, 'every room in the house was full of anxious souls, many of them deeply distressed and weeping bitterly; you could hear their sobbing all over the room. In that house many passed from death unto life'.[57] Also popular was the Sabbath school established by William Rait, a school teacher and an elder in the Bon Accord Church of Scotland. On the outskirts of Aberdeen, Mr Buchan of Auchmacoy was well known for holding evangelistic services near his home and at Woodside.

---

55. Matthews, p. 37.

56. ibid., p. 33.

57. ibid., pp. 4, 118.

Evaluation

Jeffrey draws a number of revealing insights from his detailed research on the revival in Aberdeen. The movement was co-ordinated chiefly by laymen, particularly members of the local fledgling Y.M.C.A. The spectacle of a layman preaching no doubt accounted for some of the popularity of the revival, but it also provoked opposition from a considerable proportion of the city's clergymen and/or church elders. Interestingly, the Psalms were predominantly used in services, rather than the many popular new hymns that were circulating elsewhere. Apart from this aspect, the revival in Aberdeen appears to have been very much a modern religious movement along Finney-ite lines.[58]

Jeffrey's studies reveal that only eighteen of Aberdeen's fifty-four churches (around a third)[59] were influenced by the revival.[60] This figure comprised five of the city's eleven Established Churches, and seven of the seventeen Free Churches. Jeffrey also discovered that twelve of the seventeen churches identified were less than thirty years old in 1859, and, additionally, that eight of the ministers of these churches who were successfully identified were between thirty-one and forty-two years old when the movement began. They were all in their first charge and had less than twelve years' experience of parish ministry. Indeed, three of them had been ordained for less than a year when the movement began. Jeffrey notes: 'This suggests strongly that the revival prospered under the leadership of young men who entered the ministry after the struggles of the Disruption

58. Jeffrey, pp. 61-70. Jeffrey in fact suggests that 'upon closer inspection it appears that this revival had embraced even more advanced techniques of evangelism' than those taught by Finney.

59. ibid., p. 77. The author identified all but one of these. They were Greyfriars, Holburn, John Knox and Woodside Parish Churches, the Bon Accord, East, Holburn, Newhills, North, South and West Free Churches, Belmont Street and St Nicholas Lane United Presbyterian Churches, Albion Street and George Street Congregational Churches, St Paul's Evangelical Union Church and Union Terrace Baptist Church. Methodists in the city had little participation in the movement.

60. Jeffrey makes this deduction largely from a report in the *British Evangelical* in May 1859, stating that 'out of about fifty-four churches and chapels which the city and its suburbs contain, the doors of about eighteen have been thrown open to them, and five of these belong to the National Church' (p. 77). Jeffrey does not state, however, who specifically these doors were being thrown open to. Given that revival in the city continued throughout much of 1860, there is also the possibility that some churches may have become affected by the revival only after May 1859.

years and who had been educated from the late 1840s when urban mission was becoming increasingly important in the life of the church.'[61]

Analysing the composition of those affected by the revival, Jeffrey discovered that among those whose religious background is known, more than two-thirds became new church members without the influence of another family member, suggesting that the impulses of this revival were operating 'outwith the accustomed channels, and that converts had been successfully targeted by the leaders of the movement'.[62] He also found that most revival converts came from the wealthier districts of Aberdeen, such as the West, South and East Parishes. Poorer districts were notably less affected. The revival also prospered among the skilled working class, two-thirds of which consisted of men. This group constituted a third of all those who joined churches in Aberdeen during this period, while unskilled working women made up another third. These groups largely comprised domestic servants and, especially, mill workers, the latter constituting a particularly close-knit, homogenous group. Most of the new church members were either unmarried girls between the ages of fifteen and twenty, or married men in their twenties and thirties. Although most converts were unmarried, a higher percentage of married people was revealed than in previous revivals (such as Cambuslang in 1742, where almost three quarters of those whose marital status could be determined were unmarried). Also, the revival attracted a disproportionate number of young men – around 50 per cent – in contrast to many other revivals, where 'women have usually accounted for between at least sixty and seventy per cent of revival converts'.[63] This suggests that the targeting of males undertaken by the organisers of the movement was highly successful.

Rural Aberdeenshire (1858–59)

Meanwhile, in the Huntly district of rural Aberdeenshire, the Duchess of Gordon spoke of holding special cottage prayer meetings 'for the outpouring of the Spirit' from the spring of 1858. Writing at the beginning of May that year, she said: 'We had three last week, besides

---

61. ibid., pp. 85-6.

62. ibid., p. 87.

63. ibid., pp. 95, 103.

the Wednesday prayer-meeting at the church.' At her Huntly Lodge in January 1859, a meeting of ministers was held, 'of a very searching and quickening character'. The ministers present were touched deeply and resolved to seek a closer walk with God for themselves, and to strive for an awakening in their congregations. They held similar meetings at the Lodge frequently during the year, 'and in every one of their congregations some shower of blessing fell'.[64]

Moody Stuart wrote that early in the year 1859, 'The Duchess's heart was filled to overflowing with gratitude for a remarkable work of the Lord in Huntly, in her own house and in her schools.' 'Jesus is all their cry', noted the Duchess. One young mother cried out, 'Siccan a bargain as the Lord has made wi' me. He's ta'en my son, and He's gien me His ain Son.' On March 26, 1859, the Duchess wrote:

> The work is going on, giving great joy and hope to all who desire the glory of God … the young converts are really new creatures. The giddy and vain have become thoughtful, happy, unselfish; the naughty and sulky have become happy and obedient. Old men and women, and many young men, continue to attend the prayer-meetings. There is a great movement in Drumblade parish; hardly a cottage of any size that has not a prayer-meeting in the week for fifteen or sixteen among themselves.[65]

In Huntly itself, the Duchess delighted in the fact that 'almost every day we hear of a new case of deep conviction and conversion among my people, or the young at the schools, or others'.[66] By July 1859 the Rev. Williamson of Huntly Free Church could report: 'The desire to pray seems somewhat remarkable. I can scarcely tell you the number of prayer meetings. In my own congregation alone, about six prayer-meetings among the young men, about the same number among the boys, say from ten to fourteen

---

64. Rev. A. Moody Stuart, *Life and Letters of Elizabeth, Last Duchess of Gordon*, London, 1865, p. 360.

65. ibid., pp. 361-2.

66. ibid., p. 362. In January 1860 there was a much larger conference than that of the preceding year, and drawn from a far wider circle. Twenty-four ministers slept at the Lodge, some also staying at the manse, while those from the immediate neighbourhood returned home. At a public meeting in the church in the evening, they gave 'deeply interesting and most remarkable accounts' of the work of the Lord that had taken place in their various districts (pp. 362-3).

years of age, three or four among the girls and some among the young women. The thirst for prayer is wonderful.'[67] In some other rural areas, too, revival began in the spring of 1859, as it did in Banchory, the week after the May Communion. The Rev. Robert Reid of the Free Church said that for several years the sacrament had been 'a very solemn season to their souls'. The first conversion was that of a boy of fourteen.

Here and elsewhere, the movement seems to have abated during the summer, before resuming with greater effect in the autumn (see Chapter 11). It is apparent also that the rural revival that arose during the winter of 1858 and spring of 1859 was confined to certain districts of Aberdeenshire. It did not spread outwith the region. When a deputation from Aberdeen visited Dundee in the spring of 1859, holding revival meetings under the leadership of William Patterson, spiritual awakening was not ignited, although a number of conversions were reported among the young.

---

67. Jeffrey, p. 120.

Glasgow Bridge

Rare photo of Glasgow Wynds, 1860s

Alexander Somerville

Gordon Forlong and his wife

Phoebe Palmer

CHAPTER 4

Revival Breakout: Glasgow

It was in fact news of the dramatic progress of the revival in Ulster, rather than events in Aberdeenshire, that helped spark off revival movements in the south-west of Scotland. Indeed, it was remarked that the revival spread from Ireland just as cholera would have come, crossing the Irish Sea at its narrowest point and appearing first in this south-west region.[1] Revival appears to have broken out almost simultaneously in the summer of 1859 in Glasgow,[2] Renfrewshire,[3] Ayrshire,[4] Kintyre[5] and Galloway,[6] before quickly diffusing across the whole of the country.

The above references each seem to suggest that revival in Scotland began in the particular location specified! Every reporter seemed to want their readers to believe that revival first broke out in their home district.

---

1. Professor Miller, quoted in Moody Stuart, 1878, p. 279.

2. Roberts, 1995, p. 292; Orr, 1949, pp. 60-2. The revival in Glasgow began in the Wynd Mission, according to *The Scottish Guardian*. Indeed, 'or a time it scarcely went beyond that spot...unbelief kept it from other quarters' (*SG*, 21/03/1860).

3. Moody Stuart, 1878, p. 280.

4. One writer claims that the revival was 'begun in Ayrshire through the preaching of Mr Sillars, a Free Church student, and within a few weeks made itself felt in every part of the country' (Arthur Guthrie, *Robertson of Irvine: Poet-Preacher*, PFCSH&I, Ardrossan, 1889, p. 155).

5. Particularly in Campbeltown, where people began showing anxiety about spiritual matters on hearing of the revival in Portrush, Ulster, just three hours sail away (PFCSH&I, 1861, p. 307; Orr, 1949, p. 66).

6. 'The 1859-61 revivals began in Galloway, and then affected Glasgow, spreading out to reach all Perth-shire and the north-east from the Moray Firth to the Firth of Tay' (D. W. Bebbington, *The Baptists in Scotland*, Glasgow, 1988, p. 54).

Another report states that the region around Pitcaple, Aberdeenshire, 'was the scene of the earliest of the showers' of the 1859–61 revival in Scotland. Meanwhile, John Macpherson states that the work began 'at least in its more striking manifestations in the fishing village of Ferryden', while from official returns from ministers across the country, the Free Church suggested that the mining population along with the fishing villages of the east coast were the first to show the effects of the movement.[7] Being the most populous city in Scotland, and given the widespread nature and intensity of revival activity that took place there, I make Glasgow the historical start-point of our study of the '59 revival.

Beginnings

In the months prior to the outbreak of revival in Glasgow, the general economic and social conditions of the city matched that of the nation as a whole (see Chapter 2), except that widespread poverty persisted in some areas. Considerable interest had existed amongst Glasgow evangelicals in the promotion of revivals from the 1820s onwards. Reports of awakenings in America were matters of particular interest. In 1828, the Glasgow Evangelical Corresponding Society was formed, and a special committee composed of three ministers published accounts sent by Presbyterian ministers and missionaries of outbreaks of revival in New World communities.[8]

Spurred by a fresh stream of intelligence reporting spiritual awakening across America, revival prayer meetings emerged in various churches in Glasgow from September 1858. These increased in number and size in subsequent months. The quantity of revival intelligence also gradually increased, especially, from the spring of 1859, that from Ulster. Yet, despite signs of encouragement, the multitudes were not responding. After the busy months of the second quarter of the year during which local churchmen attended biannual synods and annual assemblies as well as the monthly Presbytery meetings, all in addition to

---

7. *The Revival*, 17/05/1861, p. 271; Macpherson, 1871, p. 113; FCSRSRM, 1861, pp. 5-6, repeated in Callum Graham Brown, *Religion and the Development of an Urban Society: Glasgow 1780–1914*, Unpublished Ph.D. thesis, University of Glasgow, 1981, vol. 1, p. 774.

8. In the words of Callum Brown, 'the experience of expatriate Scottish ministers seems to have been crucial to the cultivation of Scottish Presbyterian support for revivals' (Brown, 1981, p. 419).

their usual commitments, many made the journey to Ulster to observe the revival there in progress. Coincidentally there was an increase in open-air revival preaching on Glasgow Green, and it was here, as well as in a few churches, that, in July 1859, deep distress and physical manifestations began to be observed among the anxious.

John Horner, a hardware merchant from Coleraine, crossed the Irish Sea to share with his Scottish brethren what he had witnessed of the revival in that town. He spoke at meetings in the Religious Institution Rooms (RIR), and later, in the Wynd Free Church on Sunday, July 24. As he shared detailed accounts of his own experiences of the revival, scores of people were, according to *The Scottish Guardian*, left 'in great distress. … Many were seen weeping … between fifty and eighty remained, when an invitation was given to anxious souls … some found peace. … In the case of those individuals … conviction was not produced for the first time on the evening in question. The parties had for the most part been long anxious about their souls, and gladly embraced this opportunity of unbosoming their minds.'[9] The Rev. Taylor of the Wynd Mission quickly appointed a meeting for anxious enquirers.

This account was largely confirmed in a report presented by Taylor two days later in the Religious Institution Rooms. 'Matters did not come to what appeared to be a crisis till last Sabbath (24th July)', he remarked. 'On the evening of that day, Mr Horner … addressed our … meeting, which was attended chiefly by the mission people, but also by a number of the regular congregation. The meeting was largely attended … and the address of Mr Horner must have taken effect … about sixty persons waited behind. … A similar opportunity was given to inquirers last night (Monday 25th July). I saw that the people were evidently deeply affected …'[10] After weeks and months of anticipation, revival in Glasgow had begun.

By the beginning of August, midday daily meetings were being held in the Religious Institution Rooms, which immediately became so popular that a second daily meeting was opened in another part of the building. Within a few days, this too was overcrowded, and recourse was made to the Trades Hall as a second venue. Soon evening meetings

9. *SG*, 26/07/1859.

10. Marrs, pp. 224-5.

were being held in these buildings too. On 11 August a meeting was held in the 3,400-seater City Hall, which was densely crowded for the occasion. Wednesday evening meetings were also early begun in the Mechanics' Hall on Canning Street, and these, too, quickly grew. During August, also, attendance at Sunday open-air meetings on Glasgow Green increased from hundreds to thousands.

Wynds Mission

The Wynds were located in south-central Glasgow, north of the river Clyde, and close to the Merchant city. The area consisted of 'long, narrow, filthy, airless lanes, with every available inch of ground on each side occupied with buildings, many of them far gone, yet packed from cellar to garret with human life'.[11] A Free Church had been established there as recently as 1854, with the aim of reaching out to the masses of impoverished families who inhabited the district, many of them of Irish extract. The area was quickly impacted by revival following a visit to Ulster by the Rev. Dugald MacColl, pastor of the church. Initially the meetings were mainly attended by folk from the immediate vicinity. 'The revival made no revolution on our methods of work', commented MacColl. 'We did not need new truth. ... We did not need new songs. ... Our weekly meeting for prayer became nightly; a second meeting was required when the first was closed; soon a third, and often a fourth. ... The sound as of the mighty rushing wind brought multitudes about us.'[12]

At times a dozen denominations were represented at meetings. 'We became ingenious at packing. ... Pew and passage became one solid mass', continued MacColl. 'Through it all, we still continued to give the first place to the poor of the district, especially on the Sabbath evening.' He added that although many ministers came with suspicion and scorn, 'we were happily ignorant of the critical eyes and ears, and had so little in reality to do with the work going on, ... that we were kept throughout in perfect peace as to all the conflicting views that for the first four months were taken outside.'[13]

---

11. Dugald MacColl, *Among the Masses: or, Work in the Wynds*, Glasgow, 1867, p. 23.

12. ibid., pp. 257-307.

13. ibid., pp 307-9.

Aided by *The Wynd Journal*, which gained a wide influence, the Wynd church became a centre of revival, not only in Glasgow, but throughout Scotland. Requests poured into the church to pray for specific congregations and individuals, who were especially seeking blessing. Dozens of these petitions might be read out at one single service and presented before 'the throne of grace'. By October, the Wynd church was holding around thirty other meetings throughout the district each week. In the main church itself, all rooms were fully occupied every weekday night and on Sundays from 9 a.m. till 10 p.m. or later, almost without intermission.

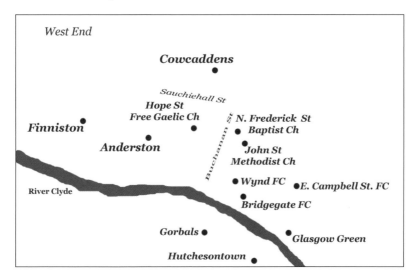

About the beginning of November 1859 it was apparent to the leadership of the Wynd church that 'the Spirit of God seemed about to be withdrawn'. Among the many who resolved to pray for this pioneering church was a group of working girls from Port Glasgow, who had been greatly impressed by reports they had heard of the work going on in that Glasgow mission. Much was their delight when their pastor, the Rev. John Duncan, reported, on his return from a visit to the Wynd church in mid-December, that he had there beheld a fresh and 'remarkable outpouring of the Spirit'.[14]

Converts were much encouraged to share their own individual experiences at church meetings but were kept under a degree of restraint; it being felt that if they deviated from simple testimony towards public

---

14. *WJ*, 24/12/1859, p. 99.

exhortation, as many sought to do, they were in danger of making misleading and even erroneous statements on doctrinal matters.

Though the Wynds district was one of the very first touched by revival in Glasgow, soon many other localities in the city were also in the throes of revival. H. M. MacGill reports a congregation other than the Wynd Church admitting 170 to its membership roll by the end of summer 1860.[15] Just a few Sabbaths after the Wynds work began, MacColl preached by request to another congregation of Glasgow. 'I came to know of nearly thirty persons awakened that morning', he observed. In addition, MacColl developed 'a large list of places', mainly work premises, where he was invited to speak, in every one of which, he believed, 'some measure of awakening ... was experienced' (see p. 68).[16]

Anderston

Prayer meetings became more numerous in Anderston Free Church throughout the 1850s, notably in 1852 (pre-Sabbath morning service), 1855 (between Sunday services) and 1858 (Wednesday lunchtime, for businessmen). Public prayer in fact reached a high in 1858 for at one point in that year it was recorded that 'the prayer-meeting held on the evening of Tuesday was filled to overflowing', and that the Wednesday lunchtime gathering attracted around 250 businessmen. Accordingly, yet another prayer meeting was begun on Thursday evenings. These were soon reported as being 'remarkable for the number of requests handed in'.[17]

By the summer of 1859 a Friday evening prayer meeting and a young men's meeting were added to the already impressive rota. By this time also, Alexander Somerville, minister of the Anderston church (who had been kept regularly informed of the American awakening by a friend in New York) had gone over to Ireland with a son to visit scenes of revival in the main centres of Belfast, Ballymena and Coleraine. He brought home to Glasgow glowing reports of the Ulster movement.

Revival proper seems to have commenced towards the close of August 1859, with a woman from the Anderston district, who, hearing news of the convicting power of God spreading through Ireland, became so

---

15. *On the Present Revival of Religion in Scotland: A paper read at the Annual Conference of the Evangelical Alliance in October 1860 at Nottingham*, London, 1860, p. 11.

16. MacColl, pp. 264-5, 288-9.

17. *SG*, 02/09/1859.

distressed about her own condition that she wakened her neighbours with her cries. Said Somerville, 'The circumstance had greater effect upon those who stayed near my church than the ringing of my church bell and all the influences connected with it for the last ten years.'[18] For, as a consequence of this one case, several other instances of deep awakening occurred. Indeed, these were now happening on an almost daily basis, so that the number of prayer meetings was increased still further, with the addition of one every night, including Sundays, from eight till nine o'clock. These meetings attracted between four and five hundred people, and at their close another was commenced to specifically deal with those anxious about their souls.

By this time, the church and its halls were open for meetings every night, and remarkably, these continued for eleven months without intermission. The meetings, which frequently began in the open air outside the church, were diversified by a variety of speakers each night. Additionally, church leaders would regularly address workers in their places of employment.[19] By means of the revival a great quickening came to the church's office bearers and helpers as well as to many hundreds within the congregation, not to mention many scores of visitors.

From that centre the movement spread out in various directions through the city and country, and a great amount of permanent fruit was reaped. By the beginning of 1860 the number of people 'under concern' and who had been spoken to totalled 234; by March it had risen to 320 with the figure still rising. Nor were the revival's effects quick to subside. The prayer-meetings remained as numerous and as strong as ever until 1861. There were twenty-two altogether, with a total attendance of 500, and all but three were the result of the movement. Most converts were established in their faith and tenderly nurtured in the Word of God by their leaders. Three other important influences of the revival were the church's crusade against public houses, care for 'fallen women' and the organising of a large team of workers to visit needy districts of town, leaving tracts and inviting the non-churched

---

18. ibid.

19. These comprised twice-weekly talks to females employed in the Lancefield Factory and weekly messages to men at the Vulcan Factory at specified times (usually for around half-an-hour), as well as addresses to workers at the Bishop Street Factory.

to meetings in the Anderston church. So marked was the latter mission that it only subsided when its work was exhausted (about 1865).[20]

Finnieston

Andrew Bonar had recently been installed as Free Church minister in the Finnieston district of Glasgow (December 1856), and at the first opportunity journeyed to see the revival in Ireland, from where he 'hurried across the water and brought the flame back to Scotland'.[21] The work in Finnieston seems to have commenced among the children, for at one Sabbath evening prayer meeting, 'a great number of Sabbath scholars waited behind to speak; six of them in bitter distress'. Then, such was the blessing attending the Thursday of the autumn Communion that Bonar felt 'once or twice … very singularly carried away as into the near presence of my Lord, and filled with hope and expectation of blessing'. Yet, while writing of this season of 'refreshing showers' in November 1859, Bonar could state that 'no week has passed since the beginning of September without awakened souls coming inquiring as to the way of salvation'.[22] Nevertheless he also noted in his diary a month later that 'as yet we have had only drops' and expressed his longing in the coming year to 'have the Spirit among us working wonderfully as in … other places' (such as Saltcoats and Ferryden, both of which the Finnieston pastor had visited, having observed in each place stirring revival scenes).[23]

Bonar's hopes for more abundant showers upon his own congregation in 1860 do not seem to have been fulfilled. The first few months of the New Year saw his son James seriously ill with scarlet fever, and also witnessed the death of his dear son Andrew. No more is heard of revival in Bonar's church during this period. And yet a work of spiritual awakening was clearly in operation. For some time later, when Bonar was asked to write a report on the revival among his congregation, the minister was able to say:

---

20. In time it was bringing out eighty families a month, with as many as 1,400 families sometimes being visited in a single month.

21. *DSCHT*, p. 84.

22. Marjory Bonar, *Andrew A. Bonar: Diary and Life*, Edinburgh, 1893 (reprinted 1961), pp. 195, 197; *SG*, 29/11/1859.

23. Bonar, 1893, p. 198.

The population of the (Finnieston) district is about 4,000, and we are able to point to dwellings in every part of it in which some soul has been born again, so far as man can judge. In the two streets nearest our church we know of fifty persons at least, regarding whom there is reason to believe that they have passed from death to life during the last three years. Last summer it was the Bible lesson in the day school that seemed to be specially owned of God to the conversion of six or seven, and to the awakening of many more. One marked case of conversion resulted from discipline in the session. Some cases of apparent and satisfactory awakening have occurred in connection with the visits of elders.[24]

Cowcaddens

Much prayer had been made on behalf of Cowcaddens, a district in north Glasgow, not least by 'a little company of householders' from that district: 'a cabman, an iron-founder, a stonemason and his wife, and another young married woman, who have lately begun to follow Jesus'. Indeed, beginnings of a movement in Cowcaddens Free Church were intimated as early as September 1859.[25] The Rev. Stevenson of Rutherglen – in the absence of pastor McGill – had been speaking to a gathering of mill-girls in Grove Street Rooms of the revival he had witnessed in Ireland. Even after he left for home, the girls did not leave, but remained behind to pray, and as they prayed, 'a great power came upon them'. Numbers began to cry and to weep for their sins, until the whole meeting was affected. The older girls leading the meeting, not knowing how to handle the situation, called for church leaders to come and assist. One who came 'saw the grace of God and was glad'. Indeed, he called it 'the most remarkable night ever this district saw'. At breakfast time next morning the same minister went to the area to preach in the open air. He was invited into the silk mill, where some of the girls he had spoken with the previous evening worked. He held 'a most solemn meeting in the dye-house, which was the beginning of many a precious time in that factory, and of meetings which were held in it for years afterwards'.[26]

---

24. *Blue Book*, 1861, p. 98, quoted in Thomas Brown, A*nnals of the Disruption*, Edinburgh, 1893, p. 779.

25. *SG*, 13/09/1859.

26. Daniel R. Kilpatrick, *The Religious History of Cowcaddens*, Glasgow, 1867, pp. 17-18.

A similar work began among prayer groups in both Silk Mill Land and Kelvin Street. One keen evangelist gave the following striking testimony:

> The work thus begun was carried on for about three years. ... One thing was very remarkable: we felt that everything must give way to the one object – the conversion of souls to Christ. We felt that we had not time for anything else. Eternity seemed very near. The glory of God, the love of Christ, the great salvation – how real they were then felt to be. Every living and Christ-loving soul was compelled to speak. They could not contain themselves, and speak they did, especially those recently converted, everywhere with new fervour and power. The minister in the pulpit preached Christ as if every word he spoke might save a soul – the elder among his people – the Sabbath School teacher in his class – all felt the need of direct and personal dealing, and (strange it seemed at the time) every one appeared to expect it. Even the godless bore to be spoken to in private, and listened with strange earnestness. They evidently felt that the grip of power was upon their hearts. Our collateral and semi-secular work, although not abandoned altogether, seemed to have lost its interest ... we felt as if it were almost a waste of time to speak of anything but Christ. Prayer meetings accordingly sprung up in almost every public work in the district. ... Some of these meetings continue to this day (several years later), and others, after being for a time suspended, are again revived ...[27]

The effect of the movement among children was said to be 'especially remarkable'. It was deemed appropriate to hold a prayer meeting for Sabbath-school pupils in church. Over two hundred attended, though only one leader. Soon a boy started weeping. Going over to investigate, the Rev. Kilpatrick found about eight boys in tears, each preoccupied with his own state. Soon, he noted, 'the whole church was a scene of weeping. ... God dealt powerfully that night'. One lad who was not from the school but who had been invited to the meeting by a pal, broke out in a prayer which 'seemed to rend the very heavens. Where did he get it? Such simple eloquence, such pleading fervour! It was the presence of God. That was the time of his conversion, and he found Christ his Saviour that night; and not he alone, but many more, I have

---

27. ibid., pp. 18-19.

reason to believe, were gathered by the Great Shepherd's arm.' For several months afterwards these meetings continued, and the good they effected was still observable years later. Looking back on the movement after a number of years, Kilpatrick, while aware of some elements which he disapproved of, nevertheless saw the Cowcaddens revival as 'a joyous spring-time of spiritual blessing' which he was absolutely certain 'nothing but divine power and grace … could accomplish'.[28]

Other Churches

The Rev. Jacob Alexander of Stockwell Free Church had paid a visit to Ireland, and on his return to his Glasgow church in mid-August, 'a great number remained in distress after hearing rousing accounts of his adventures and after he vividly described the awful doom … which awakened the impenitent'.[29] Meanwhile, since his translation as Church of Scotland minister from Errol to the recently formed Park Church congregation in Glasgow in December 1857, John Caird had attracted large audiences. During the revival period he began special meetings in his church, which 'was crammed from the hour it first opened its doors. Crowds waited in queues outside it and were thankful to obtain standing room in the packed and congested aisles.'[30]

'A great scene' was reported from North Frederick Street Baptist Church, on Thursday, 18 August. 'Men and women, young and old … were very painfully convinced of sin, and the fast-flowing tears, the heaving sighing and the earnest though not boisterous crying for mercy which could no longer be concealed plainly indicated that God was pouring out His Spirit.' Recorded pastor John Williams the next day: 'Out of a great number who felt deeply what sin was, ten to twelve had found peace this morning in Jesus.' The movement here was boosted by open-air meetings – led by Williams and other men in the church – which drew many. These took place every night throughout the autumn and winter on Dempster Street and Little Hamilton Street.[31]

---

28. ibid., pp. 19-20.

29. Marrs, p. 225.

30. Bussey, p. 97. Caird was appointed Professor of Divinity at Glasgow University in 1862.

31. *SG*, 23/08/1859; Marrs, pp. 226-7.

The Rev. Archibald MacDougall of Argyle Free Gaelic Church spent nearly four weeks in Ireland, and his account of the revival there left a deep and increasing impression on his home congregation. He wrote: 'There have been many signs of a gracious reviving work in this congregation, (which) in general is marvellously stirred up, so that fresh vigorous life and anxiety are everywhere visible. Prayer meetings have been multiplied and are numerously attended. ... Evidently the Holy Spirit is leading souls to Jesus.' This was by far the greatest blessing during the entire period of MacDougall's ministry in the Argyle Church, which stretched from 1843 to 1874.[32]

Duncan MacGregor was called from Stornoway Free Church to Glasgow's Hope Street Free Gaelic Church in 1854. 'His energy knew no bounds and in a short space of time he revitalised' the church.[33] When revival came, as many as a thousand people were known to attend a Sabbath evening prayer meeting. When the cries of one woman caused some excitement in the congregation, the minister at once asked them to compose themselves then resumed his discourse, without further disruption. Despite such outward expressions of emotion being dissuaded, MacGregor could later record that during this period, 'especially in 1859 and 1860, hardly a week passed and often hardly a day but someone came to me with the cry of the three thousand, "What shall we do?" It was a Pentecost time.'[34]

After a slow beginning, the work of revival proceeded with 'great vigour' in East Campbell Street Free Church. Wrote the minister, 'within the last eight days, we have had no fewer than thirty new cases of conviction, and almost all of them have found peace. ... It is a remarkable circumstance that all ... were stricken down, and that all thus affected professed actually to see Christ before they found peace ... last night the number of new cases was eight ...' Yet, 'all was quiet, but deeply so! There was not a word or tone calculated to lead to excited feelings.'

---

32. *SG*, 23/09/1859; Tribute to MacDougall recorded in Argyle Church Kirk Session Minutes, 6 June 1883, in Ian R. Macdonald, *Glasgow's Gaelic Churches: Highland Religion in an Urban Setting 1690–1995*, Edinburgh, 1995, p. 42.

33. In addition he applied his energies to the work of church extension to such effect that he built and established another church – the MacDonald Memorial Church.

34. *SG*, 06/09/1859; Duncan MacGregor, *Memorial of Sabbath Evenings in Hope Street Church*, Glasgow, 1864, p. 2, quoted in Macdonald, 1995, pp. 36-7.

Still, the minister saw 'six persons ... struck down and carried out to the school-house'. Two weeks later there were still several cases of 'striking down' at each meeting.[35] Meanwhile, in East Miller Street Mission Station, eight were stricken down during a prayer meeting.

Among numerous other places in the city, the Gorbals area was also 'very much revived' at this time. The East Gorbals Free Church Mission opened a Sunday school, to which only a few children came, they being regarded by the Mission's superintendent as, 'very ignorant, unruly and ungodly ... our scholars were given to swearing, lying, quarrelling and fighting with each other'. The leaders resorted to much prayer, while the church missionary visited Ardrossan and brought back an exciting account of the revival in progress there. The following Sunday, 'a few were seen in tears, and some were crying out aloud. It seemed as if the Holy Spirit had shed a life of sin in the space of a few minutes. Casting themselves wholly upon Christ, many found peace in believing, and went away with hearts overflowing with joy.' In ensuing days many parents and neighbours were awakened through the witness of their children, while attendance at the Sunday school increased considerably, due to those awakened bringing their comrades along. 'Since the movement began', explained the superintendent, 'there have been cases of conviction every night, one night as many as 24.'[36] The movement eventually subsided, but received a fresh impetus a year later, when it could be said that 'during the last two months God has again dispensed a shower from on high'. Revival also affected Chalmers Free Church on Govan Street 'in a very mixed and gratifying manner'.[37]

A 'great work' was done in Glasgow's Free St George's Mission Church. One development was a Sabbath evening meeting 'for those who do not have proper clothes to attend church during the day', although the meeting was not confined to such. It was conducted as a prayer meeting and attracted over three hundred. Many other churches and institutions in Glasgow were moved by the revival and held special meetings. These included Great Hamilton Street Congregational Church, Hutchesontown

---

35. *SG*, 26/08/1859.

36. Proceedings of United Presbyterian Church Synod 1862, p. 624; William Reid, *Authentic Records of Revival*, London, 1860 (reprinted 1980), pp. 266-72.

37. *Blue Book*, 1861, quoted in Bussey, p. 96; *SG*, 23/09/1859.

U. P. Mission, Chalmers Free Church (Govan Street), St Luke's Free Church (Calton), Kingston Free Church and Wellington Street UPC.[38]

It was reported that 'the districts occupied by the Glasgow City Mission are partakers in the gracious movement'; this largely by means of the reading of and exhorting from God's word and by faithfully dealing with people in their own homes. The work extended to all districts, 'passing throughout the city from East to West'.[39] The fact that there were fifty-seven missionaries working with the Mission gives evidence to the wide extent of ground covered and the penetrating influence of the revival movement.

A number of British evangelists pertaining to Brethren principles preached in Glasgow during the time of the revival, including Harry Moorhouse, Russell Hurditch, John Vine and Harrison Ord. Best known of all was Gordon Forlong, who hired a large canvas tent at the foot of Saltmarket Street, normally used during the Glasgow Fair week as a circus for performing horses. This location became the birthplace of many souls, and, along with operations elsewhere in the city, marked the foundation of Brethren beginnings in Glasgow.[40]

Revival in the Workplace

During October 1859 the movement continued to expand, mainly through the proliferation of revival gatherings held at places of employment. Thus it was that business establishments often became the centre of religious activity. Railway depots and stations were particularly popular because of the shift-work pattern of railway workers, who were unable to get to church services on a regular basis. For example, at Eglington Street station, a weekly meeting was held from October, attracting around fifty workers each time. In addition, churches near these locations sometimes started special revival meetings.

Dugald MacColl wrote that the 'work in workshops was one of the extraordinary and long continued effects of the revival. Daily prayer-meetings were commenced, sometimes at the breakfast, sometimes at

---

38. *SG*, 23/02/1860, 24/03/1860, 23/09/1859.

39. *SG*, 02/09/1859.

40. Not only in Glasgow, but in many places throughout Scotland, Open Brethren assemblies were the product of the revival of 1859 (Ian McDowell, *Rice Thomas Hopkins 1842–1916: An Open Brother*, unpublished paper, p. 2).

the dinner hour, in warehouses, factories, foundries, sawpits, dockyards, bakeries, smithshops, and other unlikely places. I have taken part in a prayer-meeting where at least seven hundred factory girls were present – one of the partners presiding.'[41] MacColl gave an example of how one workplace meeting started:

> One evening at our second meeting, while some friend was speaking, I went into the vestry to see some person that had been carried out. In a few minutes I heard an extraordinary uproar; and when I got back to the church I found the whole meeting in the greatest confusion, standing on the seats, and pressing towards one corner where two young men were roaring like bulls of Bashan. I first quieted the meeting by inducing them to take their seats and sing; and then I got at the young men – two apprentice carpenters, strong of limb and lung, who were then in the greatest agony, seeing, as it seemed to them, hell itself blazing at their feet. Some weeks after they found peace. One went to school, and by and bye to college, and is now preparing to enter the ministry; having already in several mission fields proved himself a worthy man that need not to be ashamed. ... The other went back to the shipyard, and proposed to the men to have a daily prayer-meeting. They at once seized him by neck and heels, held him over the ship's side and asked him, 'Do you want a ducking?' 'No', he said, half choked, and they set him on his feet. And then shaking himself into something like an ordinary state of mind and habits, he added, 'But I want a prayer-meeting!' And the prayer-meeting he got. The last time I was present, more than three years after it was started, more than three hundred were present, and I was told that then sixteen at least could take part publicly in prayer.[42]

As noted above, silk spinners at the Old Basin in north Cowcaddens held a prayer meeting every morning in their workplace, which three hundred – mainly women – attended. Similar meetings took place in some mills in the East End of the city.[43] Meetings were begun at Kingston Saw Mills three days per week, being 'attended by all the men except ... the Roman Catholics'. In a large mill and bleaching green on the Clyde, the work of revival was described as being 'extensive' under

---

41. MacColl, p. 289.

42. ibid., pp. 289-90.

43. *SG*, 26/08/1859.

the careful direction of Mr Harper of Bothwell, a man known to be zealous in missionary work. 'Detachments of the police' – about twenty proposing to attend at a time – procured the use of a schoolroom for a prayer meeting, to be held three times a week, while a twice-weekly assembly was begun among Post Office officials.[44] Students of Glasgow University also began to meet weekly for prayer around this time.

A prayer meeting and Bible class was commenced in November 1859 in a workshop in Buchannan Street. Messrs. Hay, Wilson and Co. cleared out a large apartment in their mill, in which forms and desks to seat over three hundred people were fitted. Prayer meetings were held here every morning, while in evenings it became a school, served with a properly trained teacher. Another business, Mitchell and Whitelaw, employed a missionary, who held meetings twice a week in the factory. Other companies followed their example. It is recorded that in Bridgeton, 'in one of the largest weaving mills, where 900 females are employed, besides a number of males ... for some time back the workers have been addressed twice a week, after six o'clock, in the very place where they have been working all day, and where, as many of them have said, they seldom thought of God. No sight can be more interesting – employers and employed lifting up the heart at one and the same time, to the great Father of all, for a blessing. At all the meetings God's presence has been felt; and it is believed that no meeting has been held in that mill without one or more having been awakened ...'[45]

'A remarkable movement' took place in Glasgow's Females' House of Refuge, both in the Reformatory Institute for girls and in the house for Magdalenes (prostitutes). In the former place, prayer meetings were established spontaneously in four or five wards, one of which was attended by every child in the ward. The effect of the awakening was said to have been 'apparent over the whole institute', in the complete absence of any irregularities requiring the exercise of discipline. A similar move took place in the Boys' House of Refuge in Duke Street, while in Blackfriars Street a work of grace occurred in Murdoch's School.[46]

---

44. ibid., 24/04/1860.

45. *WJ*, October 1859, p. 2.

46. *SG*, 02/09/1859, 10/01/1860.

The Palmers

Canadian Methodist evangelists, Walter and Phoebe Palmer, had been ministering throughout England during the latter half of 1859, during which time the minister of the John Street Wesleyan Chapel in Glasgow implored them to come to Scotland. They came, keen to adopt the practice that had become customary to them of inviting anxious inquirers forward to kneel at the communion rail after the service. The Palmers seemed unaware that this novelty was rarely practised in the UK, and that no church in the land, not even any Methodist church, had a communion rail installed at which to counsel seekers. Strongly advocating the usefulness of such technique,[47] the local pastor decided that quick action was called for. Carpenters were immediately sought – arriving at four the next morning to take out some pews and lay carpets at the front before the afternoon service!

There was a good deal of sobbing and crying at meetings, which were attended by people from many denominations, and shouts of praise were heard again and again, even from those not used to such expressions of excitement. Hundreds streamed to the front, ready to profess Christ or be prayed for to receive 'the full baptism of the Spirit'.[48] Church secretaries recorded 1,300 'recipients of grace', of whom around 1,000 claimed to have been born again.[49] Meanwhile, the Free Church

---

47. Ms Palmer testified that at one American church that was longing for revival, the front pews were removed at the Palmers' request, and in less than three weeks between five and six hundred people professed to find Christ, virtually all of them continuing steadfastly in their faith in subsequent months, according to their pastor (*The Revivalist*, 1860, pp. 41-2, quoted in Iain H. Murray, 1994, p. 396. Murray is of no doubt such practice was unorthodox and unbiblical, and that it represents 'full blown revivalism' rather than anything connected to genuine God-breathed revival (pp. 296-7).

48. The Palmers keenly promoted the doctrine of 'entire sanctification'. According to their biographers, they 'resisted the temptation to calculate their doctrine for the meridian of Glasgow and found the more they emphasised Christian perfection, the greater were the numbers of those professing salvation and sanctification' (Charles Edward White, *The Beauty of Holiness: Phoebe Palmer as Theologian, Revivalist, Feminist and Humanitarian*, Grand Rapids, 1986, p. 74).

49. ibid., pp. 73-5; *SG*, 21/01/1860; 26/01/1860. The Palmers also spent three weeks in Edinburgh, which visit seems to have been less notable than the Glasgow mission, although it was recorded that '450 individuals claimed to have been saved' here (White, 1986, p. 75).

synod of Glasgow found it apparent from its reports from all districts of the city that the work of revival 'is much more extensive than the public is aware of' – partly because of efforts to keep it from undue publicity.[50]

Period of Consolidation

From as early as October 1859, attendance at the City Hall began to fall dramatically. Marrs comments that this fact has rarely if ever been mentioned in any pro-revival publication, each of which, he claims, tends to be so biased as only to show positive aspects of the movement.[51] One newspaper wrote that the daily united prayer meeting in the City Hall on 24 October was 'crowded' with around 2,000 people, a rather incongruous scenario given that the Hall held 3,400! Meetings here were in fact abandoned in early December, while central daily meetings at the Religious Institution Rooms, the Trades Hall and the Merchant's Hall persisted amidst waning popularity.

The ten months from January to October 1860 was a period of consolidation. Revival activity continued unabated, but the large central meetings which had been so prominent during the previous months gave way to small local gatherings. Attendances at the Religious Institution Rooms and Trades Hall declined, while the growth of 'kitchen meetings' was dramatic. By March 1860 prayer meetings at the Wynd Free Church were reduced from being nightly to twice-weekly occurrences. In addition, where previously people had flocked to meetings in the Wynd, now 'helpers' went out onto the streets to encourage people to come into them. At the same time, the number of district meetings in connection with the Mission had grown to around one hundred. 'Kitchen meetings' were becoming increasingly popular in many other parts of the city, and in many instances were crowded to capacity. In the Anderston Free Church by March 1860, it was said that no fewer than fifty prayer meetings had been established by members of the congregation. These were scattered over the city and attended by large numbers.

Of this period, one believer wrote that on the first Sabbath of 1860, 'the Holy Spirit descended amongst us and filled all our hearts with rejoicing. I remember the exquisite joy I experienced when brought from

50. *SG*, 12/04/1860.

51. Marrs, p. 246.

darkness into the Lord's most glorious light, but the joy of that blessed Sabbath night far surpassed anything I had ever before experienced. A great many that night were deeply impressed, and some remained, anxious to be led to Jesus.' The work continued in power, then, at an evening meeting at the end of January, 'so filled were we all with the love of God, that it seemed too much for earth, while in oneness of mind and pleading with Jesus. The Holy Spirit descended, and many were in tears on account of their sins. We invited all to remain who could possibly wait, feeling that the Lord was willing to bless us all. But such a manifestation of the Holy Spirit we never before witnessed; and after pleading with God to pardon all who were earnestly asking forgiveness, everyone rose, filled with the love of God, and every mouth was filled with thanksgiving.' One prayer meeting was held in the home of a miner, formerly notorious for his wickedness. One of the converts in the district said that he had served the devil for over fifty years, but had now left his service.[52]

Fresh Impetus to the Revival

It has been suggested that there was a lull in revival activity in the summer of 1860, due to many folk being away on annual vacation on the west coast. [53] The evidence for this is weak. Those who went on holidays were chiefly from the middle classes, on whom the revival made least impact. In reality, events of a very positive nature occurred throughout the summer.

For example, additional impetus was given to the movement with the opening of the nearby Bridgegate Free Church in late June 1860. This project was pioneered by the Wynd Free Church, whose minister, Dugald MacColl, transferred himself to the Bridgegate, being succeeded in the former place by Robert Howie.[54] Around 3,000 turned up for the opening service. Over the next ten weeks, Sunday evening services here proved highly popular and one open-air meeting attracted over 7,000 people. There was an air of solemnity, 'such as has seldom been witnessed ... many (gave) evidence of deep feeling'. Many of the

---

52. *WJ*, 04/02/1860, p. 147; *SG*, 29/11/1859; 26/01/1860.

53. Marrs, p. 260.

54. By October 1861 the two churches had 1,100 communicants between them, while 200 more were applying for membership.

poor, 'who would not or could not enter a church, heard MacColl and thousands came into church after the sermons ... many having become changed persons'.[55]

Other events of a positive nature came in July with celebrations to mark the anniversary of the revival in the city, and in September, when new meetings were begun in the Joiner's Hall and at Glasgow Cross. The Bridgegate Church became, like its mother church, deeply involved in children's work. One day, 'about forty remained in distress. For about two hours the place seemed like a battlefield ... (before), by degrees, a change came as one by one obtained peace'.[56] Regular children's meetings were also held in the Religious Institute Rooms, the Wynd Church and Ewing Place Chapel. The response was often highly encouraging, but a journalist for *The Scottish Guardian* noted that at the close of a children's meeting in Hope Street Gaelic Free Church in September 1860, when the anxious were invited to meet with Messrs Radcliffe and Forlong in the adjoining Session House, 'many of the children appeared to accept the invitation merely from curiosity, or because desired to go by their parents or guardians'.[57]

It wasn't all plain sailing, however. A significant anti-Catholic element accompanied the evangelical movement in Glasgow in the second half of the nineteenth century, and this spirit at times manifested itself during the revival. Serious rioting and street fights occurred in the Bridgegate district in late August, as a result of open-air preaching by a city revivalist. The rioting was allegedly started by two men in 'clerical costumes' (i.e., Catholic priests) and led to six arrests being made after the Bridgegate Kirk came under siege by Catholic mobs. In 1861 Glasgow's Lord Provost and the Sheriff-Principal obtained an interdict prohibiting open-air preaching in the area for fear of further riots and for two years the outreach service was transferred to the City Hall.[58]

---

55. ibid., p. 262.

56. ibid., pp. 270-1.

57. *SG*, 11/09/1860.

58. Disturbances arose in other areas too. *The Scottish Guardian* reported that during open-air meetings in Pollockshaws, 'all passed off quietly until ... a company of Rome's true children met together, and tried to drown the missionary's voice by groaning, talking and laughing'. This was in spite of the fact that 'the missionaries

Meanwhile, in the Wynd Church itself, there were 'unmistakable tokens of a fresh awakening' in the summer of 1860, when there was 'an unusual solemnity ... a deep impression, (and) crying and sobbing aloud'.[59] At a Communion service in June 1860, 179 new members were admitted to the church, only a tiny number of them by certificate from other places. MacColl observed years later that, 'at least 150 cases (of conversion) were published, selected out of thousands then known to us. ... I know of only four that have had a break down, and these stood for three, four and six years respectively, and of them all I have hope still'. In the twelve months from March 1859, attendance at the Wynd Sunday School increased from 300 to 654. Another report states that in the Free Churches in East Gorbals, the Wynds and Chalmers Street, membership increased by approximately 200, 180 and 86 respectively in the year from August 1859.[60]

As many as 20,000 gathered on Glasgow Green on 19 August 1860 between 6.30 and 10 p.m. Richard Weaver[61] preached here the following month alongside Glasgow butcher /evangelist, Robert Cunningham, and numerous Glasgow ministers.[62] Each speaker was allowed just ten minutes to preach, but when the bell was rung for Weaver to stop, he turned round and said, '"Thee can ring the bell, but I'm not going to stop." I went on preaching. The Spirit came in such power that many were struck down under the word and had to be carried into a neighbouring church. There they lay on the floor as if dead. For a time they seemed to be unconscious of everything around them.' Indeed, so great was the interest on that occasion and so heavy the work entailed thereby that three of the visiting speakers,

---

have studiously avoided introducing anything whatever into their addresses relating to the dogma of the Roman Catholic faith' (*WJ*, 08/09/1860, p. 395).

59. Marrs, p. 261.

60. MacColl, pp. 255-309.

61. Though by no means a learned man, Richard Weaver was seen as a powerful speaker, and it is said that Dr Moxey of Edinburgh advised his elocution pupils to go and hear Weaver if they wanted an example of natural oratory (Bussey, p. 239).

62. As in all such cases, estimates of attendance at these meetings vary considerably, from a few thousand to 15,000 in attendance during the afternoon. *The Scottish Guardian* put the figure at 12,000, but Gordon Forlong, one of the speakers, said the number was not above 8,000.

namely, Gordon Forlong, Reginald Radcliffe and Weaver himself, all collapsed from fatigue.[63]

Initial Decline

The period from November 1860 to February 1861 was one of initial decline. During November and December, though no source stated outright that the revival was waning, diminishing intelligence from the city's churches, the fall in the number of prayer requests and letters, and the fall in advertisements, as well as shrinking attendances, all suggest that this was the case. By mid-February, *The Wynd Journal* admitted that the novelty of the revival was subsiding, but that as great or greater a work was going on than eighteen months previously, although in a quiet manner.

It was, however, at the beginning of February 1861 that awakening began in a female seminary in Glasgow. A teacher, having held her pupils much in prayer, became heavily burdened for their souls. She anonymously requested the Wynd Church to intercede for them. One day she was compelled to speak to them of eternity, urging them to decide at once whom they would serve. The whole class, one by one, promised aloud to begin serving the Lord from that moment. Cases of conviction increased daily, though there was no outward excitement; nothing unusual could have been observed by a stranger, other than occasional tears of penitence.

'For a few days the Lord seemed to have withdrawn his countenance; no new cases occurred, and those who were anxious did not seem to

---

63. Rev. J. Paterson, *Richard Weaver's Life Story*, London, 1897, pp. 131-2; Orr, 1949, p. 62. Another prominent preacher in Glasgow in the autumn of 1860 was the Rev. Thomas Toye of Belfast, who spent several weeks preaching to crowds in the Scottish metropolis in October and November. His visits occurred during a year when the minister had enjoyed two previous resurgences of revival in his home congregation, viz. January and June, 1860. It was said that Toye never remained detached from his listeners. He would open the room where he was staying so that anxious souls could visit him for counsel. So fond were his Scots friends of him that they would meet him in great numbers at the railway station on his arrival, and later return with him to the station for an emotional farewell (some even accompanying him to Belfast!). Toye returned to Glasgow at least once a year right up to 1869, preaching in the City Hall, on Glasgow Green, in theatres, in many churches and halls, and even in private homes. He made a point of keeping in touch by letter with numbers of his Glasgow converts (Toye, pp. 93, 95, 96-106).

advance. Renewed prayer was made. … A blessing followed. Seven girls professed to have found the Lord. At the play-hour nothing could be heard but praise and prayer.'[64]

Arrival of E. P. Hammond

In February 1861, American evangelist, Edward Payson Hammond was invited to conduct meetings in the city. This inaugurated a period of recovery and recession from March to August 1861.[65] For a number of weeks, Hammond conducted several meetings per day throughout the city, but he specially targeted the West End, which was regarded as being particularly spiritually cold. In fact, until his arrival, many of the suburbs, including this middle-class district, had not participated in the revival and Hammond's efforts were an attempt to remedy this situation. Indeed, ever since the first months of the revival in Glasgow, revival activity had concentrated in the less-affluent areas of central and eastern Glasgow, especially the communities stretching along either bank of the River Clyde; namely the adjacent districts of Finnieston and Anderston, along with the Wynds, Bridgegate and Calton on the northern side and Gorbals and Hutchesontown on the southern side of the river (see map p. 59). Several of the southern, northern and western environs, a number of which were predominantly middle-class areas, had hitherto known little participation in the revival.

Crowds thronged Hammond's meetings and *The Wynd Journal* reported that 'the awakening … has now reached such a crisis that … the work has become … too great to be borne alone by those emerged in it'.[66] Especially blessed was St Mark's Free Church, where many cases of awakening occurred. Despite Hammond's popularity, however, there was not quite the same fervour and intensity as existed during 1859–60.

---

64. *WJ*, 27/04/1861, pp. 37-8.

65. Marrs claimed that the invitation of Hammond to the city in effect heralded 'a new form of revival, one which was personality-led and which sought to exploit the drawing power of the preacher … the main attraction was the speaker himself' (p. 327).

66. Hammond returned to Glasgow briefly in May. Then he was presented with a gift from city ministers for his evangelistic labours. Some regarded the amount given (£256) as outrageous, given that it was many times more than most ministers earned in a year.

Hammond also addressed a number of successful meetings held specifically for children, making use of much the same content in all of his messages. One remarkable meeting saw an estimated ten thousand children gather to hear his simple, effective address. Some meetings were held in the College Hall, 'for the accommodation of the children of the better classes'.[67] Indeed, the success of the American's work among children in Scotland shaped him as a prominent children's evangelist in future years. Hammond also conducted a special service for cabmen. The City Hall was first opened to cabmen and then for any others who wished to attend. Said one, 'there could scarcely be fewer than 5,000 people within the walls – women in mutches (linen caps), scores of factory girls with bare heads, men in fustian (thick, coarse clothing), besides the trimly dressed cabmen, and hundreds of well-to-do'.[68]

Hammond had the effect of opening new centres of revival in the city, or in the case of Cowcaddens, reopening such centres. One Sabbath evening on Hammond's arrival in the area, 'the people so thronged to the places of appointed worship that when the time arrived, five churches were filled by the overflowing masses', while 'the street in front of (Dr Eadie's) church was crowded; and there, under the bright moonlight, hundreds were listening to a Christian layman who had been speaking to them for some time'.[69]

The upsurge in revival interest continued into May, when, one fine Sunday at least eight open-air meetings were held at various points on Glasgow Green, while at the South-side Park, a prayer meeting drew an alleged 1,500. It was also during this period that a string of other popular evangelists visited Glasgow. William Carter, a London chimney-sweep, came for ten days in May; Reginald Radcliffe, along with Richard Weaver and T. S. Henry, addressed a series of meetings in July; English former cricketer W. P. Lockhart arrived in August and the Rev. Thomas Toye of Belfast paid evangelistic visits in both June and August. While such names attracted considerable attention, their

67. Headley, pp. 142-78; Orr, 1949, pp. 65-6; E. E. Cairns, *An Endless Line of Splendor*, Wheaton, 1986, p. 152; *SG*, 09/04/1861.

68. Headley, p. 168.

69. ibid., pp. 169-70.

efforts did not make a significant impact on the irreligious. It was clear that the movement as a whole was coming to an end as attendance figures dropped and meetings closed.

The revival had run its course; the city had been enormously enriched by the spiritual blessing which had so powerfully graced its various quarters, and it was now time to carry forward the vision that had birthed hope and passion in so many congregations.

Glasgow Environs

Awakening commenced in Maryhill, just north of Glasgow, after a little boy belonging to the village visited scenes of revival in Ireland with his mother, where he came under saving change. On his return home he witnessed to his male friends, and several appeared to be deeply impressed. As a result, a number of lads employed in the print works and other establishments, including 'the very wildest of the juvenile population', were spiritually awakened, and began to meet together for prayer.[70]

Robert Simpson, instrumental in an awakening that occurred in Alexandria in 1838, and in the formation of a Congregational church in Bridgeton a few years later, relieved himself of the duties of a pastorate soon after, yet continued to devote himself to the blending of sacred and secular work to which he was regarded as being more adept than almost anyone in the city. As such, he preached much at 'The Five Lamps' in Glasgow's Cathedral Square during the 1859–61 revival, and also spent considerable time evangelising in Govan, where he helped begin a fellowship, also securing a building for the fledgling congregation.

The neighbourhood of Busby, a few miles to the immediate south of Glasgow, was also impacted by the revival of this period. Many of the district's youth were thereby influenced, including eighteen-year-old ploughman Robert Thomson, who was awakened via the earnest witness of his close pal, Jack, while walking to Glasgow one day. He was also inspired by the lives of three other friends, and the sudden death of one of these particularly moved him to consider eternal issues. Indeed, such conviction came upon him that his whole body would shake. Following his dramatic conversion, he became a diligent Sunday

---

70. *SG*, 23/08/1859.

school teacher and a winsome evangelist. As a result of the '59 revival a number of district prayer meetings were formed in the area.[71]

In nearby Carmunnock, the Rev. J. Oswald Dykes (later of London) established a weekly meeting in a stable, then a wright's shop. He later formed a fellowship by name of Clason Memorial Church, in Motherwell. Often Thomson would cross the hill to address meetings there, a deep impression being made on many. Numerous other communities in the immediate vicinity of Glasgow were also affected by awakening, including Thornliebank, Nitshill and Pollockshaws, where a remarkable spirit of inquiry prevailed, especially in some of the mills.

71. Rev. Alexander Andrew, *Taken from the Plough: A Memoir of Robert Thomson, a Faithful Servant of Jesus Christ*, Glasgow, n.d., pp. 34-5.

*Old photo of Gourock Ropework Factory,
Port Glasgow*

Present-day Ropework Factory Building

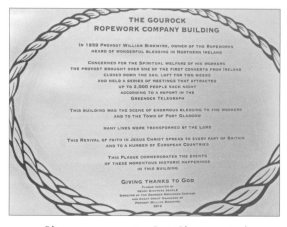

*William Birkmyre, Provost of
Port Glasgow, 1859*

THE GOUROCK
ROPEWORK COMPANY BUILDING

IN 1859 PROVOST WILLIAM BIRKMYRE, OWNER OF THE ROPEWORKS
HEARD OF WONDERFUL BLESSING IN NORTHERN IRELAND

CONCERNED FOR THE SPIRITUAL WELFARE OF HIS WORKERS
THE PROVOST BROUGHT OVER ONE OF THE FIRST CONVERTS FROM IRELAND
CLOSED DOWN THE SAIL LOFT FOR TWO WEEKS
AND HELD A SERIES OF MEETINGS THAT ATTRACTED
UP TO 2,000 PEOPLE EACH NIGHT
ACCORDING TO A REPORT IN THE
GREENOCK TELEGRAPH

THIS BUILDING WAS THE SCENE OF ENORMOUS BLESSING TO THE WORKERS
AND TO THE TOWN OF PORT GLASGOW

MANY LIVES WERE TRANSFORMED BY THE LORD

THIS REVIVAL OF FAITH IN JESUS CHRIST SPREAD TO EVERY PART OF BRITAIN
AND TO A NUMBER OF EUROPEAN COUNTRIES

THIS PLAQUE COMMEMORATES THE EVENTS
OF THESE MOMENTOUS HISTORIC HAPPENINGS
IN THIS BUILDING

GIVING THANKS TO GOD

PLAQUE DONATED BY
HENRY BIRKMYRE SEMPLE
DIRECTOR OF THE GOUROCK ROPEWORK COMPANY
AND GREAT GREAT GRANDSON OF
PROVOST WILLIAM BIRKMYRE
2012

Plaque commemorating Port Glasgow revival

Greenock

Chapter 5

West-Central Scotland

Renfrewshire

Port Glasgow

With its geographical proximity and regular ferry links to Ulster, it is no surprise that the district along the River Clyde to the west of Glasgow was one of the first in Scotland to be affected by revival in the late 1850s. Perhaps the strongest revival connections linking Inverclyde to Ulster existed in the towns of Port Glasgow and Coleraine. *The Revival* periodical observed that the union prayer meeting in New York was requested to pray for the spiritual needs of Coleraine in Ulster. The union prayer meeting in Coleraine in turn was asked to pray for the spiritual welfare of Port Glasgow. Many in the north of Ireland thus rejoiced when news reached them that revival had indeed broken out in that Inverclyde town.

More practical means were also used to light revival fires in this area. A believer from Coleraine crossed to Port Glasgow to tell his two sons of the revival being experienced back home. He held a meeting in his son's house, which was well attended. First a young girl was awakened, then the Irishman's own son. A second meeting was held soon after, and a young man was this time 'struck down'. The date was 17 July 1859.[1] The news spread quickly through the town, causing great excitement. It constituted the first known case of physical prostration to occur during the 1859 revival in Scotland.

From an early date William Birkmyre, Provost of Port Glasgow, and owner of the large Gourock Ropework Company situated on Bay Street, took a personal interest in the revival. Birkmyre was a devout Christian

---

1. *SG*, 09/08/1859.

and held the welfare of his many employees at heart. Aware that almost all his Port Glasgow workforce were of Irish birth, he decided to invite James McQuilken – considered to have been the first convert of the Ulster revival, and under whose instrumentality revival had begun in Connor six months previously – to address a meeting in Port Glasgow, opening the spacious sail loft of his Ropework store for the purpose. The invitation was accepted, and McQuilken arrived on 19 July.

From this point Birkmyre's dockside store became the centre of revival in Port Glasgow. Up to two thousand people gathered nightly to hear gospel addresses. At one, not long into the meeting, between ten and fifteen were 'struck down' and had to be carried out.[2] The most unusual case was that of a young woman, who, many hours before, had correctly specified the time when she would recover from her prostration. For the duration of her 'trance', which was witnessed by the Provost and others, the woman was blind, deaf and dumb. From the start, her eyes were said to have been, 'intently fixed on some object, which appeared to excite within her adoring wonders; her very features appeared to undergo a change, and, as if it were, a flood of light from above seemed to be poured down upon her. So instant was her gaze on this glorious object that for half an hour not an eye nor an eyelid moved.'[3]

As this meeting was being dismissed, the anxious were asked to remain for counsel. Most of the large congregation stayed for this after-meeting, during which more prostrations occurred; 'in one place three, in another four or five, and so on'. In addition, a visiting minister from Dunoon, the Rev. Paterson, noticed that 'there seemed to be thirty or forty young converts, who held fast by one another, speaking to one another of their experience'.[4]

At this and subsequent gatherings, where large numbers continued to assemble, the sense of conviction was deep. 'The cries were as piercing as anything I heard in Ireland', said one minister who made constant comparisons to the amazing scenes he had witnessed in that land. Mr Paterson of Dunoon, who had been to Ulster and had seen cases of prostration there, gave a vivid account of what he witnessed to an attentive

---

2. Orr, 1949, pp. 63-4.

3. *The Dundee Post*, 01/09/1859, quoted in Bussey, p. 286.

4. *TR*, 13/08/1859, quoted in Bussey, p. 98.

Port Glasgow audience one evening. He then described the scenes that followed his testimony: 'I just thought I was in Sandy Row, Belfast. I went back in the evening and the place was crammed. There must have been more than two thousand present. One cried out, then another, then another again, and some of the cries were as piercing as anything I ever heard in Ireland. I never heard any cries more affecting than the cries of some of the girls in the store last night. ... Till an advanced hour of the night I was visiting the persons thus struck down, and I saw a number of them this morning who found peace and were rejoicing in Christ.'[5]

On one occasion, such was the sense of holy terror that 'some even ran out of the meeting in fear'.[6] Another minister said he had seen 'strong men lying prostrate on the ground in an agony of conviction, and next morning, if one had wished to draw a picture of joy, he could not have found a better subject than the faces of these same men to whom Christ had given joy'.[7]

By the middle of August it could be reported that, although they still occurred, 'cases of violent emotion are not as common as at first'. Where they did occur at this stage, those affected were 'generally overcome in their own houses or more frequently at their work, and rarely in church or at any religious meeting', though their 'trances' were often traceable to what they heard at such places. In one day eight people had to be carried out of a local spinning mill in a state of prostration, three of whom had been similarly affected before. It was observed that the most violent cases generally occurred among those 'most ignorant of divine grace'.[8] But it was further noted by 'some of the most respectable people in town' that several unlearned people who went into a trance state, despite being unable to read, could nonetheless open a Bible and point to scriptural passages appropriate to their particular situations.[9]

By mid-August, Birkmyre required his sail loft to be returned to its normal business use, so he transferred meetings to a large store-room beside the dry dock, where crowds still flocked, until they

---

5. ibid.

6. *SG*, 02/08/1859.

7. Johnson, p. 223.

8. *SG*, 19/08/1859.

9. ibid.

were discontinued in early October. In addition, well-attended daily lunchtime prayer meetings took place in the Odd Fellow's Hall, to which many wood and iron carpenters could be seen heading in their working clothes, Bibles in pocket.

The revival influenced not only those from a Presbyterian background, but also some in both the Episcopal and Roman Catholic Churches. Indeed, among other remarkable conversions, the awakening of a Catholic woman as she scoffed at the revival while at work as a cleaner at the local police station created considerable stir throughout the town. Such was the transformation in Port Glasgow that even in Black Bull's Close – considered 'the worst locality in town' – one could hear 'the voice of praise and prayer ascending from a crowded meeting in that unlikely place'.[10] In the Orange Lodge, too, a 'happy change' was evident. Where members used to meet once a month and spend half their subscriptions on drink, now they formed a Sick Benefit Society, to which all such money went instead.

Towards the year end, some young men from Port Glasgow met together on the Greenock road, and finding that they were all in

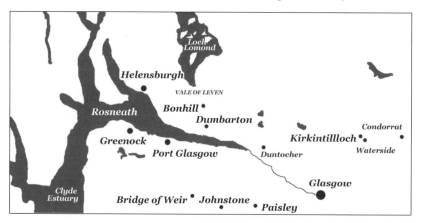

the same state of mind, decided to retire to an old quarry for prayer, agreeing to return to the same place the next evening. Keeping this appointment, they found the ground taken up by another group of young men who had also gathered to pray! The first group happily sought a Bethel elsewhere. By this stage of the revival in the district there were no more 'exciting meetings', but rather, 'a quiet and steady

---

10. ibid., 26/08/1859.

work of grace leavening the mass'. Such was the desire for prayer that nearly one hundred men were meeting to pray for an hour each Sabbath afternoon. The Rev. John Duncan related the tragic outcome of one of them, a most faithful convert, who, 'reproving and exhorting with prayer as he had opportunity, was drowned last Saturday by the ice breaking on the place where he went to skate. He was one of twins, his brother being on the ice with him, thus illustrating Luke 17:34.'[11]

Greenock

Greenock was early influenced by the revival movement, this town – along with Ardrossan to the south – being one of the chief outlets for passenger traffic between Scotland and Ulster.[12] In this town, the Seaman's Chapel became the centre of a spontaneous movement arising out of private prayer meetings, in which an estimated '1,000 people became vital Christians' within six months.[13] By April 1860 one minister could say, 'In Greenock there is one of the most striking works of grace going forward of which we have any example in Scotland.' Very few cases of the outward manifestations prominent in Port Glasgow were witnessed, owing largely to the way events were watched and guided by the town's ministers. Nevertheless, 'a very widespread and deep work of grace' was evidenced, and among all classes of the community. Its influence was seen both on those who were church members and those who were not. One town missionary had on his roll the names of nearly nine hundred individuals who have waited on him for conversation.[14]

The town missionaries were commended for discharging their duties in a truly unsectarian manner. Enquiring as to the religious connection to which parties coming to them belong, they would at once hand them over to the care of the ministers of such denomination. There were no

---

11. *WJ*, 24/12/1859, p. 100.

12. Indeed, it was returning to Scotland on a ferry from Ireland, where he had been preaching to great effect during the revival movement still in progress there, that Brownlow North conducted services onboard the steamer. His preaching produced such effect that impressive revival scenes took place amid the tossing waves of the Irish Sea.

13. Orr, 1949, p. 64; Bebbington, 1989, p. 117.

14. *WJ*, 28/04/1860, p. 242.

great union prayer meetings, and no large gatherings to hear particular preachers. Rather, 'the work has taken a safer form – the form of small private prayer-meetings'.[15]

A great number of meetings originated with and were kept up by the children themselves. One large meeting in particular was kept up by boys, being attended also by ministers or elders, who sought to ensure that everything was done decently and in order. In some parts of the town, especially Greenock's east end, a prayer meeting was said to have existed 'in almost every second house. ... And then we have prayer-meetings among the workmen in the shipbuilding yards during the breakfast and dinner hours. In one building-yard, not only has drunkenness entirely disappeared, but you will not hear anything like an oath or unseemly language throughout the large yard.'[16]

The same town minister quoted above testified to having had 'a great deal of work during the last five months, but although I have had five or six services every week, I have been far more able for my work than ever I felt before. ... Though I have had that Sabbath evening meeting for nine months, I have never preached one sermon at it. We have simply met for an hour for devotional purposes, and I have very much confined myself to reading intelligence of revivals in other parts of the country.'[17] Among those converted were a large number of sailors, sailmakers, moulders and engineers. When Richard Weaver later preached in Greenock, he marvelled to find that 'the district was moved for miles around. It seemed at that time as if the Millennium were at hand', he exulted.[18]

Paisley

As well as this well-populated Inverclyde region, many other parts of the county were also affected by this influential spiritual movement. The Rev. J. Aitken of Paisley paid a visit to Ireland in 1859, making another visit the following year. This time, finding many of the converts steadfast in their profession, he became more than ever convinced of the genuineness of the work. For several years prior to 1859, noted

---

15. ibid.

16. *WJ*, 28/04/1860, p. 242.

17. ibid.

18. Paterson, 1897, pp. 133-4; *WJ*, 15/09/1860, p. 404.

Aitken, 'the Lord had been blessing us with droppings – first one and then another being convicted of sin and brought to a knowledge of the truth'. A visit from Brownlow North was also 'very much blessed indeed'. Before long, Aitken's North Church congregation, like others in the town, was in the throes of revival, and 'many an anxious soul' was led to Christ. Wrote his biographer: 'He was so accessible and gentle in his way that inquirers flocked to him. His house was full of them from morning till night, so that those around him wondered when he got time to prepare his sermons, for he never allowed his regular pulpit ministrations to suffer from all this extra work.' Aitken also assisted at meetings in many other parts of the country and speaking of this period on his deathbed he remarked, 'my soul was very bright then'.[19]

One girl who found peace of soul in Paisley went to work the next day and became the means of awakening twelve of her fellow-workers. These twelve were later conversed with in private in their homes and all professed to find Christ. Aitken reported that many prayer meetings were held:

> Some nights I counted up twenty held on the same night. As soon as men and women are brought to Christ, they go into the work heart and soul. How fond they are of the Bible! I know about twelve young men in Paisley who have commenced the study of Greek, that they may be able to read the New Testament in the original. I may mention that there are five ministers in a district of Renfrew and Argyllshire who have arranged to have monthly meetings in each other's churches. And every one of these meetings has been blessed. One of these meetings, which commenced at seven o'clock, continued till about two next morning before it could be closed.[20]

Johnstone

In nearby Johnstone it was reported that 'a very remarkable awakening' was in progress and that 'the fire from off the altar is breaking down the wall of sectarianism'. The Rev. MacGreggor gave a detailed account of

---

19. *WJ*, 19/10/1861, p. 22; James Aitken, *Memoir and Remains of the Rev. James Aitken*, Glasgow, 1867, pp. 52-7. Aitken was often asked to publish a detailed account of cases of awakening and conversion under his ministry, but would never consent to do so, as he considered such publications injurious to the soul-prosperity of the converts.

20. *SG*, 30/08/1859; *WJ*, 19/10/1861, p. 23.

the 'fine' movement that broke out at Bridge of Weir and neighbourhood to the Free Church Presbytery of Paisley on 7 September 1859. The work began when three formerly notorious characters from Port Glasgow went down to speak there following their own dramatic conversions. After the close of one service – for which fifty converts from the town had been praying the previous evening – one could distinctly hear the sound of 'weeping and wailing by the people on the streets for their sins'.[21]

Neilston

Revival in Neilston was sparked by many from that locality visiting scenes of the extraordinary and well-publicised movement in Dunlop, Ayrshire, eight miles distant (see p. 114). A minister from Neilston spent a week in Dunlop parish, over part of which he had oversight as missionary. On the first meeting after his return home the presence of God's Spirit was evidently felt. Converts did not fail to openly avow their new-found faith – 'a new thing here', remarked the minister, 'for formerly we were culpably reserved on spiritual matters. From that night onward the work has gone on triumphantly'. It became almost impossible to get people to leave church, and many were heard to say, 'Oh, I could just stop a night here.'[22]

Convictions and conversions were not confined to one church, 'for they happen anywhere', observed the minister, 'and at anytime'.

> The worshipful, joyous solemnity that appears on the faces of the converts is truly heavenly, and generally has a strange and thrilling effect on mere onlookers. ... All are so solemnised in the awful presence of God that very few get angry at you if you ask them if they have found the Saviour. ... It looks rather strange to a mere spectator to see prayer and praise and conversation going all on in some ten different parts of the house at one time. But the moment you engage in the work, you feel entirely at ease. On our way home we often hear the sweet swell of song from different companies, as they march to their respective abodes.[23]

Meanwhile, a minister writing from an unnamed town in Renfrewshire gave, in condensed form, the following warning regarding any over-emphasis placed on the significance of physical manifestations. 'A carter,

---

21. *SG*, 11/10/185; 02/09/1859; Marrs, p. 150.

22. *WJ*, 08/12/1860, pp. 502-3.

23. ibid.

very wicked, was prostrated, dumb, deaf, blind, for twenty-four hours. Scarcely an oath was heard in the town for a month after. He began to pray, would not go to church or prayer-meetings, came several times for private inquiry, very awe-struck; said, "I have had an awful warning"; fell off, and is now worse than ever.'[24]

Dunbartonshire

Vale of Leven

Interestingly, and apparently coincidentally, just as the widespread revival of 1839–42 was preceded by a stirring movement in the Vale of Leven the previous year, so too a spiritual movement sprang up in the same valley a year before the even more extensive revival of 1859–61. Excited about reports he had heard of revival spreading through America, Henry Douglas Freshfield, a bright young minister who had been ordained to Bonhill Free Church in September 1857, began holding frequent week-night meetings for prayer and the proclamation of the gospel the following summer (1858), not just in his own church, but elsewhere through the valley of Leven. An unusual interest in divine truth was manifested by many, and the meetings were continued over a considerable period of time, with other preachers, such as Brownlow North, giving occasional help. In his labours, Freshfield received great personal blessing in bringing the good news of the gospel to others and his biographer wrote that 'that season of revival did him great service as a man and as a minister'.[25]

Helensburgh

During the summer of 1858 an aged Christian woman frequently told her Free Church minister, the Rev. John Anderson, 'The Lord has a great work to do in Helensburgh. I know it. I canna tell the time, but I'm sure it's coming.' Notable stirrings of the Spirit were apparent from as early as April 1859, months prior to the first reports of a general wave of revival sweeping over the country at large. Itinerant evangelist John Bowes spent three weeks in the town at that time, holding meetings almost every night. The chapel was often crowded, especially on Sabbath nights. Nine professed to find peace in believing and three

---

24. MacGill, p. 10.

25. H. D. Freshfield, *Memorials of Henry Douglas Freshfield*, privately printed, 1892, p. 59.

were baptised in water. Returning the following month, Bowes saw another nine people profess faith, and as many baptised, in the recently enlarged chapel. Bowes made several further visits to Helensburgh in subsequent months, when he held a fortnight's worth of meetings in October, and another series of services in March 1859, obtaining further heartwarming results on both occasions.

On hearing of the revival in America, many hearts were stirred, and union prayer meetings were held in Helensburgh from December 1859. Then, following visits by several church leaders from the town to Ireland in September 1859 (including Anderson and his missionary worker, William Mackie), an account of the Irish work was presented at the union prayer meeting. This produced a deep impression. A 'remarkable awakening' ensued, and nightly meetings were begun. Soon, 'nearly the whole town seemed for a time awe-stricken, as if the angel of death had been seen hovering over'. Evangelical churches 'laboured constantly and lovingly together' in a real spirit of unity.[26]

September was also when John Bowes made an oft-repeated visit to the Dunbartonshire town, where he frequently preached three times a day for days together. The following entries from his journal are selected:

> 21st Sept. The Ragged School was crowded; it holds 500. Many children sobbed aloud at the prayer-meeting ... several of those converted within these few days have spoken with great power. ... Christians of other churches help us in prayer. I had hoped to be off to other places, but have been detained here by this blessed work. The people are flocking to the Gospel like doves to their windows ... 22nd: Eastburn Chapel too small, overflowing almost every night, and scores if not hundreds unable to get in ... 25th: About thirty saved; scores, if not hundreds anxious. Free Church at half-past-six; about 1,500 hearers, ministers of two churches present ... 26th: (at) The Union Prayer Meeting, which we joined. The Free Church nearly full, ministers of two churches present ... 30th: Congregational Chapel overflowing ...[27]

On 5th October, the last night of Bowes' mission, the Ragged School was again packed and nine conversions were reported. This brought the

---

26. George R. Logan, *The First Hundred Years: Park Church, Helensburgh*, Helensburgh, 1964, pp. 1-2; Reid, 1860, p. 391.

27. John Bowes, *The Autobiography or History of the Life of John Bowes*, Glasgow, 1872, p. 545.

total number of hopeful conversions in recent weeks to 150, while twice as many remained in an anxious state. 'Indeed the whole town seems to be moved', noted the evangelist.[28] So grateful were the townspeople with Bowe's indefatigable labours among them that they presented him with a purse of gold valued at around £15. Bowes left the town with the heartfelt prayers and wishes of many who a month previously knew not how to pray.

Under the parlour of the Helensburgh Free Church manse was situated a large empty cellar, and this secluded venue was deemed an appropriate meeting place for a number of boys who were granted permission by the Rev. Anderson to meet there each day after school. These gatherings continued for several weeks and were conducted entirely by the young lads themselves, no adults being permitted into their sacred chamber. However, unbeknown to them, the minister and his wife delighted to hear the earnest tones of prayer that echoed from the cellar walls as well as the melodious hymns the boys gustily sang. Glad tidings came to Anderson's way in other forms too, such as a letter received in 1864 from a zealous evangelist labouring in Australia who dated his conversion to the revival in Helensburgh five years previously. At a communion held shortly after the revival, around fifty joined the Free Church alone, and it was soon deemed necessary to form a new congregation. As a result, the Park Church was opened in 1862.[29] Meanwhile, a two-day campaign in the village of Cardross, halfway between Helensburgh and Dumbarton, saw a remarkable ninety people profess conversion.[30]

Dumbarton

A prayer meeting for an outpouring of God's Spirit was commenced in Dumbarton in August 1858 by just three believers. Attendance quickly rose, and before they knew it they found themselves in the midst of a number of people anxiously seeking spiritual truth. Thankfully some

---

28. ibid., p. 546.

29. Reid, 1860, p. 400; Robert Wemyss, *The Church in the Square: A Brief History of the West United Free Church, Helensburgh*, Helensburgh, 1925, p. 17. Helensburgh's United Presbyterian Church also saw significant growth in the revival period, indeed since the induction of Alexander Duff in December 1856, and a new church was deemed necessary – this opened in 1861 (Various, *Sketches of Churches and Clergy in the Parishes of Row, Rosneath and Cardross*, Helensburgh, 1889, p. 65).

30. J. Bowes, p. 546.

Christians of greater experience joined the group, some even came from Bonhill and Alexandria. In time, 'one precious soul after another was unloosed and set at liberty'. A new venue was procured – at some cost – by way of the Abstainers Hall. A member of the group lamented the fact that some stood aloof from the work, 'apparently cold and indifferent, who might have aided and greatly encouraged us. Many have come and gone to these meetings just according to the outward appearance of the work; if there was a stirring, here they were, if there was a quiet, they were not to be found.' Nevertheless, many a soul – considered to number well over a hundred in total – was soundly converted as a result of these meetings.[31]

Then in November 1859 began 'a most decided, deep, widespread, long-continued awakening.' A few young converts from Helensburgh came to speak in Dumbarton. 'Their ardent zeal formed a striking contrast to what we had been accustomed', continued the worker; 'their appeals almost instantaneously found a response in many hearts'. Thirty or forty, chiefly young men into whose lives the light of the gospel had been beginning to dawn for some time, almost at once professed a saving change, some of whom had remarkable experiences of passing from death unto life (many of these since left the town on account of the fluctuating nature of their trade).[32]

In the spring of 1861, still in Dumbarton, the spiritual movement took a wider range, now embracing all classes and conditions of society, chiefly amongst members and adherents of the Church. Aid was rendered by various ministers from near and far. Every congregation in town was more or less directly or indirectly blessed by the revival, out of which several young men began preparing themselves for the ministry. Many small district meetings were set up in 'destitute localities', and in such areas evening-school classes were organised for adults as well as boys and girls who were at work during the day, to enable them to learn to read, write and do arithmetic.

Kirkintilloch

The work in Kirkintilloch had its origins in the Free Church Sabbath School, where on each of two consecutive Sundays, a young girl was 'struck

31. *WJ*, 05/07/1862, p. 115.

32. ibid.

down' and had to be carried into church. While the work here continued in a quieter form to which it had begun, a more prominent and noticeable movement commenced in the Methodist chapel, after Wesleyan preacher, Robert Forsyth, gave an enthusiastic account of his recent visit to Ireland. Soon one or two other groups, such as the Original Secession Church, were partaking of the blessing. An unprecedented number of prayer meetings – over thirty in all – quickly sprang up, including women's meetings, where none previously existed. Children played a prominent part in the movement and even attended the daily prayer meeting in the Wesleyan church.[33] At one meeting was a young boy of about eleven, who, when advised to go home because it was well past his bedtime, replied that he wanted to stay to see what Jesus would do for his soul. He was not disappointed, for before he left, he was 'rejoicing in a crucified Saviour'.[34]

One conservative believer was disturbed by the presumptuous manner in which conversions were being reported, stating his opinion that in the Methodist Church in particular, leaders made 'efforts to excite the public mind'. This same man could nonetheless confirm 'from long and careful observation that there is a very spectacular work of the Spirit of God in Kirkintilloch'. He suggested that where formerly many people had little time for clergymen, 'the pastor's visit is now relished'.[35]

Awakening commenced in Waterside, a suburb of Kirkintilloch, and Condorrat, a village three miles west of Cumbernauld, after a missionary labouring in Linlithgow reaped much fruit in both places. He was invited to return two months later, when more fruit was procured. 'It was heartsome', testified one witness, 'to see amongst the convicted an old, corpulent man of 92, coming forward in presence of his neighbours, heedless of their remarks.' In Condorrat, twenty-three females met one evening for prayer. They broke up at a late hour, but had no sooner left the place of meeting when the Spirit came upon them with such power that many of them were overpowered, some falling to the ground, others crying out for mercy, so that old men had to be awakened from bed to speak to them.[36]

---

33. *SG*, 11/10/1859; *TR*, 19/11/1859.

34. *WJ*, 21/01/1860.

35. ibid.

36. *WJ*, 15/09/1860, p. 403.

Duntocher, at the foot of the Kilpatrick Hills in Dunbartonshire, became 'the scene of an interesting though quiet awakening', having been spurred by narratives of clergymen who had witnessed either revival scenes in Ireland or the Wynd meetings in Glasgow, or who had visited other centres of the movement. Meetings held in the village schoolroom were crowded to excess. One individual, who exhibited some of the more marked phenomena, i.e., prostration, later testified at one of the factories, and created a widespread impression.[37]

North Lanarkshire

By the mid-nineteenth century, Lanarkshire, with its considerable coal and iron deposits, was in the grip of rapid industrialisation. Its population more than doubled in the twenty years from 1841 to 1861, from 114,393 to 241,853. It represented one of the most populous and industrialised counties in Scotland. Revival in the district coincided with a period of unemployment in the mines, and also with a severe outbreak of scarlet fever in October 1859, particularly in Wishaw, described by *The Hamilton Advertiser* as 'very bad'.[38] To what extent this influenced the revival is unclear. In Wishaw itself, revival only appears to have commenced in late 1860.

Chryston

The Rev. Burnet, later of Huntly, served as Free Church minister in Chryston.[39] His congregation received 'such a blessing' during a time of awakening that spread over the district in 1859–60. Several interesting cases of conversion caused considerable stir in the neighbourhood. The movement had lasting effect. When the Rev. Thomas Macadam served as minister there in the 1870s, he became aware of 'many in the district, whose consistency and Christian character no one can impeach'. Knowing that congregations that have once been visited with such a movement are usually quick to welcome another, his people were 'almost as one man eager for such a time returning', which was seen to have come with the 'Moody

---

37. ibid., 08/12/1859, p. 75.

38. Buchanan, pp. 24-6.

39. Born in Chryston, his son, Sir Robert William, was physician to the Royal Household from 1910 to 1919.

revival' in 1873–4 (see p. 542).[40] In the hamlet of Broomknowes, near Lenzie, a large meeting was held in a barn. There was exhibited such earnestness that a number were in tears; and it was midnight before the anxious inquirers could be at last dismissed.

Airdrie

The movement in Airdrie was especially influenced by James Innes, minister of a local independent congregation. As many as five house meetings were held on one street near the church (Johnston Street) on Friday nights, and at times the thoroughfare was crowded with folk that were unable to get into the houses. Numerous cases of prostration occurred, including that of a woman who remained speechless and rigid for many hours. The next day she sat up in bed and addressed a group of onlookers for forty minutes, before falling back into a comatose state. Everyone present was reduced to tears, the incident also having a strong effect on those who subsequently heard the story.

One open-air meeting in Airdrie in September 1859 drew over four thousand people, and nightly prayer meetings drew large crowds. It was reported by early December, however, that there had been 'a change to the revival'. In distinction to just a few weeks previously, there were now 'no crowds of eager listeners … few psalms of praise' and united prayer meetings were discontinued for lack of attendance. In addition, many who previously had stood aloof from the movement, declining either to go along with it or to discount it, had now become 'unfriendly to revivals generally'. Despite these developments, it was noted that the revival had brought considerable good to many in the town, and some people were still being blessed. In Chapelhall it was said that 'a good work is going on'. Here the Rev. Alexander Stewart was labouring 'in season and out of season', being assisted by an Irishman who was seen as being very helpful in carrying on the work in that neighbourhood.[41]

Coatbridge

It was reported around the same time that a hundred people had been converted since the commencement of nightly meetings in nearby Coatbridge. Prostrations had evidently occurred, for some weeks after

---

40. *TB*, 14/05/1874, pp. 68-9; FCSRSRM, 1895, p. 195.
41. *WJ*, 05/01/1860; 02/03/1861, p. 598.

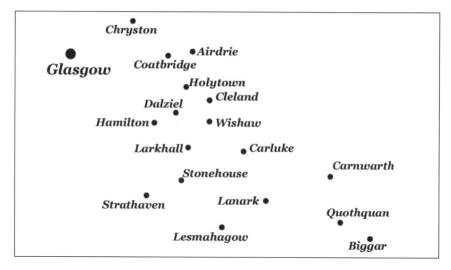

the revival's commencement the local press reported that 'excitement
has been considerably reduced. There has been no more "striking
down". However, the deep work of conviction is continuing, with
meetings in several churches and in many private homes.'[42] Out of
'revival meetings' led by Mr Inglis of Bellshill in Boyle's School, an
Evangelical Union church was formed in Munroe's Hall, and Inglis
was called as its pastor.[43] Also out of the revival in Coatbridge arose a
group of believers who were convinced of the importance of believer's
baptism (by immersion), and a small Baptist group emerged.[44]

42. *The Airdrie, Coatbridge, Bathgate and Wishaw Advertiser*, 03/09/1859,
17/09/1859 and 24/09/1859, quoted in Fred Kelling, *Fisherman of Faroe: William
Gibson Sloan*, Leirkerid, 1993, p. 51. In July 1861, Mr Sherade, an American evangelist, came to hold meetings in the Coatbridge and Airdrie region, being accompanied by Mr Buchanan, a missionary, and another American revivalist preacher,
Mr Lang. Many remained for conversation and prayer after the services. One
young man, already under conviction, who conversed with Sherade was a young
William Gibson Sloan (later renowned missionary to the Faroes), who obtained
assurance of salvation a few days later, while working in the back-kitchen of his
store (ibid., pp. 534).

43. William D. McNaughton, *Early Congregational Independency in Lowland Scotland*, vol. 2, Glasgow, 2007, p. 157. Several of the Lanarkshire Evangelical Union
churches which experienced a degree of revival blessing in 1859–61 struggled to
survive in the 1860s and were forced to close soon after.

44. Bebbington, 1988, p. 188. It was not until 1874, however, that this group came
under the direction of the Baptist Home Mission with an appointed evangelist, J.
M. Hewson.

Cleland and Holytown

On the day of the Airdrie Races in the summer of 1859, normally an occasion of great frivolity in the whole district, there was 'hardly a man, woman or boy seen leaving Cleland', six miles south of Airdrie. Formerly the inhabitants of this village were the 'first and noisiest in the crowd!' Clearly a great change had occurred in the community, influenced, it was suggested, by the quiet, ongoing work of the missionary worker stationed there.

Holytown was also affected by the revival and one or two sudden deaths made a solemn impression on the community – the hearts of many being melted and subdued. It was noted that during meetings held in the town over the course of a week in mid-October 1859, about a dozen people were affected bodily, in addition to those 'in mental distress'. It was said to be remarkable that the cases were for the most part confined to two spots – one nearest the church and the other at Omoa, nearly three miles distant. Meanwhile, at Newarthill it was said that, 'a good work is going on'.[45]

Wishaw

The Rev. William Reid attended a meeting in Wishaw, where E. P. Hammond, then stationed in Musselburgh, also laboured. Reid said he had seen nothing like the religious anxieties he then witnessed since the visit of Radcliffe and Weaver to Edinburgh. 'They seemed to hear of the living water like men dying of thirst; and many of them came to Jesus and drank.'[46] The meeting was packed, with some hundreds standing throughout the evening. About three hundred remained to the inquirers meeting, one-half of whom seemed to be awakened. These were dealt with in separate rooms, one for men and one for women. Yet, even when nearly three hours had elapsed, all the cases of awakening had not been attended to. Reid believed that Hammond was specially fitted for breaking up the fallow ground, and he thanked him from the bottom of his heart for his indefatigable labours.

One sceptic attended many revival services in order to judge the matter properly, and said he found nothing to alarm or disturb 'even the most fastidious. All was solemnity.' Five months later, the good effects

---

45. *WJ*, Nov. 1859, p. 58; 02/03/1861, p. 598.
46. *WJ*, 05/01/1861, p. 535.

were still holding fast. 'I can point to men, both rich and poor in this locality', observed another, 'who previous to these meetings were infidels, scoffers, drunkards, swearers, wife-beaters etc, and who have now become regular church-goers – sober, industrious and good members of the community. On the pay night at some of the public works, instead of men entreating one another to go and drink their wages after they get them, they go in bands and pray together till midnight.'[47]

South Lanarkshire

Hamilton

There were twelve churches in Hamilton in 1861, and as early as the close of 1858, the Established Church, United Presbyterians, Congregationalists, Wesleyans and Baptists all joined for united prayer four nights a week in response to reports of American revivals, which appeared regularly in *The Hamilton Advertiser*.[48] The United Presbyterians played a prominent role in the work here, predominantly through the instrumentality of their minister, Rev. John Inglis, who held weekly open-air services, and through the medium of invited evangelists.

Upwards of one hundred boys assembled together for prayer and devotional exercises, while a great effort was made by a number of devout women to procure a home for 'destitute females who may be disposed to turn from their paths of vice'.[49] Funds were promised to pay the rent of a house, furnish it, procure a matron, and otherwise make it a comfortable abode.

A correspondent for *The Wynd Journal*, writing in February 1860, thought it 'most remarkable', the numbers that were now engaged in conducting prayer meetings, on every evening, and in every district of Hamilton. Many were stricken to the heart. On one very wet evening, near the outskirts of the town, a man was coming to the meeting, and

---

47. *SG*, 27/12/1860; Headley, pp. 97-8. As a result of this movement, several Wishaw converts set about forming an Evangelical Union church in Young St, which operated for many decades (*Wishaw Herald*, 17/03/1921). Additional growth resulted from the secession of a number of families from Cambusnethan Free Church, whose minister had spoken out in the strongest terms against the 'new views' of the Evangelical Union.

48. *Hamilton Advertiser*, 12/03/59, quoted in Buchanan, pp. 12-13.

49. *WJ*, 14/10/1859, p. 34.

behind a hedge, thought he heard a voice. He stopped, and found three lads under an umbrella, crying to God in prayer for their conversion – thinking that no-one could see or hear them, but Christ alone. The pleas of new converts to their friends and families to come to the Saviour were also 'exceedingly touching', and had positive effects, not only in Hamilton, but in ten or twelve neighbouring towns and villages.[50]

Dalziel

The first drops of an imminent shower of blessing fell on Dalziel Free Church, to the north of Motherwell, on a Communion Sabbath in November 1860. The Rev. Ogilvy was assisted by the Rev. William Fraser of Gourock, who had taken part in the revival work in Ireland and had since done much to promote it in Scotland. His sermon that evening helped engender intense earnestness among many in the large congregation, and one person went 'rigid'. The work was given a massive boost two weeks later with the arrival of E. P. Hammond. Unconventionally, Ogilvy paraded the American visitor round the parish in a dogcart, introducing him to the public and soliciting their personal co-operation. Hammond's mission lasted a fortnight. 'The windows of heaven have been opened', wrote a journalist, 'and a shower of blessing has come down, such as we never anticipated. ... I cannot describe the state of things. ... Every night the number is swelled under Mr Hammond's solemn, faithful, loving addresses.'[51] Of the many hymns sung during the mission, 'Jesus Sought Me When I Was a Stranger' was the most popular, and the sound of three dozen young converts singing it with radiant faces, full voices and glowing hearts was described as utterly memorable.

Bravely, the Free Church minister decided to continue the meetings after Hammond's departure, and to his delight, interest increased. 'The whole available population turn out to the revival meetings', it was recorded,[52] and it was during this time that 'the principal scenes took

---

50. ibid., 04/02/1860, p. 146. However, it is possible that the revival did not leave a deep and lasting mark on the town, for when John Hambledon visited it in 1865 he recorded that 'no revival has reached this dead town for many years' (quoted in Buchanan, p. 15).

51. *WJ*, 08/12/1860, p. 503.

52. *The Mercury*, quoted in *WJ*, 05/01/1861, p. 535. Indeed, Rev. W. Reid contrasted the spiritual liveliness of the Lanarkshire mining towns to 'the deadness of Edinburgh, where Christ cannot do many mighty works because of our unbelief' (ibid.).

place, reminding one of the day of Pentecost, and rivalling anything in the history of revivals'. Remarkably, the meetings continued nightly till March 1861, and, aided by Joseph Loudon of Dalziel Parish Church, Ogilvy presided at them all, except one (on which night he was preaching elsewhere). A variety of evangelists came to speak – 'The Wynd Flesher' (Robert Cunningham) one night speaking 'the dialect of the slums', and Oswald Dykes (later Professor Dykes) 'in the most polished and gracious terms' another night,[53] but both preaching the same gospel message.

So genuine was the revival movement regarded as being that its influence – embodied in an evangelistic spirit and work – was said to have still been apparent forty years later. And so appreciated was the Rev. Ogilvy's untiring zeal in promoting the Motherwell work that in its aftermath some friends and colleagues presented him with an inscribed, elegant marble clock and a purse of sovereigns.

Larkhall

James Gilchrist, a licensed grocer and publican, was soundly converted when revival spread to the Larkhall district of Lanarkshire. He said that on the morning after his conversion when he entered his public house, 'the whisky barrels stared me in the face, and I stood condemned before them'. There could be no half-measures with Gilchrist; the barrels were rolled into the street, and the contents poured into the gutter, while the signboard bearing his emblem as a publican was painted black the same day.[54] One Sunday morning, donned in a black suit of clothes and mounted on his black horse, Gilchrist rode from Chapelton to Larkhall bearing a banner which stated, 'Prepare to Meet thy God.' On the way people stopped and gazed in solemn silence, and some declared that the Day of Judgement had surely come! Passing over the Avon Bridge and up through Millheugh, the sight of the black figure with the solemn text led to some being awakened and made to think of eternal realities in a way they had not done before.

---

53. David Ogilvy, *Historical Sketch of the Free Church of Scotland in the Parish of Dalziel from the Disruption in 1843 to the Union in 1900*, Glasgow, 1900, p. 58.

54. A similar case, vividly illustrating the work of grace going on in that district, is that of Daniel Hamilton, another Larkhall publican who, on conversion, also poured away all his liquor and closed shop. He became a bold witness and was still to be found preaching as 'a frail old man with shaking limbs and trembling voice' (David Beattie, *Brethren: The Story of a Great Recovery*, Kilmarnock, 1940, p. 208).

Larkhall was a coal-mining district, and during winter many men saw little daylight except on Sundays. Yet many of them seldom missed the evening meetings, and during winter when kitchen meetings were held, that night's preacher might be seen hurrying home from the pithead, in time to take his place in those happy, soul-winning gatherings. Meanwhile, in a bleachfield works in Larkhall, the senior partner, Mr Robson, led a daily morning prayer meeting in a separate room. Said a visitor, 'I shall never forget such a sweet sight as those men and women assembled there, about fifty in number, in their working dress, and that worthy man (Mr Robson) bending over them, father-like, imploring protection of soul and body from Him who rules in earth and heaven.'[55]

Stonehouse and Strathaven

A minister visiting Stonehouse was delighted to see the wonderful change in the village. The prayer meetings, which used to be so very thinly attended, were now held, he noted, not once a week, but every evening, and were crowded till there was not room enough for everyone to get in. A month later the visiting clergyman could report that 'the stream of spiritual influence passing through our midst deepens and widens, bearing, we trust, hundreds forward to a blissful eternity'. The revival resulted in the opening of an Evangelical Union chapel in October 1860.[56]

While coal and iron dominated much of the Lanarkshire economy, Strathaven,[57] with its plentiful supply of water, was synonymous with milling (both corn and flour). Revival finally reached the town towards the close of 1859, after some converts from Hamilton gave addresses at the long-established prayer meetings. They were followed by converts from Stonehouse, and since that time the work progressed with vigour. The revival was seen in several phases; attended, at times, by cases of prostration; on many more occasions by cases of hopeful conversion; and in general by an 'almost universal awakening'. Prominent in the work

---

55. ibid., pp. 207-9; *WJ*, 23/08/62, p. 173.

56. *WJ*, November 1859, p. 42; 10/12/1859, p. 82; Buchanan, p. 20.

57. While the revival in this county may have been predominant in some of the larger towns, Buchanan is incorrect in suggesting that 'evidence of extensive revival activity' was only to be found in two Lanarkshire towns during the period 1859–61, namely Hamilton and Strathaven (Buchanan, p. 12).

was both the staunchly conversionist Evangelical Union, where nightly meetings were held before being relocated to the larger East United Presbyterian Church, and the Church of Scotland, whose minister, the Rev. W. Barnhill was viewed as a 'tower of strength for revival work'.[58]

The Scottish Guardian recorded of Strathaven that for the two previous weeks especially the town had been 'in an extraordinary state and continues so'. There were 'severe cases of bodily manifestation' and 'the numbers are almost incredible that have been awakened, displaying great anxiety regarding their eternal safety'. Unusually, the New Year period was known for its quietness; 'the sound of praise only was heard where it used to be the sound of revelry'. One thousand people attended one Sabbath midday prayer meeting in January 1860, while that same evening 1,300 filled the largest church in town, with five hundred anxious enquirers being spoken to at the close of the service.[59]

Lesmahagow

In the parish of Lesmahagow, the Holy Spirit was 'poured out … in rich abundance, in almost every corner of it'. After many months, there appeared to be a pause in the work, so far as man could see, and 'God's people were kept down on the knee of prayer'. By the autumn of 1861, these intercessors were receiving the answers to their petitions in the form of fresh blessings poured out on some of the district meetings, more especially at Bellsfield and Coalburn Colliery, and the wright shop in Abbey Green. Two hundred members were added to the Free and the United Presbyterian Churches alone as an immediate result of the revival.[60]

Carluke

In the summer of 1859, David Drummond, pastor of Carluke's newly formed Evangelical Union Church (formerly known as Ebenezer Chapel), addressed many open-air meetings in and around the town. Deep impressions were made and numbers were converted. Soon, five or six weekly prayer meetings had also sprung up under the auspices of Drummond; these, like the Sabbath services, being attended by folk from as far away as Wishaw.

---

58. *WJ*, 04/02/1860, p. 147; Buchanan, p. 17.

59. *SG*, 10/01/1860; 13/01/1860.

60. *WJ*, 28/09/1861, p. 213; *SG*, 12/04/1860.

It was reported in February 1861 that a remarkable awakening had taken place at Orchard, a hamlet to the south of Carluke. It commenced through the instrumentality of two young brothers, who came to a knowledge of the true gospel while attending the meetings in the Bridgegate Church, Glasgow. On returning home they were enabled to get up a small meeting. One happy worker wrote: 'It pleased the Lord to help us, and He has continued to be in our midst ever since. There is scarcely a house where there has not been some awakening, less or more. In one house we can count not less than eight converts.'[61]

Rural South-East Lanarkshire

Carnwarth and Biggar

The movement in the moorland village of Carnwarth, in the south-east corner of south Lanarkshire, began when a young man from the community came under such strong spiritual influences that he felt constrained to speak with others in that rural district. Soon, upwards of thirty had undergone a great change, while the whole population was said to have been affected and church meetings were packed.

The movement in Biggar began when, riding home from the Biggar Fair, a minister came across a man in deep anxiety. After prayer, counsel and an almost sleepless night, the man found peace in believing and was soon found praying with the sick and at the prayer meetings. These were held in the manse every night, when the kitchen, passage and dining room were generally filled. One evening a woman ran out of the room crying loudly for mercy. Another was on her knees calling on God, and a ploughman burst into tears and wailing. The same two women were struck down several times after that. The ploughman found the peace he was seeking, and 'the scene was exciting and joyful to me', said the minister. 'This was the beginning', he continued, 'and for several nights numbers were stricken. Amongst these were three mothers. What a happy day for the child when the mother is brought to the Saviour! The work now goes on more quietly.'[62]

---

61. *WJ*, 23/02/1861, p. 591.

62. *SG*, 06/03/1860; *WJ*, 03/03/1860, p. 179. Strangely, *The Scottish Guardian* suggested later in the month that the revival was making little progress in Biggar (*SG*, 27/03/1860).

Quothquan

A thirty-to-forty-year-old fellowship meeting in Quothquan was brought to 'a great quickening of spiritual life' in 1860, its effects passing through parts of the quiet neighbouring country parishes in Peebleshire and Lanarkshire. One woman went through deep agony of soul. The parish minister was called on; he warned her against attending the prayer meetings and said she might end up in an asylum! Dr Walker stated that, through the secluded country districts which had been chiefly acted on by the Quothquan awakening, he knew of from forty to fifty persons who had professed either to have given themselves to the Saviour, or to be earnestly seeking Him. An interesting class of these consisted of the young farm lads – youths of thirteen, fourteen, fifteen and sixteen years of age.[63]

---

63. *Missionary Record*, 1860, quoted in Brown, 1893, pp. 775-6.

Sunset over Saltcoats harbour

Ardrossan

Vale of Garnock

CHAPTER 6

Ayrshire

North Ayrshire

Saltcoats and Ardrossan

It is perhaps not surprising that the North Ayrshire towns of Saltcoats and Ardrossan should be among the first places in Scotland to come under the influence of the revival, given not only their proximity to Ulster, but also the fact that Ardrossan, like Greenock further north, was at the time one of the chief outlets for passenger traffic between Scotland and the north of Ireland.

Ten days before revival in Saltcoats commenced, three men had got together to pray. They were each 'visited' by the Lord and the meeting they began in apprehension and fear continued in confidence and hope. Previously Brownlow North had conducted meetings in the town, which had stirred up believers and resulted in numbers repenting of their lives of sin. The movements here and in Ardrossan, just two miles distant, were further influenced by the return from Ireland of the Free Church ministers of both towns, the Rev. Davidson and the Rev. Stewart, as well as of a Free Church student – Mr Sillars, stationed in Ardrossan. Sillars at once began meetings in a harbour store in that town, which attracted up to eight hundred people. Addresses were also given by Mr Crosby and two other God-fearing captains of merchant vessels berthed in the harbour. So many flocked to the meetings that they sometimes had to be conducted in the open air, church buildings proving too small. The revival had a particular effect on Paisley Street – colloquially known as 'Little Dublin' due to the nationality of many who resided there – where a marked change became evident in the conduct of the residents.

It was said of one meeting that 'no description can give any idea of the extraordinary and unprecedented scene … especially after the anxious were assembled in the store.' Around sixty showed evidence of real conviction. In one part of the building were clusters of girls singing; in another part a whole row of boys knelt at a form and cried aloud to God for mercy. One girl was so happy that she pleaded with her parents to be allowed to stay all night in the dark store, alone with Jesus (she was, however, 'with gentle violence taken home'!).[1] At a similarly crowded meeting in the Free Church, Mr Gill of the West Coast Mission drafted off many to the United Presbyterian Church, which could not be lighted, so he addressed them in the dark! Here, the daughters of a minister, among others, were brought under deep conviction.

The Justice of Peace commented in January 1860 that such was the effect of the revival in Ardrossan that he did not have a tenth of crime cases coming before him in the last four months than he had previously. The moral reformation was perhaps greatest in the local shipyard, the town's main centre of occupation. Formerly known as 'a wicked place' and 'the ruination of the morals of the young', there was now not a swear-word to be heard, and the workmen were happy and God-fearing. The work in this town was so intense and powerful that it was said that if it continued for much longer, Ardrossan would 'soon be a town of saints'. However, while the movement in Saltcoats continued unabated, that in its neighbouring community all but came to a standstill. By the beginning of the New Year (1860) it was reported that 'there is no awakening at present; no outward manifestations. The meetings have returned to their former state.'[2]

Around half a dozen people in total from Saltcoats were bodily 'stricken' during the movement, to the extent that they were confined afterwards to bed. Such was the change in the town that in a shipyard 'some strong men who were bears in their behaviour are now like lambs'. In Saltcoats one woman who one day scoffed at the revival was before night-time stricken down – she since found peace in believing. Also prostrated was a poor Highland woman who made her cries to God in her native Gaelic tongue, before obtaining peace of heart. Indeed,

---

1. *SG*, 13/09/1859.

2. ibid., 31/01/1860.

several weeks into the revival it was said that scarcely a night passed without one or two being stricken down, though no undue excitement was managed by the speakers. Less happy was the case of several wee girls seen walking along the beach singing Psalm 23. Asked why they were thus engaged they replied, 'We are trying to find Jesus in it.' One girl solemnly added, 'But sir, we dinna think we have found him yet.'[3]

So influential was the revival in these two towns that 'a more than ordinary number of strange ministers moved about', apparently attracted to the place in consequence of the publicity obtained. A local newspaper reported that the higher classes had generally kept aloof from the movement. 'Some of them indeed were frightened, and a number actually left the place in terror.' It was, however, a case of 'out of the frying pan and into the fire' for many who left out of fear were to find themselves in places where the movement quickly spread! The same report added that the movement was now making headway among the middle classes.[4]

Garnock Valley

In the vale of Glengarnock, which carves southward from the Loch of Kilbirnie, were many mining villages containing a total population of around 30,000. 'Drops of blessing' fell on both sides of the valley when the Rev. Robert Steele itinerated there in early 1859. Indeed, so many prayer meetings rose up that he had difficulty in counting them.

Later in the year, when Steele held open-air meetings in Dalry, 'almost the whole population of the village were listening eagerly', and on one Sabbath about 3,000 heard the Word preached. However, a number of influential voices railed against the revival, not least a pub-owner who had virtually no trade on the nights of the open-air services. At an outdoor meeting during the local Fair Day, an immense crowd listened with solemn attention, in the midst of a heavy shower of rain, but they were so closely packed together that the rain could only reach their head and shoulders! The meeting was moved to a Free Church schoolroom, where, towards the close of the meeting, a working man rose, and, 'with

---

3. ibid., 13/09/1859; 30/08/1859.

4. ibid., 06/09/1859. One apparent consequence of the revival in Ardrossan was the erection of a larger church building in Bute Place (opened in July 1860) to house the Evangelical Union Church, where Peter Mather served as pastor from 1838 till his death almost fifty years later.

a heart liken to burst, poured out a most earnest prayer to Almighty God … all of a sudden the whole meeting seemed to be moved by an invisible power'. Steele said he had seen much agony in his day, including various stages of cholera, but never had he seen such a sight as this. 'A number were carried out, stricken down', he said. 'At length. … I poured out a prayer to God such as I had never uttered before.'[5]

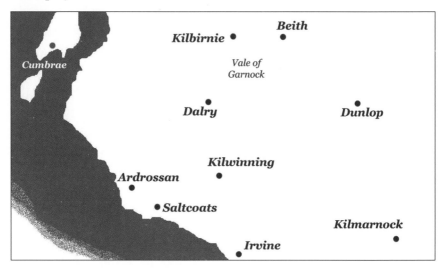

'Next morning Satan had a revival too', noted one correspondent, when people from a series of 'Romanist villages' came against the movement. Such opposition did little to dampen the revival however, and as many as 189 members were added to the Free Church near the start of the New Year, while twenty-seven weekly prayer meetings were being held throughout the extensive mission field. It was recorded that during just five consecutive days in March 1860 a total of fifty people – young and old – were 'struck down'; passing under 'that indescribable influence which renders the man unconscious of what is passing without, while the mind lives in mysterious scenes of extreme horror or of satiable joy'.[6] This included twenty-five cases on Wednesday and Thursday; seven on Friday evening at three prayer meetings; and six more at the Saturday evening converts' class – all this within just one congregation (the Free Church).

From Dalry, the awakening spread to Kilbirnie. At a meeting in the Free Church, after a young man from Glasgow gave an account of the

---

5. *SG*, 23/08/1859.

6. *WJ*, 10/03/1860, p. 187.

work he had witnessed in Ireland: 'All of a sudden the mighty hand of God was seen and felt with us and many were stricken down.'[7] The first woman to be 'struck sent up such a cry to God for mercy as caused many to start to their feet. We tried to remove her, but could not, as she had fallen under the seat, and was in the greatest agony of soul.' In less than five minutes there were ten or a dozen in various parts of the church all crying to God for mercy. One girl ran out of church, was 'struck', and had to be carried back again. The scene at this time was said to have been 'altogether indescribable. Many were in tears; some as if in a swoon, only their lips moving in silent prayer; others were sending up heart-rending cries to God for mercy. One poor girl said that her heart was as black as hell. It was truly a solemn scene. … The screams of the stricken ones were heard over the town, which brought many to church. Fear sent many who had been in the church away home. The faces of many of the scoffers were as pale as death, and some of them, strong men, had to be assisted home. It was a night much to be remembered by us … .'[8]

It was noted that several of those 'stricken, and who we had every reason to believe had found true peace', were in fact similarly affected on other occasions. Thereafter, the work in Kilbirnie progressed 'quietly but rapidly'. One unusual meeting consisted of 'twenty old men and women, many 77 or 60 years of age'. All were anxiously enquiring, 'What must I do to be saved?' Though the membership of the Free Church had remained at around 150 for many years, it jumped in the period following the revival to 226. In June 1863, for example, fifteen were admitted on profession of faith and twenty in the following November.[9]

Kilwinning

Kilwinning – where one man had had a strong premonition of a coming revival – was blessed with special services, led by Andrew Bonar, Alexander Somerville and others in early 1858. From these came 'an onward flow of spiritual earnestness', leading in the summer

---

7. In Glengarnock Iron Works, also, Steele said, 'a number were smitten' when he preached to them, 'and one young woman in a manner I never saw before' (*SG*, 30/09/1859).

8. *WJ*, 31/12/1859, p. 107.

9. ibid.; *SG*, 30/08/1859; W. J. Couper, *Kilbirnie West: A History of Kilbirnie West United Free 1824-1924*, Kilbirnie, 1923, pp. 36-7.

of 1859 to 'a very extraordinary awakening'. Initially, a considerable number of intelligent young men were awakened, this being followed by a similar work among the young women. This period was, however, 'a night of sorrow' before the dawning of 'the morning of joy' when distress of soul led to peace and joy. Said the Rev. Pinkerton of the Free Church, 'It is an easy and blessed work now to preach. God's presence is felt.' Among those influenced by the revival movement in nearby Irvine was schoolboy George Yuille, later Baptist minister and historian of the Baptist churches in Scotland.[10]

Dunlop

The Rev. William Gebbie of Dunlop Parish Church was about to cross to Ireland to witness the revival there when he was called to see a woman who had been in 'a wonderful state during the night. The Spirit of God had come down', and so sure was he that this was the beginnings of a spiritual deluge on the district that Gebbie felt he could cancel his proposed pilgrimage to Ulster. Sure enough, where previously there were drops of blessing here and there, in October 1859, 'the rain came down in torrents', and a great movement developed in the district.[11]

Gebbie was described by a fellow minister as having done more than any other man for the furtherance of revivalism in the district. The excitement extended to and affected almost the whole parish. Work was suspended – for a time little could be observed but people, conscience-stricken, 'running about seeking consolation or engaged in deep mental prayer'. 'The public houses were forsaken', observed Gebbie, 'and the keeper of the only public house in the village shut up his shop and took down his signboard. There were cases of "striking down", but I did not see them. ... Although, with some Glasgow ministers, I look cautiously upon cases of "striking", yet I do not see the necessity of suppressing one jot of the good which the revival movement has effected and is effecting. In Dunlop it has changed the face of things. The reign of Christian love may or may not last – all I say is, that it exists.'[12]

---

10. *SG*, 08/11/1860; Brian R. Talbot, *Standing on the Rock: A History of Stirling Baptist Church, 1805-2005*, Stirling, 2005, p. 52.

11. *SG*, 16/04/1861; *WJ*, 10/05/1862, p. 53.

12. *WJ*, 05/01/1861, p. 535.

A journalist attended a meeting in Dunlop at which Richard Weaver was preaching. He wrote that a young man from Stewarton 'was seized instantaneously with the mysterious visitation (of prostration), and now commences a scene among the "converts" which almost baffles description', as a state of emotional chaos broke out throughout the hall,

[The congregation was] supplied with a hymn-book, compiled by Weaver; and gathering in circles they sang portions of its contents, with frantic gestures, and in every variety of time and tune. While in one corner of the church a party was singing to the tune of 'Wait for the Wagon', another, not far distant, were enlivening the audience with 'Betsy Baker.' To persons unaccustomed to such scenes the spectacle of young men and women, boys and girls, embracing each other in transports of religious delirium – swaying their bodies backwards and forwards – standing on the seats and stamping their feet to the tune, and holding forth at the pitch of their voices: 'Christ for Me', must have been anything but pleasant to their feelings.[13]

At length, the meeting divided, because of the size of the crowd, and some accompanied Mr McLeish to the Free Church where matters were conducted with a little more propriety, but both went on until 3 a.m.[14] Conduct similar to that described above was repeated at many subsequent meetings with little variation.[15]

---

13. Weaver was not the only one to compose gospel songs. The use of modern hymns had still not become universally fashionable in Scotland, the biblical Psalms generally being the only form of worship deemed acceptable in public worship. Nevertheless, month by month, as the revival progressed, new songs and music appeared. For example, Duncan Matheson wrote many hymns, resulting in a published compilation which became highly popular. Some young people were said to have made 'amusing, though rarely malicious' parodies of a few of the hymns (Matthews, p. 63).

14. Richard Weaver himself says of this visit that upon his preaching, 'the work of the Spirit broke out in full force in the place'. The landlords of both pubs in the village were converted, and 'for a time Dunlop was without a public house' (Paterson, 1897, p. 134).

15. *SG*, 30/10/1860. John Kent in a chapter of his book, *Holding the Fort* entitled '1859: The Failure of English Revivalism', makes much of the extravagances associated with the ministry of Richard Weaver, including the Dunlop scenario (pp. 113-21). His writing, however, takes little account of the good and lasting fruit of the spiritual awakening in this Ayrshire district. One who attended numerous services in Dunlop said, 'That there were such scenes as have been described in the public press is utterly false. In performing the duties of religion, I love order and

However, notwithstanding the occasional negative report, the Rev. W. Pinkerton of Kilwinning Free Church visited Dunlop's Parish and Free churches and wrote of evidence personally gained of genuine conversions, including that of entire families, as well as the local publican. Describing Communion Monday in the Free Church he wrote: 'Brighter and better days they were even than those of Livingston and the Kirk of Shotts.' The meetings were calm and solemn – 'it is the Lord's work. ... During the past fourteen months – the most memorable perhaps in the history of Scotland's Church – I have visited many revival scenes, and taken part in many revival meetings and I feel constrained to say I have not witnessed anything so deep and widespread, and so evidently from above.'[16]

Another church leader wrote:

> As firmly do I believe that the revival movement in Dunlop was the work of the Holy Spirit, as that recorded in Acts 2. ... I have been in many revival meetings, both in the north and south of Scotland, but never did I witness more clearly the Mighty One making bare his holy arm, and doing his own work. What deep penitence, what humble confessions, what heart-felt sorrow, what gladness and joy, what zeal for the honour of Christ and the salvation of souls, was manifest there! The reality of all this struck me with such force, that I could not help repeating the words, 'Behold, I make all things new.'[17]

This minister concluded: 'I could count the converts, not by the dozen or by the score, but by the hundred, many of whom I have known for years. ... I could point you to many who would gladden your heart with a recital of their conversion, and who carry in their heart a warm love to the God of grace.'[18]

---

solemnity as well as any man, but under the present circumstances, it never occurred that there was anything wrong. Similar scenes must have occurred on the day of Pentecost' (*WJ*, 10/05/1862, p. 54).

16. *SG*, 08/11/1860.

17. *WJ*, 10/05/1862, p. 53.

18. ibid., 17/05/1862, p. 63. A minister from Montgreenan (near Irvine) also attended a number of meetings in Dunlop, as did many of his parishioners. The meetings 'had a very solemnising effect upon my mind', he wrote. 'It did not seem to me that "confusion was triumphant and chaos come again". The noise was not half so distracting to the mind, or discordant to the ear, as the hum of voices at the "conversaziones" of the Social Science Congress, and, indeed, it was neither more nor less than a religious

Many flocked from miles around to the meetings in Dunlop. A minister from Beith said he attended,

> ... for several nights in succession, and, without exception, there were weeping penitents from Beith, a great many persons, old and young, of both sexes, church members and others. In one corner of the Dunlop church were about twenty young girls from Beith formed into a little band, rejoicing that they had found the pearl of great price, and singing that beautiful hymn, 'There is Rest for the Weary.' It was a beautiful sight; the light of joy beaming in every countenance, and the eye upturned to heaven. Last week I met a great many going to Dunlop for the purpose, as one of them told me, to get a shake of Mr Gebbie's hand, through whose instrumentality they got a glimpse of the cross of Christ, and by the power of the Spirit of God, they were led to accept of Christ.

Similarly, a missionary in Neilston, who had oversight of Dunlop parish, spent a week there, 'assisting the ministers in their arduous toils. I could tell you many a wonderful sight to which I was a witness', he wrote. 'I made every effort to get as many of the people here, down to Dunlop, as I could, in order that they might catch the infection as it were, and bring the revival to our own district. The plan was entirely successful.'[19]

Diffusion from Dunlop

From Dunlop as the centre, awakening diffused throughout the wider region. The Rev. James Clugston of the Free Church in Stewarton, just two miles south of Dunlop, insisted that the movement in his own parish was 'devoid of extravagant excitement', the meetings being remarkable 'only for the deep solemnity and earnest spirit of inquiry which characterises them'. Some young girls from this district attended meetings in Dunlop, where they came under deep distress of soul, and as 'the poor little things had walked all the way from Stewarton, they were very glad to get home in a conveyance that was going that way'.[20]

---

conversazione, many of those engaged in it having the deepest conviction that God was in the midst of them.' The writer concluded that 'ministers and elders, and all who are engaged in the work are thus made to feel that they are utterly powerless and that God is exercising his sovereignty in the whole matter from first to last' (*WJ*, 24/11/1860, p. 484).

19. ibid., 08/12/1860, p. 502.

20. *SG*, 01/11/1860; *WJ*, 24/11/1860, p. 484.

The movement in Beith actually began before that in Dunlop, when a number of laymen started meetings in the Free Church schoolroom. These soon had to be transferred to the church, which, too, was packed almost to suffocation at times. Many of the local clergymen were blessed with a sound gospel ministry and had 'all along preached salvation by free grace, through Jesus Christ'.[21] But even these held aloof for a time, until the movement grew and gathered strength so wonderfully, that they seemed forced to throw in their lot. So unwilling were people to leave the church even at very late hours, that one minister was forced, from the pulpit, to ask the revivalists to leave his church, and call at his house the next morning. One meeting was addressed by Mr Frazer of Gourock, from the story of the four lepers at the gate of Samaria, 'Why sit we here and die?' 'The speaker seemed as if his lips had been touched with a live coal from God's altar', commented one who was present, and many were deeply affected.[22]

Robert Steele of Dalry also laboured in the town, visiting every week for several months. One result of this mission was that an Evangelical Union station was begun, with around seventy families giving their adhesion to the new cause. The Evangelical Union sent the Rev. Salmon to hold further meetings and a church was formed in October 1861.

Meanwhile, in Millport, on the small island of Great Cumbrae, 'an interesting work' commenced in October 1859. Four months later the movement was still in progress, the efforts of one visiting labourer in particular bringing a blessing. Wrote one witness: 'I was out today, and was greatly delighted to find so many had been awakened; some are still in great distress, others are rejoicing in Christ.'[23]

Outcome of North Ayrshire Events

A general result of the movement in Beith, according to one believer, was that the streets were much quieter, the street loungers no longer to be seen at the 'Horse Shoe Corner', and 'the movement is in everyone's mouth'. There was, however, talk of a particular 'decent tradesman's wife' becoming temporarily insane from an excessive anxiety regarding

---

21. ibid., 08/12/1860, p. 502.
22. ibid., 05/01/1861, p. 535.
23. *WJ*, 22/10/1859, p. 26; 02/03/1861, p. 598.

her husband's eternal welfare, although she soon recovered. One striking outcome of the revival was the manner agreed upon to celebrate the New Year; 'not with dancing parties and merry-makings, but by a great temperance soiree on revival principles'.[24]

In a unique scenario William Gebbie was libelled by fifty-seven heritors and parishioners for extravagances in speech and practice, and brought before the Irvine Presbytery. As well as allowing disturbing physical phenomena and hymns that were sung to 'unwonted and fantastic tunes', Gebbie was accused of using wild language that endangered sound doctrine. This included asserting the damnation of children – that is, unless they had made a definite profession of faith; for another charge against Gebbie was that he had admitted a boy of twelve or fourteen years and a girl of fifteen or sixteen years of age, to the Communion.

Gebbie was also alleged to have claimed that no man could be converted without being fully aware of the fact (he had said that it was easy for him to tell the converted from the unconverted, because he saw God looking out of their eyes), and that no unconverted man had a right to pray ('You may kneel down to pray, but you have no God to pray to – you pray to your chair'). He also reputedly said on one occasion of anyone doubting the genuineness of the Dunlop revival: 'If there is a deeper or hotter place in hell, he will get it.' One of the accusers was a farmer who had been a member of the Parish kirk for twelve years before 'being driven from the church by Mr Gebbie's teaching'. Following an apology, Gebbie was cautioned and the storm slowly subsided.[25]

Central Ayrshire

Dreghorn and Irvine

Meetings were begun in Dreghorn in central Ayrshire in the summer of 1859, in the cottages of local colliers. As interest rapidly increased, hundreds would meet to hear the gospel preached in the open air – one

24. *WJ*, 05/01/1861, p. 535.

25. *SG*, 11/02/1862; 11/02/1862; John R. Fleming, *A History of the Church in Scotland 1840-1874*, Edinburgh, 1927, p. 115; See also, *The Dunlop Heresy Case Unlocked, or Revivalism Delineated*, Glasgow, 1862.

account stating that at the beginning of September a crowd of 15,000 assembled in the fields.[26] As winter came on, the people resorted to an empty byre, until a wooden mission hall was hastily constructed. This seated five hundred and was often filled.

The Rev. W. D. Robertson of the Free Church, Irvine, where revival was also evidenced, was given strength and grace to preach at least every second night despite the recent tragic loss of two of his brothers through illness. Indeed, he was able to say, 'It is blessed work, and even in present results has a thousand times more than its reward.' Robertson described 'the crowds of eager faces seen in the cattle stalls, and likened the scene to the adoration of the magi' on which subject he had recently been preaching. Of revival in a nearby village, Robertson said that 'the women grew to look like Madonnas, and both men and women sung like angels ... it was wonderful how the spiritual light transformed the material man'.[27]

Troon

Revival affected Troon throughout the autumn and winter of 1859–60. In one church alone, there were, by October, sixteen private prayer meetings arranged for Friday evenings, with at least two people conducting each of them. As a result of the movement, a great change in moral standards became evident, most noticeably in various public works, where previously swearing was maintained to such an extent that parents were afraid to apprenticeship their sons to the different trades in case they should become addicted to 'this dreadful vice'. Now the young men in these works would not only refrain from swearing but would feel extremely sorry if ever they heard improper statements uttered either by acquaintances or strangers.

A certain 'lady of rank', returning home from a card-party, found her maid thoughtfully reading a Christian tract. The lady reproached her servant for such vain activity, but, glancing at the tract herself, was unusually impressed by the word 'Eternity' there engraved, which began to awaken her spirit. Retiring to bed, her sleep entirely left her, sighs and groans succeeding one another without intermission as she wrestled in spiritual anxiety. Around this time she also became seriously ill, but

26. Richard Owen Roberts, *Scotland Saw His Glory*, Wheaton, 1995, p. 293.

27. James Brown D.D., *Life of W. B. Robertson of Irvine*, Glasgow, 1889, pp. 183-6.

found such bodily sickness of very small consideration in the present circumstances. The outcome was that 'cards and gay company were, from this moment, wholly discarded; while her time and thoughts were entirely taken up during the short period now intervening between her approaching end and the grave, in making preparations for another world'.[28]

Ayr

'A good work' was 'manifestly begun' in the village of Newton Green, just outside Ayr, by the end of February 1860. The minister of the Free Church, around which the movement centred, was under the necessity of giving two addresses in two different houses, so anxious were the people to hear the Word. In addition, some youths in the foundry came under serious impressions and a meeting was fixed for them one Saturday afternoon. Colliers in Whiteletts, also near Ayr, held a prayer meeting every evening in their village, while in some of the pits breakfast-time prayer meetings took place; between thirty and forty regularly attending the one at Dixon pit.[29]

It was claimed that the Brethren 'lived upon revivals'.[30] Certainly this group was prominent among the numerous denominations that benefited from revivals throughout Ayrshire in 1859–60, and out of the movement five new assemblies were formed in the county (Irvine, Ayr, Largs, Dalry and Dalmellington). One of the first converts of the revival in Ayr was sixteen-year-old John Justice. A precocious individual, Justice began evangelising his friends and became uneasy that his denomination, though evangelical in doctrine, admitted those he deemed unconverted to Communion.[31] He eventually left this

28. Rev. J. Fleming, *Revivals in Troon During the Winter of 1859–60*, Kilmarnock, 1860.

29. *WJ*, 04/02/1860; *SG*, 29/03/1860; *SG*, 13/03/1860.

30. William Reid, *Plymouth Brethrenism Unveiled and Refuted*, quoted in Buchanan, p. 6.

31. Such dissatisfaction with the impurities perceived in the established churches were, according to Neil Dickson, an important catalyst in the formation of Brethren assemblies in the early 1860s and subsequently. 'Revival preaching stressed the necessity of regeneration and gave an impetus towards the concept of the gathered church, one consisting of true believers only. The newly regenerate individual looked with dismay at those who had not been similarly awakened yet who were still partaking of communion alongside him' (Dickson, 2002, p. 69).

Church in 1862. Justice was among those deeply impressed by Gordon Forlong's emphasis on studying the Bible daily and witnessing to others. He began organising weekend outreaches to the villages around Ayr, and in August 1863 he and seventeen others were baptised in the sea at Newton beach.

In Ayr itself, among the laymen who addressed meetings during the revival was a chimney-sweep turned preacher, who came to the fore in May 1861. A few months later, William Brown, a baker from Glasgow, also addressed packed meetings in the town, during which there was 'some trembling and weeping'.[32] Around this time, too, appeared on the scene an evangelist by the name of Mr Lockhart, who became especially honoured in reaching many from the wealthier class, numbers of whom were now forming prayer meetings amongst themselves.

Kilmarnock

As many as five thousand people gathered for an open-air service at Clerk's Hom, Kilmarnock on 17 September 1859. It was recorded, a few months later, that the revival in this town was 'going on in a remarkable manner'. Amongst the many converts were two young lads, aged sixteen and nineteen, who had 'formerly been ringleaders in every kind of vice'. One of them was prayed for by his father at a prayer meeting. That same evening, this son attended another meeting for the purpose of ridiculing it. But so affected was he by the testimony of a convert that he underwent a dramatic change in character. He had previously got up a dancing class, which he intended to carry on vigorously during the winter, but this pursuit he now abandoned completely.[33]

Elsewhere in Kilmarnock, the revival led to a number of young Christians being united for fellowship and the mutual study of the Bible. As each became convinced of the scriptural authority of believers' baptism, this in turn led to the formation of a Baptist Church in the town. Meanwhile, Kilmarnock's Evangelical Union congregation flourished during the entire twenty-two-year ministry of William Bathgate from August 1857. Altogether Bathgate received 892 new members in that time, an average of forty per year. The highest growth was experienced in 1860, when one hundred new members were added

---

32. *WJ*, 22/08/1861.

33. *SG*, 19/11/1859; *WJ*. 10/12/1859, p. 82.

to the congregation, during which year also a further Evangelical Union fellowship was established in Winton Place.[34] Kilmarnock's Free Church also heartily entered into the spirit of the revival, its minister, David Landsborough delivering a course of sermons on the work of the Holy Spirit with more than his usual genuine earnestness, proving a considerable source of strength and comfort to his revived congregation.[35]

Nightly meetings were held in Hurlford, to the south-east of Kilmarnock, for over two months, with upwards of sixty people evincing concern about their souls. It was said of Catrine, in East Ayrshire, in August 1859: 'Little of public interest has been happening with us for the last two weeks. The all-absorbing topic seems to be revivalism.' Further north, from Dundonald it was reported: 'The revival movement has reached us in a very marked manner. Many amongst us are anxious, while not a few have found peace.'[36]

South Ayrshire

Maybole

The revival took a firm hold in Maybole, capital of the ancient kingdom of Carrick. The town's Free Church minister, the Rev. James Moir, was aware that many in the community would be somewhat concerned at reports of stories of prostrations from other parts of the country, and indeed from a nearby, unnamed village. To counter this, he preached a sermon on the topic of revival and its manifestations to his congregation in October 1859.[37] As a result of the ensuing revival in the community in general, the Superintendent of Police in the town had no hesitation in saying that the improvement in the moral conduct of the 'middle and lower classes here has been decidedly good'. In particular, he observed that in many quarters of the town, from which he had previously received frequent complaints about rioting and other

---

34. George Yuille, *History of Baptists in Scotland*, Glasgow, 1926, p. 209; McNaughton, 2007, p. 267.

35. Robert Tulloch, *History of Henderson United Free Church, Kilmarnock, 1773–1923*, Kilmarnock, 1923, p. 34.

36. *WJ*, 15/11/59, p. 34; 13/10/59, p. 10; *SG*, 30/08/1859.

37. Published as James Moir, *The Revival, and Bodily Manifestations*, Maybole, 1859.

forms of disorder, could now be heard at nights and on Sabbaths the voice of praise and prayer, sweetly resounding from the houses of the poor. In the summer of 1861, 'interesting meetings' were still being held in Maybole and Girvan, where many were impressed and led to 'close with Christ'.[38] Amongst the young especially, a remarkable work was said to be in progress.

Crosshill

The movement also spread to nearby Crosshill, three miles south-east of Maybole, where it was claimed that in many of the most hopeful cases, the work among the anxious had been quiet; unbeknown even to their closest neighbours. Wrote one resident: 'How seldom now one hears an oath, whereas formerly you couldn't walk a few yards of the village streets without a volley greeting your ear, either from scolding mothers, gossiping and wrangling neighbours or playing children!' Of January 1st, many said that 'never was such a New Year's day seen here'. Two hundred and fifty residents, plus children, gathered in the Free Church, where, among others, a former drunkard testified and exhorted. A great many in the congregation were melted to tears by his earnest and solemn address. John McLennan, minister of that church, was delighted to see so many hold fast their profession without wavering, although he did observe that of those who were prostrated or had visions, while they continued to attend regular ordinances such as worship and prayer meetings, only a fraction of them showed evidence of saving change. This, he claimed, was because many hopeful convictions were quickly nipped in the bud by the 'deplorable charlatanry' employed by a certain unnamed group.[39]

---

38. *SG*, 22/11/1859; *WJ*, 28/09/1861, p. 213.

39. McLennan wrote: 'Those who were "struck down"' were 'hounded, courted, flattered, hung upon, honoured and coquetted with till their minds veered round to a certain point on the ecclesiastical compass. Every fresh recruit became a partisan, and one of the increasing force of enlisting sergeants who were ready at a moment's notice to swarm about any of the newly convicted, and flutter and dance and buzz about them till he or she was made one of themselves' (*SG*, 14/01/1860).

Annan

E. P. Hammond

Closeburn

Moniaive

Vale of Glencairn

Eyemouth

St Abbs

Kelso

Chapter 7

The South

Dumfriesshire

A significant revival movement began to spread across the south-west region of Scotland only after it had died down in most other parts of the country. The match that lit the fires of spiritual awakening was the arrival in the area of American evangelist, Edward Payson Hammond in January 1861. However, it would be quite mistaken to think that there were no signs of genuine revival in the region prior to that time. On the contrary, there were reports of significant stirrings in various locations throughout this vast region well over a year before Hammond ever set foot in the district.

Revival Stirrings (1860)

Ebenezer Young, pastor of the Congregational Church in Annan, was accustomed to preaching in various places in and around that town. During 1860 he became increasingly aware of the 'good work' going on in many of these settings, promoted, he felt, partly by his own sermons, but more so by the prayers and exertions of other labourers in his church. At two very crowded meetings which Young addressed in one village there existed a depth of interest such as he had rarely witnessed. Numerous members were received into his church from miles distant during that one year.

In another village where two or three meetings were now held every week, nearly twenty people had given evidence of a saving change within the year, while in a separate community, large meetings were held weekly, and many had been brought to the Saviour. Never since Young's induction to the parish in 1848 had he seen in that village anything equal to the work now in progress, which he knew was also being promoted by the minister of the Free Church. Though located six miles from Annan, members were received from this village, and even from remoter locations a good way beyond it, into the Congregational church. Sabbath schools in a number of these districts were also in an encouraging state, several of the older scholars having been lately admitted as church members. The whole number admitted during the 1860 was thirty, only one of them by certificate from another church; the rest entirely from the world.

A preparatory work had been in progress in Kirkmahoe, to the north of Dumfries, for eighteen months before the stir caused by Hammond's visit to the county. Meanwhile, in the east of the county, a minister in Ecclefechan noted, 'We have got a blessed shower now. It has begun to descend. We are getting "the former rain" moderately ... No noise or excitement, not even many tears. Only one person has been struck down; struggle very short; instant peace; just at the loom; good impression the result. The interest seems to double every week and the number of inquirers to be increased every day.'[1]

Further east still, in the parish of Half-Morton, near Canonbie, and just a stone's throw from the English border, the revival was heartily carried on from mid-February. It was said that four-fifths of households of the parish 'had a day of visitation' from the Lord, and in most of them one or two had been hopefully converted. The work also spread to adjoining parishes.

Annan (1861)

Throughout much of the period 1859–60, believers in Annan read or heard reports of God's marvellous doings all over Scotland, longing for similar showers of blessing to fall on their own community. Annan was 'almost proverbial for immorality': being under a spiritual blight right up to the close of 1860, when revival had long since drawn to a stop in other places. But then it came. And how! It has been said that probably nowhere in Scotland did a more plenteous rain of gracious influences fall in the year 1861 than in Annan.[2]

---

1. *WJ*, 17/12/1859, p. 91.

2. Headley, p. 111; D. Watt (Ed.), *A Narrative of the Great Religious Revival in Annan in 1861*, Annan, 1898, p. 4; Emilia R. Snow, *A King's Champion: Gordon Forlong, Advocate, D. L. C.: From Deism to Christianity*, Aukland, printed by author, n.d., p. 29.

One of those much aggrieved at the spiritual condition of Annan was local resident Alice Johnstone, a deeply pious woman who began a fortnightly prayer meeting in one of her own rooms in the Temperance Hotel on Bank Street. Here a few burdened souls met to plead with God to pour out His Spirit on the town. Yet two years of united weekly prayer for a blessing, along with the visit of one minister to revival scenes in Ireland and the exciting report he brought back, failed to make a significant impact on the town, 'which seemed so dead'.[3]

E. P. Hammond (1860)

It was with the arrival, on invitation, of American evangelist Edward Payson Hammond on a two-week visit from 12 January 1861 that 'true revival' came to Annan. Hammond had already actively partaken of the revival of 1857–58 in the United States, and was currently studying at the Free Church College in Edinburgh, to which distant land he had removed 'for the sake of his health and for other reasons'. His meetings in the south-Dumfriesshire town nightly grew larger and soon concerts and balls failed to attract attention and even publicans were forced to wait idly at their taps. A circus which came to the town during the awakening turned out to be a failure, folk preferring to attend meetings in church.

The pattern developed; a general meeting in the Congregational Church at 2.30 each afternoon for Bible study, praise, and the praying over of prayer-requests, for which great numbers were daily sent in and to which some remarkable answers were received. This meeting, which at first drew around fifty people, was soon attracting five hundred. A children's meeting in the Free Church at 6.30, led by Mr Drysdale, an evangelist, who in his winsome dealings with the young, 'displayed a mastery possessed by few – children delighted in him'.[4] This was followed by an adults' meeting in the United Presbyterian Church at 8 p.m., which was often so packed that folk would sit on the back of seats behind the occupants of the pews; and even then an overflow meeting in the Free Church was often necessitated. In addition, a

---

3. Headley, p. 105. Alice also kept a diary of the revival movement, and from this account and her personal letters, many illuminating details of its progress can be garnered.

4. Watt, p. 10.

Sabbath morning union prayer-meeting was held at 7.30 in one of the town's four evangelical churches on a rotation basis. Hundreds were deeply touched by Hammond's addresses, and of the singing it was asked, 'Was there ever such singing here below before?' Even some who had stood aloof declared that it was more of heaven than of earth.

One Annan minister, in speaking of Hammond's 'peculiar qualifications for an evangelist', placed in the foreground his humble, childlike confidence in the Lord: 'Believing that God has given promises, he expects Him to keep them. ... But the last among the causes of Mr Hammond's power is his peculiar sweetness of temper or disposition. He is quite a man to be loved, for he loves everyone.' *The Dumfries Herald*, however, described the evangelist unfavourably as 'the young man from America authorised by no church in this country, whose style of terrorism is obviously coarse and irreverent'.[5] It was also stated that, at the close of a meeting, Hammond was in the habit of stationing himself at the door and beseeching the people as they left.

Revival Progress

The Annan revival quickly became well known over a wide area. One minister described how 'crowds flocked to Annan from ten or twelve parishes around ... insomuch that within less than a month the awakening might be said to have embraced the whole of the south of Scotland'.[6] Almost immediately following Hammond's departure in the last week of January, a steady stream of helpers, both lay and ordained, came to assist local ministers in the work. These included, variably, Mr Sillars, a young divinity student (regarded as 'a giant in experience and power'), who left his studies to come and help; Mr Macintosh; a former missionary to Madras; Colonel Davidson of the Edinburgh Tract Society; Mr Burns of Whitehaven; the Rev. Aitken of Paisley, and the Rev. McKay and the Rev. Hetherington, both from Edinburgh. It was noted that the supply of preachers seemed to be divinely guided, for there was not one night in the course of many weeks when there was no visiting preacher in town. Lawyer and converted deist, Gordon Forlong, arrived in Annan at the close of February, and like Hammond

---

5. Headley, pp. 115-16, 284; *The Dumfries Herald*, quoted in Marrs, p. 174.

6. Headley, p. 103.

before him, laboured 'for weeks together, night after night, and day after day' in and around the town, with tremendous success.[7]

One observer noted how, 'A solemn awe seems to hang over the community'; 'from a chill dreary wilderness, it was now vernal as a garden in spring'. The revival was embraced and praised by all the town's Protestant ministers, and to one of them it seemed 'as if *all* the young men were converted'. Another added that he felt the same might be said of the young women. This clergyman also noted that often, 'sermons have not been required, and would have been quite unseasonable'.[8]

Striking Results

The Dumfries Standard reported:

> Everyone talks of the great religious change, and wonders now that so much scepticism about the revival in Ulster and the West of Scotland had before prevailed among the inhabitants of Annan. Many young sailors, who had scarcely ever attended a place of worship, have been brought to a knowledge of their Saviour; many a drunkard has deserted the public-house in horror of his previous life; the artisans of the town have abandoned the corners where they lounged in the evenings, and have betaken themselves to prayer and meditation, and even 'the Arabs' of the burgh, the boys who were forever shouting and yelling about the streets, have every evening been engaged in singing the psalms and hymns.[9]

Mr McDowall, editor of the *Standard*, visited the town to personally acquaint himself with the work there. He wrote: 'Annan used to have a full share of nocturnal revellers and offenders against the law, but these have become "beautifully less", so that the outstanding aspects of the town are influenced by and in keeping with the daily and nightly religious services.' He further observed that 'many in the higher ranks' had come under the revival's influence, so that 'we find at Annan more than anywhere else in the district extensive employers of labour,

---

7. See also Orr, 1949, p. 66. Both Hammond and Forlong were remarkably used in the Annan revival, but the biographies of each fail to make specific mention of the good accomplished by the other in this Dumfriesshire town.

8. Headley, p. 103.

9. ibid., pp. 100-1.

millowners, nurserymen, shipbuilders, etc, throwing themselves heartily into the work of revival, becoming examples to their workpeople and inducing these and others to devote themselves to it also'.[10]

Four months after its commencement, the revival was still very much in evidence. Much preparation was undertaken by local believers to ensure that the Annan Fair Day, held on Thursday, 6 May, was an influence for good on the many thousands who, more than ever that particular year, flocked to it from miles around. Over 12,000 cups of tea were cheaply supplied, in addition to other forms of 'unintoxicating refreshments', while a series of revival addresses throughout the day saw several thousand assemble, 'by far the largest congregation we think that ever worshipped God on the banks of the Annan'. This was followed by a soiree in each of four of the town's churches.[11]

Professor Martin of Aberdeen University visited Annan in the summer of 1861 and said he had not been in the town many hours before he was thoroughly satisfied that the work was real. Indeed, the revival still appeared to be in operation as late as August, a full seven months after its commencement, making it one of the longest-running revival movements in one location of the entire 1859–61 awakening in Scotland. The last diary entry of prayer warrior, Alice Johnstone, relating to the revival dates to 11 August 1861: 'The glorious work goes on', she wrote, 'very much of the spirit of prayer; much zeal and active labour. The aspect of the town is entirely changed since this commenced. Thanks be to God for this day of grace. Glory be to His holy name for his signal answers to our pleadings.'[12]

Annan was said to have been 'absolutely revolutionised' by the spirit of revival that overtook it. 'We can use no common term to describe the alteration that has been effected since January last on the appearance of the place and the demeanour of the people', remarked one observer.[13] The Rev. G. Gardiner of the United Presbyterian Church said he had personally conversed with upwards of five hundred anxious enquirers, every one of whom, with a single exception, had given evidence of a

10. Quoted in Watt, pp. 20-1.

11. ibid., pp. 24, 28.

12. Snow, p. 47.

13. Watt, p. 24.

saving change.[14] In just three months the Rev. J. Gailey of the Free Church added about the same number to his congregation. As for Annan's Congregational Church, some years previously it was in so depressed a state that the authorities deemed it 'a hopeless case'. The church began to flourish, however, particularly owing to the outbreak of revival during 1861, during which the Rev. Ebenezer Young's labours were particularly noteworthy, and the pastor was able to write soon after that, 'we have – even in our little church – received about ninety new members'.[15]

It was estimated that, remarkably, no less than three thousand individuals were hopefully led to Christ in Annan and vicinity as a result of the revival of 1861. Six years later, the town's ministers could testify that those who joined the churches as a result of the revival held out as well as any converts they ever knew. Indeed, when Hammond paid a further brief visit to Annan in 1867 it was said that, 'Hundreds who, in those days (1861), used to be seen weeping for their sins, now appear at the meetings with happy faces, and during these six years have maintained a consistent Christian walk.'[16] Many years later a more general outcome of the revival was offered – cottage prayer meetings being held sometimes more than once a week in almost every street of the town, evangelistic meetings in nearly every village in the neighbourhood and a Y.M.C.A. which right up to the close of the century was a source of much blessing in the area.

Dumfries

From Annan, and once again largely through Hammond's efforts, the quickening spread to Dumfries. Here, for about two years previously much prayer had gone up from local congregations for an outpouring of the Spirit. At Hammond's very first meeting the church was filled, and awakening began that night. Many pews were removed in the Free Church and a special platform was erected, thus providing standing room for nearly two hundred. Yet it was said that even if the church

---

14. Headley, p. 104.

15. ibid., pp. 111, 116.

16. 'At least 1,800 were crowded into the church. Many were anxious about their souls … . Though it was a late hour when we left, the under-part of the building was still filled with inquirers' (Headley, pp. 444-5).

could have been enlarged to twice its former size, it would still have been filled to overflowing, so intense and widespread was the interest felt in the services (and not only in Dumfries, but soon, in all the country around).

The movement, thus begun, continued in power. One Monday evening an estimated 1,750 packed inside the Free Church, while hundreds more stood around the doors and windows. A leader of the fellowship remarked that the scenes he had witnessed during the preceding ten days and nights were so extraordinary that he felt himself at times overcome with amazement and was almost tempted to question their reality. Hammond made use of the inquiry room to carefully advise and pray for the anxious, and some nights people had to wait more than two hours to be counselled by him.

One interesting case was that of Robert Milligan, aged forty-nine, a native of Kirkcudbright and for twenty-seven years a soldier in the 1st Regiment of Life Guards. During one service, Milligan approached Hammond and said, loudly enough to be heard over a great part of the church, 'Sir, I have been in many a battle, and received many a wound, but never such a one as I received tonight.' Hammond asked, 'Are you now then, resolved to be a soldier of the Cross – enrolled in the blood-redeemed army of Jesus?' 'Yes', was the answer, then, holding up both hands, he prayed with great fluency and unction; after which he said with modest confidence, 'I am not ashamed to own my Lord.' This impressive episode had a most touching effect upon the onlookers, many of whom sobbed aloud, while others rejoiced quietly.[17]

An interesting statistic was issued in *The Dumfries Standard*. It showed that during the three weeks from 27 January to 16 February 1860, sixty-three people were brought before the Burgh Court of Dumfries charged with 'assault, breach of peace, contravention of Police Act, drunk and disorderly, drunk and incapable, malicious mischief and theft'. In the corresponding period for 1861, i.e., during the three weeks since the revival commenced, the figure was thirty-two, a reduction of around 50 per cent.[18]

While the Free Church was the main meeting place during Hammond's visit, other church buildings were also in constant requisition

---

17. *WJ*, 16/02/1861, p. 580.

18. ibid., 23/02/1861, p. 591.

for subsidiary meetings of various kinds. Public services were held
in Maxwelltown Free Church, the Relief Presbyterian Church, the
Congregational chapel and both of the United Presbyterian churches.
Some meetings were for children only; others solely for females,
attracting up to one thousand women.

One Sabbath, a few weeks into the movement, all the churches in
which the revival was advancing were crowded beyond anything ever

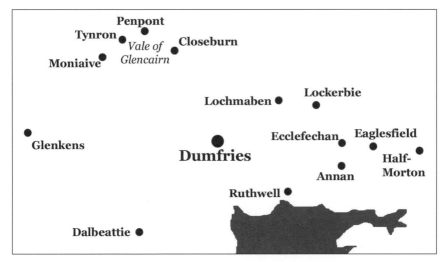

before witnessed by their respective ministers. The number of awakened
souls was greater than on any previous day. Large numbers were drawn
to the town from all the surrounding country from as far as twenty
miles distant.

The seven evangelical pastors of the town united in publishing a
testimony stating that despite the mere natural feeling and human
imperfection which no doubt were mingled with the movement, 'we
unhesitantly express our conviction that it is a very wonderful and
most blessed work ... of the grace and Spirit of God'.[19] One of these
pastors was the Rev. Robert Machray, under whose guidance the
Congregational Church increased in attendance to the extent that
an extension to the building was deemed appropriate. Another was
the Rev. M. N. Gould of the United Presbyterian Church, then in

---

19. ibid., pp. 138-9. It was reported from Dumfries and neighbourhood in March
1862 that 'all the congregations have shared in ... a remarkable awakening ... during
the last two years ... and all are reaping the fruits of it in a more numerous attendance in the various places of worship' (ibid.).

his early forties. Gould threw himself into the work and at the April Communion of 1861, after the revival had all but drawn to a close, he welcomed as many as seventy-one new members into his fellowship.[20]

Meanwhile, the Rev. James Julius Wood of the Free Church proclaimed that he had 'found people greatly changed, of whose sincerity I cannot entertain a doubt, and am ready to hold up my hands with surprise when I meet with men who persist in calling it all a delusion, and denounce Mr Hammond and others for getting up an excitement'.[21] Where the churches had initially worked together in unity, however, latterly some controversy sounded forth from Presbyterian leaders when they realised that certain 'Morrisonian' doctrines were being espoused.

Touched by so many of the poorer classes flocking to his church during the revival, the Rev. Wood afterwards decided to begin a mission work in the south part of Dumfries, so that such people could worship God without feeling inferior to the more opulent townsfolk. This proved so popular that a Territorial Mission Church was opened in the south district in 1865. This, according to Wood, was an obvious fruit of the revival. Indeed, a full five years after the revival had subsided, the Free Church Kirk Sessions testified to the ongoing reality of 'God's people being refreshed and of sinners being converted'.[22]

Dumfries Environs

One invitation after another came to Hammond from country places, three or four of which he visited for a day, or part of one. The same results attended the meetings in these places, which followed his labour in Dumfries. 'The awakening is extending through all the country round about (Dumfries and Annan) for twenty miles, at least', wrote the Rev. Wood, 'and I do not believe there is a single village or hamlet within that area which has not in some measure partaken of the awakening.'

---

20. George B. Hewitt, *1848–1948 – Hawick Congregational Church – Centenary Commemoration*, Hawick, 1948, p. 21.

21. Headley, p. 140. The Territorial Free Church (later South United Free Church) was one abiding fruit of this revival (William McDowall, *History of the Burgh of Dumfries*, Dumfries, 2006, p. 825).

22. Audrey Millar, *St George's, Dumfries, 1843–1993: The Life of our Church*, Dumfries, 1994, pp. 34-6.

Revival also spread to many other towns and villages in Dumfries-shire not visited by Hammond, and, as already noted, even in some of the places included in Hammond's itinerary, revival was already in evidence well before his arrival. Alice Johnstone wrote to a friend: 'The whole county of Dumfries was shaken, and it was indeed a solemn time.'[23] Reports came in showing that nearly every town and village in the county was experiencing revival.

Over the course of seventeen summers, Dr James Buchanan, Professor in the New College, Edinburgh, was in the habit of preaching regularly, on Sabbath evenings, in the open air in Dumfriesshire. Frustratingly, precise locations were not given. People of all denominations came to his tent, but although he doubted not that good seed was sown, he said:

> I could not put my hand upon a single case of decided conversion. Last year (1861), suddenly, and without apparently any human instrumentality to account for it, the whole district was visited with an outpouring of the Spirit of God. Now, in my immediate neighbourhood, I can point to many households where, for the first time, family worship has been established and is now regularly maintained. The whole morals of the district seem to have undergone a complete change; and, as the police expressed it to me, their office was, so far as serious crimes were concerned, all but a sinecure … the minds of the whole community have become impressed and awed by a sense of Divine things.[24]

East Dumfriesshire

Lockerbie

Towards the east of the county, a revival arose in Lockerbie, which appeared to owe its origins to the plan adopted of personally calling from house to house throughout the village during four days in January 1861, speaking to people briefly about their souls, and furnishing them with tracts. Such was the immediate impact of this effort that a correspondent found it 'difficult to write about it calmly or to attempt to describe it without appearing to exaggerate'.[25]

---

23. Watt, p. 12.

24. Brown, 1893, pp. 774-5.

25. *SG*, 31/01/1861.

Two or three months later, special services were begun. The second evening proved to be the crisis night, when as many as three hundred inquirers sought counsel. Many were in deep distress, and the Rev. Campbell of the Free Church said he had never heard such manifestations of mental anguish, especially from around thirty young women. There were few, if any, in his congregation who were not more or less impressed and in every house were one or more awakened souls. Some were sleepless for three consecutive nights. During this most 'solemn week' in the village, around one hundred people were thought to have found the Lord (out of 250-300 professions in total), and it was claimed that outward immorality virtually disappeared from Lockerbie. In the small nearby royal burgh of Lochmaben, 'a great work' was said to have been in progress.[26]

As late as September 1861, an open-air meeting in the village of Eaglesfield, near Ecclefechan, drew a crowd which was seen as very considerable indeed for a scattered rural population. Hammond spoke in Ruthwell, between Dumfries and Annan, where over two hundred waited afterwards for conversation and a significant work was begun, office-bearers being among those who made a public profession.[27]

Moffat

In February 1861, just after dark, three young lads presented themselves in Moffat, on the northern border of Dumfriesshire, having walked all the way from Locharbriggs, a distance of eighteen miles. With the consent of all the town's ministers, they arranged for a bell to be rung throughout town, announcing a meeting at 8 p.m. in the United Presbyterian Church. The building was crowded, and a deep impression was made. This was the commencement of a significant revival in the town. The second meeting attracted little less than a thousand people, the stairs, passages, and even the windows, being occupied. Next morning a number were in deep distress, and several could be heard screeching in mental agony on account of their estrangement from God. The number truly awakened was said to have equalled or surpassed the cumulative figure for the previous ten years.[28]

---

26. ibid., 06/04/1861; 16/04/1861; Free Church *Monthly Record*, June 1893, p. 144.

27. *SG*, 28/09/1861, p. 214; *WJ*, 16/02/1861, p. 580.

28. R. H. A. Hunter, *History of the Revival at Moffat in the Spring of 1861*, quoted in *WJ*, 28/09/1861, p. 214.

Mid-Nithsdale

Closeburn

Further north, revival swept through the mid-Nithsdale valley. Awakening in Closeburn was preceded by 'months of deep, heartfelt, prayerful anxiety'. Where previously there had been difficulty keeping up a weekly prayer meeting, the Free Church now had five well-attended meetings. One remarkable conversion was that of a twenty-seven-year-old man, 'at one time a poor, careless, silly creature', who was suddenly arrested by conviction on his way to a meeting. Trembling with fear, he became so weak that he had to be half-carried to the meeting place. He soon came to a place of peace in Christ, but a month later, when visiting an elder of his church, his body went rigid and he was laid in bed, where, for a full twelve hours, he sang Psalms and prayed aloud for friends and relatives. Said the Rev. Hutton, 'How hearty, how scriptural, how powerful! I never listened to such prayers before.' Soon the man regained consciousness, sat up and preached to all present on the topic of heaven and hell. After a week of exhaustion, he resumed his zealous efforts for the Lord.[29]

Penpont

The movement in nearby Penpont began in earnest in February 1861, and was said to have owed much to some godly mothers who were in the habit of meeting regularly for prayer. They also called for Glasgow evangelist Robert Cunningham to speak in the district and his visit was much blessed. A young girls' meeting was also begun around this time. The visit from E. P. Hammond gave added impetus to the work, and night after night the people flocked to the large meetings – held alternately in Thornhill, Burnhead and Penpont itself – and a 'glorious work' ensued.[30]

After leaving a meeting in the church, a group of boys retired to a field to arrange a prayer meeting for themselves. After securing a room, they invited the minister to be present to direct them. The minister came. While speaking in the kitchen to a woman, a man came in who was a notorious drunkard. While speaking to this man of the Lord, a

---

29. Reid, 1860, pp. 280-6.

30. *WJ*, 16/02/1861, 07/09/1861, p. 190.

noise was heard in the room. It was the children kneeling in prayer. The voice of a boy was heard, praying with fervour and great unction. The minister turned to look at the man. He was trembling and agitated. He hurried outside to pray, weeping bitterly. Who was it among these boys who prayed so touchingly? It was in fact that ungodly father's youngest son.

Moniaive and Tynron

In the secluded village of Moniaive there arose a great stir for some time. The prayer meetings, which were many, were well attended. One Sabbath evening not only the whole village but almost the entire parish flocked together to two meetings – one in the parish schoolhouse, and the other in the United Presbyterian Church. When meetings were first begun in Tynron, literally the whole village turned out to hear the Word of God, with the exception of an infirm old woman, in whose house a prayer meeting was held afterwards, for anxious enquirers alone, and which was filled. The revival already underway in both Tynron and Moniaive showed signs of reviving as a result of Hammond's visit to the area. Throughout the Vale of Glencairn in particular, a 'most blessed work' took place following the American's arrival. In one village, presumed to be Moniaive itself, before Hammond had uttered a word, some had to be taken away in distress of soul.[31] Nightly meetings were held for two months and much good was accomplished.

The Rev. Hall from Glasgow travelled through Dumfriesshire, and said the work was 'satisfactorily progressing. Numerous little meetings are being held throughout the villages, and at a short notice, meetings could be held at almost any place and time.'[32] Robert Hood, an Evangelical Union student from Glasgow, was sent to Thornhill for three months in the summer of 1861. Revival embers here and in many nearby communities he visited were still glowing. Hood held open-air meetings every Sabbath in some nearby community, such as Penpont, Birleyhill and Carronbridge, which invariably attracted large audiences.

A further wave of awakening was occasioned by the drowning of two other Glasgow students, both on leave from University, who had been labouring in the district; the tragedy occurring when they

31. Headley, pp. 140-1.

32. *WJ*, 16/04/1861.

went for a swim in the nearby river. The event produced a profound impact throughout the neighbourhood, and as a result, wherever Hood preached he attracted large audiences.[33]

Considerably further north, in the area bordering on Ayrshire, the ministers in Sanquhar united to welcome awakening in their district, and at one meeting five ministers were present, each busily employed in conversing with anxious ones. 'For some time past the minds of the people of Sanquhar have been powerfully impressed', having now 'found vent', one reliable witness stated.[34]

Kirkcudbrightshire

To the west of Dumfriesshire, there were numerous instances of revival stirrings in the county of Kirkcudbrightshire. To the north, around Dalry, the excitement was said to have been 'immense'. There were a number of striking cases of prostrations, thorough convictions, and 'most remarkable conversions to God'. At one meeting which was filled to overflowing, upwards of fifty remained at the close, some of whom were sobbing and crying aloud, while many others hung around the doors. One woman wrestled with God day and night, both for herself and her family, in a peat-house, which became her prayer closet. By-and-by she observed something wrong with her husband. He told her his state of mind, and 'for the first time during the twenty years of their married life they knelt down together at the Throne of Grace'.[35]

A believer from Glenkens, near Castle-Douglas, wrote excitedly: 'A few weeks ago we only heard of the revival, but now we see it!' The first convert was a young man in the Free Church congregation. Since then another and another was added to the Lord's side – 'and oh what joy has succeeded their sorrow, and they all show such love for each other. Prayer meetings increase, both in number and attendance. There is a little meeting at half-past five every Sabbath evening where *The [Wynd] Journal* is read … where souls have already been born.' More than two months later the work in Glenkens was said to be 'still deepening and extending', while 'throughout

33. David Hobbs, *Robert Hood the Bridgeton Pastor. The Story of his Bright and Useful Life*, Edinburgh 1894, p. 47.

34. *WJ*, 09/03/1861, p. 605.

35. ibid., 14/01/1860, p. 123.

the Stewartry region, there is a marked improvement in the attendance on our prayer meetings'.[36] Meanwhile, Andrew Bonar, amongst others, preached to an eager congregation of two thousand beneath Samuel Rutherford's Monument in Anworth, in August 1860. Many had travelled upwards of ten miles to attend the service at the hallowed spot.

Blessing in Kirkcudbrightshire continued in the aftermath of Hammond's missions in Dumfriesshire in 1861. In Irongray, occurred 'a great awakening'. In Locharbriggs were many anxious inquirers, while Annandale was said to have been 'thoroughly moved'. In Glenkippo, Kirkbean and Lochend, 'a promising work' was in progress.[37]

Further west, a man from Dalbeattie went to some revival services in Dumfries and returned home with two fellow-believers from the town. Awakening began in Dalbeattie on the very following night. The Rev. Brown of Castle Douglas remarked that if someone had told him six months previously that fifty to sixty of the 'better class' in the town would be attending religious meetings at 12 noon, he would not have believed it! But it happened, and many came under the quickening influence of God's Spirit.

Wigtownshire

Given the geographical proximity of Galloway to Ulster – less than twenty miles at the closest points – it is perhaps surprising that there are not more abundant evidences of revival arising in this south Scotland county. Certainly there appeared reports of early stirrings,[38] but there is comparatively little documentation of definite revival in this region, then known as Wigtownshire. That which does exist relates mainly to the pre-1861 period, such as a movement in Stranraer in late 1859.

Believers in this town had for some months been wrestling in prayer for an outpouring of the Spirit, and were on the verge of fainting

---

36. ibid., 10/12/1859, p. 83. The author of this report was, however, 'particularly anxious about Balmaghie. It is hallowed with the associations of martyr times. Martyrs lie buried in our graveyards and about three miles from where I write there is a monument erected upon the spot where four of those brave Christian heroes fell. But alas! Where is now the martyr spirit? With regard to God's special work, there is nothing special ... the people are interested, but that is all' (ibid., 03/03/1860, p. 180).

37. *SG*, 16/04/1861; *WJ*, 16/02/1861, pp. 379, 580.

38. D. W. Bebbington, *The Baptists in Scotland*, Glasgow, 1988, p. 54.

when, at a prayer meeting in November 1859, three women were struck down under deep conviction of sin. Other cases of prostration followed day after day (seven or eight at one meeting alone) till the number of these outward manifestations amounted to about twenty. To the disappointment of the workers, the revival was largely confined to the poorer classes of the town. The churchgoers were comparatively uninfluenced, many of them scoffing at the work. About thirty prayer meetings were held each week, including a nightly union meeting, led by the town's various ministers (except the parish and Reformed Presbyterian ministers, who did not join the movement).

One singular report from the later period focuses on the town of Newton Stewart, situated on the River Cree, seven miles north of Wigtown. In the spring of 1861 a revival was felt 'in all its preciousness and power' in this town.[39] The various churches held united midday and evening meetings, while, in addition, the Rev. John Walker of the Free Church commenced regular preaching – against some opposition – on a vacant piece of ground near the town centre known as the 'Angle'. Such ministerial self-effacing labours in town and country, followed by hours of conscientious personal dealing with the anxious, continued through the whole summer of 1861 and well into the winter, and, while necessitating the immediate enlarging of the church, also led to the illness which resulted in Walker's death. James Sillars, a theology student, spent several weeks in the town, and spoke each night at the 'Angle'. He and other ministers were known to be engaged till 11.30 p.m. conversing with the anxious.

The Border Counties

Broughton and Skirling

After revival reached the south-east Lanarkshire communities of Carnwarth and Biggar, it spread across the Lanarkshire border into the surrounding Peeblesshire countryside, where 'much activity' resulted. One minister in Biggar took an active part in the movement, and rejoiced that, 'The awakening and revival has also now commenced in the parishes of Broughton and Skirling, about two miles distant from this, and at Kirkund and Newlands the great work has been going on

---

39. Rev. John Walker, A *Faithful Minister; Discourses by the Rev. John Walker; With a Memoir by the Rev. James Dodds*, Edinburgh, 1864, p. lxii.

for some time, eight miles distant. Crowded meetings, were held here every night for some time.'[40]

Ancrum

The Roxburghshire village of Ancrum was once greatly blessed by the ministry of the renowned John Livingston. In the present day its Free Church minister, the Rev. John McEwan, had recently returned from Ireland where he had witnessed the revival in progress there. He was delighted to discover that in the Irish parish of Killinchy, County Down, where Livingston had later laboured for some years, no fewer than three hundred people had been awakened in the course of just a few months. The relating of such glad tidings in McEwan's own parish was one factor that helped pave the way for a 'time of merciful visitation', which, among other things, led to a marked decrease in the consumption of alcohol and increased the number of weekly prayer meetings in the district from two to ten.[41]

Steady movements were reported from both Selkirk and Hawick by the summer of 1860, from each of which, large numbers assembled nightly in private homes for prayer. Meanwhile, in the village of Bowhill, to the west of Selkirk, a steady work ensued, and a temporary building was being considered for the accommodation of the frequent meetings. However, as late as mid-October 1859, despite the existence of a union prayer meeting, there was no sign of awakening in Galashiels.[42]

Eyemouth and St Abbs

The east Berwickshire town of Eyemouth had a population of 1,500, most of whom were connected with the fishing industry. The town was said to have been in a dark place spiritually in the late 1850s. But during the last year of the decade, a work of spiritual quickening began. This progressed for a number of months before becoming very public with the occurrence of a prostration. Almost immediately, the whole town was in a state of excitement. All ministers worked in harmony, except for one who stood aloof for a time, until he visited houses and saw for himself the effects of deep conviction. The Baptists held their evening

---

40. *SG*, 06/03/1860; *WJ*, 03/03/1860, p. 179.

41. Reid, 1860, pp. 273-6.

42. *SG*, 01/05/1860; 07/07/1860; *WJ*, 26/11/1859, p. 67; 31/12/1859, pp. 107-8.

meeting at 6 p.m., the Free Church at 7, the United Presbyterians at 8, and the Methodists at various times.

One minister marvelled to see 'young careless lads sitting before you, with flushing face and heavy eye, not able to open their mouth because of their shame – and young women weeping as if their hearts would burst because they cannot see Jesus'. Three anxious ploughmen were given the Catechism to read. They came together with the minister, opened their books, and at once burst into tears. The minister told them to close their books and instead to 'read out of the book of their own hearts'. There followed a time of 'sweet counsel' together.[43]

Owing to the spiritual torpor that had previously existed in Eyemouth, John Snaith was sent to pastor the Primitive Methodist church there in 1859. It was said that his soul was on fire, and he was moved mightily by the spiritual lethargy he saw all around him. But with the commencement of revival, people began flocking to his services from miles around, including Duns, some fourteen miles distant. 'Eyemouth was born again', one historian wrote. 'The quickening was felt at St Abbs, Grant's House,[44] and the country around. Industrially as well as spiritually the fishing village rose, and finer and more industrious fishermen, with better craft and gear, it would have been difficult to find.'[45]

The United Presbyterian minister wrote in April 1860 that 'for weeks in succession I went from house to house, and during all that time I did not meet a single individual who was not impressed. Even those who confessed that they had received no saving benefit did not hesitate to acknowledge that what they saw was the work of the Spirit.'[46]

Young lads met for prayer on dark and stormy nights in boats which were tied up at the end of town.[47] Said the Rev. Peter Thomson on the effect of the revival, 'The whole town was moved just like the trees of

---

43. *SG*, 29/11/1859.

44. 'There was a considerable movement in the district of Grant's House,' noted one correspondent in early 1861. 'The converts of last year are now very useful and there have been some new and notable conversions that have greatly stirred the people' (*WJ*, 02/03/1861, p. 598).

45. William M. Patterson, *Northern Primitive Methodism*, London, 1909, p. 370.

46. Reid, 1860, p. 323.

47. Roberts, 1995, p. 299.

the forest moved with the wind. The town was all moved, and those that were not moved were desirous of like blessing.' Said another, 'The entire aspect of the population has been changed; and many have been added unto the Lord, including not a few belonging to every class of the community.'[48] Ministers were sent for to comfort distressed souls, 'just as people send for medical men when an epidemic is raging'. It was estimated by one of their number that 'not less than sixty fishermen had been born again', before the end of the year, and that 'there is scarcely a boat belonging to Eyemouth which has not one or more converted men in its crew, and in some boats the whole crew are decided for Christ.'[49]

Nevertheless, no noticeable change was effected in the life of one much-loved fisherman. His comrades told him, 'Johnny, we can't go to heaven without you!', and earnestly and frequently did they raise him in prayer to the throne of grace. Soon, to both their and his great joy, Johnny was brought safely within the fold. The Excise officer stated that during one week, the equivalent of just one bottle of whisky had been consumed in the town's pubs, considerably less than in a normal week.[50] Shortly after the revival, a large fishing boat required to be drawn up and over a hundred men gathered for the task. Payment was always made in the form of alcohol, but on this occasion the cask of whisky was left untouched, for virtually all the men had been converted and were now abstainers.[51]

---

48. *SG*, 07/01/1860; MacGill, p. 4.

49. *WJ*, 31/12/1859, p. 108. William Patterson contends that in the overall revival in the district, some 'six hundred or more souls were converted … all the churches reaped the benefit' (p. 370).

50. *SG*, 03/01/1860. It was during the 1859 revival in Eyemouth that the Rev. Thomas Salmon came to the town. He preached in the Masons Hall, ostensibly under the banner of the Evangelical Union. The cause prospered and a chapel was soon constructed, built by local fishermen in the congregation (Fergus Ferguson, *History of the Evangelical Union*, Glasgow, 1886, p. 373).

51. Reid, 1860, pp. 331-2. From just across the English border, Rev. Peter Thomson of Berwick-on-Tweed was deeply impressed by the ongoing work that he saw in Eyemouth, as well as by the piety of that town's Free Church minister, the sixty-year-old Rev. John Turnbull, who 'seemed to be deeply in the Spirit' (Turnbull was heartily involved in the revival and later wrote an account of its progress, included in Reid's *Authentic Records of Revival*.) Soon Thomson's own Berwick congregation had become greatly affected, and several men 'that were not counted careless' were crying like babies in church, unable to speak from a sense of their sin (*SG*, 07/01/1860;

Kelso and District

Smailhom and Hume

The village of Smailholm was previously noted for its want of religious observance, but was now 'completely changed' by the revival that breezed through it. In another village where, prior to the revival, only three families out of a total of thirty conducted family worship, there were now only three families which didn't![52]

While the awakening in some parts of the Merse had clearly abated – though not ceased – by the beginning of 1861, in some places this was when revival commenced in earnest. The village of Hume 'at one time appeared to be about the most hopeless of any in Scotland. It was noted as a Christless place – and it was said by one that, if Hume only a few months ago had been visited like Sodom, to try its inhabitants, there would have been found only one child of God in the whole village.'[53]

Mr Stoddart from Kelso, began meetings near the start of 1861. Crowds poured from all quarters, and many awakenings took place. Another speaker succeeded him and reaped what Stoddart had been sowing. 'He may have been reaping in tears', commented Stoddart, 'but I had indeed a reaping in joy, and had many, many sheaves.'[54] In that once prayerless village a prayer meeting was established. Every Saturday evening the villagers and farm labourers (young converts) would meet. Stoddart said that one gentleman of the district, after attending one of these prayer meetings, said he was really unable to give expression to his feelings, after hearing the prayers of these unlearned and almost unlettered men. A young farmer in the neighbourhood held two meetings weekly amongst his servants, on two of his farms. On another farm the workers met regularly every week in a loft for prayer, and the reading of the Word of God.

Greenlaw

Further north and east, at Swinton the Rev. Thomas Wright laboured with much power, and an awakening, beginning with the conversion

---

J. C. Fairbairn, *Memorial of the late Rev. John Turnbull, Eyemouth: Consisting of a Funeral Sermon, preached at Eyemouth, on 13th March 1870*, Edinburgh, 1870, p. 19).

52. *SG*, 25/08/1860.

53. ibid.

54. ibid., 16/08/1862, p. 167.

of a young man, soon spread in and around the village, with precious results. In nearby Greenlaw, there was 'a great awakening', which began at the close of the prayer union in January, and nightly meetings continued since then in the Free Church, besides many meetings at villages and farms around.[55] The Rev. John Fairbairn of the Free Church was indefatigable in the work, being aided by Mr Stoddart from Kelso, one of Horatius Bonar's missionaries, and various ministers from the district, as well as lay friends from Edinburgh. There was clear evidence of a real and widespread work, the depth of which might be judged by a report three years later, which spoke of 'abundant evidence in a goodly number of earnest and prayerful young men and young women, who are, we believe, destined to have a healthy influence on those around them'.[56]

Heiton

When one visitor began meetings in Heiton, two miles from Kelso, attendance increased from fifteen to 160 in less than a week. So sure was the visitor that the Lord was about to pour out His Spirit on that village that he urged the Rev. Bonar to send a missionary to continue the work. Mr Murray was sent, and no sooner had he commenced his outreach than the blessing came. Hundreds flocked to the meetings. 'The public houses shut us out of their hall', noted one worker, 'their trade being all but gone.' The joiner opened his shop, and the meetings were crowded to overflowing. Such an awakening had never been heard of in that community.[57]

Soon, a marvellous change had taken place over the whole district. Many men and women were soundly converted. As far as could be observed, conversions were general amongst the people of every age, including children. A clergyman, who had doubts about the genuineness of the work, met a young girl who professed Christ, and began to question her with strong theological language. Looking confused, she replied simply, 'I dinna ken, Mister, but I just tak' God at His Word.' A good work was also done by Bonar's missionaries in the village of Wark, where, 'in many cases ... there was utter neglect before'.[58]

55. ibid., 02/03/1861, p. 598.

56. *TR*, 07/04/1864.

57. *SG*, 02/03/1861, p. 598.

58. ibid., 22/08/1862, p. 173.

Towards the close of 1861, and just a year after her own conversion (see p. 39), teenager Jessie McFarlane spent time preaching in Kelso and the small villages in its neighbourhood.[59] In Heiton, where revival showers had already fallen, and where McFarlane spent the greater portion of her time, a great interest was awakened, and the largest room in the place was crowded night after night for several weeks, many expressing deep concern about their souls, and 'hungering and thirsting after righteousness'. Among the converts was a whole family who attended the meetings from a place two miles from Kelso.[60]

Among the traditional New Year festivities in Heiton was the holding of a grand ball. One night prior to the ball the local band was engaged to play lively music. In counteroffensive, Ms McFarlane and friends began an open-air service. This was commenced by singing a well-known hymn, which was no sooner begun than the band ceased to play, and instantly dispersed, many partiers turning from the music to join in the service. It was said that the presence of God was so manifestly felt that the bitterest enemies were silenced. As a result many gave up the pleasures of sin for a season and at the ball the next evening, a large number of old faces were missing. For the first time the wisdom of such New Year celebrations was questioned.

The work continued for some time, until McFarlane was called to Gallalaw, a small village in the neighbourhood of Heiton. Her labours in this place were said to have been so graciously owned and blessed that the testimony concerning it was 'the whole of the people seem converted, few unsaved souls left'. One who 'received the truth as a little child' in Gallalaw was a woman in her eighties, previously extremely ignorant of God's ways.[61]

---

59. One person converted during the movement here was Mary Binnie, a young married woman who developed a deep life of prayer. In later years, Mary was known to have prophesied a spiritual blessing on Edinburgh's then moribund Charlotte Chapel – this some years prior to the waves of revival which came to that church between 1905 and 1908 (see J. Oswald Sanders, *This I Remember: Reminiscences*, Eastbourne, 1982, pp. 92-3; Rev. William Whyte, *Revival in Rose Street: A History of Charlotte Baptist Chapel, Edinburgh*, Edinburgh, n.d., pp. 30-2).

60. H. I. G., *Jessie McFarlane a Tribute of Affection*, London, 1872, pp. 18-19.

61. ibid., pp. 19-20.

Kelso

As for Kelso itself, it seems that little in the way of spiritual revival occurred here. This despite the fact that one minister in town, the popular Rev. Horatius Bonar, was an evangelical preacher who knew the significance of times of spiritual refreshing, and constantly longed for them. Indeed, he was well-acquainted with such seasons, having experienced a powerful move of the Spirit on his congregation twenty years previously, in 1840. But no account is to be found of revival in the same church between 1859 and 1861. So, while Bonar penned an enthusiastic 'Introduction' to William Reid's compilation of revival accounts across Scotland and Ireland in 1860, he does not offer a testimony from his own parish, though contemporary records of events in Eyemouth to the east, and Ancrum to the west, are provided.[62] This may help to explain why Jessie McFarlane's biographer records that when the female evangelist arrived in the town in 1862, she found it in 'a wretched condition spiritually – lukewarmness and complete inertness prevailed, life to old and young was a mere routine of nothingness and gossiping'. Entering upon a scene of such worldliness and enmity to God, Jessie often repeated the words of St Paul, 'My soul is stirred within me to see the town wholly given to idolatry' (Acts 17:16).[63] We know that workers from Bonar's church played a part in times of awakening in other districts in the region – both in 1859–60 (see above) and again several years later (see p. 440). But it is nevertheless apparent that no significant revival occurred in the town of Kelso during the period under survey.

---

62. Similarly, in a series of pamphlets exchanged between Horatius Bonar and John Kennedy of Dingwall in 1875, on the nature of true evangelism, in which many references are made to historic revival, Bonar is silent on revival in Kelso during the years 1859–61.

63. The biographer also notes that Bonar sympathised heartily with her in her work and undertook the arrangements of meetings for her – exclusively for females – and that 'she had the joy of knowing several ... brought to the Lord' (H. I. G., p. 16).

North Berwick

Cockenzie

Longformacus

Richard Weaver

Charles Finney

Old photo of Carrubbers Close Mission

CHAPTER 8

Edinburgh and The Lothians

East Lothian

Dunbar

Scottish Church historian, John MacPherson, wrote that in 1859–
60, some communities along the Firth of Forth 'were completely
revolutionised' by the outbreak of revival among them. One of the
places notably affected was Dunbar. It wasn't long before tidings of the
deep awakening in Eyemouth reached this East Lothian town, and in a
short time, two fishermen who had been greatly used in the Eyemouth
movement, along with two men from the Coast Missionaries association,
plus several others, came to Dunbar to hold meetings. A band of converts
was gradually established, the most remarkable cases being those of
fishermen, a number of whom were transformed from their addictions
to drinking, swearing and Sabbath-breaking to being servants of God,
now meekly bearing the scoffs of former companions. These men were
invited to speak at nearby villages and farms. Particularly at Gateside
and Kirklandhill did an awakening 'so strikingly and decidedly' begin.
In each place, a granary was fitted, and several hundred people came to
hear the gospel. In the latter place eighty remained for counsel, 'most of
whom were in a state of deep spiritual anxiety and distress'.[1]

North Berwick

The work in North Berwick also began with a visit from Eyemouth
fishermen, along with that of two Coast Missionaries.[2] At the close of

---

1. John MacPherson, *A History of the Church in Scotland From the Earliest Times
Down to the Present Day*, Paisley, 1901, p. 433.

2. Messrs Murray and Fitzgerald. Also much involved in the movement along this
coast was the founder of the Coast Mission, Thomas Rosie (Rev. James Dodds, *Coast*

the second meeting in the Free Church, the congregation was dispersing without anyone staying behind for conversation. The hymn was begun, 'Oh, Won't you Come to Jesus, and Escape Eternal Fire?' All at once, wrote one present, 'the people became riveted to the spot, and they began to say among themselves, "How can we go away without Jesus tonight?"' At the close of the meeting as they were leaving for home, some came under conviction. A number returned to church and quietly seated themselves in the pews, their streaming eyes and downcast looks proclaiming unmistakably that 'the arrows of the King' had pierced their hearts. 'A band of seven spiritual physicians were for two hours as busily employed as physicians of the body going round the wards of a hospital filled with the sick and the wounded, the victims of calamity and disease. ... It was evident that the Lord had begun to work mightily in the midst of us. ... There was no mistaking the origin of such mighty movements of the Spirit. They began in the [prayer] closet.'[3] The work continued in one church every night for two months.

Cockenzie

Perhaps the most outstanding work along the southern shores of the Firth of Forth occurred in Cockenzie from the end of January 1860.[4] Meetings for prayer and exhortation were held in a schoolroom and in the Free Church. These were greatly attended, many soon beginning to show intense spiritual concern and 'to pass through the agonies of the new birth'. Many fishermen conducted their own meetings, which were carried on nightly. A visiting minister noted that 'a little degree of extravagance that appeared at first, being gently yet firmly checked, soon vanished'.[5] The work in Cockenzie was helped on by means of hymn singing. The women going about their work, and the children

Missions: A Memoir of the Rev. Thomas Rosie; London, 1862, pp. 47-8).

3. *WJ*, 28/04/1860, pp. 243-4.

4. According to W. J. Couper, 'Newhaven was embraced in March, and the Eyemouth fishermen lit the torch at Dunbar whence the light spread to North Berwick and Cockenzie' (Roberts, 1995, p. 302).

5. Rev. James Dodds of Dunbar Free Church, quoted in Reid, 1860, p. 387. Dodds, who preached in Cockenzie during the revival, scorned reports that 'the fishing population of the east coast are a comparatively rude and ignorant portion of the Scottish people, and that therefore the revival movement among them made peculiar progress. ... The fishermen of Cockenzie are an intelligent as well as a hardy class

on the streets, could often be heard throughout the day singing their favourite hymns.

The Rev. A. Lorimer, the local Free Church minister, threw himself heartily into the movement, among other things visiting the anxious from house to house and guiding these towards the way of peace. By the middle of February prayer meetings were flourishing in the neighbourhood. So numerous and remarkable were cases of conversion that an extraordinary Communion was deemed appropriate for the benefit of the new converts – these having been duly examined for credible proofs of new spiritual life.

A worker with the East Coast Mission held regular meetings in the schoolhouse every Thursday. One evening he was accompanied by an Ulster evangelist, who was visiting relatives in Cockenzie. As the Irishman asked the congregation the question, 'What think ye of Christ?', he was drawn to a mother and daughter sitting side-by-side, both showing clear signs of distress. He approached them and spoke with them at length. On realising her need for a Saviour, the mother fell to her knees, raised her arms, and cried aloud to God for mercy. The daughter was soon likewise broken in spirit, as were a number of others. These all afterwards rose from the floor or from their seats, confessing they were now at liberty in Christ.

A meeting was held the following evening in the open air, the schoolroom being occupied by a young men's Bible class. When this had concluded, the classroom was again quickly filled. Around ten o'clock, noted the evangelist:

> a remarkable wave of Divine power seemed to roll over the meeting. It was indeed a wave of richest grace, from the shoreless ocean of eternal love, and which carried back to its source the happy fruits of its gracious mission. All hearts were touched. Boys and girls, old and young, began to pray aloud for mercy. The praying brothers, and all around the desk where I stood, were weeping and sobbing heavily. At one moment nearly all that were in the room were overcome. Indeed, I would have pitied the one who was not. Still, it was quite different from the striking and screaming in the north of Ireland. There was no physical prostration. They wept much, and prayed above their breath,

of men', he insisted. 'They were by no means beneath the ordinary level either of education or character' (ibid.).

some aloud. So you may imagine the thrilling effect of such a scene. I believe it would have awed and silenced the boldest infidel.[6]

The work was still in progress in May, with accessions to the Church continuing to occur on a weekly basis. At that time Lorimer could declare that he was not aware of a single instance of backsliding: 'On the contrary, all, so far as I can see, retain the freshness and the fervour of their first love. Such gross and flagrant sins as drunkenness, profane swearing and Sabbath-breaking soon almost ceased to exist.'[7]

A weekly meeting for devotion and instruction was held for young converts, who, on almost every occasion would bring along with them some fruit of their personal missionary enterprise. Indeed, noted their minister, 'they are indeed the most effective missionaries I have ever seen engaged in the work. ... They have succeeded in inducing persons to attend public ordinances who had hitherto withstood all the influence I could bring to bear upon them for that end.' Noted Lorimer, in conclusion: 'The movement in Cockenzie has been as solid as it has been striking and decided. The fruit of it has been abundant, and it promises to be enduring.'[8]

Musselburgh

American evangelist, E. P. Hammond laboured in many places in Scotland in 1859–61. He was commissioned to supply Sunday preaching in Musselburgh's Congregational Church, near the start of 1859, which had sunk to such a low state that it was described as 'existing and nothing more'. Hammond, along with one or two helpers, would visit people from door to door, inviting people to services in the church. This they did 'again and again and again', though with little obvious fruit from it. In time he began to note a deepening of spiritual interest. Quite spontaneously, various individuals began to gather at the house he was staying in after the Sabbath evening meeting. 'Night after night, inquirers came in and crowded the house ... until the house where I was speaking was filled – every room of it ... there was no machinery of any kind to get up a revival.'[9]

---

6. *Things Old and New*, vol. 3, pp. 211-16.

7. Reid, pp. 387-9.

8. ibid., p. 389. See also *SG*, 14/02/1860.

9. *SCM*, 1860, pp. 150-5, quoted in William D. McNaughton, *Early Congregational Independency in Lowland Scotland*, vol. 1, Glasgow, 2005, p. 364.

Soon the house became too small, and the meeting had to be divided. Hammond met with the men in the church vestry, while a colleague met with the women in the house. Soon believers of all denominations were attending, and the meetings were held on a nightly basis. Both meetings attracted between forty and eighty people each.

Church meetings, too, quickly became packed and 'emotional services became daily events'. 'On Sunday nights, many', Hammond was informed, 'have been unable to gain access; every avenue of the church has been filled; and scarce a night has passed without manifestations of the convicting and converting agencies of God's Holy Spirit. ... Numbers have come from a distance ... you find them there from all classes.'[10]

Through Hammond's labours in the town – an incredible twenty-one weeks in total, almost half a year – a special work was also done among children and teenagers. Dr W. L. Alexander of Glasgow went to preach at a weeknight meeting in a church in the town and was struck by the multitude of children attending the service and seemingly taking great interest in the work going on. Later, in the vestry, Alexander came across a group of 'ragged-looking collier lads, fisher lads, and that class of young men, who, from my knowledge of Musselburgh, seemed to me really almost beyond the reach of evangelistic efforts', but who could now be seen on their knees in prayer. He continued, 'One of the party engaged in prayer ... he was a man who was pretty well known in the town as a very rough character indeed. ... I do not know that I ever felt so touched by a prayer than I was by that ...'[11]

On the same, or perhaps another occasion, also in a church vestry in Musselburgh, Alexander found a group of little girls on their knees in prayer. Tears rushed down his cheeks as he felt reproof for doubting that such a profound work could take place in lives so young and tender. The doctor wrote:

> One servant girl went down [from Edinburgh], and she got into conversation with one of those little girls ... and the little girl began to preach Christ to her as the Saviour of sinners, to the utter amazement and astonishment of this grown-up woman. She said to her, 'Lassie, where did you learn this?' After a little while the girl said, 'If you will

---

10. Carwardine, 1978, pp. 185-6; McNaughton, 2005, p. 365.

11. ibid.

kneel down, I will pray with you.' And to use the woman's own words, 'she just drappit down on her knees and I couldna but gang doun too.' And the little girl prayed; and the woman, strongly moved, when they rose up, exclaimed, 'Lassie, wha ever learned you to pray?' The child's answer was, 'Naebody learned me, I think the Lord just pits't into me.' That was the means of that woman's conversion … .[12]

Lammermuir Country

Awakening began in a district of the Lammermuir hill country on the southern edge of the Lothians at the close of the harvest season of 1860. No special means were employed, and ordinary prayer meetings in the region had in fact been suspended due to lack of interest. However, it was said that many souls were moved almost simultaneously in their own homes. On one sheep farm could be found fourteen happy converts. In subsequent months, the movement extended to a greater or lesser extent in all directions, although little outside aid was received due to the remoteness of the district and the severity of the winter weather. Yet it was said that, 'everyone who wants to help was made the bearer of a blessing and a recipient too', and the labours of Mr Rathie of the Free Church Station in Longformacus was eminently blessed in this work. He wrote: 'Opposition has assumed somewhat singular and very instructive forms. It has been a testing time for some who liked to hear of revivals at a distance. Mere formality cannot bear the real and the vital close at hand.'[13]

Edinburgh

Revival – What Revival?

Commentators diverge widely in their reporting of the depth and extent of the revival in Scotland's capital city. Revival historian, W. J. Couper was of the opinion that prior to 1873–74, Edinburgh had 'stood aloof in a somewhat marked way from revival work … the revival of 1859–1860 was scarcely felt'.[14] Likewise, an Edinburgh minister, the Rev. Reid contrasted the spiritual liveliness of the Lanarkshire mining towns during the 1859 revival period to 'the deadness of Edinburgh, where

---

12. *SCM*, 1860, pp. 150-5, quoted in McNaughton, 2005, pp. 365-6.

13. *SG*, 02/03/1861.

14. Roberts, 1995, p. 311.

Christ cannot do many mighty works because of our unbelief'.[15] Writing a century later, John Pollock stated that, 'The revival of 1859 from Ulster and the United States had blown little beyond Scottish country districts', in contrast to the 'Moody revival' of 1873–74, which, he believed, penetrated Edinburgh and Glasgow on a much deeper level.[16]

At the opposite extreme, Bussey claims that 'by the end of '59 the whole of Edinburgh was profoundly moved', stating that in one church (St Luke's), 'there were scenes of awakening almost unparalleled in any part of the country'. Bussey, however, only provides supporting evidence from a few selected places.[17] Another writer stated that 'Edinburgh very specially shared largely in the blessing' of this period.[18] In a sermon preached to his congregation in mid-November 1860, the Rev. Charles J. Brown said of the revival in Edinburgh, 'Ever since the tide of this movement has come up at length to this proud city of ours, night after night, any and every night, Sabbath and weekday alike, what spontaneous assemblies are found listening to the Word of God, not from lips of famous and accomplished preachers, but of plain men, having nothing to commend them so much as their unmistakable truth and earnestness, simplicity, fervour and longing desire to win souls for Christ!'[19]

Perhaps the strongest testimony to the existence and potency of the revival in Scotland's capital comes from James Gall, General Superintendent of Carrubbers Close Mission, who wrote that during the two years from the autumn of 1859 to the same season of 1861, 'the spiritual temperature of Edinburgh rose in a very remarkable manner. Thousands of conversions took place, not only among the lower, but also among the better classes of society, chiefly among the members of churches. Hundreds of devoted labourers were given to the Church, many of whom became ministers, evangelists and missionaries, who carried the infection of their enthusiasm to all parts of the world.'[20]

---

15. *The Mercury*, quoted in *WJ*, 05/01/1861, p. 535.

16. John Pollock, *Moody Without Sankey*, London, 1963 (reprinted 1995), p. 123.

17. Bussey, p. 107.

18. W. Keith Leask, *Dr Thomas McLauchlan*, Edinburgh, 1905, p. 135.

19. 'Revival', a sermon preached in 1860, quoted in Bussey, p. 100.

20. James Gall, *The Revival of Pentecostal Christianity: The History of Carrubbers Close Mission*, London, 1882, p. 6.

Then there are more ambivalent reports, such as from the Rev. Dr John Duncan, Professor of Hebrew and Oriental Languages in Edinburgh's Free Church College from 1843 till his death in 1870. Duncan wrote regarding the 1859–61 revival in Scotland's capital: 'We are within a very little of a general awakening among the working classes in Edinburgh', though, added his biographer, 'the tide receded before reaching its fullness'.[21] It is clearly much more difficult to ascertain the overall influence of a revival movement in a city compared to a small village or country parish. Some areas of a city may be powerfully affected, some partially, and others not at all. Certainly, while Edinburgh was still in the afterglow of the general revival movement throughout Scotland, the above-mentioned James Gall, who had previously boasted of the revival's influence in the city, now bemoaned the general state of religion in the capital. In his report dated 1 June 1861, he wrote: 'The lower population of Edinburgh is at present a sweltering mass of open ungodliness, infidelity, licentiousness and brutal heathenism, dishonouring God, scourging society, and sending down to eternal ruin thousands upon thousands of immortal souls.'[22] The overall reality appears to be that while Edinburgh was not as greatly stirred as other parts of the country, there was, in fact, as attested to above and confirmed by the following narratives, considerable awakening in numerous quarters of the city.

Carrubbers Close Mission
Situated down a narrow lane just off the High Street in the heart of Edinburgh, Carrubbers Close Mission commenced operations in May 1858 with only one member. By the end of the first year it had become a Sabbath School Institute, with thirty teachers and labourers, but also engaged in other enterprises, embracing every age and class of the surrounding population. By the summer of 1859, when the Mission's prayer meetings were starting to show signs of real spiritual life, one worker brought back reports of revival in progress in the Wynd Church in Glasgow.

It was on October 14 that, suddenly, 'the shower came on', and an 'extraordinary ... work of grace' commenced.[23] Nightly meetings were

---

21. A. Moody Stuart, *Life of John Duncan*, Edinburgh, 1991, p. 56.

22. James Gall, *Report of Carrubbers Close Mission*, Edinburgh, 1861, pp. 3-4.

23. Gall, 1882, p. 4.

held for upwards of six months and people flocked to them in droves. New premises had to be rented to accommodate the increasing number of classes and enterprises. The converts carried the revival into the workshops and homes of the people, and it became necessary to assign the workers to newly formed sections of the city and neighbourhood.

During 1860, activity at the Mission reached a crescendo. Conversions took place in their hundreds, and it was said that there was scarcely a congregation in Edinburgh that did not feel its influence. The chapel proving too small for the large crowds that were gathering, Sunday and Wednesday evening meetings were transferred to the Theatre Royal (later the Post Office), which was provided by the Government rent free. As soon as one meeting ended, another one began for those unable to gain admittance to the first. This was followed by a massive inquiry meeting until a late hour. When this, too, became overcrowded, use of the New Assembly Hall was obtained and meetings continued here for many months. But even this venue at times proved too small, and someone might have to be sent to preach to the crowds packed into the quadrangle, unable to gain admittance to the meeting place.

Operations were organised to a remarkable degree. For example, on certain weeknights when attendances were smaller, one of the workers would go to the High Street, at the head of Carrubbers Close, and preach to the many pedestrians who passed along that busy highway. After collecting an audience, he would bring them down to the Mission hall for a meeting at half-past-eight. Six preachers performed this duty in turn, being aided by around thirty canvassers. These would give out tracts and invitations, and hopefully induce people to attend the meeting. The workers would often observe a growing earnestness in the faces of individuals; others would weep, or when going to prayer, fall on their knees in an act of submission to God. Thus a number of workers acted as 'gleaners', who would watch for an opening for conversation, or when people went away weeping, the gleaners would talk with them, and hopefully bring them back to be further conversed with and prayed for.[24]

In November 1860, in concert with English evangelists, Reginald Radcliffe and Richard Weaver, a series of 'Midnight meetings' was

---

24. *WJ*, November 1859, p. 35.

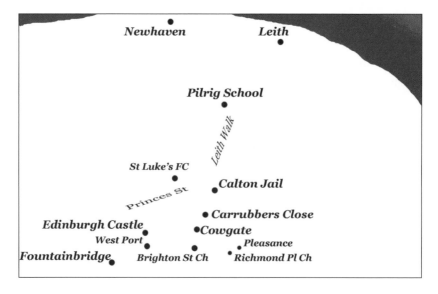

held for the city's prostitutes, of whom a remarkable 125 were 'rescued' from their lives of open sin. Of these, thirty-four were sent home to their friends, forty-eight were received into institutions, and nearly all the others were boarded in Edinburgh and Dunbar under the care of one Mrs Colonel Purves. Workers from Carrubbers Mission also did a good work among 'a number of milk-girls', whose simple and earnest appeals to the house-servants to whom they gave the milk while on their delivery rounds, were the means of bringing many of them to the meetings. One of the Mission's most active and successful labourers was a girl who hired herself out to families as a sewing-girl, and wherever she went, she readily spoke of Christ, possessing a strong burden to win souls to the Lord.

At the height of the movement there were upwards of forty meetings going on in the city and surrounding villages, and weeks of evangelism were held in churches loaned for the purpose, in addition to the nightly meetings in Carrubbers Close chapel itself. Newhaven, the Water of Leith, Stockbridge, Blackhall and other places had branch meetings begun in them. Many of these meetings were so blessed that they, too, became centres of revival. Evangelists multiplied and extended their outreach to towns and villages outwith Edinburgh. Here many souls were won, and a number of converts themselves became missionaries working for the Mission. The Rev. William Paterson was employed as the chief evangelist of the Mission and made many excursions throughout the country right up to 1863, when responsibilities were handed over to the newly formed Scottish Evangelistic Association.[25]

The movement continued well into 1861, when the Mission held a three-day Evangelistic Convocation, an all-day prayer-meeting in the Tron Church on the Royal Mile, as well as evangelistic meetings in the Corn Exchange, the Free Assembly Hall, Queen Street Hall, and a dozen churches, plus open-air meetings in Queen's Park.[26]

Jessie McFarlane (later an itinerant evangelist) wrote regarding her teenage sister Mary, during the time of the revival in Edinburgh, 'An awakening commenced among the girls of a Bible-class, of which she was a member. Several of them were led to Jesus, and she among the number. After a fortnight of great anxiety about her soul, she found such sweet rest and peace in Jesus. Being so young, and naturally very timid, I could not but wonder to see how decided she was for the Saviour, how she could tell of His love, and that now she knew He was her Saviour. I felt glad that she was safe, but began to think there was no hope for me.' But shortly afterwards, Jessie, too, went through a deep conversion experience after attending a meeting at Carrubbers Close in September 1860. Keen to grow in her new-found faith, Jessie joined a female Bible class. She said that around this time – January 1861 – 'every gospel meeting was crowded in Edinburgh and after the class was dismissed the room filled with women who came to hear of the love of Jesus from the lips of those young Christians who had found Him to be such a precious Saviour to their soul.'[27]

---

25. For additional information on the work of revival in Carrubbers Close Mission, see Reid, pp. 451-60; Sprange, pp. 138-45.

26. In addition to the work of the Carrubbers Close Mission during the three years of the revival, James Gall believed there were much wider implications. He felt that Carrubbers' labours had clearly demonstrated that Home Missions were not merely the responsibility of ministers and that the conversion of sinners was just as easily achieved through evangelistic meetings as through public worship, with evangelistic addresses taking the place of sermons. Indeed, he pointed to both the Grove Street Institute, Glasgow and St Andrew's Hall Institute in Leith as being organised on the principles of Carrubbers Mission (Gall, 1882, p. 7).

27. Mary's time as a believer in this world was not to last long. She died on 6 January 1861, 'breathing the precious name of Jesus' (H. I. G., pp. 12-13).

Revival Elsewhere in the Old Town

One church early blessed by awakening in Edinburgh was Brighton Street Chapel, situated near the University. Part of the Evangelical Union, the church was then pastored by the energetic yet controversial, Dr John Kirk. Renowned American evangelist, Charles Finney spent several days here on his intensive UK visit (which lasted from August to November 1859), preaching to deeply attentive audiences. At the close of his series of meetings he asked those who were prepared to publicly profess their faith in the Saviour to stand. At least two hundred did so, holding up their right hands in testimony.[28]

Finney later recorded: 'We had a very interesting revival in that place, and many souls were converted. Church members were greatly blessed, and Brother Kirk's hands were full, day and night, of labours among inquirers.'[29] He lamented, however, that due to 'prejudice against Brother Kirk and his view ... there was little hope of seeing a widespread revival throughout that city'.[30] Nevertheless, in Brighton Street Chapel itself, it was no uncommon sight to see as many as eighty new members receiving the right hand of fellowship on Communion Sundays. After Finney left Edinburgh, Kirk continued the meetings, and the result of these were that in 1861, 180 names were added to the roll of the Brighton Street Chapel, and in 1862, another fifty-four.

---

28. *The Revival Advocate*, 06/06/1859, quoted in Nigel Scotland, *Apostles of the Spirit and Fire: American Revivalists and Victorian Britain*, Carlisle, 2009, p. 79.

29. William Robertson of Carrubbers Close, however, paints a somewhat different (and to some extent, less accurate) picture. He says that Finney came to the Brighton Street church 'early in the month of November' and closed his mission on the tenth of that month as 'he had to leave unexpectedly for England'. Robertson went almost nightly to the meetings, but 'although large audiences attended ... there seemed to be but little interest' (Rev. R. M. Robertson [Ed.], *William Robertson of Carrubbers Close Mission*, Edinburgh, 1914, p. 20).

30. Garth M. Rosell and Richard Dupois, *The Original Memoirs of Charles G. Finney*, Grand Rapids, 1989, pp. 591-2. *The Christian News*, however, exaggerated the case when it introduced Finney to its readers shortly after his arrival in Scotland, by claiming: 'Almost all the revival spirit that has prevailed among our ministers and people is due in no small degree to the influence of his "*Lectures on Revivals*", published amongst us at the commencement of our own revival period [20 years previously]. He comes, among other things, to see the fruit of his own efforts, and the Spirit of God in him when that fruit is ripening to harvest' (*The Christian News*, 27/08/1859, quoted in ibid., p. 592).

Some of the newly formed Territorial Free churches saw the greatest moves of the Spirit during these years. From the city's West Port district, the Rev. William Tasker reported in 1861: 'At this moment I have nearly sixty candidates for communion, two-thirds of whom date their serious impressions within the last three months. At present we have at least sixty persons who hold district prayer-meetings in almost every close of the West Port.' Another congregation in Edinburgh richly blessed by revival during this period was Cowgate Free Church, whose pastor, the Rev. John Pirie, reported at the beginning of 1861: 'This time last year our communion roll numbered 177; now it numbers nearly 300.'[31]

The Rev. Thomas Cochrane reported of the Pleasance area:

> The year 1860 will be ever memorable in the history of this congrega-tion. Since last Assembly the increase in the membership is 203. At the close of the usual weekly services on some occasions four, five, six and upwards, have remained in deep concern to speak about the state of their souls. Meetings for prayer have been held by the people themselves, while not a few of the awakened and hopefully converted have taken part in these, along with the minister and others. Were the question put, 'Who have been the most instrumental in building up and adding members to the congregation?', the reply would be, 'The people themselves.'[32]

Elsewhere in the Old Town, large numbers were added to St Columba's Gaelic congregation during the period of the revival. Meanwhile, in the city's New Town, St Luke's Free Church became 'a centre for evan-gelistic work' during the awakening, continuing the blessing that had been raining on this congregation over recent years (see pp. 38-9).[33] During 1859–61, noted evangelists Brownlow North, Hay Macdowall Grant and others preached here on numerous occasions to over-whelming gatherings.

Revival among Children and Students
A remarkable work of awakening began in Edinburgh's Pilrig School, off Leith Walk, when head-teacher John Robertson and a deputy, both

---

31. Brown, 1893, p. 778; PFCSHMC, 1861, pp. 98-9.

32. Brown, 1893, pp. 778-9.

33. Leask, p. 135; Moody Stuart, 1899, p. 138.

newly converted, claimed the promise of Matthew 18:19,[34] and prayed expectantly for the conversion of six specific pupils. That same day, the eighteenth of November 1859, all six pupils came under deep conviction. As awakening spread through the school during that memorable day, the children, totalling ninety, were brought together, 'all of them either crying or with faces showing traces of tears'. Reflected Robertson: 'I can never forget, and certainly never express the overwhelming sense I had of the presence of God, the living God, as He manifested Himself amongst us. We could not but adore Him, yes really, "lost in wonder, love and praise". The holy ecstasy with which He filled us cannot be told. We seemed to be translated from the world and things earthly, and on this and subsequent occasions I thought I could not live because of the joy with which the Lord filled me. It was not easy to carry such a full cup.'[35]

A few days later all eighteen pupils of the highest class made a profession of having come to Jesus, while a new pupil-teacher was also saved. The converted pupils at once became formidable evangelists and there were many instances of peers, parents and strangers coming to faith through their efforts. For example, when Robertson went to speak in Bonnyrigg, 'The meeting that evening was a very remarkable one; there was a great breaking down on the part of both old and young.' Convinced that it was not his words alone that had been so wonderfully effectual, Robertson discovered that two girls from Pilrig had prayed behind a hedge that same evening and 'were so sure that there was to be a great blessing'.[36]

At Edinburgh University, meanwhile, and influenced by the awakening progressing in various parts of the city, and across the country, a general prayer meeting, open to all students, was commenced in December 1859, to be held every Saturday morning. Meanwhile, in the same establishment, students of the medical classes began a devotional meeting on Friday evenings.[37]

---

34. 'Again I say unto you, that if two of you shall agree on earth as touching anything that they shall ask, it shall be done for them of my Father which is in heaven.'

35. Robertson, 1914, pp. 37-54.

36. ibid.

37. One Edinburgh University graduate touched by the revival was J. R. Elder, whose thoughts were at that time turned to the ministry. So, in 1861 he went back to University and procured a Master of Arts degree which he followed up by theological studies at the New College. He subsequently served in several Free Church

Weaver and Radcliffe

Reginald Radcliffe and Richard Weaver caused a great stir when they spent six weeks in Edinburgh in the autumn of 1860.[38] On one occasion the two Englishmen preached intermittently from 7 till 11 p.m. to 1,800 people congregated in Richmond Place Chapel, while thousands more packed the street outside. Creating an unusual spectacle, the evangelists had to walk on the shoulders of stalwart men in order to alternate in ministry inside and outside the chapel! It was said that even after the services were far advanced, numbers were seen hurrying from the Old to the New Town and vice versa, in expectation of hearing Weaver.

So many crowded to hear the evangelists that they were often forced to address large open-air gatherings. Weaver spoke in Queen's Park to a huge crowd, which he estimated at forty thousand. The Rev. James Gall (minister of the new Moray Free Church from 1861), put the figure at between twenty and thirty thousand – still a vast gathering indeed. Gall said that 'no-one had stirred that city to the depths as Weaver had done'. As a result of their mission, and focusing on Weaver's ministry, James Paterson wrote: 'Not only were multitudes of souls immediately brought to Christ, but the brethren of Carrubbers Close Mission had been engaged for weeks after he had gone, gathering in the fruits of his labours.'[39]

Weaver also preached in Edinburgh's Calton Jail, where, among women prisoners alone, he had the privilege of dealing with upwards of thirty anxious enquirers. When he spoke of God's love individually to one particularly 'wretched inmate', she fell to her knees, crying, 'Thank God, someone loves me!' Her public testimony led others to cry out, 'If God can save her, He can save me!' When Weaver later preached to the men prisoners, 'the power of God was on the meeting', and there were some notable instances of conviction and conversion.[40]

---

charges, the most lengthy being in Cromarty from 1869 to 1882 and Arrochar from 1882 till his death in 1897. (P. W. Minto et al., *Memorials of the Late Rev. J. R. and Mrs Elder of Arrochar*, Edinburgh, 1900).

38. Jessie McFarlane wrote of 'a great work ... going on' in Edinburgh with the visit of these and other evangelists, 'and there were many hundreds of souls awakened at that time'. Indeed, she wrote of 'glorious times of refreshing throughout the winter of 1860-61' in Edinburgh (H. I. G., p. 9).

39. Paterson, 1897, p. 142.

40. ibid., pp. 135-6.

Another active evangelist in Edinburgh during the revival, the Rev. James Hood Wilson of the Barclay Church, was invited to preach one Sabbath evening in a large theatre in the city. His biographer said: 'The "old story" was told by him as if it were new; and it was new to himself, for he always felt afresh the wonder and glory of it. His perception of the nearness and freeness of divine grace was always very keen.' Wilson described the occasion in brief: 'A grand site; pit, first and second boxes, galleries and stage, all crowded. Was wonderfully helped, and kept my self-possession far beyond what I had hoped. If anything would fire a man, it was such an audience. After the service I met forty young women in a private room, some of them in deep anxiety. Did not get home till about eleven – not very tired after all.'[41]

Revival in the Workplace
As part of the revival movement in the city, 'A remarkable work of grace' commenced in the North British Rubber Works near Fountainbridge. One female employee conducted a daily prayer meeting in the premises, attended by two or three hundred employees. In addition, the Rev. J. H. Wilson was allowed to conduct a weekly meeting for twenty-five minutes during lunch hour among hundreds of workers, with gratifying results. Remarkably, this meeting continued for nine years. Wilson and others also conducted special evening meetings away from church for canal-men, coal-heavers, carters and slaughterhouse workers. The minister was 'quite at home with these rough fellows and moved among them frankly as a man among men'. Partly as a result of this work, the Fountainbrdge Church became increasingly a gathering place of young souls, especially of young men. Within a short time, three separate Y.M.C.A. societies had been formed with an aggregate membership of 150.[42]

In an Edinburgh factory a man deeply convicted of sin suddenly turned white of face, cried out, and then collapsed. His outburst

---

41. James Wells, *The Life of James Hood Wilson, D. D. of the Barclay Church, Edinburgh*, London, 1904, p. 215. It was immediately following a meeting in Edinburgh's Theatre Royal, 'crowded to suffocation', and during the period of the revival, that Jacob Primmer, subsequently a Church of Scotland minister, came to know the joy of sins forgiven (J. Boyd Primmer, *Life of Pastor Jacob Primmer*, Edinburgh, 1916, pp. 10-13).

42. Wells, pp. 64-5. Remarkably, membership of this church rose from just 26 in 1853 to 1,080 in 1864.

disturbed the whole factory, and a great many workers began to share the tension. Before long, prayer meetings were being held thrice a day in the building. Meanwhile, a striking and unusual movement, centring on the Canongate, occurred among many of the city's prostitutes when a medical student prayed for and spoke with them, also helping them find more suitable accommodation.[43]

In 1860 a group of believers belonging to the building trade began a weekly 'Masons meeting' for 'prayer, praise and reading of the Word'. Soon between twenty and thirty were coming together, and, noted one worker, 'we find a few of our brothers in trade brought in not only to our meeting, but into the fold of Jesus'. That same believer also made note of a social meeting which was held in conjunction with a deputation from the Joiners Prayer Meeting, 'and it was a night that will be long remembered by all present. We felt as if the Master presided himself.'[44]

Outskirts of Edinburgh

Corstorphine and Cramond

In many villages close to Edinburgh – such as Slateford and Blackhall to the south and west of the city (both of which have long since become Edinburgh suburbs), and the fishing villages of Portobello and Musselburgh to the east – prayer meetings had been established by March 1860. A deputation was sent from Carrubbers Close Mission to Corstorphine, where meetings were commenced in the open air. These soon got so interesting that the people asked the missionaries to try and secure one of the churches. The Free Church was immediately offered and so a deputation was sent to the place twice a week for a remarkable two or three years, being well-assisted by missionaries, ministers and students. If pressed for time, prayer would be held while walking by the way, one leading and the others praying.

Cramond, a fishing community at the mouth of the River Almond to the north of Edinburgh, was said to be 'like many or most of our country parishes ... in general cold, formal and lifeless'.[45] Apart from one meet-

---

43. *TR*, 15/10/1859, 26/10/1859, quoted in Orr, 1949, pp. 73-4.

44. *WJ*, 02/11/1861, p. 38.

45. *SG*, 21/01/1860.

ing irregularly led by the minister, one could search in vain to find any form of prayer meeting. With the revival movement, however, seven such prayer gatherings were in operation each week, four of them public and overflowing, the other three private and without the presence of a minister.

Leith

From Leith, ministers crossed the Irish Sea to witness the revival that was flourishing in that land, then returned and told of it before large audiences at home. Many indoor and open-air meetings were held in this district. *The Scottish Guardian* noted that 'at the Water of Leith, as elsewhere, it would seem that, literally, the publicans and harlots are entering into the kingdom'.[46]

In another publication, the case was mentioned of an old woman who kept a shoe shop in a poor locality of Leith. One day an old seaman of about seventy years came into her shop to purchase. The first pair of shoes not fitting him, he began to swear. The old woman put away the shoes, and quietly told him that she could not bear to hear her Saviour's name blasphemed, and that her practice with such people was to have no more to do with them. She reminded him that he was an old man, and how would he appear, as he must surely, before his Judge? The seaman calmed down, and besought her to supply him. She relented, he was duly fitted and went away. Shortly afterwards, however, he returned in tears, entreating her to tell him the way of salvation.[47]

Among the many who attended meetings in Leith were the entire crew of a fishing boat from Fraserburgh. Both the captain, a Mr Summers, and his crew were converted through these meetings and later became involved in revival services elsewhere in the country (see p. 252). Under the guidance of the Rev. Dr MacDonald, North Leith Free Church experienced a 'blessed season of revival' shortly after the movement first became apparent in the Lothians. One young man awakened through meetings here, and gloriously converted three months later on New Year's morning 1860, was Robert Ross, who at once became an eager soul-winner and later entered the ministry.[48]

---

46. ibid., 11/02/1860, p. 154.

47. *WJ*, 09/03/1861, p. 605.

48. Ordained minister of Forfar Free Church in 1869, Ross died suddenly just twelve years later, aged forty-one (John Ross, *Memorials of the Rev. Robert Ross, East*

Newhaven

A mile along the coast, the fishing community of Newhaven apparently had 'the worst reputation' imaginable. 'The men only quitted the sea for the tavern' and the women were 'redoubtable for swearing and cheating' as they sold their fish on Edinburgh streets. A minister in the place testified that during the winter of 1859–60 'we were visited by a veritable Pentecost'. At one meeting, 'the whole assembly was so seized with a conviction of their sins that you could hear nothing but one long sigh. For myself, overcome with emotion, I was compelled to leave the church' for a time. Another witness testified that 'extraordinary excitement' was evidenced at this meeting, which was crowded with fishermen and 'around one hundred ragged, wild-looking boys, all behaving with the greatest decorum, and at the close of the meeting there arose a universal wail for mercy'. At one point, several dozen were on the floor praying for themselves. It was said that, 'since that day hundreds of souls have been converted and this village has become like a garden of the Lord'.[49]

Recalled another observer, 'The most remarkable impression' was made. 'Soon it was in a blaze. The schoolhouse could not hold all the people that came, but the ministers opened their churches, and they also were filled. Things of eternity seemed to press upon the community; so that nothing short of salvation would satisfy the people. The children turned up the boats to have their own prayer-meetings. It was with difficulty meetings could be closed, and even then groups of people would be found outside the churches deeply anxious. They could not separate without saying, "Oh, dinna leave us till you pray again!" And when that was done the people in their anxiety would be found on their knees amid the snow.'[50]

Carrubbers Close Mission led many of these meetings, sending forth a considerable number of 'reapers', both male and female, to

---

Free Church, Forfar, Edinburgh, 1881, p. 7).

49. *SG*, 28/02/1860; 17/07/1860.

50. Anonymous, *These Fifty Years: The Story of Carrubbers Close Mission, Edinburgh: 1859 – 1909*, Edinburgh, 1909, p. 71. Evangelist Richard Hill from Glasgow wrote that 'among impulsive folk like these, strange things were said and done. "I had to ask my mates today", said one, "to take me ashore. I never saw before that there was only a half-inch plank between hell and me"' (*SG*, 28/02/1860).

gather in the harvest, i.e., to deal individually with anxious cases. The movement was still in full flow in the summer of 1860. At one meeting, for which a great many locals assembled, 'one felt that every word of the gospel vibrated in their hearts and the tears might be seen rolling down their sun-browned cheeks'. It was said that the vocal organs of the fisherwomen – who were well accustomed to singing in the streets, and who were recognisable at the meetings by their well-known costumes – resembled 'a brazen instrument', but were 'still more vigorous in singing the praises of God'.[51] Many were received for the first time into the fellowship of the Church; 'the careless have been overawed; and the entire church-going community refreshed, many of them led truly to give themselves to Christ'.[52]

Several men from the ship *Edinburgh* came under the influence of the revival while attending meetings in Newhaven; this resulted in a twice-weekly prayer meeting being established on the boat, attended by the First Lieutenant, the First Gunner, and several young men from Newhaven. *The Wynd Journal* reported in April 1860: 'A number of volunteers were to leave Ferryden for a month's drill. They were chiefly converts of the revival in that fishing village. It was a matter of earnest consideration among some of the older and more established Christians as to whether it was safe to allow these men, so young in faith, to go alone. Thus it was that a few of the older men volunteered to go, hoping also to be a good influence on board among those that were careless.' The same *Journal* remarked on the interesting circumstance that some young men from Hopeman were awakened on board this ship at the very time the work commenced in their native place.[53]

Bonnyrigg and Howgate

Initially Bonnyrigg received 'the first droppings' of God's shower of blessing; then, said one witness, 'He manifested his presence amongst us in a very unmistakable manner. ... O, what a heart-gladdening sight it was to see the youth of fourteen, side-by-side with persons whose hairs are silvered with the weight of years, earnestly looking to be guided to Christ.'

---

51. *SG*, 17/07/1860.

52. MacGill, pp. 4-5. One who oft-times laboured here 'in days of deep impression' was Rev. James Hood Wilson of Fountainbridge (Wells, p. 215).

53. *WJ*, 14/04/1860, p. 228.

Meanwhile, of the spiritual movement in and around Penicuik, the Rev. David Duncan, minister of the United Presbyterian Church of nearby Howgate, said he 'had much pleasant intercourse ... with the esteemed ministers of the Free Church in Penicuik ... in prayer-meetings and other religious services, especially during the time of revival' in 1859–60.[54]

Portobello and Joppa

From the fishing village of Portobello, James Stalker, an elder and treasurer in the local Free Church and headmaster of the village school, travelled with a friend to witness the revival in Ireland. Unfortunately he took ill on the trip, and died a few days after his return home. Prayer meetings were established in the town by March 1860.[55]

Near Portobello the first manifestation of a special work of grace commenced in cottage meetings in the village of Joppa. Joshua Coombs, inducted to Portobello Congregational Church in December 1858, found 'abundant cause for gratitude' for the 'special work of grace' in connection with these meetings. Coombs would read to the small group accounts of revival elsewhere in Scotland. Though combined with hymns, a Scripture reading, prayers and a bible-based address, the whole meeting was deliberately confined to around 45–50 minutes. In this way was interest maintained, the meetings being described as 'greatly blessed'. Both in Joppa and in his own church, Coombs also appointed an evening a week for inquirers to speak with him, while another weekly meeting held by brethren from Carrubbers Close Mission also bore fruit. Coombs was confident of a fuller imminent outpouring of the Spirit on the community, but unfortunately he didn't remain to enjoy it, demitting his charge in April 1860.[56]

West Lothian

In his study of the role of children in Scottish revival movements, the Rev. Harry Sprange noted that, compared with most other districts

---

54. *WJ*, 04/05/1861, p. 46; David Duncan, *Discourses by the Late Rev. David Duncan, Minister of the United Presbyterian Church*, Edinburgh, 1867, p. 59.

55. William Baird, *The Free Church Congregation of Portobello*, Edinburgh, 1890, pp. 111-12; Orr, 1949, pp. 74-5.

56. *The Annual Report of the Congregational Union of Scotland 1860*, quoted in McNaughton, 2005, pp. 347-9.

of Scotland, West Lothian seems to have been 'scarcely touched' by the revival of 1858–61.[57] The present author, similarly, has uncovered little of note relating to this small but relatively populous county. One noteworthy story comes from the *Caledonian Mercury*, which found there to be two classes of inhabitants in what it described as the 'dingy' mining town of Bo'ness, and nearby villages such as Newtown and Grangepans. These classes were of Orangeman and Romanists. Both classes lived in desperate spiritual darkness, and though most evangelists kept away from the area, the appropriately named Mr Tough of the Coast Mission, along with a few other Christian workers, decided to 'attack' the communities with the gospel message. Their 'success was, to say the least, astonishing'. It was not 'decent, church-going persons' who attended the meetings – indeed as a class they held aloof altogether – 'but the drunken, dissolute, ignorant and disorderly'. There was little outward expression of emotion; rather the movement was 'silent and unobtrusive'.[58]

---

57. Sprange, p. 128.
58. *Caledonian Mercury*, quoted in *SG*, 25/10/1860.

Cellardyke

Pittenweem

Cargill Parish

Bonskeid House, near Pitlochry

Glenlyon

Chapter 9

North-Central Scotland

Stirlingshire

Drumclair

Early in 1858 some inhabitants of Drumclair, by Slamannan, five miles south of Falkirk, wrote to Charles Abercrombie, a Scots teacher living in America, requesting that he return to his native land to teach the children of local pitmen. After much thought and prayer, the expatriate made up his mind to accept the invitation. He accepted the appointment as teacher in the area, while he also engaged in evangelising among miners and their families under the newly formed Scottish Committee of the Churches of Christ,[1] to which denomination Abercrombie had transferred his allegiance from the Baptist Church while living in America.

Initially, he regretted his return to Scotland, finding the 'filthy houses, degradation of the entire population', etc., almost too much to bear. But he carried on preaching both indoors and out till he was thoroughly weary. There eventually occurred some cases of conviction, and after a time six or seven were baptized in the Black Loch by the minister George Dunn. Crowds witnessed the scene in deep solemnity, and soon many more were turning to Jesus. Remarkably, a total of

---

1. The Churches of Christ was an offshoot of the Disciples (or Churches) of Christ group in America, founded by Ulster-born Alexander Campbell. Its rise in Scotland came mainly in the 1830s and, particularly early 40s, winning many new members from the Scotch Baptists. By 1842 over twenty congregations existed, mainly in central Scotland and the fishing towns of the north-east. The peak membership of 2,803 (50 churches) came in 1933, dropping markedly after 1945 (see A. C. Watters, *History of the British Churches of Christ*, Birmingham, 1947).

around eighty souls, mainly male, out of a population of three hundred, were baptised before the end of 1859 – as many as twenty-three in one day.[2] One correspondent exulted: 'The whole character of the village has been changed, radically and completely. No whisky is drunk in it, the houses are clean and comfortable and there are only eight houses without a conversion.'[3]

In 1860 a second church was founded at Bo'ness, where Abercrombie's brother-in-law, John Nimmo, coalmaster, became the leader. Soon afterwards the Drumclair teacher yielded to urgent appeals to give himself wholly to the work of an evangelist. Largely through his efforts – but sometimes in conjunction with fellow Churches of Christ evangelist J. B. Rotherham – small congregations were founded in Bathgate, Crofthead, Whitburn, and Hamilton over the following couple of years.

Campsie

The work in Campsie originated with a visit by the Rev. William Wood of the United Presbyterian Church to Ireland in September 1859 to witness the revival there. A time of prayer was intimated at a church in Londonderry, where Wood had preached, especially to pray for an outpouring of God's Spirit in Campsie. Returning home, Wood discovered that within two hours of this prayer meeting, a special manifestation of the Divine presence had occurred during a time of prayer in a Campsie schoolroom! Thus began the visible tokens of a blessed awakening in the parish, during which attendance at public worship increased strikingly, attendance at the weekly prayer meeting doubled and the number of weekly meetings in the district rose from five to twenty.[4] There was considerable awakening also in connection with the Wesleyan Preaching House, which became 'besieged with

2. *The Airdrie, Coatbridge, Bathgate and Wishaw Advertiser*, 20/08/1859, quoted in Kelling, p. 51. One of those baptised was Jane Gillon, a miner's wife from Wilsontown, a few miles south of Fauldhouse. She was midwife for the village, but 'her love for Christ and His Gospel outshone every other thing in her life', and James Anderson, a Churches of Christ evangelist, who for many years was based in Slamannan, held many meetings in her home (James Anderson, *Evangelist: An Outline of my Life, or Selections From a Fifty Years Religious Experience*, Whitburn, 1912, Chap 12).

3. *SG*, 19/08/1859.

4. MacGill, pp. 14-15.

anxious crowds; some have been in great distress, and not a few, it is believed, have found peace in believing'.[5] In 1860, a band of Christian workers in Glasgow organised revival meetings in surrounding areas. The meetings held in Campsie were attended with a measure of success, and resulted in the nucleus being formed of a Free Church Mission, which became a fully-fledged Free Church congregation soon after.

Stirling

In Stirling, Radcliffe and Weaver held a meeting in the Corn Exchange, which, Weaver noted, 'lasted all night. Far on in the morning I retired to the hotel for a little rest; but about five o'clock the watchman of the hotel called me up, and told me Mr Radcliffe wanted me to return to the Exchange to sing to those still there. I found there were yet between thirty and forty inquiring the way of salvation.' To one man who said he could stay no longer as he had to go to his work, Weaver took hold of both his and his wife's hands, and sang to them the first verse of 'Just as I am.' 'The man said, "It is done! Christ is mine!" The woman also believed. They embraced each other and went home rejoicing in God their Saviour.'[6]

Kilsyth

The town of Kilsyth, renowned in Scottish revival history, was again blessed with an awakening in September 1859. In particular, a great many were thought to have been converted over a ten-day period. The Rev. Black of the Free Church wrote that 'for three months the meetings continued. There was no excitement, certainly nothing approaching to extravagance. At our communion in November, between fifty and sixty were admitted to the Lord's Table – nearly every one of whom professed to have been brought out of darkness into light. They were of all ages, from seventeen to fifty or sixty. The tone of piety was raised among the professedly religious. The whole aspect of the place was changed, the decency and decorum of the streets presenting a very pleasing contrast to the former state of things.'[7] Indeed, it was suggested that there was now little need for a police establishment in the town as

---

5. *WJ*, October 1859, p. 18.

6. Paterson, 1897, p. 131.

7. Brown, 1893, p. 776.

many suspicious characters were showing much improvement in their walk and conversation. Proof of this was evidenced in the Procurator Fiscal's statement that criminal cases had of late decreased significantly.[8]

Strangely, James Hutchison's fascinating, detailed ecclesiastical history of Kilsyth, published in 1986, makes no mention of the 1859 revival, though it records at some length the movements of 1742, 1839 and 1866.[9] Similarly, though writing much nearer the time of the event (1866), the Rev. F. Ferguson of Blackfriars Street Evangelical Union Church, Glasgow, while recounting Kilsyth's revival legacy, makes no mention of the 1859 movement.[10] Perhaps more strikingly still, providing a detailed account of the 1866 revival in Kilsyth a year after its occurrence, but noting, too, previous spiritual movements in the town, H. W. Holland also makes no reference to the 1859 movement. It seems clear both that these and other writers were unaware of the spiritual movement that occurred in Kilsyth in 1859; but also that the awakening that took place at that time was not nearly as powerful as those that occurred in the same location in those key years, 1742, 1839 and 1866.[11]

Clackmannanshire

Tillicoultry

Clackmannanshire, Scotland's smallest county, also shared in the national outpouring of revival blessing. A correspondent to *The Wynd Journal* wrote in 1860 that the revival was progressing in Tillicoultry 'in a very wonderful manner. This place had been subject to earnest pleading for some time, and now the answer has come in showers of blessing.' One young man who was converted by means of a close friend, who himself had only recently been brought to Christ, testified to how 'a flood of light rushed into my mind; I could see that Jesus was my

---

8. *Falkirk Herald*, quoted in *SG*, 27/09/1859.

9. James Hutchison, *Weavers, Miners and the Open Book: A History of Kilsyth*, Cumbernauld, 1986.

10. ibid., p. 75.

11. A further significant outpouring of God's Spirit on the much-blessed town occurred in 1908, in what became known as the Pentecostal revival (see Tom Lennie, *Glory in the Glen: A History of Evangelical Revivals in Scotland 1880-1940*, Fearn, 2009, pp. 424-31.

Saviour. ... Oh what a happiness I felt. I cannot tell what I felt. I could not rest that night without calling in my neighbours and telling them what great things the Lord had done for my soul. We sat up till between two and three in the morning, singing and reading together.'[12]

A local clergyman, offering his version of events for a Glasgow newspaper, wrote that at the union prayer meetings, 'the deadness of the spirit and prayers for a time showed how much we needed to be revived'. When E. P. Hammond visited Tillicoultry in November 1860, the town again became, 'the scene of a rich effusion of the quickening Spirit'. Fourteen hundred packed the Popular Institute Hall, and between two and three hundred waited for the Inquiry meeting (one report puts the figure at between five and six hundred[13]), although some stayed behind through mere curiosity; and a few waited to mock. Subsequently, prayer meetings among the boys by themselves, with another group forming among the girls, sprang up spontaneously in some of the factories, while, observed the clergyman, 'false professors of Christianity are breaking down'.[14]

One church in Tillicoultry exactly doubled its membership during 1861, from 63 to 126, though the actual congregation was never below 300. The youthful and recently inducted James Strachan, whose labours were 'singly owned by God', claimed that 'revival services' held by the Rev. John Kirk and others in his Evangelical Union denomination had considerable influence in preparing the place for the late revival that had broken out amongst them.[15]

The Baptist cause was 'greatly blessed' by the labours of its minister, the Rev. Scott. In December 1859 Scott wrote: 'The Lord is still working with us. Eight have been baptized lately', making twenty additions to their number in twelve months. 'I expect to baptize four more next Lord's day', he continued, 'and there are many inquirers'. More were added over the next few months. At Clackmannan the meetings were

---

12. Marrs, p. 347.

13. *WJ*, 08/12/1860, p. 503.

14. Headley, pp. 91-3; *SG*, 29/11/1860.

15. McNaughton, 2005, pp. 293-4. Strachan was 'roused to seek the Lord and brought to personal decision for Christ' just a year previously during revival services in Leith. His ministry was short, however, as he died in July 1866, aged 31.

'remarkably well attended, and much anxiety is evinced to hear the gospel'. The movement in this county continued well into the 1860s (see pp. 434-5). In nearby Coalsnaughton, it was reported that 'the Lord has indeed opened the windows of heaven, and poured out a blessing. ... We have interesting nightly meetings. The Lord seems to be working more among the young than the old.'[16]

Fife and Kinross

Tayport

The Scottish Guardian suggested that the revival was evident all along the Fife coast from Ferryport-on-Craig (now Tayport) to the East Neuk of Fife and equally far westward along the north shores of the Firth of Forth.[17]

When a native of Tayport arrived in Dundee, he was informed by a Christian woman that revival had broken out in his home community. This was what he had longed for, but he could hardly believe it. He hastened to his home village and found it to be absolutely true. He wrote: 'Mr North has been here for about a week, and his visit has been blessed to some. ... A young lad from Maryhill came along with me, who was converted a few weeks ago while on a visit to Ireland; he and a few other young men commenced to keep meetings. ... The Lord has been graciously working among us.'[18] One minister, speaking with caution, shared his estimation that during the revival in Tayport, 'thirty or forty connected with myself have derived spiritual benefit, with all of whom I have had many meetings, and not one of whom has caused the tongue of scandal to be raised against him'.[19]

In November 1861 two years after revival had swept through these townships, a correspondent from *The Scottish Guardian* revisited several of the villages concerned. He wrote that, though the excitement had passed, 'a great change has taken place ... so strikingly apparent that it was the first thing to arrest one's attention'. Indeed the revival had

---

16. BHMS Report, 1860, p. 19; *WJ*, 08/12/1860, p. 503.

17. *SG*, 19/11/1861.

18. *WJ*, October 1859, p. 10.

19. MacGill, p. 5. *The Scottish Guardian* also remarked on the 'blessed work' in progress in Ferryport during the winter of 1859–60 (*SG*, 03/03/1860).

earned respect and reverence even from non-religious folk in these communities.[20]

Flisk and Newburgh

The Rev. J. W. Taylor, Free Church minister of the north Fife coastal parish of Flisk, stated that 'in 1860–61, the years of revival, I could count up about eighteen in one little congregation as sharing in the benefits of that awakening. Persons that had kicked against faithful and tender dealing have submitted themselves; stillness and reverence and expectancy characterise our Sabbath meetings.'[21] A little further inland, it was said of Cupar that, 'This is a district where there never has been an awakening, and when the Lord visits us, it will be quite new to most.' Earnest prayer was called upon on behalf of the town, a number of whose residents began to show 'some signs of anxiety'.[22]

A religious awakening commenced in Newburgh in November 1860 when a few believers from Perth addressed an audience of several hundred on the streets before adjourning to one of the churches for a service. At a subsequent meeting, judging from the attention with which the people listened, and the sobbing of the broken in spirit, 'it was evident that the Lord was in the midst'. The benediction was pronounced three times before the people retired. When one of the Perth men returned to his lodgings he found some twenty-five anxious souls waiting there to converse with him.[23]

The evangelists continued itinerating throughout this north Fife district, where a visit to Abernethy revealed that 'the work is progressing there very favourably indeed'. Meanwhile, a few miles to the other side of Newburgh, as 1860 drew to a close, 'a very crowded meeting' was addressed at Lindores, 'where there were many very anxious'.[24]

Cellardyke and the East Neuk

H. M. MacGill made note of a work of grace in the 'obscure village' of St Monans. One observer noted that from its harbour, scarce a

---

20. *SG*, 19/11/1861.

21. Brown, 1893, p. 776.

22. *WJ*, 10/03/1860, p. 187.

23. ibid., 24/11/1860, p. 484.

24. ibid., 05/01/1861, p. 535; FCSRSRM, 1886, p. 3.

fishing boat set sail during the revival in which religion did not form the principal topic of conversation.[25] By the spring of 1860, the flame of revival was carried to the south Fife shores of Anstruther and Pittenweem, having also extended to Kirkcaldy.[26] Further west along the south Fife coast, 'A most delightful open-air meeting' was held in the summer of 1861 on the Braehead of Buckhaven, near Methill. 'A most profound silence reigned throughout the vast assembly. There were upwards of a thousand present, composed chiefly of the fishing population.'[27]

One of the most striking revivals to occur anywhere on Scotland's coast during these exciting months took place in Cellardyke (to the east of Anstruther). It began after the loss of a boat at sea in December 1859, in which seven local fishermen perished. The community was in shock, and the Rev. Alexander Gregory was asked to lead a prayer meeting, to which two hundred people – nearly all men – attended. 'A more solemn assemblage we never witnessed', Gregory wrote. 'All seemed bowed as if under a heavy personal calamity; strong men have told us they never felt so near completely breaking down.' The prayer meetings continued weekly and a deeper earnestness and expectation pervaded the village, intensifying with reports of revival in other east Scottish ports, such as Eyemouth, Ferryden and Newhaven.[28]

In March a local youth – a member of a crew, the rest of whom were already converts – came under deep conviction while at sea. 'For three days that boat presented a scene such as probably was never witnessed in a boat before – the anguish and cries of the heart-stricken lad, the tears of his companions, the tender earnestness of the skipper, as he alternately directed him to the Saviour, and pleaded with God on his behalf.' One day the lad jumped up and declared that he had laid hold of Christ. 'An indescribable tumult of emotions at this relief, after three days of intense anxiety, filled the breasts of the crew. They could

25. MacGill, p. 5.

26. FCSRSRM, 1888, p. 4; Proceedings of UPC Synod, 1862, p. 625; Orr, 1949, p. 72.

27. *WJ*, 20/07/1861, p. 136.

28. Rev. Alexander Gregory, *A Brief Account of the Religious Awakening in Cellardyke*, Edinburgh, 1860, pp. 4-7.

attend to nothing; and how their boat drifted safely into the harbour they cannot yet tell!'[29]

Back on shore the lad's sister, too, found Christ, and crowds gathered in an elder's home to witness the scenes of shared joy. For several days that elder's home was the focus of an intense religious interest and a powerful religious movement. Indeed, ministers were called in from neighbouring parishes to help the local clergy control the surging masses of humanity in the old, narrow main street.[30]

This story was not unique. Similar intense anxiety fell on the skipper of another boat from Cellardyke while at sea. Writes Gregory: 'A brother told us that he had on former occasions seen their boat half full of water without one of the crew wincing; but that day, when he saw the anguish of their stout-hearted skipper, though they had little sympathy with his feelings at that time, there was not a dry cheek in the boat.' Back on shore, the man hid in his boat, telling his companions he would not go to sea again till he got relief from this terrible burden. Though a boat came in full of sovereigns, he would not go and take them out; the world was as chaff to him now. On his way home from a meeting, this man experienced a blessed relief; he embraced Christ and was filled with lasting hope and joy. From then, his zeal in endeavouring to bring friends and relatives to the Saviour knew no bounds.[31]

Soon nearly the entire village was moved, and spiritual matters were almost the only subjects of conversation. It was said that strong fishermen, not noted for good living, were struck down on the way to the boats by conviction of sin and were physically unable to move from the cobblestones of the streets or piers until someone could kneel beside them and bring them assurance of salvation. Many others, including married couples, also endured this 'dark night of the soul', often spending many nights on their knees and taking little food. At the close of one day's meetings, over a hundred worshippers of both sexes and all ages remained behind to talk to the minister, and at the first word that was spoken to them, they gave way to tears and sobs,

29. Gregory, p. 7.

30. ibid.

31. Reid, 1860, pp. 471-4.

presenting a most affecting sight. It was reckoned that altogether, over three hundred evinced concern for their souls (not including children), and that at least half of these found new life in Christ – many of them male and of a more mature age.[32]

As a result of the movement, a local grocer poured his stock of liquor into Cellardyke harbour, resulting in significant financial loss to his business, but leading to clarity of conscience before his Lord. Another abstinence promoter observed, 'This work has done more for temperance in a few weeks than our society had done in years.' A practical evidence of this could be seen in the method used for 'laying up', at the end of the herring fishing season, the boats not being needed for the winter line-fishing. Men were usually paid with glasses of whisky for offering themselves to this service, leading to much drunkenness during the six weeks or so taken to lay up all the boats. Now, however, a completely new 'ballot' system was devised, resulting in a more efficient and alcohol-free operation.[33]

The fishermen's Sabbath prayer meeting grew to over one hundred, while smaller meetings of a similar kind were said to abound in the town; and from many a boat, 'the voice of "holy melody", and of prayer and praise, is wafted over the surface of the deep, mingling sweetly with the singing of the wind and the murmuring of the waves'. One man said of a meeting he attended, 'I never expected to see so much of heaven on this side of time.' A fisherman declared, 'I had many a spite and grudge before … but now I love everything I see – I love the very stones under my feet.' Another commented, 'It is a different town now, and a blessed town.'[34]

The revival in Cellardyke, according to *The Scottish Guardian*, had made this 'formerly obscure' village familiar throughout the land. J. Edwin Orr described the awakening here as 'the most perfect example in Scotland of a spiritual awakening brought about by the Holy Spirit, unhindered by Satan and not imitated by the Enemy of souls'.[35]

---

32. Belle Patrick, *Recollections of East Fife Fisher Folk*, Edinburgh, 2003, p. 12.

33. Harry D. Watson, *Kilrenny and Cellardyke*, Edinburgh, 1986, p. 130.

34. Reid, pp. 461-78.

35. *SG*, 19/11/1860; Orr, 1949, p. 73. Couper, quoting one 'who was no mean judge', makes a similar claim for the awakening in Ferryden (Roberts, 1995, pp. 298-9).

Dunfermline and Kinross

In Dunfermline not a few earnest Christians had long been praying for the Holy Spirit's presence, and thus it transpired that this ancient city 'received the seal of God's blessing upon that Gospel'. Following a visit from E. P. Hammond, the Rev. Young could testify that 'the work of the Lord is going on prosperously here. On Sabbath evening the house was filled from floor to ceiling. The numbers who remained to be spoken with also increase, and many do seem to be seeking the way of salvation. We have many adversaries, but the Lord is with us, and we need not fear what men shall do.'[36]

Some men started a Sabbath evening meeting in Kinross to seek the outpouring of God's Spirit. A number were awakened through attending this meeting, which sometimes attracted over four hundred people. A Sabbath morning prayer meeting also arose at this time. Meanwhile, individuals in Glasgow and Edinburgh were communicating to their friends in Kinross how great a work the Lord was doing in these large cities, and how their own souls had been blessed. The visits of those same correspondents to Kinross in the summer of 1861, in which they faithfully testified to the saving grace of Jesus, made a further impression. As a result an awakening began in the town in September 1861. The movement attracted bitter opposition, however; an endeavour being made to stop the meetings altogether by trying to induce the ministers to interfere with it. In addition, a great many reports spread through the town, criticising the work, while many people were positively afraid of the inquiry meetings. But the gatherings could not be stopped, negative reports being countenanced by communications of the great good effected by the revival. As a result the anxious soon began to join in the inquiry meetings with hearty approval.[37]

Perthshire

Perth

While a great many church leaders, elders and lay believers travelled across to Ireland to witness the revival in progress there, very few,

---

36. Headley, p. 89. Still in Fife, but much further west, the town of Kincardine also experienced definite revival around this time (FCSRSRM, 1889, p. 3).

37. *WJ*, 21/09/1861, p. 207.

relatively, journeyed to centres of revival in Wales, much of which country had also been deeply stirred in the wake of the American and Ulster awakenings. One who did so was the Rev. John Milne, minister at St Leonard's Church in Perth. Returning from a personal visit to the Welsh towns of Abergale and Bangor in January 1860, Milne spoke in glowing terms of what God by His Spirit was doing in that land. Although hearts were stirred by their pastor's report, it was many months later, in the summer of that year, before a time of special blessing commenced among his Perth congregation.

Tuesday, 21 August was a memorable day. From early in the morning, a constant stream of people could be seen flowing from every direction to the town's South Inch, where a special evangelistic service had been arranged. One account noted: 'Some villages and parishes sent in the whole of their available population, and on the line between Dunblane and Perth such crowds besieged the different stations of the Scottish Central Railway that a sufficient number of carriages could not be got to bring them in.' Over fifty pastors and lay workers addressed a crowd which rose to an estimated five thousand by midday and which necessitated the raising of an additional platform elsewhere in the park. Not infrequently the entire crowd would kneel on the grass in fervent prayer, producing a most solemn sight.[38]

Ministers from all Protestant denominations in town, as well as the local Episcopalian minister,[39] came together in a spirit of unity to the event, causing Gordon Forlong, one of the preachers present, to write later: 'We buried sectarianism in the South Inch ... and saw no Christian weep over its grave. We were all glad to find only one heart among us. ... The gospel preached in the course of ten minutes seemed to come with amazing power ... .'[40] Reginald Radcliffe was also present, and he estimated that there were around '1,800 anxious souls in Perth that day'.[41] The addresses continued till 6 p.m., after which well over two thousand people packed into the City Hall for a further meeting, while

38. Anonymous, *Narrative of the Revival in Perth in 1860*, Perth, 1885, pp. 4-5.

39. Brian Robertson, *Perth Baptist Church: The History, the People*, Perth, 1994, p. 42.

40. Anonymous, *Narrative of the Revival in Perth in 1860*, p. 5; *TR*, 01/09/1860, quoted in Orr, 1949, p. 71; *SG*, 08/06/61.

41. *SG*, 01/09/1860. Perth's population at the time was around 25,000.

hundreds waited to be addressed outside. In addition to this, several of the town's largest churches (North United Presbyterian Church, St Paul's Parish Church, St Leonard's Free Church), as well as the Territorial Free Church and two or three small halls, were open for services at this same time, all being well filled and some overcrowded. Thus began a seventy-day period, when further open-air services drew huge crowds, and the large City Hall was crowded night after night, without exception, 'by a deeply solemnised and interested multitude'.[42] In addition, aristocrat Mrs Stewart Sandeman took charge of the City Hall side-room for women's meetings on fifty-seven of the seventy nights.[43]

John Milne delighted in the work. He wrote: 'After two years of prayer and waiting, the Lord has visited us in unexampled mercy. ... What, in ordinary times, is spread over months or years, seems now compressed into an instant, the twinkling of an eye.' He noted that on the second night of evening meetings, 'the City Hall presented a scene never before witnessed on such a scale in Perth; it was like a battlefield, a harvest field; hundreds were seeking the Lord, or rejoicing that they had found Him. ... After all our visitors left us, the meetings continued as crowded, as solemn, as earnest as before. ... Oh, it seems easy at present to be saved.'[44] During these momentous weeks, this faithful preacher was occupied from morning to night; sometimes corresponding with ministerial colleagues and friends, sometimes preparing for meetings,

---

42. Anonymous, *Narrative of the Revival in Perth in 1860*, p. 11.

43. These meetings were afterwards carried on in Mrs Sandeman's home at Spring-field on Saturday afternoons. From this date numbers increased, until, at the close of her work, the list that she kept contained 2,013 names (M. F. Barbour, *Memoir of Mrs Stewart Sandeman of Bonskeid and Springland*, London, 1883, p. 194). Through-out the revival Mrs Sandeman's house was the home for almost every evangelist who visited Perth. Her own journal contains the names of well over seventy such preach-ers, including Hay Macdowall Grant, Brownlow North, Reginald Radcliffe, Richard Weaver, Harrison Ord, Grattan Guinness, John Colville, Duncan Matheson, R. C. Morgan, Andrew Bonar, Horatius Bonar, A. Moody Stuart and H. Williamson of Huntly! It seems to have been as a direct result of these meetings that what soon became known as *The Perth Conference* was formed in 1861, an annual gathering of believers intent on receiving instruction on how to increase in practical holi-ness. Many speakers of world fame came to speak at subsequent occasions of this influential event, including Hudson Taylor, John G. Paton and George MacGregor.

44. Alexander MacRae, *Revivals in the Highlands & Islands in the 19th Century*, Stirling, 1906, (reprinted 1998), pp. 119-22.

sometimes 'smoothing down aspirates, or giving explanations to parties, who might think themselves slighted'.[45]

At Christmas, a group of local musicians known as The Guizard Boys, instead of singing their usual songs, took to singing 'Rest for the Weary', 'Christ for Me' and other hymns. Milne could further say: 'It has been a year of much blessing to the town. I have been able to rise above private and congregational feelings, and to seek the general good. God has given the blessing, by pouring out on my brethren a wonderful spirit of love, unity and self-forgetfulness. In 1840 the blessing was much confined to my own congregation; this year it has been general, every congregation getting a measure of good, and the work spreading to the country all around.' Indeed, it was said in 1860 that 'few places have been so richly watered as Perth with the dews of divine grace'.[46]

Not unnaturally, there was some opposition to the movement. Friendly critics suggested that the public meetings and the more private conferences should have been entirely separated and that they should have terminated by nine o'clock at the latest. Apart from usual criticisms against lay preaching and what was considered 'unhealthy excitement', others were annoyed that Magistrates were giving an unjust monopoly of the City Hall to one section of the community to the exclusion of others who had an equal right to it. Partly because of this, and partly because it was felt that church leaders 'cannot much longer endure the strain' of the nightly assemblies, the City Hall meetings were concluded, although the work continued, both in the churches and still occasionally in the Hall.

Many positive results came out of the revival, one being that 'the Christian man's cat and dog are the better for his being a Christian, and so, of course, are his servants, his children and all with whom he comes in contact in the house or in the market place'.[47]

Central Perthshire

Crieff and Comrie

It was reported that not only was Perth greatly affected by the revival, but that 'the country over forty miles to the north has been fired and

45. Horatius Bonar, *Life of the Rev. John Milne of Perth*, London, 1869, p. 297.

46. ibid., pp. 291-9; *SG*, 20/10/1860.

47. Anonymous, *Narrative of the Revival in Perth in 1860*, pp. 9-10.

made alive'. Indeed, it was said that 'almost every parish in the county of Perth felt the quickening influences of the Spirit' during this period.[48] After their visit to Perth in August 1860, Richard Weaver and Reginald Radcliffe journeyed to Glasgow by horse and carriage, preaching at the various towns and villages they passed through. At Crieff – where revival meetings had commenced a considerable time previously[49] – a

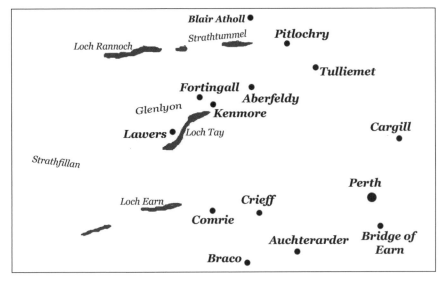

platform had been erected in a field and thousands had assembled to hear the word. After speaking, the evangelists invited the anxious to follow them to the other side of the field. To their surprise, hundreds followed. Later, many retired to the Knock (a wooded hillside behind Crieff) and 'in every corner might have been heard men, women and even children praying aloud in the most emphatic phraseology of revival times'.[50] 'We heard of whole families being kept awake all night with joy that salvation had visited their homes', observed Weaver, while at Braco 'we had a similar meeting about four in the afternoon'.[51]

Further west, in Comrie, 'God poured out His Spirit abundantly on the young. ... The village seems to be in a commotion, some being every

48. ibid., p. 12; MacRae, 1906, p. 119.

49. *The Scottish Guardian* suggests that revival here had commenced more than two years previously (18/06/1861).

50. *Caledonian Mercury*, quoted in *SG*, 06/09/1860.

51. Paterson, 1897, p. 130.

day aroused to see their lost state by nature. A great many have turned from Satan and have found peace.'[52] It was said that in some streets, with an exception or two, 'a house will not be found in which there are not some who have experienced the love that passeth all understanding'.[53]

Auchterarder and Bridge of Earn

Dunning and Auchterarder, to the south-west of Perth, were named as 'having received much' of the blessing of God. In the former place arose 'a steady, deep, progressive work' among the inhabitants. John Milne of Perth preached here a number of times, both in the open air at Holly-tree Square and indoors. 'Many true penitential tears were seen, and many a heart was made to rejoice.' Of numerous other locations around Perth, too, it could be said that, 'many of the inhabitants are now rejoicing in a deliverance from darkness into the marvellous light of the Lord'.[54]

With 'hopeful views' of the state of his congregation, a minister in Bridge of Earn, a few miles south of Perth, was told that 'all you need is to get some converts to speak to your people'. In fact, they came without his asking, when the minister was away from home on another engagement. He returned to his village 'to hear that their simple words to a score of people in the open air, on Sabbath evening last, had begun revival, and now it has reached such a height that my church is nightly filled with anxious weeping souls. Young and old – men and women, and children – are melted, broken and subdued by the mighty power of the Spirit. Now I find the harvest is greater than I have labourers for, but I am well helped by brother ministers.'[55]

Cargill

From the country to the north-east of Perth, one man wrote that 'the Lord descended in great power in Cargill and the surrounding district; and I believe within three or four weeks, hundreds have been led to seek the Lord'.[56] Cargill, was of course, a neighbouring district to

---

52. *SG*, 07/02/1860.

53. *WJ*, 14/04/1860, p. 228.

54. ibid., 18/08/1860, p. 372; 15/09/1860, p. 404.

55. *WJ*, 16/06/1860, p. 299.

56. Bussey, pp. 118-19.

Andrew Bonar's former charge of Collace. Subsequent to revival in his own Finnieston Church, Bonar journeyed to Perthshire in early May 1860. He witnessed 'remarkable awakening', especially in St Martin's Church. Bonar wrote: 'I feel the blessedness and necessity of getting far into the very presence of God and standing under His shadow. ... I think I distinctly see the answer to prayer in former days in what is now taking place at Cargill; it is God giving what He enabled us to plead before I left.' A fortnight later Bonar was back amid old scenes, revisiting Cargill 'to see God's work among the people of this neighbourhood'. He also took the opportunity to spend an hour in the wood of Dunsinane, a popular prayer retreat for the minister while living in Collace. 'I praised Him on that spot for the present awakening', he wrote, 'and whatever there is in this of the answer to prayer. And there also I asked yet more blessing for myself and my present flock, as well as more for this neighbourhood.'[57]

Highland Perthshire

Pitlochry and Strathtummel

Relating the spiritual movement that arose in Pitlochry, one local woman referred to the eager crowds that gathered in the church, or in different meeting places in the district. Some people thought nothing of walking from five to ten miles to a prayer meeting. There was an added note of urgency in the pulpit, a new sense of the presence of God in prayer, and 'more freedom in private spiritual intercourse'.[58]

Further north still, 'a very considerable work of religious awakening' was also ongoing in Blair Atholl from August 1860, as also at other places in the surrounding district.[59] Meanwhile, to the west of Pitlochry, in the Strathtummel valley, R. W. Barbour wrote that in the summer of 1859, 'a whole countryside met in eager but orderly array on a great grassy sward, rolling a psalm – the 66th, to [the tune of] Torwood, the 40th, to [the tune of] Coleshill – to Heaven, that was like the many waters of the Revelation, and then hanging rapt on the preacher's prayer or the preacher's word. ... I have seen strong men deeply moved under

---

57. Marjory Bonar (Ed.), *Diary & Life of Andrew Bonar*, Edinburgh, 1894, p. 203.

58. Anonymous, *Narrative of the Revival in Perth in 1860*, p. 8.

59. *WJ*, 24/11/1860, p. 482.

such appeals', continued Barbour. 'All the best men and women I have known in the Highlands had made a most definite response to them.'[60]

Tulliemet

During the summer and autumn of 1860, the Rev. David Grant of the Baptist Church in Tulliemet felt very much cast down in spirit – toiling on week after week, and seeing little or no appearance of good being done. He was, however, no less convinced of the lost and hardened state of his fellow-creatures around him, than of his own utter inability to arouse or save them. 'But it pleased the Lord to look in mercy upon us, and about the beginning of winter, some persons showed symptoms of concern. … My own maid-servant was the first that gave evidence of having passed from death unto life', this being followed by a number of other cases. These were all baptised and added to the church, while over a dozen more people were 'anxiously inquiring the way to Zion, with, I trust, their faces thitherward. … My weekly meetings from house to house are very well attended, and many tears are shed by the people. … I have lately composed several Gaelic hymns which I sing at the close of these meetings. Whenever the Lord revives his work, the people begin to sing psalms, and hymns and spiritual songs.'[61]

Breadalbane

Breadalbane, that vast, rugged region in north-western Perthshire surrounding Loch Tay, experienced copious showers of spiritual blessing in 1840, through the labours of itinerant evangelists such as William Chalmers Burns and John Macdonald of Ferintosh. Exactly twenty years later, in all ten congregations of the Free Church Presbytery of Breadalbane, a movement of awakening was progressing with a 'greater or lesser degree of success'.[62] In Kenmore there was hardly a family in which there was not one or more in a hopeful state. Indeed, in total, 110 communicants were received into Kenmore Free Church as a result of the revival.[63]

---

60. R. W. Barbour, 'The Gift of the Celtic Race to Religion', quoted in G. F. Barbour, *The Life of Alexander Whyte*, London, 1923, pp. 91-2.

61. BHMS Report, 1861, pp. 12-13. Grant had in fact published a one thousand copy edition of his Gaelic hymns about fifteen years previously, and they were all sold in less than a year.

62. PFCSH&I, 1861, p. 310; FCSRSRM,1886, p. 3.

63. PFCSH&I, 1861, p. 310; FCSRSRM, 1886, p. 22.

Aberfeldy

'Considerable awakening' came to Aberfeldy in October 1860. A month later and new cases of deep conviction were still occurring at each nightly meeting, and it could be said that 'the work here is most wonderful; instead of the interest diminishing, it is always increasing. ... It would indeed delight your soul to look at the multitude of seemingly saved persons as they spread themselves over the whole of the lower part of the Free Church, and who were, not long ago, darkness, but now light in the Lord.'[64] Special services continued for eleven weeks.

James Wilson, a classical scholar, was master of a school in Aberfeldy. A native of Cullen, he had heard of Duncan Matheson's work in the revival that occurred in that northern town. When that evangelist came to labour in Aberfeldy, the teacher decided to take a stand with Christ, 'and thenceforth all his learning and influence were given to the work of the Lord'. His school became a 'nursery for the church and the divinity hall'. Remarkable success attended his labours among the youths, some of whom, after a brilliant academic career, entered on the work of the ministry with much promise of usefulness. Sadly, the course of the devoted teacher was terminated 'by an early transaction to glory'.[65] The Free Church in Aberfeldy added between fifty and sixty new members as a result of the revival.

Fortingall and Lawers

From Fortingall, a great many travelled all the way to meetings in Aberfeldy, ten miles distant. The Rev. Thomas McLauchlan spoke in a packed mill-loft in the village, but due to the size of the crowd, was forced to move to a hillside, where, preaching by candlelight, 'there was manifest impression and a stillness that might be felt', to such extent that after an hour-and-a-half sermon, not one candle had gone out! A correspondent wrote: 'The whole community seems to be pervaded by the Spirit. Without there are many adversaries, and this of itself is one proof of the reality of the work.'[66] Lawers also experienced a revival in 1860–61, as testified to by the Rev. David Campbell, previously

---

64. *WJ*, 15/10/1860.

65. MacPherson, 1871, p. 121.

66. Leask, 1905, p. 137; *WJ*, 24/11/1860, p. 482.

Free Church minister in nearby Glenlyon. In at least one parish in this Presbytery where formerly prayer meetings were unheard of, there were now three in progress each week. The awakening here was seen as all the more remarkable given that the parish had not been favoured with an evangelical ministry.[67]

Strathfillan

Further west in Breadalbane, the wife of the Rev. McKinnon of Strathfillan wrote of a great awakening occurring in that area during the winter of 1860–61. Mr Fraser, a student, had been invited to speak. He preached in English while the minister translated into Gaelic. Deep concern was manifested and one man rose in the middle of an address and confessed himself a sinner before the whole congregation. In a few days there were a number of very striking cases of what appeared to be 'real conversions'. Meetings were held one-to-three times per day in various places for three weeks. Whereas formerly only the elders would pray, now there was no lack of praying men. 'The change is wonderful', said Mrs McKinnon.[68]

Glenlyon

In Glenlyon some in the Free Church had been in the habit of uniting with those of the Baptist cause for a union prayer meeting. For some reason (probably their diverging views on baptism [see below]) the Free Church members withdrew – save one person – and commenced a meeting of their own. This work prospered and in time as many as fifty-seven were added to the Free Church of Glenlyon as a result of the revival.

Neither did the Baptist work appear to suffer from the split in united prayer efforts. Donald McLellan, the Baptist missionary at Glenlyon[69] wrote that: 'Multitudes thronged, week after week, to the house of prayer' in the Baptist church, while congregations on the Lord's day were also steadily increasing. Latterly, three young men started meeting

---

67. Brown, 1893, p. 10; *SG*, 11/02/1860.

68. *WJ*, 08/12/1860, p. 503; *SG*, 19/03/61.

69. McLellan was known in Baptist circles as a powerful preacher. When he died in 1891, he was reckoned to be comparable only to Macdonald of Ferintosh as a Gaelic preacher (D. E. Meek, *Evangelical Missionaries in the Early Nineteenth Century Highlands*, quoted in *Transactions of the Gaelic Society of Inverness*, vol. 56, 1989, p. 295).

twice a week after nightfall in a wood adjoining the church. After a
time, one of them, the pastor's youngest son, came under deep soul
distress and was converted. All the rest, in a short time, professed to
have 'come to the knowledge of the Truth', and thenceforth began to
meet in the church. Many of their friends came along to the meetings,
were convicted of their sin and 'led to the footstool of mercy'.[70]

At length they felt led to hold public meetings at the Braes of
Glenlyon. So many turned up that the young converts began to fear
and tremble, thinking that they had undertaken more than they were
qualified for! But they were given courage from the Lord, and they had
no sooner begun 'than the Spirit of the Lord began also'. One here and
there began to sob and sigh, being convinced of the plague of his own
heart; then another, and another, until the whole meeting was bathed
in tears. The convicted ones could no longer contain themselves. They
were obliged to leave each one for him or herself to cry to the Lord for
mercy. 'And what a spectacle was that which presented itself to the eyes
of the originators and conductors of that meeting! In the course of a few
short hours, to see numbers whose hearts were up to that night hard
as the nether-millstone, now literally prostrate in the dust, before the
Lord, confessing their sins! One could scarcely turn a corner without
stumbling upon some prostrate wrestler.'[71] Continued McLellan:

> He who was wounded began to heal. ... Whenever one came to the
> knowledge of the Truth, he hastened in to the house to communi-
> cate the glad tidings to those who were praying within. The hymn
> 'What's the News?' was sung. They were no sooner through with it
> than another convert, with radiant countenance and eyes streaming
> for joy, came in with 'good news!' The same hymn was again repeated,
> when, lo! another and another came in rejoicing in the salvation of
> God. Thus they continued until they all, with two or three exceptions,
> professed to have found the pearl of great price.[72]

From that day onwards they held meetings almost every night, many
of them with equal success; and the great zeal manifested by the young
converts for the salvation of their companions and acquaintances, and

---

70. BHMS Report, 1861, pp. 6-8.

71. ibid., pp. 7-8.

72. ibid.

their joy when many of these friends were indeed converted, was described as 'truly extraordinary'. It was no unusual thing for bands of them to travel a distance of ten miles, there and back, on a dark, stormy night, through bogs and heather, with their lanterns in their hands, to attend the meetings. 'They frequently left my house' said the missionary, 'at one, two and three o'clock in the morning, having spent the night in prayer and praise.'[73] Then came the question of what church to join. According to McLellan:

> The Baptists were but few in numbers, and generally despised, and every means were used to prejudice minds against us. ... Tracts and pamphlets began to be circulated on both sides. We always delivered an address whenever the ordinance was about to be administered. And the Free Church minister, on the other hand, delivered a course of Lectures in defence of Infant Sprinkling. Notwithstanding all this opposition, fourteen have been baptized up to this date. Ten were baptized on one occasion, and three on another. These scenes were affecting and refreshing. For after the delivery of the lecture, the candidates proceeded in a band to the water, singing a baptismal hymn, then, following the example of the Lord Jesus, they were immersed beneath the stream, and 'went straightway out of the water', thus publicly professing their allegiance to the King of Zion.

This spectacle was witnessed by a 'numerous, yet solemn and attentive crowd of onlookers'. McLellan similarly reported the baptism of five candidates in Rannoch. That of three of them was attended by 'a great concourse of persons on either side of the river'.[74]

---

73. ibid., 1861, pp. 8-9.
74. ibid., p. 9.

Robert Annan *John Bowes* *Stephen Hislop*

Ferryden

Montrose

CHAPTER 10

Dundee and Forfarshire

Dundee

Beginnings

Of Dundee in the mid-1850s it was said that there was little outward stir in spiritual things, and evangelistic meetings were almost, if not altogether, unknown.[1] Itinerant evangelist John Bowes had been inducted to the first Christian Mission church in Dundee in April 1831, but spent a large part of his time itinerating throughout Britain. At home during August 1859, Bowes saw souls profess peace with God weekly, sometimes five in a week, and one day three. 'There has been deep feeling', he wrote, 'many tears shed, but no prostrations.' Bowes noted that among the Brethren, and apart from the many awakened who had not been conversed with, 'between thirty and forty have embraced the joyous gospel, and have been added to the church, whose numbers have been doubled this year. Thirty have been baptized, and six more are waiting.'[2]

The outbreak of revival in Dundee is more commonly dated to a work begun in the Free Church in October 1858.[3] Prayer meetings were begun early that month in a large schoolroom, but cases of conviction were not apparent till a visit from Hay Macdowall Gant of Arndilly the following

---

1. Margaret Duncan, quoted in John Baxter, *In Memoriam: Margaret Duncan, daughter of Matthew Low, Esq., Flaxspinner, Keathbank, Blairgowrie, and wife of the Rev. Arch. Ferguson*, Alyth, 1887, p. 3.

2. J. Bowes, p. 544.

3. Bussey claims that it was not until the spring of 1860 that 'the real break' came in Dundee (Bussey, p. 120).

June, when a number were in anxiety and one or two cases resulted in conversion. By October 1859, two months after the moving of the Spirit in Bowes' church, what was seen as a 'remarkable season of refreshing from God's presence' occurred at the schoolroom meetings, and there were seldom fewer than forty that remained after the general meeting, more or less in deep anxiety.[4] Soon prayer meetings were springing up all over town,[5] as well as in many factories and public works.

A significant movement among female mill workers began in November 1859 when two recently converted girls tentatively asked their boss if they could begin a meeting during their lunch hour. The manager, being a committed believer, at once consented and soon one hundred workers were attending. Within four months, fifty or sixty gave evidence of having undergone a saving change. Through these influential workers' meetings, 600 Bibles were purchased. The meetings also resulted in several cases of bodily prostration, lasting, in some cases, for several days. One evening during prayer, or shortly after its conclusion, three prostrations took place; two of the females were overpowered with an overwhelming anxiety about the spiritual condition of certain relatives. Their prayers for family members were 'incessant and affecting. The other was a case of deep personal concern, which has ended hopefully.'[6]

The Rev. W. B. Borwick of the Free Church recalled one evening when he joined with factory workers at their prayer meeting: 'I witnessed as affecting instances of the spiritual interest that they take in one another as I ever expect to see again', he said. One girl pled in prayer for five to ten minutes with an earnestness and a freedom Borwick had never heard surpassed. 'I felt that my warmest utterances were cold, and that, if this were not wrestling with the Angel, I despair of knowing what it is.' In time, the girl was 'taken from the fearful pit ... and is now on the Rock'.[7]

---

4. Reid, 1860, pp. 183-4.

5. In distinction, claimed the Rev. W. B. Borwick, to the revival during McCheyne's and Burns' ministries (1839–41), when prayer meetings were numerous only 'over a portion of the town' (ibid., p. 178).

6. Reid, 1860, p. 187.

7. ibid., pp. 178-9.

Variety of Operations

The Kirk Session minutes of Lochee Free Church offered a note of thanks for the 'outpouring of the Holy Spirit on the congregation and district' under the longstanding ministry of the Rev. T. B. Dodds. Meetings were held in the schoolroom and were frequently crowded, and during one week alone, forty anxious souls waited to converse with the minister.[8] Meanwhile, Duncan Matheson spent much time in Dundee during the period of the revival, preaching mainly in the Hilltown Free Church. Hundreds were thought to have been saved through his efforts there. The most prominent Dundee convert was Robert Annan, a mason and former drunkard and army deserter, who was profoundly convicted on hearing both Matheson and George Campbell (of Aberdeen) speaking in Kinnaird Hall. Annan spent the next thirteen hours in a hayloft, flat on his face before God, pleading for mercy. Soon he was led to cast anchor on Christ, and thus it was that 'the grace of God obtained a victory over this stout-hearted sinner'. Immediately he became a zealous evangelist, fearlessly testifying to God's grace both within and without the city.[9]

In March 1860 Bowes baptised a further seven converts in his Dundee church, raising membership to 140. Around that time revival meetings were being conducted each night by visiting evangelists over a number of weeks, at each of which some new converts rose to testify and exhort. Bowes also held revival meetings at Lochee. By April it could be reported that 102 people had been added to the Christian Mission in just seven months, most of them 'from the world'; and ninety of these were baptized within the following two months. Meanwhile, conversions continued on an almost weekly basis and membership soon exceeded two hundred.[10]

---

8. McGregor, *A Short Sketch of the History of Lochee Free Church*, p. 10.

9. John Macpherson, *The Christian Hero: A Sketch of the Life of Robert Annan*, London, 1867, pp. 15-21. It was, however, on his return to Dundee in 1864 from a period spent in Aberdeen, that Annan's labours were 'most signally owned by God' (p. 36). In Gourdon also, where Annan resided for a time, his landlady spoke of him wrestling for whole nights in prayer for an outpouring of the Spirit, to the extent that many a night he scarce got any sleep and his bed remained untouched (Hector M. Adam, *James Jolly, Minister of Dr Chalmers' Territorial Church, Edinburgh: Memorials of an Earnest Life and Faithful Ministry*, Edinburgh, 1888, p. 20).

10. J. Bowes, pp. 548-9.

In the autumn of 1860, open-air services were held in Dundee's Barrack Park. On the second evening, a number of ministers and others, fearing that there might be no blessing, retired in great heaviness of spirit to pray. Kneeling on the grass, they continued in intercession for nearly two hours. By and by, the darkened sky began to pour down torrents of rain, and the mass of people, with most of the speakers, were dispersed. About three hundred, however, continued in prayer and praise, sensing that a climactic and spiritual breakthrough might be imminent. An observer noted that as the rain began to die away and the sun again appeared, 'an extraordinary sense of the Divine Presence fell upon the whole assembly. Suddenly the Christians were filled with great joy. Simultaneously many of the anxious found the Lord, and began to speak of the Saviour he was seeking or the Saviour he had found. On passing through the whole company, we did not find one who was not either rejoicing in Christ or seeking Him with intense earnestness. The cloud of glory rested there for a season, and no visible signs or miraculous gifts could have added to the blessed consciousness and most veritable certainty of the immediate presence and gracious working of God.'[11]

Distinctive Features

Speaking some months after the outbreak of revival in his midst, the Rev. Borwick reported, 'There has not come within my knowledge a single case of an individual that gave evidence of having been joined to the Lord in the perpetual covenant that has drawn back. ... The persecutors, in many cases, have left their ranks – the persecuted Christian never.' One consequence of the revival was that a Sabbath school was begun for the more neglected children of a destitute neighbourhood. Where previously this initiative had utterly failed due to the ungovernable nature of the children and their inability to read, now it proved a great success. 'The schoolroom is filled. They can now read the Bible with ease ... and give evidence that they are at the feet of Christ, clothed and in their right mind.'[12]

Prior to the revival there was thought to have been 'scarcely any Christians' in a large lodging house containing over two hundred lodgers. But when a minister from Ireland, the Rev. J. Simpson of Portrush, visited the place in 1860, 'several very decided cases of

11. Bussey, pp. 125-6.
12. Reid, 1860, pp. 177; 181-2.

conversion' occurred, with many more lodgers coming under deep concern. A fellowship meeting was commenced, which continued on a nightly basis. In addition, regular 'exercises and instruction' were begun, while 'closets for secret prayer' sprang up throughout the building. As a result of the spirit of awakening among them, it became evident that there arose 'a few very remarkable trophies of Divine grace in the house, and they bear the reproach of Christ with meekness and cheerfulness'.[13]

Some unusual incidents occurred in regard to the revival in Dundee. One day in August 1860 Mr McChon, a labourer, was charged in court with throwing stones or other missiles at revival preachers the previous evening. Owing to lack of proof, however, the accused was discharged. Around the same time another young man (aged twenty-two and a member of Hilltown Free Church) was dismissed from work due to what was described as his 'absolute insanity' as a result of being involved with the revival in the city. It was noted that he had formerly had a decidedly 'weak intellect'. After a period of rest at home, it was hoped that his mental state was beginning to improve.[14]

Longevity

In the spring of 1861 the Brethren were still holding 'revival meetings' almost every night except Saturdays in both central Dundee and Lochee. One day in March John Bowes baptised seven people in front of 'the largest assembly he ever had at an immersion'. The following month a further twelve were baptised, including Bowes's seventeen-year-old son. During seven months in 1861, a total of 102 people were added to the assembly, coming 'chiefly from the world'. Ninety were baptized in the same period, raising membership to 201.[15]

At a meeting of the Free Presbytery of Dundee as late as the early autumn of 1861, attention was drawn to the various mission stations in the area. The Rev. McGilvary stated that he had recently preached in the open air at Lochee to about a hundred people. It was there intimated that anyone who wished to speak to a church leader could go to the schoolhouse, and this was soon filled. 'The people were thirsting for religious knowledge', and McGilvary saw 'a very healthy work going

13. ibid., pp. 186-7.

14. *SG*, 01/09/1860; 13/09/1860.

15. J. Bowes, pp. 548-9.

on there'. Someone else mentioned a meeting in Westfield, which only three adults and four children had attended. Refusing to give in, the worker tried again, and he now gathered over one hundred people week after week. The meetings were held in an old mud barn, and several of the people, who had not been in the habit of going to any place of worship told him that they blessed God for the old mud barn, for to them it was an ivory palace. At another place, 'the most wicked in the whole district, where he was twelve months ago, and could not get a

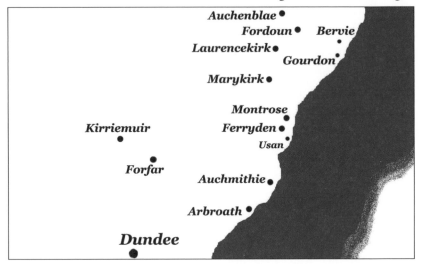

meeting, he tried last night, and the place was crammed with the very people whom it was most desirable to meet'.[16]

Arbroath

Following a visit to Arbroath, Stephen Hislop, a Scots missionary home on furlough from India, wrote that many of the factory, as well as the fishing population there, had been deeply blessed. In two small fishing villages in the neighbourhood, in particular, with a population of 150 families, about thirty persons, ranging from fifteen to seventy years of age, were said to have surrendered their lives to the Saviour, and were seeking to bring others to Him.[17] The Rev. John Gillies said that the fishing population of one of these villages, Auchmithie, as well as that of Arbroath itself, 'have been to a considerable extent awakened from

---

16. *WJ*, 19/10/61, p. 22.

17. ibid. The Baptists in Arbroath also received an impetus from the revival and moved to larger premises, viz. the Temperance Hall (Yuille, pp. 1, 58).

the spiritual stupor of generations. How that has been, as to human agency, cannot well be told. The devoted missionary now labouring among them has informed me that not a little of the awakening cannot well be traced instrumentally to his labours.' Rather, Gillies offered by way of part-explanation the fact that fishermen were a people that dwelt alone, and so the channels of sympathy between them and the rest of the population were few and narrow. However, they were comparatively many and wide between one fishing village and another. Hence, in all probability, revival, when originated in one village, may legitimately find its way along those channels to another, and hence the flow of revival blessing to places like Auchmithie.[18]

Forfarshire

Ferryden

The revival that occurred in the seafaring community of Ferryden, in the Forfarshire parish of Craig, was one of the most dramatic to arise anywhere in Scotland in the late 1850s. Some have sought to account for the mass turning to God that took place here by showing that materially, the summer of 1859 was a particularly poor season for the fishing industry all across the north-east of Scotland. The fisherfolk of Ferryden were as much affected by this as anywhere else, while in addition, storms affected efforts later in the year. Locally, large shoals of dog-fish were reportedly eating the bait put on the lines to catch saleable fish, so that families were making a loss. Further, the annual soup kitchen in Montrose opened early that year in view of the volume of disease in the town. As has been noted elsewhere, however, poverty in itself does not lead to spiritual revival – it is simply one factor that often helps facilitate its occurrence.[19]

First Fortnight

In the summer of 1859 some local believers had formed a special group to pray for revival in their community and to witness to their friends. The meeting became crowded, and a great spiritual thirst was evinced, especially following the invitation sent to some laymen from Montrose

---

18. Annual Report of the Congregational Union of Scotland 1860, pp. 9-10, quoted in McNaughton, 2005, p. 196.

19. See the section entitled 'Facilitators of Revival' in my book, *Glory in the Glen*, pp 442-4.

who had visited scenes of revival in Ireland to come and speak (see p. 214).[20] Interest and soul concern continued to increase.

Then in the first of two remarkable weeks in November 1859, Hay Macdowall Grant visited the town and held public meetings, also speaking to people in their homes. There arose deep, widespread conviction of sin, during which the people were, in their restlessness, constantly going into each other's houses, speaking of their burdened and intolerable state, and declaring that they could not live if they did not get Christ. By this means, the people reached such a state of general excitement that an 'unrestrainable outbreak' occurred at a meeting led by Grant on 12 November, when five fell down under conviction.[21] This served to attract many more of the curious and inquiring to the meetings. When Free Church minister Hugh Mitchell preached a few nights later, a fisherman found himself seized with a terrible shake and sank into a semi-comatose state for a quarter of an hour, before finding spiritual release. On the following evening during a calm address, when there was 'as little to excite as in the ordinary preachings', men and women were 'overwhelmed, crying out, and falling down'. By now, the entire population of the village seemed aroused.[22]

The following week proved a week of deliverance as the first had been one of conviction. On the conversion of one woman, others flocked to her house where, according to William Nixon, they 'gazed on her emancipated state and contrasted it with their own continued and terrible bondage. She was thus the most powerful of all sermons they heard. ... Every successive hour (of that second week), ministering angels seem to have got fresh messages to carry to the courts above, concerning the repentance of another and another sinner, which fills all heaven with gladness. And ere that second week had passed, many a heart that had been bursting with its sorrows, was breaking out in songs of rapturous joy.'[23]

Visitors
Partly in response to the numerous bodily prostrations and trances which were reported, many came from other districts to witness the

---

20. William Mitchell, *A Brief but Bright Wilderness Journey: A Memoir of William Guthrie*, Edinburgh, 1860, pp. 7-8.

21. Nixon, 1860, pp. 14-15.

22. Gordon, pp. 135-6.

23. Nixon, 1860, pp. 9-10.

remarkable movement in progress. Among those who came were three young men from Kirriemuir, 'determined ... to ascertain for ourselves the reality and extent of the work there. We came across an old fisherman, preparing his lines, who was full of it. "See there", he said, pointing to his dwelling, "is my hoose; there has been hundreds of souls born again in it. They have come from far and near, lots of them scoffers, but they got inside and we prayed for them, and God heard our prayers and they went away rejoicing".'[24]

Other visitors included a host of ministers from near and far who came both to witness and assist in the work,[25] particularly during the sickness of Mitchell; although it was observed that 'the work has actually increased with the absence of any minister whatsoever'. Interestingly, the labours of two Episcopalian clergymen were also spoken of as being greatly blessed.[26] There was scarcely a day without a packed evening meeting right to the end of December, and for a time, business was suspended, the salvation of the soul being the all-absorbing topic of conversation. Indeed, for a few weeks, says Bebbington, 'Ferryden was the talk of Scotland.'[27]

Stephen Hislop was assigned the duty of supplying services throughout February 1860, during Mitchell's continued convalescence. Hislop sought with great care to 'master the facts' of the awakening. He personally studied every individual case of visions and prostrations, and concluded, 'I do not like the visions; but they are nervous, not Satanic. No doubt much is due to weakness of body and nervous excitability. And when the attacks are frequent, I think they are far from desirable.' Regarding prostrations, many described them to Hislop as 'a weight at the heart' or 'a mountain of darkness before their eyes, which came

---

24. Matthews, pp. 79-81.

25. Among these were Joseph Wilson, Abernyte; James Hood Wilson, Edinburgh; A. Moody Stuart, Edinburgh; and Andrew Bonar, Finnieston. Bonar noted in his diary in December 1859: 'Called to visit Ferryden, where the Lord is working wonderfully. It is like the breath of warm sunshine upon ice and snow; the souls of men here are melted down everywhere' (Bonar, 1894, p. 203). A number of lay preachers, including Gordon Forlong, also spent time in the village.

26. *SG*, 14/02/1860.

27. D. W. Bebbington, *Revival and the Clash of Cultures: Ferryden, Forfarshire, in 1859*, private paper, 2004, p. 4 (later published in Dyfd Wyn Roberts (Ed.), *Revival, Renewal and the Holy Spirit*, Milton Keynes, 2009, pp. 65-94).

nearer and nearer until it knocked them over'. Peace in Christ usually came shortly after, which was generally proved authentic by a subsequent fruit-bearing life. With these, therefore, Hislop felt little unease.[28]

Analysis

Professor David Bebbington brings to light a number of interesting features of the revival at Ferryden from a booklet written by William Nixon, former Free Church minister of Montrose. The booklet consists of a short history of the revival along with twenty-four interviews with local residents who professed conversion as a result of the movement. Nixon's account, which was originally designed to help direct revivals in other fishing villages along the Scottish coast, was also, according to Bebbington, 'an effort to stamp his own moderation on events at Ferryden'.[29] The booklet included a four-page critique on prostration, which Nixon saw as having no connection whatever with a special work of grace. (The local *Montrose Review*, which was aligned with the Free Church, also criticised the prostrations, and generally downplayed the revival, deploring the tendency of visitors to turn the revival into a spectacle.) Nixon shows that some of the most compelling experiences during the awakening took place when men were at sea. Even for those awakened at home, the great waters were a common source of imagery used to express their experiences. Further, the perils threatening seafarers were a significant factor in fostering a sense of ultimate issues, more so indeed than the fear of hell itself, which place, like heaven, was mentioned in only two testimonies. A strong solidarity among crew-members, and the tight-knit community life of Ferryden, proved contagious settings in which revival fostered. Similarly, the family structure of the village led to numerous converts being swayed by words and experiences of relatives. In particular, the commitment of wives to bringing their husbands to Christ shines through some of the narratives. And, although sixteen of the twenty-four cases in Nixon's collection were female, only two of the six prostrations, two of the four visions and one of the four auditory experiences were reported by women (although it is possible that Nixon was selective in the

---

28. George Smith, *Stephen Hislop, Pioneer Missionary & Naturalist in Central India from 1844 to 1863*, London, 1888, pp. 295-300.

29. Bebbington, 2004, p. 39. ibid., p. 38.

narratives he chose in order to diminish any sense of gender bias). His findings suggest that revival was not gender-exclusive; it was more a family concern.[30]

Results

Among the many changes induced by the revival, it was said that no swearword had been heard in the village for months, and one notorious blasphemer said he couldn't swear now even if he tried! Where previously there had been much enmity between neighbours, everyone now eagerly sought reconciliation. Children were also treated far more 'reasonably, affectionately, quietly, christianly, and they are not like the same creatures'. Theft, so prevalent before, was now non-existent. Even on the boats, men disentangling lines used to help themselves to fish from the lines of their neighbours. All this had ceased, 'and they are become rather ready to give what is their own, than to take what belongs to others'. The poor used to 'loudly proclaim their wants'; now they submitted cheerfully to the Lord's will. One house which furnished 'a meeting place for low and depraving amusements' was now utterly abandoned. Such had been the solemnity among the people for months that every day was now as a Sabbath-day; they showed 'little concern for anything compared with the things that belong to their peace' and one felt that the intrusion of ordinary conversation would be 'offensive trifling'.[31]

With a population of around 1,100 in Ferryden itself, it was claimed that 'nearly one-half have come under the power of the revival'.[32] Church elders and others in Ferryden modestly suggested that over two hundred had come under the power of saving grace. According to George Smith, 'the immediate result was the addition of 104 names

---

30. ibid., pp. 14-17.

31. Nixon, 1860, pp. 8-11.

32. MacGill, p. 5. One outstanding convert was the youthful William Guthrie, who was led to faith through the witness of peers in his Bible class. Though naturally shy, Guthrie immediately became a spiritual firebrand – 'the glory of God and the salvation of souls were his chief, his only desires'. Over the following three months he led two of his sisters to faith, as well as many in his Bible class, and others. His soul-winning efforts were short-lived, however. Tragically, Guthrie, naturally of a weak constitution and delicate frame, passed away before 1860 had drawn to a close (Mitchell, 1860, pp. 67-70).

to the Free Church Communion roll in November 1859, and of forty in June 1860, so that 430 men and women were members of that one congregation out of a gross population in the parish of 1,930 souls, old and young, adherents of the Established as well as of the Free Church of Scotland'.[33] The figures excluded, of course, the many new converts who were already church members, and the many who had not yet applied for membership.

And the fruit abided, a large percentage of converts being found to stand the test of several decades. In the early 1880s George Smith visited the town in the interest of foreign missions. The whole adult male population was about to sail, towards midnight, for the fishing in the North Sea. Yet, in all his decades' experience, Smith had 'never seen a gathering more inspiring, devout, enthusiastic'. Indeed, as late as 1888, Smith found that the parish still bore 'fruit of the foreign fields from the seed which Hislop there sowed'.[34]

Montrose

Two ministers and several laymen from Montrose,[35] directly across the South Esk river from Ferryden, brought home accounts of the revival in Ireland in the autumn of 1859. This, along with influences from the work in both the Mearns (see p. 217) and in nearby Ferryden, led to a deepening of interest throughout the following eighteen months. Indeed, during this period hardly a week passed without several conversions, generally with little outward demonstration of feeling. Many gave 'unmistakable signs of being offended at the work', especially because of the prominence of laymen who led the meetings in town.[36] Despite this, the movement advanced. Open-air meetings became highly popular, with an estimated six thousand attending one, while two buildings, seating 2,500 cumulatively, were often simultaneously filled for evening services.

At one meeting not fewer than a thousand remained for conversation, many of them deeply smitten with conviction of sin. 'There were young

---

33. Smith, 1888, p. 299.

34. ibid., p. 300.

35. The laymen comprised a worker from the Montrose Home Mission, surnamed Mudie, and a group of friends from the area.

36. Mitchell, 1888, p. 2.

men from the mechanics' shops and the building yards, from the shops and the counting houses, as well as two or three students from college. There were young wives with their children, with domestic servants and workers in the factories, as well as young ladies connected with the most respectable families in town. It was a night had in remembrance by many.'[37] H. M. MacGill wrote: 'Not fishermen so much as persons of various conditions and ages, but especially young females, mill workers, household servants, and young men in a similar position in society, to the number of five or six hundred, have experienced a marked spiritual change; not to speak of cases to which no publicity has been given.'[38]

The *Scottish Congregational Magazine* reported 'a more intense thirsting for the word of God than has ever been known in the community'. There were about fifty meetings for prayer held in private houses (nearly always filled), beyond those immediately under the superintendence of churches.[39] These were mostly conducted by recently converted young men, of whom from thirty to forty divided the town into districts, and became vigorously employed in seeking to win sinners to Christ. One woman stopped attending the prayer meetings because, she said, they were becoming disrespectful due to the number of 'drunkards and worthless folk' that were packing into them![40]

William Mitchell said that a prominent feature of the movement was assurance. 'Of all the converts ... we have not met with one who questions the personal interest he now has, and will ever continue to have, in the great salvation.' Mitchell also believed that the town's two United Presbyterian churches were 'most greatly blessed', and 'remarkable conversions took place among them'.[41]

As to numerical fruits of the movement, membership of the Free Church trebled in just one year, while there were fifty-five additions to the Montrose Congregational Church in the months following the start

---

37. *Scottish Congregational Magazine*, February 1861, quoted in McNaughton, 2005, p. 189.

38. MacGill, p. 5.

39. *Scottish Congregational Magazine*, February 1861, quoted in McNaughton, 2005, pp. 187-90.

40. PFCSHMC, 1861 p. 97; Sprange, pp. 159-160.

41. Mitchell, 1860, p. 2.

of the revival. That denomination's Annual Report of 1862 revealed that the Bible class was still regularly attended by about 120 students.

The revival also affected the congregation of the Parish Church in Craig. Its evangelical minister, the Rev. Robert Mitchell, had served in the church since the Disruption, and was keen to assist when revival broke out in his community; indeed he even considered issuing a pamphlet about it. A prostration in his congregation on Sunday, 20 November caused 'much excitement', not least because such manifestations were very uncommon in Established Church settings. Meanwhile, and still within Craig parish, it was noted that in Usan, a tiny fishing village near Ferryden with a population of just 120, where formerly resided only three professors of religion, no fewer than 33 adults were received into the Church in just a few weeks near the beginning of 1860.[42] At least fourteen of these were brought to faith during a visit from Stephen Hislop during the month he spent ministering in the Ferryden neighbourhood.

Kirriemuir

Three young Christian lads from Kirriemuir went for a weekend to Ferryden to witness the revival there.[43] Greatly encouraged and blessed by all they had heard and seen, they came home to find friends eagerly awaiting their arrival. In church, their testimony produced a profound impression, and several conversions resulted, also beginning 'a more forward moving of spiritual power'. From both town and country, there was no difficulty in getting people together to hear the Word, even amidst the very bitter hostility to the movement which often came from churchgoers. 'Young converts had a very trying ordeal to pass through; all manner of Scriptural difficulties were magnified; still they proved faithful through it all.'[44]

One young man from Kirriemuir became 'troubled in soul' after hearing a sermon by the Rev. D. Whyte in the Free Church of Airlie,

---

42. *SG*, 21/02/1860.

43. Kirriemuir was the birthplace of Scottish divine, Alexander Whyte. Presumably referring primarily to the showers of blessing that fell on that town in 1859, Whyte, on encountering the atmosphere of revival as a student in Aberdeen that same year, later said that he 'felt at home at once; for I had been born and brought up in a town which had been blessed with an evangelical ministry, and with successive times of refreshing from the presence of the Lord' (Matthews, Chap 1).

44. ibid., pp. 79-81.

whose preaching had been notably affected by a personal visit to Ireland to witness the revival there. The young man was to become a great witness in the town and throughout the district. Everywhere, he had no difficulty in either securing houses, or filling them even to standing room, so eager were the people to hear. Such was the case at a meeting held in a tailor's house in Airlie, where the young man used to work. At least four conversions took place that night and 'the kitchen of Carlingwell' became one of the centres of the revival, 'where many were rescued from a careless life. ... Conversions were frequent among the ploughmen and villagers, and clear evidence was given of the nature of the change.'[45] Close to Kirriemuir, revival was also experienced in the Congregational Church in Forfar.

Howe o' the Mearns

In the autumn of 1859 there was 'a considerable revival of religion' in some of the districts of the Mearns (the former county of Kincardine).[46] The principal means to its spread in the region was the return from Ireland of a number of laymen from Montrose and neighbourhood who had witnessed the work of grace in Belfast, Ballymena, Coleraine, Lisburn and other Irish towns. According to one report, Auchenblae was the first place in the Mearns district where the revival manifested itself. Several remarkable conversions took place, while, at the same time, deep interest was awakened in Laurencekirk, Marykirk and other locations.[47]

The movement centred on Laurencekirk, where no attempt had been made to 'get up' a revival – no great preachers had visited the place – and no means were used except the communicating of reports of revivals in other places, along with the fervent prayers of a few earnest Christians. Noting the increase of anxiety among his parishioners, the Rev. Andrew Noble arranged a united prayer meeting. 'The prayers were most refreshing, some of them overpowering', he wrote. 'At the close of the meeting we found from thirty to forty persons in deep distress of soul'; many of whom 'professed to find peace before they went home. ... For some

---

45. ibid., pp. 75-8.

46. *SCM*, February 1861, quoted in McNaughton, 2005, pp. 187-8. Eager to spread the fires of revival, some of the young converts from these localities addressed meetings in nearby Montrose, which soon became a centre of awakening.

47. Mitchell, 1860, pp. 1-2.

time the commotion in the village was very great. Some were weeping over their sins; some were rejoicing over the conversion of their children, their pupils, and their neighbours. Some were standing aloof, shaking the head, and wondering whereunto this might grow, while some were scoffing, and others openly blaspheming.'[48] The Congregational Church gained twenty-nine members as an immediate result of the revival, while over a dozen prayer meetings were started in and around the village.

Free Church minister in Marykirk, the Rev. William Munnies, an Irishman, did not delay in making the journey to his homeland to see for himself the remarkable revival of which so many uplifting reports had reached his ears. Back in Scotland, he threw himself into evangelistic work with uncommon energy. His preaching now carried a new unction, and was blessed to the conversion of many, and to the quickening of many over a large part of the county. A fifteen-year-old lad in the village by name of James Jolly was one of the hundreds who came under serious conviction in the revival that ensued. He was led to the Saviour some months later, in the summer of 1860, when Munnies invited Duncan Matheson to hold some meetings in Marykirk, in 'the little church in the woods'.[49] The next day, his first day of new life in Christ, Jolly made a point of speaking to a relative about her soul's concerns, and invited her to a meeting, which issued in the woman's conversion. Indeed, while Jolly became a lifelong friend of Matheson, he also caught and retained that same zeal for the salvation of souls that marked that most doughty of evangelists.

Revival was also experienced in Inverbervie, where a Mr Collie laboured; this was succeeded by a similar season of revival at nearby Gourdon. Here it was said that, 'a visible change has come over the place. Many of the most careless have been deeply impressed.'[50] As many as twenty-eight weekly prayer meetings were taking place in the Bervie/ Gourdon district. A few miles inland from Bervie, the Rev. Philip of Fourdoun shared in the revival work with eagerness and dedication.

---

48. Annual Report of the Congregational Union of Scotland 1860, pp. 10-11, quoted in McNaughton, 2005, pp. 244-5.

49. Adam, pp. 18-20. The details of Jolly's conversion are recorded in the biography of Duncan Matheson.

50. *WJ*, 31/03/1860, p. 210.

Huntly Castle grounds

Strathbogie

Rhynie

Chapel of Garioch

Inverallochy

Fraserburgh

*Elizabeth – last Duchess
of Gordon*

Cliffs at Bullars o'Buchan

Old photo of Footdee (1859)

CHAPTER 11

Aberdeenshire

Introduction

The Rev. H. M. Williamson of Huntly, looking back on the years prior to the 1859–61 revival, gave a rather depressing picture of the spiritual condition of the north-east of Scotland prior to the spiritual awakening that soon afterwards graced the land. 'Any profession of personal salvation as possessed and enjoyed was branded as presumption, hypocrisy, or self-righteousness. The district was called spiritually, "The Dead Sea". The preaching of morality instead of grace for half a century had covered large districts with immorality, illegitimacy, drunkenness, and covetousness.'[1]

Thus it was that for some years before the revival commenced in rural Aberdeenshire a number of people, especially in the Free Church, had begun to grapple seriously with their responsibility for evangelism in what was becoming an increasingly irreligious society. A number of lay evangelists were invited to hold meetings throughout the area. The spiritual interest that this nurtured, along with ongoing dissemination of news of revival in America and subsequently in Ireland, created a strong atmosphere of expectation among the churchgoing community. Prayer meetings sprang up all over the region. According to Kenneth Jeffrey, Free Church session minutes for this period repeatedly describe the 'remarkable spirit of prayerfulness that overcame rural congregations. ... Across the north east of Scotland in countless parishes, men and women gathered in homes and barns, indeed wherever they could find room to meet together, and prayed earnestly for revival.'[2]

---

1. Radcliffe, p. 67.

2. Jeffrey, pp. 119-20.

Prayer groups became the centres from which the movement permeated whole communities and formed the context within which many of those who were affected were converted. Prayer meetings, indeed, lay at the very heart of the movement.

It was within this context that the revival began to disseminate in country districts. This was achieved by four principal means: a) groups of young men who had been influenced by the movement in Aberdeen going out from the city to hold revival services in rural districts; b) people travelling into Aberdeen to attend revival meetings; c) by contact with fishing communities who had come under the influence of the revival along the coast. This was particularly the case regarding communities situated near to the coast, e.g. Deskford and Millseat. d) via the agricultural towns of Huntly and Banchory, both of which became important revival centres from which the movement dispersed to surrounding districts.

Thus the revival was diffused to a considerable extent by converts who were keen to share their faith with family, friends and anyone they came into contact with. It was also disseminated, as already noted, by itinerant evangelists who laboured faithfully in this vast county, in particular Brownlow North,[3] Duncan Matheson and Reginald Radcliffe. Matheson in particular, traversed almost every parish of Aberdeenshire, and the district around, everywhere preaching the gospel, and being aware of significant blessing.

Of greatest significance of all was the role played by ministers of the Free Church within the region, within which denomination the revival was most prevalent.[4] These men dominated and exercised a profound influence upon the course of the revival. Such ministers were, on the

---

3. By this time, in an overture of the Free Church General Assembly (May 1859), North had been recognised as an 'evangelist extraordinaire', despite his lack of ministerial qualifications. The overture bore, among many others, the signatures of Robert Candlish, George Smeaton and James Begg.

4. Jeffrey specifies four of those who became 'key organisers' of the movement. Robert Reid of Banchory, William Ker of Deskford, Henry Williamson of Huntly and Archibald Gardner of New Deer. All except Reid (who was 48) were aged between 27 and 36 at the time of the revival and had been ordained into their first charges between 1852 and 1856. Hence they were young men who had become ministers during a period when the Free Church was becoming increasingly engaged in active evangelism.

whole, staunch Calvinists, who held traditional, conservative views on the conversion process, which they felt should ordinarily be a protracted, agonising ordeal that could last for weeks or even months. Because conversion was not seen as a spontaneous, immediate act of a person's own will during the excitement of a religious service, special after-meetings for anxious inquirers were not a feature of the rural movement as they were, for example, in Aberdeen. Thus the awakening unfolded itself in the country areas of Aberdeenshire in a steady, undramatic manner, and generally – in keeping with the character of the farm-folk and the guidance of their ministers – with an absence of religious excitement. For manifestations that appeared at public meetings were relatively quiet and not infectious, but more often the farm-folk were affected in their homes.

The farm-folks' daily lives also had an impact on the assimilation of the revival into the rural hinterland of north-east Scotland. Farming life was, of course, governed by a clear seasonal pattern. Late summer was the busiest time of year, while winter afforded more free time. It is interesting to note, then, that while revival began in some rural areas in the spring of 1859, it abated during the summer, only to re-emerge with greater poignancy during the autumn. Meanwhile the most significant period of the movement lasted from October 1859 to February 1860, thus corresponding to the period when farm-folk had most free time. The revival in country areas was also influenced by key dates in the agricultural calendar. For example, revival prospered on the occasions of the biannual feeing markets – held during the terms of Whitsunday and Martinmas – when revivalists seized the opportunity provided by the fact that farm-folk were relatively free from the demands of work (see pp. 229-31).

Of greater significance still was the connection between the revival and the traditional communion season. These long-established five-day religious festivals were knitted into the annual rhythms of the farming calendar and had a profound influence upon the timing and manner in which the revival appeared in Aberdeenshire. Regularly the high points of the movement coincided with these great rural occasions, which became the means by which the revival prospered and was sustained. Furthermore, the open-air field services, which became perhaps the most important feature of the revival among the farm-folk, were often planned in order to coincide with the local communion seasons.

Upon their return from visiting scenes of the Irish revival, ministers from Aberdeenshire began to hold these outdoor meetings in their parishes. During the autumn of 1859 they were held almost every evening in the principal agricultural towns of the north-east. The 1860 Huntly rally appears to have injected a fresh burst of enthusiasm into the movement, and that summer/autumn, open-air services were even more popular than in the previous year. This type of meeting was still quite common in the early summer of 1861, when another series of open-air meetings was held in places like New Pitsligo, Banchory Teman, Chapel of Garioch, Aboyne and Fyvie.[5] Large open-air audiences could easily be had in almost every district. This was in strong contrast to just a few months previously, when religious meetings outside of church walls were virtually unheard of. Because of the extent to which the north-east was influenced by the revival, we shall give a reasonably comprehensive region-by-region survey.

Strathbogie

Huntly

Duncan Matheson was especially adept at open-air preaching, and it was he who initiated and led special two-day evangelistic gatherings at Castle Park, near Huntly.[6] He was invited to use the grounds by the God-fearing Duchess of Gordon (1794–1864), a great supporter of the work. The Duchess had of course been witness to heartwarming revival stirrings in and around Huntly throughout the spring and summer of 1859 (see pp. 51-3). Said her biographer in regard to the proposed rallies: 'The Duchess was by education and habit averse to novelty, and all her feelings were against publicity for herself. There was no light cross involved in such a step, with the scoff of the world, and the opposition of some valued friends. But her eye was single, she believed it to be the will of God, and gave herself to it with her whole heart and soul, and the Lord aided his blessing abundantly.'[7]

---

5. Jeffrey, p. 135.

6. ibid., p. 125; Orr 1949, p. 70. James Turner spent a few days preaching in Huntly in May 1860, and a visitor to a cottage meeting there a decade later, marvelling at 'such a wondrous measure of divine unction as quite took me by surprise', discovered that several of its members were converts of Turner's labours in the area (Elizabeth McHardie, *James Turner: or, How to Reach the Masses*, Aberdeen, 1875, pp. 29-30).

7. Moody Stuart, 1865, p. 364.

The rallies were held over four summers from 1860 to 1863 and attracted many thousands annually by road, rail and footpath, to gospel ordinances. (Indeed, they led to Huntly quickly becoming a centre of the revival movement in the north-east.) It had rained for weeks prior to the first event, in 1860, so earnest prayer was made to God. Remarkably, the rain stopped just before the people drew together on 25 July. It was said that 'though the clouds hung low all the first day, as if they must break at every moment, not another drop fell. The second and great day of the feast was bright and cloudless, and the rain recommenced only after the forenoon train of the day following had borne away the last of those who had lingered to the close of the blessed assembly.'[8]

The hand of God seemed apparent in every detail of the occasion: 'The fears of the timid even for the injury of the place were wholly disappointed; not a plant on the grounds was injured.' Further, the Duchess wrote that 'my housekeeper greatly feared the things that were to be sent to the schools would not keep, especially the milk and the meat of which an ample supply was required. But she told me with grateful amazement that both were preserved twice as long as they had been for some time previously. Truly there was not one thing out of place or unseemly.'[9]

It was estimated that during that first year, the majority of adults attending were converts, but that around half of these were believers of less than a year's standing. *The British Herald* reported that on the Thursday, 'the power of God seemed to rest more particularly on the services in the open air', where six or seven thousand were assembled. The attention of the people became so riveted at the great meeting that, even when the awakened were requested to repair to the tent that they might be conversed with as on the previous day, comparatively few availed themselves of the opportunity, choosing rather to remain where they had been wounded, 'expecting, no doubt, that the power of the Lord, which was so manifestly felt, would be present to heal them. And we believe many were filled by the God of hope with all joy and peace in believing.' Of the unsaved, between three and four hundred were spoken with during the weekend on account of the

---

8. ibid., pp. 365-6.

9. ibid., pp. 366, 369-70.

anxiety of their souls. On one farm near Huntly as many as ten people were awakened.[10]

This first year the number of people present was estimated at seven thousand, and in some of the subsequent years, at ten thousand. It was said that believers who shared those never-to-be-forgotten times, told how, under the 'arousing appeals' of Duncan Matheson and Brownlow North, the 'stripping and searching ministry' of Dr W. P. Mackay of

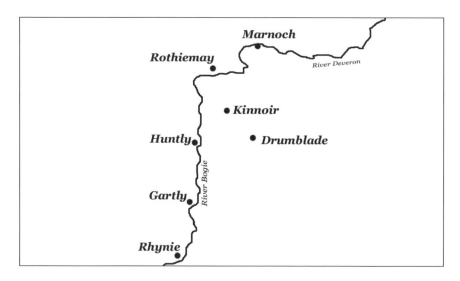

Hull and the 'full-orbed death, resurrection and union with Christ's gospel' of J. Denham Smith, 'hundreds passed out of darkness and bondage into the light and liberty of the kingdom of God, seated on the great sward or under the canvas tent where, all day long, anxious ones awakened on the field were pointed to the Saviour'.[11]

Just a week after the open-air conference at Huntly Lodge, and partly as a result of its success, the Duchess of Gordon could report that 'most of the small places between Pitcaple and Huntly are calling for help very urgently. But the most remarkable awakening was in a farm not far from here. Mr Williamson (Free Church minister of Huntly) went there on Sunday evening; I am told that thirty out of fifty in the barn were most deeply impressed, and many went away rejoicing ... there is no excitement,

10. *The British Herald*, quoted in Headley, pp. 82-3; *SG*, 31/07/1860.

11. Ross (Ed.), *Donald Ross: Pioneer Evangelist*, Kilmarnock, 1890 (reprinted 1987), pp. 165-6.

but so much depth of feeling and earnestness.'[12] Indeed, Williamson said of the awakening in some inland towns and villages he visited (Huntly, Keith, Marnoch, Grange, etc.), 'there is scarcely a house in which at least some members of the family are not deeply moved'. A visitor to Huntly in the summer of 1862 found that 'our prayers have been answered in that the principal inn, and some of the smaller ones, are now closed'.[13]

Kinnoir

Revival in Kinnoir (about three miles north of Huntly) began when a small cottage prayer meeting grew in interest and intensity until several young men were brought to peace in Christ. Similar meetings were begun in other houses in the district. The Duchess of Gordon sent Duncan Matheson, Sergeant Hector Macpherson, and John More, a butler in her service, to speak there. The meetings at Kinnoir were so well attended that neither barns nor houses would hold the people. The Duchess therefore decided to put up a wooden church that would hold three hundred. The Kinnoir Kirk opened soon after, 'the people greatly delighted, and many much impressed'.[14] Alexander Whyte was appointed missionary here in the summer of 1861. He wrote: 'It is the audience that does the preaching. Farmers, shepherds, farm servants and others gathered in that little (newly built) wooden church and we had rare evenings there. A group of young men in Strathdon who found a new source of power in the revival often went miles across the moors in parties of two or three to hold a kitchen meeting in some remote township.' One believer said that his local church was always full – those who were not saved were the exception.[15]

Feeing Markets

A number of evangelists took opportunity to preach at the country feeing markets during which farm servants hired themselves out to local farmers. Held twice a year, they were seen as great public festivals, attracting large crowds and invariably resulting in much revelry and drunkenness. Donaldson Rose spoke of the Huntly feeing market of

12. Moody Stuart, 1865, p. 369.

13. Roberts, 1995, pp. 300-1; *WJ*, 26/07/1862, p. 138.

14. Matthews, pp. 96-7; Moody Stuart, 1865, p. 370.

15. G. F. Barbour, pp. 97-100; Matthews, p. 100.

November 1859 as 'one of the most remarkable days in my life – perhaps one of the most remarkable days I will ever see in this world'. He saw 'old men and young lads and intelligent tradesmen – all assembled together, and the room crowded over and over again by the anxious, many of whom had been arrested in the market ... those solemn meetings and solemn dealings will never be forgotten'.[16] Two houses were opened in the Court House located on the main square to receive inquirers. There were several rooms for men, and four rooms on different floors for women. Here hundreds during the day came under deep conviction. Several women were at work all day with tracts, and Reginald Radcliffe, H. Williamson and others, were engaged in addresses publicly and privately. 'Such a day has not been seen here before', testified one witness.[17]

Meanwhile, when Duncan Matheson and others went to speak at a feeing market in Potarch, to the west of Banchory on Deeside, they met with almost complete indifference, despite much previous prayer. The men, around a dozen in number, moved to the edge of the crowd, and knelt down with uncovered heads, to entreat God 'to have mercy on those who have no mercy with themselves'. Amidst this humbling scene, 'Satan appeared let loose'. Some danced, whooped and yelled around the circle, while one man knelt down beside Major Gibson and spat in his face. At length the men got up and returned to the centre of the camp. 'Then we got an audience indeed, and the Word seemed to be with power.' Some were stricken with great conviction of sin, and Matheson continued preaching, even from his conveyance as he was about to leave the ground.[18]

Yet again the Duchess of Gordon described how, during the revival, 'The market at Insch was something wonderful; so different from former

---

16. 'A Report of a Conference on the State of Religion and Public Meeting, held in the Free Church, Huntly, January 5, 1860', p. 21, quoted in Jeffrey, p. 133.

17. *WJ*, 03/12/1859, p. 75. This may have been the same occasion recalled by Rev. Alexander Whyte, who spoke of two vastly differing personalities who preached during the revival in the north-east, 'on an improvised platform in the centre of a "Feeing Market" crowd – Williamson of Huntly, one of the most handsome and best groomed men in the country, a stately Presbyterian divine, alongside "The Brigget Butcher" (Robert Cunningham) with face that might have been hewn out with his own meat-axe, minus an eye, which he had lost in one of the fights of his unregenerate days, and a voice like a bull of Bashan' (Matthews, Chap. 1).

18. Johnson, p. 232.

years. The eagerness to hear of Jesus was most earnest, the solemnity great, with the warm pressure of the hand of all around. The hall taken to speak to anxious ones was filled all day. The greatest wonder is that they did not see one intoxicated person, nor hear one bad word.'[19]

Gartly

In Gartly, near Huntly, Radcliffe and others spent a whole morning in prayer in the Free Church manse before the evening meeting. At night, the church was packed with men; 'but it was also filled with the presence of God. The Lord had gone out before us'. The Scriptures were preached with power. The subject was the raising of Lazarus from the dead. The whole address did not occupy above twenty minutes; but it was said that the people were 'melted like wax before the presence of the Lord. Many a Lazarus came forth from the grave of spiritual death, and afterwards sat at meat with Him, and some of them went forth to preach the Gospel.'[20]

Rothiemay

When Radcliffe preached in nearby Rothiemay, there was a notable absence of spiritual power. Radcliffe suddenly paused; and with head lifted up, poured forth his soul in prayer. As he prayed, 'the house was as if shaken; every heart was moved; a great awe of God fell upon all, and God wrought mightily'. As the hour was late, Radcliffe announced a meeting of inquirers early the next morning. 'The Lord rebuked the weak faith of many, and honoured the faith of His servant, by filling the church the next morning with inquirers after God and His salvation.'[21] The revival in this district continued for some time after it had quietened

---

19. G. Gordon, *The Last Dukes of Gordon and their Consorts, 1743-1865*, p. 217, quoted in Jeffrey, p. 133.

20. Radcliffe, p. 68.

21. ibid., pp. 68-9. Rev. J. More recalls this same (or perhaps another) occasion in Rothiemay, when during his message, Radcliffe seemed to 'stick. He covered his face with his hands as if ashamed, and the silence for a few minutes was oppressive. Then he burst into tears, and exclaimed in a voice trembling with emotion; "Oh dear friends, how can a poor worm like me describe to you the glory of my Lord Jesus Christ?" His mouth was opened, and for twenty minutes the truth poured from his lips like a torrent. At the close of the address hardly anybody left ... these hard-headed unemotional people were sobbing all over the place, and were literally asking, "What must I do to be saved?" It was an easy and grateful ministry for

down elsewhere (see p. 443). Bestowed on Marnoch and Drumblade, also, were 'precious and wonderful results that can never be forgotten'.[22]

Rhynie

Centred on the small upland village of Rhynie, a church social meeting had been held twice a year for some time. Latterly the topical focus for discussion had been 'Revivals'. The unanimous outcome of these talks was the belief that a main requisite of a revival was persistent prayer. The Rev. Nicol and another minister in the district started meeting together every two weeks or more to pray for an outpouring of God's Spirit on their community. In time they observed how folk were coming out more to hear the Word, and the main prayer meeting increased greatly in attendance. Some young men commenced a prayer meeting on Sabbath mornings – all of these were soon spiritually awakened and each came through to a place of peace. From then on, the revival went on unabated, and when Nicol visited homes in which he expected to find no regard to divine things, he was delighted to encounter anxious souls.

Radcliffe laboured in Rhynie 'with very considerable success' during two open-air services. In total between seventy and eighty turned to God in a relatively short period of time, mainly within the age bracket of twelve to forty, and mostly young men. With enquiry it was found that the main means of awakening was preaching on the Cross. At prayer meetings between twelve and twenty young men were willing to pray who before would have scoffed at the thought of even being present on such an occasion. The Independent Church in Rhynie also felt the living breath of the revival and there were many conversions, resulting in nineteen additions to membership in 1860.[23]

Garioch

Pitcaple

The Scottish Guardian reported that for the twelve months up to the end of August 1860, 'an important religious movement' had been in progress in most parishes of the Garioch district of Aberdeenshire. Near

---

anyone who knew anything of the way, to point stricken souls, such as these, to the Saviour' (ibid., p. 82).

22. Brown, 1893, p. 80.

23. H. Escott, *A History of Scottish Congregationalism*, Glasgow, 1960, p. 59-61.

the start of 1860, the Free Presbytery of Garioch could report 'a work of awakening more or less among the congregations within their bounds'.[24] Revival in the region appeared to begin with a dramatic outpouring occasioned by the preaching of Duncan Matheson in the Free Church of Garioch, by Pitcaple, on 4 August 1859, this ironically at the time when the minister, the Rev. George Bain, was in Ireland, drawn over by accounts he had heard of the great revival there. Mrs Bain records

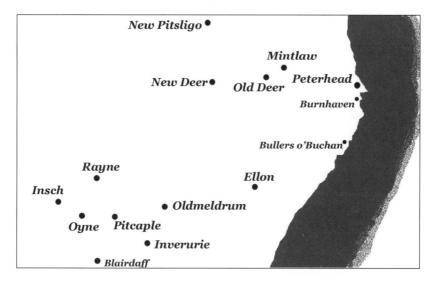

that Matheson was given 'most valuable assistance on that remarkable night of the outpouring of the Holy Ghost on the people gathered from the surrounding district, Duncan's previous knowledge of not a few of them giving him an advantage in dealing with the many souls awakened on that memorable occasion'.[25]

Reginald Radcliffe was another who was invited to preach in Pitcaple while the parish minister was over in Ireland. Mrs Radcliffe records that when Bain returned home on the Saturday, he found that there had been a great awakening. The next evening, Radcliffe preached on the hillside, for the church could barely have held a third of those who came to hear him. From there, many inquirers went into the church to be spoken to by Radcliffe; but a large congregation remained, who were addressed by Mr Bain. It took hours to deal with the anxious,

24. *SG*, 28/08/1860, 07/02/1860.

25. Macpherson, 1871, p. 116.

many of whom were among the fifty new communicants admitted at the sacrament held on the first day of 1860, this being in addition to a number of existing communicants who were also converted during the revival in the district.

John Gordon of Parkhill laboured with success in Pitcaple, while Radcliffe returned to the place, along with Duncan Matheson and others, in August 1860 for an all-day open-air service. Well over a thousand attended, some walking up to twelve miles to be there. Once again, many were awakened and hopefully converted, while, at times, especially when the assembled worshippers unitedly knelt on the hillside in prayer, the scene was said to have been both 'impressive and unusual'.[26] The biographer of Matheson records of this occasion: 'The power of God was manifest on the souls of many', especially one Sunday afternoon, when a prolonged meeting was held after the church service on account of the agitated state of some young persons. Outside, Mrs Bain found a young Bible Class boy, previously 'entirely hard and careless', trembling and pale. Both he and his sister, also awakened, were spoken to at length and after a period of deep distress, both came through to a place of peace in Christ.[27]

Writing in 1865 Bain stated that seventy new communicants were added to his congregation as a result of the revival and there had been little going back among them. At a recent election of elders, five of the seven men chosen had been converted during the revival movement. Subsequently they had an election of deacons, and of the eleven elected seven were the subjects of the recent awakening. Others had become Sabbath-school teachers, and some young men were studying for the ministry. A number of persons had been reclaimed from drunkenness. Another fruit of the revival was that the young men had undertaken the support of a native catechist in China, and the young women the education of a girl in India.[28] Duncan Matheson said of Radcliffe's work at Oyne, just two miles from Pitcaple, that he knew of a hundred people brought to Christ through him there.

---

26. Radcliffe, pp. 84-5; *WJ*, 18/08/1860, p. 372.

27. Macpherson, 1871, pp. 116-17.

28. Brown, 1893, pp. 784-5; cf. 1865, pp. 18-19, quoted in Muirhead, Ian A. 'The Revival as a Dimension of Scottish Church History' in *RSCHS*, vol. 20, 1980, p. 195.

Rayne

To the north of Pitcaple, the parish of Rayne was also signally favoured. Here, the work was conducted in such a quiet and unostentatious manner, and with no involvement from any well-known preacher, that it was little known outside the region. Special services were held on the fourth anniversary of the opening of the church. A case of prostration occurred at an evening meeting, so affecting the whole congregation that hardly a dry face could be seen. An open-air meeting was then held in an 'elevated position in the centre of the parish', which, though unadvertised, drew over two thousand people from all directions, in 'vehicles of every description, from carriage and pair, down to the farmer's common box-cart'. The anxious proceeded to a nearby barn for counsel; this building plus another barn was filled with inquirers, while small groups retreated for prayer into surrounding fields and adjacent houses. Older folk present commented that 'there was never such a day as this seen in Rayne'.[29]

Inverurie

The market town of Inverurie was also moved by events of 1859–60. The Session records of the Free Church, under direction of the Rev. Thomas Gray, reported that a 'marked effect' was produced within its bounds. 'There is a growing feeling of earnestness and solemnity in the congregation at large. There are tokens of the Spirit's power and presence such as have not been seen or felt for years past.'[30] In particular there was much awakening among farm servants.

Meanwhile, in Blairdaff, a few miles south-east of Inverurie, it was said, 'a great work has gone on'. A sermon preached on the barren fig tree led to the awakening of an elder and his wife, as well as that of a deacon and his wife, each of them feeling that they figuratively represented this tree. A governess was converted after pondering on the significance of three deaths in her family, as too was a 'very wild young man, a poacher', who, after going to visit his minister in the middle of the night and still finding no relief, finally found peace in the wood on his way home as he knelt down and came 'just to Christ

29. *SG*, 28/08/1860.

30. Rev. Alex S. Crichton, *Annals of a Disruption Congregation in Aberdeenshire: Being the Story of Inverurie Free Church*, Aberdeen, 1943, p. 14.

himself'. Then again, at Insch, in the flax mills, a significant work was done. Additionally, three farm servants, each formerly quite careless, were awakened, and could now be regularly seen, during part of their dinner hour, holding a meeting in the stable.[31]

Oldmeldrum

When Reginald Radcliffe preached at Oldmeldrum, to the north-east of Inverurie, the large Free Church congregation was unimpressed by his simple, unadorned gospel address. There was no response to the appeal at the end of the service and the people began to make their way homeward. The workers gathered around Radcliffe in dismay, but he said, 'Friends, have faith in God. Let us ask him to send them back.' Their prayer was quickly answered. Arrested as if by an unseen hand, the congregation began to return to the church in ones and twos, and later in crowds, until the big kirk was again one-third full. The cold indifference was now gone and the simplest words melted their hearts until the whole assembly was in tears. The elderly Rev. Garioch was said to have been 'transported. His face shone like an angel's.'[32]

Another said of this occasion, 'The cloud of Divine mercy burst upon us in such a manner that I can only wonder and adore. I am as one that has dreamed, and often I ask myself, "Can it be real what has passed before us these last few days?".' Dr R. McKilliam, who was present at these occasions, could reflect several decades later: 'For many, many months we continued to reap, and the place was literally changed ... croquet parties, social evenings, etc, were set aside for prayer-meetings and Bible readings, and we never for a long time came together without expecting manifest blessing ... for well-nigh forty years we have never quite lost the practical results (of the revival) from our life and ministry.'[33]

Old and New Deer

New Deer

The work in the sizeable parish of New Deer began around the beginning of October 1859 and was preceded by much prayer. The Wynd Church

---

31. *WJ*, 07/01/1860, p. 114.

32. Shearer, pp. 101-2.

33. *WJ*, 10/12/1859, p. 82; Radcliffe, pp. 72-3.

in Glasgow was requested to pray for the people of this community, and the very following Sabbath New Deer believers began to notice a change in the spiritual atmosphere. A sermon preached from John 9:1 – on the theme of Jesus of Nazareth passing by – was the means of much awakening. For weeks after, the Rev. Gardner came across people who traced their first serious impressions to that day. At one united prayer meeting, three young men came forward and told, 'with great simplicity and modesty', the diverse means by which they individually came to Christ. These statements made a deep impression on the audience, and all the more so because it was seen as the first incident of the kind that had ever occurred there.[34] The movement advanced steadily, although perhaps more slowly and with fewer notable incidents as in some other places. Yet on one November Sabbath, about seventy waited at the late meeting, the majority in spiritual anxiety.

Open-air meetings were held in barns and schoolrooms, as well as in churches, and great earnestness was apparent everywhere. When severe storms affected the north in late February 1860, it was feared the good work would be interrupted. But it was proved that 'the Lord can carry on His work in all weather', for during a visit from Gordon Forlong, the storm, in which there had been a lull, commenced with renewed severity.[35] High wind and drifting snow rendered it dangerous to be far from home. Despite this, at the Sabbath evening meeting, much to the astonishment of the organisers, the church was almost full, and a deep impression was made by Forlong's address.

Old Deer

In Old Deer considerable effort was undertaken by the different denominations in the hope that the Lord would bless them also with His refreshing showers. They were almost in despair, when at a prayer meeting towards the end of January 1860, a young man was brought under serious impressions. He began to sob during the first prayer. After a while he sank down on the seat, and then fell upon the floor, crying, 'Lord Jesus have mercy upon me.' This was the beginning of days of blessing. In meetings held in nearby Mintlaw in August 1861,

---

34. *WJ*, 21/01/1860, p. 132; 14/01/1860, p. 123.

35. *WJ*, 10/03/1860, p. 186.

considerable impression seemed to be produced; the inquirers' tent was filled, 'and it is trusted that the day's services were blessed to not a few'.[36]

New Pitsligo

Students from Aberdeen University's Marischal College led meetings at New Pitsligo. On the eighth night, 'gloriously was prayer answered. The house was full of the presence and power of God. ... In and around the village, in the schoolroom, hall or barn we continued for months almost nightly holding gospel meetings, and seldom without souls inquiring and finding the way of salvation.'[37] The *Banffshire Journal* described a typical summer's evening open-air service at New Pitsligo in 1859: 'It is something impressive to hear the earnest voice of the preacher, and romantic to behold large groups of women with babies in their arms, and workmen, in working dress, seated around him in the grass sward, on our village square, devoutly listening to the word of truth.'[38]

One result of the movement here was the formation of a Congregational Church in 1861. Within this neighbourhood, a scoffer was brought to Christ. She had come to scoff, but gone away to pray. She returned, and was asked why she was there again. 'Ah', she said, 'I like to see the laddies on their knees.' Another person from the same district, a young man, 'caught the flame himself' and was then the means of 'setting the family on fire'; each member was converted, from the very youngest up to the head of the family.[39]

Skene

An 'evident work of God' began in Skene after the return to his Free Church parish of the Rev. Robert Ireland from Saltcoats, where he had been assisting his brother-in-law, the Rev. Davidson, in the surprising work of revival there. Open-air gatherings took place in the summer of 1860 on the lawn at Kirkville, Kinmundy, and at the other extremity of the parish, the Letter of Skene. The next day, believers went out two-by-two throughout the parish holding open-air services in different places.

---

36. ibid., 31/08/1861, p. 181.

37. Matthews, p. 132.

38. *The Banffshire Journal*, quoted in Jeffrey, p. 135.

39. *WJ*, 12/07/1862, p. 125.

No less than twenty Saturday evening prayer meetings were held every week in cottages, conducted by the people themselves, for the purpose of praying for blessing on the following Sabbath services. Sunday evening meetings were held in the Lyne school, and here, following a testimony given by the local 'carrier', many souls were touched. That same night, in the woods near to the schoolroom where the meeting was held, many people in anxiety prayed till past midnight.

The increase in financial collections was quite striking during this period, out of which much good works were effected. For example, Ireland established two schools in the district, and significant improvements were made to the manse. Very many who later became part of the Skene congregation were the fruit of the revival, and Ireland looked upon his parish as 'a field which the Lord has blessed'. His own work in the revival was seen to be all the more remarkable given that he was a man in whom any appearance of excitement rarely manifested itself, 'ranting fanaticism having no part in his nature'.[40]

The work in Skene was revived in the summer of 1861, with added impetus from the renowned Huntly meetings, when services were held by the edge of Loch Skene. Folk came from miles around – including a band of workers, clerical and lay, from Kintore – to hear Ireland preach,[41] as well as a host of visiting speakers (mainly from the north-east, but including Robert Cunningham from Glasgow). As many as 1,600 gathered for one meeting, when, during an interval in the afternoon, a prayer meeting was held. Wrote William Baird: 'The Spirit came down with such sensible power that the multitude became immediately broken into groups, who retired in different directions and cried to God for mercy. It was a scene never to be forgotten.' One minister noted that he had 'never seen such marked evidences of the Lord's power'.[42]

Duncan Matheson said he witnessed on this occasion, 'the awful solemnity upon our spirits, when it seemed as if we felt the immediate power of God in our hearts, and were almost afraid to speak, as if one felt near the very gates of heaven. Some of us felt so at Skene. And when we saw the Lord working, and the slain so many, we lifted

40. William Baird, *Free Church Congregation of Portobello*, Edinburgh, 1890, pp. 151-5.

41. Ireland removed to serve as Free Church minister in Portobello later that year.

42. Baird, 1890, pp. 153-4.

up our hearts and sang "Hallelujah", "for the Lord God omnipotent reigneth".'[43] At an evening meeting in a local church, seven men from a single farmhouse four miles distant were awakened within two hours.

The Rev. Davidson of Saltcoats paid a visit to Aberdeenshire in 1861. One district, which he claimed had been amongst the darkest in the county at one time, was now the 'scene of a very remarkable awakening'. Entering one farmhouse he found a couple with five grown-up daughters. All had been converted during the previous year and each in a different way. Not only so, but each girl had been almost entirely ignorant of the change in each of her sisters, although each was aware that the others had previously appeared anxious about something! None had spoken to the others about spiritual matters until all were savingly changed.[44]

Deeside

Banchory and Maryculter

Jeffrey seeks to show that the single most significant factor in the dispersing of the 1859 revival across the north-east of Scotland was the recently improved communications network in the region, particularly the new railway lines, such as the Deeside line which reached Banchory in 1853 and the Northern line which arrived at Banchory a year later. These links, noted one journalist, 'wrought a complete revolution in all our travelling arrangements'. Thus it is, Jeffrey claims, that 'all the villages on the railway line from Aberdeen to Banchory, which included Cults, Murtle, Milltimber, Culter, Drum, Park and Crathes', were influenced by the revival movement that was spreading across the county.[45]

The Rev. William Selbie laboured with great diligence in the parish of Maryculter. It was usual for him to preach at Maryculter on Sabbath morning, at Bourtreebush in the afternoon, and to hold a kitchen, farm, or open-air meeting in the evening. People from the surrounding neighbourhood attended in large numbers. One who was

---

43. *WJ*, 19/10/1861, p. 22. As well as this parish to the south-west of Aberdeen, parishes just north of the city also came under the influence of the revival, e.g., Newhills, where Rev. Cravan laboured faithfully, and Belhelvie (Matthews, p. xv; FCSRSRM, 1888, p. 4).

44. *SG*, 17/08/1861.

45. Jeffrey, p. 165.

deeply impressed at one of these open-air meetings, 'D. M.', went on to serve as a city missionary for thirty-four years.

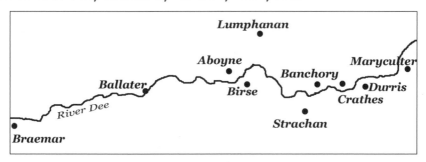

In Banchory a revival movement had begun in the Free Church with the spring Communion in May 1859 (see p. 53). The Rev. Robert Reid stated that a shorter 'extraordinary' Communion was held in August, and another in January 1860. In regard to this the session minutes recorded, 'There has been a truly wonderful awakening … there were more communicants added to the roll (50) than there was during the whole past nine years of the minister's incumbency.'[46]

Many interesting cases of conversion took place, including those of two Sabbath-school teachers. Even the Episcopal Church shared in the blessing. One ardent worker in Banchory was Colonel Burnett Ramsay, and he gladly assisted at meetings with local lay-preachers, be they even his own groom or gardener. Many field meetings were held on the grounds adjoining his Banchory Lodge; one held in the summer of 1860 attracted as many as three thousand people. A navy pensioner was among those who were dramatically awakened through these events, and some six hundred people were drawn to his testimony meeting on the evening of his conversion.[47]

Westward Spread

Banchory became a centre of the movement in the wider area and Reid became 'the inspiration of the revival' from the city eastwards to Durris,[48] south to Strachan, north to Lumphanan, and as far west as Birse, Aboyne and even Braemar, some forty miles distant, while adjoining districts 'all partook of the gracious influences'. Over the course of fifty years one

46. *Wynd Journal*, reported in Sprange, pp. 173, 134.

47. *Monthly Record*, 1893, p. 213; Matthews, pp. 121-4.

48. An open-air service here in 1860 attracted between three and four hundred people.

local believer met with men and women in many different districts of South Africa who came from these Aberdeenshire parishes, and who were led to Christian decision at these homely, informal evangelistic services. The same man knew of five converts from the region who went on to become overseas missionaries.[49]

Some young girls from Ballater came to Aberdeen, where they were awakened and converted. One of them invited her mother to come and see her in the city, she and her friends having prayed that her visit would be blessed. The mother came, went to church, heard a gospel message, but remained unmoved. However, as she was leaving church, a person put his hand on her shoulder and asked if she was saved. 'It was enough, the arrow went home, she returned to Ballater and told others.' Soon there were five or six prayer meetings in operation, but a curious observation was noted in the fact that 'only one-half of the village has been visited; in the other half not one case of an anxious soul is to be met with'.[50]

Meanwhile, eight miles west of Ballater, by the entrance to Balmoral Castle, a revival meeting was held near the suspension bridge at Crathie in the autumn of 1861. The attendance was large and included several gentlemen of rank from the nearby castle. The Rev. Cobban of Crathie Kirk said at the same time, 'The Lord has been blessing us greatly, and the work is still going on. The population is small, but relative to it the work is really great.'[51]

Coastal Aberdeenshire

St Combs

James Turner, a fish-curer from Peterhead, created considerable stir when, in December 1859, during a slack period in business, he moved from place to place along the north-east coast, directly and forcibly declaring a contextualised gospel message to the attentive crowds who gathered to hear him.[52] The first phase of Turner's mission was to Fraserburgh and

---

49. Jeffrey, pp. 122-4.

50. *WJ*, 07/01/1860, p. 114.

51. *WJ*, 19/10/1861, pp. 22-3.

52. Jeffrey, pp. 199, 192. Turner had become increasingly engaged in evangelism in the Peterhead area over the previous six years; now his ministry was to extend

the scattering of fishing villages located at each side of it. Awakening broke out in St Combs, a village of ninety-four families, a few miles east of Fraserburgh, at the start of December. On Turner's second evening, around four hundred packed into the church. 'What a night of the power of God!', jotted Turner in his Diary. 'The meeting was kept up until morning. A great many did not sleep that night, neither did I.' The next night God again 'came down with such power', and indeed to such transforming effect that as long as fourteen years later it was without difficulty that a journalist could obtain 'testimony after testimony of the successes and triumphs of divine grace, as wrought out in personal experience – blessing, blessing, blessing on every side, in awakening, in conversion, in the raising also of God's children from a state of bondage and fear to a spiritual level so high that, unmoved by changing circumstances, through all these intervening years, their hearts have never ceased to sing a doxology to Jesus.'[53]

A moving example of the work in St Combs was that of a mother, who, along with her eldest daughter, was already a Christian. This woman saw several of her sons turn to Christ for salvation under Turner's labours. Her husband, an alcoholic, appeared to undergo a degree of reformation also, but shortly after fell back into 'open, stout-hearted rebellion' and made the home-life of his family a living hell. However, even then, as he later testified, 'I was mony a time seeking the Lord amo' the braes, oot o'sicht.'[54] Soon, he underwent a period of deep spiritual distress, which was by-and-by turned into a joyful testimony of salvation.

A daughter of this man kept away from Turner's meetings because she thought herself a righteous woman. Having suitable accommodation, however, she invited Turner to stay with her during his St Combs campaign, and she couldn't fail to hear the evangelist's midnight pleadings in prayer night after night as he wrestled for souls alone in his closet. This told upon her spirit far more than his preaching could have done. So, too, did the conversion of a brother much the same in character as herself. Deeply convicted, she moved around the village seeking help, but wherever she went she found 'everybody … rejoicing

---

further north and west, but almost always confined to fishing communities.

53. McHardie, p. 21, pp. 52-3.

54. ibid., p. 48.

in God'. After a long, hard struggle, she gained assurance of faith while kneeling in the ben-end of her house, and indeed became quite overpowered, lying for some time insensible on the floor, her body and mind exhausted, but her soul unutterably happy. The news of her transformed life delighted her husband, who was at sea and who had become a new creature in Christ shortly before!

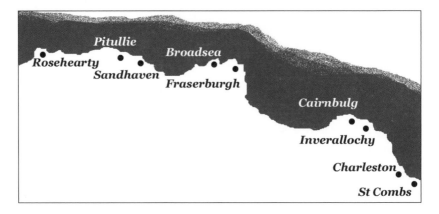

Turner met with considerable opposition in St Combs, as he did almost everywhere he journeyed along the north-east coast – this came often from those who might have been expected to take his side. The opposition, noted Elizabeth McHardie, came 'right into their midst not only with the suddenness of some blazing meteor, but the destructiveness also of a bomb-shell, spreading death and devastation around him in every direction; and though it was among the enemies of the King, the spiritual force was so new and terrible that some seemed afraid and kept aloof from it, while bolder spirits did what they could to subdue it.'[55]

Turner also went from house to house in the tiny village of Charleston, close to St Combs. 'For ten days I laboured in these two places', he wrote, 'and God saved young and old, drunkards and fighting men. What a sight to see men of seventy years crying on the streets for mercy! From 400 to 500 were led to feel their lost estate. What a work of God!'[56]

Cairnbulg and Inverallochy

Turner then moved along the coast to the twin villages of Cairnbulg and Inverallochy. In the former place he observed that on the third

---

55. ibid., p. 52.

56. ibid.

night, 'The Spirit of God came down on a great many, and God gave me great power.' People came an hour and a half before the start of the evening meeting to ensure they got a seat. 'Numbers come to me every day in concern about their own souls, or about the souls of others who are dear to them. ... If the work goes on the whisky shops will soon be without customers.'[57]

'Equally surprising results' were obtained in Inverallochy, Broadsea, Pitullie and Rosehearty. In the former place, the effects of the awakening produced by Turner's labours were still drawing souls to 'the Light of Life' many years afterwards. In 1875 a young girl came to trust in Christ, awakened by means of the sudden death of her uncle, who drowned at sea along with all other crew members just days before. This man, along with another uncle and her own father, had been converted in Inverallochy through Turner in 1860 and all had lived consistently godly lives ever since. Two brothers converted at the same time were also lost on that Inverallochy boat, while the girl could name numerous other locals whose lives had been similarly changed through Turner's visit.[58]

Fraserburgh

Strangely, Fraserburgh does not feature prominently in accounts of revival along the north-east coast during 1859–60. Nevertheless, according to both Robbie and McHardie, the town, like its neighbouring villages mentioned above, 'fell under deep conviction of sin' with Turner's visit in December.[59] One girl from Findochty talks about attending Christian meetings in Fraserburgh during the herring-fishing season in the summer of 1859. The meetings were led by a curer, Mr 'G. B.', and were composed mainly of young women. The young girl in question was awakened through these meetings, but only received assurance of faith on Turner's visit to her native village some months later. It is unclear whether revival was in progress in Fraserburgh at this early stage or not. In any case, the fisherfolk of this town lived predominantly in Broadsea, an area located in the north of the town, and it is in this 'seatown' community, which was also visited by Turner, that revival would have been most prominent.

---

57. ibid., p. 22.

58. ibid., p. 55.

59. W. Robbie, *The Life and Labours of the Late James Turner of Peterhead*, Aberdeen, 1863, p. 93.

Peterhead

There is some debate over the extent to which the other large town in the area, Peterhead, was affected by the ever-extending revival movement. *The Wynd Journal* reported that in the summer of 1859, the gatherings at the open-air meetings in the town were 'extraordinary'. Immediately at the end of the herring fishing (normally mid-September), some of those who had 'got good' went home and commenced prayer meetings in their own villages.[60] Reginald Radcliffe, Gordon Forlong and other evangelists subsequently preached here on different occasions during the autumn and winter of 1859–60, drawing considerable crowds, but having no spectacular effect. Orr, however, suggests that revival did occur in the town and could be dated to the summer/autumn of 1859, quoting a journal that noted the effect of a united prayer meeting which, over the course of a year, had seen around fifty conversions. Jeffrey, however, viewed these events as a preparation to embrace revival, rather than as revival in itself.[61]

In fact, Jeffrey devotes an entire chapter of his study of the revival movement in the north-east to 'The Relative Failure of the Revival (of 1858–62) to affect Peterhead'. He states that when the movement broke out with unprecedented influence along the coast between February and April 1860, there was 'no sign whatsoever that it appeared in Peterhead. The town is not referred to in a single report of the revival during this period.' On the contrary, in March when other fishing towns and villages were literally ablaze with religious excitement, the local press described the spiritual atmosphere in the town as being indifferent and tiresome. Peterhead appeared as the only settlement along the coast of north-east Scotland between Aberdeen and Inverness 'that did not embrace this religious movement'.[62]

Jeffrey provides several reasons for the revival's limited effects in Peterhead. First, he gives evidence to suggest that most of the town's clergy were not favourably disposed to the revival. The only group which identified itself firmly with such cause were the Baptists, and they were only a small group. Further, unlike most towns and villages along the north-east coast where revival flourished, Peterhead had a relatively large, and therefore

---

60. *WJ*, 19/10/1861, p. 23.

61. *The Revival*, (17/08/59), quoted in Orr, 1949, p. 71; Jeffrey, p. 234.

62. ibid., p. 235.

diverse, population. There were numerous industries in the town other than fishing, which, in 1840, only employed an eighth of the workforce. Thus there was greater social diversity and a number of men were of the professional class, particularly within the churches. As a result, there was less receptivity to the emotionalism of revivalism, which was gladly embraced elsewhere. This was the attitude, also, of the local newspaper, the *Peterhead Sentinel*, which adopted an alarmist, unsympathetic reaction to reports of revival in other places, particularly in regard to physical manifestations. Thirdly, the more cultured people of Peterhead were averse to a religious movement led by a local, unordained, Methodist fish-curer with outspoken views and an overzealous attitude to religion.[63]

Certainly, as late as April 1860, after seeing revival blaze along the Moray and Banffshire coast, Turner bemoaned the indifference to divine things in his native town, calling it 'a stronghold of the devil'. Revival prayer meetings had been started in Peterhead, but there was some furore when Turner used them to speak against and pray for unconverted ministers and office-bearers, some of whom were themselves present at these gatherings! The meetings were stopped and Turner became much ostracised. Undaunted, he started holding meetings with his brother in their own building, a capacious barrel-making edifice which he modified so it could accommodate around two hundred people.

At last, in July 1860, Turner could report: 'The blessed Spirit is working here ... we had resolved to hold meetings in our co-operage on the nights that the boats were not at sea. We have now these meetings every night, and the Lord is saving souls. Last night was a great night, many crying for mercy, and four were struck down under strong convictions of sin. I think some were saved, but a few got frightened and ran out – the devil in them could not stand it. On Sabbath we had a remarkable time of the Spirit's power ...'[64]

It is reported that frequently, when Turner's coopers (barrel-makers) arrived for work in the early morning, they had to wait until a prayer meeting had broken up from the previous evening and the fishermen had gone to their own homes. On occasions, when he preached, some were so convicted of sin that they rolled on the earthen floor, pleading with God to forgive them. The meetings continued to be held for nearly

63. ibid., pp. 237-40.
64. ibid., p. 31.

eighteen months. Sometimes there was but little appearance of fruit, and at other times 'the quickening Spirit was vouchsafed in a very remarkable manner'. Still the meetings were carried on, and that humble and hallowed spot, it is believed, became the 'birth place of souls'.[65]

The two small fishing villages lying at either end of the town, Buchanhaven and Burnhaven, both came under the influence of the revival, though not until the end of April 1860, and seemingly without the direct influence of Turner. The *Aberdeen Free Press* reported on 8 June that in Burnhaven a prayer meeting for revival had been in progress for many weeks in the Congregational Mission Chapel; and that following a sermon by the Rev. R. H. Smith around four weeks previously, an 'awakening commenced, and has since increased steadily and quietly'. At Buchanhaven the work was more recent. 'About a fortnight ago', the newspaper continued, 'after a week-evening service by Mr Smith, a number were impressed and the work commenced'.[66]

Bullars o'Buchan

The village of Bullars, to the south of Peterhead, was more firmly held in the grip of Episcopalianism than virtually any other north-east community at the time. When two unnamed evangelists arrived in the village and began to preach in the wide space that existed between the two rows of houses, they got no congregation. Consequently, the visitors determined to make house-to-house visitation, and began at the home of Jake Alexander, the lay spiritual leader of the township by dint of his moral life, knowledge of Scripture and assertive religiosity. Other locals followed the evangelists into Jake's home, to hear him bluntly refute the evangelists' assertion that the Lord called them to witness in the area. 'Ay, and sae did the seven sons oo'Sceva, the Jew', retorted Alexander. 'They thought they could tak' the Lord's name in the mou' like Paul did; but when yon lad cam' oot upon them he let them see anither story.' Jake's interlocution somewhat confounded the visitors, who resorted to informing him that he was on

---

65. James Cordiner, *Fragments From the Past: An Account of People and Events in the Assemblies of Northern Scotland*, London, 1961, p. 16; Robbie, p. 95.

66. The *Aberdeen Free Press*, 08/06/1860, quoted in Jeffrey, *When the Lord Walked the Land*, pp. 235-6. Jeffrey implies that the movement here was stimulated by two local fishermen who drowned while crossing Dunnet Bay, but the evidence suggests that the awakening had started before this accident (p. 185).

his way to hell. To this remark a neighbour responded, 'Judge not, my bonny lad, or ye'll hyae a fair chance to be there afore him.'[67]

In a nearby fishing village, also an Episcopalian stronghold, Lucky Cairney, the granddaughter, daughter, wife and mother of successive generations of fishermen, was looked upon as the people's spiritual leader after the death of her husband. Remarkably strong in character, she had utmost confidence in the providential ordering of God. It was said that 'nothing daunted her; she looked upon it as the burden laid upon her back by her heavenly father, who would remove it, or her, when his will was accomplished'. Yet even in the face of such formidable leadership, this village (as also Bullars) became deeply swayed by the evangelical witness that challenged it during the 1859 revival. Cairney herself was quoted as stating that whereas around thirty families previously walked each Sunday from her village to Bishop Jolly's Episcopalian church in Peterhead, virtually no one went following the revival. Even her own relations, both there and at her married home, had deserted their mother church for the more exciting evangelicalism. 'Revivalists, Plymouth Brethren and such like had scattered them to the wind.'[68]

Aberdeen

Second Revival Phase (1859–61)

Revival had broken out so manifestly in Aberdeen as early as 1858 – the progress of this unique movement being provided elsewhere (see p. 43). Signal blessing continued into the spring and summer of 1859, but it was upon Radcliffe's return to Aberdeen in the autumn of 1859 that the revival entered a second period of intense activity. Crowded meetings were held for several months in the newly opened Music Hall which was able to accommodate up to three thousand people. The meetings were held each Sabbath evening, and the first gathering, addressed by Radcliffe, attracted 9,000 people, only a third of whom were able to gain admittance. During these months, according to Professor Cowan of Aberdeen University,

---

67. Rowan Strong, *Episcopalianism in Nineteenth Century Scotland*, Oxford, 2002, pp. 59-60.

68. ibid., pp. 61-2. Strong also notes other reasons for the decline in the Episcopal Church among north-east fishing communities in the mid-nineteenth century, such as the denomination's inability to supply local clergy, resulting in considerable defection to more stable churches, such as the Church of Scotland.

writing in 1910: 'the whole community seemed to feel the influence at work ... a feeling of solemnity seemed to pervade the life of the city'.[69]

In November 1859 Charles G. Finney, on his second visit to the United Kingdom, came to Aberdeen at the invitation of the Rev. Ferguson of the Evangelical Union Church in St Paul Street. Finney reported that after initial apathy and discouragement, 'a very interesting change was manifestly coming over his congregation and over that city'.[70] Thirty-four additions to membership were made in Ferguson's Church in 1859 (which may not have included the majority of converts from Finney's visit), and eighteen in 1860, compared to twenty-one and seventeen in 1857 and 1858 respectively.

The revival in Aberdeen appears to have entered another quiet period through the first three months of 1860, during which time it was raging uncontrollably along the Moray Firth. However, a third season of revival activity came into being towards the end of the summer of that year, when a two-day conference held at Huntly in July had the effect of injecting the work with a fresh impetus. George Campbell, minister of the Free North Church, reported in October how, 'in the past six or seven weeks in Aberdeen we have seen a work of more power than we saw before. Since the Huntly meetings there seems to have been a new impulse given to the work. ... The Spirit of the Lord seemed to come down upon the people as he had not come before.'[71]

By the end of 1860, however, the fervour of the revival was beginning to abate once again. In May 1861, the *Aberdeen Free Press* reported the occurrence of only a 'few special religious services. These consisted of a series of nightly prayer meetings held in various places of worship, a week at a time in each church. Attendance at these varied depending on where they were held. Reginald Radcliffe, along with Richard Weaver, continued to conduct revival services during the summer of 1861 in Aberdeen. A Mr 'R. J.' spoke of 'very large' gatherings of people attending Sabbath evening open-airs on the Broadhill in August 1861, and it was through one of these that he was led to Christ. A coal-shed became his prayer closet, while, additionally, other 'outhouses, pattern-

69. ibid., p. 113.

70. Rosel and Dupois, p. 596.

71. Jeffrey, p. 58.

lofts, hillsides and sandpits were often afterwards antechambers of the King's Palace'. 'R. J.' spoke of 'almost indescribable persecution' at his workplace, especially from one who was a church member. Life became very busy for this and other keen converts, and during the winter it was not uncommon for them to address two, three, or even seven cottage meetings in one week.[72] By this time, however, the movement appears to have slowed down considerably. Although evangelists continued to visit the city and meetings were arranged until 1864, the dramatic scenes of revival had disappeared. Revival in Aberdeen had ebbed and flowed in various phases over the course of two-and-a-half years.[73]

South Aberdeenshire Villages

Footdee

The North-East Coast Mission was founded in 1858 by Thomas Rosie, an Orcadian, who had been responsible for other similar missions in the south of Scotland and who went on to found a seaman's mission in Bombay. Donald Ross became the Mission's first secretary and superintendent. He, along with around twenty assistant missioners, was responsible for the stretch of coast between Ferryden and Thurso. He was described by one commentator as 'strict and rigid in doctrine, blunt and fearless in expression'.[74]

In the mid-nineteenth century Footdee was a fishing village situated at the east of Aberdeen harbour, quite distinct from the city proper. When Ross preached in the squares of Footdee in 1859 and for at least once a fortnight for the whole of 1860, this fishing community was said to have been hearing the gospel for 'almost the first time in its history'. Ross saw little fruit from his labours however, so he began to pray for a storm, so that the fishermen would be kept at home! Towards the end of January 1861 the storm came. Tragically, its ferocity led to

---

72. Matthews, pp. 85-6.

73. One lasting fruit of revival in the city was the Seabank care-home, which was started in Diamond Street.

74. Morgan, *The Villages of Aberdeen: Footdee and her Shipyards*, Aberdeen, 1993, p. 73. A native of Alness, Ross-shire, Ross grew up in a pious home, his family 'coming out' at the Disruption. He served for a short time with the Free Church in Newmains, Lanarkshire, before taking over as leader of the North-East Coast Mission.

the capsizing of a boat, drowning four Footdee fishermen and leaving fifteen children orphaned. 'The scene on the pier at the time', reported the *Aberdeen Journal*, 'where the whole community of Footdee was congregated, was indeed heart rending to witness.'[75] Ironically, the tragedy was to act as a stimulus for the much-prayed-for awakening which followed.

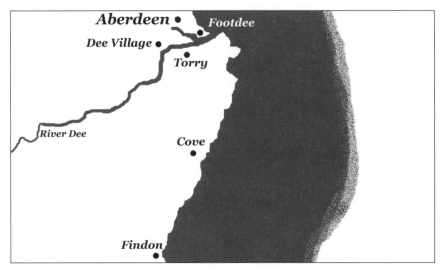

Wilson Summers, a sea captain and an earnest Christian, along with some of his crew came to help Ross with meetings in the Footdee hall. By the third night between two and three hundred were gathered. Even the rafters were occupied. One man testified, 'The windows of heavens soon opened in blessing; the village was inundated; and the Spirit of God brooded over the face of the waters.' Another recorded: 'Men and women who were addicted to drink were converted; cursing and swearing were exchanged for prayer and hymn singing. The whole place became a veritable garden of the Lord.' Around a tenth of the community's population was said to have been converted, and Ross 'nourished these, his children in faith with a jealous care'.[76] One of these 'children' was David Fowler, later a leader in the Brethren, who was said to have been saved chiefly through hearing his brother, with tears streaming down his cheeks, praying for him in public.

---

75. *Aberdeen Journal*, 01/02/1860, quoted in Jeffrey, p. 185.

76. Diane Morgan, *The Villages of Aberdeen: Footdee and her Shipyards*, Aberdeen, 1993, p. 73; Ross, pp. 126-7.

Dee Village

One revival convert spoke of an 'extraordinary meeting' at Dee Village, just south of Footdee, where a Young Men's Christian Association had recently been formed. The schoolhouse was packed, and even before the Rev. J. C. MacPhail gave out the text of his sermon, 'the entire meeting broke down. The sound of weeping and sobbing was so loud that no ordinary speaking could have been heard … the feeling of solemnity was almost overpowering; for the realisation of the presence of the Spirit of God was such as to overawe us so much, that we did not dare to speak except in whispers as we tried to point those in agony of soul to the Saviour. You could no more have doubted the presence of the Spirit of God than you could have doubted your own existence.'[77]

Torry

The revival also extended across the Dee estuary, to the community of Torry. Alexander Whyte, then a student at Aberdeen University, said, 'It was the revival atmosphere that kept some of us alive in those days. Many were the Sabbath evenings that I (and others) went over to the fishing village (as it then was) of Torry. We had splendid evenings with the fishermen.' Whyte spoke of the unique 'mystical depth and spirituality of life' which 'thoroughly converted' fishermen revealed. 'We refreshed our souls in Torry, and came back again strengthened for the next week's work.'[78]

These young men also testified that 'on Sabbath, when the bells were ringing for church, only two were seen to leave the village and they did not seem to be going to church. That was enough; visits were made, and never-to-be-forgotten meetings held. On weeknights, if a storm was blowing, some of the lads went down to the village, and the sound of the little bell soon filled the hall with an earnest audience.' In the summer, these same lads regularly visited the fishing villages along the coast to Stonehaven, and 'good fruits resulted'.[79]

---

77. Matthews, pp. 89-90.

78. Barbour, pp. 90-1.

79. Matthews, pp. 60-1. Colonel Ramsay of Banchory and Duncan Matheson came often to Stonehaven, where, as a young boy, W. S. Bruce heard the latter give illuminating addresses to the young from the steps of the Court House door. 'It needs high spiritual instincts to reach the standard of the Good, the True and the Beautiful', Bruce wrote. 'But the fishermen at the harbour as well as Duncan Matheson found it possible to climb to it; and we boys did our best to follow' (Matthews, pp. 4-5).

Meanwhile, the Rev. Davidson of Saltcoats, on his way home from a visit to Aberdeenshire in the summer of 1861, preached in an unnamed fishing village in the county. The menfolk were all at the herring fishing, so of the over two hundred who attended almost the entirety were women, many of whom professed awakening and conversion.[80]

Cove and Findon

Some Footdee converts became earnest evangelists. Others travelled much with Ross – and his small pony – to such southern fishing villages as Burnbanks, Portlethen, Cove and Findon. In the latter two places, significant spiritual blessing was experienced, similar in intensity to that felt in Footdee. Indeed, the revival that broke out in Cove, in particular, was described as being 'very memorable'. The women 'sang the songs of Zion with rare feeling', often to worldly tunes. A much-respected elder, accompanied by his daughter, used to walk every Sabbath afternoon from Aberdeen to the village, where he was in the habit of holding meetings. The daughter, on her eighteenth birthday, entered a church she hadn't been to before, and heard the text, 'Ought not this woman, whom Satan hath bound lo these eighteen years, be loosed from her bonds on the Sabbath day?' 'The fetters fell, a brief but happy life and an abundant entrance gave testimony to redeeming love.'[81]

This example was followed by young men whose meetings were greatly blessed. On one occasion, in a fisherman's house, the whole gathering broke down and many were deeply moved. The place became too strait, and of their savings they bought wood, and erected a meeting house in which to worship. There 'the blessing God commands – life that shall never end', came to many.[82]

By 1861, reported one authority in the village, 'with the exception of the ship-pilots, who remain what they were, if not worse – there is a great change. I do not suppose there has been a single bottle of whisky drunk this year at the launching of their boats – while there used to

---

Though it did receive 'some droppings' of blessing during the 'Moody revival' of 1873–74, Stonehaven was long 'regarded as hopelessly dead in spiritual matters' (*TB*, 24/09/1874, p. 378), and did not feature prominently in the 1859–61 movement.

80. *SG*, 17/08/1861.

81. Ross, pp. 127-8; *WJ*, 19/10/1861, p. 23.

82. ibid.

be a whole fortnight of drinking and fighting. There was not formerly a single family that had family worship, but now there is not a single family except those of the pilots that have it not.'[83]

Awakenings in Unnamed Districts

Several striking occasions of spiritual awakening occurred in Aberdeen-shire districts, where, frustratingly, the exact location is not revealed. The Free Church congregation of 'P' experienced a 'wonderful outpouring of the Spirit and a great awakening and ingathering into the kingdom'. The minister began to take an interest in what was then called 'dark D', and sent ministers and evangelists to visit the place. One of the first to come was the Rev. Donald Grant. On his arrival, and in order to get to his meeting place, Grant had to walk past a large barn in which a dance was being held. He entered the barn and asked to say a few words, but this was refused and he was ordered out. 'But before doing so, he held up his hands, his pale face beaming with a heavenly smile, and said "One thing is needful – the salvation of the soul", and further, with awful solemnity he added: "Oh, how dreadful to see you all dancing to hell!". Some were pierced with conviction on the spot, and from that night the movement began to spread throughout the parish, bringing a large number under the power of the gospel.'[84]

One convert spoke of great antipathy to the revival within his home, and following his conversion his father ordered him to give up religion or to get out. At once the lad chose the latter option, a step which indirectly led to his studying for the ministry. He later said, 'We could not meet for prayer in any of our own homes, but night after night, during the dark autumn evenings, some twenty young lads met in a wood, under a large beech tree, and there poured out our hearts in prayer and song.'[85]

The Rev. John Robertson related the story of a young woman who lived with her mother and sister in an Aberdeenshire village. Having been recently converted, this woman enthusiastically moved from house to house pleading with people to open their hearts to Jesus. Her mother and sister, ashamed of such enthusiasm, deduced that the girl was mad,

---

83. ibid.

84. Matthews, pp. 139-40.

85. ibid.

and called not only the local village doctor but also the physician of a neighbouring village. After consultation, both expressed the same opinion and signed a paper for her to be admitted to a lunatic asylum! The night before her scheduled incarceration, both mother and sister began to have second thoughts, and started to wonder whether it was Mary who was mad or themselves! Her referral to the asylum was dismissed. Sometime later, Brownlow North had tea, not just with members of this family, but with the relatives on both sides – twenty-three in all – each of whom, through Mary's pleading, had been led to Christ.[86]

Meanwhile, elsewhere in Aberdeenshire, it was reported that in one strath, ten miles long, there was not a house in which there was not someone awakened, and there was believed to be not a family in the villages scattered over that district in which the worship of God was not established.[87]

---

86. Johnson, pp. 235-6.

87. *SG*, 09/12/1859.

Cullen

Portknockie

Findochty

James Turner

Portessie

Portgordon

Gardenstown

CHAPTER 12

Moray and Banffshire Coast

Introduction

Perhaps the most dramatic manifestation of the 1859–61 revival in Scotland was among the tight-knit fishing communities of the Moray and Banffshire Coast, a people-group generally unchurched and irreligious. Following the retelling of accounts of awakenings in America and Ireland by local ministers and visiting evangelists, a strong desire and expectancy for revival had been engendered among the people of these communities in the months before revival proper began. One source suggests that the first indications of a work of God along the north-east coast was as early as the spring of 1859, immediately after a sermon preached by the Rev. Mr Bain, Chapel of Garioch, in the Free Church of Rathven, from the words, 'My Spirit shall not always strive with man.'[1]

Revival along this stretch of coast seems to have appeared in several distinct waves. The first wave forcibly struck the shores of Cullen near the start of 1860, immediately spreading west, rocking each of the five nearest townships in its path – Portknockie, Findochty, Portessie, Buckie and Portgordon. A second stream emanated from Banff in March, flowing eastward to Macduff, Portsoy, Whitehills, Gardenstown and Crovie. A third pulse of revival appeared in the Moray town of Hopeman around the same time, diffusing westward to Burghead and

---

1. *WJ*, 19/10/61, p. 23. Novelist Neil Paterson wrote depreciatingly of north-east Scotland being 'devastated' by the 1859 revival, which 'swept like a tidal wave' over its villages, leaving in its wake 'a great sense of piety and moral exaltation, a form of insanity known as mania, and a sharp rise in the birth-rate' (*Behold Thy Daughter*, London, 1950, p. 139).

Findhorn, eastward to Lossiemouth, and inland to Elgin. In the closing months of 1861 a fourth wave of revival power struck Portgordon, also affecting Findochty, Portessie, Portknockie and Banff. The ministry of James Turner was directly influential in the appearance and spread of at least three of these potent spiritual currents.

Cullen

The Rev. John Mackay of Cullen insisted that it was in his town of ministry that the Moray-Banffshire work of revival began. 'It was at the usual weekly meeting conducted by myself, a few days after my return from Ireland, and after giving some account of the work there, that the first cry of soul-distress was heard.' That startling cry came from a young man, who since found his Saviour.[2] Then, 'early in 1860, the whole place was moved as by an earthquake. ... At first the awful shadow of an angry God coming to judgement fell on many, and it seemed as if there was one dead in every house. Awakening was followed by conversion. The thunder of Sinai gave way to the peaceful sunshine of Calvary.'[3] James Turner spoke here; so did Reginald Radcliffe. But the one most associated with the Cullen revival is Duncan Matheson, who preached frequently in both the Free and Independent churches. Nowhere, he repeatedly testified, 'did the work appear to him to be of a more solid and substantial character' than in this town.[4]

Matheson especially made his mark on the young men of the town. His biographer said of him:

> His broad, free, genial manners captivated their hearts; his talents, magnanimity and uprightness commanded their respect. Many of them were converted at this time; and it was pleasing to see the finest youths of the place sitting in a company round about their father in the faith, and receiving his counsels as from an angel of God. For the young men he had a peculiar love; they were his joy, and as his very life. ... In particular he ever urged upon them entire consecration. 'Be out and out for Christ', he would say, 'nail your colours to the mast, labour for God, and live for eternity' ... One of them is now an ordained missionary in China; another labours in Turkey, a third

2. *WJ*, 17/10/62, p. 20.

3. Macpherson, 1871, pp. 118-19.

4. *WJ*, 17/10/62, p. 20.

preaches the gospel at home, a fourth is preparing to take the field as a medical missionary, and others are occupying their talent in the quiet corners of the vineyard.[5]

James Jolly, converted in the village of Muirkirk in Forfarshire in the summer of 1860 through the ministry of Matheson, felt called, sometime later, to visit Cullen, the home town of two of his closest friends, James Simpson and William Duffus, who both later became ordained ministers. Simpson wrote of Jolly's visit to Cullen: 'God was pleased to give him a remarkable outpouring of the Holy Spirit. He had been praying much for this, but it came to him as a blessed surprise. He was addressing a meeting with a most painful sense of his own deadness and hardness of heart. Suddenly remarkable manifestations of God's presence and power began to appear in the audience. A great work of grace broke out, in which many professed to be brought to the Saviour.'[6]

Jolly returned to Cullen some months later to find many people mourning over the death of a young local fisherman, who had been brought back from the Stornoway fishing in a coffin. 'The whole Seatown was lying under an impression', wrote Jolly. As a sign of respect for the dead man, none of the boats went out to sea during his wake. Taking advantage of the opportunity, Jolly held an open-air meeting in the evening. 'Without exception', he noted, 'this was one of the most solemn meetings I ever was present at. I got liberty in speaking on the subject of death, judgement and eternity, and the people dispersed in a state of great anxiety.' Jolly held a number of further meetings in the town, to which the fishermen, attracted to him for his friendly, down-to-earth character, were drawn in large numbers. One memorable open-air service was conducted from the top of a brae, and another from inside the Public Hall, when 'many cried aloud and many more lifted up their hearts in silent prayer'.[7]

Portknockie

Further west along the Moray Firth coast, revival hit Portknockie and adjacent villages with the suddenness and force of a tropical

---

5. Macpherson, 1871, p. 121.

6. Adam, pp. 27-8.

7. ibid., pp. 29-32.

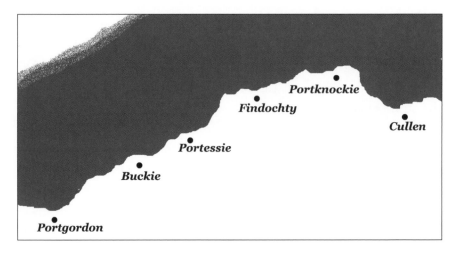

thunderstorm in February 1860, with the arrival of James Turner. Said one writer, employing another metaphor: 'The whole place was moved as by an earthquake. Fear took hold on the sinners of Zion; trembling seized the hypocrites.'[8] Thus began a dramatic wave of revival along the fishing villages of the Banff and Moray coast. Three men from Portknockie had been praying together for an outpouring of God's Spirit for three months when Turner arrived at the door of one of them and asked if he could hold a meeting. One of the trio, James Wilson, went through the village ringing a bell, announcing a meeting that night (4 February) in the hall, to which three hundred came. The following night, meetings were adjourned to the larger Free Church. Wrote Turner of the Sabbath-night meeting: 'The Holy Spirit came down with great power on the people. Strong young men were smitten down and became weak as water. This continued till morning, and many souls were saved. I went to bed for three hours. Called a meeting after breakfast and from 300 to 400 people met with me. The power of God came on man, woman and child, and many found the Saviour.'[9]

After-meetings for the anxious were held in 'Findlay's hoose', which was packed with distressed souls crying aloud for spiritual light on their burdened hearts. An unheard-of phenomenon, several cases of prostration engendered great alarm, and on the third night in particular,

---

8. Macpherson, 1871, p. 118.

9. ibid., p. 23. In Portknockie Turner formed a Temperance Society and above eight hundred signed the pledge, including the township's three whisky sellers.

'the people were falling like sheep a' round aboot'. Someone ran for Findlay, himself a recent convert, who had gone to a nearby house, and cried, 'Rin! Rin! Finla', for they are a' either deed or deeing in your hoose!'[10] Everyone in Finlay's home on that particular evening was more or less deeply affected.

Two people, in their state of prostration, had dramatic views of hell before being gloriously converted, while a third person, objecting strongly to the meeting, left in disgust, but before running many yards, fell prostrate in the snow – some two feet in depth. Someone came to speak with her and before leaving that spot, she too rejoiced in conscious salvation. Even Findlay himself looked scared by what was taking place all around him and in his own home. Turner, recognising his doubts, turned to him and said, 'My brother, you've been praying for the work of the Spirit of God, and now that it's come ye dinna believe it!'[11]

Indeed, many found peace that night, as had, by three in the morning, most of those remaining, and so the house was cleared. Instead of going home to bed, the new converts went to knock up friends and relatives to tell them the great things which God had done for them. When morning dawned the converts were going up and down the streets and lanes praising God. 'Portknockie had never such a sun-rising!', noted McHardie.[12]

Sadly, on a one-day, follow-up visit to Portknockie around the end of February, Turner did not find things as he wished. 'The dear people were not going back', he insisted, but neither were they 'attacking Satan's camp'. The evening meeting was stiff at first, but then 'the Lord sent the Holy Spirit down. What a night of power! Many cases of prostration and loud cries for mercy.' The meeting was kept up till around five o'clock the following morning.[13]

Meetings were held publicly and privately, all day and every day, as well as every evening, for six weeks, during which time no boat went out to sea. 'Yet though a people that had to work day-by-day for daily bread, they lacked nothing ... many interesting stories could be told of

10. McHardie, p. 90.

11. ibid., p. 91.

12. ibid., pp. 90-1.

13. ibid., p. 26.

how the barrel of meal never wasted, nor the cruse of oil failed, while these Pentecostal scenes continued. ... Not only houses', said one, 'but the very holes and caves in the rocks were full of people crying for mercy – even the very hen-houses were filled with the children in like condition.' Indeed, children 'could not be tired of praying and singing hymns'.[14]

One morning in the school, while devotional exercises were being conducted prior to the day's lessons, such was the ardour with which these were entered into that even there cases of striking down commenced, and spread rapidly. One man who was sent for reported that when he arrived the whole school was prostrated at one time – about twenty pupils.[15] The headmaster of the institution, Mr Fraser, was also deeply affected by events of these days, and at one meeting he received a vivid vision of angels in heaven playing their harps before the Throne. Being musically inclined, the beauty of the music he heard fascinated him, and he put out his hands as if taking hold of a harp, working his fingers up and down as if drawing forth its sweet sounds.

One of the three original praying men of the village had been converted as early as 1844, but had lived in and out of sin until the year prior to the commencement of revival, when he and his two colleagues began meeting together to pray in earnest. But even after Turner's momentous visit, this man continued to entertain doubts. He went into a cave by the shore to pray the matter through, determining he would not leave till he knew his salvation was a reality. In these dark, musty surroundings, he experienced a profound vision which served to completely remove his doubts. 'For four years after', he later wrote, 'I scarcely ever ceased, when awake, to leap for joy and praise God.'[16] .

A report was issued against the Free Church missionary at Portknockie, Mr Manson, by two Presbytery ministers who had gone to witness the revival in the village. The charge was that Manson had shown a lack of sympathy towards the movement. In his defence Manson made a long statement in which he asserted that he only vindicated the forms of worship authorised by the Free Church and resisted innovations that

---

14. ibid., pp. 90-1.

15. *The Banffshire Journal*, 28/02/1860, quoted in McHardie, p. 91.

16. McHardie, p. 104.

led, if anywhere, to Methodism. After a good deal of discussion it was resolved to proceed no further with the charges.

Findochty

Expectations ran high with reports from Turner's mission all along the coast, and in Findochty and Portknockie in particular this flaming evangelist found that 'not only has the spirit of God been preparing me to go round the coast, but has also been preparing the people for me'. When Elizabeth McHardie visited Findochty a decade later, she was able to record the testimonies of hundreds of local fisherfolk who had remarkable stories to tell of the 1860 revival and later movements in their community – merely a tithe, she noted, of what could have been gathered from among them.[17]

Turner arrived in Findochty on 7 February and as he opened the first meeting in prayer, a woman cried out for mercy. In a short time nearly all present were doing the same. 'My voice was completely drowned', Turner wrote. 'I never saw such a scene in all my life. I question if some of the dear people could have cried louder though they had been in hell. ... This scene continued for four hours, and to this date – Tuesday February 7th 1860 – a great number of the inhabitants of Findochty date their conversion.' Another meeting was arranged for 9 a.m. the following morning. Joseph Flett's rhythmic means of describing this memorable event was: 'The cries of the lost ones / The yells of despair / And loud hallelujahs / All met in the air!' A man who had loudly boasted before going in that no power would make him cry out was heard above everyone else shouting, 'I'm a whited wall. I have nothing to cover me but leaves!'[18]

By this time a deep solemnity had pervaded the whole village, and there was barely a single individual in it but manifested tokens of concern. 'Even the cooking of victuals is much neglected', noted one. One woman came under such conviction through Turner's visit that she felt she must have committed the unpardonable sin. No one could comfort her, so, thinking she was mad, a doctor was called. But despite a charge of nearly five pounds for treatment, there was no change in her condition. A very strong impression came to her, 'A doctor cannot deliver you, my Son hath died', and shortly after, upon hearing Turner

17. ibid., p. 117.
18. ibid., pp. 23, 118-19.

a second time, she came through to a place of profound peace, as too did all of her family bar one.[19]

While in a state of prostration a girl received an impression to tell the minister of the United Presbyterian Church to preach a sermon on 'The Lord is my keeper'. The message was duly delivered, as in turn was the sermon – and with great unction, so much so that the minister had to ask some people afterwards whether he had spoken the truth, and in a coherent manner, for he had been under such an extraordinary influence that he hardly knew![20]

A fisherman who was a professing Christian came under such conviction when a crew-member insisted he wasn't yet a true believer that he considered throwing himself overboard. Instead, he dropped into his bunk and had a vivid, detailed dream about a boat with a white sail. The next day he saw that very same boat as they sailed into the village harbour. He found the crew of this boat to be all Christians and imbued with a revival spirit. Soon after, truth flashed upon his spirit's eye and he became a new man in Christ. Speaking years later he could still say, 'though all the men in the world were to try to shake my faith in that foundation that I know to be laid in Zion, they could not do it'.[21]

One man converted during Turner's first meetings in Findochty claimed to have been so filled with the Spirit of God that he fell unconscious for twelve days on end, to the extent that he 'could not tell whether in the body or out of the body'. When at the herring fishing at Fraserburgh, a fisher-girl from Findochty found herself returning again and again to the nightly meetings being held there. One night she was so distressed she stayed out in the fields praying till four in the morning. She remained under deep conviction for four more months, before the light suddenly dawned on her following Turner's visit to the village. Although she owned a Bible, she felt utterly ashamed that she could not read it. Sorely tempted by the enemy one night that she was still unconverted, the girl opened her Bible at random and decided that if she could read the verse her finger rested on she would never doubt her salvation again. The Bible opened at Psalm 103, and she found that

19. *SG*, 16/02/1860; McHardie, pp. 120-1.

20. ibid., p. 121.

21. ibid., pp. 122-4.

not only could she read the verse immediately before her, but the next verse and the next, right to the end of the Psalm. Further, the truths of these verses brought her much encouragement and she felt the presence of the Lord so strongly that it was 'just as if He was in the house beside me. ... An' someway or ither', she said, 'everything appeared to be new; every little picture on the wall; everything in the house seemed to be that lovely. I went out to the door, and the very sea, and the rocks, appeared to be quite different, and I just praised the Lord, for I was that happy I didna ken what to dee.' [22]

Some local fishermen expressed great disappointment at not being able to attend Turner's meetings, as they needed to take advantage of the good weather and go out with their boats. Turner quietly responded that there was a work to do in the village and that no boat would go out from Findochty that day – this despite the fact that throughout the morning there appeared no sign whatsoever that the day would remain anything but fine. Yet, sure enough, by two in the afternoon the sea and wind were in such a state that no boat could venture out. Thus it was that for a whole fortnight the fishermen were free for the Lord's service. [23]

On meeting a young mother with her baby, Turner asked pointedly whether she could give up that child for God. It took some time and encouragement before at last the woman replied in the affirmative, whereupon Turner dedicated the child to the Lord. That boy 'grew up a remarkable child; it seemed as if from that time the Lord had taken possession of him by His Spirit ... prayer was preferred to play', and he longed to be told about heaven, to which 'bonny place' his soul departed at a tender age. [24]

It was said that 'at Findochty ... with but few exceptions, the whole village may be said to have found the truth'. [25] Interestingly we're informed that immediately following Turner's visit, and perhaps somewhat alarmed at the excitement created by the Peterhead cooper, several experienced Free Church ministers, notably, Robert Shanks

---

22. ibid., pp. 127-30.
23. ibid., p. 134.
24. ibid., p. 135.
25. MacGill, p. 11.

from Buckie, the Rev. Williamson, Huntly and the Rev. Bain, Chapel of Garioch, came to conduct meetings in Findochty, 'soothing the poor people', and having the effect of 'very much allaying the excitement'.[26]

The Findochty converts immediately became conspicuous for their holy zeal. 'In them burned a fire restless to seize upon everything that came within its reach. This they carried with them wherever they went, and set hearts all around them in a blaze. If they crossed the sea it went with them. If in the prosecution of their calling in other villages, towns, or even crowded cities, still it went with them and made them burning and shining lights.' Indeed, through Turner's instrumentality, a work of God, such as had rarely taken place anywhere, was brought about in Findochty, and in no place that he visited was the work said to have been of a more abiding and permanent nature. [27]

Portessie

There being no church or hall in the village to gather in, Turner's meetings in Portessie were held in an unfinished house, consisting of walls and a roof but no doors or windows. Planks were set out to seat folk, and the more fit climbed up onto the rafters. But many more stood outside in the deep snow, with a biting wind coming in from the ocean, just yards from the house – it being a season of unusual severity. While most men were out at sea, it was felt that 'not one man, woman or child left in the village was wanting' from the meetings held here.[28] A meeting which commenced on Friday evening at six o'clock lasted till four o'clock the following morning, and was resumed at 10 a.m.

One elder, having been in deep anxiety for three days, 'was born again on the mighty deep. The whole boat's crew sat around me', he said 'and when the change passed, I began to pray. And the prayer-meeting went round from ten o'clock a.m., until six in the morning, and before that time three of them gave evidence of being born to God.' It was said that 'prayers, praise, cries and groans' could be heard throughout the night during the movement.[29]

---

26. David R. Rose, *The Great Revival of 1859: The Happenings Along the Moray Coast*, Aviemore, n.d., p. 6.

27. McHardie, p. 115; Robbie, pp. 58-61.

28. *SG*, 21/02/1860.

29. McHardie, pp. 143-4.

A woman who came under such soul distress that she would leave her young child at home to go and hear Turner speak, found liberty one night after resisting an impression of evil that assaulted her in bed. Overjoyed, she ran to the meeting place with nothing on but her night gown, marched right up to the pulpit and exclaimed, 'Rise, all of you and praise the Lord for saving me!' The whole house rose in a spirit of praise, after which the ecstatic woman, having donned more suitable clothing, went to virtually every house in Portessie 'tellin'' them what the Lord had done for my soul; especially did I go to those who had any grudge at me, or me at them, and to all sects and parties I went alike. And from this arose a new stirrin' up, and many were led to go to the meetin's.'[30]

An elder and Sabbath-school teacher, fully aware he was unconverted, followed a young man from Findochty out of a meeting, who was on his way to tell his parents of his recent conversion. 'He was just running along by the side of the houses like a bird, and as I looked at him a shaking came over me, I could not understand the meaning of it. When I turned round to make for the house, my sight went away, I thought the rocks were split right open to swallow me up; and I made a tremendous leap over the chasm to get into the house.' He later made it to the home of this man's parents, only to find the son singing at the top of his voice, 'I'm not ashamed to own my Lord; Nor to defend his cause. ... His parents were wringing their hands. When I went in, my burden fell off', said the elder, 'and down at once I went on my knees and began to pray for his parents. The house filled in a trice, and there was a great power of the Spirit.' Like so many other converts, overjoyed at their new-found salvation, this man, on his way home, went into the houses of all those he knew to be as yet unconverted, and warned them of their careless living. Arriving home, the elder found his little daughter, 'a girl of fourteen, preaching, and the house full about her. The ablest men in the place were trying to confute her, but in vain ...'[31]

Fishermen returning home from the west coast were astonished to find the town turned upside down – drunkards having become praying men, and men who had formerly spoken for Satan, now speaking for God. They

---

30. ibid., p. 144.

31. ibid., pp. 146-7. A day or two later this elder's son was converted, as was his wife on Turner's second visit to Portessie some months later.

never had such a welcome, for when the boats came in sight, the whole town turned out to welcome them in with the hymns. At one particularly powerful meeting, 'Old John Macintosh' stood up and cried, 'You that are against the work, come and see if this be chloroform', for whenever James Turner began to speak they 'tumbled down like sheep round about him, and all through the meeting'.[32] The reference to chloroform arose owing to the inability to adequately explain how the prostrations occurred; hence a rumour spread along the coast that they were brought about by chloroform poured onto a napkin, which Turner kept in his pocket, and with which he secretly infected the anxious when he prayed for them or walked past them, by blowing the handkerchief across their faces.

One fisherman testified that as a result of the revival, 'about fifty of the men were so full of faith, and had such clear minds and simple hearts, that for about four years, with them it was only to ask and receive – even three of them were sufficient to obtain the blessing. Three of them have sometimes gone to a corner of the hall where the worst people were, and have had the house filled with power.'[33]

A converted man, deeply concerned that his wife remained in darkness of soul, returned home from a meeting around midnight, and urged her to yet go to the meeting hall, while he stayed home and prayed for her. She went, and he prayed earnestly, retiring to bed at two in the morning. His wife returned home four hours later, a new creature in Christ. Unable to keep the good news to herself, the wife obtained a horn, and with a friend went through the village for seven days in a row, sounding it forth and announcing a meeting in her home.

One woman, annoyed at hearing Turner witness to her son, told him in no uncertain terms to leave him alone as he had been a Christian since birth. Unable to remonstrate with her, Turner boldly informed her that she was a Pharisee. The words stung her sharply, but she went to the meeting that night, confessed that it was indeed so, and both she and her son gave their lives to the Lord. Wonderfully, four other members of this family were brought in shortly after, but tragically all were lost when a Portessie boat was sunk soon afterwards. In the same boat was another young man and his father, both converts of the

---

32. McHardie, p. 153.

33. ibid., p. 156.

revival, and another man who, along with his wife, had also received saving grace through Turner's ministry. Two of the drowned men had in fact been due to be married on the very day their boat went down.

The revival was seen as a truly spontaneous movement, which no one but the villagers themselves had guided. It was estimated that one sixth of the entire population of this town – around 150 people – turned to the Lord during this movement, many of whom joined the United Presbyterian Kirk.

Buckie

Turner arrived in Buckie on Sunday, 12 February and preached in the Free Church the following evening to well over a thousand people. A number of Portessie people placed themselves in the seats occupied by the choir with the view of leading the congregation in the singing of revival hymns that had proved popular in their own community. When Turner led in the singing of one of those hymns, the Free Church minister, Robert Shanks, objected, remarking that no one could pen anything as good as the Psalms.

Then there followed the early occurrence of several prostrations, raising such a tumult among the multitude assembled, both within and without the building, that Turner lost all control over the audience. Appalled at these scenes, Shanks ignored a deacon's remonstrations and called for a constable to close the meeting. Before he could arrive, Turner closed the meeting himself and adjourned to the brand-new United Presbyterian Hall Indeed such had been the commotion in the Buckie Free Church that its leaders never opened their doors to Turner again. Turner was made most welcome in the United Presbyterian Church, and meetings, over several nights, were 'blessed in a very remarkable manner'.[34]

One local minister, the Rev. McGill, in an attempt to describe the effects of the revival in Buckie, recalled

> … a series of scenes which it is impossible to narrate, and which, for those who witnessed them, shall never be forgotten. Men and women of every age and character of mind were affected in a manner that, in recalling the past, to many seems now entirely unreal. Tears, tremblings, groans, loud outcries for mercy and failings of bodily strength were all witnessed at one and the same time among those who constituted that

---

34. Robbie, pp. 64-5.

large assembly. Night after night, for upwards of ten days, such manifestations were witnessed and although now these physical effects have very much subsided, still we cannot look upon that congregation without observing visible traces of the awful ordeal through which it has passed.[35]

A feature of the Buckie movement was the public confession of sins by both men and women – 'confessions so awful', wrote one, 'that it would be an unpardonable breach of the rules of morality and common decency to repeat them' – but which included fornication, adultery and even an instance of murder.[36]

A native of the town wrote of events: 'The people have almost to be forced away from the meetings … they would remain day and night, if allowed; and I believe that a good many who have been here for some days from villages to the east of this, have taken but little food since they came. … I have tried to judge of this movement as calmly as possible, and one of its most important features is that almost every individual in this place, both young and old, has been brought under concern about their soul's everlasting welfare.'[37]

When one Buckie woman obtained spiritual peace after seeking Christ, she somewhat tactlessly turned to her yet unconverted friend and said, 'I've naethig adee wi' ye noo. … I must join my ain company', and she left her friend weeping for her sins.[38] Four young Buckie men, anxious for their souls, went to speak with Turner privately. Dropping to his knees to pray for them, Turner soon appeared to receive assurance that his entreaty was answered, for he turned to the men and stated his belief that by noon that day the soul of each would be at liberty. They all went to the morning meeting, and sure enough, before it had ended, Christ had revealed Himself to each individual, and all four went home rejoicing.

No record exists of Turner's own impressions of his initial meetings in Buckie, but on paying a brief second visit to the town two or three weeks after the first, he expressed disappointment that he needed to

---

35. *SG*, 29/03/1860.

36. Rose, p. 8. Some who knew these people well, however, insisted that some of the sins confessed, coming from those in an excited state of mind, had no basis in fact.

37. McHardie, p. 24.

38. ibid., p. 189.

reignite the cooling fires. Yet he was able to say before he left, 'A great work of God is getting on there.'[39] This work continued against huge opposition – more formidable than at any other point in all his labours. Yet in time this was fully overcome. At some meetings as many as sixty anxious souls could be found in the vestry weeping and crying for mercy.

A number of church leaders received much blessing at Turner's meetings in Buckie. The Rev. William Barras of the United Presbyterian Church said he got more good in just one meeting than he did during years spent at theological college.[40] Another U.P. minister 'came to Buckie for James Turner and took him away in a gig, and on the road that cleric was brought to the saving knowledge of the truth.'[41]

Perhaps the most notable of all Turner's converts was James Riach. He went on to become a fearless and most useful evangelist all over the north coast of Scotland. The Rev. Green, a later minister in Buckie's U.P. Church, called him 'one of the most Christ-like men, in humble life I have ever been privileged to know. What the late Robert Murray McCheyne was among ministers, James Riach was among the fishermen of our Scottish North-East Coast.'[42]

It was said of the four contiguous villages, Portknockie, Findochty, Portessie and Buckie that by the end of summer, 1860, 'not less than a thousand have undergone a radical change'.[43] Three young men belonging to one congregation, and converted in the revival, gave themselves to the service of the Lord and immediately entered into study for the ministry. The membership of that same congregation was trebled, and the Sabbath school rose from fifty to five hundred, while there also arose a movement for raising money for missions, as a memorial of the revival.

---

39. ibid., p. 26.

40. However, this minister was said to have soon after turned against Turner and his fervent evangelistic approach. He even 'interdicted the young men from preaching as they used to do'. It wasn't long before he gave in his resignation, to the great delight of many of Turner's Buckie converts (McHardie, p. 191).

41. ibid., p. 190. Mr Mangles, the Wesleyan minister in Portessie said he 'learned more among the white caps and blue jackets than ever he had learned during his course of preparation for the ministry' (ibid.).

42. McHardie, pp. 199-201.

43. MacGill, p. 11.

Portgordon

Around 1850, a native of the village had predicted that 'the Lord would send an ambassador to Portgordon, who would turn it upside down ... the angels were wanting to pour out wrath, but Jesus was pleading to have patience with it until He sent the ambassador.' This came a decade later in the form of James Turner, who was invited to the place by an aged woman with whom James' brother, George, had lodged previously. Many in the community had already heard the good news, being constrained to go and hear Turner in nearby Buckie. Even prior to his arrival in Buckie and Portgordon, the evangelist was given assurance through prayer that 'the Master is to deliver them into my hand'. On his arrival in the latter village on 17 February, he noted, 'I have faith for this place.'[44]

After an uneventful first meeting, Turner spent almost the whole of the next night wrestling in prayer. At breakfast he announced, 'The King will be here in His beauty tonight, and the Spirit of God will prowl through every corner of Portgordon.' It turned out, noted his host, just as he said, 'The whole town that night seemed to get a special call.'[45]

Most meetings were held in a 'none-too-sizeable' room in the school, commencing around four or five in the afternoon and closing at anything from one to four the following morning. At one meeting, which was described in detail by a local correspondent, as the people gathered, Turner led around sixteen boys in the singing of hymns – 'all in knots of three, four and five, and in the centre of each a well-worn hymn-book, which they clustered around, and from which they were singing at the top of their voices, and with much greater rapidity than regularity.' The room soon 'got heated almost to suffocation', and in this state the meeting was kept up for nine and a half hours, many

---

44. McHardie, pp. 213, 223, 225. One who met Turner in Portgordon described him as 'a man of small stature, some five feet six, and proportionately slender, wrapt in a dark grey top coat of the sack fashion, his neck protected by a dark woollen cravat; with dark brown hair, carefully combed, and in his very regular features nothing which could strike one as likely to convey the impression of any particular ability. They indicate at first a fairly balanced, rather than a vigorous mind, but on coming into closer contact, an excitable, dreamy temperament becomes manifest (*Banffshire Journal*, quoted in Rose, p. 8).

45. McHardie, pp. 210-1.

people remaining there for the entire duration without food or drink, including several young women with babies at their breast.[46]

One Portgordon lass, intrigued to hear of the man who was 'pardoning folk's sins', made her way to Buckie, returning eight nights in succession to the meetings there. During all that time she testified that she 'scarcely either ate or slept' until she came to peace in Christ. Another testified that 'the bitterness which a man feels for the loss of his first-born was nothing to the bitterness with which I was made to weep for my sins'. One twelve-year-old boy 'got the blessing' after being sent to a meeting by his believing mother, although it was only with repeated visits to the meetings that the boy became established in the faith. Soon he was witnessing publicly for the Lord and helping run the meetings after Turner's departure, while he also began a young men's meeting, through which much good was done.[47]

Prior to Turner's visit several Portgordon natives, having attended his meetings in Buckie, called along an old man in their village, who everyone took to be a Christian, but who was completely unable to help them and who in fact was under as deep conviction as they were. The man continued in this condition for over six weeks, until he became affected physically, and grew quite ill. The doctor was unable to help and the man was left to die. But following a vivid dream in which he was powerfully spoken to, the invalid was at once restored to full health and soon he also found spiritual healing through a work of grace accomplished in his soul. But although now free in Christ, the man felt unable to witness for his master because he had financial debts. He prayed earnestly into this matter one day at sea, asking the Lord to take his burden. To the man's utter amazement, 'In about fifteen minutes my nets were full. My hair almost stood on end. That night my debts were paid, and since that time, by His grace, I have stood in the forefront of the Lord's battle.'[48]

At least one public house in Portgordon closed down as a result of the Spirit's dealings with its landlord. However, another publican refused to hear Turner when the evangelist paid him a visit, so Turner warned him faithfully before shaking the dust off his feet. In a short time the

46. Rose, p. 8; *SG*, 01/03/1860.

47. McHardie, pp. 210, 221-3

48. ibid., pp. 225-6.

publican and his family were turned out of their lodgings and the man died in despair, while his wife, years after, continued to be bitter at anything Christian.

Banff

Fifteen miles further east along the coast, towards the end of 1858, four godly lads from Banff began to meet in a nearby wood after work, where they would plead in prayer for a youth of similar age until that lad too joined their ranks, which he invariably did. By intertwining branches of adjoining trees, the youths constructed a comfortable booth in which they continued to pour out their souls, until, in October 1859, early storms drove them from this hallowed Bethel to more sheltered confines. During the winter months, their numbers increased to about forty, most of them still being without peace of soul.[49]

With the arrival of Turner in Banff on 5 March 1860, what was regarded as a second wave of revival began. A climax was reached on the fifth night of his eight-day mission, which meeting lasted from 7 p.m. till 6 the next morning. One man described that Saturday night as 'a night never to be forgotten. It seemed as if there was a pitched battle between the powers of light and darkness. Up till nearly 12 o'clock it was something awful. A clog hung on the meeting. ... The battle was won about midnight – then came a glorious morning when victory was declared on the Lord's side.'[50]

Eight or nine young men in their late teens prayed in succession; the prayers of two of them being accompanied by 'an elevation of sentiment and feeling that seemed to border on ecstasy'.[51] One man said of the meeting, 'It was just like a field of battle after victory, and many were the slain of the Lord upon it. I am sure from twenty to thirty were to be found lying all at one time completely prostrate, and by the time that these arose like men from the dead, the same mysterious power had as many more

---

49. James Stark, *John Murker of Banff; A Picture of Religious Life and Character in the North*, London, 1887, pp. 146-7.

50. McHardie, pp. 73-4. One eyewitness of these events fifteen years later remarked: 'Not a few are there alive, scattered abroad as evangelists throughout the world, who can look back with joy and gratitude and date their conversion to God from that time' (William Henry Harding, *James Turner*, London, 1912, p. 8).

51. Rose, p. 16.

levelled to the dust in like manner. Thus it became utterly impossible to clear the meeting until six o'clock in the morning.' Out of the seven hundred assembled, at least one hundred were thought to have been brought to Christ on that momentous occasion, and, noted one fifteen years later, 'I scarcely have heard of any belying their profession.'[52] In all, from two to three hundred were alleged to have been converted through Turner's ministry in Banff, though some believed this estimate too low.

Other meetings were equally noteworthy. At a prayer meeting held in the Free Church, 'a boy of seventeen or eighteen prayed most fervently for the conversion of his brother, who was in a distant part of Scotland. There was simplicity, a beauty and a pathos about the prayer really affecting. At its close scarcely a dry cheek was to be seen, although the church was crowded.' The Free Church minister, the Rev. John Murker, decided to investigate the matter, and found that 'in the very same hour that the prayer was offered in Banff, the brother, then more than two hundred miles away, was brought to a sight and sense of his sinfulness, and led to consecrate himself to the Lord.'[53]

Another striking case was when several young men, the worse for drink, started to disrupt a revival meeting in the United Presbyterian Church, and though quietly admonished, would not stop. At once the Rev. Murker called to all present, 'Mark these men and see what their end will be.' He then spoke of a young man who opposed the work at a village some miles away from Banff, and who, three days after, came to an untimely end. At another village he visited, two young men raised a disturbance, and within a week both men were laid in the grave. It was said that none of these Banff men, with one exception, was alive at the end of the year, although at the time of meeting they were in the prime of manhood and apparently in perfect health.

A similar incident involved six or seven men who regularly attended the meetings, choosing to stand about the passages or lean against the pillars instead of taking seats. A climax was reached when one of them, a doctor, knelt down and pretended to cry out for mercy. Turner immediately discerned the mockery and warned them before all that if they failed to repent, 'My God, before a twelve-month, will sweep you

---

52. McHardie, pp. 74-6.

53. Stark, pp. 154-5.

off the face of the earth.' Remarkably, this prophecy was fulfilled to
the letter, for all of these unrepentant men met untimely deaths within
the prescribed period.[54]

The Rev. Thomas Baxter had been converted at the age of eighteen
but by his own confession had fallen into spiritual indifference. Now
under deep conviction, he called on Turner to visit him at a meeting in
his home. Turner suggested they go to their knees to get a baptism of
the Spirit. Baxter did so, 'and the Spirit of God so fell on all, rather all
but one, and on Mr Baxter especially, that he never rose from that chair
until four o'clock in the morning. At times he appeared to be quite in
an ecstasy.' All in the room shared in the mighty baptism except one,
though he, too, was later converted.[55]

A woman who entered the home while these things were happening
was in such distress that the kitchen floor became literally wet with
her tears. A man who later showed up and entered the room where the
Spirit had fallen, but who knew nothing of these events, immediately
exclaimed, 'The Lord's in this room. It's full of the Holy Ghost!' From
that night on, this home became open for meetings until the inhabitants
built a large extension onto it for the sole purpose of spiritual gatherings.
Here many a soul was brought to Christ.

An elderly woman was in the habit of meeting with other believers
to pray for Turner and the Lord's work in Banff. On the last day that
she managed to get to the meeting (with help) she fell down through
weakness. Even as she lay on the floor, she still found the grace to
earnestly lift up many loved ones to the Lord. She then prayed, 'Lord
I'm not able to carry the burden of souls any longer. I leave them all
at the mercy-seat, trusting that I will meet them all at Thy right hand.'
As she lay still breathing out 'Glory! Glory! Glory!' a daughter who
was present saw with her spiritual eyes three glorious crowns above her
mother's head. Looking again she saw the room full of angels. Then a
bright vision of heaven, which returned to her daily for a time. The glory
surrounding the Throne of God appeared so exceedingly bright that the
woman's sight was often impaired for a while after gazing on it.[56]

---

54. McHardie, pp. 77-8.

55. ibid., pp. 65-6.

56. ibid., pp. 69-70.

Banff was noted for both the amount of conversions and 'the sanctification and power dwelling in believers' souls'.[57] The steadfastness and
progress of these converts, over a period of several months, served to
confirm the conviction regarding the amount of good accomplished.
A great work was also done among the boys, who held prayermeetings
of their own, which were 'exceedingly well conducted … the flower of
the youth of the town are on the Lord's side', it was said.

The young men, now one hundred strong, began conducting prayer
meetings in the town and surrounding districts. These quickly became
crowded and soon many more prayer groups arose, as many as ten to
sixteen being conducted simultaneously in Banff alone.[58] The Sabbath
School in just one church – the United Presbyterian Church – rose
from fifty to nearly two hundred in just two months. Deeply involved
in the work here was Sheriff Pringle, who held a meeting prior to the
main Sabbath morning service. Murker said of the revival in Banff that
'prostrations of every phase have been numerous, but no evil seems to
have arisen from these'.[59]

By June 1860, revival meetings were still being held as frequently,
and attended as numerously, as formerly. In fact, instead of abating, the
ardour of those who were brought to the knowledge of the truth seemed
rather to increase.

Macduff

From Banff enthusiasm diffused to Grange, Whitehills, Portsoy, Fordyce
and Macduff, following a visit from Turner to each place. In all these
locations, similar results were witnessed as in other places.[60] Ministers in
Macduff had long united in prayer with their colleagues in nearby Banff
for an outpouring of the Spirit on their communities. Fifty years later,
the Rev. MacPhail remembered, 'as distinctly as if it were yesterday',
the weekly prayer meeting of the Macduff Free Church, and 'the late
Rev. Mr Leslie reading a summary of the American and the beginning
of the Irish awakening. Macduff and its neighbour town, Banff, were

57. *TR*, 21/08/1861, p. 79.

58. Stark, p. 149.

59. Matthews, p. 74; William D, McNaughton, *Early Congregational Independency
in the Highlands and Islands, and the North-East of Scotland*, Glasgow, 2003, p. 348.

60. Stark, p. 151..

early the scene of much of the presence and power of the Spirit', he said. Duncan Matheson laboured in Macduff at the same time as James Turner was working in Banff, while shortly after, Turner, too, visited the town, which became thoroughly soaked with showers of blessing.[61]

Portsoy and Whitehills

In Portsoy, as in many other places where revival flourished, there had been a previous preparation. Through the instrumentality, for example, of evangelists such as Radcliffe and Brownlow North, many had previously been led to make earnest enquiry. The Rev. Reid, noting that the work in his Free Church had been very quiet and gradual, went on to give details. 'The teachers of our Sabbath school have had a special prayer-meeting on behalf of the children under their instructions. One evening after addressing the children, I wished

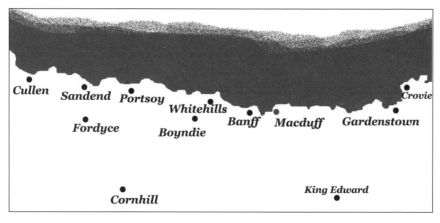

to give an opportunity to any who wished to speak with myself or their teachers. So many remained that I invited them to come up the following day to the manse, when thirty or forty came. Many of the little ones were melted into tears, and were reluctant to leave after engaging with them again in prayer.'[62] The relatively unobtrusive work became more public with the arrival of Turner in the spring of 1860, whereupon 'the Spirit's power was manifested in a very remarkable manner and ... many souls have been saved.'[63]

---

61. Matthews, Chap 1; Sprange, p. 177.

62. *WJ*, 21/01/1860, p. 132.

63. McHardie, p. 27. It is surprising therefore, that word was handed down to later generations that both James Turner and Duncan Matheson laboured in vain in

Awakening in Whitehills commenced with folk travelling three miles to Banff, where Turner was speaking. Quickly, 'the whole of the little town was astir', one witness noted. One evening a group of women asked for the village chapel to be opened. 'As many people were waiting round it as filled the chapel at once.' Praise and prayer proceeded till nine o'clock, when the first cry for mercy was heard. The work thus begun continued for six weeks, during which time the boats stood on the shore. Nothing was done except that which helped secure the salvation of souls. On Turner's visit to the community, two churches were filled. One who went from one church to the other observed 'great concern being manifested by many'.[64]

Gardenstown and Crovie

Interest had been created in the eastern villages of Gardenstown and Crovie by news of revival in townships further west. On one occasion eleven fishermen from the two villages, anxious for their souls, went over to Banff, where Turner was leading a house meeting. All of them went home converted men and were still standing firm over a decade later. Prayer meetings were started in the two close-knit villages. In general, however, prior to Turner's visit in the winter of 1860, these communities were 'in the same state of spiritual death and wickedness for which they had been noted', with the result that some were 'positively hostile' to the Peterhead evangelist. Shortly, however, the meeting place became 'so densely crowded before the hour, and the people so loathe to separate, that, on different occasions, [Turner] had to enter by the window, and go out in the same way'! It was noted that two male converts, one from each village, 'have left their boats and nets to become fishers of men, and are now pursuing the ordinary course of study in Glasgow'.[65]

Added impetus came from the visit of four fishermen from Portknockie. The visitors claimed that at one forenoon meeting,

---

Portsoy during the 1859–61 revival (Jackie Ritchie, *Floods Upon the Dry Ground: God Working Among Fisherfolk*, Peterhead, n.d., p. 99).

64. McHardie, p. 75; Robbie, p. 90.

65. ibid., pp. 98-102. Both later became prominent spiritual leaders in their community. The nearby village of Pennan was not nearly so moved by Turner's preaching, though even here, 'a good number were in a somewhat anxious state' (ibid., p. 102).

'nearly the whole assemblage were struck down at once'. They said they had seen nothing like it in 'the west'. Some people lay prostrate till 5 o'clock in the afternoon and one who lay prostrated for some thirty-six hours resulted in a genuine case of conversion. The Portknockie men also conducted a meeting that evening, which continued till midnight. Subsequently, they separated into pairs and officiated in two houses 'so that all could benefit from their services'.[66] They also engaged in door-to-door visitation during the day, following Turner's own methods.

'W.W.' and 'J.F.' found many wonderful fruits of Turner's labours in Crovie. At one meeting they beheld six women engaged in prayer in succession, all of them Turner's spiritual children. 'The influence of that meeting was felt over the whole town.' The general aspect of Gardenstown was said to have been markedly changed for the better, and with long-lasting effect. Drink, the besetting sin of so many north-east communities, was almost given its death knoll. Said one villager, 'There is not half the number of public houses in the district that there was formerly, while in the village of Crovie not a drop of spirits can be had.'[67]

Inland Banffshire

King Edward country

In the early summer of 1860 a group of young male converts from Banff began 'labouring with the greatest zeal' in different parts of the inland country district (Banffshire and north-west Aberdeenshire). It was reported that, 'Boyndie, Castleton and other parts of King Edward country have been frequently visited.' Two deputations were sent into the Millseat district, and several meetings were held at and around that place, and within two or three miles of it. 'Considerable impression has been made there, and numbers are in a state of anxiety.'[68]

The Rev. James Murker, who itinerated in the counties of Banff and Aberdeen during 1861–62, observed that 'wherever young men had gone out, from Banff especially, there you would see the fruits of their labours'.

---

66. *The Banffshire Journal*, quoted in Orr, 1949, p. 70; *SG*, 12/04/1860.

67. McHardie, p. 98; Harding, p. 11.

68. *WJ*, 30/06/1860, p. 317.

At some of the meetings Murker had been 'struck with astonishment at the remarkable interest and earnestness that had been excited'.

> [At] one meeting in particular, which might be taken as an instance … there was a host ready to take part in the proceedings, and after the meeting had been drawn to a close, and as they were going out, there might be seen a little company conversing anxiously in the courtyard, another by the dykeside, another going home singing praises. It was about half-past twelve – it was a beautiful night in the month of May. They said, 'let us linger here a while and enjoy that moonlit scene, and listen to that sound.' It was something they had not been accustomed to – here was the low murmur of prayer, there the sound of heart-felt praises being wafted home to heaven on the midnight breeze.

Murker also mentioned an instance where he found a prayer meeting being held in an outhouse among the turnips and straw.[69]

Fordyce

James Turner visited Fordyce, a few miles inland from Portsoy, in March 1860, where at once a meeting was arranged in the Free Church. The place was crowded and 'a very deep impression' was made on many hearts. The same spiritual power was displayed on successive nights, where at times, 'night fled into early morning like a dream before the multitude left the hallowed spot'. One who was present wrote: 'Turner seemed to enjoy a more than usual serenity of soul, as he moved gently among the people, sometimes raising the song of praise then charging the undecided to yield up their whole hearts to God, cut every tie, and close with a freely-offered Saviour.' Shortly afterwards, Turner spent two nights in Grange, near Keith. 'The second night I was there', he said, 'about three hundred remained to speak with me about their souls.' [70]

Cornhill

When in November 1860 Turner arrived in Cornhill, a few miles further inland from Fordyce, he laboured incessantly for four days, speaking from twelve to fifteen hours per day, and getting just a few hours' sleep each morning. From the start the Free Church, where he held his meetings, was packed, not a single scoffer was encountered,

---

69. ibid., 12/07/1862, p. 125.

70. McHardie, p. 27.

and Turner said he knew that 'the Master was indeed present. ... On Saturday night and Sabbath morning the Spirit's power was particularly present. Many found the Saviour, both old and young. What a sight to see old, grey-headed sinners weeping and laying hold on Jesus. It was nearly five o'clock before I got to bed, and that same day I had to preach three times in Banff.'[71]

Open-air gatherings less prestigious than those at Huntly or Skene were commonplace around this time. One witness describes a 'remarkable' meeting in a moss in the Ord district near Cornhill in the latter days of the revival. 'The moss is surrounded by the humble dwellings of a mass of peasantry, many of whom have been converted. ... In an undulating slope, sheltered from the coldness of the afternoon, several hundreds sat to hear of salvation and holiness through the blood of the Lamb. After a time the multitude arose, and many retired to a humble barn, singing as they went, having felt that it was good for them to have been there.'[72]

Later Wave of Blessing

Portgordon

A further wave of blessing swept over some north-east coast villages in the last six weeks of 1861 when Turner again passed through them. The evangelist was in an extremely poor state of health before he even commenced this mission. Although he had spent most of March, April and May of 1861 resting on the Isle of Wight on the advice of his doctor, his health took a further downward turn after his return to Peterhead, made worse by a haemorrhage of the lungs. He arrived at Portgordon merely to say farewell to his former converts there. But once in the midst of so many people thirsting for the word of life in the very place where such power had formerly accompanied his preaching, the burning desire to speak could no longer be restrained. The frailty of his body was lost sight of – thoughts of consequences to it were set aside, and once more he plunged headlong into what was his natural passion, that of winning souls to Christ. For several weeks he went from village to village as before, speaking with as much power and unction as when comparatively a strong man.

---

71. ibid., pp. 31-2.
72. *WJ*, quoted in *TR*, 21/08/1861, pp. 79-80.

In Portgordon 'his words were like fire, searching and burning the spirits of the people'. Sadly, even since his first visit just a year or two previously, many were already in a backsliding condition, though it was these who were now particularly affected, many of whom cried out in conviction of their sin. An elderly man converted through Turner on his first tour along the Moray coast vividly describes the most notable scenes from his second visit:

> The second night was the memorable one. The Spirit of the Lord was present in an extraordinary manner. There was nothing visible to the eye, but there certainly was a mysterious sound – as of a mighty rushing in at one corner of the school – onward it swept over all the school from that one corner to the others. Everyone in that room was conscious of the presence and working of some mysterious power, all were moved by it, simultaneously moved, to decision for God. One young girl alone of all that was in that room, resisted the spirit of God. Every heart was melted that night but hers, and James Turner made the remark that she seemed to be possessed with seven devils.'

At the close of his message, Turner was exhausted, yet he continued to exhort the Lord's people in the way forward. A class meeting was spontaneously arranged, and as Turner left it at two in the morning, the broken-hearted were kneeling on the streets praying for mercy. Clearly, the movement was as strong and general as during Turner's first visit to the village.

A woman nicknamed 'Aunt Bell' received 'a great blessing' during this second visit from Turner to Portgordon. 'I was on my knees', she recalled, 'and the power of God on me was so strong that I could not get up from my knees until about two o'clock in the morning – I felt as if nailed to the earth. It was a time of extraordinary workings of the Holy Spirit. That night as in the days of old, He came as with a mighty rushing wind into our midst and filled the place, and so conscious was I of His operations on my spirit, that they seemed more physical than spiritual.'[73]

Portessie and Findochty

In Portessie Turner recorded in his diary: 'There were signs of the blessing, even at the commencement of our first meeting, but before we separated the Spirit seemed to be poured out on every soul in the meeting, and the people bowed themselves down before the Lord, and

---

73. McHardie, p. 233.

a great cry for mercy went up from old and young.' Next day was the Sabbath, when around six hundred assembled for a meeting at 4 p.m. One night, Turner asked for five minutes of silent prayer, during which 'the Holy Ghost came like a mighty rushing wind and filled the place'. Turner broke the silence with the words, 'Now we have the power' and sure enough, a mighty work began. At another meeting the same thing was repeated, and around twenty conversions resulted, which were proved real 'by long years of fruit-bearing'.[74]

From Findochty James Wilson recorded: 'The same power was manifested. I could not describe the scene there, as broken-hearted penitents, many backsliders (who had) returned unto the Lord, and the people of God were all weeping for joy. This continued for a day and a night, out and out; but I slipped out of the meeting leaving the people with the Master himself, and went on to Portknockie', and Banff, both of which places also received a fresh anointing.[75]

These were Turner's last public addresses. While his heart continued to burn for Christ and for souls saved, his body gradually weakened further, and he passed away on 2 February 1863, aged forty-four.

---

74. ibid., pp. 36, 156.
75. ibid., p. 96.

Burghead

Lossiemouth

Deskford

Elgin

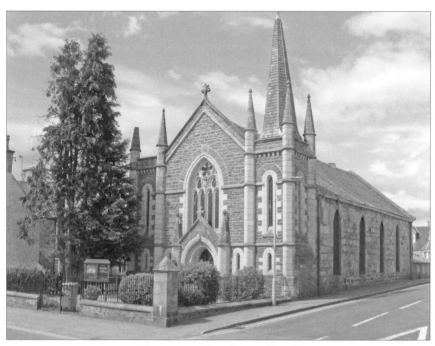

Grantown-on-Spey Baptist Church

CHAPTER 13

Moray

Hopeman

Further west in the county of Moray, a separate wave of coastal blessing
began in Hopeman during an ordinary prayer meeting one Monday
evening in March, in the home of a fish-curer. The meeting lasted till
3 a.m. The excitement increased and rapidly diffused over the village,
and similar meetings took place in the home of a Mr Slater during
the whole of the next day and evening, again continuing till early the
following morning. This pattern was repeated over the next few days,
overflowing also to other houses, which too became overcrowded. On
the Friday, the Free Church schoolroom was secured for a meeting,
becoming filled in a matter of minutes by around three hundred people;
many others having to stand patiently, though anxiously, about the
door and windows. During the course of the meeting a young boy of
ten 'voluntarily stood up and prayed with great fluency and earnestness
– confessing his own sins, beseeching an outpouring of the Holy
Spirit and pleading for a number of his relatives'. This made a strong
impression on all present, and 'a deep wail filled the building'.[1] Many
cried aloud for mercy; some swooned and were carried out; others
exulted in new-found peace and joy. One who witnessed the scene said
he could compare it to 'nothing short of a mixture made up of 150
persons who had been witnessing the death-bed of some near and dear
relations, and the same number of persons who had with infinite joy
received these back from the graves again'.[2]

---

1. *SG*, 20/03/1860.

2. *Elgin Courant*, 16/03/1860, quoted in Rose, p. 27.

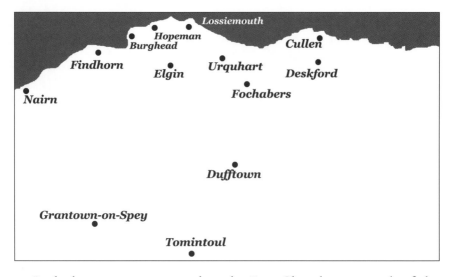

Packed meetings continued in the Free Church over much of the next week, day and night, and right on till 2, 3 or even 4 in the morning. On the Wednesday night, many were entirely prostrated during the services. At one meeting, continued till early the following morning, a number of people who had previously gone home to bed, were forced to rise again and return to the meeting place, owing, they said, to an uneasiness in their souls from which they could find no peace. These were prayed for, and many were deeply affected emotionally. The meeting was carried on till three in the afternoon, under direction of the Rev. Dr Brander and the Rev. C. F. Corbett of the Established and Free Church respectively. The people could only be forced to leave at four o'clock to partake of some food, on condition that the meeting resume two hours later. On resumption, one particularly moving prayer was offered, which had the effect of reducing almost everyone in the church to tears – their heads generally down upon the seats. On their feet again, another prayer led to the entire assembly rocking back and fore 'like a field of corn when the wind blows upon it'.[3]

Visiting ministers officiated at some of these meetings, which tended to result in rather less excitement being produced. The Rev. Henry Williamson, Free Church minister of Huntly, generally very wary of emotional display, said that he had never seen more anxiety of soul

---

3. Rose, p. 28.

than he witnessed 'on the first day he was at Hopeman; which had been quite awful, so that he could imagine nothing like it except the Judgement'. A number of young men from Hopeman were about to go south to train as naval volunteers. Normally great revelry preceded this step, but due to the influence of the revival, in 1860 the men resolved to spend the evening prior to leaving in united prayer.[4]

The *Courier* stated that no attempts were made to 'get up' this movement. There were no special 'revival meetings; the movement seems to have been purely spontaneous'.[5] For a time in the village, business was said to have been 'almost altogether suspended'. One newspaper correspondent wrote that 'there is scarcely a house in the whole village where some are not anxious about their souls.'[6]

It was from Hopeman that revival spread to Burghead, Lossiemouth and Elgin. Following the initial intensity of the movement, it was noted that 'the people have been induced, partially, to return to their ordinary avocations, which, during the heat of the excitement, had been totally suspended, time being scarcely taken to attend to the simplest necessities of nature'.[7]

Burghead

In Burghead revival was preceded by a prayer meeting in the home of a Christian woman, bedridden for thirty years, whose constant prayer request was for 'the outpouring of the Spirit' on the town.[8] In a more immediate sense the movement was sparked by some villagers going to witness the revival which had already commenced in Hopeman.

---

4. Moody Stuart, 1865, p. 369; *SG*, 03/04/1860. One effect of the revival was seen at a wedding in Hopeman in December 1860, when some of the most prominent features of the time-honoured 'penny-wedding' were dispensed with. After the meal, 'a cheerful and harmless conversation took place, during which several services of fruit and cake were handed round, followed by the singing of a few favourite anthems. Then, the cloth being removed, prayer was engaged in right earnestly, and individual after individual did so engage with increasing solemnity and fervour up till a little past ten o'clock, when all separated quietly, and it was hoped not a little profited' (*WJ*, 05/01/61, pp. 535-6).

5. *The Elgin and Moray Courier*, 16/03/1860, quoted in Sprange, p. 200.

6. Rose, p. 33; *SG*, 20/03/1860.

7. ibid., 27/03/1860.

8. MacGill, p. 3.

At meetings there, several were 'stricken down', although, during the subsequent movement in Burghead, there was less external excitement, and few if any bodily prostrations. This lack of extravagance, among Free Church adherents at least, was largely due to the direction of the Rev. D. Waters, who was deeply anxious to avoid the excesses that had cropped up elsewhere, yet who felt it most improper to hold aloof from the movement.

The people knew that Waters was not a man to be trifled with, and that no mere effervescence of feeling without practical result would deceive him. During the revival his 'outspoken speech and somewhat abrupt manner told with a force what no other form of appeal could have done'. He was particularly anxious to guard those influenced by the movement against unsound doctrinal teaching, and his efforts to secure this were unsparing. Two services were held daily for sixteen days consecutively, which, Waters remarked, 'were just like as many Sabbaths'.[9]

As a result, a large proportion of the people came under deep and serious impressions in the town, and one could frequently see 'burning briny tears chasing one another down furrowed cheeks'.[10] Meetings were also held in the United Presbyterian Church, sometimes simultaneously with those in the Free Church, it being estimated that united assemblage amounted to at least one thousand people. As in other fishing communities affected by the movement, the revival in Burghead was largely confined to the fishing portion of the community. Their worldly employments were completely given up and the week or ten days when the revival was at its height was to them like one long Sabbath, spent entirely in religious exercises. During intervals of public worship, and sometimes during the entire night, prayer meetings were held in private homes.

Three cases of prostration occurred on the 19th and 20th of March, none of them in church. One young woman, struck down in her home, 'became perfectly dumb, shook like an aspen leaf, and, when any consolation was offered her, furiously sprang on her comforters. In this state of mental derangement she has continued ever since'.[11]

---

9. Various Contributors, *Our Church Fathers: Being Biographical Sketches of Disruption Fathers in and Around the Presbytery of Elgin*, Elgin, 1899, pp. 41-2.

10. *SG*, 20/03/1860, 27/03/1860.

11. *The Moray Advertiser*, quoted in Rose, p. 31.

Meanwhile, two young brothers, deeply convicted at the same time on the street, immediately ran home. One fell on his knees in his room while the other knelt by his mother's side and poured out his soul in prayer. It was said to have been impossible to go into any house almost, day or night, in which you did not find the family, or some of its members, engaged in prayer. It was also said to be almost impossible to get people to leave church even after four or five hours of religious services, while some individuals were said not to have been in bed for four days and nights in a row.

Lossiemouth

Three fishermen from Hopeman carried the revival to Lossiemouth in mid-March 1860. In no time, prayer meetings were being held 'at all hours, all day and all night'. Said one, 'Cases of striking are common, chiefly among the fishing class, as well as prayers – rather incoherent – and the most awe-striking ejaculations imaginable. This is the case among males and females, from those of adult age down to the lisping child.'[12] Some, however, considered the juvenile meetings held in the Free Church to be most irreverent. When several seasoned believers sought to sensitively point out the errors in which the young people were persisting – such as protracting their meetings to unsuitable hours – and tendered them much helpful advice, the ardent youths carried on regardless, even praying vehemently for their paternal advisers, that their hearts might be softened and that they might be forgiven for trying to shut the doors of mercy upon them.[13]

In like disapproval, *The Elgin Courant* correspondent spoke against the liberal and imprudent use with which the word 'converted' was being used among believers. 'Others, again, of a peculiarly loquacious turn of mind, and who are evidently bent, in season and out of season, on using, as they think, every possible opportunity, seem to take an infinite delight in asking every person they meet in our streets their usual question, "Have you found Jesus?" The motives of such may be pure', noted the journalist, 'but it is for the intelligent public to judge as to the propriety of such a course.'[14]

---

12. *SG*, 20/03/1860.

13. *The Elgin and Moray Courier*, 30/03/1860, quoted in Sprange, p. 204.

14. *The Elgin Courant*, 06/04/1860, quoted in ibid.

At one meeting the Rev. Vassey of Elgin Baptist Church suggested that women should restrain their feelings while in church, or at least refrain from attempting to address the meeting or pray audibly. 'The most praiseworthy decorum in the circumstances was observed throughout' the remainder of the service. But at midnight, many made their way to the Free Church, where, during the course of the next three hours, they gave full vent to their emotions, with 'shrill, piercing shrieks of females voices', and 'agonising implorations for mercy'.[15]

By mid-April the meetings were becoming more thinly attended, although the 'frantic like and irreverent' praying, and the beating of feet to the hymnal music still made one witness 'fancy that he beholds a company of wild bacchanalians'. By this time, wrote another, 'extravagance had subdued to something like the wonted equilibrium – the hallowed stillness attending on the welcomed cessation from manual labour on that sacred day seemed as if from sympathy to produce a corresponding serenity and sober calm'.[16]

At the request of some lads from Kingston, at the estuary of the River Spey, some youngsters from Lossiemouth also visited that coastal community, whose population belonged almost exclusively to the Free Church. They remained here for a couple of days, and 'by their presence and conversation produced a certain impression of the reality and greatness of the work going on', and influenced many for their spiritual good.[17]

Findhorn

Yet further west along the Moray coast, in Findhorn – the population of which was around one thousand – by March 1860 daily meetings were being held in the church, the schoolroom and in private homes. In all of these a greater degree of order and decorum prevailed than in other places hit by the revival. Soon there were 170 to 200 cases of deep conviction. Thomas Davidson, a young ministerial student with the United Presbyterian Church serving in Forres at the time, described how the revival in the district began in that small port: 'For some days the work of the school there could not be carried on. The excitement

---

15. *SG*, 20/03/1860.

16. *The Elgin Courant*, 13/04/1860; *SG*, 27/03/1860.

17. *The Banffshire Journal*, 10/04/1860, quoted in Sprange, pp. 206-7.

broke out among the boys, and that still more remarkably than among the adults – forty cases among them. The teacher … has been very active in the work, and has aided the minister very much. I thoroughly believe in the genuineness of it all; it is the most remarkable event in the history of Christianity since Pentecost.'[18]

Unusual Physical Phenomena

A notable feature of the revival along the Banffshire and Moray coast was the occurrence of unusual physical manifestations, particularly fainting and trances, which especially affected women and children. These occurred particularly at crowded protracted meetings, which often began in the early evening and continued till between four and six o'clock the following morning. Such meetings were usually led by laymen who imposed little constraint upon external excitement.

Writing in 1880 the Rev. Ker of Deskford accounted for the unusual physical phenomena he witnessed among the fisherfolk of the northeast coast saying:

> In 1860 there was great spiritual ignorance and very little knowledge of the Scriptures, and thus the superhuman power which came upon them had little to work upon, and their self-consciousness evolved of necessity many strange things. Bodily prostrations were frequent; visions and dreams were striking and peculiar; religious excitement became intense and disturbing. In the midst of all this, however, the reality of many true conversions was made to appear more and more evident. The whole life of the population was awakened into practical action, and they gave evidence, increasing in strength year by year, of a people arising into a new life from a previous state of spiritual, moral, and intellectual death. The Word of God became to them their daily study, and the personal interest in its living truth led them through it into a spiritual knowledge of the person of the Living Word Himself.[19]

---

18. James Brown, *The Life of a Scottish Probationer, Being a Memoir of Thomas Davidson*, Glasgow, 1878, pp. 57-8.

19. *The Christian*, 10/06/1880, p. 7. In later awakenings, Ker observed, it was mainly younger people who were influenced, 'and though they had themselves no saving knowledge of Scripture truth until the quickening power came upon their minds, yet there had been so much more familiarity with it during the intervening years, that there was substance upon which the superhuman could work, and hence none of the former strange and stumbling things have now occurred [i.e., during a revival

While it is true that the majority of cases of striking down occurred in the heat of emotional church services or crowded house meetings, a number of people were affected when alone, in the ordinary course of daily life. A woman in Buckie was struck down while sitting at the front of her house making a net during daytime. A girl was laid prostrate while lighting the fire. Others were struck down while walking along the street. Dr Haynes of Buckie examined a number of cases of people having been struck down. He found 'the pulse in all cases undisturbed, the heart's action quite natural; and in no case have I seen a train of symptoms analogous to hysteria; males, females, ignorant and educated, weak and strong minds, are alike susceptible'.[20] This particular phenomena became known as 'The Happy Sickness' because in most cases those affected were, after a time, restored to soundness of mind and physical health.

It was suggested that a number of people who were prostrated in the early part of their spiritual experience returned to things of the world, giving opportunity for the unbeliever to pour scorn on their experience as being a puff of emotional release with no underlying value. The reason sometimes offered for such backsliding was the fact that those who had been prostrated were often looked upon de facto as having also been converted, allowing them to trust more in their physical and emotional experience than in the Cross of Christ.[21]

A notion arose among some people that they were required to wait to be 'struck down' before the Holy Spirit could possibly work in them, and that He would never begin to move upon any community without some conspicuous sign of His coming. Some instances of striking down were dealt with by the dangerous action of thrusting knives or spoons into the mouth in attempt to prevent lockjaw.

While these phenomena occurred also in numerous other places, they were most prominent in fishing communities, whose inhabitants were seen to be more excitable than other classes of the Scottish

---

movement that spread along the Banffshire coast in 1880]. To my mind, so far as I have been able to form a judgement upon it, this fact serves to explain a great deal of what seemed to be mysterious and unaccountable, and for which many plausible theories and explanations were given at the time.'

20. *Inverness Advertiser*, 16/03/1860.

21. ibid., p. 242.

population (although some fishing communities reported few or no physical prostrations). They also chiefly occurred during the early phase of revival in a district. Jeffrey goes as far as stating that 'a large proportion of those who were converted, especially women and children, experienced strange physical manifestations'.[22]

The United Presbyterian Church conducted a fascinating survey of the awakening across the length and breadth of Scotland. Fifty-three answers were received relating to places where the revival has been 'most conspicuous'. Of these, twenty-eight reported that there has been no case of prostration. Of the remaining twenty-five, one minister said they occurred in hundreds; one specified sixty; another named twenty or thirty; another fifteen. Two said the instances were 'numerous'; seven mention that such cases were 'few'; three say that there were 'some'; five specify two or three; and three state that there was only one.[23]

Even of meetings in Glasgow's Wynd Church, which early experienced a powerful move of the Spirit, Dugald MacColl could write: 'Not more than perhaps a dozen persons were affected with entire physical prostration. These were all young girls; one or two seemed, from their violent convulsions and outcries, as if possessed; the others, some of whom were well educated, remained for hours calm but unconscious. We attached no value to these physical manifestations. They were evidently connected with great mental emotion. Some of these cases were followed by conversion, and some were not. We had only one case of a trance.'[24]

It is apparent in general, then, that prostrations were relatively few in number, except in certain fishing communities, and were particularly rare among men. And while they certainly brought reproach from many institutional clergymen as well as from the Press, nothing like the degree of controversy regarding the manifestations developed in Scotland as arose in Ulster.[25]

---

22. Jeffrey, p. 228.

23. A Glasgow congregation, where apparently, 'bodily prostration in hundreds of cases accompanied the awakening' (MacGill, pp. 6-7).

24. MacColl, p. 293.

25. For more on physical manifestations during the Ulster revival of 1859, see William Gibson, *Year of Grace: A History of the 1859 Ulster Revival*, Railton, 2009.

Evaluation of the Coastal Revival

A correspondent writing to the *Aberdeen Free Press* in March 1860 had no hesitation in speaking of thousands having come to 'a saving knowledge of truth, full of heavenly joy and love' along the Banff and Moray coast, without, to his knowledge, a single case of backsliding. This despite the 'snares and temptations being deliberately set' in the path of the young converts, 'in a malevolent attempt to lead them astray'.[26]

It was no coincidence that the movement along the north-east coast occurred in winter, when boats were generally tied up and the fisherfolk had more time to devote to religious concerns. In a number of places, work was abandoned for days on end. In Findochty, the meetings 'continued for more than a week, night and day, with only a few hours of interval'. In Burghead, a particular week was described as 'one long Sabbath, spent in religious exercises'.[27]

Many commentators, while approving of the revival in general, deeply deplored the more overt manifestations that were allowed to accompany it in some quarters. At the tail end of the movement along the Banff and Moray coast, a Banff minister, the Rev. Bremner, claimed that immorality had increased since the revival began, and that 'prayer-meetings among us have degenerated into midnight revels, where every last corner is entitled to go beyond the speaker who preceded him in excitement and extravagance'. Bremner was also critical of prayer meetings held in farm houses and in the private homes of the fisherfolk.[28]

Another wrote: 'There is such a thing as zeal without knowledge, impulse without a particle of judgement, strong convictions without any intelligent principle to guide them.' The boisterous and irregular conduct of some caught up in the excitement of the moment, he felt, was in no way helpful in leading others to serious reflection about their souls' concerns. On the contrary, 'Their riotous conduct will scare people away, and so allow their ill-trained skill and impetuous zeal to collapse.' It was essential, this man stated, that discernment is used to distinguish between fanatical proceedings and the general movement. No great

---

26. *Aberdeen Free Press*, 09/03/1860.

27. Jeffrey, p. 205.

28. Norman Campbell, *One of Heaven's Jewels: Rev. Archibald Cook of Daviot and the (Free) North Church, Inverness*, Stornoway, 2009, p. 165.

revival had ever occurred, he opined, without the accompaniment of such fanatical disturbances. 'It is a common trick of the enemy, when he finds that he cannot arrest the progress of truth by a determined opposition, to aim at damaging it by the introduction of a counterfeit, or raising up adversaries from among its indiscreet abettors.'[29]

At a meeting of the United Presbyterian Presbytery of Banff, the Rev. Forrester of Keith gave a report of the spread of revival along the coast, making the following salutary comment on cases of extraordinary manifestations: 'I hold it to be a dangerous and illogical policy for Protestant bodies to coquet with miraculous powers. These prostrations are not only no proof that this work is of God, but, above all things, they are not to be desired.' He was also concerned at the loose and incautious style in which conversions were spoken of. 'When one thinks how far it is possible for a man to go in religion and not be religious, what affections he may cherish and still those affections be false, there is a necessity of caution.' These disturbing elements, Forrester considered the chaff of the movement. Despite these objections, the Moderator was still of the opinion that the wildest enthusiasm was infinitely preferable to the death of spiritual unconcern.[30]

Entire villages were morally and socially transformed by the revival movement, which radically affected virtually every coastal community between Aberdeen and Inverness. George Gardiner of Banff wrote of the overall effects of the revival on north-east communities: 'The whole face of society in those villages is so changed that those who have known them before are struck with wonder.'[31] (For more on the lasting changes resulting from successive waves of revival movements in north-east fishing ports, see Chapter 16).

Inland Moray

Deskford

The remarkable conversion of a veterinary surgeon in Deskford in March 1858 exercised considerable influence throughout the district, and helped prepare the way for the more extensive movement which followed. Fifteen

---

29. Rose, p. 25.

30. Rose, p. 37.

31. ibid., p. 19.

months later, the Rev. Ker, on the seventh anniversary of his ordination, urged his church to pray for and expect the coming year to be 'a year of Sabbath rest'. Immediately upon this, in September 1859, 'more evident tokens began to appear'. Ker said that he had known his congregation thoroughly for seven years, and he could mark at once a mighty change wrought by the Spirit of God. As in every other case, there was a gradual preparation. 'It came suddenly on those not thinking of the matter; it was long prayed for and expected, but he might say it came suddenly upon himself, for the mighty conviction that took hold of so many was extraordinary.' The weekly prayer meetings became more largely attended, servants in the manse being the first brought under deep conviction.[32] Previously, Ker 'had great difficulty in keeping up a weekly prayer-meeting with anything like a decent attendance'. But now, for several weeks past, they had had prayer meetings every night, very largely attended indeed, and though these meetings were continued during the heavy snow storm, it did not interfere with the attendance.[33] Latterly, nightly meetings, instead of being held in the church, took place in people's homes throughout the district.

Four months into the work, fresh interest was aroused on news of the remarkable revival in nearby fishing villages. Noted Ker, 'This effect appeared most strikingly throughout the series of meetings on eight successive nights in the church, while the special shower of blessing lasted.' Many who had been previously awakened were wonderfully quickened. Meetings were not protracted 'as a means of securing a blessing', though they were prolonged on two occasions out of necessity, to deal with the large number of anxious cases. Many came from neighbouring parishes, and special meetings were also held in these areas, an evident blessing from the Lord resting upon every one of them.[34] Ker was at pains to emphasise that nearly all the conversions, rather than being attached to

––––––––––––––––

32. An unusual incident, without physical accompaniment, also occurred around this time. A stranger, with no connection to the revival meetings, came into Deskford parish and 'was suddenly overcome on the road by a feeling like bodily illness, instantly followed by great spiritual anxiety'. A few hours later he met Rev. Ker, who directed him to the Saviour. 'Soon after, he was visited with affliction in the death of a child, during which the reality of a blessed change in him was apparent to all who came into contact with him' (Reid, 1860, pp. 356-7).

33. *WJ*, 21/01/1860, p. 132.

34. Reid, 1860, pp. 349-58.

human agency, were 'marked by nothing beyond the natural effect of the application of the truth of God, by the Spirit of life gradually and most surely leading the burdened soul to find peace and rest in Christ.'[35]

As a result of the revival that gripped Findochty, a group of young fishermen from that village travelled to nearby communities to share their new-found faith. In Deskford they found little to encourage them, for a dance was being held that night; moreover the ground was two feet deep with snow. Undaunted, they began an open-air meeting right outside the dance hall, singing, praying and giving a short address. The party-makers held out for a while, but curiosity got the better of them and soon every one came out to the impromptu service. 'I never felt more of the Divine presence than I did that night', said one fisherman, and by and by several were found to be under deep soul concern. When this fisherman met some of these same people a decade later he rejoiced to hear that they had received their first start in the Divine life that very night.[36]

Elgin

'Extraordinary Proceedings' was the unexaggerated headline *The Courant* used to describe events in Elgin during a weekend in March 1860, when a group of young 'revivalists' from Lossiemouth, including a number of children, came to hold meetings. The local newspaper journalist reported what he observed, 'Hymns were sung apparently with ecstatic joy and three boys prayed with great fervour, producing excitement', especially among the juveniles. 'The extraordinary sight of mere children rising up and praying in a full church, as best they could, astonished all, and their fervour, by sympathy, appeared to pervade the congregation.'[37]

When the meeting was finally concluded near 10.30 p.m., 'the more affected' moved to the Baptist chapel, singing hymns on the way. This building was at once crowded to excess, the audience being composed chiefly of young men and women in their teenage years. 'Girls as well as boys spoke, some crying one thing and some another, and praying, singing, sighing, weeping, and incoherent exclamations, accompanied by strong emotion characterised the meeting', which continued till four the

---

35. Brown, 1893, p. 777.

36. McHardie, p. 133.

37. *The Elgin Courant*, 30/03/1860, quoted in Sprange, pp. 311-12.

next (Sabbath) morning. 'The service was extravagant, and occasionally approaching to ridiculous, but when laughing was seen the cry was "pray for the scoffer". The leading juvenile revivalists seemed delirious, and much was said and prayed so surprising and so extravagant as to confound and astonish every calm onlooker that was present.'[38]

Like services were again commenced in the Baptist chapel on Sabbath and kept up during a great part of the day. *The Courant* wrote of that day's activities: 'Hundreds, drawn together by curiosity, could not obtain admission to hear the children praying and lamenting over the great sinfulness of our city.' This meeting, which was adjourned to a private house, went on till midnight. The next day, finding the Baptist church closed by members concerned at 'such unseemly proceedings', hundreds of children were to be seen going up and down the street seeking for places of meeting. To one house the police were sent for, and had to interfere. A room was crowded to suffocation, and in the midst of children praying and singing and saying extraordinary things, two girls fainted. 'The sensation was great; they were supposed to be "struck", but a few minutes and a little water restored them to consciousness.'[39]

Both of Elgin's newspapers spoke disapprovingly of these astonishing and unorthodox meetings. *The Elgin and Morayshire Courier* said that they were 'felt by the great bulk of the community to be an outrage of public decency and Christian propriety' and blamed not the children, but those who made them 'a public spectacle' and in effect 'sanctioned these proceedings'. *The Elgin Courant* was even stronger in its disapproval, and suggested that 'a few nights such as that of Saturday last would be followed by some losing their reason, and being sent to lunatic asylums'. It continued: 'We have had union prayer-meetings in our city for a considerable time past, no doubt productive of much good, but they have been conducted by rational and Christian men, not by thoughtless boys and girls, encouraged to acts of extravagance by a few whose zeal has blinded their judgement and made them forget that common sense and the good order of society will not tolerate midnight meetings of the young of both sexes in any church in our city.' It concluded: 'In one word, the revivals, such as we have seen them in Elgin, should be curbed by the

---

38. ibid.
39. ibid.

sensible part of the community for they are becoming a disgrace to that pure and peaceable religion which is gentle, retiring, contemplative and rendered more engaging when accompanied with superior intellect, and observed in accordance with the rules of well-ordered society.'[40]

The Courier did concede, however, that as the movement progressed, 'a regard for Christian decency and propriety has begun to assert its supremacy, and at least some of those who at first encouraged these excesses have felt it necessary to disown and discourage them'.[41]

Meanwhile, it was said of the Rev. James Morrison of the Free Church of Urquhart, five miles to the east of Elgin, that he was a preacher of rare power and soon came to be ranked among the best preachers of his day. While eminently successful throughout the land he was no less so in his own congregation where he was 'cheered by several remarkable times of blessing, as in 1861-62 – when no fewer than sixty-two joined the church for the first time.'[42]

Fochabers

Just prior to the first open-air conference at Huntly Lodge, the Duchess of Gordon wrote that 'there is an awakening in Fochabers', a town of much interest to her Grace as she had lived at Gordon Castle in that vicinity for about twenty years during her husband's lifetime. As a result of the fresh wave of the quickening Spirit, the Duchess delighted to observe that, 'Mr Dewar (the minister) has grown young again.'[43]

Jeffrey's research suggested that 'the western region of Morayshire, that had the largest Roman Catholic community in the whole north east Scotland' and as far as Protestant presence was concerned was occupied

---

40. *The Elgin Courant*, 30/03/1860, quoted in Sprange, p. 313.

41. *The Elgin and Morayshire Courier* quoted in *SG*, 03/04/1860. Goings-on of an unorthodox nature in Elgin's Baptist Chapel were to occasionally reappear over the next few years. In April 1863, the *Inverness Advertiser* reported allegations of 'irreverence' and 'fiery spirits' at a meeting in the church. A Mrs Tenant from Banff, along with an unnamed young man, were said to have prayed with 'great vehemence', and prayer times were sometimes interrupted by a hymn, while there was an outburst of prolonged clapping by one person present. The meeting was finally brought to a close by the pastor pronouncing the benediction and the simultaneous cutting off of the gas lighting! (N. Campbell, p. 166).

42. Various Contributors, *Our Church Fathers*, pp. 99-100.

43. Moody Stuart, 1865, p. 369.

by the Church of Scotland alone, without Free Church or other religious denomination, 'was unstirred by the revival'. Meanwhile, the kirk session minutes of many nearby inland parishes that did have a Free Church presence make little or no mention of the revival at all, and their records show no growth during the period of the general movement.[44]

Dufftown and Tomintoul

At one convenient stage during the progress of the general awakening in Aberdeenshire, Reginald Radcliffe, Duncan Matheson and others did a missionary tour of the vast district to the west of Huntly. 'At Dufftown, at Glenlivet, at Tomintoul, which was most interesting, there were meetings till late at night, and early in the morning, and along the roadside in picturesque glens, old and young and middle-aged coming out to stop the carriage, because they wanted to know if they could know that they were saved.'[45] Said Radcliffe following the visit to Dufftown, 'We were rejoicing last night over strong men healed on the spot, and through their tears then instructing one another. The Lord granted the shower at once.' The Duchess installed a permanent mission-station at Tomintoul, her biographer noting: 'Mr Anderson, who was selected by her for the work, was remarkably owned by the Lord, and she greatly rejoiced in the good that was effected through his devoted labours.'[46]

Just a few miles to the north Hay Macdowall Grant, laird of nearby Arndilly House, was keen to itinerate personally and also to invite fellow soul-winners to evangelise along the villages and hamlets that dot the banks of the River Spey and nearby communities. So successful were their efforts that it was said that 'for several years grace flowed like a river all along the region, bearing many into the kingdom of God'.[47]

Grantown-on-Spey

It seems that revival came to Grantown-on-Spey prior to visits from either Reginald Radcliffe or 'two earnest and godly ministers of the Free Church in Huntly'. Peter Grant, Baptist pastor in Grantown, took

44. Jeffrey, p. 159. He found the same to be true of less-populated western areas of Aberdeenshire (see map, ibid., p. 158).

45. Radcliffe, p. 76.

46. Moody Stuart, 1865, pp. 371-2.

47. Obituary to Charles Morrison in *The Christian Worker*, 1916.

great pleasure in noting that in April 1861, 'the year that some called the year of prayer may now be called the year of salvation: the Lord in mercy visited us with a time of refreshing, the Church was revived, many of the most careless became concerned about their souls, without being stricken down or fainting ... the simplest and plainest way in which the Gospel of Christ could be stated, the more it was blessed of God to give rest to the weary soul'.[48]

Some anxious souls crossed the high hills of Cromdale – a distance of ten miles – to attend meetings, and an amazing sixty-one candidates were accepted for baptism in the year from April 1860. Grant noted the existence of 'prayer-meetings everywhere, and great awakening in some of the out-stations'. Throughout the region, numerous prayer meetings, Bible classes, Sabbath schools and meetings for inquirers were held each week, as well as the three services each Sabbath in the chapel in Grantown. In these demanding duties, seventy-six-year-old Grant was aided by his son, William, who bore much of 'the burden and heat of the day'. Grant continued, 'most of the families connected with the Church have been visited in mercy, mostly young people, six of them my own grandchildren ... . As the harvest became great, the labourers increased. Several of the young men are very active in leading souls to Christ, and our old men are not idle.'[49]

A further thirty-four people were added to the church in the year from April 1861, with more in the waiting, thus raising church membership – even after a considerable loss in numbers for various reasons – to 291. 'In many places the mountains have been thrashed, a shaking came among the dry bones, and a great army arose; and now that some time has been given to winnow the corn, it was found that there was not so much chaff as was expected, and that many who with weeping went out with the precious seed of the gospel have returned rejoicing, bringing their sheaves with them ...'[50]

Among those who joined the church were four husbands and three wives; most of the rest were young and unmarried, including two who went to study at the Baptist College in Glasgow. Over one hundred

48. BHMS Report, 1861, pp. 10-12.

49. ibid.

50. ibid., 1862, pp. 12-13.

people were baptised in total during the period of the revival. And noted Grant in April 1863, 'only in a few instances our hopes have been disappointed'. He also stated that he was not aware of any 'prayers, or prayer-meetings or efforts made in the time of the awakening, but have continued to this day'.[51]

With 'doors opening on every side', Peter Grant's son, William, took many extensive evangelistic tours from Grantown-on-Spey during 1861 – through Ardclach, Knockando, Glenrinnes, Glenlivet, Strathdown, etc. 'In all these places there is a great awakening', Grant senior reported, 'and sometimes he requires to continue till midnight praying or preaching, and in places, of which we formerly often said "can these dry bones live?", the Lord is breathing now the breath of life into their souls. A good number of them have come over the mountains and hills and a great distance, to be baptized, in obedience to their Lord and Saviour, from places where opposition is strong, and the rubbish of prejudice still remains.'[52]

---

51. ibid., 1863, p. 25.
52. ibid., 1862, pp. 13-14.

PART 2

The Big One –
The Highlands and Islands

Introduction

While many places in the Highlands of Scotland were stirred by revival during the period 1859–61, it cannot be said that revival was pervasive across this vast territory. Thus, the Rev. McLaughlan of the Free Church overstates the case by suggesting that, 'almost over the whole Highlands there was more or less of a spiritual movement', going on to suggest that where there was no marked outbreak, one would often find that a good work had been going on quietly in the congregation.[1] Some parts of the Presbyterian Highlands, however, were not strongly influenced by the 1859–61 awakening. The participation of laymen such as Brownlow North (albeit specially licensed) and Hay MacDowall Grant may have been one factor that helps explain why. For example, during the very year revival commenced, the Synod of the Church of Scotland issued a statement against lay preaching during public services, although some leading ministers, including the Rev. Norman Macleod, bitterly opposed such ruling. The United Presbyterian Synod of 1859 also ruled against unlicensed persons preaching in their pulpits, and this point was strongly pressed at each subsequent meeting of the Synod. In some cases, however, such ruling was overlooked, e.g., when James Turner was invited to speak at the United Presbyterian Church in Buckie. The Free Church was the Presbyterian body most open to lay preaching within its churches, although one or two Synods, such as that of Moray, decided to disallow such liberty. In other areas, however, it was often within Free Church walls that men like Brownlow North, Hay Macdowall Grant, Duncan Matheson, etc., delivered their gospel addresses.

Indeed, preaching by converted lay speakers occurred to such an extent that the 1859–61 movement in general became known as 'The Laymen's Revival'. As well as the theological argument against their employment, 'the general lack of education, brusqueness and

---

1. Free Church General Assembly, 1861, quoted in *WJ*, 08/06/1861, p. 86.

irrationality of lay preachers' were particular irritants for some people. One correspondent complained of a certain lay preacher, that he 'murdered the Queen's English and committed grammatical havoc – not to speak of crying offences against good taste, common sense and sound logic'.[2] There is little doubt that some ministers also had misgivings about the negative impact that the encouragement of lay preaching and extra-denominational meetings would have on clerical authority and denominational allegiances.[3] These anxieties surfaced again, with more vocal prominence, during the Moody campaign of 1873–74 (see Chapter 22). Bussey over-generalises the situation in 1859–61 by suggesting that once the opposing Highland communities 'understood' the revival and the importance of lay preaching, 'they took it to their hearts, and in few places have there been more satisfying results'.[4]

Association for Religious Improvement

A very generalised picture of the spiritual work in progress across the Highlands and Islands in this period comes from The Association for the Religious Improvement of the Remote Highlands and Islands, which was told at a meeting in December 1859: 'Several of the schools of the Association have shared in the work of revival which has been going on in some parts of the Highlands, and very interesting accounts have been received from the teachers of prayer-meetings being established among the young, and of hopeful signs of conviction and deep impression.'[5]

The Eleventh Annual Report of the Association (1861) records:

> During the last six to eight months there has been a decided work of revival in many parts of the Highlands, and in no districts of the country have the young more largely shared in the blessing. In some places the young alone have been seriously impressed; in others, the movement began among the children, who were engaged in reading their Bibles and tracts whilst herding on the hills, and met together for prayer in the barns in the evening, till the attention of the older people was awakened, and they also were made partakers of the blessing. So

2. Marrs, p. 173.

3. Such doubts were, for example, expressed by ministers in the Ulster revival of 1859 (J. Holmes, p. 72).

4. Bussey, p. 154.

5. *Inverness Advertiser*, 06/12/1859.

great has been the thirst for hearing the Word, that young women have been known to walk twenty miles on Sabbath, besides standing during the service in the crowded places of meeting; and children of ten or twelve years old have walked regularly for months seven miles to church and prayer-meetings, both on weekdays and Sabbaths; sometimes in groups, with one reading aloud by the way, or singing psalms and hymns, one giving out the line, and all joining. During the summer, they remained for evening service, passing the interval in the woods, in little groups, engaged in prayer and singing.[6]

In one school at least forty were known to have been awakened, and, so far as could be properly judged, appeared to be truly converted, whilst as many more seemed seriously impressed, who had not openly expressed their feelings. The teacher's house was crowded for several weeks with anxious inquirers, both day and night, and ministers who preached there described the scene as one of the most affecting and delightful they had ever witnessed, even little children of five or six years old eagerly listening to the Word of life and showing how deeply they felt their need of a Saviour. Meanwhile, it was reported that in one area in the north of Scotland where the population had been *en fête* on the occasion of the founding of a savings bank, the proceedings were wound up with a religious address, the people enjoying that as 'the best part of the festival'.[7]

---

6. *TR*, 01/02/1862.

7. *SG*, 12/07/1860.

Campbeltown

Gunpowder Factory Buildings, Millhouse, Cowal

Oban

Ardnamurchan

John Colville

Portree

Gravir, Lewis

CHAPTER 14

Argyll and the Western Isles

South Argyll

Campbeltown

In Campbeltown, on the south of the Kintyre peninsula – one of the closest districts, geographically, to the dramatic scenes of awakening that had so powerfully impacted Ulster – each of the five Protestant churches united in the revival that swept through the fishing port. In a town with a population of around nine thousand, it was estimated that on one weekday evening an aggregate congregation of five thousand met for prayer in various churches. The following Saturday night, according to *The Glasgow Herald*, the twenty public houses sold only seven gills of whisky between them, far less than usual.[1] People came from a distance of up to twenty miles to the meetings, and 'towards evening the various roads leading into the town are thronged with rustics bending their steps towards the house of prayer'. One preacher spoke at a meeting which was packed full an hour before the scheduled time of commencement. 'There were upwards of twenty young men and young women affected', he wrote, 'and O! I never felt anything so heartrending as was this scene; their cries were most dreadful. The ministers of the Free Church came to our help, and were deeply interested. We wanted home today, but the people are all holding us, so we have resolved to remain till Thursday morning, as there is no boat on Wednesday.'[2]

Another man described a revival meeting in the Gaelic Free Church, where, 'such a crowd, I never saw in Campbeltown', upwards of two

---

1. Orr, 1949, p. 67.

2. *WJ*, October 1859, p. 18; 22/10/1859, p. 26

thousand attending. The crowd filled the porches and far outside of the doors, and were hanging on the windows and dykes of the church and wherever any glimpse or sound could be got of the meeting. Several girls were struck, and were taken out to the schoolroom after the large meeting. It was estimated that 'there cannot be less than the half of the population of this place present at those interesting meetings every night'.[3]

John Colville, a native of the town, took great delight in dealing personally with the anxious. A female friend wrote that in one home, 'the two rooms and passage were crowded, and the most affecting sight I witnessed was to see the strong policeman kneeling in the lobby, when Mr Colville was at prayer, beside a very little boy, and another very wicked woman, all with broken hearts on account of sin, seeking forgiveness. The policeman was a scoffer when the work began in the town, and now he is brought low. He could not contain his feelings.'[4]

A number of prostrations occurred in Campbeltown, including that of one man who was 'struck down' while proceeding along the road on horseback. Previously, no more than twelve or fifteen people would attend a weeknight prayer meeting during the harvest, and in recent years the meeting was given up altogether in that season. Now, however, attendance at the Free Church prayer meetings, harvest time notwithstanding, was between four and five hundred.[5]

Rural Kintyre

In the large rural region that comprises Kintyre, the work, though not as marked as in Campbeltown, was nonetheless notable. *The Argyllshire Herald* recorded in late November that in Drumlemble, during one of the meetings held, as many as a dozen people cried out; whilst at Southend, the number was 'considerable'. Progress of the movement on western Kintyre was described as 'onward', with some instances of conviction occurring at Clachan, and also at Tarbert. The awakening here began in Tarbert Free Church during the November Communion, 1859, at which the Rev. James McPherson of Killean assisted. During

---

3. ibid.

4. Mrs Colville, *John Colville of Burnside, Campbeltown, Evangelist: A Memoir of his Life and Work*, Edinburgh, 1888, p. 94. See also Orr, 1949, pp. 66-7.

5. *SG*, 21/01/1860; *WJ*, 13/10/1860, p. 435. It seems, however, that there was nothing like the same degree of blessing in Campbeltown's Argyle Free Church.

the action sermon, delivered in Gaelic, many were deeply affected. Then, at the evening service, some cried out in agony of soul while the minister prayed. It was said that one hundred were awakened on that and subsequent nights. The movement continued into the New Year. Said one witness, 'The revival, and stories connected with it, and the changes wrought on some individuals in neighbouring districts, are in every persons mouths. ... I hear none speak against it.' It was noted that 'the spiritual guides of the parish are doing all in their power to forward the good work'.[6] The Congregational Church at Whitehouse in north Kintyre also experienced revival around this time.

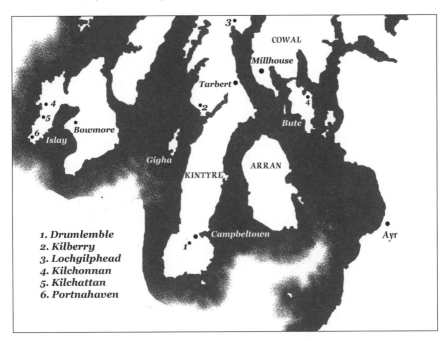

1. Drumlemble
2. Kilberry
3. Lochgilphead
4. Kilchonnan
5. Kilchattan
6. Portnahaven

McPherson also preached further west in Kintyre, at Kilberry in western Knapdale. Here, a girl aged sixteen got such a view of her danger that she sunk in her seat as if unconscious. 'A great crowd gathered round; she addressed them in Gaelic about their insensibility and hardness of heart, and also prayed. She slept none that night, but she found peace in Christ the following day. You may well believe that this incident made a great impression.'[7] McPherson revisited the area

---

6. ibid., 03/12/1859, pp. 75-6; *SG*, 29/11/185.

7. *The Argyllshire Herald*, 02/12/1859, quoted in Sprange, p. 126.

in March 1860, when seven or eight individuals – chiefly young people – were awakened. Meetings were held every night since.[8]

Lochgilphead

Awakening began in Lochgilphead in the autumn of 1859, but had died down somewhat. Then, in the following spring it 'burst with renewed vigour' following a visit from James McPherson in late March. The Killean minister spoke nightly in the Free Church, which, he noted, was 'not able to contain the crowds of people who throng to it long ere the appointed hour, eager to procure seats. It is almost impossible to describe the impressions produced upon the people nightly. Suffice it to say that the outward physical signs observed in other places where the revival movement has taken place are realised here to the full.'[9]

On the other side of Loch Fyne, in the Kerry district on the south-west peninsula of Cowal, many flocked to the home of local farmer and lay preacher, Archibald Campbell, who, despite the heavy demands of his work, spent almost entire days searching the Scriptures for truths to share with his hungry hearers each Friday evening. His house outgrown, meetings were moved to the church at Millhouse, near the centre of the peninsula, where they continued for two years on end. While there was no undue excitement, such was the earnest feeling realised that when the attentive audience dispersed from the packed church, 'they left the pew-desks wet with their tears'. Opposition to the movement took the form of employees of the Millhouse Gunpowder works planning to disrupt a New Year meeting in church. On Hogmanay, a horrific explosion in the factory resulted in the deaths of many workmen and an awe-stricken community assembled the next day to hear Campbell speak from the words of Psalm 46:10, 'Be still and know that I am God.' The plot had dramatically backfired, resulting instead in an even more 'profound impression ... upon the countryside'.[10]

Inverary

The local ministers of both the Free and United Presbyterian Churches worked in hearty sympathy with the revival movement that broke out

---

8. *SG*, 08/03/1860. From 1859, John Colville also travelled throughout the country districts of Kintyre on his 'Missionary pony ... in search of the sheep and lambs of the fold' (Colville, p. 96).

9. *SG*, 27/03/1860. See also Bussey, p. 150.

10. G. N. M. Collins, *Principal John Macleod D.D.*, Edinburgh, 1951, pp. 251-2.

in Inverary, largely in connection with the visit to the area in November 1859 of two young male converts from Ireland. 'The entire community was deeply moved', noted Alexander Macrae. 'Night after night there were fresh cases of conviction and of conversion. Many were added to the Lord and became members of the different churches.'[11]

James Chalmers, a young lawyer's clerk, colluded with some pals in an attempt to interfere with the revival meetings, and to prevent the so-called 'conversions'. He was constrained, however, by the urgent appeal of a young friend, to attend one of the first meetings. 'It was raining hard, but I started, and on arriving at the bottom of the stairs … they were singing "All People that on Earth do Dwell", and I thought that I had never heard such singing before – so solemn, yet so joyful. I ascended the stairs and entered. There was a large congregation, and all intensely earnest. The younger of the evangelists was the first to speak … and he spoke directly to me. I felt it much, but at the close hurried away back to town, returned the Bible to McNicoll, but was too upset to speak much to him.'[12]

Chalmers went to another meeting a few nights later, when he was 'pierced through and through and felt lost beyond all hope of salvation'. The following day, however, the United Presbyterian minister led him 'to kindly promise and to light'. Chalmers at once made public profession of his faith. He joined the UPC in 1860 and became a teacher in its Sunday school. He also became a bold and tireless evangelist and was used by God to the conversion of many. In 1866 he set out as a missionary to the South Seas, and through his later labours in New Guinea, became famous throughout the world.[13]

Argyllshire Islands

Islay

It was estimated that prior to the outbreak of revival on Islay on 23 August 1860, out of a population of about fourteen thousand, there

---

11. MacRae, 1906, pp. 51-2. The changes were lasting. Years later, Rev. Robert Rose would count those of his own Free Church congregation who had been savingly blessed during the revival, and who had been called home before himself (ibid.).

12. Cuthbert Lennox, *James Chalmers of New Guinea*, London, 1902, p. 6.

13. ibid., Robert Louis Stevenson termed Chalmers, 'The Greatheart of New Guinea' (*Missionary Record* of the United Free Church, June 1901).

were not more than one thousand who could be called 'regular hearers of the gospel'. In distinction, there could now be seen 'the unexpected spectacle' of six thousand people meeting together on a weekday, to hear the preaching of the gospel. The movement began in Bowmore, the island's principal community, and was accompanied by 'terrible excitement, such loud lamentations that the clergyman's voice could not be heard'.[14] A teacher in the Gaelic School Society marvelled at the turn of events: 'Our meetings ... are a scene indescribable, with weeping, crying and fainting. I might have given you the number of those affected, but suffice it to say that you would be astonished at the enumeration.' This worker also pointed out that one could observe 'great thirst for hearing the Bible wherever you go. The like was never seen in this island before. In almost all parts of the island the work is seen, although nothing of it among the English hearers.'[15]

Children as young as eight were awakened in the movement. One Sabbath was Communion day in both the small town's churches, and 'the largest assemblage of people ever seen in Bowmore' attended the services. The following day, preaching in Gaelic took place in a tent, while in the church nearby a service was held in English. In the tent, 'the Lord came down upon the people and many were smitten in heart'. The cries of some were so loud that they could be heard from within the church while the minister was preaching.[16]

Just days after the movement broke out in Bowmore, twenty miles away, at Kildalton, when the Rev. McKenzie had spoken only one sentence of prayer during a service, 'there was the like occurrence (of awakening)'. A few days later, in the Rev. Cameron's church at Kilchoman, 'there was a similar awakening'. In this church, where recently the congregation amounted to less than sixty, there were now nine hundred regularly attending the prayer meetings every day.[17]

In the fishing village of Portnahaven prayer meetings were held twice a day, during which 'some very striking cases' occurred. The excitement and distress was described as 'extreme, and the whole population of

---

14. *WJ*, 15/09/1860, p. 404; 08/06/1861, p. 86; *SG*, 11/08/1860.

15. Appendix to GSS Report, 1861, p. 13.

16. *WJ*, 18/08/1860, p. 372; *SG*, 06/09/1860.

17. *TR*, 22/09/1860, p. 58, quoted in Orr, 1949, p. 67.

the island appear so far interested that they come in great multitudes to attend to prayer-meetings'.[18]

Profligate characters ridiculed the movement and boasted that it couldn't affect them. They, however, were among the first to be brought under powerful conviction of sin in their respective districts.[19] When the Free Church minister of Campbeltown visited the island, at a time when folk were busily employed in the harvest, 'scarcely an individual about the place ... did not leave his work to come and hear the gospel'.[20] Indeed, where formerly prayer meetings had attracted less than a dozen people and were latterly abandoned altogether, now four to five hundred islanders flocked to the prayer meetings in the Free Church.

Mull

Parts of Mull were also 'visited with an awakening breeze'. Christopher Munro was ordained into the Free Church at Tobermory in 1857, and his very first sermon was blessed to the conversion of one of his hearers. During 1859–60, records Alexander MacRae:

> Tobermory was favoured by a season of blessing unsurpassed anywhere by intensity of feeling and depth of devotion. The weekly prayer-meeting grew into a nightly one. The meeting place, at the foot of the brae, was packed night after night by an audience gathered from the town and the surrounding districts. An eyewitness relates that, though he had gone to Tobermory from the stirring scenes in Glasgow and neighbourhood, he had never felt such intensity of spiritual power as in Mr Munro's meetings. The prayers were a passionate outpouring of the heart before God for individuals and for the community. The singing was equally impressive, and Mr Munro's addresses, while quiet and undemonstrative in delivery, were charged with spiritual power, every word of which quivered with emotion and life. Again and again the entire congregation was swept by a tide of spiritual emotion which left no one untouched.[21]

Also in Tobermory, considerable effort was undertaken to stir up the Baptist congregation. Ageing pastor Alexander Grant paid a visit to the

18. ibid., 13/09/1860; *WJ*, 15/09/1860, p. 404.

19. *SG*, 09/10/1860.

20. MacRae, 1906, p. 52-3.

21. Appendix to GSS Report, 1861, p. 12; MacRae, 1906, p. 58.

Irish towns of Belfast and Banbridge, so that he could give a first-hand report of the Ulster awakening to his home church. But even before he returned home, prayer meetings for an outpouring of the Spirit were started in different parts of the village and these continued for many months. In addition, recently instated assistant pastor Duncan MacFarlane went to witness revival scenes in Glasgow and Greenock. Both men, on their return, gave a course of lectures on the revival 'to large and attentive audiences' in a large schoolroom belonging to the Established Church, which was readily granted to them on occasion of their own building being too small for the numbers that wished to hear.[22] The community was blessed as a result.

So appreciated were the services of one Gaelic School Society teacher in Borg that people of the townships around, as well as folk from neighbouring islands, came for him on some evenings and alternate Sabbaths to conduct prayer meetings. 'A very considerable religious awakening' broke out in connection with these meetings, leading to several young men and women being 'in a very promising state'. From Torloisg, in the west of the island, the Rev. Donald Corbet wrote that the 'awakening breeze' caused 'much subdued impressiveness', except when that was occasionally broken by sighs and groans, and bitter weeping. 'The thing seems to be still progressing', observed Corbet. 'I saw an old woman of 70, whose concern for salvation seems to have dated no farther back than Sabbath week.'[23]

Bute

Rothesay, on the island of Bute, was visited early in 1858 by Brownlow North, his ministry being followed up by that of another 'Gentleman' preacher. Edwin Orr tells us: 'This leader became a student of theology, and visited Ulster as such, returning to Rothesay's Victoria Hall in July 1859 to tell of his experience in Ireland and to urge the people to repentance. Some one hundred or more inquirers remained behind, and a movement began which spread throughout the county of Bute, which includes two islands, Bute and Arran.'[24]

---

22. Donald E. Meek, *Sunshine and Shadow: The Story of the Baptists of Mull*, Edinburgh, 1991, p. 12.

23. Appendix to GSS Report, 1861, pp. 9, 12.

24. Orr, 1949, pp. 62-3.

Of a meeting on Bute in mid-August the same year it was said, 'We had a glorious outpouring of the Holy Spirit such as never has been witnessed in Rothesay before. … Some were in the most intense agony of soul. Many were on their knees praying. We sang several hymns which allayed the excitement and soothed many a heart.' Touchingly, the converts of the richly blessed 1858 missions were seen 'praying for the newly awakened'. One Sabbath, three thousand people gathered in Mill Park for an address, while the average attendance at the nightly prayer meetings was nine hundred. A number of petitions were read at these, such as, 'Seven young men anxiously seeking Christ, but who have not found him, seek to be remembered in prayer.'[25]

The Rev. Robert Elder kept short notes regarding sixty-two persons who conversed with him in 1858 and 1859, 'under more or less concern'. Eighteen years later he wrote: 'Of many of these I can now find no trace. A considerable number, I grieve to say, went back from their impressions, and some lapsed into open wickedness. But a large proportion turned out well, giving hopeful evidence of a saving change. A few I have attended on their deathbeds, and have been cheered by the hope that they have gone to be with Christ. A good many are away from this place, and settled elsewhere; but many are still living here, and are earnest and consistent members of my congregation, some of them being active and earnest workers on the Lord's side.'[26]

From Rothesay the blessing spread to Tarbert, Kilchattan, Kamesburgh, Birgadale and elsewhere on the island. In the summer of 1861, when Rothesay was crowded with holiday visitors who annually streamed into the place during the Glasgow Fair, open-air meetings were held over several days within the walls of the old castle. The Rev. Dr Buchanan preached there one evening to an audience estimated at five thousand.

Iona

Located off the Ross of Mull is the tiny island of Iona, one of the oldest Christian centres in Western Europe and the cradle of Scottish Christianity. An article written in April 1860 gave the following report: 'The revival movement has at length reached this sequestered spot – the ancient luminary of Caledonia, when "roving barbarians" and savage

---

25. *SG*, 19/08/1859, 02/09/1859.

26. Moody Stuart, 1878, p. 305.

tribes derived the true light of Christianity at a time when almost the entire world was lying in the moral darkness of heathenism. In this lone Isle of Iona, there are at present many anxious souls seeking the way to Zion. The movement is making general and unostentatious progress. The work is not confined to one class – the old, as well as the young, are brought under no ordinary seriousness and concern.'[27]

Gigha

On the small, sparsely populated island of Gigha, the most southerly of the Hebridean isles, nightly prayer meetings had been held for some months, and though the weather was described as being 'exceedingly wet and stormy', the people came from all parts to the meetings. During these, a number were visited with 'striking conviction of sin and danger'. Many others were silently impressed, showing a remarkable change in conduct. 'The island has become an Island of Prayer', noted one correspondent. 'Little boys on their way home from these meetings, though the nights be dark and stormy, remain among the rocks and hills, praying alternately till a late hour.'[28]

North Argyll

Few held high expectations of an extensive awakening spreading through the expansive terrain of north Argyll. A correspondent writing to the *Inverness Advertiser* around the start of 1860 said in regard to Oban and Fort William: 'There are few places so dark as the surrounding country, and it is very much to be hoped the revival may spread to these places. We have not heard that it has done so yet. Some of these districts, such as Morar, Arisaid, and Knoydart, are very difficult of access, and the people are very dark and ignorant.' Similarly, a report in the *Wynd Journal* claimed, as late as October 1861: 'The mainland districts of Ardnamurchan, Arisaig, Knoydart, Moydart, Morrer, Lochaber and Strathglass are chiefly peopled by Roman Catholics. No missionary efforts have yet been made in their behalf, except where the Ladies' Association (of Edinburgh and Glasgow) have established their schools.'[29]

---

27. *West Highland Journal*, 27/04/1860, quoted in *SG*, 01/05/1860.

28. *Argyllshire Herald*, 25/11/1859, quoted in *SG*, 29/11/1859.

29. *Inverness Advertiser*, 20/03/1860, p. 3; *WJ*, 19/10/1861.

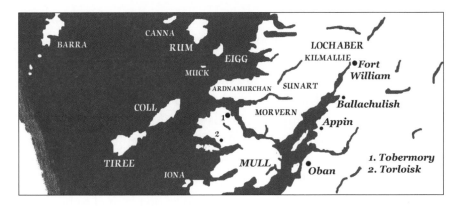

Oban

Despite such perceived spiritual darkness extending over much of this inhospitable region, showers of spiritual blessing were in fact bestowed on a number of favoured locations. Revival services, led by the Rev. Campbell of Tarbert, were begun in Oban in the winter of 1859. Meetings were held in the Established, United Presbyterian and Free Churches, those in the latter building taking place every night in English and Gaelic alternately and being regularly crowded to excess. A witness noted, 'All the usual outward manifestations of revivalism' were evident, including several cases of 'striking down'. 'At every meeting many cry out and shed tears. The whole village is in a state of excitement.' Nearly all the shopkeepers adopted the 'early closing system' so they had opportunity of getting to the evening prayer meeting. Meetings were still going on in early 1861.[30]

Ardnamurchan and Sunart

In regard to the remote Ardnamurchan peninsula the Rev. Grant of Tobermory Baptist Church, having gone to Ireland to witness the revival in progress there, crossed to this expansive area shortly after his return home. He wrote: 'I remained ten days, and preached nine times in different parts of the country. The people come out better to hear than usual. Indeed, I have not seen such large audiences in that place during the last fifteen years', this despite the fact that the people were 'still waiting for the outpouring of the Spirit'.[31]

---

30. *SG*, 13/01/1860, 13/03/1860, 19/02/1861.

31. BHMS Report, 1860, p. 11.

The revival movement in the extensive Sunart and Lochaber districts of Western Argyll was said to have been of 'a very sound character'. Gaelic services were conducted throughout the whole area by the Rev. MacQueen. The group of elders in the Kilmallie kirk in the 1870s were to a large extent the fruit of this revival, and it was said that 'a finer or worthier Session no minister of his day had in the whole Highlands'. One well-known convert from this area would regularly pray on the hillside above Corribeg where he lived and his splendid voice could be heard across Loch Eil in Ardgour. His public prayers were noted for their considerable length, and on one occasion he had to be gently requested to stop after having prayed on his feet for an hour![32]

Ballachulish and Fort William

Two Irish converts, who had previously been labouring in Oban and Inverary, began meetings in Ballachulish, Fort William and Kilmallie, from the beginning of February 1860. Their labours God blessed 'in such an extraordinary manner', and these places were visited with 'an outpouring of His Spirit, and in such measure that we are as men who dreamed'. A minister from Fort William wrote that the churches in all three places were,

> all at once … crowded with earnest and attentive audiences. The Spirit of prayer was poured out abundantly – God's people were revived – the work of conviction and conversion began chiefly among the young men and women, and O! when I think that some of my own family are among the number what shall I render to the Lord for all His gracious benefits? It is impossible to state positively the number of converts as I believe there are not a few hidden ones, known only to the Chief Shepherd, but I think I am within the mark when I say that upwards of 150 at least have been brought to a knowledge of the truth in the parish, including Balla-chulish. There are no outward manifestations such as striking down.[33]

---

32. John Macleod, *By-Paths of Highland Church History*, Edinburgh, 1965, pp. 51-2, 59.

33. *WJ*, 18/02/1860, p. 163, 07/04/1860, p. 219. This contradicts another report from this area, which states that 'at many of these meetings, cases have occurred where the parties are "struck down", and unable to go home unassisted' (*Inverness Advertiser*, 20/03/1860, p. 3). The *Wynd Journal* had to correct a previous article which led some to believe that 400 people had been converted in the district. What their West Highland correspondent had actually stated was that 'about 400 had been led to think seriously about their souls' (*WJ*, 16/06/1860, p. 299).

Some received peace and joy in a few hours, then came once again under deep distress, 'from which they emerge to get fresh and more glorious views of the Son of Righteousness'. Others remained in anxiety for weeks, 'hoping and praying on, but yet unable to say that they have found the Saviour'. The moral change in the area was marked – with drunkenness and swearing not being seen or heard for over two months. The Fort William minister expressed the good hopes he entertained regarding four Roman Catholics, who, he said, continued attending meetings 'in the face of every opposition, and I heard one of them engage in prayer'. Well-attended prayer meetings arose where previously there were none. 'We have daily meetings for prayer in this village and there is a young men's meeting. ... It is the most interesting meeting I ever attended in my life. The earnestness, the soundness of their views, and the effect is truly marvellous. Old people are moved to tears and I confess I never felt so much humbled as when listening to their simple petitions.'[34]

A Glasgow visitor wrote regarding the Lord's Supper celebrated in Fort William on 2 September 1860: 'It was a precious time to many a soul. The Gaelic service was on the outside on the burial ground, and it was indeed very solemn to see the thousands gathered there. Never were there so many communicants before. A few were awakened. It was a solemnising thought to be sitting by the cold dwellings of the lowly dead, to commemorate the dying love of Him who took the sting from death.'[35]

Appin

Congregational minister, the Rev. Charles Whyte reported that 'considerable awakening' had broken out in the quiet district of Appin, on the shores of Loch Linnhe. Ten or twelve had been hopefully converted in that small community, and a number more were under deep conviction. Throughout the previous twelve months there had been a considerable thirst for hearing the Scriptures, and one or two cases of deep conviction and hopeful conversion had occurred. It

---

34. *WJ*, 07/04/1860, p. 219. The work in Ballachulish is also referred to in FCSRSRM, 1888, p. 3.

35. *WJ*, 29/09/1860, p. 421.

wasn't, however, until the district was visited by two young converts from Ireland that 'the power of God ... was so signally manifest'.[36]

The two Irishmen referred to, Messrs. Stirling and Dickson, had been invited to Appin by the Rev. W. S. McDougall of the Free Church, following reports of their success in other towns in the West Highlands. But in this church, too, before any special meetings were held, several came repeatedly to the minister under deep concern of soul. Stirling came for a fortnight, holding meetings every night. The people came out in crowds, and a considerable number were deeply affected. Dickson came for a week following the departure of Stirling, and there were new cases of awakening every night. A few weeks later McDougall wrote: 'March 9th was a blessed night with us, our church was a Bochim. There were many new cases of awakening and very much weeping among men, women and children. This continued for a succession of nights. A goodly number, of whom I have retained a list, have come to converse with me, some under deep concern of soul, whilst others have peace and joy in believing.'[37]

Inner Hebrides

Skye

This section refers almost exclusively to awakening in Skye, there being an absence of documentation of revival movements on other Inner Hebrides islands during 1859–60, such as Coll and Tiree. Among the Baptists in the latter island, where tokens of blessing had been received as recently as 1856–57, 'from 1860 to 1874 [Duncan] MacFarlane saw the membership of the church decline from 71 to 45, as emigration once more took its toll'.[38] In Eigg and Canna, too, where there lived a high proportion of Catholics, only a few conversions here and there were reported. Nevertheless, these places were not altogether bypassed by the '59 revival, for Alexander MacRae records that 'Eigg, Rum and Coll

---

36. William D. McNaughton, *Revival and Reality: Congregationalists and Religious Revival in Nineteenth-Century Scotland*, in RSCHS, 33, 2003, p. 212.

37. John S. McPhail (Ed.), *Memorials of Rev. W. S. McDougall, With a Sketch of his Life*, Edinburgh, 1897, pp. 20-1.

38. Donald E. Meek, *Island Harvest: A History of Tiree Baptist Church 1838-1988*, Tiree, 1988, p. 15.

felt the influence of the signal blessing given to Tobermory' – although he gives no examples.[39]

By the late 1850s a considerable number of ministers, elders and godly believers on Skye were earnestly praying for another season of revival – at the congregational meetings, in private houses, and at meetings led by the Gaelic teachers. Some travelled to Glasgow, and others even across to Ireland in 1859, giving stirring accounts of the work of revival they had seen on their return. In time, over the island generally, 'droppings from on high' were beginning to be felt. Soon a 'great awakening' was in progress, commencing – as had the famed revival of twenty years previously – in the north, and like that revival too, gradually extending until it had pervaded the whole island.[40]

Beginnings in Arnisort

Its first appearance seems to have been in the schoolhouse of the northerly parish of Arnisort, on the Waternish peninsula, part of Roderick Macleod of Snizort's charge. It had been customary for some time to read to the scholars accounts of revival in other places, and two weekly meetings were kept for that purpose, to which anyone that chose might come. At the ordinary prayer meeting on 1 February 1861, an unusual number of people, as if moved by a sudden impulse, attended. The teacher, Mr Ferguson, was somewhat taken aback by this level of interest, and felt at a loss as to what to say. So he picked up his copy of John Angell James's *Anxious Enquirer*, read the first part of it, and afterwards the sixteenth chapter of John's gospel.

'During the meeting an uncommon solemnity was felt; one young girl broke out in cries for mercy, and two young men could hardly stand at prayer, and thus commenced a movement which for many weeks kept the school-house more like a hospital than anything else, many sleepless nights being passed there, and so many going to and fro that it was a matter of wonder and thankfulness that Mr and Mrs Ferguson stood it so well. In school the children were often in deep distress at their Bible lessons and in singing psalms and hymns.' Forty-six of the scholars under the age of sixteen were 'more or less impressed during

---

39. *WJ*, 19/10/1861; MacRae, 1906, p. 58.

40. *WJ*, 27/04/1861, p. 39; PFCSH&I, 1861, p. 307.

that blessed season', many of whom were found to be 'walking as to inspire the best hopes'.[41]

Joyfully, the converts would walk over twelve miles to meetings in Portree, singing praises to God as they returned the same evening. Roderick Macleod and his colleague, Mr MacPhail, had just returned from a meeting in Portree one evening, when, in the words of the former, they were 'suddenly arrested by the sound of vocal music passing the

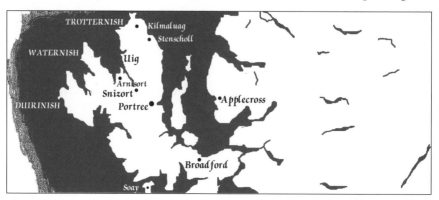

house. ... It was the Arnisort party, chiefly scholars, returning from the meeting at Portree, and intensely interesting it was to hear a manly voice giving out the line, and then the whole party bursting into full chorus, loud enough to be heard a mile away; at such an hour of night it was even sublime.' Macleod added, however, that 'many of the children were often in deep distress because their parents would not allow them to come to church in the rags they usually wore'.[42]

Trotternish

The Rev. Macleod further noted that the school at Kilmaluag, in Uig parish, was also 'visited with a large measure of awakening power. No fewer than ten girls and six boys, one-third of the whole number

---

41. PFCSH&I, 1861, pp. 309-10; Steve Taylor, *Skye Revival*, Journal, Winter 1999, pp. 1-3; MacRae, 1906, p. 67.

42. Steve Taylor, *The Skye Revivals*, Chichester, 2003, p. 118. A Free Church report makes mention of a 'great revival' in Duirinish, north Skye, between 1861 and 1886. This was under the ministry of Rev. Alexander MacColl (formerly and latterly of Lochcarron), probably in 1859–61, and certainly before 1877, when he moved to Fort Augustus (RFCSR&M, 1886, p. 35). One convert of this 'season of evangelical revival' on the island was Norman Campbell, who went on to live a most fruitful Christian life until his death in 1905 (PFCSH&I, 1908, p. 60).

attending', were 'seriously impressed, and their conduct hitherto is giving general satisfaction', much to the comfort of the local school-teacher there, notwithstanding the amount of labour to which he had in consequence been subjected. Of the twenty-six young women attending the 'industrial school at Stenscholl ... as interesting a looking batch' as ever Macleod saw, 'about one fourth, have been so impressed as to give every hope that the true peace of God is in the hearts of some of them at least'.[43]

Snizort

When Roderick MacLeod preached at a communion service in 1860, 'a large number of the people fainted'.[44] In the evening, when Dr Thomas McLauchlan 'spoke on the love of God in Christ Jesus, the whole audience seemed to break down under an overwhelming sense of divine grace', and the minister found it almost impossible to close the service.[45] The Rev. John MacRae of Lochs, Lewis, was also much used in this revival, and the congregation of Snizort presented him with a yacht, *The Wild Duck*, to help him in the pastoral oversight of his vast Lochs parish, where roads were rough and few, and also to make it easier for him to cross over to Skye.[46] The small isle of Soay also came under influence of the revival, the movement here being led by the teacher, Murdoch McCaskill, who later became Free Church minister of Dingwall.[47]

During the last three months of 1859, when revival was at its height in Glasgow's Wynd Church, much prayer was made there for Skye, especially the localities of Portree and Snizort. Roderick Macleod himself visited this Glasgow congregation around this time, from where

---

43. Taylor, 2003, p. 118.

44. This provides a degree of evidence that the revival began earlier than 1861. Earlier still, and certainly before any mention of revival on the island, Henry Alford, Dean of Canterbury, on holiday in Skye in August 1859, spent a Sabbath in Portree. Here he witnessed 'a most curious sight, the Free Kirk Sacrament, 2,000 persons sitting all day in a field opposite our window' (Henry Alford, *Life, Journals and Letters of Henry Alford*, London, 1873, p. 292).

45. Leask, pp. 137-8.

46. Macleod, *The Beginning of Evangelical Religion in Skye*, Aug/Sept. 1995, p. 21.

47. Laurance Reed, *The Soay of our Forefathers*, Edinburgh, 2002, p. 35.

he returned to his remote island home to seek more earnestly than ever like blessings for his own parish. Many months later, revival came; and in June 1861 the *Wynd Journal* reported that 'in three different parishes [revival] is recognisable, but especially in Snizort'. This paper further testified that 'the church is crowded to the door. Many of the people sending up heartrending cries to God for mercy, and all seeming under deep impressions.'[48]

In 1859 a believer from Glasgow had urged a friend in Skye, a 'man of respectable, humble life', to begin a meeting to pray for revival on the island, and so it was that, the following winter, a special meeting was begun in Portree among a few laymen. The lowland believer was delighted when revival finally came to the island, but bemoaned that 'the town of Portree continues as inert as ever. If God's people would be but faithful, the work of revival might in Skye be complete, and not one village on these low shores, nor so much as one hamlet among these purple mountains, where the Sun of Righteousness might not rise with revival on His wings; and from a dreary wilderness in the midst of the sea, it might be flourishing as a garden of delights.' Sure enough, within a short time, specific mention could be made of an 'awakening at. ... Portree'.[49] It was reported a quarter of a century later that many office-bearers then serving in the Portree Free Church were the fruit of the 1859–61 movement.[50]

Summary

Providing a summary of the results of the Skye revival at the Free Church General Assembly in May 1861, the Rev. Reid of Portree noted:

> Throughout various parts of Skye, the revival has been progressing in a remarkable way. Sometimes there were no visible instruments. Some were awakened sitting by their own fireside, some on returning home. Some after leaving the meetings apparently very little concerned would be overpowered on the way home, so as to be found rolling on the road crying for mercy; and there had been a few cases of persons awakened at midnight both from their spiritual and natural sleep, by perhaps

---

48. *WJ*, 08/06/1861, p. 86.

49. ibid., 27/04/1861, p. 339; Rev. McLauchlan, addressing the Free Church General Assembly in 1861, quoted in *WJ*, 08/06/1861, p. 86.

50. FCSRSRM, 1886, p. 35.

some single text they had heard the night before coming home with power to their hearts. The blessing had been chiefly confined to those between the ages of sixteen and twenty-four – though there were some aged persons converted – and some of their schools had been remarkably visited. The fruits of the revival had been very satisfactory. The outflowing of love for each other among the converts was great; open sin had disappeared, such as Sabbath profanation; family worship is all but universal where it was scarcely known before; and there is a great thirst for the private reading, as well as the public hearing of the Word of God.[51]

Outer Hebrides

Lewis

Lewis has long been regarded as Scotland's 'Island of revivals', given the multitude of spiritual movements that have graced its shores. The 1859–60 revival is undoubtedly the island's 'forgotten revival' of the nineteenth century. A number of accounts of Lewis's spiritual history make no mention of it at all;[52] most others ascribe to it just one or two sentences. The island was affected by revival from the autumn of 1859.[53] Two recent events on Lewis had been the means of leading the people to think about eternal things. In the late summer of 1859, a boat's crew was lost at sea not far from the island's shores. About the same time a woman lost her life by falling over a cliff. So great were the effects these occurrences produced among the people that prayer meetings were immediately commenced. So well attended was the one held in the church that meetings had frequently to be held outdoors.[54]

Start and Spread

One of the first places affected was Garrabost in the parish of Knock, when the Rev. Peter MacLean preached at a Communion service. 'A breeze of Pentecost passed through the congregation', noted Norman

---

51. *WJ*, 08/06/1861, p. 86.

52. e.g., Alexander MacRae, who recounts several other instances of revival in Lewis and Harris (MacRae, 1906, pp. 69-80), makes no mention of the 1859–61 movement on this island.

53. Richard Owen Roberts says November (1995, p. 293).

54. *SG*, 10/02/1860.

Macfarlane.[55] Donald Murray was the Free Church minister there at that time. Macfarlane describes him as being 'great in prayer, and he was surrounded by a fine set of godly and praying men and women. Their spiritual education under the Rev. Duncan Matheson[56] was of Pauline type, deep, thoughtful and thorough, and it now bore fruit under Mr Murray, whose own spiritual influence resembled Matheson's, with a touch of St John added. There was a remarkable work of grace among the boys and girls of the congregation. There were many other seals of Mr Murray's ministry, and the sheaves of harvesting embraced men of strong character.'[57]

A work commenced in Ballalan in October, deep interest being taken in the prayer meetings established there. According to a report in *The Wynd Journal*, by December the movement had apparently extended over 'the whole island', with 'prayer-meetings numerous and numerously attended' in most of the island's churches. The same publication tells of a young Lewis man who had been recently converted in the Wynd Church and who 'had his joy increased by hearing almost immediately of several of his companions brought to Christ at home.'[58]

Stornoway

Movements in Barvas and Carloway were said to have been 'equally encouraging', but there was thought to have been more concern in Stornoway than in any of the rural parishes. Having been involved in two previous revivals, Free Church minister, the Rev. Peter Maclean welcomed the movement, 'with more than a Highland

---

55. Norman C. Macfarlane, *Apostles of the North: Sketches of Some Highland Ministers*, Stornoway, 1989, p. 69.

56. The previous Free Church minister in Knock, who left for Gairloch in 1844. It is perhaps ironic that his former flock embraced the revival so warmly; Duncan Matheson was said to 'dislike everything sensational and even emotional, and revivals in which there was excitement he spoke strongly against'. Opined Macfarlane, 'Whether he thought that there could be any widespread revival without excitement it is now impossible to say, but, human nature being what it is, a great movement must move greatly. There was no great movement in Gairloch during Mr Matheson's ministry, but the solid foundation he laid there led to a rich blessing in after days' (ibid., p. 48).

57. ibid., p. 87.

58. *SG*, 25/10/1859; *WJ*, 26/11/1859, p. 67.

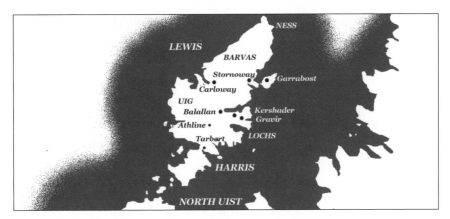

welcome. ... Maclean's wings spread out to this breeze. He gloried in revival, and the island was now in its sweep. He threw himself body and soul into it and laboured to the top of his bent ... Zeal for his Lord burned in him like a fire.' On the Sacrament Day a large congregation gathered in the Green, and as the wind had changed that morning the preaching box had to be shifted so that the voice might be carried with the wind. On the change being effected, Maclean cried out, 'Oh, come ye people, and sit in front, for I have good news for you today.' He gave out his text: 'I have blotted out as a thick cloud thy sins.' He preached with unusual power. 'He had come from the presence of his Lord and his voice trembled with emotion. To the great congregation he seemed like an angel straight from heaven', and that sermon was easily recalled by many fifty years later.[59]

Maclean's labours among his immense congregation were very abundant before the revival arrived: preaching three times each Sabbath, and conducting two or three meetings during the week, along with other pastoral duties. Now, however, there was on the part of the people a greater thirst for the means of grace. To meet this demand weekday services were multiplied, and an assistant had to be engaged for a season.[60] Such was the cry of souls in his ear all day, his constant toiling in prayer and his preaching in season and out of season, that his health broke down in 1861, and for two whole years he was laid aside by the serious breakdown that now resulted from this incessant strain. For the

---

59. Macfarlane, 1989, pp. 69-70.

60. J. Greig (Ed.), *Disruption Worthies of the Highlands & Islands – Another Memorial of 1843*, Edinburgh, 1877, p. 218.

remaining years of his life he was said to have been 'never far from the edge of physical disaster', and he died in March 1868.[61]

In Steinish, near Stornoway, an evening-school class had to be cancelled because those who normally attended were now flocking instead, every night of the week bar Saturday, to church services or prayer meetings. Soon a class of married men was formed, eager to attend evening school in order to learn to read, whereby they might conduct family worship in their own homes. This pattern was repeated throughout the island.[62]

Ness

In Ness, where the spiritual ingathering was especially great, the Free Church minister had to shorten one service owing to the outbreak of sobs and crying. 'Many strong men are struck', he stated, 'and unable to suppress their grief. ... It is difficult to deal with cases, and answer many startling objections.'[63] The teacher of the Gaelic School Society in the Ness district of Lionel wrote of 'an extraordinary movement, especially among the young, here'. In 1861 the Ness Free Church communion roll was about fourfold what it was in 1843.[64]

'A considerable revival' commenced in one parish with one or two individuals being led into deep seriousness, resulting in remarkable changes in their conduct and character. This, without making 'any communication with living man about it', made a profound impact on their colleagues. Soon twenty men and as many females were 'wonderfully changed', and many others were thus brought to awakening state. Meanwhile, in a formerly godless fishing village, in 'which it would be painful for any religious man to enter on a Sabbath evening', several individuals were 'led to walk in His ways', having such effect on other villagers that it could be said, 'there is now no idle gossiping or Sabbath profanation seen'.[65]

---

61. John Macleod, *A Brief Record of the Church in Uig (Lewis) Up to the Union of 1929*, Carishader 2001, p. 15.

62. GSS Report, 1860, p. 12; 1861, p. 9.

63. Colin and Mary Peckham, *Sounds from Heaven: The Revival on the Isle of Lewis, 1949-1952*, Fearn, 2004, p. 30; *SG*, 16/12/1859.

64. GSS Report, 1860, p. 13; PFCSH&I, 1861, p. 310.

65. GSS Report, 1860, p. 11-12. As also with several other accounts of the 1859-61 revival in Lewis, the specific location where these events occurred is not stated.

Lochs

With news of the outbreak of revival in Ireland, 'Big' John MacRae of Lochs (MacRath Mor), while preaching from Psalm 68 on 'Gifts for men', said, 'Perhaps the Holy Spirit is crossing the Irish Channel at this moment. God grant we may feel his power.' On a following Sabbath 'Lochs was in a thrill. The Spirit came like a mighty rushing wind.' The crowds on the Sabbaths were so great that the church could not contain them. Services were held in the open. Often the sobbing of the congregation stopped MacRae in the middle of his sermon.[66]

Wrote Norman Macfarlane: 'There were great times. Forty young men joined the membership of the church – a large number considering the Highland reticence as to joining. When the winter came the large gatherings still met in the open. Storms did not daunt them. Sometimes the snow fell and whitened the congregation, but they sat on, warmed by inner fires.'[67] Macfarlane also records that within this expansive east Lewis parish, 'Gravir was a favoured garden where grew many a tree of God's planting. The ministries of Robert Finlayson and Big MacRae bore glorious harvests in the parish of Lochs, and Gravir was one of its choicest spots where the desert rejoiced and blossomed like the rose.'[68]

It was further recorded of the revival movement in Lochs that it 'appeared in almost every school in the parish. The teachers felt they could not make any comment on a passage of Scripture without the children being affected. One teacher said he did not feel teaching to be such a toil in 1859–60, although he had a great many more scholars. A teacher of the Gaelic Society recorded that in Kershader schoolhouse, during a Bible class for ten-to-twelve-year-olds, when reading about Christ's suffering in John 19, seven of them fell down on the floor, shedding tears and crying out. When asked what was the matter with them, they answered that they were crucifying Christ with their lives. A few nights later, during a meeting at the schoolhouse, seventeen

---

66. Macfarlane, 1989, pp. 11-12.

67. ibid. See also G. N. M. Collins, *Big MacRae: The Rev. John MacRae, (1794-1876): Memorials of a Notable Ministry*, Edinburgh, 1976, p. 38; Rev. Norman C. Macfarlane, *Life of Rev. Donald John Martin: Preacher, Soul Winner, Social Reformer*, Edinburgh, 1914, p. 55.

68. Norman C. Macfarlane, *The 'Men' of the Lews*, Stornoway, 1924, p. 128.

scholars began to shed tears, and to cry aloud, and some of them were not able to go home without the help of others.[69]

Two 'children' of the revival of 1859–60 in Lochs were John and Alexander Macleod. The spiritual birth of John, a fisherman and merchant at Kershader, was protracted and painful. But when he came to a place of peace, he, like his brother Alexander, a fisherman and crofter at Habost, were out-and-out for Christ. John owned a boat, which became known as *The Gospel Ship*, for it carried full loads of worshippers to Crossbost on Sabbath days to hear '*Big*' MacRae transcendently declare the Word of God. It also ferried MacRae to Kershader and other ports when on his preaching tours.

John Macleod had a tent made of boat sails for the ministers' meetings, and boats from every quarter converged on Kershader to hear the great preacher. 'From every one of these boats, as from barges of melody, arose the strains of holy Psalms as they sped their way over the waters.'[70] Alexander Macleod's quaint thatched home was often crowded with people who came to hear him conduct family worship, such meetings leaving a strong spiritual fragrance in the lives of those attending. Indeed, the home got the name of 'House Beautiful', and to godly people it was a magnet. Two of Alex's sons became ministers, while a third served as a missionary in China.

Two further revival converts of 'MacRath Mor' during the 1859–61 revival were Alexander Maclean, formerly a stable boy employed by the Lochs preacher, and John Montgomery, a tailor by trade. This duo was known as the Jonathan and David of Lochs – 'lovers of the inseparable type'. When MacRae moved from Lochs to Carloway, Maclean and Montgomery often crossed the moor to hear their spiritual father – a walk of thirty-six miles there and back. Maclean later became a teacher, while his friend served as a missionary in South Uist and at Laxdale.

Yet another convert of John MacRae during the 1859–61 revival in Lochs was Hector Morrison, a merchant sailor and a native of Gravir. After a prolonged period of deep conviction, he at last found peace – 'like entering a room which the electric switch suddenly illuminated in a blaze'.[71]

---

69. *SG*, 05/01/1860; GSS Report, 1860, pp. 12-13.

70. Macfarlane, 1924, pp. 72-86.

71. ibid., pp. 130-2.

His Christian walk was subsequently one of much influence in the area. Malcolm Morrison of Melbost, a soldier's son, was converted to Christ as a boy. The place of his conversion – the foot of a cliff in Valtos, in Uig parish – became to him a very Bethel. In this location he often returned to renew the prayers of his youth. Having failed at attempts to work as a blacksmith or as a fisherman, Malcolm turned to teaching Gaelic and to winning souls to Christ. He was teacher at Kershader during the time of the 1859 revival, when his devotion to soul-saving was extraordinary. It was said there was no man in the Lews who was more honoured of God in bringing men to the Redeemer; his earnestness, labours and testimony being 'heavenly voices that sounded like a great gong'.[72]

Carloway and Uig

In 1858 the Rev. John MacLean became the Free Church minister in Carloway (which was disjoined from the parish of Lochs in 1844, becoming a parish in its own right). A year or two later, revival swept across this district also, and the area became as 'a field which the Lord had blessed'. As with many periods of spiritual awakening, a strongly emotional and at times even hysterical element became attached to the 1859 movement in Lewis. Nevertheless, it could still be said that 'when the emotionalism subsided a core of true converts was left'. One of these was thought to have been twenty-five-year-old Jessie Macdonald (Bean Aonghais Ruaidh), a native of the area and daughter of devout Christian parents. Jessie did not make public profession of her faith till some time after her conversion, but when she did, she became possessed of a profound assurance of personal salvation and was a source of strength and spiritual support to many around her, becoming particularly well known for her astonishingly accurate gift of prophecy regarding the lives of people who lived near her.[73]

In Mangersta, Uig, the revival was said to have been 'general', as it was too in 'the neighbouring district', as well as throughout the parish. In one community, silent weeping and a manifest solemnity marked the

72. ibid., pp. 163-4.

73. Collins, 1976, p. 41; Annie Morrison, *Christian Women*, Lewis, n.d., p. 24. Ms Macdonald was especially noted for her predictions that children, yet unborn, would become 'servants of the Lord', for which the author provides several significant examples of these prophecies being fulfilled.

meetings for nearly two years. Women attending cattle on the 'shealings' met morning and evening in a bothy for worship, while fishermen did likewise on their boats. One minister rejoiced in the aftermath of the awakening in his parish, because he now had no bother in selecting as many as twenty-eight office-bearers from recent converts.[74]

Summary

An unnamed Lewis minister gave a brief but most illuminating summary of the revival in Lewis to *The Scottish Guardian* towards the end of January 1860: 'The revival was a hundred fold more extensive than that which visited the island in 1812. There are none of the excesses of that period; still there is frequently agitation of body, with sobs and outcries. Many strong and hale men have been brought under the influence. Places which were formerly used for people meeting in and spending the Lord's day in a careless manner are now deserted. The young attend the prayer-meetings in large numbers.'[75] Equally enlightening are the words of John MacRae of Lochs, who, speaking at the Free Church Assembly of Lewis in 1861, stated that nine years previously 'there were only four ministers in the island; now there are fifteen churches, eight of which belong to the Free Church; and the improvement in the religious feeling of the people, which began earlier than the recent revival movement, has been great'.[76]

Athlinnie

Returning home from Tarbert, Harris, in early November 1859, where he was assisting with the sacrament of the Lord's Supper, John MacRae preached in the open field at Athlinnie in North Harris, from the words, 'The sacrifices of God are a broken spirit; a broken and a contrite heart Oh, God, thou will not despise.' Said one who was present:

> There was scarcely an individual hearing that sermon who was not more or less impressed, outwardly at least. We have never listened to a sermon which more fully set forth the doctrines of the Redeemer's

---

74. GSS Report, 1861, p. 9. Appendix to FCSRSRM, 1874, p. 11. John MacLeod makes no mention of revival in Uig during these years in his *Brief Record of the Church in Uig.*

75. *SG*, 10/02/1860.

76. *WJ*, 08/06/1861, p. 86.

sacrifice, repentance in the broken and contrite heart, and its power over souls, obtaining a view of Christ as the surety. So deeply did we feel our indebtedness to the Lord for the privilege of listening to it that, we believe, we should have willingly walked home on our knees, a distance of forty miles to the west side of the Island of Lewis. ... We should give all the sermons we have ever heard or read to possess this one as it was spoken by its distinguished author.[77]

Tarbert

Meanwhile from the parish of Tarbert itself, came, at the beginning of 1860, 'the appearance of great awakening'. While anxious inquirers had been observable at the above-noted November 1859 Communion, this was 'principally confined to parties from Lewis'. At the start of 1860 meetings were held nightly in different places, and one who helped lead them confessed, 'I never saw in my life such a sight. ... I thank the Most High that I have been spared to see such a day. ... Wherever a meeting would be mentioned, we might be sure of having a full house, and more than full sometimes. ... And surely it would cause the heart of every lover of Zion, and faithful disciple of Christ, to rejoice on seeing the powerful effect of the Word of God upon the consciences of sinners. Scores were crying in great distress of soul, "What shall we do?"'[78] Still on Harris, one earnest believer observed that by February 1860 the revival was,

> exerting its benign influence over the masses of the youths of this island, more especially over those who are destined to be the mothers of the next generation. At Tarbert there is a prayer-meeting held every Wednesday evening presided over by the Free Church catechist, a man of deep Christian experience and extensive knowledge of the truth, and many come long journeys eager to hear the Word, the place of meeting being invariably crowded. At some of these meetings the congregation become quite excited and cry and sob aloud for salvation. I have even found it difficult to hear the expositions of the preacher under those perturbations.[79]

---

77. Nicol Nicolson, *Reverend John MacRae (Mac-Rath Mor – Big MacRae) of Knock-bain, Greenock and Lewis: A Short Account of his Life and Fragments of his Preaching,* Inverness, 1924, pp. 38-41.

78. GSS Report, 1869, p. 13.

79. *Inverness Advertiser*, 10/02/1860, quoted in Sprange, p. 72.

Later in the year came a report from the Rev. John MacLeod regarding the school children in Marig, who, he said, were 'deeply affected and impressed with a sense of their sins whilst reading their lessons. Parents who were careless about their souls are now seeking the way to Zion, attending regularly on the means of grace, and thirsting for the water of life.'[80]

The Uists and Benbecula

The teacher of the Gaelic School Society in Hogary, in North Uist reported in 1860: 'The Lord is showing mercy to the people here by His own word. My Sabbath morning school is attended very well, and one morning lately so much of that power was amongst the people that I could hardly get one to sing, for weeping and crying. May the Lord be glorified.' Disappointingly, little else is known of revival in the Uists or Benbecula at this time.[81]

A correspondent to the *Wynd Journal* claimed that in South Uist, Benbecula and Barra, there were 6,000–7,000 Roman Catholics, 'sunk in great ignorance and spiritual darkness … . Although there are a few solitary souls seeking the Lord, yet the multitude are fast asleep in the fetters of unbelief, worldliness, ignorance and superstition. In most of those islands the means of grace are very limited, and altogether inadequate to the wants of the people. Districts might be named where the people seldom hear a gospel sermon, and where prayer-meetings are never thought of, or if desired by the people, have been discountenanced by the ministers.'[82]

Somewhat more encouraging tones came from the West Coast Mission, which noted for the year 1863–64 simply that in Benbecula, 'Mr Robert McMillan is labouring with apparently much success.'[83]

St Kilda

In 1860 it was arranged that a minister should visit the totally isolated archipelago of St Kilda, by far the most western of Scotland's Western

---

80. GSS Report, 1861, p. 10.

81. ibid., 1860, p. 12. In his section on 'Revivals in North Uist' in *When God Came Down*, John Ferguson makes no mention of revival on the island during 1859–61.

82. *WJ*, 19/10/1861.

83. Annual Report of the West Coast Mission, 1863-64, p. 10.

Isles, located some forty miles off North Uist. Here he was to take a Communion service and bring up the arrears of baptism and marriage since the last ministerial visit some three years previously. The Rev. Reid of Portree Free Church was appointed, and was transported, along with two elders,[84] on the *Porcupine*. The ship arrived in St Kilda in late May and a Communion service was quickly announced. One man who accompanied Reid on the trip was John Hay Maxwell, Secretary of the Highland and Agricultural Society of Scotland. Maxwell noted how the native folk, who had been very chatty when the boat arrived on their island, filed into church shortly after 'with the most reverential demeanour' and in 'deepest silence'. The church was filled, both with islanders and with crew and passengers of the *Porcupine*. Maxwell proceeds to give a personal and critical, yet very revealing account of the progress of the service he witnessed:

> I managed to get a seat close to the door, and too close to Miss Christie McLeod the Idiot, who insisted on patronising me and offering me a share of her Gaelic Bible which neither of us was capable of reading. Mr Reid, when I entered, was exhorting the congregation preparatory to administering the Sacrament, and the scene was one of no small interest, more particularly in connection with revivalism. Had he been like too many of his class he could easily have returned to Skye with accounts of the wonders he had worked, and the revival he had stimulated. The work was ready to his hand, but to his credit he would not take advantage of the excitement under which many of these before him laboured. He strove on the contrary to calm and soothe them, and did not proceed with the Communion till he had succeeded in doing so. I, of course, could not understand him, but his tone and demeanour clearly showed what his object was, and my impressions were confirmed afterwards by the Uist gentlemen. Notwithstanding his creditable conduct, we were in expectation of hearing 'the cry' at any moment and of being required to carry out some of those affected.

---

84. One of these was christened Judas by the crew of the ship that took them to the island. John Hay Maxwell described him as 'a long, lanky figure, a lanthorn jawed cadaverous countenance, a mouth destitute of teeth except a couple of fangs, an expression of sanctimony and self-satisfaction, a long cloak and a black staple hat, all reminded me of the notorious "Men" who exercise so unbounded and tyrannical a spiritual sway over the ignorant people of Sutherland and Caithness' (Michael Robson, *St Kilda: Church, Visitors and "Natives"*, Port of Ness, 2005, pp. 430-1).

The class who were so [affected] corroborated all the most reliable accounts of such scenes. The weaker the intellect, the greater was the emotion. There was none visible among the men – comparatively little among the married women, a few of them were moved, but many of the girls were bending and twisting their bodies, and groaning piteously. It may seem irreverent to record it but it is perfectly true, that, of all present, my neighbour Miss McLeod was most saturated with revivalism, and had the movement been encouraged by the preacher, she was the first who would have required assistance.[85]

85. ibid. Given St Kilda's geographical and social isolation, it seems doubtful whether the events here described, though occurring amidst the nationwide awakening of 1859–61, were directly influenced by the revivals occurring elsewhere in the country.

Daviot Church

Archibald Cook

John Kennedy

Matthew Armour

Chapter 15

The Far North

Inverness-shire

Inverness

Beginnings

A number of evangelistic initiatives sprang up in Inverness during the 1850s which, combined, helped to pave the way for a spiritual awakening to overtake the town. In late August and early September 1858, the *Inverness Advertiser* carried two lengthy articles, favourable in tone, on the revival taking place in America, both written by the Free Church minister of East Kilbride. This was followed in June 1859 by detailed accounts of the Ulster revival. A correspondent writing to *The Scottish Guardian* claimed that the movement that later came to Inverness did not have its origins in the American or Irish revivals, but with a visit from Brownlow North, who, along with Hay MacDowall Grant, conducted a preaching tour of the north in the autumn of 1858. One Sabbath evening North had preached in the East Church 'to an immense crowd', the building being 'thronged in the stairs and passages'. The audience had been 'eager to hear the powerful and impressive expounder of the Gospel',[1] whose address had made 'a decided impression' on the community. Young Christian men were revived and commenced district prayer meetings in destitute parts of the town, also forming a Y.M.C.A. in May 1859. These non-denominational prayer meetings took place in both the early morning and early evening, at 7 a.m. and 7 p.m. respectively. A minister arriving

---

1. Norman Campbell, *One of Heaven's Jewels: Rev. Archibald Cook of Daviot and the (Free), North Church, Inverness*, Stornoway, 2009, p. 164.

in Inverness in March 1859 was quick to notice that 'a measure of new religious interest had been awakened' as a result of North's visit.[2]

The first half of 1859 saw a number of further beneficiary measures, such as a series of lectures on the 'prevalent sins of the day' delivered by local ministers in the town's churches; the 'Eighth Annual Appeal for United Prayer' being advertised in a local paper and endorsed in its editorial; the targeting of the town by the newly formed North-East Coast Mission, which organisation aimed to soon have a resident missionary agent in the town as one of ten districts into which its directors had divided the coast; and the induction to the Free High Church in March of the Rev. Donald Fraser, a respected preacher and a keen supporter of revival. Perhaps partly as a result of these initiatives, in May 1859, in regard to Inverness and the north-east, increased prayer meetings were observed, as well as a more marked seriousness on the part of communicants and a far greater than normal number of admissions to the Lord's Table.

Inverness Town Mission

A highly significant factor in the development of revival in Inverness was the formation of the Inverness Town Mission in 1850, and its employment of a full-time evangelist in Duncan MacBeth from Applecross. MacBeth, who was quickly praised for his 'singular earnestness, perseverance, judgement and faithfulness', set a pattern of visiting hundreds of families not in the habit of attending church. A great many of these were poor and resided mainly in Merkinch and other areas west of the river. By 1855 MacBeth noted that initial opposition had gone and in some houses there was 'a longing for my return'. By 1857 people were flocking to his prayer meetings, the one on Sabbath evening being 'crowded to the door'. Such interest continued to grow and by 1858 the missionary was holding five weekly meetings as well as visiting over 1,700 families annually and holding hundreds of small meetings 'for prayer and simple exhortation'.[3]

By this time MacBeth could report, 'Many souls that had lain for years in spiritual death have become anxious inquirers, and not a few

---

2. Edward Duncan Hughes, *What God Hath Wrought: The Story of the YMCA, Inverness*, Inverness n.d., p. 13; N. Campbell, p. 166.

3. ibid., p. 175.

are at this moment under deep soul concern.' The year 1859 saw further instances of spiritual fruit from his work. His meetings were now so popular that people 'were crowding about the doors and windows' to hear his stirring addresses, and there was considerable 'obedience rendered to the outward call of the Gospel Truth'. MacBeth refused to enumerate conversions till 'their profession be somewhat tested', but he was aware of many promising cases. By 1860 attendance at meetings surpassed that for previous years, and a good number were also now attending regular church services. 'It is a token for good to souls when we behold a moving amongst the dry bones', MacBeth rejoiced. 'The Lord only can command the breath of spiritual life to enter into them in His own good time and way, and to Him be the glory.'[4]

It should be noted that the ministry of MacBeth was conducted largely independently of the revival work that developed elsewhere in town, which progressed in a general spirit of evangelical ecumenism amongst the town's ministers.[5] For the Highland evangelist was wary of people professing conversion too soon, and there seems little doubt he would have deplored the revivalist methods – such as instant 'decisions', the 'Inquiry room' – of Reginald Radcliffe, Richard Weaver and others who came to the Highland capital during the period of the revival. One who came around to views similar to MacBeth was the Rev. Cameron of nearby Ardersier, who expressed regret that he had 'not taken a firmer stand' against some of the lay evangelists, in the light of some of the doctrines he had heard them expound. Donald Fraser of the Free North Church, while holding reservations regarding revivalist methodology, nevertheless 'rejoiced if good was done, by whatever instrumentality'. Many other conservative believers, too, were concerned at the easy faith displayed by converts of popular evangelists who visited their town. Donald Fraser noted that the zeal of these young converts 'was

---

4. The work of the Town Mission continued to flourish, with MacBeth stating in the spring of 1863, 'There is no abatement, but rather an increase, in the attendance at all the meetings' (ibid., p. 178).

5. Yet Rev. Sutherland of the East Church felt that there was an inclination in the joint services conducted during the revival to 'ignore the great doctrines of Calvinistic theology'. This tended to force Free Church ministers to put their distinctive of the Headship of Christ 'in abeyance'. While he welcomed several lay evangelists into his church, Sutherland nevertheless sensed that the overall effect of their preaching was 'to Arminianise the Church' (ibid., p. 167).

accounted presumptuous by not a few Christians of the old school, and there was some danger of a breach between the young spiritual efflorescence on the one hand and the Church usages and authorities on the other'.[6]

General Movement

It seems that revival had become general in the town by September 1859, by which time a 'considerable awakening' had developed, 'without noise or extravagance'. The daily morning prayer meetings begun in 1858 were a mainstay of the movement, and were still active fifteen months later. Donald Fraser noticed that they were being maintained by young men in the town and that they acted as a kind of spiritual gauge – as the meetings rose or fell, so did the work of God among them. He further observed that about the end of September 1859 anxious enquirers began to converse with ministers. Many got relief from the burden of their souls, not at meetings but after they got home, while pouring out their hearts in private before God. Overall, Fraser believed that 'a good many young people had begun to believe with their hearts, and wished to confess with their mouths the Lord Jesus', as a result of the revival.[7] He sought to give counsel to those awakened, and received some as communicant members. He also directed them into service at the Sabbath school and asked them to pray in public.

Prayer meetings were held every morning in the Free High Church and nightly at Fraser Street Chapel, also several times a week in the United Presbyterian Church, East Free Church, North Free Church and the Wesleyan Chapel, as well as several schoolrooms. Additionally, weekly prayer meetings were being conducted in at least twenty private homes throughout the town.

Revival converts from the townships along the Banff and Moray coast were quick to testify to the transformation in their own lives whenever they sailed to ports elsewhere in the north of Scotland. In Inverness, a Findochty believer went into a barber-shop. The owner had himself been converted shortly before, through the ministry of James Turner and he was so overjoyed at meeting a brother from Findochty that he felt unable to shave anyone who came in! Instead he shut up

6. ibid., p. 166-7.

7. ibid., pp. 166, 168.

shop and took his fisherman friend to a meeting he had organised. Sometime later, when again in Inverness, the Findochty fisherman was pleased to find that the barber was still keeping the meeting going. 'Whenever he saw me he came to ask … have you gathered in any souls for the kingdom?'[8] Another convert of Turner's in the Highland capital was a meal-seller, who quickly became 'a noble champion' for the Lord's cause, addressing meetings in Clachnaharry, just outside Inverness, on every occasion he had opportunity.

A few boys who had been 'a nuisance in their neighbourhood' became little missionaries during the revival and went through the town distributing tracts. A good number had been brought to speak to the ministers by those of their own rank and age, to whom otherwise the ministers would have had no access. Open-air preaching was conducted almost every night in various quarters, while in Muirtown a large wooden building was converted into a preaching station. 'The sound of preaching invariably gathers a good congregation', noted one Inverness correspondent, adding that such audience would remain attentive for hours.[9]

'Large devotional assemblages' gathered in the Free High Church and the Free East Church, which were open every night, and one minister said he conversed with 150 inquirers. An altered appearance was observed on the streets, especially on the Sabbath, when hardly a drunkard could be seen. The Rev. Sutherland of the Free East Church wrote a letter to be read out at the massive open-air rally in Huntly in 1860 which stated that he had seen 'more fruit attending the ministry of the gospel during the last year than during eighteen years in my previous ministry; and I am not aware among those who make an open profession of a single case of external backsliding'.[10]

East Coast Influence

As previously inferred, the movement in the Highland capital was given added impetus in March/April 1860 with the visit of some fifty or sixty Buckie fishermen. Morning and evening meetings were conducted each day, to which crowds attended. This was a seasonal visit from the east coast dwellers, to procure mussels for bait at the river mouth. Most of

8. McHardie, pp. 133-4.

9. *Inverness Advertiser*, 12/01/1860; *SG*, 09/09/1859.

10. ibid., 21/10/1859; *WJ*, 21/01/1860, p. 132.

them had come under the influence of the religious revival which had lately spread across north-east ports, and noted one Inverness local, so changed was their lifestyles that 'one has difficulty except from outward appearance in recognising the same men who have visited us for so many years past'. Instead of wasting their time drinking and swearing, they now held prayer meetings in various parts of town, dressed in their ordinary fishing attire. The first of these meetings – in the Free High Church – went on till a late hour, but was 'of the most orderly description ... the fishermen sang and prayed at intervals in their own earnest manner – one individual giving a simple but accurate description of the revival which had been so much blest in their neighbourhood'.[11]

James Turner led meetings in Inverness's Methodist chapel in June/July 1860. He wrote movingly in his diary: 'I have been four nights in our chapel here, and it has been filled to the door. Last night even the passages were crowded, many crying for mercy, and I trust not a few finding it. It was daylight this morning before I got to bed, it being about one o'clock a.m. before we could leave the chapel, and the house continued nearly full up to that hour. On Friday, Mr Parker went with me to the Infirmary, and nearly every person we spoke to was moved and melted down, and I hope some really found peace of believing. A backslider on his deathbed has been restored.'[12]

Although the revival in Inverness had peaked many months previously, spiritual excitement continued into the summer of 1861, when thousands attended great open-air meetings during the annual Wool Fair in mid-July. Special trains brought people from Keith, Elgin and other places along the east coastline. The venue was Farraline Park, not far from the town centre. It might have been a wholly Presbyterian gathering, with several of Inverness's main Presbyterian church leaders taking part (as well as a number of laymen), but among the ministers speaking was Ferdinand Dunn, a Baptist from Fortrose, meeting the largest congregation of his life.

Star attraction at this gathering, though, was Robert Cunningham, the converted butcher from Glasgow, who ranted and railed against

---

11. *Inverness Advertiser*, 03/04/1860, p. 2.

12. McHardie, p. 30.

publicans and against 'decent church-going folks who sat listening to ministers whose religion was all doctrine stowed up in the garrets of their heads'.[13] His discourse made a deep impression on many. Meanwhile, round the corner at the same time, a similar service was being conducted in Gaelic. Total assemblage at the two services was estimated at four thousand. Meetings continued well into the evening, and for a further two days.

Heightened spiritual interest continued into 1862, in the autumn of which year Brownlow North returned to Inverness to preach to large crowds in three of the town's churches. Hundreds of people were turned away because of lack of room. As late as November 1864, when Richard Weaver held a week's mission in several churches in town, 'these large buildings were all crowded to the doors'. Weaver's discourse was occasionally interrupted by 'loud sobbings and audible exclamations from individuals in the audience, but there were not violent "revival" demonstrations'.[14]

Other Districts

Nairn

A correspondent writing for the *Wynd Journal* informed readers towards the end of autumn 1859 that, 'a great religious movement' had been going on in Nairn for several weeks. Communicants were no longer satisfied with being members of the church; 'they found that they must be born again'. There were interesting cases of children getting their parents up during the night to pray for them. One young person, speaking in Gaelic, testified, 'I would not take upon myself to say I am a Christian; but there is one thing I feel now, that I am all wants and Christ all fullness.' The movement was said to have been similar to that in Inverness, with 'signs of quickening in some of the country parishes around'. In Nairn (and in Keith) it was observed that 'children, apprentices and maid-servants have their stated prayer-meetings'.[15] Kenneth Jeffrey also refers to this Catholic stronghold, noting that

---

13. *Inverness Advertiser*, 12/07/1861, quoted in Norman Newton, *The Life and Times of Inverness*, Edinburgh, 1996, p. 107.

14. N. Campbell, p. 170.

15. *WJ*, 21/01/1860, 13/12/1859, p. 132; *SG*, 21/10/1859.

the (then Nairnshire) parishes of Nairn and Ardclach were to some extent influenced by revival.[16]

Daviot

The Rev. Archibald Cook had transferred to Daviot from Inverness in 1844 and remained there till his death in 1865. A new Free Church building was opened in the parish (at Dalvourn, Farr) in 1859, and Cook preached three sermons every Sabbath, one in Gaelic. His preaching was highly esteemed and people flocked to his services from all over the parish and from as far away as Glenurquhart and Strathspey. Local tradition speaks of nine hundred gathering on the moor beside the Free Church at Farr because the building sometimes could not contain the numbers attending. A 'remarkable revival of religion' commenced in Daviot in the late summer of 1859. Given the stirring evangelical ministry of Cook, it seems likely that the Free Church participated in the awakening, although no record survives of Cook's involvement in, or views on, the movement in his parish.[17]

In any case, where previously the area had been stigmatised 'Dark Daviot', now there were four preaching stations in the area apart from the church, and all were well-attended. In the church itself, numerous sermons were delivered every week to crowded audiences. These came from the local minister, as well as visiting preachers – laymen included – who came to assist in the work. By early 1860 the movement was still as active as ever, although weekday meetings had been restrained for a time due to the recent storms. Even at this late date, a suitable site was being sought for the construction of a hall for united prayer meetings to be held in.

Laggan

Duncan Campbell of Kiltearn was involved in the revival in the south Inverness-shire parish of Laggan. Recalled the Rev. Dugald Shaw, 'He was in the habit of coming every year to the Communion, for at least

---

16. Jeffrey, p. 159.

17. *Aberdeen Free Press*, quoted in *SG*, 22/11/1859. However, his opinions on man-centred revivalistic methods are more than hinted at by a comment made at a communion in the early 1860s, when he said, 'They are today shouting "Awakening". What awakening is that? It is a kind of natural affections, with nothing at the root, something far more dangerous to you than your sins' (N. Campbell, p. 172).

fifteen years, till latterly he became so frail that he could not venture so far. Here, as he used to say himself, he had much of the Lord's gracious presence in secret and public, much tenderness, liberty, and spiritual power in the pulpit. That was the case particularly in the years 1860-61, when there were two revivals like what [sic] took place at Loch Tayside more than fifty years ago (1816–17). Mr Campbell himself, we doubt not, received a fresh baptism of the Spirit in Laggan during the Communion of 1860, and his sermons were blest to many souls. … Indeed, after the heavenly dew rested on the soul of Duncan Campbell, none excelled him in preaching Christ in His fullness and freeness. I had a goodly number of excellent ministers assisting me on Communion occasions, but there was none of them whose services were attended with such quickening power as those of our esteemed friend.'[18]

Fort Augustus

Everywhere the Banffshire and Moray fishermen set sail to on their fishing trips, they were keen to boldly speak up for the Lord. Docking at Fort Augustus one morning, two converted brothers, keen evangelists, began a meeting at seven o'clock with the singing of a hymn. 'In the course of a few minutes we had a great meeting of men, women, girls and boys', said one of the fishermen. 'At the close of it I never saw so many souls seeking Jesus at once.' Some generous souls came up to the visitors and offered them money, to which came the response that it was souls, not coins, they were after. When they came to leave, the quay was so crowded they could scarcely get away. 'It seemed as if they would have taken us in their arms and kept us', enthused the fisherman. 'It was the only place where we met with no opposition.'[19]

Ross-shire

That there was no general revival movement in Ross-shire during the period 1859 to 1861 is evidenced by remarks made by the Rev. Malcolm Macgregor of Ferintosh, who served for twenty-three years as co-presbyter to Duncan Campbell in Kiltearn parish. In July 1874 he wrote: 'Alas! Since the revival of 1841 and 1842, there has been no manifest and extraordinary outpouring of the Holy Spirit upon Ross-

---

18. Duncan Macgregor, *Campbell of Kiltearn*, Edinburgh, 1874, pp. 86-9.

19. McHardie, p. 133.

shire, melting the souls of the community into overwhelming and irrepressible earnestness in seeking Christ and salvation. Nevertheless', remarked Macgregor knowledgeably, 'in no part of the church is the gospel more faithfully and powerfully proclaimed. The people of God are fed with the finest of wheat. ... The cause of Christ is advanced, the kingdom of God cometh, though "not with observation".' [20]

There were, however, at least a few days of 'observation', such as a Communion Sabbath in June 1858, when Campbell gave an address which 'was felt by not a few to be singularly powerful and solemn. An aged Christian said that with the exception of a sermon preached by Campbell at Tarbat during the Revival time (of 1840), it was the most solemn he had listened to from him.' [21]

Tain partook of 'some drops of those blessed showers' that descended on the country from 1859. In November of that year, Hay MacDowall Grant preached here with some unction during the minister's absence and dealt with crowds of inquirers. Nightly meetings were commenced. Children were especially blessed, 'eagerly inquiring the way Zionward'. In the Sabbath school, a worker noted that 'uncommon stillness and awe pervaded our meeting, and many of the little ones were bathed in tears'. [22]

In Munlochy and district, prayer meetings were held nightly, some of which were sustained until near daybreak the following morning. An army Major by name of Corman laboured for a while in the area, being assisted by several ministers from adjacent parishes as well as some laymen from Inverness. There were even several cases of striking down reported from the Munlochy region. [23] The Congregational Church in Avoch also experienced a revival around this time, during the ministry of David H. Philip. [24]

---

20. D. MacGregor, pp. 99-100.

21. ibid., pp. 67-8.

22. *SG*, 25/10/1859.

23. *Banffshire Journal*, quoted in Rose, p. 39.

24. McNaughton, 2003, p. 212. Ferdinand Dunn of Fortrose, pastor of the then only Baptist Church in Ross-shire, preached in Avoch during 1862, to 'the largest congregation I have preached to in the open air in this quarter. It was truly a delightful service, both young and old heard with marked attention' (BHMS Report, 1863, p. 15).

The participation of laymen such as MacDowall Grant, however, may have been one factor which helps explain why many parts of Presbyterian Ross-shire were not strongly influenced by the 1859–61 revival, although this was probably not the only reason.[25] It is possible that the county at large had early developed a dislike of emotionalism through the influence of the much-respected Rev. John Kennedy, who laboured in Dingwall Free Church from his ordination in 1844 till his death forty years later.

However, we know that one of Kennedy's Free Church colleagues in Ross-shire, the Rev. John H. Fraser of Rosskeen, took part in revival services in Burghead,[26] so Fraser was clearly not averse to the revival movement, and possibly held special meetings in his own church too, though the short 'Memoir' written of him mentions nothing of this. His situation appears to have been similar to that of his colleague, the Rev. Campbell of Kiltearn, who was also used in revival elsewhere in Scotland in these momentous years, but apparently not in his own county.

John Kennedy had early visited Ireland during 'the great revival season' there, with an ardent 'panting to find the best accounts that I had heard to be true'. However, as with other revival movements he knew of, 'where I expected a "wilderness" to be changed into a "garden of the soul", I have only seen a desert becoming more a waste than before'.[27] Thus he was left with the impression that in connection with

---

25. Some believers in Ross-shire even criticised revival in other parts of the Highlands and Islands where there was no lay preaching. Norman Macfarlane records that 'on one occasion Angus Maciver and Kenneth Ross were at a Communion in Easter Ross. On the Question Day, Angus stole in unnoticed and covered his head with his plaid. He wished to listen and not to speak. One of the "Men" opened out and thundered against revivals and particularised the revival in Lews. Angus threw the covering from his head and sat bolt upright. He was soon observed, and the minister in charge called upon him to speak. The Lews revival was fortunate that day in its defender. *MacRath Mor* (Big MacRae) called the faultfinders the "black crows of Easter Ross"' (Macfarlane, *The "Men" of the Lews*, p. 60). G. N. M. Collins suggests that the Lewis revival in question was that in Lochs in 1859–60, but it was clearly an earlier movement, as Maciver died in 1856, well before the start of the '59 awakening (Collins, 1976, pp. 38-9).

26. *Inverness Advertiser*, 23/03/1860, p. 3.

27. Kennedy said of his visit to Ireland, 'I had ample opportunity of examining the first results of the movement. I was present at a converts' meeting. There was a desk for preaching practice at one side of the hall in which they were assembled.

revivals with which he was personally aware, there was, to a greater or less extent, a genuine work of grace, but that this was not infrequently covered out of sight by a superficial excitement, which alone caught the eye of the public.[28] In their efforts to increase such emotionalism, men were, he believed, 'unconsciously working out a design of the enemy, who would fain implicate in it the honour of vital godliness, that he might, by proved failures, bring discredit on the Spirit's work, and thus confirm the unbelief, and deepen the sleep, of worldlings'.[29]

Sutherland

That the revival – at least in its early stages – had little influence on Sutherland is evident from a notice from the Sutherland correspondent

---

One after another mounted it, and delivered a discourse. I heard four of these, but in none of them was there any reference to the law, to the necessity of regeneration, to the Divine person or atoning blood of Christ, or to any of the Divine perfections but love. Vague declamations about the danger of unbelief, and the desirableness of peace and joy in believing, was all that they contained. I thought then, and I still think, that the themes ignored by those speakers could not be passed over in a true converts' address; and I was not unprepared for the answer given, two years thereafter, by an Irish minister, to my question, when I asked, "What is now the result of the revival in your district?" His reply was, "During that wonderful movement I laboured with all my strength, and at such a pitch of hope, that I thought none around me would remain unsaved; but, at this moment, I know no result besides the spread of Plymouthism, and a prevalent contempt for the stated means of grace, the last of those whom I regarded as converts having recently gone back to the world' (John Kennedy and Horatius Bonar, *Evangelism: A Reformed Debate*, Portdinorwic, 1997, pp. 113-14).

28. Thus it is that, though regarded as 'the prince of Highland preachers', who made a profound impression on his hearers, Kennedy's ministry in Ross-shire does not seem to have been marked by any great spiritual movement, being, in the opinion of a later minister in the town, 'marked rather by correct doctrine than spiritual life' (Rev. J. R. MacPherson, in *A Wave of Blessing in Black Isle and Easter Ross*, Glasgow, 1906, p. 40).

29. Kennedy and Bonar, pp. 114-15. Kennedy's biographer, Norman C. Macfarlane, opined: 'It was more than a surprise that the ardent admirer of Dr John Macdonald should oppose and almost scoff at revivals. The Pentecostal and Sychar revivals of the New Testament might have given him pause. This was one spot in his fine mind which went lame. The Highlands followed him into this and other desert places' (Macfarlane, 1989, p. 103). Rev. Donald Beaton argued, however, that Kennedy did not oppose revivals as such (Rev. Donald Beaton, *Some Noted Ministers of the Northern Highlands*, Inverness, 1929 [reprinted 1985], p. 276). See Chapter 20 for Kennedy's reaction to the Moody mission.

to the *Inverness Advertiser* in April 1860: 'Whether it be that we Sutherland folk are more hardened than our Caithness neighbours, or whether we are to be "left to ourselves", are questions not easily answered. We only know that while a revival is going on within a few miles of our border, here there are no signs of one. There can be now little doubt that this movement is productive of good. We ourselves know parties who were not remarkable for much good, who have lately turned from their evil ways to seek the Lord, and we sincerely hope that the changes wrought may be permanent.'[30]

The county did not remain totally aloof from the movement, however. A gentleman from Ewing Place Chapel in Glasgow travelled to the far north during 1861 and laboured in various places. He wrote:

> In one village a real work of the Spirit, so far as man can judge, appears to have been commenced. Indeed, several young men there have been wonderfully changed, and from all accounts that have reached me, the change seems to be real. One night I attended a prayer-meeting held by these young men, and it was most pleasing to hear the prayers which were offered up by eight or nine of them, one after another. A few elderly persons have also been blessed, and still the work goes on. Nowhere did I find so much warmth manifested since leaving Glasgow, as at the prayer-meetings in that village.[31]

The Glasgow evangelist confessed to there arising considerable opposition in some places to the revival meetings. This, he felt, stemmed 'in some cases from ignorance, and in others from direct hostility to aught that savours of revivalism'. He hoped such prejudice would soon vanish as people became more enlightened in regard to the real nature of the work. Considerable difficulty was even experienced in obtaining a place to meet in, with prior application having also to be sent to the Duke of Sutherland (who was then in London). Notwithstanding the varied

---

30. *Inverness Advertiser*, 10/04/1860, p. 2. Free Church records also suggest that the north of Sutherland, at least, did not experience revival blessing during 1859–61, nor again during the 'Moody revival' of 1874–75. However, spiritual awakening did appear in this region latterly: a number of townships along the north Caithness-Sutherland coast all the way to Cape Wrath receiving a shower of blessing during 1897–98, when missionaries from the Highland Committee visited the area (Lennie, 2009, p. 73).

31. *WJ*, 31/08/1861, p. 182.

objections strongly urged by many, the hall was granted, this by the Duke himself. 'It was a complete triumph over all who opposed the work', wrote the visiting evangelist. 'I think we had about twenty meetings altogether, and at some of them the Lord's presence was truly felt. The last meeting, more especially, was a most successful one, and I do not despair of hearing in a short time that the Lord has commenced a blessed work there.'[32]

Speaking at the Free Church General Assembly in 1862, Captain McKenzie of Nairn referred to a visit he had made to Sutherland. He said that the call that drew him there was 'grace, an effectual call'. He went to the schoolmaster and asked for use of the schoolhouse as a place of meeting. The headmaster agreed to allow him use of the building 'for the sake of Nairn'. 'But I don't want it for the sake of Nairn' said McKenzie, 'I want it for the sake of Christ.' His request was granted. Asked if there was anyone who could go through the community and introduce him to the people, the headmaster pointed to the corner. There the visitor found 'a child of God groaning and weeping at the altar of grace. I went from house to house, and there was not a single person to take an interest in the matter, but next evening we had about twenty or thirty weeping souls before us'.[33]

Hugh Buchanan, a native of Londonderry, came to Scotland in 1859, in an attempt to spread the influence of the mighty Ulster revival. He took an active part in the progress of the revival movement and travelled north, where he settled in the Sutherland district of Lairg. Here he conducted evangelistic meetings in various parts of the county.[34] Meanwhile, in the parish of Creich, which was blessed with a strong evangelical heritage going back to 1810, Alexander Murray, born in 1853 and later an eminent elder in Creich under the ministry of Gustavus Aird, recalled, as a youth in the early 1860s, being able to count no less than eight prayer meetings being held on a Saturday evening in an area of some three square miles around Badbea.[35]

---

32. ibid.

33. ibid., 12/07/1862, p. 125.

34. George Macdonald, *Sketches of Some of the 'Men' of Sutherland*, Inverness, 1937, p. 138.

35. Iain H. Murray, *The Life of John Murray Professor of Systematic Theology, Westminster Theological Seminary, Philadelphia, Pennsylvania 1937-1966*, Edinburgh, 1984, pp. 6-7.

Caithness

The experiential Christianity of many Caithness believers in the mid-nineteenth century was renowned.[36] Accounts of revival in the county in 1859–61 come predominantly from a particular stretch of the east coast and from the two main towns, Thurso and Wick. It is probable that other parts of this expansive county, like neighbouring Sutherland, were much less affected. Hay Macdowall Grant returned to Caithness in August 1859, after his highly successful visit there twelve months previously in company with Brownlow North (see Chapter 3). This time he was assisted by his seventeen-year-old nephew, William Hay Aitken, later to become a Canon in the Church of England. Grant addressed the adults, and Aitken the children, amongst whom a considerable work soon began.

Thurso

A crowd estimated at four thousand gathered in Thurso to hear the preachers. The work went on right through the week, and the following Sunday 'the power of God seemed to come down upon the place'. Upwards of four hundred souls were dealt with as inquirers, and more than half of these were believed to have become members of the different churches – the vast majority joining Thurso First Free Church.[37]

The Rev. Walter Ross Taylor of that church said that by May 1860 upwards of two hundred communicants had been added to the Communion roll, which included previously just three hundred names. The yearly additions previously, he noted, 'arising partly from the peculiar state of feeling in the Highlands on this subject – were only about twelve; surely it indicated a remarkable change to find ten times the number of applicants coming forward'.[38]

Over fifty years later, in 1909, Canon Hay Aitken reminisced about this time in Thurso: 'The whole place was stirred, as I think I have

---

36. One Argyllshire believer who journeyed through the far north in the late 1860s concluded somewhat simplistically that people in Ross-shire lived on the faith of their grandfathers; those in Sutherland on the faith of their fathers; while in Caithness 'he fell in with a people who had a godliness of their own' (quote in N. Campbell, p. 65).

37. C. E. Woods, *Memoirs and Letters of Canon Hay Aitken*, London, 1928, p. 83; Gordon, 1876, p. 132; MacRae, 1906, pp. 138-9.

38. *WJ*, 08/06/1860, p. 86.

never seen a place stirred before or since.'[39] The mission, he said, 'did more to shape my future career than perhaps any other event in my life … seldom in the intervening fifty years have I witnessed more remarkable manifestations of the power of the Holy Spirit, affecting a whole population, than I did then'.[40]

Wick and Pultneytown

An 'association of prayer' had been set up in Wick in 1859 to bring people of different congregations together to pray for an endowment of God's Spirit in power upon their northern community. Controversy soon attended the movement, however, for the Rev. Charles Thomson of Wick Free Church promptly withdrew from the group as soon as the Established Church minister, Dr Lillie, joined, insisting on the necessity of guarding what he saw as Free Church principles.[41] Despite this degree of disunity, revival nevertheless came to the town in the first days of 1860. The Rev. G. Stevenson said of the fishing community of Pultneytown,[42] just across the harbour from Wick: 'The second week of the year [1860] was a remarkable one in this place, as well as in many other parts of our land … the Holy Spirit came down in great power on the congregation.'[43] Two persons were in such distress that

39. Gordon, 1876, p. 133. Alexander MacRae, too, states that 'probably no place in the north of Scotland was so deeply moved by the revival of 1859-60 as the town of Thurso, though he gives but scanty details of its progress there' (MacRae, 1906, pp. 138-9).

40. George E. Morgan, 'A Veteran in Revival': R. C. Morgan: His Life & Times, London, 1908, pp. 133-4.

41. He stated, 'I cannot, even to promote outward association in prayer, recognise as evangelical a backsliding denomination which, whatever it may profess in words, denies in deeds that the Lord Jesus Christ, who purchased the Church with his blood, is the sole Head of the Church' (N. Campbell, p. 268).

42. The revival here centred on the Pultneytown Free Church. Wick Free Church played a less prominent part in the movement, although its minister, Charles Thomson, had gone to see the work in Ireland and had participated in services in various places there. On his return home, 'he associated himself with others of his brethren in prayer-meetings for a like blessing, that were continued for six months, and not without evidence of gracious results' (Greig, pp. 140-1).

43. Strangely, it is not until the end of March 1860 that a Caithness correspondent for the Inverness Advertiser can say: 'The revival movement has now come to this side … signs of revival manifested themselves some time ago, but it was not until Sunday last that it assumed the true revival type' (30/03/1860, p. 3).

although their house was near, they could not walk home but had to be taken into the session house.[44] From that time, cases of awakening occurred regularly. Numerous letters were also sent to the minister from anxious souls and relatives interested in their friends' salvation. Twelve members of one family – husband, wife, brothers, sisters and nephews – were brought to Christ.[45]

A separate notable work began among Pultneytown school children on 6 February. One little girl spoke of some cases of conversion after Scriptures were read out during the morning's Bible lesson. Those around her began to weep aloud about their sins. The Rev. Stevenson arrived and addressed the pupils, and soon there was loud weeping in all parts of the school. The children went home crying at lunchtime and upwards of a dozen boys held a prayer meeting together before returning to school in the afternoon.

Since then about a dozen separate children's meetings arose sponta-neously – some of them numbering forty or fifty – taking both teachers and parents by surprise. When the minister preached a sermon to the

---

44. Both subsequently came to peace in Christ. Rev. Stevenson said of the husband, 'He has for several months been appointed missionary to the tinkers of Caithness, and follows them from place to place, exhorting them, reading the Scriptures, and praying with them' (Reid, 1860, p. 439).

45. Stevenson made it clear, however, that 'the number of those who have come under religious impressions is a mere handful compared with the community at large … . We have had some droppings of Divine grace; but the ground all around us is still very dry and barren' (ibid., p. 450).

children on the evening of March 1st, another veritable *Bochim* (place of weeping) ensued. Three or four times the blessing was pronounced, when a further address had to be given and it was only when Stevenson promised to preach to them the following evening that they could finally be persuaded to leave the church. Some went home to their closets and continued most of the night in prayer – many, it was believed, being savingly impressed that evening. One lad found peace on the fifth day after he was awakened. He testified that he now felt 'as if one were beating me' when he heard his peers swearing.[46]

Altogether in Wick and Pultney, 'a harvest of souls was gathered in'. Whenever the Moray-Banffshire fishermen arrived in the place, they would compel their Caithness comrades to come out of their boats so they could hold meetings among them, some marvellous conversions ensuing. One giant of a man, and 'very wild', was arrested by the Spirit and led as a lamb to the feet of Christ. He became 'a wonder to the place, a standing witness for God, and a gallant worker'. He began a regular prayer meeting and became so trusted among locals for his piety that he was often called on to pray for the sick and dying. Indeed, all this man's family were converted and became bold witnesses, including a brother, William (Henderson), another hulk of a man, who was so ferocious and wild that fishermen were afraid to go out to sea with him. He, too, like a little child found his way to the Cross and remained a glorious witness for Christ after his conversion. Another man who came to these meetings was converted only after a great struggle. In the heat of his zeal, he approached his minister and chided him for not informing him of his hitherto state of spiritual darkness. He then pleaded, 'Can you feed me now that I am converted?'[47]

Towards the tail end of the revival, a fishing boat from Portknockie came into Pultneytown harbour. On the boat were two saved men, one of whom had two and the other three unconverted brothers as part of the crew. These two believers felt an uncanny burden for their unsaved brothers and had spent many hours at sea pleading for their salvation. On one occasion they had been on their knees for three hours in prayer, when they heard someone singing a hymn on the deck above. It

46. MacRae, 1906, pp. 160-4.

47. McHardie, pp. 150-1.

transpired that one of those for whom they had been praying had found peace and was now singing songs of praise! At a meeting in Pultneytown, 'that same mighty power was manifested' and another crew member, along with several others present, were able to exclaim, 'Another sinner saved by grace. Glory to God!' Since that time all the crew bar one were brought into the fold, each continuing strong in his faith.[48]

Lybster

Further down the Caithness coast, it was reported that 'at various points of the coast where Buckie men have been fishing, an awakening has taken place'. Remarked an April report in regard to Lybster: 'Real revivals only began recently when three crews of Buckie fishermen one day took shelter in that harbour.'[49] With Bible in hand, they proceeded to the marketplace and openly addressed their fellow fishermen with spiritual words seasoned with grace. They started a prayer meeting in the local school, and the first the minister, the Rev. Mackay, knew of it was when he was roused out of his bed to come and minister to the anxious!

A good work commenced, and during the course of these meetings, 'several people were "stricken down"'. Mackay added, 'There is truly a great movement here, over which I rejoice with trembling. We have had prayer-meetings twice a day and for the past week little else has been done or spoken about. There is certainly a great change produced upon many, and I pray it may be permanent and saving.'[50]

Latheron

The Rev. George Davidson of Latheron found himself 'in powerful sympathy' with the revival – he 'cherished it, guided it and strenuously endeavoured to extend its influence'. As early as autumn 1859 a thrice-weekly prayer meeting was held in the Latheron schoolroom. Attendance grew to around four hundred, the people 'actually thirsting for the Word, and drinking it in greedily'. In early February 1860, the Moray fishermen arrived for their spring white-fishing season. The utter transformation in the lives of these men astonished everyone. Whereas in former years the average whisky account of each fisherman

---

48. ibid., p. 97.

49. *SG*, 17/04/1860.

50. *Inverness Advertiser*, 30/03/1860, p. 3; *WJ*, 07/04/1860, p. 219.

during the season was about thirty shillings, now, marvelled one local, 'During the whole season not a man has passed a glass of whiskey to his lips. Amid storms of wind, rain, snow and sleet', in their 'arduous and toilsome vocation', the men 'have been totally abstinent, at sea and onshore'.[51] Where formerly many pounds were spent on liquor, now not even a few pence was given towards the demon drink.

The report of their altered habits greatly strengthened the impressions already existing as to the reality of the work. Meetings now became nightly, and where formerly there had existed a subdued feeling with tears and sighs, now there was a degree of 'violent agitation', and a few cases of prostration. 'Many of both sexes were wont to stand up in rapid succession, as if under an irresistible impulse, and to utter the most earnest and fervent supplications.' A few of the 'boisterous' kind 'evidently spoke for effect', and had to be checked.[52]

In any case, calm and order was restored after just a few nights, and among the unsaved a solemn awe spread over the whole district, especially where the revival movement had taken hold. *The John O' Groats Journal* noted that 'some of the Portknockie crews on their way to Lewis the other day engaged in worship in their open boats in early morning. The singing of hymns and Psalms could be heard distinctly around the quays, rather novel sounds in our harbour and presenting a striking contrast to the bacchanalian orgies which used to be indulged in on like occasions.'[53]

In Latheron, considerable opposition came against the work. Two 'men of reputed piety', though not members of the church, nor regular churchgoers, 'openly and unscrupulously denounced' the work, being 'greatly instrumental in limiting, if not arresting' its progress. They held meetings by themselves, and a few who had been awakened at the revival meetings went to consult them, 'but were speedily relieved of their impressions, which were pronounced "utter delusions". ... And yet they have themselves never attended a meeting, nor witnessed a really serious case!' 'A still greater hindrance' came from two of Davidson's elders, who withdrew from the meetings because of 'the unwonted manner in which convictions seem to be produced, and the

---

51. *SG*, 26/06/1860.

52. Roberts, 1995, pp. 301-2.

53. ibid., p. 302.

extraordinary excitement that attended them'. One was also a catechist of much 'piety and zeal', and the minister said that despite reasoning with him, 'his apparently conscientious scruples were so great that I could not prevail'. Their discountenance of the revival had the effect of 'staggering many in their opinion of the work'.[54]

Nevertheless, a quiet movement did proceed, and produced the most positive results. Looking back, Davidson could say that 'never was there seen or remembered a more quiet, sober and orderly fishing season than the last, over the whole of this coast'. Eighteen were added to the Parish Church roll at the next Communion, and all of them, said the minister, 'as well as others who have since joined us, continue steadfast in their profession. They manifest such zeal for the cause of Christ, love to one another, delight in divine ordinances, meekness and humility in their deportment, and an example deserving the imitation of all. The language of their lives and conversation is, like that of Moses of old, "Come thou with us, and we will do thee good, for the Lord hath spoken good concerning Israel".'[55]

Forse

Four Banffshire crews had been located at the small fishing community of Forse, situated between Lybster and Latheron, since the beginning of February 1860. Here they remained till the end of June, in preparation for the herring fishing. All of the men had been brought under the influence of the revival and it was stated that 'not only has their conduct been becoming of their profession, but, as might have been expected, their example has had a very beneficial effect on the locality'.[56]

Some other Moray fishermen got use of the local Free Church, and, wrote one worker: 'For three months held meetings twice-a-week, walking four miles to it, and scarcely held one meeting without souls being brought to the Lord. In one, a deacon of the Church was converted and confessed it openly, and does to this day; and Mr Davidson, the good old minister, also professed to get great good.' But, throwing his all into the revival, as Davidson did, there was a counter-effect. For

---

54. Alexander Mackay, *Life and Times of Rev. George Davidson, Latheron*, Edinburgh, 1875, pp. 177-9.

55. ibid.

56. *Northern Ensign*, quoted in Rose, p. 40.

although he was 'greatly refreshed and enlarged in his own spirit', his 'robust and vigorous constitution began at last to give way', his physical health suffering somewhat from overactivity.[57]

Dunbeath

A few miles down the coast from Latheron, a respected elder of the Free Church in the village of Dunbeath wrote of 'a wonderful movement' having taken place,

> ... within the last eight or ten days. A few crews of fishermen from Buckie who annually frequent the place during the winter months, engaged in their calling, and who were looked upon as pests to society by their loose lives, fishing on the Sabbath, profane swearing, drunkenness, etc, but now they hold meetings for prayer in their temporary erections on the beach, some of the inhabitants joined with them and found Christ. These meetings extended to the Free Church and school, where they are conducted every night instead of being held formerly on the Sabbath evenings only. Both Church and school are crowded to overflowing from six at night to four in the morning, and numbers struck down both at the meetings, and in their own houses. Boys from six to twelve years of age stand up to pray uninvited and can scarcely be got to desist. A number have found the Saviour, and not a few of them the most debased in the place.[58]

As noted above, these meetings were first held in the fishermen's wooden sheds, to which local people flocked to hear testimonies, prayers and the Word of God. The meetings were then transferred to the Established Church school, and then, when that became overcrowded, the Free Church of Dunbeath was granted them. 'The Lord went with us, and the power went with us', noted one Buckie fisherman. [59] The Free Church schoolmaster's daughter was the first to be brought to the Lord, and having received the spirit of Christ, she became greatly desirous of healing the longstanding breach between the Established and Free Churches in the district. This she accomplished with good effect, and the ministers of both churches were soon reunited as friends.

---

57. Alexander Mackay, *Life and Times of Rev. George Davidson, Latheron*, Edinburgh, 1875, pp. 156, 179, 195.

58. *WJ*, 07/04/1860.

59. McHardie, pp. 195-6.

Berriedale

Another Buckie fisherman told how the Berriedale Church of Scotland was granted to the zealous evangelists to hold meetings in. One fisherman elaborated: 'In the first meeting in the Established Church, there were about forty crying out for mercy. Mr M. led the meetings, while we fishermen spoke and prayed.' Here also, the cases of striking down were pretty numerous, and at the prayer meetings, which were continued nightly, several cases occurred.[60]

The Orkney Islands

Sanday

Revival in Orkney began somewhat dramatically on the north isle of Sanday, when 'a glorious manifestation of a remarkable kind' occurred. The Free Church here was pastored by the somewhat fiery and controversial Matthew Armour. Many months prior to any outbreak of revival, a meeting was set up specifically to pray for an outpouring of God's Spirit on the island.[61] During 1860 Armour also paid a visit to Carrubbers Close Mission in Edinburgh, where awakening was already in progress.

Back home, Armour set aside Sunday, 14 October 1860 as a time of waiting 'for the promise of the Father'. There was much earnest feeling and on the way home the people were weeping and crying, 'Lord, have mercy upon us.'[62] When the children later assembled for the Sabbath school, a deacon gathered them at the door and addressed them. Many cried bitterly and during the whole time of the Sabbath school such weeping continued.

Things came to a head during the November Communion, when at the close of the Monday service, some were seen outside the Free Church,

> ... leaning against the wall, crying for mercy. The vestry was crowded with persons in deep earnestness. ... On entering the church, the scene baffles description. ... A feeling of awe at seeing so many human beings groaning and crying, and strong men writhing in agony under

---

60. ibid., p. 153; *Inverness Advertiser*, 30/03/1860, p. 3.

61. Rev. John Paterson, *Memoir of Robert Paterson, D.D. Kirkwall*, Edinburgh, 1874, p. 319. The previous summer there had been an acrimonious split in the Free Church congregation, with ninety-one members petitioning the presbytery for alternative ministry, as they claimed that Armour's ministry was inadequate.

62. *Orkney Herald*, 20/11/1860.

a sense of their guilt. Some, who had newly found peace, were singing. ... Young and strong men were shouting with an almost superhuman voice, declaring 'what God had done for their souls'. Many
were lying prostrate round the pulpit and all through the church,
so that it was hardly possible to move without treading on some of
them ... it was between four and five o'clock in the morning when they
finally dispersed. Many declare that they slept none that night, but
went to their houses and gathered in groups for prayer; and they say it
was the happiest night they ever spent in their lives.[63]

The Rev. John Paul of Sanday's United Presbyterian Church described
the following evening as 'in some respects, still more astonishing'.

> [The revival was] more striking and wonderful than any revival I have
> read or heard of, unless it be that which has taken place in some parts
> of Ireland. ... I think I can restrain my feelings as well as most peo-
> ple; but on this occasion I was completely overcome. I laid my head
> upon the desk and sobbed awhile. ... Some were on their knees pray-
> ing, and others lying on their faces moaning in agony; some running
> about apparently wild with joy; and others in groups singing hymns
> and psalms of praise. The session-house had been set apart for those
> who wished to retire but to be there was no great retirement, for it
> was crowded during the evening with praying people, and so were
> the porches of the church and the back seats of the gallery, and many
> were found prostrate on the floor of the church,[64] between the seats,
> and in out-of-the-way corners, in great mental agony; and I have seen
> two little girls, apparently about eight or ten years of age, kneeling on
> the floor, with their faces on the seat-board and one of their number,
> about the same age, praying most earnestly over them and for them;

---

63. ibid.; *The Revivalist*, January 1861, pp. 14-16. See also Sanday Free Church
Session Minutes, 02/11/1860, 06/02/1861.

64. Paul said that at a subsequent meeting, no fewer than seventeen people were
carried out of the hall in a state of prostration. He continued: 'These prostrations
seem quite unaccountable. A person will be sitting in the church, under no apparent
excitement, when suddenly he will fall down insensible. They know nothing that
is passing around them at such time; but they sometimes speak, or sing, and they
always come out of it in a joyful state of mind. While in this state of prostration
the pulse beats regularly, and the colour remains in the face; but if one pinch them,
or scream close to their ear, or dash water in their face, there is no sign of sensation.
The length of time they continue prostrated varies from half-an-hour to fourteen
hours' (*Orkney Herald*, 28/01/1861).

and there were many such instances of juvenile earnestness. ... On going out. ... I found many about the church and dykesides, some of them standing, but many of them kneeling on the cold, wet ground, praying earnestly, and most of them audibly.[65]

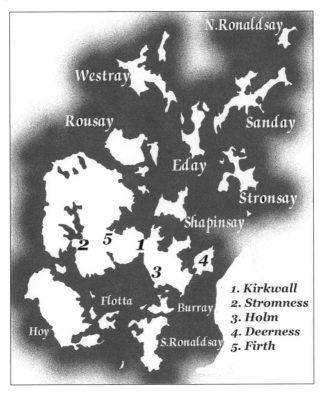

Some were of the opinion that the Sanday revival was largely a result of Armour stirring up enthusiasm by his emotionally charged preaching. *The Orkney Herald* complained of the 'unseemly concomitants' of the hysteria Armour aroused. It regarded 'the desire for physical manifestations ... as an unhealthy symptom, which could easily be traced to the same source as the passion for balls and theatre'. It is noteworthy that in several other Orkney locations which Armour visited, e.g., Papa Westray, Rousay and Kirkwall, emotional manifestations, previously unknown in these places, were an immediate result of his preaching. A correspondent for *The Orcadian* felt that 'those under conviction should be cautioned not to give way to any violent or unrestrained exhibition of their feelings'. He observed, interestingly,

---

65. ibid., 04/12/1860.

that in Sanday 'it is not those who are under concern for their souls that make the loudest noise (for the noise is at times tremendous), but those who declare that they have found joy and peace in believing. And it is painful to think that when you ask some of these the grounds for their exceeding great joy, they cannot tell. Some plainly say that they do not feel that they are the children of God ... .'[66] More caustic still was Dr Stephan, the Roman Catholic missionary, who wrote to his superior: 'In Orkney the Protestants begin to be mad from revival humbug. A man of their kind was put to the lunatic asylum at Edinburgh. ... Many other people have lost their senses, amongst them a minister of the Free Church and the medical man told me yesterday that this minister will be sent probably to the same lunatic asylum.'[67]

By the start of the New Year, it was said that 'the excitement is kept up to an extraordinary degree'. The work was still in progress several months later, when there existed 'a great number of small meetings in every corner of the island'.[68] It was during this period that Sanday folklorist, Walter Traill Dennison, took a break from chronicling island stories to write his ten 'Sanday Revival Hymns', which were subsequently published.[69]

Eday

From Sanday revival spread to every one of Orkney's other north isles. In Eday there had existed 'for several months past ... a remarkable degree of solemnity and tenderness': this due to the periodical circulation of news, in both written and oral form, of the progress of revival in America since its commencement. Nevertheless, it was

66. *The Orcadian*, 12/01/1861, p. 3.

67. A. Gray, *Circle of Light: The History of the Catholic Church in Orkney since 1560*, quoted in Jocelyn Rendall, *Steering the Stone Ships: The Story of Orkney Kirks and People*, Edinburgh, 2009, pp. 164-5. This appears to be a reference to Rev. Armour, who in fact, was never sent to an asylum.

68. *The Orcadian*, 12/01/1861, p. 3; 02/03/1861. After the revival, Paul's congregation increased considerably. By 1878 membership had risen to 566, with five Sabbath schools, 39 teachers and 220 scholars scattered throughout the island. A new church, seating 800, was built in 1880 (David M. N. Tinch, *Shoal and Sheaf: Orkney's Pictorial Heritage*, Kirkwall, 1988, p. 157).

69. Dr Stephen Clackson, 'Centenary of a Radical Kirk Minister: The Life of Rev. Matthew Armour' in *The Orcadian*, 06/03/2003, p. 31.

following reports of the work in neighbouring Sanday that revival began in earnest. Hundreds were regularly attracted to joint public meetings. The minister of the United Presbyterian Church provided graphic details of the events at one such service: 'An unwonted silence prevailed, but all at once, as if the pent-up emotions of the audience could no longer be controlled, loud cries for mercy and groans of agony, not unmixed with joyful acclamation, burst out in various parts of the church. Many fell down on their knees and prayed aloud, others retired to the gallery and vestry, and some to the outside of the building for the same purpose.'

> [The minister] was standing before the pulpit in deep anxiety, whether to tolerate or attempt to restrain such an unwonted scene of excitement. But conscious that there had been nothing unwarranted by the Divine Master in the preceding services, and observing many, who had formerly been careless and sermon-proof, now sobbing and shedding tears in deep concern for their eternal interests, I concluded that the movement was from above.[70] Numbers were struck down so as to be unable to rise, even strong men had not only to be lifted up, but also supported and kept from falling, by their friends. As I proceeded from place to place for the purpose of giving instruction and direction to anxious inquirers, I found every one willing, almost eager, to converse about the interests of their soul, as if the hope that maketh not ashamed had already been imparted by the Holy Spirit.[71]

By this date, district prayer meetings were in operation throughout the island, and seven numerously attended meetings were held one November evening. Meetings were also held on the tiny island of Pharay (long since uninhabited), and when two visiting ministers crossed from Eday in a small rowing boat, they were greeted most enthusiastically by the Pharay people, almost the whole island making preparations to attend the service which the visiting clergymen were to lead.[72]

---

70. A visiting minister concurred, but was deeply concerned that 'hollow, unnatural incoherent declamation should be avoided, which tends to terrify the weak, and can be of little use except to produce a transient and not very desirable sensation' (*Orkney Herald*, 11/12/1860).

71. ibid.

72. ibid.

North Ronaldsay

At a meeting in a large barn in North Ronaldsay, which was completely filled, two boatmen gave an account of the religious awakening in Sanday. Many were 'visibly and deeply impressed'. The following night three hundred attended the Parish Church, the largest building on the island. At one point, 'one of the boatmen calmly inquired, "Has Christ no friends here?" Then he engaged in a short prayer, and was very impressive. A deep silence ensued: it was evident that there was a power working in the midst of them. Their sighs became audible, and at last some got up weeping and crying for mercy.' Meanwhile, 'in the session-house and outside the church multitudes were on their knees praying; and some were crying out in extreme agony'.[73]

For ten days, it was said, 'all work was suspended except what was absolutely necessary for the preservation of their own lives and those of their animals'. For a while district meetings were held almost every night, every family wishing it to be held in their own house, that some long prayed-for family member might be blessed. It was also claimed that there was not a single home on the island in which the altar was not erected, 'and upon which is not placed the sacrifice of morning and evening prayer'. One man said, 'If all this is not a work of God, I know not how to designate it.'[74]

Westray and Papa Westray

First appearance of the revival in Westray occurred at a meeting in the Baptist Chapel at Pierowall, when about fifty persons, adherents of the various churches on the island, were, said the minister, 'as deeply affected under the conviction of sin as any I had seen before'. Some, especially the young men, 'trembled violently, readily acknowledging their guilt, and cried for pardon'. For a while union meetings were held in each of the three churches in regular nightly rotation. On Tuesday evening, 27 December, a meeting was held in the United Presbyterian Church, and though the ground was 'covered with snow, and the frost keen … and the roads were also very bad, the church was crowded at an early hour'. Indeed, it was said that 'nothing seems now to satisfy the people but a meeting every night', and that 'nothing is talked of

---

73. ibid., 08/01/1861.
74. ibid.

throughout the island but the revivals'. On one occasion, 'the people would not allow the ministers to leave the place of meeting, but took hold of them, and cried out that if they left, they would be lost'.[75]

It was a tradition in Westray on New Year's Day, as in many other parishes in Orkney, for a large crowd of men and boys to play 'The Ba'– a rough, rugby-type ball game with only the very minimum of rules.[76] However, on New Year's Day, 1861 (Monday, 14 January), not a person turned up for the game, although no efforts had been made to stop it. Indeed, it was said that 'the aspect of the day was completely changed from its usual appearance ... no amusement of any kind was engaged in. Presently the salvation of the soul is the great object of attention; every other object is considered of minor importance.'[77] It was noted that 'even young men in bothies read and pray together'.

A Westray schoolteacher 'felt as if God was converting sinners all around and was passing by the children of this school'. Soon, however, some here were also affected, and both a boys' and a girls' prayer meeting were voluntarily commenced – to the scorn of other pupils. In January 1861, the teacher wrote:

> I observed an unusual appearance of silent weeping among a number of boys who had previously been careless. ... Then almost all instantly gave vent to their anguish of soul. Tears flowed freely over their young blooming faces, while their deep-toned cries revealed their agony of soul. Now a scene exceedingly affecting and one that cannot be described took place. The little band at once found work congenial to their nature. With tears of sympathy flowing freely they ran to their afflicted school-fellows with their Bibles in their hands, entwining their arms around their necks, and whispering into their ears the invitations of the gospel – the very words which gave themselves comfort. I felt the scene before me uncommonly

---

75. ibid., 06/01/1861, p. 3.

76. John D. M. Robertson, *Kirkwall Ba': Between the Water and the Wall*, Edinburgh, 2005, p. 265. The tradition in Westray continued up until World War 1 but still continues in Kirkwall to this day.

77. *Orkney Herald*, 22/01/1861; Harcus, p. 87. Jocelyn Rendall records that this 'mirthless New Year was never repeated; 1862 was brought in in traditional fashion' (Jocelyn Rendall, 'The Orkney Revivals', in *The Orkney View*, 1994, pp. 24-5. See also Rendall, 2009, pp. 163-5).

affecting. I tried to pray with them, but from my deep emotion I could hardly utter a word. I sent for Mr Reid (the headmaster), who came in to witness the solemn scene. He was also deeply affected. He spoke to them and prayed with them. We spent the rest of our time in directing them to suitable passages of Scripture, and when the hour of dismissal came they asked leave to remain to hold a prayer-meeting. On this occasion two boys were absent, and to my surprise next morning they were both struck with deep conviction of sin, which being observed (for they seem to know this by instinct), they ran to them and embraced them.[78]

In Papa Westray, just off Westray, 23 December 1860 was observed as a day of thanksgiving to God on the Tri-centenary of the Reformation, and 'for His goodness in the late harvest'. The sense of solemnity was almost tangible, and some came under conviction of sin, thus inaugurating a time of revival on the island. From the 6 to the 14 January 1861 meetings were held every evening and were numerously attended for upwards of three hours. Children, too, met in different parts of the island to pour out their young hearts to the Lord, and some children on their way home from school were known to pray together in boats on the beach and by the dykesides. Then, with a visit from the Rev. Armour of Sanday, 'a revival broke out in its most aggravated form'. It was claimed by one present that thirty people were affected 'with more or less violence' and that 'that reverend gentleman's eloquence has had its effect in bringing matters to a climax'.[79]

Stronsay, Rousay and Shapinsay

Stronsay also shared in the revival, which first appeared at a meeting in Whiteness village on 2 January 1861. New Year's Day (old style, i.e., 14 January) 'which used to be a day of much intemperance and ball-playing, etc, passed away without anything of the kind'.[80] Over a dozen well attended prayer meetings arose, and on at least two occasions meetings in the Established Church were so crowded that some could not get seats.

---

78. *Orkney Herald*, 05/02/1861. A deep movement, with events strikingly similar to those in the Westray classroom, occurred also in Holm school (See *The Orcadian*, 05/03/1861).

79. *Orkney Herald*, 05/03/1861; *The Orcadian*, 30/03/1861, p. 3.

80. ibid., 02/03/1861.

A 'gradually growing earnestness' developed in Rousay, with no external manifestations till the visit of Matthew Armour in January 1861, which, in keeping with this evangelist's ministry during the period of the revival, 'was productive of very remarkable excitement'. The three congregations worked together in admirable unity, and some attended the meetings from the neighbouring isles of Egilsay and Wyre, where meetings were also held. Around forty Rousay residents applied for membership to the Free Church alone at the April 1861 Communion, 'all of whom', it was said, 'seem to have come to Jesus'.[81]

The movement in Shapinsay began at a prayer meeting in Balfour village. A few weeks later it was said that 'nearly the whole of the inhabitants, more or less' were under its power. A setback came when the Presbytery of the United Presbyterian Church decided to withdraw from the union prayer meetings, which were attracting many. Still, meetings of between four and five hundred were known, and so universal was the interest that a marriage party, which met at 6 p.m. for their ceremony, did not fail to turn up for the prayer meeting at 7.30![82]

Orkney Mainland

On Orkney's mainland, many parishes were affected, including some that never before or since were visited with revival. In Kirkwall, weeknight meetings took place in all the Protestant churches, which attracted many hundreds. In particular, the Rev. Dr Robert Paterson of the United Presbyterian Church threw himself into the work, and quickly also became a keen promoter of the dramatic revival in Sanday. In the latter months of 1860, some young men (a number which grew to over twenty) regularly held prayer meetings in a room at the shore, most of these belonging to the working classes. Larger services were also held at the shore, and it was said that 'the gatherings are so large that no place can be got to contain the crowds ... . In other parts of the town, also, more private meetings are held in unwonted numbers.'[83]

---

81. *Orkney Herald*, 28/01/1861; *The Orcadian*, 02/02/1861, p. 3, 02/03/1861.

82. *Orkney Herald*, 22/01/1861, p. 3; *The Orcadian*, 12/01/1861, p. 3.

83. *The Orcadian*, 26/02/1861. James Nicolson was staying at a farm near Kirkwall at that time and 'witnessed some strange scenes amongst a few of the farm servants'. He went to hear Rev. Armour preach in the Free Church and later wrote that 'it was a time of strange excitement, and [Armour's] manner rather tended to keep it up.

Of the south mainland parish of Holm at this time it was reported that 'a silent manifestation of serious thoughtfulness ... has swept over almost the whole parish ... . The general aspect is one of silent weeping, with very little noise. There are few families, we believe, where this manifestation has not appeared; and those families most careless are now the most contrite. The movement is a great mystery to human reason ... . The prayer-meeting of boys has about seventy persons present. A great change of feeling seems to pervade the parish.'[84] During his speech at a wedding celebration in March 1861, the local minister, the Rev. John Pettigrew poured scorn on parties where everyone got 'roaring fou' (drunk), or would 'run up and down for the purpose of amusing others, often to the injury and even the danger of their own life'. He believed that such a solemn ordinance as marriage should be marked in a more appropriate manner. Pettigrew sat down to a round of applause. 'Fruit and cake' was served, the minister gave another address; and after a concluding prayer of thanks for the 'singular happiness all had enjoyed', the people separated, with no music or dancing having taken place. Other mainland parishes touched by the revival included Deerness, Tankerness, Firth, Evie, Rendall and Stromness.[85]

Revival in Unnamed Locations

A prayer meeting 'for the coming of the Holy Spirit' was begun in an unnamed Scottish town by a bedridden woman and some friends in April 1858. Over nearly three years the numbers augmented till the church to which they adjourned was filled from night to night. When, early in 1861, a minister 'met his class of about thirty persons, the place was a very Bochim; they could do little but weep over their own guilt and danger'. Ministers blessed in revivals elsewhere came

---

But that he was in earnest no one doubted. To me who had come to the knowledge of the truth by calm and deliberate thinking, the whole thing seemed strange, but that it left permanent results I do not doubt' (Rev. Alexander Goodfellow, *Two Old Worthies of Orkney, or the Sayings and Doings of John Gerard and Matthew Armour*, Stromness, 1925, p. 172).

84. ibid., 05/03/1861.

85. ibid., 23/03/1861, p. 3. The south isles of Burray and South Ronaldsay were also affected by the movement, although parishes in the south-west of the county – Stenness, Orphir, Hoy, Flotta – appear to have been little moved.

to preach, resulting 'in the salvation of scores, if not hundreds'. Fifty people joined one church during a single Communion. 'For weeks it was difficult to get the crowd to dismiss from worship.' They would plead, 'Do, minister, let us have a wee bit o' prayer, we like it so.' The gracious change was said to have been 'proportionately as extensive and conspicuous among the more easy and educated as among the working classes'.[86]

A minister in a rural district had become thoroughly discouraged with the low spiritual state of his congregation. Despite years of faithful preaching their hearts remained hard, and even news of revival elsewhere in the country seemed to leave them unmoved. One day he suddenly decided to abandon the preparation of his sermon, and to devote himself to prayer. On entering the pulpit the next day, the conviction seized him that something remarkable was about to happen. The people were unusually attentive, their faces betokening solemnity and awe. 'When the service came to an end several persons were broken under the Spirit's influence. That service proved to be the beginning of a genuine and permanent revival. The stagnant pool disappeared, making way for the pure, life-giving stream of the Water of Life.'[87]

In November 1861 the *Wynd Journal* reported:

A village in a distant part of Scotland has been the scene of a remarkable awakening during the last eighteen months. It would occupy too much time to tell about the first drops that fell from heaven, but it may be safely stated that conversions have been so numerous as to change the character of the entire Protestant population of the district. One who has been present at many of their meetings would bear witness to the wonderful prayers poured forth by these young disciples. Such a gushing flow of love towards the blessed Redeemer – such a tenderness of compassion towards those who are still far off, and so much apparent expectation of an answer from the Hearer of prayer, is not often met with. This favoured spot is visited in the summer season by many strangers, and amongst them were some who felt it a privilege to help on the work.[88]

---

86. *TR*, 28/09/1861, p. 99.

87. Johnson, pp. 239-40.

88. *WJ*, 02/11/1861, p. 38.

The Journal continued: 'These friends, on returning to their homes, have frequently sent back an assurance of continued interest in the progress of the revival, begging themselves to be remembered at the throne of grace. Many places thus prayed for have shared in the blessing. Some of the strangers, however, cared for none of these things, but happening to enter the little church, were pierced by the arrows of the Great King.'[89]

---

89. ibid.

Mary Slessor

James Chalmers

William Robertson Nicoll

John McNeill

Christina Forsyth

CHAPTER 16

'1859 Revival' – Appraisal

Convergence of Revival Traditions

The observation that three main revival traditions have emerged over time, each with its own distinct features and theological assumptions, is explored in the introduction to my *Glory in the Glen*.[1] The earliest of these traditions takes the form of community-based rural revivals that generally arose through the faithful preaching of Scriptures by the parish minister. They were fairly protracted and orderly affairs. A second stream became popular among Methodists, Congregationalists and other independent groups, often arising as a result of the fervent appeals of local lay preachers. With a 'new birth' experience that was sudden and climactic, these revivals were short in duration and involved spontaneous and noisy outbursts of religious enthusiasm. A third revival form emerged with the advent of well-organised evangelistic crusades in urban settings, led by professional itinerant evangelists. These invariably made use of the 'anxious seat', 'enquiry room' or space at the front to encourage public 'decisions for Christ'.

What occurred during the 1859–61 revival was the emergence for the first time of all three schools of revival in one country – even in one county – at the same time. For example, Kenneth Jeffrey's in-depth study has shown that the revival's expression in the rural north-east of Scotland in general followed the older revival genre, consisting of

---

1. Lennie, 2009, pp. 26-8; c/f 2014, pp. 27-8. For Jeffrey's original discussion on this theme see Jeffrey, Chapter 1. David Bebbington explores this concept further in his excellent, *Victorian Religious Revivals: Culture and Piety in Local and Global Contexts* (Oxford, 2012). He identifies five 'patterns' of revival emerging over time – Presbyterian, Congregational, Methodist, Synthetic and Modern (pp. 4-15).

community-based movements led by the parish minister. The majority of those influenced in these places had been invited to church by a relative, and converts were typically unmarried, female and young, the greater proportion being in their teens. Jeffrey concluded that these factors were consistent with the outworking of the traditional form of revival. The experience of spiritual awakening elsewhere in rural Scotland during these years fits the same pattern, this being especially true of movements in Argyll and the Western Isles.

Perhaps the majority of spiritual movements surveyed in this book conforms to the second revival tradition, or, more particularly, to the *synthetic approach* identified by Bebbington.[2] The initial, sudden outbreaks of revival in towns along the south-west coast fall into this category, almost universally accompanied – as they had been in Ulster, from whence they jumped the Irish Sea – by spontaneous outbursts of strong emotion. The same is true of the revival's manifestation in fishing ports up and down Scotland's east coast, from Eyemouth and Cockenzie in the south, to the coastal communities of Aberdeenshire, Banff and Moray, and right up to the Caithness ports of Pultneytown, Lybster and Latheron. Such outlets of emotional revivalism could be found, too, in a surprising number of other locations at this time, such as the market towns of North Ayrshire, and across the north isles of Orkney.

The third model of revival was clearly in evidence in some of Scotland's large towns and cities within the same time period. The movement that sprang up in Aberdeen in 1858 was co-ordinated chiefly by laymen, particularly members of the local fledgling Y.M.C.A., who engaged wholeheartedly and in a business-like fashion in the work. Many of the preachers involved were also laymen, such as Reginald Radcliffe, Brownlow North and John Gordon. Jeffrey shows how evangelists fitted their services around the working and social patterns of the population, especially those of young men, who were particularly targeted. Everything was done in a highly organised and efficient manner, from the distribution of religious tracts and Bibles to the advertising of revival meetings, and to the way in which the

---

2. A pragmatic and largely homogenous evangelical approach to awakenings that developed in the nineteenth century, retaining some elements of typical Methodist revivalism, but recruiting many Presbyterians, Congregationalists and Baptists to the cause (Bebbington, 2012, pp. 11-13).

anxious were dealt with. Conversion was presented as an instantaneous experience that simply awaited the decision of an individual's will. Meetings were also designed to be calm and controlled, and there was a notable absence of the physical manifestations that were notorious in nearby fishing communities. All of this is suggestive of the more modern model of religious revival.

In Glasgow, too, organised methods were employed by Walter and Phoebe Palmer, who invited anxious inquirers forward to kneel at the communion rail after the service. Later, E. P. Hammond specially targeted the West End of the city, hitherto untouched by revival, and which was regarded as being particularly 'cold'. It was in Glasgow also that Hammond began to hold meetings specifically for children. None other than 'new measures' pioneer Charles Finney himself addressed meetings in Edinburgh in 1859, asking those willing to publicly profess their faith in Christ to stand and hold up their right hands in testimony. Meanwhile, revival leaders in Perth arranged a massive evangelistic service at the town's South Inch. Lay evangelists, Radcliffe, Weaver, Forlong and others gave addresses throughout the day, after which thousands packed into the City Hall for a further meeting. Each of the above scenarios is suggestive of the Finneyite, 'use of the appropriate means' type of organised revivalism.

This third stream of revival of course showed itself more prominently still in the 1870s, with the arrival in Scotland of Dwight Moody. Moody and Sankey's methods took organised evangelism to a whole new level, epitomising the planned evangelistic crusade that was hitherto unknown (and to many, unthinkable) in Scotland. This became a pattern of mass evangelism in the years to come – notable, for example in Torrey and Alexander's Scottish campaign of the early 1900s, and most famously of all, Billy Graham's stadium rallies in the 1950s.

Extent and Influence of the Revival

As clearly evidenced by the abundance of historical data in this book, the revival of 1859 and the 60s was very widespread, constituting the most extensive evangelical revival in Scotland's history. Its influence extended to every one of the nation's counties.[3] The vast majority of

---

3. Shetland, Orkney, Caithness, Sutherland, Ross-and-Cromarty, Inverness-shire, Argyll, Nairn, Moray, Banffshire, Aberdeenshire, Kincardine, Forfarshire,

Scotland's Western Isles were touched by revival during these years. From Lewis in the north to Arran in the south, and including most of the island communities in between: Harris, North Uist, Benbecula, St Kilda, Islay, Mull, Bute, Great Cumbrae, Iona, Gigha, Skye, Soay, Eigg, Rum and Coll. To the north of Scotland's mainland, virtually every one of the north isles of Orkney witnessed revival scenes. As well as these, many of Orkney's mainland communities were also affected, as too were some of the south isles. All of Scotland's large cities – Glasgow, Edinburgh, Aberdeen and Dundee – came under the influence of the awakening, as did each of the major towns – not least Inverness, Perth, Stirling, Ayr, Greenock, Paisley, Motherwell, Hamilton, Kilmarnock, Dumfries, Dunfermline and Elgin.

A fine example of the permeation of revival into one Scottish region is provided by Jeffrey, who gives substantial evidence to confirm the influence of the awakening in a great many rural parishes, towns and villages in north-east Scotland, and in the principal city, Aberdeen – as well as in the fishing communities that dot the region's coast. Before 1859 had drawn to a close, *The Scottish Guardian* said the revival had penetrated 'almost every parish from Tomintoul to Banff, and every town and village shared more or less'.[4] Duncan Matheson said in the autumn of 1861 that he did not know 'perhaps one place in the county of Aberdeen where there are not living witnesses to the power of God's grace, and to the might of His Spirit'.[5]

James Murker of Banff said that during the course and immediate aftermath of the revival in the north-east, he had been honoured to hold meetings in twenty-seven or twenty-eight different parishes in the counties of Aberdeen and Banff, and that, 'with the exception of one place, he had seen no difficulty'. At one meeting in November 1861, attended by about forty individuals, Murker discovered that only three

---

Perthshire, Kinross-shire, Fife, Clackmannanshire, Stirlingshire, Dunbartonshire, Renfrewshire, Lanarkshire, West Lothian, Midlothian, East Lothian, Ayrshire, Berwickshire, Peeblesshire, Selkirkshire, Roxburghshire, Dumfriesshire, Kirkcudbrightshire and Wigtownshire.

4. By the beginning of 1860, similarly, the *Wynd Journal* was 'credibly informed that there is scarcely a town or village between Aberdeen and Inverness that has not been visited by the quickening power of the Spirit' (*WJ*, 07/01/1860).

5. *SG*, 29/11/1859; 19/10/1861, p. 23.

people could trace their conversion further back than two years. He was proud to say that 'in these northern parts there is a noble army of living men and women who had come forth to do battle for the Lord'.[6]

With regard to Aberdeen, although it was commonly believed that 'the whole city was deeply moved' by the revival,[7] Jeffrey's pioneering study reveals that only about one-third of the city's congregations were significantly influenced by the movement. In other words, while marked revival blessing was experienced in different parts of Aberdeen, the entire city was not moved. Yet a minister who visited Aberdeen thirteen years after the revival remarked that the work of 1858–60 must have been 'very profound and widespread as he had met many decided Christians in the city who had been converted at that time'.[8]

The same is true of other principal centres of population across Scotland. Marrs found that revival meetings were held in a total of fifty-five (39.5 per cent) of Glasgow's Protestant churches between 1858 and 1862.[9] Yet there were a number of other ministers whose churches were not included in the above figure of fifty-five who yet spoke in favour of the movement,[10] and it is possible that they too held special revival meetings. In addition to this, of course, is the correspondence from many (Free Church) congregations which did not report a 'decided revival or awakening' yet where was evidenced 'the manifestation of an increased interest in spiritual things, and a great willingness to hear the Word'.[11]

It is true that some areas witnessed little stirring, especially districts where there was no evangelical witness. Referring to Scotland in general,

---

6. *WJ*, 12/07/1862, p. 125.

7. Shearer, p. 100.

8. Blaikie, p. 156.

9. Of these, Marrs claimed, 27 were involved during 1858–59, with a further 8 being added in 1860, and another 20 in 1861 after the arrival of Hammond. This comprised 28 of the 40 Free Churches in the city, 13 of the 38 United Presbyterian Churches, 4 out of 6 Congregational/Independent Churches, 3 of the 39 Established Churches, 3 of the 6 Baptist Churches, 2 of the 3 Methodist Churches and 2 of the 3 Relief Presbyterian Churches.

10. e.g., Rev. Norman MacLeod of Barony Church of Scotland; Rev. Dr Matthew Leishman of Govan Church of Scotland.

11. FCSRSRM, 1861, pp. 4-12. A number of Marrs's findings are provided in the section covering Glasgow (Chapter 4).

The Wynd Journal stated that 'a large proportion of the church-going community has been outside this great work ... many have scarcely wished it otherwise ... the great proportion of our settled well-to-do congregations have been on the whole unmoved'.[12]

Again and again, revival reports of 1859–61 testify to sectarianism being broken down, as members of various denominations united wholeheartedly for prayer meetings and revival services. Evangelical ecumenism was indeed a prominent and salutary feature of the movement, although Carwardine perhaps more accurately reflects the situation in saying that the more committed evangelical wings of the different denominations '*often* worked together',[13] as does Bussey in stating that '*for a time* sectarianism was practically obliterated' (both emphases mine).[14]

The perception is that such harmony among the denominations did not always continue so strongly after the revival subsided. This is clearly reflected in a statement made by a correspondent to *The Revival* periodical in 1862 that, 'Sectarianism and want of unity are murdering their thousands in this city.'[15] It is interesting to note, also, that in regard to the union negotiations entered into by the Free Church and United Presbyterian Church in 1863, no primary or secondary source identifies the revival as influential.

Comparisons to Previous Revivals

Repeatedly in revival reports, one finds the claim that the 1859 revival in a particular community was more influential than a previous movement that had affected that locality. Comparisons, including the four given below, generally refer to the geographic extent of the revival in question, and only occasionally to its overall clout. For example, during the 1859 revival in Dundee, prayer meetings began to spring up all over the city. This, claimed one prominent town minister, was in distinction to the famed revival that overcame Dundee during the ministries of Robert Murray McCheyne and William Chalmers Burns

---

12. *WJ*, 21/04/1860, p. 236, quoted in Jeffrey, p. 77.

13. Carwardine, 1978, p. 99.

14. Bussey, p. 236.

15. Marrs, p. 337.

two decades previously, when prayer meetings were numerous over only a portion of the town. A similar observation was made of the town of Perth. The Rev. John Milne observed that in 1840, revival, potent and vigorous as it was, was largely confined to his own Free Church congregation; whereas in 1860 it was much more general, every congregation receiving a measure of blessing, and the work spreading to the country all around.

Dynamic and of enduring impact was the evangelical awakening that shook Uig parish in Lewis in the third decade of the nineteenth century, before ricocheting around much of the island. Notwithstanding the influence of this revival, one island minister gave his strong belief that the 1859–60 revival was 'a hundred fold' more extensive than that earlier movement. Meanwhile, the surprising opinion of one Free Church minister on visiting a Communion occasion in Dunlop during the 1859 revival was that, 'Brighter and better days they were even than those of Livingston and the Kirk of Shotts, the most memorable perhaps in the history of Scotland's Church.'[16]

Counting Converts

Worldwide revival authority, J. Edwin Orr, claimed that out of a total Scottish population of slightly over three million, there were 300,000 revival converts. This estimate has been quoted again and again over the decades, and is accepted by many as authoritative. But there are major problems with Orr's calculation.

First, it is generally acknowledged that a great many converts were already in customary formal membership of the Church – these were seldom noted as accessions, as they were unlikely to request the removal of their name from the register in order to resubmit it on the basis of a more thorough experience. Yet, while making note of this fact,[17] Orr then goes on to use membership growth as a basis for estimating the number of converts. As evidence, he provides data which shows that 477 of Scotland's United Presbyterian congregations added 15,314 new members in 1859, an increase of 10 per cent.[18] Orr assumes that

---

16. *SG*, 08/11/1860.

17. Orr, 1949, p. 76.

18. *United Presbyterian Magazine*, 1860, p. 371.

all of these were 'presumably in the latter months of 1859', and as a direct result of the revival. But he gives no evidence to support this assumption. In any case, it is probable that a great many revival converts of the second half of 1859 were not formerly added to the Church until after the year end.

Secondly, Orr completely overlooks the fact that a large number of mission stations established by the United Presbyterian Church in the mid-1850s were given formal sanction around 1860. As a result, those attending mission stations were suddenly eligible for inclusion in national statistics. This might account for a considerable portion of the increase in growth of the United Presbyterian Church during the revival period.

Thirdly, and perhaps most significant of all, additions to church membership or professions of faith do not in themselves equate to genuine Christian conversion. Many included in such statistics may, after the initial excitement of their 'conversion experience', or after a time of testing or peer pressure, fall away entirely from their short-lived faith, though still be shown as church members.

Orr also concluded that because the Presbyterian Church of Ireland had 'incompletely reported' an accession of ten thousand members in the first three months of the Ulster revival,[19] representing a membership growth of 10 per cent to that denomination,[20] and that this was compatible with statistics from the United Presbyterian Church in Scotland, therefore 'this percentage may be considered typical of the Presbyterian bodies'.[21] But given that the movement in Ulster took on a different form to that in Scotland, one cannot make deductions from one to the other. It is also unreasonable to suppose that all Presbyterian denominations in Scotland shared equally in the revival blessing. There is much evidence to suggest, for example, that the Established Church,

---

19. His source (Gibson, 1860, p. 256) in fact says that the vast majority of those included in this figure were added during the first Communion subsequent to the revival.

20. A statistic echoed by Alfred Russell Scott (*The Ulster Revival of 1859*, doctoral thesis submitted to Dublin University, 1962, p. 189; cf. p. 168), but contradicted by John Weir (*When Heaven Came Down: The 1859 Revival*, London, 1860 [reprinted 1987]), who said that the Presbyterian Church numbered 'nearly half a million people' (p. 113).

21. Orr, 1949, pp. 77, 201.

the largest in this group, did not, as a whole, enthusiastically endorse or embrace the movement. Thus, one main value of Orr's efforts is that they serve to illustrate the difficulties and complexities involved with statistical evaluation and assessment of revivals.

Another problem with using statistics showing growth in congregational membership as a mark of the revival's influence is that this ignores the growth rate prior to the revival. From 1848, a new period of church extension in the cities, especially Glasgow, was championed by the Rev. Robert Buchanan of the Free Church, being similar to the efforts of Thomas Chalmers a few decades earlier. It was sought to combine this type of 'territorial church' with an 'aggressive' system of evangelism to bring the working classes to church. Other denominations caught the initiative and followed on a similar path. As a result, a number of churches showed considerable growth in the years prior to the revival.

The Wynd Free Church maintained an influx of about one hundred members for each of the five years preceding the movement. Indeed, such was its success that since 1857 the ambition had been to build the even bigger Bridgegate Free Church. During the same period Wellpark Free Church showed annual gains of 130, while Greyfriars United Presbyterian Church averaged 127 additions each year for the three years from 1857.

With respect to the United Presbyterian Church, at the annual meeting of their Glasgow Mission churches in April 1862, their persistently increasing membership rolls were deemed to be the fruit of ten years' missionary work. No mention at all was made of the revival. Sunday-school statistics for Glasgow show similar signs of growth just prior to the revival.[22] Congregational accessions during the period of the revival have to be seen in the light of these considerations.[23]

The number of converts from the 1859–61 revival in Scotland remains unknown and completely unverifiable but is universally considered to have run into at least numerous tens of thousands. The influence of

---

22. Indeed, the increase in UPC rolls among children between the ages of five and fifteen totalled 4,811 in 1859, followed by further increases of 2,935 and 2,281 in 1860 and 1861 respectively. These compare to 3,087 in 1856, 2,075 in 1858 and 4,343 in 1866 (with similar increases during both previous and later decades).

23. In addition, some areas showing high rates of church growth during the revival were densely populated districts, such as the Wynds and the Gorbals, each with a population of about 22,000.

the revival is seen in the number of references in subsequent decades to ministers, elders, evangelists and missionaries who dated their conversion to this period of blessing.

Prominent Converts

Among the most prominent converts of the 1859 revival in Scotland were:

Mary Slessor – led to Christ in Dundee through the faithful witness of an old widow who described to her the eternal torment facing those who didn't know Christ. Aged twenty-eight, Mary set off to serve as a missionary in Calabar, south-east Nigeria. Living among those she worked with, Mary learned the local language and fought tirelessly for the social needs of the natives. To many Nigerians she became known as 'The mother of all the peoples'.[24]

James Chalmers – converted in Inverary in 1859. He served as a missionary in the Cook Islands for ten years before moving to New Guinea. Here he received acclaim both as an explorer and as a missionary, and aroused widespread interest in the island among Westerners by his lectures and publications.[25]

Robert Annan – converted, following a wild and reckless youth in Dundee, through the preaching of Duncan Matheson. Annan immediately became a fiery evangelist, labouring ardently for souls, especially among the roughs and drunkards he formerly associated with. An accomplished swimmer, Annan reputedly saved eleven people from drowning, but tragically died saving a young boy from the river Tay in 1867 (see also p. 475).[26]

John Anderson – converted during the time of the revival; he became the first Principal of the Bible Training Institute in Glasgow, serving from 1898 to 1913, when he was succeeded by David McIntyre. Anderson also founded the Southern Morocco Mission.

Alexander Mackay – converted in the aftermath of the revival in Rhynie, Aberdeenshire. Mackay served as a missionary in Uganda from 1878

---

24. W. P. Livingstone, *Mary Slessor of Calabar: Pioneer Missionary*, London, 1915.

25. Richard Lovett, *James Chalmers: His Autobiography and Letters*, London, 1902, pp. 26-8.

26. Macpherson, 1867.

till his death from malaria in 1890. During that time he made the district a centre for the evangelisation of Africa, cultivating the friendship of its savage tribes. In addition to teaching the gospel, he worked as a farmer, carpenter, bridge and road builder, schoolmaster, printer and translator. This created a spirit of deep respect, causing Ugandans to call him, *Muzungu-wa Kazi* – 'white man of work'.[27]

William Robertson Nicoll of Auchindoir, Aberdeenshire – an indirect product of the revival, coming under the influence of the Huntly rallies organised by the Duchess of Gordon when he was just nine years old. Nicoll founded and was editor of the *British Weekly*, a prominent non-conformist periodical. A much-respected author, he also acted as chief literary adviser to the publishing firm, Hodder & Stoughton. He was knighted in 1909.[28]

James Gilmour of Carmunnock, to the south of Glasgow – he moved to Mongolia in 1870, serving with the London Missionary Society. Sharing the primitive life of nomadic Mongolians, Gilmour had to wait for fifteen strenuous years before seeing his first baptism. His persevering faith inspired many, and his books opened Western eyes to the hitherto unknown territory of the Gobi Desert.[29]

John McNeill – converted in the afterglow of the Scottish awakening. He preached alongside both Spurgeon and Moody, and was nicknamed the 'Spurgeon of Scotland'. McNeill became one of the most prominent evangelists of his time, travelling widely, but also serving for many years as a pastor of churches in England, Canada and America.[30]

Christina Forsyth of Glasgow – became a Christian at the age of fourteen after being invited to a meeting in Bridgegate Free Church, where 'a workman in rough clothes told how he found Christ'. She became a missionary in 1878, serving among the Mfengu people of the Xolobe Valley (Fingoland) in the Eastern Cape of South Africa. Regularly

27. Orr, 1975, p. 89.

28. T. H. Darlow, *William Robertson Nicoll. Life and Letters*, London, 1925.

29. Richard Lovett, *James Gilmour of Mongolia: His Diaries, Letters and Reports*, London, 1892.

30. Alexander Gammie, *Rev. John McNeill: His Life and Work*, London, 1933.

visiting people in their homes, through loving service over thirty years, Forsyth gradually won a great many to the Christian faith.[31]

James Orr – born in Glasgow and converted during the revival, he shortly afterwards entered Glasgow University. He became Professor of Church History at the theological college of the United Presbyterian Church in 1891, and later of theology and apologetics at the Free Church College in Edinburgh. Orr lectured widely in Britain and America.[32]

There were numerous other notable converts of the 1859 revival, including William Gibson Sloan, famed missionary to the Faroe Islands (see pp. 419, 591),[33] the Rev. John Mackay of Cromarty, later Free Church evangelist to the Highlands,[34] and Professor James Simpson, obstetrician,[35] to name just a few.

Denominational Results

A United Presbyterian Church Report for 1861 reads: 'There is little reason to suppose that at any time previous to 1860 or 1861 such an accumulation of testimonies to the felt quickening and sanctifying presence and power of the Holy Spirit throughout all districts of the Church, could have been produced.'[36] It was suggested that as a result of the revival normal Sunday attendance at United Presbyterian Churches increased by over 50 per cent.[37]

A resolution of the Church of Scotland spoke of the effects of the revival by way of 'gratifying evidences manifested in many counties,

---

31. W. P. Livingstone, *Christina Forsyth of Fingoland: The Story of the Loneliest Woman in Africa*, London, 1918, p. 6; J. Edwin Orr, *Evangelical Awakenings in Africa*, Minneapolis, 1975, p. 81.

32. *DSCHT*, pp. 638-9.

33. Kelling, pp. 53-4.

34. Rev. Alexander Mackenzie, *The Rev. John Mackay, M.A., Student, Pastor, General Assembly's Highland Evangelist*, Paisley, 1921, pp. 22-4.

35. *DSCHT*, p. 774.

36. Proceedings of the U.P. Synod, 1857–63, p. 422, quoted in Bussey, p. 140.

37. Brown, 1981, p. 428. For a possible alternative reason offered for such rise, see Chapter 16. Interestingly, however, Marrs's work shows that, for Glasgow, the United Presbyterian Church was not greatly impacted by the revival, with only thirteen of its thirty-eight congregations holding revival services, six of which were not commenced until 1861.

of an increased anxiety about the salvation and deepening interest in religious ordinances, followed in so many cases by fruits of holy living'.[38]

Many Baptist congregations benefited from the revival and saw their numbers rise, while a number of new congregations arose in the aftermath of the movement, for example in Kilmarnock, Lossiemouth, Cambridge Street (Glasgow), Bervie and Mintlaw (though the latter two were fairly short-lived). Arminian and Calvinistic Baptists were united in favour of the revival. Records one Baptist historian: 'In the context of revival blessings from God, the theological differences between Baptists, and those between Baptists and other evangelical Christians, appeared to be much smaller than had previously been thought. ... The growth in the churches at this time would act as an incentive to further untied efforts in prayer and evangelistic activity',[39] one obvious result being the formation of the Baptist Union of Scotland in 1869.

J. Edwin Orr, speaking of Britain as a whole, claimed that 'the Brethren gained more from the revival than any other body'.[40] F. R. Coad, in his history of the Brethren movement, claims that the independent Brethren received an impetus from the revival movement that within three decades transformed both their character and influence.[41] The revival acted as the foundation of Brethren beginnings in many Scottish locations, notably Glasgow.[42] Their success, says Andrew Buchanan, 'was principally because of their ability to absorb converts'. In 1864 the editor of *The Revival* noted that 'many of the converts of the revival have become either Plymouthists or Baptists' and he believed that those who 'complain of this have, in most cases, themselves to blame for it'. The ability of the Brethren to, what Buchanan calls, 'mop-up' after revivals was also commented upon by their critics. P. Mearns stated in

---

38. Acts of the Assembly of the Church of Scotland, 1860, p. 62, quoted in Marrs, p. 140.

39. Brian Talbot, *The Search for a Common Identity: The Origins of the Baptist Union of Scotland 1800-1870*, Carlisle, 2003, pp. 297-8.

40. Orr, 1949, p. 203.

41. Quoted in Buchanan, p. 9.

42. The Salvation Army was another church body that was to rise from the 1859 revival in Britain.

1875: 'Eager to proselytise, Plymouth Brethren are found in the wake of religious awakenings as constantly as sharks follow ships.'[43]

Towards the close of 1860 Free Church officials sent a questionnaire to all its congregations asking whether any recent religious awakening had taken place in their parishes and if so, to give details of such movement. From these the Rev. Dr Julius Wood concluded that in two-thirds of the church's presbyteries distinct revival was reported, with increased signs of spiritual life being reported from many of the remaining presbyteries. Specifically, 169 returns were received (out of a total of 882 congregations). Eighty-six of these reported 'a decided awakening and revival, more or less, in their districts and congregations'.[44] These came from forty-two different presbyteries. Of the remaining eighty-three returns, however – spread across twenty-four presbyteries[45] – almost every one was able to claim 'the manifestation of an increased interest in spiritual things, and a great willingness to hear the Word'.[46] Indeed, several of these eighty-three congregations subsequently declared that a definite work of grace had since occurred in their localities, while 'many congregations where there has been revival ... (have) not reported to us'.[47] It is much to be regretted that none of the congregations who made returns are identified in the Report.

The Free Church Committee on the State of Religion and Morals conducted an identical review the following year, reporting to the General Assembly of 1862. On this occasion, Dr Julius Wood reported that fifty-seven congregations had responded but only eighteen confirmed the presence of revival in their midst. However, none of these eighteen congregations had claimed revival in 1861. Wood concluded that for the years 1860–62, 'the Committee ... has returns ... showing a work of revival in 104 of the congregations of the Church'.[48]

---

43. ibid., p. 47.

44. FCSRSRM, 1861, p. 5.

45. Thus replies came from 66 Presbyteries (42+24), out of a total of 71 throughout Scotland. The 5 Presbyteries who submitted no returns were Jedburgh, Wigtown, Lanark, Nairn and Lochcarron.

46. FCSRSRM, 1861, p. 5.

47. ibid., pp. 4-12.

48. FCSRSRM, 1862, pp. 4-5.

Two years later (1864), a further Circular drew in reports from around two hundred Free Church ministers which strongly confirmed that an extensive and powerful revival movement had taken place throughout the land. Being compiled several years after the peak of the movement, the responses are of particular significance, and show that in every case lasting fruits of the revival were still in evidence at that later date, while incidences of backsliding were very few.[49] A still later Free Church report provides further testimony to the lasting impact of the general awakening of the late 1850s. In 1887 the Free Church Assembly reported: 'Our deputies have often noted the fact that they have found ministers all over the country, who thank God for faithful fellow-workers in office, who were brought to the knowledge of Jesus Christ during the revival and evangelistic labours of the years 1859–1860.'[50]

Opposition

There were, of course, those both within and without the Church who spoke against the revival. One journalist noted, wryly: 'So far from wishing a revival of God's work, many churchgoers have done their utmost to quench the first appearance of religious earnestness in their own homes.'[51] Some were scornful of meetings continuing till late at night; and occasionally employers complained of absenteeism from work.[52] Artisans and the self-employed were, in the words of Callum Brown, 'also hostile, disliking the disruptive and "rude" quality of the awakening'.[53] The main charge was the high degree of emotionalism prevalent at some meetings, and the corresponding manifestations with which some folk were affected. One learned sheriff ascribed to the revival 'a vast increase in the number of lunatics' and even, implausibly, in the number of petty thefts.[54]

---

49. ibid., 1864, pp. 3-8; FC Proceedings, 1864, pp. 320-3.

50. FC Proceedings, 1887, p. 75, quoted in I. Muirhead, p. 195.

51. *WJ*, 21/04/1860, p. 236, quoted in Jeffrey, p. 77.

52. Callum Brown, *The Social History of Religion in Scotland since 1730*, London, 1987, p. 147. The 1742 Cambuslang revival was also condemned by several landowners for the loss of farm work which they claimed it caused.

53. Brown, 1981, p. 427.

54. From a statement from the Rev. Dr Bisset of the Established Church, relayed to his General Assembly, quoted in Kent, *Holding the Fort*, p. 114.

Many church leaders across the country deplored the methods employed by some colleagues, who went to considerable lengths to encourage displays of emotionalism in their services. Church of Scotland minister, Donald Macleod, while generally most sympathetic to revivals, was dubious of the means employed by a Free Church colleague in Lauder, Berwickshire, in 1859, which, he felt, encouraged emotionalism. 'Instead of preaching the Gospel he indulged in realistic descriptions of revival scenes where people were "struck down", and strong men "felled to the ground like oxen". Following on this, he asked all to engage in prayer. For a few minutes he remained silent, until one felt the tension of suppressed excitement, and then he began, "O Lord, do it – do it now".'[55] Meanwhile, at the 1860 General Assembly of the Church of Scotland, the Rev. Dr Robert Lee was singular in querying the validity of taking up time discussing the revival taking place throughout the country. He said that he considered it 'most undesirable ... to enter into [the] wide, difficult and intricate problem of revivals'.[56]

Some members of the middle classes complained that revivals tended only to have a temporary effect on aspects such as church attendance, drunkenness and immoral behaviour amongst the working classes. United Presbyterian minister, John Kerr of Glasgow, wrote in 1869: 'There is surely something that can be done for this [working] class better than either spasmodic revivalism or wax candles' (Roman Catholicism).[57] Indeed, Sabbath desecration increased markedly in the 1860s, particularly after the 'Sabbath War' of 1865–6, when the churches lost the struggle to prevent the Sunday running of trains. However, according to Callum Brown, the strength and influence of the churches did not decline immediately as a consequence of events at this time.[58] Marrs summarised the opinion of some historians (such as John Kent and Richard Carwardine) in saying that the 'vast majority of conversions emanated from within the Christian community or its

---

55. Sydney Smith, *Donald Macleod of Glasgow: A Memoir and a Study*, London, 1927, p. 76.

56. ibid.

57. Brown, 1981, p. 442.

58. ibid., p. 449.

fringes and were predominantly from the middle classes and those working classes who were skilled or enjoying regular employment'.[59]

The strongest attack against the lay preaching employed in the 1859–61 revival came from the magazine of the Original Secession Church, a conservative remnant stemming from the first secession from the Church of Scotland in 1733:

> In defiance alike of all the warnings that past history teaches, the dec-
> larations of the Word of God, and the warnings of eminent ministers
> of Christ, we are told by some persons that all hopes of the elevation
> and conversion of the masses, and the revival of religion, depend on
> the ministrations of lay-men, thus virtually ignoring both a regular
> ministry and the government of the Church by Kirk advertisements
> that 'The Converted Sweep' – 'The Fisherman' – 'The Flesher' – 'The
> Young Evangelist' ... will address public meetings on the revival of
> religion. The opinions of the following eminent ministers of Christ,
> it is fondly hoped, may, by the Divine blessing, tend to check an evil
> which is fraught with most appalling results, if the future history of
> the Church is to resemble the past ...

... to which there followed extracts from the writings of Calvinist thinkers like Samuel Rutherford, David Dickson, William Gurnall and John Lowe.[60]

Newspapers were often biased for or against the revival. *The Glasgow Herald* at first spoke favourably of the movement, but changed its stance markedly during its progress, to the extent that it doubted if any permanent good had resulted from it. *The Scotsman* also took a stand against the revival and virtually ignored it for weeks. Then, in August 1859 it brought readers' attention to 'the revival disease' that was spreading through the land. It also termed the awakening an 'epidemic' and 'a preaching madness ... '. Whenever the longest of revival sermons have been taken

---

59. Marrs, p. 169.

60. Nicholls, p. 6. Nicholls believes that the 1859 revival was a factor in the 'demise of the old Reformed church order' in Scotland and its replacement by 'modern evangelicalism'. But he puts much of the blame on preaching from within the Scottish Presbyterian ministry itself, because it had become so 'learned and refined as largely to lose its cutting edge ... . Gripping and bitingly relevant in its language and applications, it certainly was not, as an hour's browsing through its published specimens will reveal' (ibid.).

down, they are found to be stupidity itself ... the history of revivals is the opprobrium of religion'. Richard Weaver was also strongly criticised by *The Record* for being too sentimental in his addresses and pleas.[61]

While the Catholic *Free Press* urged opposition to revival meetings, all the Protestant denominations participated in the revival,[62] although the Established Church generally retained a somewhat ambivalent attitude to the movement.[63] The Free Church and the United Presbyterian Church were perhaps the most notably impacted.[64] In the former denomination, 477 congregations added over 15,000 new members in 1859 alone, while the number of prayer meetings doubled and normal Sunday service attendance increased by over 50 per cent, remaining at that level for many years.[65]

Crime Reduction

A number of police authorities reported a notable reduction in crime in their districts, along with less drunkenness and quieter streets. A report from the Police Superintendent of the Ayrshire village of Maybole stated that as a result of the revival in the community in general, he had no hesitation in saying that the improvement in the moral conduct of the 'middle and lower classes here has been decidedly good', with a notable reduction in regard to 'rioting and other forms of

---

61. Marrs, p. 51; Kent, 1978, pp. 119-20; Paterson, 1897, p. 134. The same reporter claimed that most conversions that took place under Weaver were short-lived, though he provides no evidence to support this (more info? p. 119).

62. Including Baptists (Bebbington, 1988, pp. 54-5), Congregationalists (McNaughton, *A Few Historical Notes on Early Congregational Independency in Scotland*, Kirkcaldy, 2000, p. xxviii), Brethren (Dickson, 2002, pp. 61-3), UPC (Proceedings of UPC Synod, 1862, pp. 620-8), and the Free Church (FCRHMC, 1861, pp. 96-100; PFCSH&I, pp. 307-12).

63. See Andrew L. Drummond and James Bulloch, *The Church in Victorian Scotland 1843-74*, Edinburgh, 1975, pp. 185-6. Callum Brown suggests that 'during the three centuries after the Reformation, revivalism had never been supported by the Church of Scotland. Individual clergy, however, did offer their support .... Missionary work was designed to achieve peaceful conversions by educational rather than emotional methods' (Brown, 1981, p. 420).

64. Within the Free Church, one or two prominent leaders, most notably James Begg, originally regarded the revival as the long-expected breath of heaven, but later modified their position due to its excesses, and even became bitter critics of the movement.

65. Orr, 1949, p. 77; Drummond and Bulloch, p. 185.

disorder'.[66] Further north in Ayrshire, the Justice of Peace in Ardrossan commented in January 1860 that such was the effect of the revival in that town that he did not have a tenth of crime cases coming before him in the last four months than he had previously.

As to the moral effects of the revival in Edinburgh, James Gall of Carrubbers Close Mission wrote: 'The diminution of drunkenness in the city was so remarkable as to appear in the police reports as more than triple what had been effected by the Forbes McKenzie Act (1853), which Act forced the closure of pubs in Scotland on Sundays, and reduced closing time to 10pm on weekdays. In 1859 the convictions for non-criminal drunkenness were 4,883,

In 1860	3,830	1,053 less
In 1861	2,952	878 less
In 1862	2,571	381 less
In 1863	2,235	336 less
In 1864	2,195	40 less

In all, 2,688 cases less, or over 55% less in four years.'[67]

A similarly interesting statistic was issued in *The Dumfries Standard*. It showed that during the three weeks from 27 January to 16 February 1860, sixty-three people were brought before the Burgh Court of Dumfries charged with 'assault, breach of peace, contravention of Police Act, drunk and disorderly, drunk and incapable, malicious mischief and theft'. In the corresponding period for 1861, i.e., during the three weeks since the revival commenced, the figure was thirty-two, a reduction of around 50 per cent.[68] The Dumfries police force expressed to one church leader during 1861–62 that so far as serious crimes were concerned, their office was 'all but a sinecure'.[69]

Further testimony came from a chief constable of 'one of the largest counties in Scotland', containing a number of populous towns, to the effect that, during the revival period, there was a considerable diminution of all classes of criminals.

66. *SG*, 22/11/1859; *WJ*, 28/09/1861, p. 213.

67. Gall, 1882, p. 6.

68. *SG*, 23/02/1861, p. 591.

69. Marrs, however, claims that national crime levels had in fact been decreasing throughout the 1850s and thus had nothing to do with the revival.

In regard to sexual immorality, in a total of eight of Scotland's largest towns and cities (including Edinburgh and Glasgow), there was an increase of sixteen illegitimate births in 1860, compared to an average annual increase of fifty-one in previous years. Taking all of Scotland into account, the illegitimacy figures show a fractional rise year by year, except in 1860, when it was stationary – indicating the effects of the revival.[70]

Community Transformation

Dr S. R. MacPhail, writing in the early 1900s, said that he personally knew 'towns and districts which to this day remain entirely different from what they were previous to that revival'. Annan was said to have been 'absolutely revolutionised' by the season of blessing that overtook it. The revival in the East Fife fishing port of Cellardyke, according to *The Scottish Guardian*, had made this 'formerly obscure' village familiar throughout the land. J. Edwin Orr described the awakening here as 'the most perfect example in Scotland of a spiritual awakening brought about by the Holy Spirit, unhindered by Satan and not imitated by the Enemy of souls'.[71]

W. J. Couper makes a similar claim regarding the awakening in the Forfarshire fishing village of Ferryden,[72] which had a population of 1,100 in the late 1850s. It was claimed that around a half of this number came under the influence of the revival and that at least two-fifths of these had come under the power of saving grace. And the fruit abided, a large percentage of converts being found to stand the test of several decades. As late as 1888, visiting evangelists were struck by the devotion and enthusiasm of the Ferryden converts. One historian claimed that these striking factors 'set it in the forefront of religious movements … in Scotland within the last half-century'.[73]

Effects of the awakening in the north-east of the country were even more pronounced. There was scarcely a town or village between Aberdeen and Inverness that was not visited by the revival. Entire communities were morally and socially transformed by the movement. George Gardiner of Banff wrote of the overall effects of the revival on north-east townships, 'The whole face of society in those villages is

---

70. Registrar-General Returns, quoted in Orr, 1949, pp. 181-2.

71. *SG*, 19/11/1860; Orr, 1949, p. 73.

72. Roberts, 1995, pp. 298-9.

73. Moody Stuart, 1899, pp. 141-2.

so changed that those who have known them before are struck with wonder.'[74] The Rev. Barraclough, minister of the Wesleyan chapel at Banff, stated that if the revival along the Moray coast was not the work of the Holy Spirit then he was unable to consider that the Spirit was at work anywhere on the earth.

As a result of the significant bouts of revival to impact the Aberdeen harbour village of Footdee during the 1860s, a report written the following decade remarked upon how the whole village had become 'a picture of tidiness such as is seldom to be met with among classes of the population reckoned higher in the social scale ... this external order is only the index of a still more important change in the habits and character of our fisher town, the population of which has within the past few years undergone a remarkable change for the better in a moral point of view'.[75]

Perhaps nowhere in all of Scotland were the positive effects of ongoing revivalism more pronounced than in Portgordon. The village underwent a whole succession of seasons of spiritual quickening during the 1860s and early 70s, each of which rocked the community. The overall effects were striking. Prior to 1860 there were ten public houses in operation in Portgordon, all doing a good business. By 1875, following the latest movement, every one of these drinking establishments had closed down, it being said that the families had 'gone to ruin – some are in America, after failures – and all are in low circumstances'. Four open houses rose up in their place, although each was considered to be 'far down in business'. The converts of the various revivals that swept through the community, the majority being products of James Turner's racy missions of 1860 and 1861, were said to have been 'a most sober industrious people, and their families growing up in decency, and in order, serving the Lord'.[76]

An article in the *Elgin Courant* in October 1874 reported that other than public houses, business in Portgordon was in a very flourishing condition, with particular increase in regards both to shipping and

---

74. Rose, p. 19.

75. Anson, p. 142.

76. McHardie, p. 250. It has been generously estimated that Turner was 'the means of converting more than eight thousand persons' in just two years (P. F. Anson, *Fishing Boats and Fisherfolk*: *Fishing Boats and Fisherfolk on the East Coast*, London, 1930, p. 45).

fishing. At that time the village boasted 1,695 registered tons of shipping, as well as seventy large, and over thirty small fishing boats, all manned by local fishermen. The community's total floating property was valued at around £45,000. Portgordon also claimed twenty-six captains who had passed the Local Marine Board examination while under thirty years of age, all of whom were now in charge of vessels. Additionally, around a dozen young men had passed as first mates and were about to become captains. The author of this report stated his confidence that there could be very few towns of similar size that could say the same of its seamen.[77]

Of Portgordon and the plethora of nearby fishing ports, W. J. Couper wrote in the early twentieth century: 'No one who travels today along the southern shores of the Moray Firth can avoid being struck with the apparent material comfort of the fishing communities. The housing accommodations are excellent and there is an air of thriving plenty which is too often conspicuously absent in similar townships elsewhere. The prosperity has been traced directly to the [1859] revival [and subsequent moves of the Spirit in these villages]. Revival is a reality here. You can see it, you can touch it, you can measure it, you can go into it and be sheltered by it, and taste some of its material sweets.'[78]

Enduring Impact

The main lasting effect of the 1859 revival could be testified to in the subsequent lifestyles of many thousands of individuals across the country whose lives were transformed, or whose spirituality was revived, as a result of it. In many cases so potent was the revival's influence that the social fabric of the community was at least temporarily altered in a positive manner, the effects of which generally continued for a period of some months or in a few cases, years. In select localities, as we have just observed – notably the fishing ports of the north-east coast – communities were radically altered with lasting effect as a result of the successive waves of revival movements that swept through them.

But nationally, the revival was not an 'awakening' in the sense spoken of by some academics, notably William McLoughlin, whereby cultural transformation is achieved through a major reorientation in

---

77. *Elgin Courant*, quoted in ibid., pp. 250-1.

78. Roberts, 1995, p. 305.

the population's belief-value system. The 1859 revival did not lead to significant changes in societal structure. Nevertheless, it is at least a little surprising that as early as 1866, one Lowland minister felt it appropriate to write an eighty-page book, which, making no mention whatever of the extensive and dramatic revival of just a few years previously, bemoaned the desperate spiritual and moral conditions in Scotland and urged believers to call out to God for an outpouring of His Spirit on the land.[79]

What is true of Scotland as a whole is also true of specific locations, not least the nation's largest cities. That many areas of Glasgow were powerfully affected by revival from the summer of 1859 is easily attested to in the section relating to that urban centre (see Chapter 4). Yet, of course, by no means was the entire city moved, and nor were the spiritual and social benefits achieved by the spiritual quickening of a lasting nature. Thus, as early as 1862, just a year after the revival had drawn to a close, a correspondent in *The Revival* periodical referred to 'the awful state of the city', to the tens of thousands who never heard the gospel, and to the thousands to whom 'the glorious liberty of the children of God is not preached'. The writer claimed: 'The love of mammon, the love of fine Roman Catholic-looking Gothic buildings, and formalism and sectarianism are rampant in Glasgow.'[80]

In the same year, even Dugald MacColl of Glasgow, referring to revival meetings in places other than his own Wynd Church, admitted that 'When revival came to congregations or places, in not a few instances the work came to a speedy end. Some of those who reaped more in a week than they had done in a series of years were contented with their week. And thus to a large extent the work of Revival, although it has everywhere left its individual results in conversion and renewed life, has not everywhere left a very much larger surface of cultivated land, or a greatly improved husbandry.'[81] Note that he is not suggesting that the revival was merely a flash in the pan, with little or no positive, lasting effects. He is stating that in certain cases the revival was cut

---

79. John Henshelwood, *The Revival of Religion: The Want of the Times*, Edinburgh, 1866.

80. Marrs, p. 337.

81. *WJ*, 26/07/62, quoted in ibid., pp. 337-8.

short before it was able to reap its fullest potential. That not in every scenario did the roots of revival go deep. This notwithstanding, the favourable effects of the revival from various quarters of the city were still in clear evidence long after the movement had subsided. Writing towards the close of the nineteenth century, Dr Stark could state of the 1859 revival in Glasgow, 'Much of the Christian philanthropy that has been in our city for the last thirty years owes a great deal to the impulse received at that time.'[82]

Some of the main outcomes of the revival were noted as being: Church membership increasing markedly, as the majority of converts quickly associated themselves with the Church; partly as a result of this, a warmer family atmosphere was imported into Christian fellowships; preaching became more practical, dealing more with the present life and its needs; and a greater emphasis was also placed on sin and the need of conversion. Other consequences of the revival were the increased emphasis placed on prayer, on evangelistic missions, both home and abroad, and the establishment of Sunday schools in needy areas.

A report issued in 1865 noted that the effects of the revival had continued to make themselves felt across Scotland right up to that date in regard to 'the spread of vital religion'. All classes of the population had been influenced by the movement, and only in its earliest stages was it accompanied by excitement. Both lay and clerical agencies had been effectively used to spread the revival, by means of united prayer, expository preaching and direct witness. The report noted that the revival resulted in the quickening of believers, the increase of family religion and the decrease in cases of discipline in congregations throughout the country.[83]

Writing near the beginning of the twentieth century, one author makes the striking claim that 'All the mission movements – home and foreign – philanthropic schemes, and measures for the alleviation of human suffering, have been mainly manned and maintained during the last fifty years by the converts of the revival of 1859 and the sixties, and those who sympathised with it.'[84] Men's minds turned increasingly

---

82. Roberts, 1995, p. 305.

83. Orr, J. Edwin, *The Light of the Nations*, Grand Rapids, 1965, p. 138.

84. Matthews, p. xii.

towards the social needs of the less privileged. As a result, a number of social and philanthropic societies and projects emerged – facilitated largely by personnel who had been converted during the revival – to help with slum clearance and welfare of the poor, the reclamation of prostitutes and the rehabilitation of alcoholics and criminals.

Scores of new endeavours started up with lasting and powerful effect, while, additionally, many existing Christian societies were thoroughly revived. For example, the National Bible Society of Scotland was established in 1861; William Quarrier commenced his orphan homes in Glasgow in 1864; the Children's Special Service Mission (C.S.S.M.) was established, spurred by E. P. Hammond's work among children; The Edinburgh Conference of the Y.M.C.A. laid the foundations of the modern Y.M.C.A. in 1864; Seamen's Friends Societies were independently set up in Aberdeen, Greenock and Glasgow in the early 1860s.[85] There also arose, as a consequence of the revival, the North-East Coast Mission, the Bible Women's Association and numerous other philanthropic institutions.[86]

---

85. See John L. Duthie, *Philanthropy and Evangelism*, in *The Scottish Historical Review*, 1984, pp. 155-73.

86. Marrs, however, insists that many such schemes, even those that came into effect during the revival period, were in fact initiated prior to the outbreak of the general awakening.

PART 3

Revival Afterwaves
1862–72

Introduction

The revival fires that burst into flame across the country during 1859 and 1860 had, in the majority of instances, begun to subside before the close of that latter year. Still, in a number of locations the embers continued to burn well into the following year, and, indeed, in some places it was not until 1861 that the flames of revival were first lit. By the close of that year, however, it was almost everywhere apparent that Scotland's most extensive spiritual awakening had essentially run its course.

No sooner was this perceptible, however, than a succession of further pulses of spiritual awakening began to resonate across the country, both among communities which had experienced revival during the period 1859–61 and in districts which missed out on the blessing of those years. In one or two instances – notably Alloa – blessing received in the early sixties appears to have been simply a continuation of the revival begun in the same locality during 1859–61. In the vast majority of cases, however, it was a fresh and distinct wave of spiritual reverberation that came to each township and not merely an ongoing experience of a previous occasion of spiritual outpouring. There appears to have been three distinct currents. First are the revival reverberations which flowed copiously in the immediate aftermath of the 1859–61 movement, particularly affecting localities completely overlooked by the earlier movement (notably many Shetland districts, along with Peterhead), as well as other districts that previously were only partially moved.

Just a few years later, a further, more substantial resurgence of revival swept through many Scottish villages, towns, cities and parishes. This occurred within the wider context of a more general, but almost completely unrecognised movement to quicken the United Kingdom in these years – for notable revival influences were also felt in England, Wales and Ireland. Communities were affected from as far north as Shetland and Orkney to southern Wigtownshire and along the Scotland-England border in Roxburghshire. The movement was

411

general in Fife, South Lanarkshire and parts of central Scotland, and was also prominent in the town of Kilsyth, renowned in Scotland revival history.

Yet another wave of religious revival was apparent in the early seventies, being most distinct in a number of north-east fishing communities – as had indeed the two previous waves of sixties' revival blessing, notably Portgordon – and in rural Aberdeenshire, where arose a fascinating wave of blessing among the Brethren between 1870 and 1872.

William Gibson Sloan   *David Sandeman*

Tobermory

Rothiemay

CHAPTER 17

Revival Reverberations 1862–65

Shetland

Lerwick

While, by the spring of 1860 there were eight special prayer meetings in progress in Shetland, no general movement occurred until November 1862 – more than three years after its sudden appearance in many localities on the Scottish mainland. An evangelistic campaign was begun in the parish church of the main town, Lerwick, by John Fraser and Dr Craig of Elgin. In no time the meetings were overcrowded, night after night. Nearly all the town's evangelical churches, though especially the United Presbyterian and Congregational Churches, participated in the work. The meetings continued week by week right into the second month of 1863, when private prayer meetings became more dominant. By this time also, the revival had spread from the town to many country areas: first in a southerly, then westerly, and latterly northerly direction, until it could be said that 'the greater portion of the Mainland has been permeated with its influence'.[1]

Cunningsburgh and Sandwick

South of Lerwick, it was noted that 'the shower of blessing has watered in a copious and refreshing manner almost every cluster of hamlets' all the way south to Sumburgh Head, on the southerly tip of the island. Throughout this entire portion of the island the converts were said to be very numerous, some of them rare instances of the power of divine grace.'[2]

---

1. *TR*, 05/03/1863, p. 113.

2. ibid.

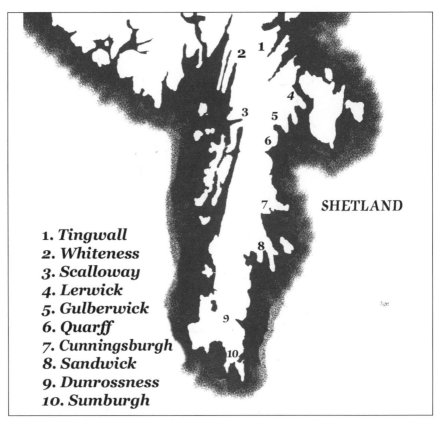

1. Tingwall
2. Whiteness
3. Scalloway
4. Lerwick
5. Gulberwick
6. Quarff
7. Cunningsburgh
8. Sandwick
9. Dunrossness
10. Sumburgh

SHETLAND

'A few drops of the shower of the divine blessing' fell on Cunningsburgh from an early date. The life of one local was so transformed that his spiritual enthusiasm attracted the attention of many. At one meeting he addressed fellow sinners in an excitable and forceful manner. The large audience was melted to tears and a considerable number were physically prostrated, having to be removed from the meeting place. This man quickly arose as leader of the revival party in his area, and many were influenced by his exhortations. Not only in Cunningsburgh, but in Lerwick and other places did they spread their demonstrative form of revivalism. Some saw this as being so much at variance with the former 'noiseless and irreproachable nature of the work as carried on by the pioneers and fast friends of the general movement, that cause has been given to the enemy to speak derisively of the work as a whole'.[3]

The movement in Sandwick proceeded on more balanced grounds. A group of young men entered heartily into the work, commencing a

3. ibid., 19/03/1863, p. 138.

course of tract-distribution, house-visitation and prayer meetings all across the wider district. In Gulberwick 'a great moving of hearts took place'. In nearby Channerwick and, especially further north in Quarff, known for its spiritual coldness, the converts' efforts quickly stirred up the hearts of believers and greatly arrested the attention of the ungodly, who now flocked to the meetings in the Free Church. 'A great and good work of God has obviously broken out here', exulted one witness.[4]

Dunrossness

Further south on this elongated south Shetland peninsula, 'union meetings' were commenced in Dunrossness by a visiting evangelist from Inverness. The Established, Free and Baptist churches all shared in these, while the Methodists 'rather stood aloof'. Sinclair Thomson said he knew of no one who had 'shared more richly in, I hope, divine unction, from the beginning of these meetings, than the parish minister. For some months now, when he is in health, he has a public meeting for divine worship in some corner of the parish, every evening in the week, except Saturday, and on Sabbath two or three, in as many different places.'[5] Revival spread rapidly over the district and on a few occasions, a number of people (on one occasion 'a great many' people) had to be carried out of one church 'in all the weakness of helpless infancy', where they had to wait for a considerable time before they recovered strength sufficient to walk home.[6]

Just four years previously, Dunrossness Baptist Church had experienced considerable revival (see pp. 41-3), after which 'seasons of comparative dullness' followed. In the spring of 1863, 'times of refreshing from the presence of the Lord' once again fell upon the fellowship. In April, Sinclair Thomson – known as 'The Shetland Apostle' – then approaching the age of eighty, 'immersed ten persons, several of them taller and heavier than I ever was, standing in the cold lake without boots for about seven minutes while I did so.' Thomson added, 'I was not in the smallest injured in strength or health more than had I never been from my own fire.'[7]

---

4. ibid., 26/02/1863, p. 101; 05/03/1863, p. 115.

5. Letter dated 11/04/1863, quoted in BHMS Report, 1863, p. 10.

6. *TR*, 15/01/1863.

7. BHMS Report, 1863, p. 11.

By the end of the year, another eighteen people had been baptised and added to the church, making eleven males and seventeen females in all. Thomson hoped well of several more, believing them to be 'as on the way to the fellowship of the saints'.[8]

Walls and Sandsting

In the westerly parish of Walls, packed services were held in both the parish and the Free churches. These were, said John Craig, 'ordinary services … with the exception of the singing of revival hymns. There were no alarming presentations of the judgements of God, or the threatenings of God against sinners; but merely a simple and earnest pleading with the people to receive Jesus as the only Saviour.'[9] Craig added that these kindly addresses seemed to be more powerful in melting the hearts of the people than anything he had ever seen. As a result of the movement, there were forty-eight additions to the Congregational Church and around the same number to the Methodist chapel.

Believers from the Baptist Church in nearby Sandsting had been praying and longing for a revival of religion around them and were thus overjoyed when there arose 'a considerable awakening among the dead in trespasses and sins'. Within this parish, services were also held in the Independent chapel of Sand. The Rev. Fraser of Reawick often felt little option but to dismiss the meeting sooner than scheduled, due to the manifestation of feeling that began to overflow. 'I saw strong men weeping like children', he wrote. 'Individuals were awakened from a thoughtless to a thoughtful state, sitting in their own houses, while walking by the way, or lying in their beds, on whom and for whom no special efforts had been put forth. … The reaction which commonly follows times of awakening has not overtaken us. … Since last summer about sixty have been added to our fellowship.'[10]

Whiteness and Weisdale

Across the bay from Sandsting, 'the whole parish of Tingwall, formerly desolate and dry', was said to have been 'watered, in some measure, with

8. ibid., 1864, p. 9.

9. McNaughton, *Early Congregational Independency in Shetland*, Lerwick, 2005, pp. 96-7.

10. McNaughton, 2005, p. 97.

dews of the divine Spirit'. In the Whiteness neighbourhood of this parish, 'the manifested influences of the Spirit were most extraordinary'. There was said to have been scarcely a house 'without its trophy of Divine grace … a feeling of devout thankfulness seems to pervade the whole district'.[11]

Lanarkshire-born evangelist, William Gibson Sloan saw the Spirit move powerfully through his ministry in the Weisdale area, north of Whiteness in July 1863. Having visited most homes in the area, large numbers turned out at the meetings, forcing a rescheduling of meeting place from schoolhouse to large barn to the open air! On one beautiful

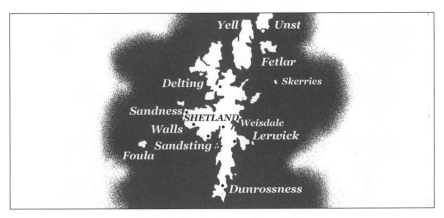

moonlit night, most of the people accompanied Sloan on his journey home. 'We sang together as we went', exulted the pastor; 'I felt happy. It reminded me of the Plains of Heaven where the Glorified roam. We sang joyfully, prayed together and parted.' On another evening, 'the power of God was evident. In singing the last hymn with the line, "When shall we all meet again", many were in tears and some had to sit down. Many waited behind to be spoken to about the way of salvation.'[12]

Still in the west of Shetland's mainland, in the fishing village of Scalloway, what gave the Rev. Nicol Nicolson of the Congregational Church assurance from the start that the movement in his parish was genuine 'was the absence of arousing speakers of any kind'. Forty-five new members, aged between fourteen and seventy, were added to his

---

11. TR, 15/01/1863, p. 35.

12. This was just a few years after Sloan's own conversion in Lanarkshire during the revival of 1859–61 (Kelling, pp. 51-4, 74-7).

fellowship as a result of the movement, all of whom, six months later, 'seem to be living epistles, laying themselves out as far as can be for the salvation of others'. The latter time of the movement was the season when the young men set out to sea. Nicolson received letters from Liverpool and other ports, indicating that 'the good the Lord has of late been doing may reach to distant parts of the world'.[13]

The movement here seems to have been in contrast to that which arose in Scalloway Baptist Church, where 'a considerable excitement of a professedly religious nature' was evident. Pastor Robert Scott was somewhat concerned, however, that the way the meetings were being conducted appeared to be 'quite aside from the sound scriptural order of the Word of God'. In his opinion, therefore 'as in similar cases, a sad reaction is to be dreaded'.[14]

Delting and the North Isles

In the north-mainland parish of Delting many were said to be 'rejoicing in the peace of believing, and prayer-meetings are springing up into existence on all hands'.[15] Revival extended to Sullam, where around twenty members were admitted to the local church in twelve months. By the summer of 1863, Papa Stour, along with the three most-northerly inhabited Shetland isles – Unst, Fetlar and Yell – were all affected by the stirrings of revival that had recently spread across the county's main island.

Even more isolated communities were likewise moved. The small island of Foula is situated twenty miles west of the Shetland mainland, and considered one of the United Kingdom's most remote, permanently inhabited islands. Since the death of the Congregational minister at the close of 1862, one or two lay preachers had visited the church there, sharing accounts of the revival elsewhere in Shetland as well as delivering biblical addresses. Then in the summer of 1864 a series of protracted meetings was held, and 'a considerable awakening' was the result. Fifteen were added to that fellowship. It was suggested, remarkably, that more than half the island's population of 280 were converted altogether.[16]

---

13. *TR*, 15/01/1863; McNaughton, 2005, p. 98.
14. BHMS Report, 1863, pp. 8, 14.
15. *TR*, 19/03/1863, p. 139.
16. ibid., 1863, pp. 98-9; Orr, 1949, pp. 69-70.

Answered Prayer

In one place a few converts gathered to pray for the conversion of two 'singularly godless families', the members of which opposed the revival work in every way possible. At the very time the converts were praying, a little girl in one of the households lifted a copy of the Bible and read aloud a few verses. 'The effect was extraordinary. Every heart was smitten and melted under the power of communicated grace, and with tears rushing from their eyes and on bended knees the whole household was heard crying aloud for mercy. The feeling and influence were communicated to the next dwelling, and there too the stout-hearted sinners were subdued, and with their distressed and anxious neighbours, sent for the young men who had been praying for their conversion to speak a word of comfort to their agitated and awakened souls.'[17]

In another place some young women met together to pray. This aroused the interest of several young men, who, unknown to the ladies, sought to obtain access to an adjoining room, from where they could hear the females' earnest entreaties. As the men listened to 'prayer after prayer ascend to heaven, perfumed with the sweet incense of Jesus' name, from lips touched with a live coal from off the altar', in no time their hearts were smitten with conviction.[18] This in turn became a source of much encouragement to the praying ladies, who thought their prayer cries were being heard by God alone.

Lasting Results

The good work was still in progress as late as the autumn of 1864. Two evangelists who spent ten days on the islands at that time said they had 'never seen anything more satisfactory than the work of God in Shetland. Well-nigh a thousand persons would assemble at midday, in a solitary church on a moor, where you could not count more than a dozen houses, so earnest are the people to hear the glorious gospel of Christ.'[19]

One visiting evangelist, James Adam, spoke of well over two thousand anxious souls in total coming forward to be spoken to at meetings

---

17. ibid., 19/03/1863, p. 137.
18. ibid.
19. ibid., 06/10/1864, p. 217.

he held throughout the islands. As late as the winter of 1864, Adam was holding two meetings daily. He would trudge at least ten miles each day from place to place, often crossing hills in treacherous weather. 'I have twice lost my way on the hills', he wrote, 'the snow being so deceiving, that I had to wander about for hours before I got right again, many a time going nearly over the head in holes that were filled up with snow. Yet I was as happy as could be. The Lord was with me, and when I would get to the chapels where I was speaking, I would find them full; and just as I was, wet and wearied, I would go up to the pulpit, and we would not be long begun when the fire from heaven would descend, and all wet and coldness would fly away.'[20]

The Earl of Cavan visited Shetland towards the close of 1864, and noted, 'There appeared an awe of God upon the people of these islands. The countenances and behaviour of the inhabitants were striking. Those who were converted in 1862 stand fast, and none are said to have gone back.'[21]

Ross-shire

Garve

'A great sensation' was elicited by the intimation of 'revival meetings' in the Ross-shire village of Garve, at the head of the loch and the foot of the strath of the same name, in the autumn of 1862. The stir was owing to the fact that the meetings were to be conducted by a female evangelist. This was Mrs Thistlethwaite, an elegant but novice evangelist from Ireland, whose husband had recently leased the shootings at nearby Loch Luichart. Since their arrival in the district, the couple had quickly become known for their generosity to the local poor. Services were held in the Free Church preaching station/school, a partition in the hall having to be removed to accommodate the crowds that sought admission. In fact, dozens of vehicles and scores of pedestrians flocked to the remote spot from long distances, to the extent that a large number of people had to be turned away. Those allowed entrance were so impressed with the meetings, which continued over several nights, that news quickly spread throughout Ross-shire and far

---

20. ibid., 02/03/1865, p. 136.
21. ibid., 19/01/1865, p. 37.

beyond of such novel proceedings in this long-established Calvinist stronghold.[22]

Certainly the Rev. John Kennedy used the opportunity to speak against the practice of women preaching, taking care not to refer to Mrs Thistlethwaite or the Garve meetings by name. He insisted he did not wish to 'repress the Scriptural development of a Christian lady's zeal'; he just didn't want to see such enthusiasm being misdirected.[23] In response Mrs Thistlethwaite stated that she was not technically preaching, but rather 'prophesying and edifying', for which, in regard to women as well as men, there were biblical precedents.[24]

Western Isles

Mull

Duncan MacFarlane of the Baptist Church in Tobermory reported in March 1864 that 'it pleased the Lord to pour down His Spirit in one or two of the stations that I visit (between eight and sixteen miles from Tobermory). MacFarlane stated that the 'awakening commenced and the Spirit came down' as a result of a young man from Islay crossing over to Mull on a preaching tour, when he preached at several of these stations. Four young women and a lad of fourteen professed to be changed, each requesting to be baptised. On 3 January, after preaching to a great audience in a large barn, MacFarlane led his congregation to the riverside, and in the presence of many witnesses, 'these five converts followed their Saviour into the water'. Although the day was

---

22. Further promotion was afforded by a short article describing the services sent to the *Inverness Courier* by three young businessmen from Dingwall who had been impressed by Mrs Thistlethwaite's preaching.

23. The Garve meetings also came to the attention of Dr Begg of Edinburgh, who wrote to the *Inverness Courier* saying it was 'good to see higher classes converted', but that there was 'no plainer text in the Bible than "I do not suffer women to preach"' (William Simpson, *A Famous Lady Preacher: A Forgotten Episode in Highland Church History*, Inverness, 1926, p. 8).

24. ibid., pp. 5-10. After moving south to enjoy considerable evangelistic success in places like Hampshire, London and even Paris, the defiant evangelist appeared to antagonise John Kennedy further by returning to Ross-shire in August 1866, even to his own charge of Dingwall. Here, during the local Communion season, on the Thursday 'Fast Day' of that sacrament, three hundred people gathered, many out of curiosity, to hear Mrs. Thistlethwaite preach in the open air outside the local hotel.

very cold, the pastor noted, 'I spoke a little at the waterside, and deep impressions were made, several shedding tears, not only from what they heard, but also from the scene itself. In the evening we retired to the barn and I preached to a large crowd, among whom the Spirit of God was evidently working. I again preached in the neighbourhood the following evenings.'[25]

At the end of the month, MacFarlane found another five or six professing faith, and four were baptised before over three hundred onlookers. 'I found and felt the presence of the Lord wonderfully', noted the island minister. 'I have no doubt whatever that His presence was felt by many in that crowd, for they all seemed to be in perfect peace.' A further two were baptised in like circumstances a month later, while numerous others remained under concern of soul. Concluded MacFarlane, 'it would rejoice your soul ... to see the glorious meetings, the happy conversations and the evident tokens of God's presence we have had for the last three months'.[26]

East Coast Fishing Communities

Footdee

In the fishing community of Footdee, which had experienced revival in early 1861 (see pp. 251-2), nightly meetings continued without intermission for two whole years. Donald Ross, Superintendent of the recently formed North East Coast Mission, led the work, receiving help in his labours from several Aberdeen ministers and others. Early in 1862, 'there was another remarkable and gracious and far more reaching moving of the Spirit of God' in the closely knit community.[27] More excitement prevailed than in the previous year's work, and there was probably 'a greater proportion of stubble', said Ross. Indeed, referring to the biblical parable of the wheat and the tares, Ross sometimes said

---

25. BHMS Report, 1864, pp. 7, 13-14.

26. ibid. There appears to have been a pronounced season of blessing in Mull just two years later. When two evangelists visited the girl's school in the summer of 1866 and spoke of the love of Jesus to all, 'the first indications of the glorious work that God has done among us appeared' (*TR*, 16/08/1866). One can only echo Harry Sprange's sentiment that, 'infuriatingly ... no further details' are given! (Sprange, p. 295).

27. People both worked and lived cheek by jowl, most of the small houses in this compact village being occupied by at least two families.

that he could not believe a work of grace to be really of God unless there was chaff. News of the mighty work spread over the wider area, Ross hoping that it would act as an incentive 'to those who laboured for souls to faint not'.[28]

Pultneytown

'Soul-reviving seasons for nearly three months' took place in the fishing community of Pultneytown, Wick, in the autumn of 1862, when Methodist lay preacher John MacDonald came to preach both indoors and 'in the streets, lanes and high-ways'. A group of females, whose souls were 'on fire with the love of God', joined MacDonald for a special prayer meeting in the north-Caithness township of Mey, to pray God's blessing on the place. 'Every heart was melted, and every soul set on fire by the Holy Spirit.' Assurance was given them that God's work would be revived, and souls saved. The following Sabbath, the meeting place was packed, and 'the showers of grace descended copiously'. One old man became prostrate and soon 'found peace, and many others enjoyed the peace of God that night'. At a woman's prayer meeting, 'every soul felt a divine influence, and was indeed baptized with the Holy Ghost'. People walked miles to meetings, and from one meeting to another, singing all the way, thus attracting many strangers whose interest was aroused by the singing. Alexander Henderson, who wrote a report on the work for *The Revivalist*, described the trek from Staxigo to Wick, as 'the happiest three miles' walk that ever I had in my life'. About seventy professions of faith were recorded. In the opinion of Henderson, however, the movement would have been 'far greater but for the underhand opposition which was set to work by parties who ought to help forward the cause of the Lord'. Such opposition was apparently meted owing to MacDonald's life of great sin before his conversion, and a time of backsliding subsequently. Many, however, were in no doubt that 'he really is a noble champion for His Master's cause'.[29]

---

28. Ross, 1890, pp. 128-9. So significant was the 1862 move of the Spirit in Foot-dee that around the year 1865 Ross and 'a representative Footdee fisherman' were invited to speak in Drumblade, near Insch, to speak of what God had wrought during that time.

29. *The Revivalist*, November 1862, pp. 171-2.

Portessie, Findochty and Portknockie

Converts from the 1860 revival in Portessie, most of whom had continued strong in their faith in the days following, arranged to hold a prayer meeting on New Year's Day 1863, to petition God for a fresh outpouring on their community. Aware that this day was normally spent 'in the service of Satan', it was deemed appropriate to give it entirely to the Lord's use. Thus they gathered at nine in the morning, and continued right through to midnight, with a two-hour interval in the afternoon. 'God wrought graciously and powerfully in their midst', the Rev. Ker of Deskford Free Church wrote, 'and the whole place became alive to the importance of eternal realities.'[30]

Two miles along the coast, revival began in Findochty just days later, when some young lads met for prayer among the rocks and came under 'deep and overpowering emotion'. They went through the village proclaiming the gospel from house to house. Others joined them and they met for prayer again by the walls of an unfinished church. After a time they all came under deep conviction of their sinful state, and several cried out in agony of mind. The noise of their distress reached the ears of some believing adults who exhorted them with such effect that almost everyone became affected and 'a general spirit of prayer was poured out'. From this place they went to a hall already filled with people. 'There also the Lord wrought graciously in pouring out such a spirit of concern that the whole place became affected.'[31]

Some of the young men went to Portknockie, and there also the same work was manifested. Here, the majority of those who came under spiritual conviction were led by what Ker termed 'individual exertion'. The anxious were directed to go from the large meetings to small private meetings in people's homes, 'and there the Lord oft spake peace' – often through the 'experience-telling' (testimonies) of recent converts.

Portgordon and other villages also shared in the blessing, largely through the work of a deputation from the Evangelistic Association of Scotland, who addressed crowded meetings every night. The deputation was privileged to see 'much of the power of God' and to experience for themselves 'something of the refreshing rain that had descended on

---

30. *TR*, 05/03/1863, p. 111.

31. ibid.

these places'. Continuing the analogy, *The Revival* reported that 'the latter rain has been as refreshing as the former'.[32]

Work stopped for sixteen days in the area – virtually all other activities being laid aside. Food was in general 'disregarded or forgotten, or only taken at snatches of time'.[33] A young lad who had an impediment in his speech, was soundly converted. All of a sudden he began to pray

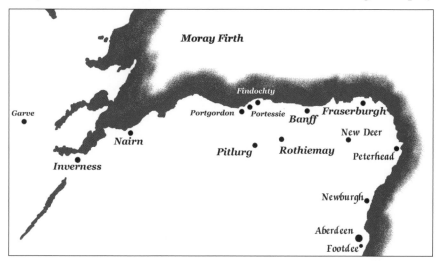

with much fervour and fluency, and even addressed meetings, without any indication of his defect. Everyone was moved by the lad's healing, though such transformation was by no means a singular case.

A boy of eight years of age, under strong convictions, spoke at one meeting, and his words made such a deep impression that more were convicted and converted in those moments than on any other occasion during the revival. One Christian worker visited Findochty at this time, having heard that the village 'was overshadowed by the Holy Ghost, and we found it so in very deed. We had never seen anything like the power that was here manifested in prayer, and that by illiterate but pious fishermen. It had a most humbling effect on me', the worker continued. 'The people were gathered together to hear us speak for the Master, but speak I could not.'[34]

---

32. Robbie, pp. 72-3.

33. *TR*, 05/03/1863, p. 111.

34. McHardie, p. 235. The Rev. William Birrell was ordained into the newly formed Findochty United Presbyterian Church – which had formerly been co-joined with

It was reported that, owing to the 1860 and 1863 revivals, the entire village of Findochty now professed to be converted, with the exception of five or six individuals 'who keep close together and apart from the others. They fear contact with God's people, knowing that some who, in their boldness, went to drag their children away from the meeting, have been arrested on the spot, and seized with overwhelming terrors, have cried out for mercy.'[35]

Ker reported that as a result of the revivals of 1860 and 1863, 'those on the Lord's side are the majority in most of these villages'. An obvious difference between the two movements was that physical prostrations were almost entirely absent from the more recent awakening. In general, most observers considered that 'the latter movement was far more satisfactory than the first. The apparent commotion is much less, but there is a deep, solemn and earnest feeling pervading all classes.'[36] Indeed, Ker saw 'what seemed to me a higher stage of the Christian life reached at that time', which 'seemed to bring greater stability and a deeper conviction of divine truth'.[37]

St Ninians

James Flett and all the crew on his Findochty fishing boat were Christians, converts of the 1859–61 revival along the Banffshire coast. The scales had fallen from Flett's eyes at a meeting for the anxious during James Turner's visit to the fishing village in February 1861. 'Then out of the meeting I got, and went round all my relatives telling them what God had done for my soul. At the meetings after that, I had in particular great power with God in prayer, and on the spot obtained direct answers.'[38] Flett soon went through a time of testing, however, and for a while lived a powerless Christian life.

---

the Portknockie congregation – in March 1862, and 'from first to last seemed to enter with much ardour into revival work'. Unhappily, he was deposed for confessed immorality in September 1866 (Robert Small, *History of the Congregations of the United Presbyterian Church*, Edinburgh 1904, p. 131).

35. McHardie, p. 235.

36. *TR*, 05/03/1863, p. 111.

37. In a remarkable change of mind, Ker afterwards spoke of this movement as being 'a delusion of imaginative men' (*'The Christian'*, 10/06/1880, p. 7).

38. McHardie, p. 118.

When at the small community of St Ninians, Flett and his crew attended church meetings, where Mr MacDonald, the East Coast Missionary, had asked Flett to take his place one night. Terrified at the prospect, and sensing a satanic onslaught, Flett held tenaciously onto God. 'He lifted me wholly out of myself', Flett later recalled. 'The Spirit took possession of me.' Flett spoke of the experience as being like 'a second conversion, which stripped me completely from fear of man. I spoke truly as He gave me utterance and that night upwards of one hundred souls professed to come under conviction. The work begun that night went on' and news of the movement spread all over the east coast.[39]

Fraserburgh

Up to 1862 there was no record of a powerful revival having broken out in Fraserburgh. It was not that the town had been completely overlooked by the spirit of awakening sweeping across the country during 1859–60. Many had come under conviction, while earnest believers were praying for a more substantial shower of God's Spirit on the town. One resident in Fraserburgh, however, was deeply concerned that the town was as if 'blindfolded … which the devil is rocking away in his arms, hushing its inhabitants asleep on the very mouth of the pit; and he will continue rocking them in the cradle of self-righteousness and formality, till he rocks them into hell, if they don't look alive, and awake out of their God-dishonouring and devil-pleasing state'.[40] Prayer increased over the months, and as the summer of 1863 wore on, expectancy grew of an imminent move of the Spirit in the town.

One correspondent received much information that 'the Lord is pleading His cause in that town. I expect to hear of a great blessing upon it soon, if they keep declaring the Word and walk consistently.' The eyes of the people of Fraserburgh, were, the correspondent noted, fixed upon the fisherfolk from Findochty and Portessie who had converged on the town during the busy herring season and who had been caught up in the revival movement that had recently spread through their own communities. The work in Fraserburgh, he believed, depended largely on the witness in life and talk of these converts, although the bold

39. ibid., p. 118; cf. p. 154.
40. ibid., p. 181.

witness of some of these 'had been cooling down a little'. It appears that a revival was indeed triggered off in the busy port, for Elizabeth McHardie notes that at the close of the season, the fishermen from the Banffshire coast 'returned home with hearts all on fire', sparking off 'one of the special seasons of revival with which the Banffshire coast has been visited'.[41]

Peterhead

Peterhead, which largely (and singularly)[42] missed out on the dramatic outbreak of revival fever which spread along the north-east coast in 1860, partook of a late share in the blessing in 1863. The loss of three fishermen when their boat capsized first produced a deep impression on local communities. 'Frequent religious services' were immediately held, which a great many attended, and in connection with these an awakening appeared.[43]

This inspired a visit from Miss Graham, a young evangelist from Edinburgh. There developed 'such a season of awakening as has never before been witnessed in Peterhead ... every Sabbath night hundreds go away that cannot get in'. It was during the after-meetings 'that we see the working of the Spirit ... there was no noise ... all was done decently and in order'. After Miss Graham left town, up to four hundred continued to meet each evening. The evangelist returned in February 1864 and once again led gatherings that attracted a large response.[44]

The following month, just when some in the town were praying for a helper to come and nourish the new converts and build them up in their new-found faith, another female evangelist, also from Edinburgh, arrived on the scene. Jessie McFarlane seemed fitted for the task in hand, and, as she engaged in Bible studies based on St John's Gospel, 'the converts went on from strength to strength, growing daily in the

---

41. ibid., pp. 183, 180.

42. Although see above regarding Fraserburgh.

43. *The Revival*, 23/07/1663.

44. ibid., 28/04/1863, quoted in Jeffrey, p. 236. News of Peterhead being visited 'with the power of the Holy Ghost' is also found in the personal correspondence of one particular fisherman, who wrote: 'It is a blessed thing that life is manifested somewhere; and we have reason to praise God that Peterhead, the native place of dear Mr Turner, who now walks the plains of light, is being revived' (McHardie, p. 184).

Divine life. Such lessons were learnt', noted her biographer, 'and so much real teaching received on all hands, and the habit of searching into the word of God enforced, that the blessing which attended her labours cannot be estimated.' One person who frequently heard her preach in Princess Street Hall said, 'She simply expected God to bless His own word.' It was found, in particular, that every single night, on singing the final verse of 'There is a Fountain Filled with Blood', which verse Jessie insisted on having repeated three times, at least one soul 'believed in Jesus', and so McFarlane 'won the hearts of many'.[45] Peterhead was graced by a further wave of blessing later on in the sixties (see p. 452).

Newburgh

A number of evangelists came to hold meetings in the Aberdeenshire coastal village of Newburgh in the 1860s, including a retired soldier, and Donald Ross of the North-East Coast Mission. Ross held after-meetings in one of his landlady's rooms; this was often packed to the door, where Ross stood asking everyone as they passed out how it was for eternity with them. His landlady was the first to be saved, followed by the daughter of a Free Church elder.[46]

Following services led by a Mr Taylor, 'a most blessed revival' broke out in the community at the start of 1865. Many girls awakened by the visit of the old soldier were brought to Christ, and some became wives of devoted preachers. The whole village was 'most graciously stirred', and 'some very notorious characters, drunkards, and infidels' were converted, and were soon to be found preaching in the open air. Converts included the future wife of evangelist, James J. Scroggie, who testified, 'The Lord loved and gave, I believed and have.' One evangelist followed another to the village, 'and still the wave of blessing rolled on'. Converts formed a prayer group and took to visiting every home in the neighbourhood. Said one, 'My district lay among the fisher folk, and for each one individually I prayed and laboured, and praise God, one after another were brought to Christ.'[47]

---

45. H. I. G., pp. 25-7.

46. Ross, 1890, pp. 172-4.

47. James Scroggie first came to Newburgh in 1866, the first of numerous visits where he was 'greatly used in the conversion of souls' (Jeannie Scroggie, *A Life in the Love of God*, London, 1908, pp. 11-19).

Banff

The revival begun in Banff in 1860 continued in ebbs and flows right through to the close of 1862. One evangelist said at that point that 'the proportion of young men who profess to be the Lord's is greater than anywhere we have been.'[48] An impression was produced in the town a couple of years afterwards, in the late summer of 1865, under the preaching of William Hay Aitken, being intensified by a two-day visit from his father, the Rev. Robert Aitken of Pendeen in Cornwall, an Episcopalian clergyman with a powerful ministry under which many hundreds had been converted. In Banff the blessing deepened. Hay Aitken felt compelled to stay on longer than originally intended, and meetings were continued for nearly three months. Much fruit bore forth, and the Christian Association doubled its membership to nearly one hundred.[49]

Many years later, Hay Aitken wrote regarding this evangelistic campaign: 'Upwards of a hundred young men professed to give themselves to God. A good Christian man who resided there, and had helped in the movement, came to see me a year later, when I was a curate in London. He was a cautious Scot – a man whom I should never expect of exaggeration; but when I eagerly asked him how the young men were standing, he replied, deliberately enough, "They are standing right weel! There be jist twa that I'm nae sae sure aboot, but a' the rest are holding on grand!"' Portsoy, too, shared in this blessing, and 'a band of faithful workers' from Banff came along to help Aitken and his uncle Hay Macdowall Grant in the work.[50]

Nairn

Grant and Aitken helped also in the awakening that began fifty miles further west along the Moray Firth in October 1865, among the fishing population of Nairn. The movement followed six years of prayer by a group of believers in the town, who had earnestly interceded for such a blessing. Twenty-eight members were admitted to the Free Church during the year, after thorough examination.[51] 'Babes-in-Christ',

---

48. *TR*, 06/11/1862, p. 213.

49. FCSRSRM, 1866, p. 4; *TR*, 17/05/1866, pp. 270-1.

50. William Hay Aitken, quoted in Johnson, p. 4; Gordon, 1876, p. 333.

51. FCSRSRM, 1867, pp. 7-8.

departing to the seasonal herring fishery on the Continent, 'earnestly begged their Christian friends to remember them at a throne of grace.' The good work continued at home into the summer of 1866, at which time also 'a very decided movement' commenced among little boys and girls, from the age of ten to fourteen years. It was said that 'some of them seem to have truly laid hold of Jesus, and have little prayer-meetings among themselves'.[52]

The Rev. James Morrison of Urquhart parish in Moray referred to a 'gracious work in our midst' in 1862, after which he was pleased to find that the vast majority of those who professed Christ continued strong in their faith. Subsequently, Morrison compared the movement to that which occurred in his congregation twelve years later, in 1874 (see pp. 565-6).[53]

Inland Aberdeenshire

Rothiemay

In some parts of inland Aberdeenshire, the influences of the 1859 revival lingered, and blessing was experienced, well after other districts had reverted to their 'wonted calm'. Such was the case in Marnoch, Rothiemay and neighbouring districts. One young man who attended many meetings in this locality was John Smith, who later became a Free Church of Scotland minister. Smith had become seriously awakened during the earlier part of the revival movement, to the extent that his whole life was altered, but he was conscious that he was still unconverted. On 6 January 1863, Smith attended a soirée in the Free Church in Rothiemay. After the meeting he spent some time in the adjoining schoolhouse, then set out, with two friends, on the eight-mile return journey home. 'The subject of conversation was chiefly the Lord's work and the revival then going on in the district', he said. It was the death of one of these friends just a few weeks later that helped lead, over a year later, to a complete breakthrough in Smith's spiritual struggles, whereupon, he exulted, 'I could scarcely come down my stair for joy.'[54]

52. *TR*, 17/05/1866, pp. 270-1.

53. ibid., 04/06/1874, p. 116.

54. John Smith, *Memorials of the Rev. John Smith*, Edinburgh, 1888, pp. 7-8.

Pitlurg and New Deer

Jessie McFarlane returned to the north-east eighteen months after her popular visit of 1863, when, in May 1865, she held meetings in a number of places. Her work was especially blessed in Pitlurg and New Deer. In the latter place, says her biographer, 'a great awakening ensued; many were converted ... the work was of God and grew mightily'. New Deer had been touched by revival in 1859–60; but now, wrote McFarlane, 'the few who were found faithful and had not denied the name of Jesus' were quickened and brought into fuller liberty during this 'time of refreshing from the presence of the Lord'.[55] One woman who attended McFarlane's meetings spoke years later of how she 'longed to hear her sweet voice leading the praise of Jesus'.[56]

Fife and Clackmannanshire

Auchtermuchty

A correspondent for the *Wynd Journal* reported in April 1862 that there has been 'a real awakening' felt at Auchtermuchty and Drumshelt under the fervid prayers and powerful appeals of a female evangelist from Edinburgh, thought to have been Miss Graham. This evangelist, noted the journalist, 'has been more owned for the last six months to arouse careless souls than any one I ever heard of. She is now at Cockenzie among the fishermen, and the same effects are following her labours. She never opens her lips to tell of the love of Jesus but souls are struck, for the hand of the Lord is with her.'[57]

Alloa

An awakening relating to the Baptist cause in both Alloa and other parts of Clackmannanshire began in 1859 and continued well into the 1860s (see p. 184). In June 1862 James Scott wrote: 'The Lord's work is still progressing here. ... I am engaged every night, and when the weather is good

---

55. By this date, McFarlane, though from a Presbyterian background, had come to accept Brethren ecclesiology and adventism, and was noted for being the first to introduce these ideas to this part of the country.

56. H. I. G,. pp. 28-9; Dickson, 2002, p. 75.

57. *TR*, 12/04/62, p. 21. In the same month, elsewhere in Perthshire, the *Blairgowrie Advertiser*, in an article titled 'Hypocrisy Unmasked', brought attention to the fraud and forgery perpetrated by a young man in Blairgowrie who had set himself up as a 'revivalist' (N. Campbell, p. 166).

I speak in the open air, as we get more to hear us in the open air than when we meet indoors.'[58] Twelve converts were added to Scott's church in a few months, while in December 1863 the meetings were 'still being kept up with encouragement', and 'excellent meetings' were being held in the house of a family, all members of which – father, wife and eldest son – had been recently converted and baptised. Scott also spoke with three young women from Clackmannan, who all 'seem to have passed from death unto life'. He added: 'There may be a number more there whose hearts the Lord has opened to receive the truth.'[59] A number of folk in Alva also came under impressions during the duration of the movement.

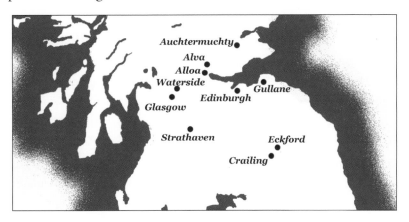

Alva

Meanwhile, in the spring of 1863 a further time of awakening commenced in Alva, at the foot of the Ochil hills, where evangelist John Colville, was preaching. The keynote was struck in a sermon given by the Rev. John Young in the United Presbyterian Church on the text, 'Be troubled, ye careless ones'. The next night the Town Hall was filled to overflowing and the meetings continued nightly for five weeks. Recorded Colville's wife: 'The work was, to a large extent, one of revival, many of God's hidden ones being brought to light, and many who followed afar off being led into the "closer walk". Many young people were quickened.' Colville presided at all the meetings and Duncan Matheson also preached here. A list was kept of young people who 'woke up to eternal realities' during these weeks of blessing. Of these,

---

58. BHMS Report, 1863, p. 30.

59. ibid., 1864, p. 24.

one became a minister, several became ardent evangelists or missionaries, while some passed away, 'whose dying beds were illuminated gospels'.[60] Each springtime after this, Colville found his way back to Alva to hold meetings, though these never equalled in intensity those of 1863.

Mid and East Lothian

East Lothian ports

Towards the end of 1862, nineteen-year-old evangelist Jessie McFarlane spent some months labouring in East Lothian. Aberlady, Dunbar and the proximate village of Bellhaven were all visited, but most of her efforts were concentrated on the village of Gullane. There was considerable opposition to women preachers in Scotland at this time. Women were not expected to preach theology nor were they considered good at it. Indeed, the Edinburgh church that Jessie attended threatened to revoke her membership because of her involvement in preaching.[61] In attempt to somewhat alleviate the controversy, McFarlane, in the active months as an evangelist since her conversion in 1860, had preached only to women. When asked why she did not admit men to her meetings, McFarlane's response was, 'I cannot yet see that the Lord would have me to do so.'[62]

However, in Gullane matters came to a head. The desire to hear her speak was so strong that many young men – 'principally post-boys, horse-trainers, etc' – surrounded the windows of the room in which she was speaking and begged to be allowed to hear. Their earnestness was indeed well tested, but when reminded that the souls of men were as precious in the sight of God as those of women, McFarlane could no longer accept the responsibility of refusing them the opportunity of hearing the gospel. From this time on her meetings were thrown open to those of both sexes. The work in Gullane grew mightily – 'men and women, old and young, were gathered into the fold of the Good

---

60. Colville, pp. 129-30.

61. J. Holmes, p. 116. Holmes, in her chapter on female preachers in times of revivalism in Victorian Britain, noted the opinion of one observer who stated that McFarlane's 'forte lies in the picturesque and illustrative rather than in powerful reasoning and logical sequence' (p. 117).

62. H. I. G., pp. 21-2.

Shepherd, and an abundant reaping-time was the result of earnest prayer and self-denying labour'.[63]

Edinburgh

McFarlane also preached for eight Sabbath evenings in Edinburgh's large Music Hall. Sometimes the doors had to be closed before the starting time of the meeting, shutting out hundreds, who were addressed outside. Similarly, in the summer of 1863, and again in July/ August of the following year, this young evangelist spoke repeatedly in Glasgow's City Hall. The people gathered in such large numbers that hundreds were turned away, although the hall, when packed, could hold from three thousand to four thousand people.[64]

Still in Scotland's capital, Carrubbers Close Mission, near the city centre, was started with the intent of reaching out to children in the neighbourhood, for no Sabbath school existed in or around that area. Well into 1860, the dramatic awakening that had arisen months before (see Chapter 8) was still going on. With the good work continuing, there came news a few years later – in 1864–65 – of an unusual movement among Sunday school pupils at the Mission – chiefly the elder boys. The youngsters began holding prayer meetings among themselves in their houses in different parts of the town.[65]

Glasgow and Dunbartonshire

Waterside

A work commenced in Waterside on the outskirts of Kirkintilloch in 1860 (see p. 95) was given new momentum in 1862, when a visiting believer got use of the village school, and 'sent through the town drum for a meeting at 3 p.m.' Although it was daytime, the school was nearly full of men and women who left their work to spend an hour in prayer. 'You would have seen the men with their aprons on', noted one correspondent, 'and women with their children, met to hear the words of eternal life. Many were seen to weep, and since, we have reason to believe, bowed at the feet of Jesus, clothed and in their right minds.' A fortnight

---

63. ibid.

64. ibid., pp. 22-3, 35.

65. *TR*, 22/06/1865; 17/08/1865. Unfortunately, nothing more is known about this movement.

later the evangelist returned, and the school was crowded once again. Many since that time gave evidence of 'their union to Christ'. A visit to Kirkintilloch revealed that here, too, 'a good work is going on'.[66]

Glasgow

It was said of Glasgow that the work of revival underway in the city since the late summer of 1859 received a fresh impetus in April 1862, when a great blessing attended the Communion season in several places. A great many converts were added to the various churches, mainly the fruits of the previous revival. Believers were also stirred to increased prayer and labour. This was said to have been shown in the efforts put forth at the 'various successful meetings now being held'.[67]

Also in Glasgow, a quiet but extensive awakening was experienced in the two congregations at the centre of the Wynd Mission in 1864–66. This followed the popular weekly open-air services on Glasgow Green and those at the Glasgow Fair led by the Rev. James Wells and the Rev. Robert Howie, the latter, 'a man of fervent piety and extraordinary evangelistic power'.[68] The Wynd Church grew to such an extent that in June 1864, a new congregation was formed in the newly built Trinity Church in Charlotte Street, with Howie as its minister. Out of the 720 Wynd members, 430 accompanied him to form the nucleus of this fresh congregation. Within two years there had been 885 additions to membership, while the Wynd Church admitted seventy-one at the November 1865 Communion. In both cases, nearly all new members had previously been living in neglect of the means of grace.[69] Outstanding growth in the Wynd Church was to continue right through to 1869 (see Chapter 18). Elsewhere in the metropolis, as a result of an exciting movement in Blackfriars Street Chapel during the late summer and autumn of 1864, itinerant evangelist John Bowes, who paid several visits to the church during that time, was able to baptise seventy converts.[70]

---

66. *WJ*, 09/08/1862, p. 156.

67. *WJ*, 12/04/62 p. 21.

68. MacColl, p. 318.

69. FCSRSRM, 1866, p. 4; MacColl, pp. 362-74.

70. J. Bowes, p. 555.

Hillhead

'A considerable movement' was experienced in the mining community of Hillhead, on the outskirts of Glasgow, in 1865. Here, Duncan Matheson wrought night after night 'amidst striking displays of divine grace'. Matheson reaped where others had sown, not least the saintly David Sandeman, who had sometimes tarried before God all night, crying, 'The whole district, Lord, the whole district! I cannot ask for less.'[71] The Rev. James Jolly acted as Free Church missionary in Hillhead, and when William Robertson of Carrubbers Close Mission first went to help him, couldn't but remark on the significant number of miners that had been 'brought to the Lord'. The strong feeling in the place was indicated by the words on the lips of many, 'It's just heaven or hell.' Some men were even awakened as they drank in the public houses; others were dealt with in the mines.[72]

The South

Roxburghshire

Further south, in the Borders region, upon one stretch of the Teviotdale valley, notably the parishes of Eckford and Crailing, a few miles south west of Kelso, which had 'hitherto been dry and barren as the heath in the desert', came, during early 1862, 'a very gracious rain' of the Holy Spirit, so that it became 'like a well-watered garden of the Lord'. The first tokens of blessing appeared in a barn at Eckford Mill, in which a laymen's meeting had been held for some months previously. With the aid of a lay missionary, meetings were held at other farm places, 'during which very deep awakening took place, and very many are now rejoicing in Jesus'. Meetings were latterly translated to Crailing Free Church.[73]

---

71. Macpherson, 1871, p. 173.

72. R. M. Robertson, pp. 121-2.

73. *WJ*, 05/04/1862, p. 14. Further west, in Ayrshire, for many years the membership of Kilbirnie Reformed Presbyterian Church stood at around 150; this was still the case in 1864. But the following year 'an extraordinary advance' was recorded, when membership jumped to 226, an increase of 50 per cent. This may have been the result of a spontaneous revival in the congregation, although I know of no record of this having taken place. Certainly much earnest work was being done among the lapsed and careless around this time. But it seems that the personal popularity of the incumbent minister, the Rev. Peter Martin, inducted to the charge in 1863, may have had something to do with the rise in membership, for soon after he left for Ipswich in

Spiritual blessing in this county continued the following year. In the village of Smailholm, Peeblesshire-evangelist Robert Steele began meetings in the schoolroom. These became packed, forcing people to meet in a large granary, in which seat-less venue people were more than happy to stand for hours on end. At times, tears flowed in abundance from beginning to close of the meeting, and it was with difficulty the preacher could make himself heard. Horatius Bonar and his missionaries aided in the work, while the Rev. Paterson of Carrubbers Close Mission had to extend a visit he paid to the district, describing the atmosphere as 'quite remarkable'. 'The whole district round Kelso seems more or less awakened', wrote one correspondent. 'The Lord has graciously smiled upon it, and there are abundant tokens of blessing.'[74]

1869, membership dropped back to the norm of past years (W. J. Couper, *Kilbirnie West: A History of Kilbirnie West United Free 1824-1924*, Kilbirnie, 1923, pp. 36-7).

74. *TR*, 29/01/1863, p. 53; cf. 19/02/63, p. 87.

Crovie

Boddam

Donald Ross

Haddington

Duncan Matheson

Kilsyth

Wolfelee

CHAPTER 18

Resurgence of Revival 1866–69

Revival in England, Wales and Ireland

A definite resurgence of revival was observable in many parts of Scotland during the years 1866 to 1869. Outbreaks of revival were not unknown in other parts of Britain during this period too. Regarding a season of localised awakenings in Wales in 1866, it was noted: 'The spread of cholera produced great alarm, and the people flocked to the meetings which were held almost every evening for six months.' [1]

In February 1868, at the little mining village of Arkengarthdale in the North Riding of Yorkshire, a revival first appeared in the Sunday school and the children then sought to convert their elders. Hardly a sermon was preached during the entire eleven weeks in which two local preachers conducted special services. It was said that the cries of anguish and shouts of triumph heard as the long prayer meeting finally broke up brought the inhabitants out into the streets in astonishment.[2]

Across the Irish Sea, it was suggested that the great work of grace manifested in places like Ballycregagh in 1859 continued in power for a long time afterwards. But it appears that a fresh work was making itself felt in this community towards the close of 1866, at which time the Rev. William Montgomery Spears, so active in the earlier movement, translated there. 'Prayer-meetings were held in the homes of the people every evening throughout the week and the crowds who flocked to them were addressed by ministers and converts with an earnestness

---

1. Eifion Evans, *The Welsh Revival of 1904*, London, 1969, p. 10.

2. R. B. Walker, 'The Growth of Wesleyan Methodism in Victorian England and Wales', in *Journal of Ecclesiastical History*, vol. 24, 1973, p. 275.

which seldom failed to have glorious results. The good seed sown sprang up unto an abundant harvest, and on every side one heard nothing but songs of rejoicing.'[3]

A couple of years later, in September 1869, on the last of the Rev. Thomas Toye's annual preaching visits to Glasgow, he was accompanied back to Belfast by two evangelists from Scotland whose labours had been greatly blessed (one of them had visited Toye's church in 1859 and became one of his most esteemed friends). They held revival services in Toye's Great George Street Church every night for a week. After they left, Toye continued the meetings. 'It was', wrote his wife, 'a time of great awakening and refreshment to many.'[4]

Scope of Scottish Movement

Returning to Scotland, a Free Church Report of May 1867 makes note of the 'real and very remarkable work of the Spirit of God in a number of places', one of various seasons of revival which seem to 'pass over the Church like the tides of ocean, now setting in with a mighty flow, and anon passing away with an ebb'.[5] A year later came further mention of this 'religious movement so remarkable in the present day. ... One of the striking features of the times is the widely diffused manifestation of an interest in religious subjects. From the Houses of Parliament to the meeting for Bible reading in the cottage kitchen, multitudes are thinking and speaking about religion. Over and above the ordinary services by the stated ministry, religious meetings are being held, literally in hundreds, both in town and country. In some instances these meetings are attended with a real, deep, extensive work of the Spirit of God, as no one can reasonably doubt who truly knows them and their results.'[6] The accounts in this section comprise some of the most significant awakenings of this period.

It is interesting to note that the start of this revival surge coincides with the fourth cholera epidemic of the nineteenth century, although in none of the following narratives is any connection made between the

3. R. M. Sibbett, *The Revival in Ulster, or The Story of a Worker*, Belfast, 1909, pp. 95-6.

4. Toye, pp. 104-5.

5. FCSRSRM, 1867, p. 2.

6. ibid., 1868, p. 7.

outbreak of cholera and the awakening which took place in the area.[7] That it caused many to consider eternal issues, however, is evident from narratives such as that which appeared in the *Scottish Congregational Magazine* in 1866: 'The prevalence in this land of a grievous pestilence among cattle, and the threatened approach of cholera, naturally turned the minds of men not only to seek natural means of cure or prevention, which have not as yet been found, but also led the devout in their conscious helplessness to turn to God and to implore his aid.'[8]

By January 1867, *The Revival* could speak of 'about twenty large towns and country villages' where great numbers had been brought to the saving knowledge of gospel truths. The movement was advancing surreptitiously. 'Little comparatively has been said about it, but it will leave its mark on this and succeeding generations.'[9] James Balfour, an elder present at a Free Church conference that discussed the general revival across the country, stated at its close, 'I have been at every Assembly since the Disruption, and I never remember anything so interesting and affecting. The testimonies that have been borne by ministers from such a variety of places, of the presence and power of the Holy Ghost in our land, ought to be both humbling and encouraging and demand from us a most reverential and grateful acknowledgement.'[10]

The North and Western Isles

Shetland

William G. Sloan, insisting he had taken care not to exaggerate anything, reported an awakening in Upper and Nether Sound, just outside Lerwick in early 1866. 'This place was noted for carelessness, and, during the great awakening about three years ago, was little affected by it, but now the Lord is making bare his arm and plucking

---

7. Just prior to a movement in Forfar in 1866 (see pp. 456-7), Duncan Matheson did note that 'cholera is not apparently decreasing. The voice is loud and solemn, yet in the same paragraph he wrote: 'the place is hard, and the people sadly indifferent ... few are seeking God; few are caring for God' (Macpherson, 1871, p. 177).

8. McNaughton, 2005, p. 319.

9. *TR*, 17/01/1867, p. 31.

10. The General Assembly of the Free Church of Scotland, *The Present Work of Grace: Being Notes of a Conference Held by The General Assembly of the Free Church of Scotland on Thursday 27ᵗʰ May 1869*, p. 8.

brands from the burning.' People were unwilling to leave meetings, even after three hours. Sloan also visited all the families in their homes and spoke to many who were anxious. Apparently, before Sloan's visit, a young man had been converted at sea, came home and was the means of awakening many of his neighbours. 'Although he could not speak much in public, his heart was filled with joy in the Lord.' Sloan noted that another 'dear Christian brother belonging to the place, who has long laboured there, has been fully engaged in the good work, and is now rejoiced to see the work of the Lord prospering around him'.[11]

Orkney

In Orkney, 'a deep undercurrent of religious feeling' ran through Westray during the summer-autumn of 1866.[12] 'The ditches were all cut, the ramparts of the enemy were all honey-combed, and it required only the word of command for the soldiers to march up and take the citadel.' Onto the scene appeared evangelist Rice T. Hopkins, who held a number of meetings on the island in December 1866 (and again two months later). 'The third night I spoke in the Baptist chapel', Hopkins observed. 'Several were weeping aloud, and from that time, large numbers remained behind to all the after-meetings. The second week, so many stayed, I scarcely knew where to begin; men and women, in every part of the place bowed beneath the power of the Word.'[13] Revival ran deep and as many as sixty additions were made to the Baptist Church. However, when Hopkins returned to Westray in June 1868 with firmly established Brethren tenets, he invoked a deep and longstanding rift in the church, two-thirds leaving to form a new assembly.[14]

---

11. *TR*, 15/03/1866, p. 145. Fred Kelling, in his biography of Sloan, makes no mention of these events.

12. Harcus, pp. 91-2.

13. Neil T. R. Dickson, *Revivalism and the Limits of Co-operation: Brethren Orkney Origins in the 1860s*, private paper, p. 5.

14. Harcus, pp. 94-6; Dickson, *Revivalism and the Limits of Co-operation*, pp. 3-11. Hopkins had begun to lean towards Plymouthism a year or two previously, and though he had raised some suspicions among the Westray Baptists on former visits, they saw little that was decidedly objectionable. Now, however, he was fully convinced of the 'new' teaching, and took advantage of current dissent within the Westray congregation regarding a separate issue. He visited many churchgoers in

In between these visits – in January 1867 – Hopkins, accompanied by Donald Munro, preached over the course of two weeks in the Orkney mainland parish of Harray, people sometimes walking through heavy snow to get to the services. William Corrigall, a member of Harray Congregational Church, who in his youth had heard James Haldane preach, had a dream of two strangers bringing revival to the islands, and he later recognised Hopkins as one of the men in his night-vision.[15] Revival indeed broke out, and over a year later, the parish's Congregational minister could say, 'We are still reaping the fruits of the revival of last year. The interest which was then awakened has in no way abated, but is still growing ... during the past year, many have ... openly professed faith in the Lord Jesus Christ. ... The parish of Sandwick, as well as that of Harray, has enjoyed a shower of divine blessings.' Other denominations in the region also benefited numerically from the movement.[16]

Lewis

The Rev. John ('Big') MacRae translated from the Lewis parish of Lochs to that of Carloway in 1864[17] and served here for seven years to great popular acceptance. It was said of him that 'what Christmas Evans was in the Welsh pulpit, John MacRae was in the Scottish. There were the same powers of imagination; the same gift of vivid description; the same lightning flashes of the things of the Spirit of God; withal the same strain of Celtic mysticism, and the same power of appeal as they laboured to commend to lost sinners the Saviour who came to seek and save that which is lost.' Although in his seventies, much good was done during MacRae's ministry

---

their homes, and, when an address was given in the church denouncing Brethren doctrine, two-thirds of the congregation left to form a Brethren assembly. The Baptist minister, utterly heartbroken at the decimation of his beloved congregation, left the island for America shortly after (Dickson, pp. 83-4; Harcus, pp. 94-6). Sadly, evidences of division between the two rival factions were still apparent in Westray decades later.

15. Untitled biography of Hopkins, in Dickson, *Revivalism and the Limits of Co-operation*, p. 5.

16. W. D. McNaughton, *Early Congregational Independency in Orkney*, Unpublished paper, 2000, p. 52.

17. Not 1866 as stated in Collins, 1976, p. 41.

in Carloway, especially during two particularly blessed seasons. In one of these upwards of fifty names came forward as new communicants within eighteen months – an action not taken lightly in these parts.[18] Said the Rev. Nicol Nicolson, a schoolboy in Carloway while MacRae ministered there, 'We have listened more than once to Dr Mackintosh of Dunoon; Dr Mackintosh Mackay of Harris; Dr John Kennedy; Mr Roderick Macleod of Snizort; Mr Spurgeon, and many other eminent men, but, in our opinion, he [John MacRae] surpassed them all in point of substance, animation, power, fullness and impressiveness.'[19]

North-East Coast

Introduction

Since its inception in 1858, considerable work was done all along the extensive east coast of Scotland, from Arbroath right up to Wick, by deputies of the North-East Coast Mission. Mission Superintendent Donald Ross spoke of 1866 as having been a time of 'general ingathering in all the towns and villages of the coast, excepting Johnshaven, Stonehaven, Muchals, Newtonhill, Rosehearty, Pennan, Garmouth and Kingston, Campbeltown (Ardersier) and Golspie'.[20] For that one year alone, the Mission reported 'a revival of religion' in 'Orkney … Wick, Rosemarkie, Nairn, Findhorn, Lossiemouth, Buckie, Portessie, Findochty, Portknockie, Cullen, Portsoy and Boddam', though not always occurring as a direct result of their efforts alone.[21] At Findhorn the work prospered so much that the Coast missionary described his lodgings as being besieged by inquirers. Ross said of the Mission in November 1866, 'Never since 1858 has the work ceased on our coast; it lived and burned brightly somewhere. At present it is alive

---

18. ibid., p. 3; FCSRSRM Appendix, 1874, p. 17-18. G. N. M. Collins refers to 'the bursts of brilliance' that marked MacRae's Carloway ministry (Collins, 1976, p. 41). Nicol Nicolson says: 'The days spent in this parish were no less blessed for the awakening of many of all ages, than any other period of his ministry' (Nicolson, p. 25).

19. Nicolson, pp. 29-30.

20. *TR*, 29/11/1866, p. 304.

21. *SG*, 19/03/1868, p. 155. Frustratingly, no further details are provided in the Report of the progress of revival in each, or any, of these ports.

at Wick, where a great number since the middle of September have been brought to Christ.'[22]

Meanwhile, when Robert B. Wallace, who had previously served with the Coast Mission in Thurso, came in 1867/68 to the district of Mey/Scarfskerry, some twenty miles from Wick on the north Caithness coast, a revival ensued. Around eighty conversions took place, many of which were followed by baptism in a nearby 'geo' (inlet of sea between the sheer cliff edges) as induction into the local Baptist church.[23]

Portessie and Findochty

Since the revival of 1859, much prayer had gone up in Portessie for a further, similar outpouring on the village. As early as 1864 and for over two years thereafter, more than forty Methodists met privately to pray weekly at a set hour. Public prayer meetings also arose, as many as ten occurring in one week. At length the answer came, and, according to Wesleyan minister, Henry J. Pope, 'so powerfully that even devout men were astonished'. For, towards the close of December 1866, 'God poured out His Spirit upon both Portessie and the adjoining village of Findochty in an extraordinary manner … . Meetings were held in both places every evening, conducted for the most part by the fishermen themselves, some of whom were remarkably qualified for exhorting people …' The twenty-third of December was especially memorable, being the opening day of the new Methodist chapel. An 'experience meeting' began at two in the afternoon, when many testimonies were given, most dating their conversion to the awakening six or seven years previously. The misery of the many unsaved in the hall soon became insupportable, and the occasion turned into a 'penitent's meeting', which lasted for several hours.[24]

During a 'tea meeting' the following evening, the customary speeches by ministers of the various denominations were felt by nearly all to be out of place, for among the people there was 'no relish for the ordinary topics'. A time of prayer and exhortation commenced, and all of a sudden 'more than twenty persons, chiefly men, pressed through

---

22. ibid., 29/11/1866, p. 304.

23. Yuille, p. 102; Bebbington, 1988, p. 313.

24. McHardie, pp. 173-4.

the crowd, and came forward to the place appointed'. Their testimonies thrilled the congregation. Many others came under deep conviction, including prominent office-bearers in neighbouring churches, and some who were there only because it was a tea meeting, who would never normally venture into a church building. As the meeting closed, 'many small companies might be seen in the moonlight wending their way homeward by the sea-side, to some neighbouring village; but amongst them all, there was only one theme of conversation – they glorified God, saying, "We never saw it in this fashion".'[25] The Rev. Major wrote:

> The excitement was intense. For nearly three weeks men forgot their worldly business, and attended to that of saving their souls. Meetings were held day and night with only three or four hours' intermission … . Men, who for hours stood with their hands in their pockets coolly surveying the scene, in one moment would be pierced with strong conviction of sin, and would literally roar aloud for mercy. It was no unusual thing for persons to go to bed to sleep away their misery, but unable to do so, rise and come to the meetings in an agony of distress … scores of persons would be crying for mercy at the same time, and this too, after hours of quiet waiting, and with as much suddenness as a thunder shower.[26]

At least twenty hopeful cases of conversion were reported among drunkards in Portessie alone. The publican was one of the first to confess his sins. He went home from the meeting and pulled down his sign, gathered together his glasses and smashed them among the rocks, then opened the largest room in his house for a young men's prayer meeting. 'Without doubt', said Major, 'more than a thousand persons were under conviction', while 'the numbers of the saved amounted to more than 600 persons'. In Portessie alone, at least one-sixth of the entire population, or 150 persons, was said to have 'turned to the Lord', a quite remarkable number given that this was, for the most part, in addition to the hundreds that had professed conversion during the earlier revivals of 1860 and 1863 in the village. The membership of the Methodist Church at once increased from sixty to 140, while in Findochty, between sixty and eighty young men and old converts,

25. ibid., pp. 175-6.
26. ibid.

belonging to the Presbyterian Church, formed themselves into classes, and were generally met weekly by members of their own denomination. In addition, with this amazing spiritual providence, all the financial difficulties of the new chapel were at once overcome.[27]

Whitehills

Elizabeth McHardie noted that there were 'three special times of revival' in the Banffshire coast village of Whitehills (in the Grange district) between Turner's visit there in 1860 and the year 1875. Frustratingly no dates or details are given, except that 'one began by Mr S., who, if not one of James Turner's converts, was at least led out to work for the Lord through him. The second and third also [came] through those who had directly or indirectly received their working impetus through the instrumentality of James Turner.'[28]

Macduff, Gardenstown and Crovie

A local minister wrote in connection with the labours of a North-East Coast missionary in the townships of Macduff, Gardenstown and Crovie that he knew of scores who were brought to Christ from the start of 1868. Some, when initially visited in their homes, were 'inveterate in their hostility against anything spiritual', and were quick to tell the

---

27. ibid., pp. 177-8. Ker did not look favourably on this movement along the Banff-shire coast, nor on that which occurred a few years later, in 1870 (see p. 488). Writing in 1880, he said these seasons were 'accompanied by great intensity of emotion, which stirred the community, and awakened a spirit of expectation in the country districts. There were, however, no such evidences of spiritual power as had before been so undoubted (i.e., in 1860). The human elements were the most marked, and thus, even though the efforts made to extend the influence of them were greater than ever before, they failed entirely to bring any conviction to the minds of discerning men that the same power from heaven had been at work among them. There was earnestness enough, and a consuming religious zeal, but no proof of anything higher than what may arise from earthly sources. ... This became the means of securing practical objects in connection with church organisation, but it did not indicate more than an increase of religious earnestness and activity. The fact of these repeated occurrences of renewed animation among only one class of the community has tended to discourage the spirit of believing expectation in the country districts, and to make men slow to believe in the present work of saving grace (i.e., what he believed was a genuine move of the Spirit along the same coastal villages over a decade later, in 1880), whose features are so very different from these, until the lapse of time shall have demonstrated the reality of the change' (*The Christian*, 17/06/1880, p. 7).

28. McHardie, p. 80.

evangelist to clear off! By his gentle perseverance, however, a sea-change occurred. Indeed, the minister said that of all the genuine moves of the Spirit he had personally witnessed in the preceding nine years, he knew of none as genuine as that in these three places, especially Macduff. 'It would not be believed were I to utter my full opinion of the results of the efforts of last winter', he concluded.[29]

Peterhead and Environs

In and around Peterhead, the largest halls quickly became crowded in an awakening that began at the start of 1868. 'The work here is something extraordinary', said one worker. Upwards of fifty seamen, besides many others, were said to have been converted. On the tiny island of Keith Inch, opposite Peterhead harbour, and constituting the easternmost point of mainland Scotland, a meeting kept up for years with apparently little fruit was now seeing whole families converted. A hitherto thinly attended cottage meeting in the Roanheads district was now unable to contain the inquirers. The Cholera Hospital was granted as a meeting place, and 'many souls have been converted there'. In Buchanhaven, just north of Peterhead, many were 'crying out for mercy'. In Collieston, 'the whisky-bottle has given place to the Bible and the hymn-book'. Of the fishing community of Boddam to the south, long considered 'barren as a desert ... the whole village is moved'. The awakening in Peterhead was compared to that of 1863 in the town, except that natives of the district, rather than outside evangelists, were now the chief agents of the work.[30]

Fraserburgh and Environs

In the fishing villages to the east of Fraserburgh, and to a lesser extent in Fraserburgh itself, an extraordinary work took place. One man, entering St Combs, was able to assemble a congregation of 250, mainly men, within half-an-hour of his arrival. This was achieved by sending a boy through the village blowing a horn, thus calling the people 'to hear the blowing of the gospel trumpet'. At one after-meeting at Cairnbulg, 'there were from thirty to forty young men and women all broken by the power of God's Spirit, crying to God to save them; no tongue

29. *TR,* 11/06/1868, p. 328.

30. ibid., 20/02/1868, p. 106.

could describe it … . There is no end to the work.' A local newspaper confirmed that 'during the last two or three weeks, [Cairnbulg] has been visited by the most extensive and influential religious awakening by which it has ever been blessed in all its former history … The people have, as by mutual consent, given up the thought of everything else but the salvation of their souls … . The common house of meeting, which is capable of containing upwards of 400, has become quite insufficient for the crowds that are thronging to it thirsting for the word of life.'[31]

Footdee

Between the time of the 1862 revival in Footdee and the end of the decade, there had been 'but scant and occasional droppings from above' on the village. That is, until February 1869, when two deaths in the community touched the consciences of many. One afternoon at Sunday school, to the astonishment of the teacher, all the children broke down – crying, as they were, for salvation. Donald Ross, a year before his resignation as superintendent of the North-East Coast Mission, came quickly on the scene as 'the "zymotic disease" of soul-trouble soon swept over the village'. The fishermen, because of deep inward conviction, were unable to go to sea; indeed their fleet of yawls lay uncared for for five or six weeks. 'Men, women and children were seen at all times of the day dropping on their knees – indeed oft-times lying full-length – on the snow-covered ground, crying for mercy.' Ross and a worker converted in the area in 1861, 'preached with unction to a nightly overcrowded "school", while to those unable to gain admittance (for the Aberdeen townspeople flocked to the village) the gospel was proclaimed in several of the fishermen's houses'. After the evening meeting, Christian men and women retired separately to adjoining houses for prayer, while the anxious were spoken to in the hall – only workers in whom Ross had the fullest confidence were allowed to converse with them. At least three meetings were conducted simultaneously each night during March and April, and, remarkably, about six hundred souls were said to have been converted.[32]

---

31. ibid., 11/06/1868.

32. Ross, 1890, pp. 129-30; FCSRSRM, 1870, p. 6. Then as at other times, Ross was said to have underestimated results (Ritchie, *Believer's Magazine*, April 1903, p. 47, quoted in James Hervey, *Donald Ross: A Soteriological Retrospective*, December

A Free Church minister in Aberdeen spoke most enthusiastically of this 'very remarkable work of the Spirit' ongoing in Footdee and neighbourhood, although he admitted he had had no direct connection with the work, beyond giving all the aid in his power to the labourers more directly engaged in it. He did say, however, that he had had 'some little experience in such work, in many places. ... I can truly say that I have never seen any revival of religion, whether in Ireland or elsewhere, so deep and so real, and so universal within its limits. There is scarcely an individual above twelve years of age in the village who does not make a credible profession of being converted. There is no excitement with which any judicious person acquainted with such work could find any fault.'[33] As a result of the revival, the 'Fittie' folk successfully petitioned the Town Council's Links and Bents Committee for a site on which to erect 'a building for religious meetings and general purposes'. Thus, a large new Mission Hall, colloquially known as the 'Schoolie', was built in the centre of North Square, being opened in November 1869. Originally the Mission represented a Free Church presence in the area and meetings were regular and crowded.[34]

Torry

Shortly after the outbreak of this remarkable revival, on the other side of the river Dee a similar movement sprang up among the fisher-folk of Torry. The Aberdeen minister quoted above in connection with the revival in Footdee noted, 'A very remarkable proof of the power and sovereignty of God' in the fact of its rapid extension. Much prayer had been offered Torry, he stated,

> ... day and night. Now the people of this village viewed the work with much suspicion, and, I may say, contempt. They deemed themselves

---

2009, p. 6). For a year after the revival Ross conducted a Bible class for converts. This was continued for some years further by his successors in the Coast Mission. Some forty young converted fishermen accepted responsibility for the weekly Gospel service – three for each meeting, the triplets being rotatory. All three public houses in Footdee were closed down in a few years (Ross, 1890, pp. 131-4).

33. The General Assembly of the Free Church of Scotland, *The Present Work of Grace*, Edinburgh, 1869, p. 6.

34. Diane Morgan, *The Villages of Aberdeen: Footdee and her Shipyards*, Aberdeen, 1993, p. 73.

a superior race, physically and intellectually; and they refused to be instructed or spoken to on the subject by their neighbours; in short, they resolved, as it were unanimously, that such a work should not prevail among them. But prayer was made to God without ceasing; and after hope had almost fled, God appeared in power, and melted their hard hearts and bowed their proud wills, and at the present time a very gracious and deep work of God is in progress among them also.[35]

'For a short time almost the whole grown-up population manifested a very deep anxiety' of soul, and among those who found new life in Christ there was no decline in spiritual interest months later, when weekday and Sabbath meetings were as well-attended as when the movement was at its height.[36]

Rural North-East

Huntly

Huntly was a centre of revival in the north-east during the movement of 1859–61, and many were converted there. 'It needed only to get them well together', reminisced Dr R. McKilliam years later, 'to have the embers burst forth into fires, which burned up much dross and warmed the hearts of many who had grown cold. This God did very specially for us about six or seven years after that first revival of 1859–60, in a manner which turned Huntly upside-down, and continued with more or less blessing for three years.' Reginald Radcliffe returned to Huntly on more than one occasion during this period, his special work now being more in the line of 'stirring up the missionary enterprise'.[37]

Dufftown and Aberlour

Hay Macdowall Grant of Arndilly shared in the work of a revival in Dufftown in the summer of 1868. Among the many souls awakened was one young man so convicted of sin that he began to shake uncontrollably. A year later nearby Aberlour was likewise visited with 'a wave of His loving power' following the visit of two evangelists. One man sat with his hand on his mouth 'to conceal the emotions which

---

35. General Assembly of the Free Church, p. 6.

36. FCSRSRM, 1870, p. 6.

37. Matthews, pp. 146-7.

were springing from a heart full of joy in the Lord'. One whose life was radically changed at this time was local Charles Morrison, who had heard Macdowall Grant preach with power in the district some years previously, but was not at that time converted, though several members of his family were.

Soon after, converts experienced a further 'wonderful manifestation of His presence ... a foretaste of heaven's glory' which they found worthy of comparison, not to a previous work of revival, but to the biblical scene of the Transfiguration![38] It is this movement that D. J. Beattie is referring to when he notes that towards the end of 1869 there was 'a remarkable work of grace' in Dufftown and Aberlour. The movement resulted in over twenty believers publicly confessing Christ by being baptised in the River Spey. A keen evangelist himself, Morrison was one of many converts who chose to adhere to Brethren principles and, on the first Sabbath of 1872, he helped Donald Ross found an assembly in Aberlour parish.[39]

Other parishes in north-east Scotland also experienced quiet, reverent spiritual awakenings in 1868–69, including Forres, where, night after night for several months, the Free and United Presbyterian churches were alternately filled, and meetings for prayer were held in two schoolrooms in the town. Macdowall Grant was just one of the laymen who came to help here, shortly before his death at the age of sixty-three.

Forfarshire

Forfar

'A fearful place. No tongue can tell its sin.' Yet, much in his prayers, Duncan Matheson said, 'When I die, you will find Forfar written on my heart.' In September 1866 the tireless evangelist laboured earnestly in the Forfarshire town, aided by similarly useful soul-winners, Rice Hopkins, Harrison Ord and John Colville. Amidst much apathy and verbal abuse, the Spirit moved, and over a thousand people would gather to the open-air meetings. Matheson records on

---

38. Gordon, 1876, pp. 356-7, 359-60.

39. This Brethren assembly was still meeting almost a century later (Obituary to Charles Morrison in *The Christian Worker*, 1916; Beattie, p. 268).

various dates, 'The very first night not a few were smitten, and it has gone on ever since. ... A great crowd gathered round. They listened breathlessly. ... I have seldom seen such a solemn meeting on the streets.' By October, Matheson could say, 'The work here is a very decided one. ... Last Monday night will never be forgotten; the vestry was like a hospital.' Many became 'rooted and grounded in Christ, who will be a leaven in a place over which many have sighed, wept and lamented'.[40] The Rev. MacPhail had begun his ministry in Forfar just a few months previously and was naturally thrilled at the work of grace he witnessed. Night by night for six months the work went on apace. Duncan Matheson ultimately broke down under the strain. From that time, MacPhail testified, 'my way has ever been in similar work, though, alas, not with similar results'.[41]

The village of Letham was blessed with spiritual awakening in November 1867, during which the entire Congregational Church Bible Class made profession of faith, the majority of whom also officially joined the Church. In the spring of 1868, signs of awakening became evident in another village and surrounding district in Forfarshire.[42] It was not until the end of autumn, however, that meetings were held. But at once a deep impression was made – men, women and children all sharing the blessing. At the close of one of the sermons in February 1869, all those who had derived benefit from the work were asked to remain behind. Between 120 and 130 did so. Yet these, it was believed, did not amount to half of those who had been truly awakened. The blessing 'descended manifestly' on some of the farms in the neighbourhood. On one large farm there was 'scarcely a family which had not been moved, besides two or three of the young ploughmen in the bothy'.[43]

Ferryden

Ferryden, scene of a dramatic revival of religion in 1859–60, was location for another move of the Spirit in the autumn of 1867. In the intervening period, much prayer had gone up from intercessors at

---

40. ibid., 15/11/1866, p. 269; Macpherson, 1867, pp. 177-9; *TR*, 15/11/1866, p. 269.

41. Matthews, Chapter 3.

42. Annoyingly, the authors of the Free Church report deleted the exact location of this awakening.

43. Brown, 1893, p. 777: FCSRSRM, 1869, pp. 1-2.

cottage prayer meetings, whose voices often battled with the noisy waves
of a troubled ocean, as they pled with God to revive His people again.
Macdowall Grant, the immediate instrument in the earlier awakening,
along with the resident East Coast missionary, conducted meetings in
the open air and in the large schoolroom. The young, for whom much
prayer was made, became the first tokens of the work, especially young
women who had hitherto been 'more than ordinarily an occasion for
anxiety and sorrow to the godly in the village'. Soon all ages and classes
were being encompassed by the blessed work, particularly during the
second week of October, when more were found to be spoken to outside
the meeting place than could be contained within. Among country
labourers from the adjoining district also, 'grace has been gathering
its trophies'. The work continued for a number of weeks at least, and
was noted for being deeper, broader and more comprehensive than the
revival of six years previously.[44]

From Arbroath, too, it was reported: 'A great many of the young
have been brought to know the Saviour and are showing this by their
walk and conversation. There are about thirty-four young men who
meet for prayer every Friday; their ages are from eleven to eighteen.'[45]

Fife
Several Free Church congregations in East Fife recorded powerful
spiritual movements in the years 1866–1868, including those in Carnbee,
Anstruther, Strathkinness and St Andrews (among the fishermen). The
report which brought light to these movements also stated that, beginning in 1860, 'Anstruther has been visited by a succession of awakenings,
recurring every seven years up to the late '80's.'[46]

St Monans
Revival came to St Monans in 1867, the result of the earnest labours of
'some Christian fishermen from the north'. Revival stirrings continued
over the following year or two,[47] and it was reported in the *East of Fife*

44. *TR* 14/11/1867, p. 639; '*Monthly Record*', January 1868, p. 16.

45. *TR*, 13/06/1867.

46. FCSRSRM, 1888, p. 4.

47. ibid.; FCSRSRM, 1870, p. 15.

Record of 1869 that three line boats from the community were out in the Firth of Forth, roped the boats together and held an extempory religious service for two hours, during which they engaged in singing from Richard Weaver's hymn-book. When the wind freshened, each man had again to take his own boat.

The revival was a source of concern to some in the kirk and the *East of Fife Record* reported in 1870 that 'the absence of fishermen on the coast of England had created an unsettled state of the religious community, owing to sectarian movements', of which there were many in

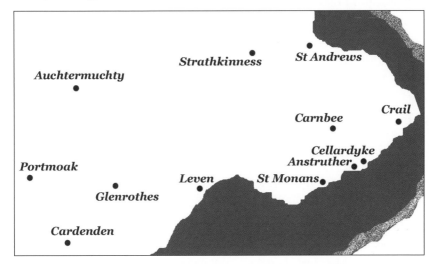

the locality.[48] Indeed, a native of St Monans described his home village during the nineteenth century as the 'Holy City' of the East Neuk of Fife, with a 'polyglot of sects'. These included the Church of Scotland, Baptists, Catholics, Congregationalists and four brands of 'fawn-overcoated and bowler-hatted' Brethren who 'hell-fired at you in the streets and summoned you to judgement through your letter box'.[49]

In an attempt to come in line with this competition, the Free Church Fast Day, usually observed in November, had been abandoned. In response to this 'remarkable interest in divine things, manifested in St Monace and ... the absence of any regular labourer there of any denomination', the Rev. Walter Wood and the Kirk Session of nearby Elie Free Church decided to initiate a new congregation in St Monans.

48. Brown, 1987, p. 216.

49. Christopher Rush, quoted in ibid.

In a remarkably short time sufficient funds were raised to carry out the
£1,000 project, which was formally opened in September 1870. By 1874
St Monans Free Church had a congregation of around two hundred
communicants and the parish had to be divided into four areas for ease
of administration.[50]

General Movement

Meanwhile, it was following the setting aside of a meeting of the
Free Church Synod of Fife in October 1867 entirely for devotional
exercises and prayer for revival – though not necessarily solely through
such intercession – that stirrings of awakening occurred in numerous
communities in the centre and west of the county, such as Cellardyke,
Portmoak, Auchtermuchty, Crail and Cardenden.[51] The General
Assembly of the Free Church of Scotland held a half-day conference
in May 1869 on 'The Present Work of Grace' which they felt had been
and still was taking place in many parts of the region.[52] A member of
the Synod of Fife claimed that he had information showing that there
were spiritual movements in twenty or twenty-one localities within the
county. Fishing villages, agricultural districts and mining communities
were all visited with the shower of blessing. Revival stirrings had also
broken out in more than one district which had for many years lain
under the blight of moderate preaching, and where the people had little
opportunity of hearing a pure gospel, until some godly laymen began to
work in the area. The Synod member felt as if 'the Spirit of the Lord was
only waiting for more prayer and more effort on the part of His own
people, in order to engirdle the entire province with a band of fire'.[53]

One Fife minister spoke regarding 'a considerable village' within his
district where in 1869 there was 'an undoubted religious movement.

---

50. Aitken Fyall, *St Monans: History, Customs and Superstitions*, Edinburgh, 1999,
pp. 229-31.

51. FCSRSRM, 1870, pp. 15-16.

52. Individual reports from this conference are detailed in the convention notes.
Frustratingly, in no case is the precise location of the 'work of grace' given, although,
thankfully, in a few cases, such as that of Footdee, Torry and Wolfelee (though
nowhere in the country of Fife) the location can be deduced from information
gathered from other sources (General Assembly of the Free Church, p. 8).

53. ibid., p. 3.

It began very quietly, and without assignable cause, some months ago, and has now become much more prominent, chiefly owing to the visit of some strangers, one of whom – being "very commendable" – has been much blessed in the effect of his addresses. They have had nightly meetings, and a good deal of excitement. … More recently the work has still been going on, and the number of those interested has greatly increased.' While only 'comparatively few' had shown evidence of having undergone a saving change, and although 'they have very much need of being instructed in the way of God more perfectly … they do seem to be willing to listen, and it is pleasant to have to address such attentive ears'.[54]

Still in Fife, though from a small town at the opposite side of the county, another minister spoke in May 1869 of 'a movement of a revival character' having taken place within his bounds. During the previous twelve months, numerous open-air evangelistic meetings had been held in the summer, these having been transferred to the Free Church in the winter time. These had proved successful, with anxious souls requiring to be conversed with at almost every meeting, and those brought into living faith said to be 'walking consistently'. Prayer was very much the power behind the movement. Weekly district prayer meetings were led by deacons along with recent young converts, while the congregational prayer meeting was still largely attended and sometimes packed, with some finding the need to remain behind to converse about concerns of their souls.[55]

Perthshire and Clackmannanshire

Tullibody

'An interesting and extensive work of grace' arose in Tullibody in Clackmannanshire in May 1867, through the plain preaching of the gospel by the Free Church minister, the Rev. Goldie. 'I let God speak his own truth in naked simplicity and power,' he stated.[56] Interest deepened with every sermon. The rapid growth of converts in proportion to the time they had previously been 'under the secret training of the

---

54. ibid.
55. ibid.
56. *TR*, 26/09/1867, p. 539.

Lord' astonished the minister, who also confided, 'There is such entire sympathy between us. I know their spiritual state so well, that I often feel myself to be saying the very truth that is suited to them.' Six months later, conversions were still occurring among anxious souls, and tears were still being shed in church. Goldie cautiously estimated around sixty conversions, though some put the figure much higher – to around 150, which included 'a considerable number' of children. From neighbouring Perthshire came 'gratifying accounts' of a movement in Auchterarder in the same period.[57]

Dunkeld

A young minister from the Free Church Presbytery of Dunkeld said in May 1869 that he

> … felt no liberty to question the reality of an apparent work of grace which, for many months past, had been going on among his people. He had been deeply impressed by a word spoken to him when a student: 'If souls are not saved, reckon your ministry a failure.' Ever since he became a minister, he had tried to set this before him. About two years previously, he had from time to time had special meetings for prayer, with friends to assist him as he had opportunity. The interest in these meetings did not abate. Last summer it deepened; but it was not till on a Monday in last October (1868) that there seemed any move among the people.
>
> The first night nothing very special appeared; but, on the second, deep impression seemed to be made in the case of one or two. He now felt as if a cloud of blessing were resting upon his people, and that forthwith it would break. On the following Thursday, at the meeting, there was deep solemnity. At the close, twenty anxious souls remained, desiring to be spoken to. The meeting was dismissed but the people would not go away. Among them were many of the young. The scene in the vestry of the church that night he said he would never forget – parents and children weeping about their souls. They sang, 'There is a Fountain Filled with Blood' before they went away.
>
> At the end of the week it was found impossible to stop the meetings. They went on for five weeks, and were better at the close than at the beginning. At this time many of the children seemed really to have given themselves to the Lord. They had prayer-meetings among

---

57. *Monthly Record*, January 1868, p. 15.

themselves. One little fellow was heard saying to a companion, 'It is your turn to pray this time'. The answer was, 'I canna pray, but only two or three words'. 'Oh', said the other, 'that'll do very weel, but, mind, ye maun put a' your heart into them'.[58]

The agency used in this work had been chiefly ministers. There was nothing of a startling or sensational kind; rather, the work had, in its character, been very quiet. The conviction of sin in cases of apparent conversion was generally deep; indeed the deeper the conviction, the more real and satisfactory the cases afterwards usually proved. The young minister concluded by referring to the gracious fruit still remaining, and expressing his hopefulness for the future.

Elsewhere in Dunkeld Presbytery came news of another 'deeply interesting movement'. A young man, recently converted during a time of absence from his native village, approached the Free Church minister requesting that special meetings be held. Equally keen for anything that might awaken his people, and especially as Communion weekend was approaching, the minister at once arranged a week of special meetings, to be held alternately in the church and in a hall in the village. The 'tokens for good' were most encouraging, and the people attending were 'like a blind fire, waiting for the match to be applied'. So the meetings were continued, and indeed went on for around three months, during which time 'drops of blessing were constantly falling, and the impressions extending'. Everything was done in a 'quiet and orderly manner' so that no evil could be justly spoken against the work. The minister found that it was in his 'visitations from house to house that the real character of the work was best seen'. For it was in people's homes that many of those whom the minister considered to be of exemplary character (as did also the people consider themselves to be) were found to be wanting in matters of salvation. The pastor emphasised the importance of classes for the young, which he felt was 'like placing fuel on the altar waiting the divine fire to come down that will, in due season, kindle it into a bright and glowing flame'. Thus, he found that among children attending 'our weekday schools are some as interesting cases of what appears to be real conversion as I have

---

58. General Assembly of the Free Church of Scotland, pp. 5-6.

anywhere witnessed. The members of my Bible class, without a single exception, profess to have undergone a saving change', he remarked.[59]

Central Scotland

Linlithgow

Considerable awakening spread throughout central Scotland between 1866 and 1868. In Bathgate a youth of seventeen from Glasgow, converted during a visit by Richard Weaver to that city, held ten nights of meetings in May 1867, during which numbers made profession of faith. In nearby Linlithgow a more spontaneous and powerful work emerged around the same time. By the start of April 1867, the Bible class in the Town Mission hall rose from about twenty to 105, with attendance averaging between eighty and ninety. Great earnestness often prevailed among the children, and as an evidence of the Spirit's work, a small group began to meet for prayer each Sabbath evening after the Bible class. Attendance kept increasing until at least ten people aged between eleven and fourteen had 'joined themselves to the Lord'.[60]

Haddington and Gladsmuir

'A gracious movement of a very remarkable kind', lasting many months, breezed through the market town of Haddington in East Lothian, which had been, a correspondent noted, 'in a fearful state since the time of John Knox'! This followed a visit from Thomas Holt and George Geddes of the Scottish Evangelization Society at the start of 1866. The conversion of a notorious female drunkard stirred the whole community. The work continued 'almost imperceptibly to deepen and to extend, silently permeating all classes of the community, and infusing fresh life into all the churches in the town'. Surrounding villages were also moved and several hundred people were brought under conviction.[61]

---

59. ibid., pp. 6-7.

60. *TR*, 16/05/1867.

61. *TR*, 08/03/1866, p. 131; 17/05/1866, p. 277. See also *TR*, 06/09/1866, p. 131; 25/10/1866, p. 229. Little impression, however, was made on the village of Ormiston, between Edinburgh and Haddington. Here in 1545 Scottish Reformer George Wishart was betrayed, thus, some believed, placing a curse upon the place. No revival was known to have occurred here in the centuries since that time (W. H. Clare, *Pioneer Preaching or Work Well Done*, London, n.d., pp. 48-50).

Several such villages were located in the parish of Gladsmuir, to the west of Haddington. The work here seems to have been unconnected to that of the Evangelization Society, but rather commenced 'while the incense of the Week of Prayer was ascending to the throne of God' at

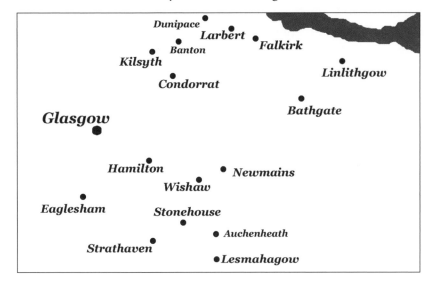

the start of 1867. Following deep intercession during that week, 'almost immediately the blessing came down in copious showers', and the large schoolroom at the ironworks was soon crowded with anxious enquirers. It was reported that for two or three miles around, 'there is scarcely an individual who is not either professing to have been converted or to be in an anxious state of mind'.[62]

In Penston, scores were said to have put their trust in Christ, 'and the religious aspect of the whole village is entirely changed'. One visitor told of his joy of hearing locals pour out their hearts to God in their mother tongue, and to hear their employers and neighbours testify to the genuineness of the change that had passed over them.[63]

Falkirk and Larbert

A season of refreshing arose in the border districts of Stirlingshire, North Lanarkshire and Falkirk in August 1866. The awakening began in Cumbernauld, where visits from Harry Smith and E. Asbrown, also of the Evangelization Society, had produced 'an excitement they

---

62. *TR*, 13/07/1867, p. 329.

63. ibid.

could not manage'. The work here proved deep and genuine, and soon spread west to Kilsyth and east to Dunipace and Larbert, where fervent, consistent prayer for revival had gone on for years, intensifying on news of movements elsewhere in the region. From Larbert awakening spread further east to Camelon and Falkirk, where the work, supported by a number of churches, continued into 1868.

Evangelist John Bowes, then in his early sixties, came in contact with this 'gracious work' on his own extensive travels throughout Scotland. He wrote, in February 1868, of 'hundreds ... being converted at Falkirk, Bainsford (just outside Falkirk), Stenhousemuir, Denny, Kilsyth and several other places', and evangelists such as Geddes, Holt, Sommerville and Henderson being greatly used of God.[64] The Rev. Macpherson of Larbert Free Church reported that in twelve months he admitted over one hundred new members, 'the great body of whom give encouraging evidence that they have accepted of the Saviour and his salvation'. Two years after the revival, Macpherson further reported that virtually all converts remained steadfast in their faith and that there had been 'a large accession to the staff of our elders and deacons of pious and devoted men, whose qualifications for their respective duties I trace to the revival movement'.[65]

Eaglesham

Showers of blessing were experienced in the village of Eaglesham, ten miles to the south of Glasgow, following the transfer to the Free Church station there in 1867, of Robert Thomson of Busby, dramatically converted during the revival of eight years previously (see pp. 79-80). Remarkably, given his lack of formal education, Thomson was at this time a divinity student at Glasgow University, but he threw himself into the work at Eaglesham. He wrote: 'Tremblingly was I brought to this place – this valley of dry bones. But it has been a precious winter to me, and I believe to all my fellow worshippers. ... I believe that souls through all eternity will look back to it from the heights of celestial bliss, as their time of espousals, their time of love, their merciful visitation.' The reading of the life of evangelist James Shaw Sillars fired Thomson up with a fresh zeal, and he instituted district prayer meetings wherever

64. J. Bowes, p. 584.

65. *Monthly Record*, January 1868, p. 16; 1867, pp. 4-7; 1869, pp. 4-5.

there was an opening. For three months he preached virtually every night, and three times on the Sabbath. For several months nothing very special happened, until one evening in the Bible class (numbering thirty), Charles Glass (of Glasgow) proposed to have an inquiry meeting. Seven or eight remained behind in tears. 'This was the beginning of better days.' Fresh cases appeared almost every night, until nearly all the class became the subjects of serious impressions.[66]

'What wonderful days we are having now at Eaglesham', exclaimed one local believer. 'Our young minister is being so manifestly helped that we can't but feel that the Lord has sent him to us. There is such a power and such an unction from on high.' The Rev. Alexander Andrew of Busby Free Church loved visiting Eaglesham, especially during Communion seasons. He called Thomson's time there 'nothing less than a season of revival during the whole three years of his stay'. It was in the midst of this period of refreshing that Thomson made a full, deliberate dedication of his life to Christ's service, resolving 'to be Thine now, and Thine for ever – Thine to live and Thine to die!'[67] Thomson was an effective soul-winner in the townships south of Glasgow till his premature death in January 1874, aged thirty-two.

Kilsyth

According to Methodist preacher, the Rev. H. W. Holland, Kilsyth in the mid-1860s 'was considered to be, morally and religiously, about the worst town in all Scotland. The percentage of illegitimacy was high; the public houses were thronged; men spent their wages in drink as fast as they earned them; the heads of some families were unmarried, many of the children were unbaptized, and most of them insufficiently educated. Many homes were wretched, and the uncleansed lanes (for there is nothing in the place worthy to be called a street) were made hideous by midnight brawls.'[68] The Police Act had never been adopted in the town, the inhabitants of which numbered around 7,500, and the sanitary, social and educational conditions were said to have been appalling.

---

66. Rev. Alexander Andrew, *Taken from the Plough: A Memoir of Robert Thomson, a Faithful Servant of Jesus Christ*, Glasgow, n.d., pp. 41-2.

67. ibid., pp. 38-9.

68. H. W. Holland, *The Kilsyth Revival (Scotland)*, London, 1867, p. 8.

Various preachers had spoken in Kilsyth over the past ten or fifteen years, including the venerable W. C. Burns, home on furlough from China.[69] The revival is thought to have started in the home of the deeply devout Janet Cowie, who had seldom missed a church service in Kilsyth in the past forty years, to which she had to walk the nine miles round trip from her country cottage. She regularly held prayer meetings in her home, and a number of conversions occurred just a few weeks prior to the start of the revival. These converts carried their newly kindled zeal and influence to the open-air meetings in Cumbernauld, and from thence the work passed to Kilsyth.

Here, a two-day visit from English Brethren evangelist, Harrison Ord in August 1866, along with the arrival from Cumbernauld of fellow-soul-winner, Henry Smith, meant that very quickly, 'the whole place was stirred, church after church was opened' for nightly meetings over three months, and hundreds professed conversion. The Established, United Presbyterian, Free, Congregational and Methodist churches were all open for weeknight services, the latter chapel alone holding meetings every night for more than eight weeks. Among the Methodists, too, over two hundred hymn-books were purchased in a few short months, and four new fellowship classes were formed. Even the opening of nearly all the town's churches seemed insufficient to meet the needs of the people, 'for every day crowds stood in the streets to hear the preaching of the word'.[70]

Holland claimed that no cases of prostration or even overexcitement occurred during the duration of the revival. The congregations were so quiet and orderly, he said, that a stranger would hardly know, from what he saw or heard, that there was any unusual work going on. Even sudden conversions were a rarity; most of the converts being in a state of 'genuine penitence for about a week before they find peace with God'. Holland regarded the expression on the faces of those whom he preached to as indicating 'an intellectual awakening, a mental earnestness, softened and spiritualised by the infusion of a highly-devotional element'.[71]

69. This, in 1854, was his first and only furlough, and lasted less than a month.

70. Hutchison, p. 74.

71. Holland, pp. 18-19.

Other evangelists took part in proceedings, and ministers from Edinburgh, Belfast, Glasgow and elsewhere also came to assist, and in almost every case commanded large audiences. Some of these workers also engaged in door-to-door visitation, such as the Rev. McDowall of Saltcoats, who spent a week or two in Kilsyth at the height of the revival. He called at a certain house making enquiry for a woman whose name he had received. Another woman in the house exclaimed, 'I have more need of you than she has. She found Christ last night, but I have not found him yet!' That woman found rest in Christ later that same evening.[72]

Another testimony came from a young convert who attended a meeting so as to be of aid to the anxious. He climbed over some seats and sat next to one whose face was buried in his hands as he sobbed for his sins. To his surprise, he found it was his own brother! As they bowed their heads to pray together, someone else sat beside them. This turned out to be their father! 'Then we three wept and rejoiced together', remarked the emotional convert.[73] Among others, the captain of the Kilsyth Rifle Corps was very active in the movement, and a rifle-corps prayer meeting was held once a week, to which volunteers attended in large numbers.

Said one evangelist regarding the town, 'The tide of blessing has swept over it ... in unprecedented power.' The Rev. Josias Jago of the Congregational Church went as far as claiming that the revival was 'as fruitful of good as any with which the village has been favoured in former years' – an incredible claim, given the fame of two particularly powerful seasons of revival this town had previously enjoyed (1742 and 1839).[74] Even more remarkably, Holland claimed that the work was 'more substantial and solid than all similar movements that have gone before it in the same town'. It took 'hold of the inhabitants of Kilsyth to a much larger extent than was the case in 1742 or 1837'. He believed, too, that it affected all classes equally, in proportion to their relative numbers (the majority being working class). However, scarcely any of the 'very young, or of the very old' were among the converts; rather, most were married working men, from thirty to forty

---

72. *TR*, 11/10/186, p. 200; Hutchison, p. 75.

73. ibid., p. 74.

74. *TR*, 25/10/1866, p. 230, quoted in McNaughton, 2005, p. 281.

years old, and many had previously been 'notoriously and awfully wicked'.[75]

Several newspapers bore witness to the remarkable change in the town, describing 'the inquirers at Kilsyth eagerly poring over their much neglected Bibles' and 'hurrying to the house of God, not only on Sabbath day, but on every night of the week'. Altogether, Holland estimated, nearly eight hundred people were brought to a living faith, including many who came from outlying districts, such as the villages of Condorrat and Banton, both of which also received a share of the blessing.[76] Even the sizeable Romanist Irish colony 'seem to be overawed and held in check'; indeed, two or three Irish Catholics came under the influence of the revival, notwithstanding the maledictions of the parish priest. A notorious poachers' gang was broken up when eighteen of its twenty members were converted. The coalpits were also transformed. Of the eighteen men working in one pit, all underwent 'a great moral change, except one, a Roman Catholic'. To many the terms 'breakfast hour' and 'dinner hour' had more reference to spiritual food than to the supply of their bodies, and among those who met together were a group of colliers, who started a lunchtime underground prayer meeting.[77] Following the awakening, managers of the town's public houses – of which there existed as many as twenty-six! – complained of the lowest trade in twenty years. A local publican complained that never in that time had she known a Sabbath with no custom, as was now regularly the case. One man testified, 'they may say what they like against this revival, but the very horses are the better for it.'[78]

Before the end of the year, the Congregational Church had gained seventy-three new members, the Free Church, over fifty, the United Presbyterian Church, around eighty, the Methodist Church, seventy, and the Evangelical Union Church, forty.[79] This latter group, which

---

75. Holland, pp. 23.

76. *TR*, 13/09/1866, p. 145; McNaughton, 2005, p. 282.

77. FCSRSRM, 1867, p. 2. See also *TR*, 13/09/1866; 11/10/66; 25/10/66.

78. Holland, p. 26.

79. The gains stated for the UPC, Methodists and Evangelical Union Church were quoted by the Rev. Fergus Ferguson of Blackfriars Street Evangelical Union Church

established a church in Kilsyth in 1863, co-operated heartily in the revival work, but became 'so dissatisfied with the instructions often given to the anxious that they unanimously resolved to open meetings in their own hall'.[80] The Established Church, so blessed by revival less than thirty years previously, was conspicuous by its non-participation in the revival in regard to either labours or harvest. Josias Jago stated that during 1867–68, some converts, many of whom were previously 'openly irreligious' and 'utterly negligent of the ordinances of God's house', fell away 'through the power of strong drink … but many continue with us, and, as far as we know, live Christian lives'. Summing up the effects of the movement Jago stated, 'The outward aspect of the village is again much as it was previous to the revival, sin and wickedness being rampant; but the number of God-fearing men and women is considerably increased, and all the churches are stronger and wealthier, spiritually, than they were before the revival.'[81]

South Lanarkshire

Hamilton and Stonehouse

Blessing spread throughout Lanarkshire via the labours of Thomas Holt and George Geddes, the Scottish Evangelization Society workers whose labours had already proved so fruitful elsewhere in central Scotland. The duo broke new ground in Hamilton in August 1866, in which town, 'a little band of believers' had been meeting together for six weeks successively, and praying for a blessing. 'Widespread awakening' was also experienced in Strathaven, especially in the Free and United Presbyterian Churches, and John Colville was called to help in the work here.[82]

---

in Glasgow, which church was visited by a band of converts from Kilsyth in November 1866. Ferguson's memory of the results of the revival were sketchy, and therefore the figures he quotes cannot be taken as authoritative. However, they do confirm the very considerable impact of the movement on most of the town's congregations.

80. Around eighty professions of faith were recorded, and 'the church and congregation greatly increased'. Soon thereafter, however, discouragement set in, the minister was removed, and by 1870 the church had ceased to exist (*Evangelical Union Annual*, quoted in McNaughton, 2005, pp. 283-4).

81. McNaughton, 2005, p. 282.

82. Colville, pp. 171-5; FCSRSRM, 1867, p. 9.

A work commenced in Stonehouse in the autumn of 1866, prior to the arrival of Holt and Geddes. The enthusiastic Free Church minister, the Rev. Hamilton, shared his pulpit with a wide range of evangelists; for example, in August of that year, on the occasion of the Stonehouse Fair, Mrs Poole (wife of 'working class, Fiddler Joss') addressed his congregation. The meeting was described as a 'place of weeping'. Holt and Geddes arrived in December and soon meetings had to be transferred to the larger United Presbyterian Church. Apparently, a remarkable 213 letters were received by the evangelists telling of blessing received in that place during their short visit. Members of the Scottish Evangelistic Association held a series of meetings in the Free Church, as well as in the open air, in 1867. By March of that year, the total number thought to have come under a 'saving change' had risen to between five and six hundred.[83]

Wishaw and Newmains

But it was the Brethren who benefited most from these revivalist efforts, and many new assemblies were formed. 'Showers of blessing' came to Lanark and the Wishaw and Newmains area from 1866 to 1869.[84] From 1859 the Open Brethren in Wishaw and Newmains co-operated in organising revival services most Sunday evenings, both inside and outside the Wishaw public school. As many as 400–500 would meet. There were 150 apparent conversions between September and December 1866 following a visit from Holt and Geddes. By January 1867 the Newmains Brethren assembly contained 120 members, but converts were also relocated to other areas, resulting in the commencement of a meeting in Holytown in August 1867 (where fourteen were in fellowship) and in Rosebank two months later (with eighteen participants). Such practice was described as 'God's way of extending his church by loving branches'.[85]

Although meetings in Wishaw were conducted by local Brethren members, particularly John Wardrop, they were arranged to appeal to a wide social spectrum. Rare appearances by 'Mr Watson, the converted sweep' and 'Mr Ewing, the converted slater', were designed to appeal

---

83. Clare, p. 54; Buchanan, p. 21.

84. Dickson, 2002, p. 75.

85. Buchanan, p. 23.

to a working-class audience. Several women also led revival meetings, many attending on the first night out of curiosity to see such novelty.[86] A large Brethren hall was built in Wishaw in 1869, and Samuel Blow, a noted English evangelist (who once preached 'Eternity Eternity where will you spend eternity?' to the Prince of Wales), held a six-week mission here without a break, during which 'a marvellous wave of blessing rolled over the town and neighbourhood, leaving scarcely a house without some token of blessing. In some cases whole families were converted'. As a result, a further 150 people were converted, making 300 altogether.[87] There appears to have been a lack of church provision in Wishaw at this time. Though containing a similar population to Hamilton (around fourteen thousand, five hundred), the latter town had twelve churches, compared to Wishaw's five. Buchanan suggests that it was largely because other denominations were not highly active that the Open Brethren were noticeably successful in Wishaw during this period.[88]

Lesmahagow

In the wake of the 1859 revival, a group of believers dedicated to Brethren principles started meeting together in a workshop in Lesmahagow. Amidst 'intense persecution' from 'prominent businessmen' in the neighbourhood, aided by a 'rather officious policeman', the group engaged in open-air evangelism. By September 1868 it was reported that several hundred enquirers were 'anxiously drinking in the truth' at these afternoon occasions, while some evening meetings were also held outside as no venue big enough could be found. Such meetings continued until dark. 'The Lord was

---

86. ibid., p. 24.

87. Samuel Blow, *Reminiscences of Thirty Years' Gospel Work and Revival Times*, Kilmarnock, 1890, pp. 85-6; Buchanan, *Brethren Revivals*, pp. 80-1.

88. He contrasts this to the experience in Stonehouse, where the Brethren failed to benefit from the revival of the mid-1860s, and in Hamilton and Strathaven, where there was similar Brethren inactivity during the period 1859–61. He concludes: 'Therefore, with the exception of Wishaw, the Open Brethren failed to take advantage of what was a significant religious revival in Lanarkshire between 1859 and 1870. The Open Brethren were certainly not repelled by the prospect of a revival and readily welcomed itinerant evangelists common to this movement. Yet their commitment to activism was impaired by their negative attitude towards existing denominations' (Buchanan, pp. 23, 26).

working in our midst', observed one participant. 'Many, under deep conviction of sin, refused to go home. Anxious ones were led into the hall and pointed to the Saviour.'[89]

A time of revival had begun, and for twelve months two evangelists – Pattinson and Henderson – preached every night on the streets or in the hall, where there were many remarkable cases of conversion. The opposition continued, and one minister denounced the group of local, 'unlearned, ignorant yet well-meaning baptists', from whom some strong criticism was delivered. Replied one of the brethren, 'We have not time just now to engage in discussion. Like Nehemiah we are doing a work for the Lord and we dare not come down to the plains of Ono in case the work should cease.'[90] An outstanding feature of the work of grace at that time', one witness noted, 'was the remarkable number converted through the instrumentality of Mary Peterson and Mary Hamilton', two unmarried believers. During this period of blessing, the Lesmahagow assembly saw remarkable growth.[91]

John Bowes reported 'A great work in hearts and homes has gone on' in the tiny village of Auchenheath, to the north of Lesmahagow, between 1869 and 1870. On a visit there in May 1870, Bowes held large and attentive meetings both in the schoolroom and in the open air. 'Sinners continue to believe and live', he wrote in his journal, noting also the case of one man who, only sometime after joining a local church, became awakened to his spiritual need. In a state of anxiety he called on his minister, who, disturbingly, advised him to read some of Burns's poems or a Shakespeare play to help assuage his fears! Aware that such indulgence would avail him little, the man began instead to read the New Testament and was gloriously converted. Noting that there were many in his neighbourhood who were still under conviction, the new believer felt it his duty to call again upon the minister, to warn him against providing such ungodly and unhelpful advice to others. The minister was outraged at such an act of humiliation, and promptly dismissed evangelicals as 'quacks'! Apart from this particular church leader, Bowes was encouraged to find that in and around Auchenheath

89. Beattie, pp. 210-12.

90. ibid.

91. ibid.; Buchan, p. 26; *TR*, 26/03/1866, p. 168.

and Lesmahagow there were around a dozen evangelical ministers who were well able to 'show the way of salvation'.[92]

City Work

Dundee

A most interesting movement spread through parts of Dundee during 1867. While it began earlier in the year, it appears to have been largely promoted by the death of popular evangelist, Robert Annan, who tragically but dramatically drowned at the age of thirty-three while helping save a boy who fell into the river Tay.[93] It was said there had never been such weeping in Dundee for one man, and his death became the means of an awakening in the town. 'In the East end of Dundee it was as if there was someone dead in every household. ... The man who had been despised and opposed by men was now the object of their lamentations.'[94] The movement was widespread across the city. Chalmers Church (pastored by the Rev. Bell), the Reformed Presbyterian Church (Rev. Riddell) and the Westgate Church (Rev. Duke) all saw crowded meetings and marked blessing.

Yet another church in the city, Hilltown Free Church, saw several hundred anxious enquirers dealt with, one by one, in one week. This was the church of which Annan was a member. Nearly three thousand gathered in a field to hear his funeral sermon on the Sabbath following his death. It was even said that this 'Christian hero' accomplished more

---

92. J. Bowes, p. 587.

93. *TR*, 02/05/1867, p. 243; 06/02/1868, p. 70. The boy was rescued but Annan took cramp and drowned in the strong current. Added poignancy is added to the story in light of the belief that he might have survived had he let the boy go. Annan, though a powerful swimmer, had in fact previously saved at least six or seven lives through similar acts of self-sacrifice and was awarded the Dundee Humane Society silver medal for his heroism. Annan had worked in a woodyard, and twenty-four hours before his death he was guiding a raft of logs along the Tay. Oddly, he had said to a friend that he had experienced 'a wonderful manifestation of the Lord to my soul out there on the water'. The spot he pointed to was the very spot where he drowned the following day. Interestingly, also, a friend of Annan's, while noticing how the evangelist became much more tender and humble in the years following his conversion, felt he also increased in 'zeal and realisation of the shortness of time, as if the Lord were ripening him for his own presence' (Adam, p. 20).

94. J. H. Hudson, T. W. Jarvie, and J. Stein, *Let the Fire Burn*, Dundee, 1978, p. 38.

by his death than by all the labours of his life. 'As you listened to the weeping, you were made to feel the utter impotence of human instrumentality – a feeling not unmingled with a sense of joy and awe in the presence of the Divine Worker.' Some, who since the 1859–61 revival had prayed incessantly for unsaved relatives, now rejoiced in the long-waited response.[95]

It was around this time that James Jolly, a young evangelist converted in the revival of 1859–60, came to Dundee – which he described as 'surely the most wicked town in the country' – and began a mission connected with Chalmers' Church under the ministry of a Mr Bell. A number of believers from other churches in town were enlisted to assist Jolly in home visitation, tract distribution, and pressing everyone to attend church or Sabbath school. Open-air preaching was also engaged in at the West Port. 'A blessing rested on the work', noted Bell. There were many hopeful conversions, and membership of the church rapidly increased, to the extent that galleries had to be erected in the building.[96]

Glasgow

Bridgeton Independent Church was admitted to the Evangelical Union in 1861 and in the following year Robert Hood became its pastor. Initially, despite the church being packed to capacity on his induction, and many having to be turned away, he was ostracised by neighbouring pastors, owing to deep suspicions regarding his denomination. Soon, however, the barriers began to break down and he became esteemed by all the churches, including even the Roman Catholics. Progress during his first year was small, but by the close of the second year his eighty members had become 136.

By 1866, the church was able to assert, 'Our general audiences have considerably increased. Notwithstanding our disjunction, caused by death, removal, etc, the roll of membership has been further augmented. A marked wave of religious awakening has just flowed in upon the Sabbath School, and a few precious souls have been hopefully converted to Jesus.' Three years later, the membership had been 'still further increased', and in 1871 it had risen to 258, and by 1877 to 487, by which time a new building was deemed essential. Another Evangelical

---

95. Macpherson, 1867, p. 110. See also *TR*, 21/11/1867, p. 653; 06/02/1868, p. 70.

96. Adam, pp. 34-5.

Union church to see remarkable growth in Glasgow in this period was East Howard Street Evangelical Union Church, which grew in membership from its formation around 1865 to three hundred within a couple of years.[97]

An inauspicious prayer meeting was begun in a home in George Street, in Glasgow's deprived Mile End, being attended by only two or three people. In a short time a 'thirsting for the living water' began. The dwelling-house overflowed and permission was granted to use a nearby schoolroom, which soon also proved too restrictive, owing to the 'great numbers who were falling at the foot of the cross'. Many, it was reported, cried out for mercy and took shelter 'under the wing of our blessed Saviour'.[98]

Between March and May of 1867, showers of blessing fell on the children and youth at Andrew Bonar's Finnieston church in Glasgow when American evangelist, E. P. Hammond, came to assist. By this time Hammond was beginning to narrow his focus of ministry towards children. Among the converts were Isabella and Marjory Bonar, Andrew's own daughters. Gordon Forlong claimed that due to the success of the 1859–61 revival, there were now hundreds of laymen labouring in the city, many 'holding meetings of their own and doing a great work'.[99]

John Riddell came to Glasgow in 1867 to serve as the fourth minister of the celebrated Wynd Church, the centre of the most remarkable and sustained Home Mission venture in the Free Church's history, and scene of an almost continual revival movement since 1859 (see Chapter 4). His three predecessors had all left in an atmosphere of complete goodwill to form new congregations; Dugald MacColl, in 1860, to the Bridgegate; Robert Howie, in 1864, to Trinity Church, Charlotte Street; and James Wells, in 1867, to the Barony Church in the High Street, each taking a large contingent of the Wynd folk with him to form the nucleus of a new cause. In each case, with the arrival of a new minister, the congregation began to flourish anew, with striking church growth.

---

97. David Hobbs, *Robert Hood, the Bridgeton Pastor. The Story of his Bright and Useful Life*, Edinburgh, 1894, p. 184-5; McNaughton, 2007, p. 120.

98. *TR,* 13/12/1866, p. 329; 24/01/1867, p. 45.

99. M. Bonar, p. 261; *TR*, 22/03/1866, p. 165

Similarly, the early part of Riddell's four years at the Wynd were memorable, the church being filled to overflowing, and the bulk of the people coming from the immediate vicinity. Many of the poorest and most depraved in the city were brought to Christ during these months, and in after years the minister was to say that he could not recall a Sunday on which souls had not been saved. The church, it was said, was in a state of constant revival, while the Wednesday night prayer meeting, one of the most remarkable in Glasgow, was crowded with 'the poor, the maimed, the halt and the blind', who listened eagerly to every word which fell from the preacher's lips.[100]

A movement commenced in Kelvinside Free Church with the arrival of William Ross Taylor,[101] a native of East Kilbride, who was inducted to the Glasgow charge in June 1868. Previous to that date, membership of the church had for some years been stationary or retrograde but it increased dramatically in the years 1869, '70 and '71 with eighty, 103 and 106 new members being added to the roll in each year respectively.[102]

---

100. D. P. Thomson, *Personal Encounters*, Crieff, 1967, pp. 48-9. In 1878 Riddell, then minister at Augustine Free Church, responded to an 'SOS' from the disheartened remnant of the old Wynd congregation, facing a totally new situation in an area which had been completely transformed by demolition and depopulation. Rising to the challenge, and with the generous help of friends and well-wishers in every part of Scotland, Riddell created on a new site what was at that period the most remarkable range of Home Mission activities centred on any one spot in the city, including a Deaconess Home, Medical Mission, ample hall accommodation, together with a convalescent home in another part of the city. Riddell remained pastor at the Wynd Church until the 1910s. Due to its ongoing pattern of planting new churches with a nucleus from outgrown existing congregations, over just a few short decades, remarkably, the number of churches in Glasgow which owed their existence directly or otherwise to the work in the Wynds was at least twenty-four, many of them comprising the strongest that the city contained (N. Walker, *Chapters From the History of the Free Church of Scotland*, Edinburgh, 1895, p. 88).

101. Taylor became Moderator of the Free Church General Assembly in 1884 and again in 1900–1, which later position gave him the honour of constituting the first General Assembly of the United Free Church of Scotland in October 1901.

102. Membership continued to flourish in subsequent years, most notably in 1875 (a year of growth in many Glasgow churches), when 77 new communicants and 116 members of other churches were added to the roll. By 1877 the church was regularly full, every pew having been let and occupied, and by 1878 membership stood at a record 783. By 1878 a number of new congregations had formed in and

Edinburgh

Meanwhile, the Evangelical Union Annual Report for 1867 reported 'a considerable amount of interest' in Edinburgh's Brighton Street Evangelical Union Church. Through the ordinary labours of the Rev. John Kirk and other agencies, sixty-three names were added to the membership. Still in Edinburgh, Horatius Bonar received a call from sixty communicants in Edinburgh's Free Church extension charge at Grange, and he was inducted in June 1866. Within a year there were seventy-four additional communicants, while ten years later the figure was seven hundred. These official figures would almost certainly have been considerably less than numbers actually attending. Impressive growth also attended the induction of William Adamson to Buccleuch Evangelical Union Church in September 1868. Admissions to membership during the following year were twenty-eight, more than doubling the existing figure. The Sunday services increased in even greater proportion, while a Theological Class which Adamson commenced in a side-room of the church quickly prospered, and was soon attracting three hundred students of both sexes, including many from Edinburgh University. The classes were so successful that they continued for eighteen years.[103]

A minister in one of Scotland's cities spoke of 'a quiet work of grace' in his Free Church congregation during 1868–9. While extra outreach meetings were held, always being successful, the work was mostly in connection with the ordinary services. An evangelistic meeting on the Sabbath evening did great good in the way of bringing out the results of the day's work. During a period of little more than three years, over one thousand had joined the church – half of them for the first time, and most of them giving tokens of being hopefully converted. The minister felt that 'plain, earnest preaching' played a significant role in the movement.[104] While seeking to prepare with care, he studied to avoid all unnecessary elaboration, and endeavoured always to give a

---

around Kelvinside, including three more Free Churches, and to these many from Taylor's congregation moved in the late 1870s and early 1880s.

103. Iain H. Murray, *Scottish Christian Heritage*, Edinburgh, 2006, p. 180; McNaughton, 2005, pp. 229, 331.

104. General Assembly of the Free Church of Scotland, p. 4.

frank and familiar statement of truth. Further, he gave opportunity to all under concern to come and tell their difficulties. One Sabbath he intimated that he would be waiting for such purpose for an hour in the evening. That night thirteen anxious souls came to him. Additionally, the minister spoke of young converts being very zealous, and doing good service in the way of bringing companions and friends under the influence of the gospel. In this way a large number of young men and women had themselves been blessed, and in turn were made a blessing to others.

Southern Scotland

Stranraer

In Wigtownshire, Murray McNeil Caird, law student turned evangelist, saw an awakening take place in Stranraer in 1866 and 1867, in which latter year, a more general 'gracious shower of blessing' occurred in the town. Stranraer witnessed another movement two years later (1869), when 'resolute sinners, coming to the services determined to resent every effort for their conversion, were suddenly arrested by the power of the truth, and remained deeply distressed, seeking salvation, and, before twenty-four hours had passed, rejoiced in Christ their Saviour'.[105] An impressive range of meetings in Dumfries for prayer, exposition and preaching were well attended and in just three years the church roll rose from thirty-five to 220, the greater number of them persons who had previously fallen away into 'habits of utter carelessness, or who else had never known what it is to attend on ordinances'.[106]

Garnock Valley

An inconspicuous awakening occurred among the Ayrshire miners of the Garnock Valley at the turn of 1867–68. This followed regular evangelistic support from the owner of the works till his death in 1866, and district meetings conducted by 'a band of devoted working men ... in their working clothes'. One enthusiastic witness said, 'It was refreshing to join with these new-born babes in singing "If ever I loved Thee, my Jesus, 'tis now".' The village of Reddance, near Dalry,

---

105. ibid., 28/11/1867, p. 669; 28/10/1867, p. 668.
106. FCSRSRM, 1868, pp. 5-7; *Monthly Record*, January 1868, pp. 15-16.

containing several hundred inhabitants, was also said to have been 'deeply moved. In every house some are inquiring the way to Zion.'[107]

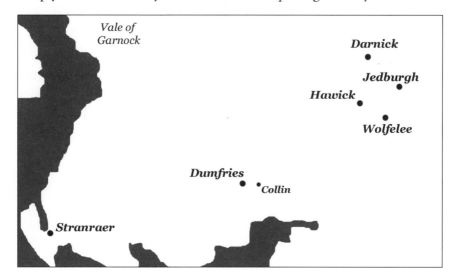

Darnick

Seeking to recover his health after a period of illness, evangelist Duncan Matheson journeyed from his home in the north of Scotland to the Borders' community of Darnlee, to the west of Melrose at the beginning of 1868 to stay with friends. His biographer wrote: 'Here again the fire burned. He could not rest. Gathering together the people of Darnick, a village in the neighbourhood, he indulged once more in the luxury of preaching Christ. Immediately there was a sound and a stir among the dry bones. The Spirit of God began to work gloriously among the dead. The movement, though confined within the narrow limits of the village and adjacent country, was a remarkable one; men and women were brought to the Lord.' Asked how he, who was suffering from a terrible malady, could do so much work, Matheson replied characteristically, 'Ah, the Lord saw that I was very weak, and just worked all the more Himself.'[108]

Hawick

In Hawick, a concert of prayer was begun in January 1867, where 'interesting details of the Lord's work all over the world were constantly kept before' the faithful intercessors' minds. By spring, open-air work

---

107. *TR*, 16/01/1868, p. 37.

108. Macpherson, 1871, pp. 226-7.

showed unusual blessing from the very start and nightly church meetings began. These lasted more than six months. 'Where for a generation very rarely were there to be found inquirers', now there were hundreds; and where it was previously difficult to obtain the services of an evangelist, now they came uninvited! By the end of 1867, it was seen that all classes had been reached, other than children and young men. These were thus earnestly and specifically prayed for, and soon 'a great work began among the lambs of the fold' while 'scarcely was there a business in town ... in which some young men were not savingly' changed.[109]

Collin

Believers of all churches in the parish of Collin, to the east of Dumfries, had long prayed for a blessing on their spiritually dry community, and by the autumn of 1867 'a shower of blessing' had begun to descend. The small chapel, located just outside the village, was soon crowded to overflowing and could have been filled twice over. The work was greatly revived the following autumn, by which point 'a very deep and widespread work of God' was said to have been in progress in the district.[110] On some farms, most of the servants became recipients of grace, which revolution was said to have been all the more noteworthy given that previously they had all been completely devoid of the fear of God.

Wolfelee

Much prayer was offered during the summer of 1868 for a spiritual outpouring on Wolfelee, an entirely rural charge along the Rule Water valley, to the south-east of Hawick in Roxburghshire, and not far from the English border. There followed 'a very remarkable awakening' later in the year, amidst suspicions by some who doubted 'whereunto it would grow', and opposition from others who insisted that conversion was unnecessary or at least that it should not occur in church! 'Tokens of His gracious presence' first became apparent during special meetings that began on 20 December. Numbers attending were large, especially in proportion to the population of the parish. These were therefore continued week by week, with, on average, four meetings being held

---

109. *TR*, 28/05/1866, p. 302.

110. *TR*, 28/11/1867, p. 668.

each week until the end of March 1869, besides the Sabbath evening service, which was the best attended of all.[111]

During the height of the awakening, seventeen meetings were held in nightly succession. Inquiry meetings also proved profitable, the anxious at first consisting almost exclusively of young men, one or two of whom initially trembled and were unable to speak. Utmost care was taken in conducting these after-meetings – only ministers and evangelists were allowed to converse with the anxious, and such were spoken to individually rather than as a group. Fully sixty professed salvation in eight weeks and thirty-two communicants joined the small Free Church congregation before the year-end. Around seventy-five persons of all ages had been spoken to by the end of March – many of them frequently – from which time meetings were limited to Sunday and Wednesday evenings. During its entire course, the movement was 'remarkably free from excitement' – the people listened 'with solemn silence and earnest attention while the Word seemed usually to fall on them like dew on the grass. ... A solemn awe pervaded the population of the parish during the awakening' as a result of which it could be said that 'in so far as we know, none of those who professed to come to Christ have dishonoured their profession'.[112]

People of all ages and connected with various churches in the parish and neighbourhood attended the meetings in Wolfelee, and thus the blessing was in a corresponding measure diffused. In a nearby unnamed village, a quiet yet powerful spiritual movement began in December 1868, following visits from a number of evangelists, one of whom also shared accounts of the awakening in Wolfelee. All major denominations participated, and while it seemed that 'a considerable number appear to have fallen from their first love', as a whole the fruits of the awakening remained strong and consistent.[113]

---

111. FCSRSRM, 1869, pp. 3-6.

112. ibid.; General Assembly of the Free Church of Scotland, pp. 4-5.

113. FCSRSRM, 1869, pp. 3-6.

Eyemouth

Findochty

Portgordon

Wick harbour, late 1800s

Garioch Parish and Bennachie

CHAPTER 19

Revivals of the Early 1870s

East Coast Awakenings

Eyemouth

Significant spiritual movements continued into the 1870s. An awakening began in Eyemouth in the summer of 1869, continuing into 1870–71, as the result of the loss of two local fishing boats and five lives in the North Sea off Tyneside. When the news of the tragedy was telegraphed home to Eyemouth, special prayer meetings immediately sprang into operation, and a spirit of awakening spread throughout the community.[1] In the words of one reporter, the town was visited with 'a quickening work of the Holy Spirit, by which the whole place was moved, and precious souls brought out of death into life'. Some who had been touched by the revival of 1859–61 but had since lapsed into former habits now returned to the pews. A local chronicler wrote that the change produced by this 'outburst of what is called revivalism' was 'unmistakable. These rude, unlettered fishermen ceased to visit the public-houses, refrained from the use of oaths, and instead sang psalms and said prayers.'[2] The interest in spiritual things continued over a considerable period and lasting good to the community followed. It appears to have been in the midst of this 'extensive revival of religion' in Eyemouth that the health of one dedicated worker, Matthew Dick, a student of the Evangelical Union Academy, broke down. After a time of recuperation, Dick left Scotland for Australia, where he served as a Congregational minister.[3]

---

1. ibid., 1871, p. 1; Peter Aitchison, *Children of the Sea: The Story of the Eyemouth Disaster*, East Linton, 2001, pp. 182-3.

2. FCSRSRM, 1871, p. 1; *The Scotsman*, 22/12/1921, p. 7.

3. F. Ferguson, p. 373.

Findochty

The year 1871 began with a 'descent of the Holy Ghost' upon the people of Findochty, a spontaneous movement which had a powerful effect on this community. One local believer wrote of the work in the village:

> It is very difficult to find words to describe it, for the same features or manifestations of revival work were never known here before. It seems to me as if a cloud of glory were hanging down, hovering over the whole village – the whole of it I may say is blessed. ... Nothing is attended to but praise to God, which never ceases night nor day. I can see groups of men, women and children, through every part of the village, dancing before the Lord for whole days. ... J. S. has been filled these three days, and marvellous to relate her deafness is all gone. And many other cases, which have been confined to their beds for a considerable time can now be seen on the streets, every day and at any hour, dancing before the Lord and shouting His glorious praises with all their might, from a heart filled and ready to burst with the love of God.[4]

A month later, on 6 March, that same Findochty resident rejoiced that the work was still 'going on satisfactorily. The tone of our meeting is still rising. The high blessing is almost universal in our village. ... Fear and shame are quite gone, and with a holy boldness they will do anything and everything for the glory of God and for the good of souls. And while I write these few lines, the sound of praise is rising from every part of our village and never ceases but when the people are asleep. For me to describe the work and what accompanies it is, I confess, impossible. It far surpasses my knowledge, and to what I cannot understand, I bow in humble submission. I am lost in wonder at the mighty working power of my God and Father ... .' It was said around this time that as a result of the various sporadic revival movements that had overtaken the place, 'there is not a young man, religious or non-religious, in the village of Findochty, that would go into a public house to take drink – they have more self-respect than would do it'.[5]

---

4. McHardie, pp. 136, 140-1.

5. ibid., p. 135.

Gospel Procession and Dance

A climax of the revival along one prominent stretch of the coast was a holy procession engaged in by many hundreds of converts. A significant number dressed for the occasion and made banners inscribed with biblical quotations. From Findochty the long train of converts marched westward, each member with uplifted heart shouting forth the praises of the God who had so gloriously filled their lives with His love. Reaching Portessie, the group gathered in a large circle at the east end of the village, waiting for additions from that place to fill their ranks. This done, onwards they stomped to Buckie, where a brief halt was made for refreshments. Local resident, William Smith wrote that as they began their homeward march from Buckie, 'a powerful effect' was produced upon onlookers from that town. Not only so, but the power of God on the marchers 'waxed stronger and stronger amongst them. Many were overcome by the mighty power of God and began to exhibit such manifestations as we had never before seen. Men and women were to be seen in numbers, from one end of the village to the other, who, to a stranger, would have appeared to be under the influence of drink. All appeared to be moved by one great but common impulse, and with a quick pace their long irregular train moved on, multitudes now having joined them without any preparation, dressed just as for household work.'[6]

Returning to Portessie, 'the people of God in that place caught the flame and came under the same power'. Here had existed for some time a disturbance in the minds of many believers, who had been told that without baptism by full immersion their conversions counted for nothing. This had caused great anguish among many, but with the arrival of the gospel procession, a mighty influence seemed to spread like lightening through the place, causing many to literally run to join the merry band, saying, 'No more water for me. Nothing but the blood of Jesus!'[7]

Onward to Findochty the growing ranks of converts proceeded, where, gathering more on board, they moved to Portknockie, 'preaching the gospel to every creature they could get at, without doors or within.

6. ibid., pp. 137-8.

7. ibid.

And such was the powerful effect of these simple means, wielded by the Holy Spirit, that the whole of the people were awakened, and for several days there were great convictions of sin, and many seeking the way of salvation – and praise God, many found it, and almost all who spoke their experience at that time testified to the power that accompanied the demonstration.'[8]

The emergence of dancing, referred to above, was peculiar to the revival along the north-east coast at this time, although it was to become a longstanding custom in the area. 'It was never for once dreamed of', continued Smith. 'It's first appearance was among the children, and then among persons more advanced in life, and perhaps stranger still, many advanced in the Christian life also came under its power, and in many cases irresistible power. And the persons thus engaged showed symptoms of the greatest joy – and truly their very appearance bespoke them to be under a high divine impulse.'[9]

More often than not, what was described as the 'gospel dance' was little more than gentle synchronised swaying in time with hymns being sung. Mr Macdonald, a banker from Buckie, was curious to observe this procedure, so he attended a meeting in Portessie one Saturday evening. Around three hundred were present and he was pleasantly surprised to see that the meeting was conducted in a most orderly fashion. As he lingered around the door at the close of the meeting, Macdonald watched a group of between thirty and forty people, women mostly, gather in a corner of the hall, where they sang a lively hymn. Their motion seemed to speed up as they continued, and 'latterly it was so simultaneously and gracefully done' that Macdonald, from a distance, took it to be a dance. But as he got nearer them, indeed almost joining them in their activity, he noticed that each had their eyes closed and their countenances were 'as if wrapt with heavenly joy'. Macdonald's

---

8. ibid., pp. 137-9. Similar processions were made as far west as to Portgordon and as far east as to Portsoy.

9. ibid., p. 137. See also James McKendrick, *What We Have Seen & Heard During 25 Years of Evangelistic Labours*, Arbroath, 1914, p. 127; FCSRSRM, 1871, pp. 1-3. This tradition of 'gospel dance' soon developed further; whereby a person newly converted at once went to share the good news with relatives, who would immediately rejoice with public prayer and praise, joining hands to sing a lively hymn, to which they kept time with their feet.

conclusion was that these were women who had maintained a good Christian character, and one should not hurriedly condemn them for their quaint bodily expressions of worship.[10]

It appears to have been somewhat less frequently, and only among the young, that the application of dancing took on more demonstrative expression in the form of leaping and other overt bodily movements. One believer, seeing this activity in Portknockie U.P. Kirk, sought to remonstrate with one so engaged, whose spontaneous response was, 'Stop I cannot, for the love that I have got into my heart is boundless, inexpressible. I must dance for joy, and praise God.' Perplexed, the inquirer sat down to ponder and pray. If this same joy could be his experience also, then he longed for it. Reading Jeremiah 31 about the restoration of Israel with attending joy and dancing, all at once the man sprang to his feet, leaping and praising God. 'Every particle of our body, every faculty is redeemed', he realised. 'We are entirely consecrated to God. In Him we live and move. Why should we not praise and leap for joy?'

A Portknockie publican – 'one of the devil's drill-sergeants' – was among those laid hold of by the Spirit at this time, while the entire crews of four or five boats were also converted. For a time, meetings were held in Portknockie 'day and night – no stops'. This left the leaders of these meetings utterly exhausted, but they were kept going by their unity of purpose – 'nothing but the salvation of souls'.[11]

Buckie

The work in Buckie originated with a lay preacher from Portgordon coming to speak in the Buckie mission hall. Here, James Riach – regarded as the most notable of all of James Turner's converts – along with the East Coast Mission and others, had been labouring zealously and with good effect. Indeed, it seemed now only to require the slightest fanning to put all in a blaze. At both the afternoon and evening meetings, anxious souls stood up and cried aloud to God for mercy. A local minister from another congregation also rose up, and strongly objected to such emotional scenes, which he said were 'nothing but witchcraft and hysteria'. Soon the place was in an uproar, with

10. McHardie, pp. 141-2.

11. ibid., pp. 112-13.

those who supported the minister 'standing on the tops of the seats, gesticulating dreadfully, and others beside them were pulling them down', while all the time others continued singing. Eventually the minister left the hall in a rage, and 'the work of God seemed marred, every soul was downcast'.[12]

The meeting continued, but in a notably subdued tone. Efforts were made to revive the atmosphere, 'but with little apparent effect, every soul seemed wounded, thus Jesus was pierced in the house of His friends. One prayed after another, but there was no power.' The people's faith exhausted, it was decided, it being near midnight, to pronounce the blessing. At this point, recalled one church leader, while the parting hymn was being sung:

> The mighty power of God came down, as a mighty rushing wind; never shall I forget it nor do I wish to forget. Of all the sights I ever looked upon in this world, to me it was the most solemn and interesting. I saw about forty men and women all at once, at the pitch of their voices, weeping, as they cried for mercy; the men, strong men, bowed down, or rather lent back, for their hands were outstretched upwards, with their faces, full of agony, looking heavenwards, and their backs bending backwards. Such was their desire for mercy, each called for himself or herself, and all at one time, none heeding the prayer of his neighbour. ... Although there were eight or nine of us there, willing to work, or direct anxious souls, our services were not required. The Lord seemed to say, 'Stand aside and behold My glory.' For a considerable time this went on without the slightest intermission, and without interruption, for none of us dared put a hand to it to guide it the one way or the other. We were in no fear of the Ark of God, although it seemed to rock to and fro, and to suffer from apparent confusion and want of order, we were all fully persuaded this was the work of God, and it was perfectly safe in his own keeping.[13]

The meeting, which had begun at 7 p.m. was finally brought to a close at 3.40 the following morning.

The movement, thus begun, continued in power. James Riach wrote of 'three or four meetings in different places every night; the mission

---

12. ibid., pp. 236-7.

13. ibid., pp. 237-9.

hall crowded to overflowing, and many outside. … It will astonish you to hear that "A. R.", filled with the Spirit, is, preaching the gospel right and left, and today (March 13ᵗʰ) was the means of awakening five souls.' Riach also preached 'on the street to Papists and all sorts, and had this, that, and the other objection thrown in my teeth … the Papists are wild, but I believe the truth has laid hold of some of them, although I have not heard of any decided case yet'.[14]

Portgordon

A young girl from Portgordon was 'laid down in a state of complete prostration' at a meeting in Portessie, undergoing a mighty struggle before she saw Jesus approaching her and giving her 'a drink of the living water'. In her vision, Jesus told her to go and testify to those in her home township. She had to be led there by her sister for her sight was taken from her until after she had delivered her message. At the close of a meeting in Portgordon Free Church, the girl stood up and shared her remarkable testimony. The Lord 'shook Portgordon that night. The meeting-place was crowded with people anxiously enquiring how they could come to Jesus, and many found the way to Him … . In about a week the whole place was in a flame, and even drunkards had not only become new men in Christ Jesus, but were out preaching the good news to others … . Many backsliders also were restored', including one who wrote, 'The state of the town reminded me of the retaking of Mansul, for the ungodly were forced to hide themselves, and I among the rest, for if you went out some young soldier of the cross was sure to attack you about your soul.'[15]

That same man, before being restored in the faith, became so troubled in conscience by the omnipresence of the revival spirit in Portgordon that he fled to Cromarty, ostensibly on business, where he resolved to stay till the revival had ended. But he found himself completely unable to forget what he was running from. He was reminded of Jonah going down to Joppa in retreat from the Lord, especially when the first person upon whom he called in regard to his business at once asked, 'How is the work in Portgordon? If I had the time to go down, I'd go right away.' The words weighed heavily on the man's heart, and he resolved to

14. ibid., pp. 207-8.
15. ibid., pp. 243-4.

return home without delay. The first sight to greet him as he approached his home village was a great procession of converts, 'some preaching, some praying, all rejoicing'. He made a detour to get home without bumping into them, but his sister's first words upon entering his house were, 'Oh brother, what a work has been done here since you left us.' And she began to relate case after case of conversion.[16]

One story involved an entire crew of reprobate fishermen who had entered a local bar one day to get drunk. The barmaid pointed to a cask of whisky, newly delivered, but unopened, because she had lost all her patrons owing to the revival. Somewhat taken aback, the captain at length declared that since everyone else was caught up with their spiritual condition it was time he was too, and he got up to leave the pub, the rest of the crew following obediently behind him. The men went out to sea, but at the first port they called in to, they all went and signed the temperance pledge. Having laid down the weapons of their rebellion, the men, on returning home, began attending the meetings and all 'gave their lives to the Lord', in which faith they joyously continued as sanctified and sober men.[17]

After a time it was intimated that their meeting place in the Portgordon Free Church was to be taken from them if the revival meetings were not stopped. An unsavoury split ensued, in which the Methodists, who had kept the meetings going, were joined by a considerable number from the Free Church, and these began to meet in a garret owned by local fisherman, John Hendry. In this sanctuary, a Methodist Church was later established and Mr Purves from Newcastle was called as pastor. Purves later wrote of one memorable service in that hallowed garret, when in the prayer meeting that followed the Sabbath meeting, 'The mighty power of the living God came down on us and filled every soul. The effect was the same as in the early days, we all praised God.'[18]

It was around this time that a young boy commenced meetings for his own group of peers. These were greatly blessed, as many as six boys being brought to the Lord in one meeting. A nine-year-old girl

---

16. ibid., pp. 244-5.

17. ibid.

18. ibid., pp. 245-7.

called Susan began to meet with these young ones and soon also came to a place of spiritual rest. When she later hurt her leg and had to be pushed around in a perambulator, Susan remained an active evangelist, reproving sin or speaking words of encouragement to all she met. Her illness increasing, Susan was confined to bed. But this failed to restrict her labours, for she asked to be carried to the garret meetings, where she openly pled with God to bless those in attendance, and with such assurance of faith that 'often the meeting was brought to groan with uncontrollable emotion, so near did this little one, by her pleadings, bring them to the source of love and light'.[19]

One girl convicted of sin, but who failed to find peace due to unbelief, was laid prostrate. On the second day she spoke, saying her eyes, which were turned up, would not be opened till the eighth day. This happened as she had prophesied, but she was still unable to move. Instead, she lay, playing as it were on a wind instrument, occasionally laughing and at other times shuddering and crying, 'Hell, Hell!' At one point she said that she saw the father of the local minister, the Rev. Brown, in heaven, and others also, whom she named. Greatly intrigued and knowing that the girl could never even have seen a photo of this elderly man, who had lived all his life in England, the minister retrieved his photo album and asked the girl to pick out the man in question. The album pages were turned one by one with nothing said until at last the girl stated matter-of-factly, 'That's him.' The minister was astonished, for her judgement had indeed been correct.[20]

A woman who had been converted through Turner's labours in 1860 had since fallen away, but was reawakened some years later when, in an accident at work, her arm was severed from her body. As great as her physical pain and discomfort was, she suffered even more from her wounded spirit – and literally roared in pain from the discomfort she suffered. After finally retrieving the peace of heart she once enjoyed, this woman soon fell back into her selfish ways, until, during the awakening of 1871, she went to Portgordon to observe the revival work. Here, in her unbelief, she was struck down, remaining in this helpless state for several hours.

---

19. ibid., pp. 251-2.
20. ibid., pp. 249-50.

On recovery, she decided to remain in Portgordon for a further week, during which time she was prostrated several times more, also receiving some remarkable glimpses into the unseen world. An accompanying angel spoke to her and answered her questions.[21] She later gave vivid descriptions of heaven, its golden streets, the river of life and the names of various people with different-sized crowns on their heads, whom she recognised as having lived godly lives on earth (including James Turner). After viewing the seven vials and golden censer mentioned in Revelation, the woman was allowed to view hell, the description of which those who heard felt too terrible to repeat. Lastly she saw some Portgordon residents with cloaks on. That of one person, whom she named, looked perfect in appearance until she held up her arms, when a hole became distinctly visible. Strangely, that same woman, who had been regarded as having an exemplary character, soon after lifted her arm against God, in that she did all she could to oppose His work.

Spread of Revival along the Coast

The movement along this stretch of the coast continued for months, and as late as the end of June 1871 it could be said that 'Portessie is subdued almost to a man'. As well as Portessie, Findochty and Portgordon, the communities of Cullen, Scotstoun, Portsoy, Banff and Macduff each also received a large share of the blessing, which was said to be more persuasive and general than anything that had preceded it. Physical manifestations were decreasingly in evidence at this time, as too was the performance of the 'gospel dance'. Not all supporters of revival, however, spoke favourably of this period of spiritual awakening.[22]

The movement also spread westward to Lossiemouth, Burghead and Hopeman. This area was also visited by James Riach, who 'in heavy sea boots and fisher garb stood up and spoke the words of life to listening hundreds'. It being intimated that a deep work of grace was in progress, the school in Hopeman was opened and on half an hour's notice several hundred people collected. Meetings were held each forenoon and evening and after some months 107 people were enrolled

---

21. Several other people, in their state of prostration, also received visions in which 'a conducting angel' accompanied them.

22. Rev. Ker of Deskford spoke of it as being more a work of man than of God (see p. 451).

in a communicants' class. One minister said he had 'never seen any work more manifestly the work of the Spirit than this has been'.[23]

Further Wave of Revival – Portgordon

The building of a new chapel was commenced in June 1872, the stones for it being brought by fishermen in their boats, and each one prayed for as it was laid. At its opening nine months later, in February 1873, came yet a further shower of blessing on the expectant congregation. On the opening Sabbath the new minister delivered a sermon of great unction, but he wept at the close of it. Indeed he was hardly able to go on, so upset was he that no obvious results from his message were apparent. In the afternoon a love feast was held at 3 o'clock, when so manifest was the power of God, and so overflowing, that half of those present were unable to share their personal experience before 5 p.m., the hour of dismissal. At the evening service at 6.30, 'every soul seemed as if face-to-face with God'. The prayer meeting began two hours later, when there was 'such power in the prayers of each child of God as proved the downfall of the devil's kingdom in many hearts, hitherto unmoved by all the previous seasons of revival that had passed over Portgordon'.[24] Many present had rarely, if ever, witnessed anything like it. It was said that 'at least ten souls found the Saviour' on that memorable day, and many who had been separated by previous division were brought back within the fold of the merry band of believers.

'To give an account of this meeting after this is simply impossible', observed one who was present. 'Souls were seeking God in every corner throughout the chapel', and this went on till after midnight.[25] A woman of about twenty became anxious early on in the meeting and was spoken to gently and beseechingly by several in the congregation. She remained on her knees for hours, sobbing freely, but refusing repeated appeals to petition God for mercy on her soul. When she then became prostrated, some took it that she had been laid out between the powers of heaven and hell. She was carried home at six in the morning and remained in this state for eight days. When she eventually came

---

23. McHardie, p. 20; FCSRSRM, 1871, pp. 3-4.
24. McHardie, pp. 240-1.
25. ibid., pp. 241-2.

around, it was pointed out to her that she had been prostrated because of her disobedience and that she needed to accept at once the salvation offered her by Christ. This she did, and she turned out a gentle but bright Christian, and mighty in prayer.

By the end of the first week, 'a blessed revival had broken out' and it was decided to keep the chapel open night and day. This was almost continuously filled with seeking souls, between four and six people being brought to the feet of Jesus every night, many of whom had stood against former times of awakening in the village. A great work was also done among the young, so that there was formed a class of converts on trial, till they came of age to be received into full membership. In that one week membership of the fledgling church rose from 56 to 103, virtually all of which number instantly became, 'burning and shining lights', strong enough in faith to be able to take part in any meeting.[26] Among this number was the entire family of the above-mentioned Susan, all of whom were won to Christ through the young girl's unceasing, believing prayers for her loved ones and for an ongoing blessing on the work carried on in the new chapel.

A great many others were added to the church at this time, it being said that 'people more powerful in prayer it would be most difficult to find in any church. A united loving people they are.' Portessie and Buckie were further moved and the Presbyterian churches were constrained to 'throw open their doors'. The movement continued well into 1874 (see Chapter 21) and many conversions were recorded.[27]

Caithness

Fishermen from Banff and Moray spread the blessing in progress along those shores to the harbours dotted along the Caithness coast. In Wick, noted one Findochty man, 'Every night we were there we were taken out to the meetings and many were seeking the way of salvation. Our general mode of procedure was to start from our boats in one band and sing all the way to the meeting place "With Steady Pace the Pilgrim Moves" or some other favourite hymn. The people seemed panic-stricken, and a great many were seriously inquiring about the reality of the work of God in our coast, and I am glad to say some

---

26. ibid., pp. 248-9.

27. ibid; *Methodist Recorder*, 20/03/74; 30/03/74.

have got the blessing, and apparently a good work is begun, glory be to God!'[28]

Further south in Caithness, over six hundred attended meetings in both Dunbeath and Berriedale, in which latter place 'forty persons cried aloud for mercy' at the first meeting. The labours of the saintly James Riach of Buckie, especially, were considerably blessed in Wick, Pultneytown, Dunbeath and Helmsdale. Baikie observed that, 'between the Wick converts and the Banff fishermen great friendship ruled, and their united believing efforts resulted in a great harvest of souls'.[29]

Brethren Movement in Aberdeenshire

Inverurie and Kemnay

The establishment of Brethrenism throughout the Garioch district of Aberdeenshire dates to the years 1870–72, and the itinerant labours of Donald Ross (who had recently relinquished his charge as superintendent of the North-East Coast Mission) and other evangelists sympathetic to the Brethren cause. As a result of their efforts, times of spiritual quickening were reported from various parts of this vast rural district.

In the spring of 1871 the evangelists were active in Inverurie. Local resident John Ritchie dated his spiritual birthday to 2 April 1871. He later wrote: 'The little inland town was stirred to its depths.' Within a fortnight, 'there were some twenty or thirty new-born babes in Christ all in the glow of their early love, hungering and thirsting for the Word'. Ritchie continued, '"The Revivals" – as we were called until another name was found – were the one topic of conversation in all the countryside.'[30] Great opposition was raised against the work and those who were converted had a good deal to bear. 'Several were threatened, a few shut up in their homes, and the bulk escorted along the streets to and from the meetings by bands of scoffers singing songs.' Howling crowds assembled outside the hall, and often roughly handled both preachers

---

28. McHardie, p. 141.

29. One source has it that Turner himself spent a few days in Wick, where 'some have got the blessing and apparently a good work is begun' (Baikie, pp. 59-61).

30. John Ritchie, quoted in Ross, *Donald Ross*, p. 146. Ritchie became a prominent evangelist for the Brethren in Scotland, also establishing himself as a prolific writer, editor and publisher, based in the town of Kilmarnock (see Henry Pickering, *Chief Men Among the Brethren*, London, 1931 [reprinted 1996], pp. 307-10).

and converts, but the work went on and increased. From outside the hall also, 'urchins were encouraged … to throw in stones, sticks and old cabbages, and occasionally live crows would be pushed through a broken window pane in order to disturb the worshippers'. Some of the opposition came from thoroughly suspicious ministers, some of whom held imitation evangelistic services to counteract the work of these 'New Prophets'.[31]

In Kemnay, hundreds of granite workers in the quarries – mostly 'very ungodly men' – were reached; and amid the usual opposition – which in this case took the form of taking the tiles from the roof of the meeting place and dropping stones through the aperture on the heads of the preachers – many were converted. Frequently bands of young believers walked up from Inverurie, and sometimes returned in the early hours of the morning, 'singing the songs of Zion'. In the villages of Oldmeldrum, Oyne, Insch and Rhynie, a 'continuous work' was carried on for months. 'Hundreds were awakened and saved and many old believers got such a rousing up that they were wont to speak of it as a "second conversion".'[32] The whole countryside was stirred.

Old Rayne

One main hub of activity was at Old Rayne, where, on 23 April 1871 some converts came together to celebrate Communion outwith the jurisdiction of any denomination – 'the first of its kind we had ever seen', noted Ritchie. They met in the workshop of Sandy Stewart, a joiner who had prayed earnestly for blessing with his two companions. The walls had been whitewashed and the congregation sat on wooden planks. 'There was true worship, such as has to be shared to be understood: it cannot be explained', continued Ritchie. 'Never before had we heard such singing – possibly never shall we hear it again till we go to heaven – not the music,

---

31. ibid., p. 152; Cordiner, p. 73; One of the very few ministers who attended any of the meetings (albeit elsewhere in Aberdeenshire) was from the Free Church. He became 'enraged to the utmost degree' at what was said from the front, and stood up to express his feelings. Apparently, during the revival of 1859, he had taken 'an active part in the work, but had become, through sectarian bitterness and prejudice, as barren and dry as the heath in the desert' (John Ritchie, quoted in Ross, 1890, pp. 148-9).

32. Ross, 1890, pp. 165, 181. It was at the age of ten and under the 'hell-fire preaching' of Donald Ross in Rhynie in 1873 that Alexander Anderson, later a medical missionary in China, was converted. Sprange states that 'a few months later two other Brethren evangelists, William Murray and John Scott, had a revival in Rhynie and an Assembly was formed' (Sprange, p. 256).

but the heart that was in it – true melody, produced by the Spirit operating in the hearts of the worshippers.'[33] Within two years the numbers meeting in this informal manner at Old Rayne had swelled to fifty-nine.

At a meeting in Huntly, 'the fury of the enemies waxed hotter, until they threw off all religious disguise, and rushed to the platform, knocking the preachers to the floor and shamefully abusing them'. An attempt was even made to toss one of the preachers over the bridge into the River Bogie. Such tactics were considered by one report to be 'without parallel, even among Roman Catholics in Ireland', and reached such a pitch that some tormentors were charged by the authorities and fined. Nevertheless, it was claimed, 'Some wonderful trophies of grace were won' and 'the fruits of the work are to be found over the face of the whole earth, and some who then opposed the truth have since, through grace, been conquered by it, and become themselves witnesses to its saving and sanctifying power'.[34] In total, between 1871 and 1873, no fewer than twenty-eight Brethren meetings were formed across the north-east of Scotland.[35]

Other Movements

Communion in Creich

Believers at the 1872 summer Communion in Creich in Sutherland were so sensible of the gracious Spirit of God in the ordinance that one old man from the parish of Reay prayed publicly on the Monday morning for grace to endure the pain of separation. The services on that Sabbath began at eleven in the morning and, with an interval of one hour, continued till half past nine at night. After the services the people refused to disperse and continued in praise and prayer till midnight. The following day they gathered again at seven in the morning.[36]

Communion seasons had of course played a most significant role in the religious life in the north of Scotland for over two hundred years. As late as 1885, the biographer of John Fraser of Rosskeen could state:

---

33. ibid., p. 157.

34. Cordiner, p. 74; pp. 165-9.

35. For a list of these, see Dickson, 2002, p. 97.

36. See Murdoch Campbell, *Gleanings of Highland Harvest*, Stornoway, 1958 (reprinted 1989), p. 97.

Our sacramental seasons in the North, especially in Ross-shire, have from time immemorial been blessed seasons, to which true religion owes much. No man can thoroughly understand or appreciate the religion of the Highlands who is ignorant of the influence which these solemn seasons have in moulding the religious character of the people. ... Such seasons in Rosskeen, especially in summer, during the ministry of Mr Fraser, have proved an unspeakable blessing to many precious souls which gathered there in crowds from all the surrounding parishes. The great multitude in the Grove, especially on the Communion Sabbath – the long white Communion Tables – the solemn stillness, only broken by the voice of the preacher, and the indescribably rich and plaintive Psalm-singing – was altogether a beautiful sight. This was of course in addition to the crowded English congregation in the big church. To be present in Rosskeen on the 'Question day' and hear the 'Men' – a whole college of venerable elders and other intelligent members – discussing Christian experience and marks of grace, was a rare treat. The preaching at Communion seasons in the North is perhaps, on the whole, not excelled in any church or country in the world ...[37]

Grangemouth

Following longstanding prayer, an awakening in Grangemouth Free Church in the winter of 1872–73 dated from an unusually solemn November Communion. Due to many awakened consciences, fewer than usual participated in the holy sacrament. The movement that ensued continued for six months, affecting chiefly women, but, like a similar awakening within the same denomination around the same time – in the Dumfries-shire village of Langholm – was, said the minister of Grangemouth Free Church, 'so quiet ... that I believe few comparatively in the town were aware of any unusual interest in divine things'.[38]

Galashiels and Hawick

The labours of the youthful south Scotland evangelistic duo, Messrs. John M. Scroggie[39] and W. D. Dunn, were richly blessed in Galashiels

---

37. Alexander Cameron, *Memoir and Remains of the Rev. John H. Fraser, Rosskeen,* Inverness, 1885, p. 5.

38. FCSRSRM, 1873, pp. 1-4.

39. *The Christian,* 07/06/1906, p. 17; Bebbington, 1988, p. 120. Dunn, a native of Bowsden in the Borders, was converted around the age of twenty through the preaching of John Thomson, a fisherman/preacher from Cockenzie. He quickly

in the autumn of 1872, greatly stirring the entire community. Indeed, Galashiels was the first campaign in which the two evangelists laboured together, a pairing that proved highly fortuitous, for the two men continued to minister in tandem for the following fifteen years. The blessing in Galashiels began 'before the first Gospel word was spoken'. In the rooms that the evangelists occupied, a prayer meeting was held on the first night. On the following morning word was brought up from the house below that a woman there had been awakened and converted the night before through the prayer meeting held in the flat above! From the opening of the mission, 'the converting power of God revealed itself', and hundreds were hopefully converted in campaign that was continued for fifteen weeks.[40]

A similar work of grace was effected in Hawick the following year, where the same two labourers, aided by numerous other workers, preached nightly for several months during the winter. For the first few weeks the tide seemed as if it would not rise but in the third week, it assuredly did so, and so much blessing was poured out that this mission, too, was extended to fifteen weeks. Several hundred people were thought to have shown hopeful evidence of conversion in that Borders town. Indeed the Galashiels and Hawick missions proved to be just the beginning of the remarkable work that these two brethren did throughout Scotland. For quickly the fame of those missions went out far and wide and resulted in invitations pouring in from throughout central Scotland and northern England (see pp. 548, 589).

---

became possessed of a passion to reach out to others with the gospel message, engaging initially in colportage work in the Borders and Northumberland. Scroggie had laboured as a missionary agent for Walter George Hepburne-Scott, ninth Lord Polwarth. The two men first met while engaged in evangelistic work in Kelso.

40. *The Christian*, 07/06/1906, p. 17; FCSRSRM, 1873, pp. 4-5; Bebbington, 1988, p. 121.

PART 4

The 'Moody Revival' 1873–75

Introduction

Historians have contrasted the revival which began to spread throughout Scotland from November 1873 to previous religious awakenings in the country. Says William Couper:

> The revival of 1859–60 had its way prepared for it. The sound of its coming had been heard for many months before it actually reached the shores of Scotland … . It was otherwise in 1873–74. There were no particular indications that the land was to be specially visited.[1] Doubtless there were many anxious souls upon the watchtowers. … Several places did have preliminary meetings once the work was begun and before its influence reached them, but on the whole, there were no general preparations, no special desire over the country, and no special expectancy among the people. Moody and Sankey came to Scotland almost as Whitefield had come long before, unheralded and unknown and with the same result. The people were in the midst of a revival almost before they knew it.[2]

All this is even more remarkable given that on their arrival in Scotland, Moody and Sankey had little understanding of the Scottish Church, its history, theology or current conditions.

Wrote Professor A. H. Charteris of Edinburgh University early in 1874: 'If angels had told us six months ago that our still and decorous city would be stirred to its depths by two strangers we would not have believed the tale.'[3] Such assessment is true, although it should be noted that Moody was not totally unknown when he arrived in Edinburgh

---

1. It is apparently the case, however, that the Rev. R. S. Candlish, minister of Free St George's Edinburgh, shortly before his death in the autumn of 1873, prophesied a great blessing on the land.

2. Roberts, 1995, pp. 307-8.

3. James F. Findlay, *Dwight L. Moody, American Evangelist, 1837-1899*, Chicago, 1969, p. 155.

in November 1873. Robert Morgan of Morgan and Scott, the London publishers of the revival magazine 'The Christian', helped prepare the way throughout 1873 by publishing a series of articles on the man and his work in America. Morgan also supported Moody from the outset of his arrival in the UK. Yet while it might be thought there was a certain degree of expectancy in the Scottish air regarding the Americans' visit, in reality this was minimal, for no one knew the evangelists were in fact coming north of the border.

Henry Drummond

Horatius Bonar

George Adam Smith

Dwight L. Moody

Ira D. Sankey

Corn Exchange, Grassmarket, Edinburgh

Moody and Sankey at Botanic Gardens, Glasgow

CHAPTER 20

The Scotland Mission

Edinburgh

Introduction

Despite two previous visits to England by Dwight L. Moody[1], when he and singing companion Ira D. Sankey arrived in Britain in 1873, they were practically unknown men. While engaged in evangelistic work in the north-east of England they were invited to come and preach in Scotland by the Rev. John Kelman of Leith,[2] who had personally travelled to Tyneside to see the Americans and was deeply impressed by what he witnessed.[3] The Moderator of the United Presbyterian Church claimed that 'weeks before Messrs. Moody and Sankey came to this city the revival work had begun. Some months before, it would have been impossible to assemble in this Queen Street Hall, out of all Edinburgh, a hundred people at the weekly prayer-meeting.' But within a week of the meetings beginning in a classroom, they became crowded out, and had to be transferred to the Queen Street Hall, where hundreds flocked to them.[4]

---

1. In 1867 and again in June 1872. While this latter visit took Moody as far north as Glasgow, it was following a sermon in a north London church that a time of spontaneous spiritual blessing broke out among the host congregation. This caused considerable stir in the community, though nationally neither it nor the American, who helped inaugurate it, provoked much attention. However, it was in part this revival that enticed Moody back to the UK the following year.

2. Drummond and Bulloch, alone among commentators, suggest that James Hood Wilson was largely responsible for the coming of Moody and Sankey to Scotland (Drummond and Bulloch, p. 9).

3. From the ranks of the United Free Church, Dr Kelman later took an active part in the Union controversy of 1900.

4. *TB*, 21/05/1874, pp. 87-8.

With the minimum of preparation, the two Americans began daily services in the capital city in November. Attendance grew quickly, and three or four of the city's largest churches and halls were constantly in use. Eventually, the Corn Exchange in the Grassmarket – the largest public hall in the city, seating six thousand people – was rented, and even this often became overflowing. Other principal centres of the movement in Edinburgh (from most of which places Moody preached on more than one occasion) included Barclay Free Church, Viewforth Parish Church, Fountainbridge Parish Church, the Free Church Assembly Hall, the Established Assembly Hall, St Stephen's Parish Church, Free High Church, Tolbooth Parish Church, Free North Leith Church and Free St John's Church.

Moody and Sankey

One immediate reason for the success of the 'Moody Revival' was the personalities of the American evangelists and their particular style of delivery. Moody's physical appearance, his strong Southern drawl, his warm, winsome personality, and his use of striking anecdotes were all considered highly novel to Presbyterian Scottish audiences, and many were won over by his charm. One observer noted that Moody 'never began to preach until he had gathered his audience into almost perfect rapport with himself. From the time he came before his vast audiences, to the moment when he rose to preach, he kept the entire body absorbingly occupied with something interesting.'[5]

However, even supporters of Moody could work up little enthusiasm for his preaching ability itself. Professor W. G. Blaikie, with whom Moody resided while in Edinburgh, said his messages were 'plain, honest, somewhat blunt'.[6] Another supporter of Moody, Principal George Adam Smith, also admitted, 'Moody said some crude things, as an uneducated man must. While some of his addresses were powerful, others were very poor. But men felt themselves in presence of a Power, towards whom their obligations and opportunities were not to be weakened by any defect in its human instruments.' It became evident that it wasn't so much Moody's preaching power, but his copious supply

5. ibid., p. 100.
6. Roberts, 1995, p. 319

of illustrations, anecdotes, and personal reminiscences, that touched people most.[7]

Whole congregations were swayed, too, by Sankey's attractive, though untrained, baritone voice, self-accompanied on his 'kist o' whistles' (a small cabinet organ). 'Slightly rough, but round and full and with that quality of sweetness much prized in his age', the tone of Sankey's vocals had, writes Pollock, an 'indescribable quality which, with his sympathetic nature, seldom failed to reach the most hidden recesses of the heart. ... It was this capacity to create spiritual longing, soften prejudice, bend wills, that was Sankey's distinctive gift. He racked the hearts of all classes, rich and poor.'[8]

Edinburgh in the Throes of Revival

Within a short time the whole city was said to have been moved to its core. All the leading evangelical personalities of the time were to be found giving their support, either on the platform or in the inquiry room[9] – only a few high-and-dry churchmen holding aloof. All classes, including aristocrats, the destitute and especially young men – including University students – found their way to the enquiry room. 'For all the month of December', wrote one correspondent, 'nothing else was spoken of in Edinburgh. The work, the meetings, and the men were spoken of at breakfast, at dinner, on the streets, and even in the ball-rooms. What does it all mean? What is all this about? At certain hours there seemed no one in Princess Street who did not carry a hymn-book, the tramway cars were full of hymn-books, and often it happened that nearly everyone in them was interested in the same subject, and pleasant Christian fellowship was exchanged.'[10]

---

7. ibid.; George Adam Smith, *The Life of Henry Drummond*, London, 1899, pp. 56-7.

8. Pollock, pp. 144-5. According to his own testimony, Sankey received his first impressions of saving truth from a Scotsman at a Sabbath school he attended (Andrew A. Bonar, *James Scott: A Labourer for God*, London, 1885, p. 14).

9. These included Professor Charteris, Marshall Lang, John McMurtrie, George Wilson, Lord Polwarth (Church of Scotland), Robert Rainy, James Hood Wilson, John Kelman, Horatius Bonar, William Arnot, Alexander Whyte, James Balfour (Free Church), Professor Henry Calderwood, Andrew Thomson, James Robertson (United Presbyterian), David McLaren (Congregational), Thomas Knox Talon (Episcopalian). See J. R. Fleming, *A History of the Church in Scotland 1843-1874 (1875-1929)*, Edinburgh, 1927–33, p. 235.

10. 'Narrative of Awakening' pamphlet in *TB*, 1874.

Principal George Adam Smith attended one meeting where 'hundreds of men stood up in witness that they had found salvation'. He claimed that 'never before in the history of Scotland has such a work of grace been done among its young men'. At another meeting, composed of sixty-six young men, it is recorded that all but six made a profession of faith before they left the place. In particular, considerable stir ensued over the dramatic conversion of Donald McAllan, chairman of an Infidel Club in the city, who initially had bitterly opposed the work of the Americans.[11]

Centres of Education

It was said of students at Edinburgh University's New College that they 'had gone into the movement nearly in a body'. Professor MacGregor testified to the great blessing which they had received, and, as an illustration, said that though he had been trying for some time to get from amongst them 'a very good situation filled up', he had been unable to do so, because they were all 'so much bent on evangelistic work'. A group of believing students from Edinburgh University distributed letters to fellow students who had recently 'passed from death to life', requesting that they join them in helping 'to promote the cause of the blessed Lord Jesus in the various Universities of our land'.[12]

Other centres of education in Edinburgh also shared in the harvest. Over two months after Moody left Edinburgh one source reported: 'We could tell of institutions where the pupils appear en masse to have been impressed and changed. The Children's Church for the waifs of the Canongate has experienced great benefit from a wonderful accession of spiritual life and power which has come on the pupils, males and females, of the Teachers Training College in Moray House. ... We could tell of equally remarkable changes in connection with various gatherings of young persons where the influence seems to have passed on four-fifths or five-sixths of the whole.'[13]

During his time in Edinburgh Moody and his wife stayed in the home of Professor W. G. Blaikie of New College, while the Sankeys stayed with Horatius Bonar. It was said that the period of this revival

---

11. Roberts, 1995, p. 319; W. R. Moody, *The Life of Dwight L Moody*, London, n.d., p. 175.

12. Smith, 1899, p. 64; *TB*, 28/05/1874, p. 110; 19/11/1874, p. 510.

13. *TB*, 18/04/1874.

was perhaps the happiest in Bonar's life, 'when his whole nature seemed to mellow and broaden'.[14] Dr Blaikie believed there was hardly a congregation in Edinburgh where a very remarkable experience was not to be found, 'in regard to spiritual things; prayer-meetings and Bible classes filled with new interest; and greater readiness to speak and hear on the most tender points, on which formerly they had been silent'. The professor went as far as suggesting that 'never, probably, was Scotland so stirred; never was there so much expectation'.[15]

Churches and Ministers Affected

Alexander Whyte, minister of Free St George's, threw himself heartily into the work and as a result saw an exceptionally large communicants' class the following year. He also saw his Tuesday night prayer meeting move from the church hall into the sanctuary itself. Another minister, the Rev. John McMurtrie, of St Bernard's Parish Church (later editor of *Life & Work* magazine and Moderator of the General Assembly of the Church of Scotland), wrote in 1874 that he had 'never known so happy a winter as last, during the whole course of his ministry'.[16]

In Dr McLauchlan's Gaelic Church forty-one new communicants were admitted at the spring sacrament of 1874, a remarkable number considering traditional Highland reticence in coming forward to make that step. Some 'excellent people' in his congregation who were formerly very doubtful about the value of the work confessed that their doubts were now removed and they now 'gave thanks for that which formerly they viewed with suspicion'.[17]

The Rev. James Robertson of Newington had long been highly cautious of the exuberances of 'zeal without knowledge' in revival meetings.[18] Yet before Moody had been a week in Edinburgh,

---

14. Robertson Nicol in Various Contributors, *Memories of Dr Horatius Bonar, by Relatives and Public Men*, Edinburgh 1909, p. 103.

15. *TB*, 28/05/1874, p. 110; Moody, p. 168.

16. Warren W. Wiesebe, *Living with the Giants: The Lives of Great Men of the Faith*, Grand Rapids, 1998, p. 130; Smith, 1899, p. 60.

17. *TB*, 28/05/1874, p. 110.

18. He particularly deplored the practice, quite common during the Moody campaign, of attempting to count the number of supposed conversions at a meeting. When specifically requested to attempt such enumeration at one after-meeting where

Robertson was perfectly satisfied with the nature of the mission and threw himself with his whole heart into the meetings, seldom missing one, although there were generally three in a day. His short five-minute addresses were said to have been 'often very precious, having about them a great dash of genius, combined with uncommon fervour'. Another recorded that that winter, the ministry of Robertson was 'greatly blessed to many, and his labours were owned of God to the ingathering of not a little of the abundant fruit of that time of blessing'. During 1874 he visited many places, either with Moody, or following up his work. Some of Robertson's parting words in public to Moody before the latter left Edinburgh were, 'I am meeting from day to day with older Christians who wish they were young again – who wish they had been children at such a Christ-finding time as this. This very morning a father told me with deep emotion, how his young people had on recent evenings been coming home from the meetings saying there is beauty in Jesus, and wondering that all the world didn't see it too, and that they themselves had not seen it sooner.'[19]

Altogether, across the city, many hundreds of converts were counted, especially among nominal church members. Children, too, were greatly moved. The Rev. John Hood Wilson, who 'gave himself up entirely' to the work, went to conduct worship at the Boys' Industrial Brigade. He jotted in his diary: 'There has been a very interesting work going on. About one-third of the boys are said to be under deep impression. ... Did not get home for two hours after the service. Had a meeting for inquirers: eleven came.'[20]

One observer noted that 'from the time he came before his vast audiences to the moment when he rose to preach, Moody kept the entire body absorbingly occupied with something interesting'. Sometimes this took novel forms. A black American singing group happened to be in Edinburgh during part of Moody's campaign in the city. At one

---

he was speaking with the anxious, Robertson point blank refused, retorting, 'When God the people writes, He'll count!' (M. H. M., *James Robertson of Newington: A Memorial of his Life and Work*, Edinburgh, 1887, p. 209).

19. ibid., pp. 206-10.

20. James Wells, *The Life of James Hood Wilson D.D. of the Barclay Church, Edinburgh*, London, 1904, p. 218.

meeting Moody had them concealed in the gallery, and at a given signal they began to quietly sing 'There are angels hovering around'.[21]

Closing Days

The Watch Night service at the close of 1873 was a highly memorable evening of praise and testimony. One writer said: 'There has seldom been a meeting at which the power of the Holy Spirit was more felt. It lasted for four hours, and they seemed to be so short. During the last ten minutes the vast audience that crowded the Free Assembly Hall knelt down and engaged in silent prayer.'[22]

On the first Sunday of 1874 Moody and Sankey, often independently, conducted no fewer than six meetings in as many hours. A day conference held a fortnight later drew 150 ministers. The American evangelists' farewell meeting was held in the fields on the slope of Arthur's Seat, there being no building which could accommodate the multitudes who wished to pay their respects to these American brethren who had brought so much blessing to their city. Charles Spurgeon, who apparently visited Scotland's capital shortly after Moody and Sankey's visit, said, 'The gracious visitation which has come upon Edinburgh is such as was popularly never known before within the memory of man. The whole place seems to be moved from end to end.' Fourteen hundred was quoted as the number of people professing conversion as a direct result of the Edinburgh mission.[23]

It was said that for months after the Americans left Edinburgh there was not 'the slightest abatement in the numbers of inquirers and converts ... the work is less centralised; that is the only change, and is penetrating more and more into corners hitherto unreached'. People were encouraged to send in slips of paper asking questions, and relating problems. These were then answered by experienced ministers and laymen, allowing for counsel and teaching to be adapted to people's needs. Indeed, such was the level of organisation that it was reported that 'twelve hundred converts, who gave their names in Edinburgh, were visited every fortnight for the next two years'.[24]

---

21. Coffey, p. 100; Kent, 1978, pp. 162-3.

22. M. H. M., pp. 209-10.

23. Quoted in Roberts, 1995, p. 324; Scotland, p. 145.

24. 'Narrative of Awakening' pamphlet in *TB*, 1874; Smith, 1899, p. 60. Largely through the influence of Henry Drummond the *Gaiety Club*, named after the Gaiety

Glasgow

Glasgow in an Uproar

While Moody and Sankey were still in Edinburgh, a group of 130 evangelical ministers in Glasgow eagerly united in heart and mind with aim of encouraging the work. A weekday prayer meeting was initiated, which from the very start was crowded to the uttermost. The American evangelists moved from their strikingly successful mission in Edinburgh forty miles west to Glasgow in early 1874, where they were based for ten weeks. Three thousand Sunday-school teachers surrounded the evangelists in the City Hall at the first meeting, while an hour before the time for the services such a crowd had assembled that four large churches in the neighbourhood were filled by the overflow. Meetings during the day were generally held in local United Presbyterian, Congregational and Free Churches, while evening meetings continued to be held in the City Hall, the churches being used only for overflow meetings and as locations for the inquiry rooms.

Support for Moody and Sankey was general among Glasgow denominations, although the Church of Scotland remained somewhat aloof. It was said that 140 churches in the city backed the Moody campaign. The clergy of Free and United Presbyterian Churches in particular gave almost unanimous support to the awakening, by appearing beside the evangelists at meetings, by conducting the smaller prayer meetings, and by advertising the revival from their pulpits. Because meetings were conducted at various times of day during the week, Moody and Sankey were often seen rushing from venue to venue. A good number were held between noon and 1 p.m. in the city's West End for the benefit of professional and clerical staff during their lunch breaks. The Ewing Place Congregational Church became a main focus of the revival in the city, also serving to attract many young men to the Y.M.C.A. meetings held there. Moody was particularly interested in the work of the Y.M.C.A., and devoted considerable time to preaching at its meetings.[25]

Music Hall in Edinburgh where its first meetings were held, was set up, in order to foster and continue the kind of practical Christian work that Adam Smith saw as a positive aspect of the mission.

25. Brown, 1981, pp. 438-9.

While Moody was in Glasgow a small team of male students began their own nightly meetings with the purpose of helping each other in the work of evangelism, or as Henry Drummond put it, learning how to 'buttonhole' the man in the street. Soon Drummond and several other young converts were taking revival meetings on their own and travelling to other places that Moody visited, to work with the new converts there (see p. 539). A pattern eventually emerged for these meetings; they were begun once Moody's main evening meeting was underway, and continued after the main service, often in a separate venue.

In Glasgow, despite (or because of) opposition and newspaper controversy raging high, enthusiasm and earnestness were even greater than in Edinburgh. Meetings were held in the streets and squares of the city; parents met to pray for the conversion of their offspring, while children's meetings were also held. One convert wrote that the revival became the absorbing topic of conversation, even in circles where religious subjects were usually considered entirely out of place. 'I have myself been present on more than one occasion in the billiard saloon', he noted, 'where the coin has been tossed to decide whether the evening was to be spent at "Moody and Sankey" or the theatre.'[26]

Furthermore, it wasn't just Glaswegians who attended the meetings. People came in their throngs from surrounding districts eager to hear the two foreigners about whom so much fuss was being made. One day as many as five hundred people made the journey from Kirkintilloch to hear Moody preach in Glasgow's capacious Circus Hall, some having walked the thirteen miles to get there. Among these was a group of seven, two of whom were already Christians. Wonderfully, and no doubt partly owing to the prayers of these, the other five committed their lives to Christ during that evening's meeting.

Finnieston Free Church

Among the many churches that reaped a rich harvest in the blessing of this time was Finnieston Free Church, which became a centre of the work in the city. Not content to wait till the American evangelists arrived in Glasgow, Andrew Bonar, the church's pastor, made several trips to Edinburgh to see the work in progress there. 'The tide of real

---

26. Alexander Gammie, *Pastor D. J. Findlay: A Unique Personality*, London, 1949, p. 15.

revival in Edinburgh has been stirring up all of us', he jotted in his diary on New Year's Day 1874. By 10 February, Bonar could note that Glasgow, 'has been at last visited' by the move of God, which he likened to the revival days of 1839–40, 'but there is more now than then'. Almost every day in March Bonar heard of someone in his congregation or neighbourhood who had been brought to Christ; while by April he exulted in 'souls getting salvation so easily, and all so solemnly too. There is deep gladness; no excitement. It is a day of visitation assuredly. I have fifty-four coming to the Lord's Table for the first time.'[27]

Yet all the while this devout minister was seeking 'a new baptism' for himself, feeling 'my own soul is not lifted up in the ways of the Lord as it might be. I need more compassion for souls.' Bonar longed for an increase in 'power from on high', all the more because, at the age of sixty-four, he felt this might be the last time he witnessed genuine revival. His prayer was wonderfully answered during the following fortnight, when on more than one occasion Bonar, 'felt the nearness of the Lord more than usual. At one time I seemed to myself to be so near Him that I might have passed within the veil.' By mid-May Bonar knew of more than seventy souls under his own care who had been converted since Moody arrived in town. On top of that not less than one hundred had been awakened in the Sunday school, most of which cases Bonar considered very hopeful.[28]

Anderston Free Church

A number of difficult issues had developed in the Anderston Free Church by 1873; one was of a financial nature, another related to a school begun by the church twenty years previously, while the third was in regard to the resident population around the church being increasingly displaced due to the rapid encroachment of business enterprises upon the area. The strain of these issues was to an extent relieved by Moody and Sankey's visit, for it was in Anderston that Moody found his most active Glasgow helpers.

---

27. M. Bonar, p. 293.

28. ibid., pp. 295-6. From this point the movement in Finnieston seems to have ebbed off, although Bonar was caught up again in the excitement of revival a year later, when in the summer of 1875 he assisted Moody in his London campaign.

The Rev. Alexander Somerville, in particular, threw himself into the work, and in humility realised that his preaching needed to be remodelled somewhat along the lines of Moody's. Thereby, with an increased zeal and using a fresher and less ecclesiastical vocabulary, he could, he felt, give greater evangelical force to proclaiming the gospel message, thus being more able to win over a new generation of young people while still fulfilling his duty to build up their fathers in the faith. There were many additions to church membership as a result of the awakening in the Anderston church, and the Kirk Session recorded 'the unprecedented position of having so many more young men in training for the ministry'.[29]

Somerville seems to have been significantly revived by both Moody's message and Sankey's music, and he followed the campaign up, not just in his own church, but throughout Scotland and beyond, travelling with Moody on his visits to Dundee, Aberdeen, Inverness, Wick and Thurso, Elgin, Oban, Belfast, Dublin and other places. Even more energetically for a man now in his sixties, Somerville entered the 'most remarkable era in a singularly useful life', becoming something of a world missionary, and conducting evangelistic campaigns in India, North America, Canada, Australia, New Zealand, South Africa, Russia, Turkey and all over Europe during the remaining fifteen years of his life.[30]

The Hundred-and-One

One remarkable young men's meeting held in Ewing Place Church soon became popularly known as 'The hundred-and-one night'. Moody, though present, never preached; instead Dr Cairns of Berwick delivered a powerful address on immorality, then a deputation of five students from Edinburgh spoke, one after the other. Adam Smith recalled:

> As the meeting proceeded, the spiritual power was such as I have never experienced on any other occasion; and when Mr Moody, at the close, ordered the front seats to be cleared, and invited those who wished to be prayed for to occupy the vacant pews, a hundred-and-one came forward. As the evangelist pleaded, and that solemn stream began to gather from every corner of the church, the sense

---

29. Thomas Adamson, *Free Anderston Church, Glasgow*, Glasgow, 1900, p. 43.

30. Biographical sketch in A. N. Somerville, *Precious Seed Sown in Many Lands*, London, 1890, p. xx; *DSCHT*, p. 787.

of Divine power became overwhelming and I remember quite well turning round on the platform and hiding my face in my hands, unable to look on the scene any more. Yet all was perfectly quiet, and the hundred-and-one were men of intelligence and character, who were not carried away with excitement, but moved by the force of conviction.[31]

Several of the converts of 'The hundred-and-one night' were connected with Free St Stephen's Church in north Glasgow. Full of fresh zeal, these sought to commence a work in the much-neglected north-west district of their parish. Thus was founded the Springbank Mission, which commenced operations with a forenoon Foundry Boys Religious Society, a Sabbath school and an evening service for adults. Numbers of children were soon gathered in, and a work of grace followed. Within a short period of time, as many as seventy-five young people were noted as not only having made a profession of faith, but as having given evidence of a changed heart. Mr Stewart, superintendent of the Sunday school, followed up these cases with peculiar interest, and rejoiced to testify that in no single case were his hopes disappointed.[32]

Hillhead

In the spring of 1874, 'The Spirit of God began manifestly to work' in the mining district of Jordanhill and Hillhead, to the immediate north-west of Glasgow, a district noted in the past for being the recipient of spiritual blessing. The Hillhead meetings were held in Kelvinside Free Church throughout the entire month of March. Moody occupied the pulpit in the forenoon, while Brownlow North followed in the evening, invariably preaching 'with rare freshness and power' to an overflowing congregation. At the close of each Sabbath evening service, as many as four hundred to five hundred remained

---

31. Smith, 1899, pp. 64-5.

32. George Ernest Philip, *Free St Matthew's Church, Glasgow: A Record of Fifty-Five Years*, Glasgow, 1898, pp. 104-6. In the late 1870s the work of the Springbank Mission was taken over by neighbouring Free St Matthews Church. The work here expanded greatly in subsequent years. By 1887 the Foundry Boys' Meeting was drawing an average attendance of 683 boys with crowds sometimes passing 900 (Charles D. Cashdollar, *A Spiritual Home: Life in British and American Reformed Congregations, 1830-1915*, Pennsylvania, 2000, p. 194).

to continue in prayer for a blessing, and at the close of these second meetings inquirers remained in increasing numbers for conversation and counsel. Kenneth Moody Stuart was minister of the church at the time and believed that many were enabled to yield to Christ, while in the course of pastoral visitation he found that 'others, who did not visit as enquirers, shared in the same blessing. It was altogether a memorable harvest time.'[33]

Glasgow Converts

One young man then working in Glasgow as an apprentice-draper and converted around this time was nineteen-year-old Dugald Christie, later a medical missionary to Manchuria. David Findlay, prominent preacher at St George's Cross, Glasgow (and to whom Findlay's Memorial Church remains a tribute), was also converted at this time, when he heard both Moody and Dr Alexander McLaren – whom Moody termed 'the best minister in Europe' – preach in Glasgow.[34] As a young man, Duncan Main was converted to Christ in April 1873, several months before Moody's Glasgow mission. He gloried in the opportunities of service during the Americans' campaign, such as preaching at open-air services, which were many in number during this period. Main became a lifelong friend of David Findlay and went on to serve as a missionary to China.[35]

Perhaps the most prominent of all those impacted by Moody's campaigns in Glasgow in terms of the influence he went on to exercise, was Keir Hardie, a teenage miner of non-believing parents from Lanarkshire. Three years later, in 1877, then aged twenty-one, Hardie wrote in his diary: 'Today I have given my life to Jesus Christ.'[36] He joined the Morisonians but also took an active interest in social welfare and politics and went on to become the founder of the Labour Party,

---

33. Moody Stuart, 1878, pp. 427-9. North's labours were blessed in other churches of the city around this time, as they were too in Dumbarton, where between 300 and 400 responded to his appeal for commitment to Christ (*TC*, 23/07/1874). Further blessing was received when the evangelist returned to Kelvinside Free Church at the beginning of 1875, just months before his death later in the year.

34. *DSCHT*, p. 171; Gammie, 1949, pp. 15-16.

35. Alexander Gammie, *Duncan Main of Hangchow*, London, 1935, pp. 17-18.

36. Donald Carswell, *Brother Scots*, London, 1927, p. 164.

and a patriarch in Labour's history. Towards the end of his life, in 1910, Keir wrote: 'The impetus which drove me first of all into the Labour movement and the inspiration which carried me on in it, has been derived more from the teachings of Jesus of Nazareth than all other sources combined.'[37]

In Glasgow it was noted, 'For some time past a good work has been going on amongst our sailors.' Open-air meetings were held at the corner of the Sailors Home, which attracted the attention of this class of men, 'who are always loitering about'. Adjourning to a room in the Home, a believing sailor would lead the gathering with hymns, testimonies and a short address, before 'anyone who wishes to be specially prayed for is asked to signify it by holding up his hand. Sometimes as many as six or eight will do so.' Through these meetings, a number of seafaring men 'appeared to receive Christ into their hearts'.[38]

Farewell Meeting

At a farewell meeting in May solely for young converts of Moody's five-month Glasgow campaign, the number present, apart from workers, was 3,500, this being by no means all who were blessed during this period.[39] At a closing meeting, held in the vast Crystal Palace in the city's Botanical Gardens, between twenty and thirty thousand people crowded around the Palace well before the scheduled hour to hear Moody preach, which had the effect of preventing the evangelist from gaining admittance! Instead Moody preached from the vantage point

---

37. Stephen Timms M.P., 'Christianity and Politics', quoted in *The Bible in Transmission*, Autumn 2001. As a missionary in the West Indies in 1879, Mary Dyer came across a backslidden convert of Moody's Glasgow campaign, working as a sugar-plantation manager. Under Dyer's instrumentality, the man fully rededicated his life to Christ (George Dyer, *Christhood: As Seen in the Life Work of Mary Dyer*, London, 1889, pp. 96-8). Lachlan MacLean, evangelist and missionary to St Kilda from 1906, was another who, as a young man, was influenced by Moody's Scottish meetings (Tom Steel, *The Life and Death of St Kilda*, Glasgow, 1975, p. 103). Meanwhile, a further convert of Moody's Glasgow mission was sixteen-year-old Isabella Murray, who later, with her husband Dr Morrison, served as a missionary in India (Isabella Morrison's unpublished *Memoirs*, held by her great granddaughter, Mrs Young, Inverallochy).

38. *TB*, 19/11/1874, p. 506.

39. ibid., 21/05/1874, pp. 90-1.

of the top of the coachman's box of his carriage, while the choir sang from the roof of a nearby shed, and Sankey rendered a number of his own melodic and emotionally charged compositions.

An 'Evangelistic Movement' was formed in the aftermath of Moody's visit, and an 'Evangelistic Tent' set up on Glasgow Green, where daily and nightly meetings drew thousands. The 'Tent Breakfast' served excellently the purpose of bringing in the poor and outcast, who would not normally be induced to attend a gospel meeting. It also gave birth to several other organisations immediately associated with it, while leading in turn to a number of other initiatives, such as Boarding Houses of the Young Women's Christian Association and an Industrial Feeding School.

Moody's Travels Throughout the Land

What has not been widely recognised is the breadth and depth of awakening that occurred throughout much of Scotland during this exciting period. Publisher, Robert Morgan acted as a significant promoter in the Moody revival by mailing complimentary copies of *The Christian* to hundreds of Scottish ministers when it became evident that the Moody mission was progressing so successfully. He also recruited workers for revival meetings through his periodical, and published Moody's speeches and writings, Sankey's hymns and tunes, and various books on the revival written by clergy.

In 1876 a Free Church commentator reported: 'All over the country, though not in every congregation, and not even in every district, a great change has taken place ... religion is dealt with as a reality. The solemn and awful importance of its truths and of their issues is recognised ... coldness and formality (have) been broken in upon, and living active religion taken their place.'[40] In *The Christian* newspaper of 19 March 1874, Andrew Bonar cites awakening across Scotland from Lockerbie to Aberuthven. More recently, Harry Sprange gives ample evidence to back his claim that 'From April 1874 onwards reports appear from all over Scotland, and from every denomination, of a wide-spread awakening.'[41]

---

40. FCSRSRM, 1876, p. 1.

41. Sprange, p. 244.

While Moody was still in Edinburgh, a circular was sent to every minister in Scotland, calling attention to proceedings in the capital, and asking for united prayer that the work would spread widely. This effected, among other things, invitations from church leaders all over the country for the American duo to hold meetings in their localities. Thus, Moody and Sankey's travels took them all over Scotland; from Ayrshire to Caithness, from Oban to Arbroath; and wherever they preached they did so with great success.

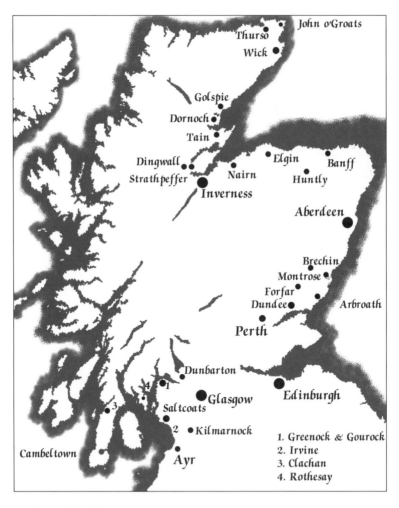

Central Scotland

The evangelists spent two and a half weeks in Dundee between their grand Edinburgh and Glasgow campaigns. Towards the close of this time, upwards of four hundred people applied for 'young converts' tickets', professing to 'believe on the Lord Jesus Christ'. Large additions were made to the membership of the many churches, in some congregations as many as one hundred and upward. The Americans paid a second visit to Dundee in June 1874, when they made a special effort at reaching young men, a policy continued after the evangelists left the town. It was said that 'In the Post and Telegraph Offices alone there are some twenty young men and lads who have come over to the Lord's side, and are zealous in His service.'[42] It was further reported: 'A powerful undercurrent of spiritual influence is plainly seen to be at work among the youth' of Dundee. 'In many quarters the tide is fairly turned, and is setting in steadily in the right direction.' Regarding the work among the children, the same correspondent remarked: 'We have never before seen so much precious fruit in the same space of time.'[43]

From Glasgow, the American evangelists visited Greenock, Gourock and Dumbarton. Many in Greenock's Free North Church 'were spiritually blessed'. On a personal note, the devoted and modest Rev. Boyd wrote: 'These past weeks have been more precious to my soul than any former time of my ministry ... . For months before (Moody and Sankey's visit), I was stirred up to greater prayerfulness, more earnest desires for growth in grace and usefulness in the ministry. But now I have far more vivid views of the love of Christ to a poor sinner, and such a joy of assurance as I never experienced before.'[44]

The Rev. James Kerr of Greenock's Reformed Presbyterian Church said that such was the popularity of the American visitors that he was

---

42. *TB*, 04/02/1875, p. 681.

43. ibid., p. 682. In many towns the evangelists travelled to, detractors spoke out against them. George Gilfillan was a long-established and well-respected Secession minister in Dundee, having been inducted there in 1836. He had spoken out against previous revivals in the town and elsewhere, but had less sympathy still for the Moody and Sankey campaign, which form of revivalism he viewed as merely emotional Christianity. He not only denounced it, but ridiculed it, perhaps without sufficient discrimination. This brought upon him severe criticism and no little abuse. He received one letter addressed simply to 'George Gilfillan, Devil of Dundee'. Such insensitivity hurt him deeply, but failed to deter him from speaking out his honest convictions. To him steady religious training was far more profitable than people being converted 'straight away' (David MacRae, *George Gilfillan: Anecdotes and Reminiscences*, Glasgow, 1891, pp. 27-8).

44. Anonymous, *Memorial Sketch: Free North Church, Greenock, and its First Minister, David Boyd*, Greenock 1900, pp. 32-4.

one of only two church leaders in the town who refused to 'dance attendance upon them' as other ministers were doing, nor did he look on them as Jupiter and Mercury, 'gods come down to us in the likeness of men'. Instead he felt it proper to 'try the spirits', and in so doing he found Sankey's hymns, in particular, to be lacking in scriptural warrant (see Chapter 22). Although he felt his criticism was clear, logical and impersonal, it brought on him a 'great deal of odium and hostility' from 'the Sankeyites', many of whom, Kerr felt, were violating their own ordination vows in so doing.[45]

Next, Moody and Sankey travelled to the Ayrshire towns of Kilmarnock, Saltcoats, Irvine and Ayr. At 8.30 on a late May morning, 1,750 packed Kilmarnock's Low Church for a special address by Moody to office bearers and other church workers, not just from the town, but from districts miles distant. Of this meeting it was said: 'Seldom has any audience been more impressed; for more than an hour he held them spell-bound as he discoursed on Christian work.'[46]

It was now time for Moody to penetrate the central Highlands of Scotland. He began by journeying to Perth, where for a week he led daily meetings in each of three venues (his last message to a crowd estimated at over seven thousand). Then it was over to Stirling. This town's Erskine United Presbyterian Church became packed to capacity, hundreds being turned away from Moody's meeting in the town. From the second day, 'a very decided work of God' took place. Some hundreds, from nearly all classes, professed to be brought to the Lord, and it was believed that 'on the whole Stirling has seldom, if ever before, enjoyed such a year of blessing'. Nearby Bridge of Allan was likewise touched.[47]

The North

From Perthshire, the American duo proceeded to Aberdeen, where they stayed two weeks. This was the only city of which Moody said that his words seemed to come back to him when he preached.[48] But

---

45. A. Holmes, *Memorial Volume to the Rev. James Kerr, D.D.*, Glasgow, 1906, p. 47.

46. ibid., p. 122.

47. ibid., 22/10/1874, p. 442; FCSRSRM, 1876, p. 5.

48. John K. Maclean, *Triumphant Evangelism: The Three Years' Missions of Dr Torrey and Mr Alexander in Great Britain and Ireland*, London, 1906, p. 29.

his time spent here was by no means fruitless. Involved in the work in the Granite City was (Isa)Bella Darling, a seventeen-year-old girl from Dalkeith who had been converted five years previously through the ministry of Brownlow North at Edinburgh's Carrubbers Close Mission. A member of Broughton Place United Presbyterian Church, Bella, along with her two sisters, went forward for personal counselling at one of Moody's meeting in Scotland's capital. Bella learned from Moody how to deal with anxious souls, and her frank, open manner and tender compassion quickly secured the confidence of burdened souls. Encouraged and eager to help others, Bella travelled to Aberdeen to attend Moody's meetings there. She was quickly singled out by the evangelist, who appointed her to work in the inquiry room. For ten days she laboured thus, preserving the names and addresses of no less than forty people who had accepted Christ under her personal dealing – while she also sang in the choir. Of equal significance, Bella kept very full notes of Moody's addresses both in Edinburgh and Aberdeen, and these were later published.

Next the two evangelists paid a flying visit to the Forfarshire towns of Montrose (where Sankey received the criticism of having a complacent attitude to his own singing), as well as Brechin, Forfar and Arbroath, before moving on to the Highland capital, Inverness.

'Not since the days of Dr Macdonald', claimed Alexander MacRae, 'were the Highlands so profoundly stirred by the Spirit of God as they were during the visit of the honoured American evangelists, Moody and Sankey, in the summer of 1874'.[49] The Highland Railway Company ran special trains in connection with the meetings, giving facilities to many outside Inverness (and indeed other northern centres at which the meetings were held) to attend.

However, in general the strongly Calvinist northern Highlands were closed to the Americans.[50] John Kennedy of Dingwall produced a 31-page booklet entitled, *Hyper-Evangelism: 'Another Gospel', Though A Mighty Power, A Review of the Recent Religious Movement in Scotland*

49. MacRae, 1906, p. 86.

50. Callum Brown states that the Moody revival affected 'practically all of Scotland', including parts of the Highlands not affected by the revival of 1859–61 (Brown, 1981, p. 437). He does not, however, specify any Highland location, nor am I able to in my own research, of which this is true.

(Edinburgh, 1874), in which he aired his emphatic views on Moody's 'Arminian' methods (in essence, an emphasis on faith rather than the sovereignty of God),[51] by which means, he believed, the life of the Free Church was 'departing, the result of revivals got up by men'.[52] In the same year, Horatius Bonar responded to Kennedy's allegations with a 78-page booklet, *The Old Gospel: Not 'Another Gospel', but the Power of God unto Salvation* (Edinburgh, 1874).[53] Kennedy in turn responded to this with *A Reply to Dr Bonar's Defence of Hyper-Evangelism* (Edinburgh, 1875). The Highlander's stance helped ensure strong prejudice against the evangelists in the north of the country, as did contents of a letter

---

51. Though it is possible that he rarely, if ever, met one, Kennedy painted a totally unflattering picture of a typical Moody convert, as a 'molluscous, flabby creature without pith or symmetry, breathing freely only in the heated air of meetings, craving to be pampered with vapid sentiment, and so puffed up by foolish flattery as to be in a state of chronic flatulency, requiring relief in frequent bursts of hymn singing, in spouting addresses as void of scripture truth as of common sense and in belching flippant questions' (quoted in Douglas Ansdell, *People of the Great Faith: The Highland Church 1690-1900*, Stornoway 1998, p. 119). Yet hundreds of these converts went on to become members, and some even ministers, within Kennedy's own denomination.

52. Kennedy's main charge that Moody's message constituted 'another gospel' Bonar knew to be completely contradicted by the many testimonies of ministers, Sunday-school teachers and parents regarding the changed lives of individuals personally known to them. Kennedy also made a number of sweeping generalisations, such as that Moody never made a call to repentance. This was utterly repudiated by Bonar, who had heard Moody preach on many occasions. Central to Kennedy's argument was his disapproval of Moody's emphasis on 'immediate salvation'. Bonar felt he was not compromising his Calvinism in supporting Moody's insistence that gospel preaching should look for an immediacy of response. He also supported the need to counter a 'lurking distrust of the generosity of God in the free offer of salvation', which was so prevalent in Calvinistic Scotland. He thus believed that Moody's emphasis on the love of God to all sinners was the right one. Kennedy deplored the adoption of inquiry rooms, which, he felt, were used to make public profession easier. Bonar, too, disapproved of 'hasty or premature announcement of conversions', and did not expressly disagree with Kennedy on this point. Iain H. Murray's views on this topic are pertinent. He writes: 'It cannot be doubted that the endorsement that Moody gave to the public appeal was to contribute to a significant long-term deterioration in evangelism. Conversion was to become identified with an instant decision made at an evangelistic meeting' (Murray, 2006, p. 196).

53. Interestingly, despite Bonar's strong approval of the Moody movement, there does not appear to have arisen a prominent awakening in his own parish of Kelso at this time.

sent to Kennedy from a lawyer in Chicago, which cast aspersions on Moody's character and business dealings.[54]

After an eventful week in Inverness, the Americans made a detour north to Tain. To this Ross-shire town people walked, rode, drove or came by special train from as far away as Helmsdale and Inverness to hear Moody preach in Academy Park and – when it was wet – in the Free Church. Nearly five hundred rose to be spoken to and prayed for regarding their salvation one afternoon, while 'whole families were to be seen sitting side by side, all anxious about their souls'.[55] Moody said that he had never seen such a result anywhere from twenty-four hours work. From Tain, Moody and Sankey returned to Inverness, stopping for a day in Strathpeffer, and then heading to Nairn, Huntly, Elgin and Banff.

The Americans came to the popular spa-town of Strathpeffer at the invitation of the Rev. W. S. McDougall, Free Church minister of Fodderty and Contin. Moody preached 'three stirring and thrilling sermons', two in the open air to audiences of two thousand and about four thousand respectively, and one in the Free Church to an audience of eight hundred. Some members of McDougall's own family were among those 'led to decide for the Lord' at this time – all family members still presumed to be standing in their faith twenty-five years later.[56]

---

54. Kennedy had circulated the letter among Scottish ministers for almost two months before Moody discovered what was happening. The American at once wrote to his Chicago patron and friend, J. V. Farwell, asking him to endorse his work, and to get local ministers to do the same because 'the man has threatened to publish the letter if I come on to the north of Scotland and I have promised to go and shall if nothing happens' (J. Holmes, p. 70). The local organising committee also wrote to Moody expressing its concern, but the letter of recommendation from Chicago soon arrived and the controversy died away. Thus, what could have been huge damage to Moody's reputation was avoided.

55. MacRae, 1906, pp. 91-2.

56. Moody visited the Strath again on his next trip to Scotland in 1881–2, when among those manifesting concern were three of the Manse family, in whom Mr McDougall had good reason to hope that the Holy Spirit had begun His saving work. Whether these were the same individuals, or other siblings, within the McDougall family, is unclear. Any dissension between McDougall and John Kennedy of Dingwall – which parish was adjacent to McDougall's – over inviting Moody to his church proved of temporary duration, for, on Kennedy's death in 1884, McDougall preached at the funeral of his 'beloved friend and nearest brother-minister' (ibid.).

Moray and Banffshire

To the Castle Park in Huntly, 'all sorts of vehicles brought their living freights of both sexes, and the number of pedestrians from neighbouring localities was altogether unprecedented. The village of Aberchirder almost emptied itself',[57] and the same thing could be said of numerous fishing villages along the coast, the exodus from which was so great that the resources of the railway were severely tasked. At least fifteen thousand people were computed to have attended one afternoon meeting.

A work of grace seems to have commenced in Elgin prior to the visit of the two Americans, who spent five days in the town. With their arrival, folk came from all around. A crowd reckoned between fifteen and twenty thousand filled the Market Green to overflowing while 'the whole hillside, for a great distance up and round about, was covered with the dense multitude that presented, with their varied dresses, a most imposing spectacle.'[58] A year later the Rev. Dr MacPhail of the Free Church said he had added 110 communicants to his church roll the previous year, most of whom ascribed their conversion to the seven months of concerted effort surrounding Moody's visit. In addition, he knew of at least as many more who could soon take the same step. MacPhail's strongest testimony related to his Bible class, which by the winter of 1874–5 exceeded his class of the previous year by well over one hundred, now numbering 431, of whom 213 were males and 218 females.

MacPhail sought to give more insight into the makeup of these statistics. For instance, of ninety-six individuals who met at a special meeting which he called, all of whom professed to have been brought to the Lord the previous year, the minister found there were fifty-two who had not yet made a public profession. Of the ninety-six mentioned, fifty-three were engaged in active Christian work; while several more were practically occupied in caring for young families. Of these ninety-six, twenty-four were previously members of the congregation, showing

---

(John S. McPhail, *Memorial Sermons of The Rev. W. S. McDougall, with a Sketch of His Life*, Edinburgh, 1897, p. 23).

57. Rufus W. Clark, *The Work of God in Great Britain under Messrs. Moody & Sankey, 1873 to 1875*, London, 1875, p. 151.

58. ibid., p. 154.

that the work was not confined to the young. Indeed, of the young communicants specified already, several were about forty years of age, and a few above sixty. MacPhail found that a vast proportion of those savingly blessed were so changed as a result of the special services, but he believed that fully two-thirds 'received good' previous to Moody's visit.[59]

For months before Moody arrived in Banff for an eight-day visit, there had been marked interest in religion; church services and Bible classes overflowed and many made their way to the manse to talk with the minister on spiritual matters. The arrival of the famed evangelists brought things to a head. From every town and village from miles around they came; every hotel and lodging house being occupied. Fishermen came from Buckie, Fraserburgh and other ports, and slept in their boats overnight. Regularly two thousand packed into the Parish Church while fifteen thousand gathered in Lord Fife's park on one occasion to hear Moody preach. Sankey's ministry of song had an equally dramatic effect. The American first sang a little-known hymn. Years later the minister wrote:

> I have never, I say it carefully, seen an impression on a large audience like it. ... My choir broke down and could not sing the next paraphrase. ... Following Sankey's rendition of 'The Ninety and Nine', every head was bowed. No one looked up. We remained for five minutes in silent prayer, and then recovered ourselves. ... I never in my life saw a congregation so swayed to a man's voice.[60] ... My whole choir that night gave their hearts to God. Over eighty young men and women, as I afterwards learned authoritatively, were won to Christ. ... And best of all, the converts stood. The work was deep; it was rooted in clear conviction and intelligent grip.[61]

---

59. *TB*, 18/02/1875, p. 711.

60. 'The Ninety and Nine' was written as a poem by Elizabeth Clephane, daughter of the Sheriff of Fife, in 1868. Sankey read the poem in a newspaper while travelling by train in Scotland. He put one verse to music spontaneously while at a meeting in Edinburgh shortly after. The Lord 'gave me again and again the same tune for all the remaining verses, note for note', Sankey later remarked. Half the audience was, along with both Moody and Sankey, in tears. From then, 'The Ninety and Nine' swept Scotland, and instantly became Sankey's most popular hymn (Ira D. Sankey, *My Life and Sacred Songs*, London, 1906, pp. 247-51; Pollock, pp. 139-42).

61. W. S. Bruce, *Reminiscences of Men and Manners During the Past Seventy Years*, Aberdeen, 1929, pp. 176-8. One man who went on to become a Member of

The Far North

From Elgin and Banff the Americans went south by Keith to Aberdeen, where they had previously spent a fortnight preaching, and thence by sea to Wick and Thurso.[62] Preparatory meetings were arranged immediately prior to Moody's visit to Thurso, at which preachers from Dingwall,[63] Glasgow, London and elsewhere assisted. At one, three quarters of the congregation – between eight hundred and nine hundred people – remained for inquiry, every one deciding to yield to Christ. Thus when Moody arrived the following week, 'the ground was prepared for him'. And after he left the town, the meetings were carried on for some time, thanks largely to the energy and zeal of Charles Taylor, a student at Edinburgh's New College. 'A movement of a very earnest and gladdening kind' was begun in a quarter of the town known as the 'Fisher Biggings', a degenerate area, of which many inhabitants were known to be careless and even hostile to any influence of a religious kind. Nightly meetings were held in the 'Bethel', a hall connected to the Scottish Coast Mission, as well as, on the Sabbath, in the Town Hall, whose five hundred seats were nearly all taken in just a few minutes. Each place, recorded one worker, 'has indeed been a Bethel-house to many … whose hearts we believe the Lord has touched'.[64] The churches, the Y.M.C.A., and every religious and philanthropic institution in the town and neighbourhood were said to have been inspired with new life and energy as an outcome of the movement.

While in Caithness, Moody and some friends paid a visit to Duncansby and John O'Groats. News of his presence spread rapidly

---

Parliament, received 'a new turn to my life' at these meetings, which led many others into the ministry and the mission field (ibid., p. 175).

62. By this time Sankey had parted with Moody and returned to join his family in Edinburgh, where he rested before accompanying his colleague on their Irish tour.

63. This was the Rev. John Kennedy. It seems remarkable that this staunchly Calvinist preacher should involve himself in such a mission (his text was 'I am the Bread of Life'), given his strong antipathy towards the whole Moody campaign. Kennedy later wrote of the movement: 'I heard the leading teacher repeatedly' (Kennedy and Bonar, p. 17). It is unclear whether he was referring to the Thurso meetings, where Kennedy had preached a week *before* Moody arrived in the town, or to his home town of Dingwall, where Moody preached – in the Established Church – in late August 1874 (*TB*, 03/09/1874, p. 332).

64. *TB*, 22/10/1874, p. 444.

through the district and soon a considerable gathering of men and women, attired in their Sabbath dresses and with Bibles in their hands, assembled at John O'Groats House, and pleaded with him to speak a few words to them. The local newspaper reported that he spoke for twenty minutes, 'rousing the audience to a deep conviction … standing as he did on the northmost mainland of Britain, with the blue waters of the broad Atlantic rolling between him and his home, seemed as a link building the two nations together in that unity and brotherly love which are the main characteristics of his doctrine. This was probably the first sermon preached from John O'Groats House.'[65]

Last Days of Mission

From Thurso, Moody moved south, holding open-air and church meetings before large crowds in Golspie, Dornoch and Dingwall, and then back to Inverness, where he hosted a one-day convention. Then on his twelfth wedding anniversary, Moody, accompanied by his wife and family, steamed down Loch Ness and the Caledonian Canal to preach in Oban, where much preparatory work had been done during the two preceding months by Andrew and Horatius Bonar. Next day the Americans sailed through further glorious scenery and on towards Campbeltown, where a work of grace had been ongoing for several months past (see pp. 572-3), and where the evangelist's visit was now 'crowned with remarkable blessing'. En route to Rothesay in early September, Moody stopped at Clachan for a single meeting. He is on record as saying that Clachan was one of the best meetings he had anywhere in Scotland – the Holy Spirit being so evidently working on the hearts of the people.[66]

Moody's last meeting in Scotland was held in Rothesay. The large West Free Church quickly became densely packed and oppressively warm, so the meeting was adjourned to the Esplanade. Quickly, an immense crowd of no less than three thousand assembled round the preacher. An eyewitness wrote: 'For fully an hour he riveted the attention of his large audience, narrative, metaphor, parable, illustration and appeal following each other in quick succession and agreeable variety.

---

65. ibid., 27/08/1874, p. 314.

66. J. M., *Recollections of D. L. Moody and his Work in Britain 1874-1892*, Edinburgh, 1905 (published privately), p. 46.

Towards the close of the service the scene was one never to be forgotten. The firmament was cloudless, and myriads of stars shone brilliantly (for by this time night had fully set in), and were reflected in the Bay, beyond which lay the Cowal Hills, dark and massive in the distance. Every now and again the houses in the Gallowgate, and the spire of the West Free Church, were lighted up by flashes of street-lighting.' Deeply impressed, evidently, with the position, the scene, and the circumstance that he was addressing probably for the last time a Scottish audience, Mr Moody concluded a discourse which 'for point and power ... had not been on any former occasion surpassed'.[67]

Generally, Moody and Sankey stayed no more than a day or two in any one place, and, as we have observed, frequently the work grew in intensity and effectiveness after their departure. This was certainly true of Berwick-on-Tweed, Edinburgh and Tain where the movements the evangelists helped inaugurate continued well into 1875.[68] For example, the Rev. John Hood Wilson recalled speaking at a meeting in a hall in Edinburgh in 1875. 'It was a wonderful gathering. I suppose there must have been about two thousand young ladies, mostly at school. I gave the second address on "Taste and see that the Lord is good". I fancy that there was never a meeting exactly like it.'[69]

---

67. Clark, pp. 161-3; *TB*, 10/09/74, p. 348.

68. Roberts, 1995, pp. 313-14; *The Christian*, 15/07/1875, pp. 14-15; 29/07/1875, p. 8; 15/04/1875.

69. Wells, p. 222.

Drumblade Church

Drumblade Parish

Marnoch Free Church

Gartly, Strathbogie

Kennethmont

CHAPTER 21

Revival *sans* Moody

Significant awakening was also evidenced in scores of towns and villages around the country where Moody never set foot. In such cases, quickening was generally preceded by the reporting of events elsewhere and by the setting up of special prayer meetings. In addition, deputations of young men from Edinburgh travelled from the city to hold special meetings throughout the nation. These aroused much interest and led to many making commitments of faith. On one occasion, Edinburgh University students, George Adam Smith and Henry Drummond, set off by train to go and preach in the Highlands. Unsure as to where to go, they tossed a coin for it. Smith went to Inverness, Drummond to Nairn or Elgin. Wrote Smith regarding his colleague: 'As matters turned out, this decision was very important, for, where he went, there was such a blessing that he felt called to devote himself more absolutely to the work; and he used to speak of this occasion as one of the turning-points by which his subsequent work was determined.'[1]

Edinburgh and Environs

Edinburgh

That a spirit of awakening, especially among the young, continued in Edinburgh well after the departure of Moody and Sankey is evident from a number of reports dating from the spring and summer of 1874.

---

1. Smith, 1899, pp. 65-6. On hearing of his success in the north, Moody requested that Drummond went, with two other Scottish students, on a short mission to the Newcastle/Sunderland area in Northumberland. The deputation 'went for three days and stayed a fortnight, with still less hope of getting away, for the work grew past all belief and spread to the neighbouring towns' (ibid.).

During a fortnight of children's meetings held in Stockbridge in March, an eyewitness testified, 'Many, if not all, were deeply convinced of sin. There was no special preaching to that effect, and yet such was the state of the case. We have seen the head bent low, the lips quivering and the eyes wet with tears, because of a sense of sin. But when Christ was set forth as the sinner's substitute, we have seen the eyes gleaming through the tears ...' [2]

A Congregational report in April claimed that 'all the churches and Sabbath schools had felt the awakening, and the work seemed to be spreading among the young like leaven – nothing could account for it – it must be of God'. Around the same time another account speaks of 'whole schools bending under the influence of the Almighty Spirit', and of 'the ragged school children, and those of the first boarding schools, yielding up their hearts to the Lord of Love'.[3]

Dalkeith

The influence of the revival movement in Edinburgh was early felt in Dalkeith, and special prayer and evangelistic meetings proved most popular, churches and halls being at times crowded to excess. Summarised the Rev. Bannerman: 'For very many of us, that old Secession church, with its simple furnishings, has become in these weeks a place of hallowed memories – a place where the gospel of our Lord Jesus Christ manifestly proved itself the power of God unto salvation – a scene not only of offered, but of answered prayer.'[4]

Old Craighill

Special services were held at Millerhill and Old Craighill, a few miles south-east of Edinburgh and just north of Dalkeith, shortly after Moody's Edinburgh campaign. This resulted in, 'by the gracious influences of the Holy Spirit, a precious revival of religion in this locality'.[5] Deeply engaged in the work was the devout teenager Bella Darling (see p. 529). Having a deep love for children, Bella had become

---

2. *TC*, 02/07/1874, quoted in Sprange, p. 319.

3. *TB*, 30/04/1874; *TC*, 07/05/1874, quoted in ibid., pp. 318-19.

4. *TB*, 18/04/1874, pp. 15-16.

5. Samuel MacNaughton, *Joy in Jesus: Brief Memorials of Bella Darling*, Edinburgh, 1876, p. 24.

involved in the Millerhill Mission in 1871 as a Sunday-school teacher, and quickly became highly distinguished in dealing with youthful souls. Although also involved in missions in the Infirmary and in the closes of Edinburgh, Bella found time to hold special services, being aided by her father, and on occasion, the redoubtable Henry Drummond.

Further east, the loss of a boat in a strong gale, with four young Dunbar fishermen on board, had softened the minds of many and prepared them for the reception of gospel truth. The resulting awakening proved to be of a genuine character and was productive of precious fruit, it being said that 'so far as is known, there have been no cases of flagrant backsliding'.[6]

Glasgow Environs

Govan and Anniesland

In the early months of 1874, while Moody and Sankey were so busy labouring in various parts of Glasgow, Brownlow North was at work in some of the large and populous suburbs which girdle that city – namely Govan, Partick and Hillhead. Reports of the remarkable results which followed the meetings in Govan were shared at the daily noon meetings in Glasgow city centre and tended greatly to encourage the hearts of believers to abound in prayer for a still larger blessing.

In the Anniesland coalpit, five of the fifteen miners, all Christians, began to meet during their breakfast hour to intercede – sometimes with tears of compassion – for their unsaved colleagues. Their hymn singing attracted notice and soon others came to join them in their small 'temple', 150 yards underground. On the first Saturday of the meetings, two miners found rest in Christ, followed by another the following day. Altogether twenty souls were brought to the Lord, including one whose eyes were opened after being sensitively spoken to following the death of his four-year-old child, to whom he was much attached. These brethren, accompanied by others, began outreach to five nearby villages and 'every night some soul has been wounded by the arrows of the Mighty One'. At one place the house was so crowded that two leaders of the meeting were unable to get entrance. Meanwhile, an elderly man on horseback, as he came along the road, heard the

---

6. *TB*, 01/04/1875, p. 812.

singing, stopped, entered into conversation, and before he left for home 'seemed to discover the way to New Jerusalem'. During the third week a work also began to appear among the boys and girls, many of whom were awakened.[7]

Chryston

In Chryston, to the north of Glasgow, there seemed to be no special preparation in the way of increased spirituality up till a week or two before the movement commenced. Indeed it had been deliberately stated from the pulpit that the spiritual condition of the congregation had not for years been at a lower ebb. Nevertheless, some godly folk were praying, and with news of revival in Edinburgh, prayer meetings were commenced during the national 'Week of Prayer'. The Rev. Thomas Macadam wrote: 'The Christian people seemed to get a new life – a very taste of heaven upon earth. Those who were present will never forget that fortnight. God's Spirit was felt to be present. The very place seemed sanctified.' The following week many came under deep conviction and 'between sixty and seventy were personally spoken to about their souls. ... Our Communion fell on the following Sabbath. Of the preciousness of that day I shall not speak; for though the members of the congregation would feel that I was not overstating the reality, others might think I was exaggerating did I attempt to describe the tenderness and sweetness of our fellowship with Christ on that occasion.'[8]

Nightly for nine weeks the meetings were continued, with no abatement of attendance or interest, yet with an absence of excitement. Notwithstanding the influence on church members, fifty professing converts were admitted at the following dispensation of the Lord's Supper; while twenty more had joined the communicant's class, but left the district before admission, and a good many joined other congregations. Macadam suspected at the time, however, that a considerable number of the anxious were merely under the influence of a temporary excitement, or the delusion that somehow they might be saved in 'a cheap and easy way, without being willing to part with their sins'. Of course it was no surprise to find these falling away after a time. Despite

7. ibid., 11/06/1874, p. 136.

8. ibid.

this, the minister, believed, 'a large proportion of the whole did profess to accept the Saviour'.[9]

Macadam noted further that there was, among some converts, a lack of 'constant Christian instruction and supervision'. This was particularly noticeable among the mining population in districts some distance from church. 'Many who made a profession have been entangled in the tide of abounding iniquity around them.' Nevertheless, at a later Communion near the start of 1875, the minister noted, 'Fully every fourth face was that of a recent convert. On a very sober estimate, nearly one-third of those who sat at the Lord's table had professed Christ within the year.'[10]

Outreach was extended to a village two miles distant, 'where, in proportion to its size', noted Macadam, 'there have been remarkable fruits. At present, in another village, there are numbers of new inquirers at every meeting, and every prospect of the blessed work still going on.' In all, three hundred people under soul concern were spoken to, while 'among the most careless men working in some of the neighbouring pits there is not a little awe, and in many cases outward reformation, though they have not been brought to the Lord'. Professed converts were noted for being of 'most satisfying character' as well as for their 'teachableness and modesty'.[11]

Bargeddie and Ballieston

The village of Bargeddie was one of many mining villages near Coatbridge, in the parish of Old Monkland. The indulgence of strong drink was greatly aggravated owing to a recent general rise in wages. Accordingly Christians were summoned to increased concern, and, noted one, 'much public and secret prayer went up to heaven for a

9. ibid., 25/02/1875, p. 729.

10. ibid.

11. Macadam, who furnished the report on the Chryston movement, noted that 'humanly speaking, the great strength of it has been the fact of the awakening here about 1860 under Mr Burnet, now of Huntly (see pp. 96-7). There are many in the district, whose consistency and Christian character no one can impeach .... My own congregation, who had received such a blessing at that time, were almost as one man eager for such a time returning; for it is a noticeable thing that congregations that have once been visited with such a movement are always ready to welcome another' (*TB*, 14/05/1874, pp. 68-9).

blessing on our moral wilderness'. Open-air meetings were arranged, which led to 'a conversion now and again, like a flower in the desert'. Then, as the sacrament of the Lord's Supper drew near, the interest in spiritual matters deepened – 'the drops began to take the form of a shower. It rained at last.' Since then many striking conversions took place, while, 'the ordinary channels of usefulness have also been flooded'. In nearby Ballieston, too, a good work was done, and many anxious souls filed from open-air services to after-meetings in the 'iron church' at Swinton.[12] Of Coatbridge itself it was claimed that 'never, we think, in the annals of Christian work in this town has there been so great a movement'.[13]

Shotts

A native of Ayrshire, Robert Gilchrist quickly discovered his evangelistic gifting following his conversion, and laboured for some time with the Glasgow City Mission. He also established a mission under the supervision of East Gorbals Church, which was so successful that it was sanctioned as a congregation, with Gilchrist its first pastor. Ordained as minister in Shotts Free Church in 1861, Gilchrist rejoiced at the news of Moody and Sankey's signal success in Edinburgh and Glasgow in the winter of 1873–74. A preacher of more than ordinary power, at once the Shotts pastor sought the extension of that great work of grace in his own district. One means was the publishing of a number of gospel tracts, some of which made reference to the revival in progress in the district. According to Gilchrist: 'There was an unusual influence accompanying the word of God read and preached, which took hold of the hearts of the people and drew their attention to the great concern. The word of God was a living instrument in the hands of the preacher.'[14]

---

12. ibid., 27/08/1874, p. 316; 24/09/1874, p. 177.

13. ibid., 01/10/1874, p. 388.

14. Robert Gilchrist, *The Life-Story of Hugh Morton, Newmilns: A Worker for Christ*, Ardrossan, n.d., p. 152. Gilchrist spoke of being on the isle of Arran in the autumn of 1874, with friends from Newmilns and Galston. All three of these men had recently experienced touches of revival in their home districts, so it is no surprise that they were, in the words of Gilchrist, 'a very congenial company. Sankey's hymns were sung, and the salvation of souls was the theme of conversation. Mr Morton was just in his element …' (ibid., p. 153).

Many young men and women were caught in the tide of the local revival that ensued, a number of whom became zealous workers in the Lord's vineyard both at home and abroad. Among these were Andrew Thomson Miller (later minister in Dunfermline, and Clerk to the Presbytery of Dunfermline and Kinross), Dundas Erskine (who left Scotland in 1886 as a missionary to South Africa, where he laboured for the following twenty-five years) and Samuel Mathers (a worker with the Glasgow City Mission, then minister at Greengairs, before his early death soon after). Such was the success of the revival in Shotts that it necessitated the erection of a new church, which handsome eight-hundred-seat structure was opened in 1878 by Andrew Bonar.[15]

Dumbarton

Meanwhile, the Rev. C. White of Overtoun, just north of Dumbarton, said that 'Showers of blessing' had descended upon Dunbartonshire, not in connection with the visit of Messrs. Moody and Sankey, but prior to their visit. Thus, when the Americans arrived, 'they saw that the Spirit of God had been working there'. White's own Bible class, he believed, had yielded at least thirty converts.[16]

Inverkip and Paisley

John McNeill was a nineteen-year-old railway servant living in Inverkip, on the Renfrewshire coast, when Moody was preaching in Edinburgh and Glasgow. He wrote: 'Quiet little village, quiet little Free Kirk; worship of the quiet stereotyped sort. No frills, certainly not. When suddenly there's a stir! Our minister (the Rev. Peter Douglas) has been to Edinburgh; he has heard a preacher, an American called Moody, and a singer called Sankey, and according to him Edinburgh's on fire! There's a revival on – whatever that may mean. The sough of it is on our minister's breath, his prayers and his preaching. We young folks begin to talk to each other, quietly, about the deepest things; we begin to seek, and we find.' The minister called a 'testimony meeting, on a Sunday night; unheard of thing in our wee quiet village. Folks mightily stirred; gathered round the doors.' McNeill and two other lads got up

---

15. J. M. Dewar, *After Sixty Years: A Historical Sketch of the Free (now United Free) Church in Shotts*, Shotts, 1911, pp. 32, 38, 76-86.

16. *TB*, 04/06/1874, p. 126.

in turn. 'They hammer and they stammer, but they're out with it. They have taken Christ to be their Saviour, and mean henceforth to live for Him.' All three remained sturdy Christians. John McNeill in particular became one of Scotland's most prominent evangelists of his time. His early success, interestingly, was achieved in tandem with Moody during the American's third British tour, though he later preached in many locations across the world.[17]

Meanwhile, the spiritual impression produced in Paisley in the spring and early summer of 1874 was said to have been 'very profound'. This was especially true in regard to the young. Boys' prayer meetings spontaneously arose in both the town's principal schools. In one, as many as thirty-six boys met twice a week for prayer and the reading of Scriptures.[18]

The South – Ayrshire

Maybole and Dalmellington

Parish minister, Roderick Lawson, led the movement in Maybole, Ayrshire, although all the churches united in the work, for it was believed that this ''not only swelled the numbers but disarmed the opposition'. The village was said to have been as stirred as anywhere else in Ayrshire, despite little help being received from outwith the immediate locality. On a single Sunday, one preacher had to address no fewer than ten meetings. Out of this time of awakening came *The Maybole Evangelist*, a weekly tract founded by local banker and lay-evangelist William Shaw, and distributed throughout the area.[19] An August edition of the tract reported an increased interest in the various evangelistic meetings which were held three or four times per week. It also referred to a converts' meeting the same week, which drew over

17. Pollock, pp. 128-9. Strangely, Gammie's biography of McNeill, while recounting the story of his conversion, makes absolutely no reference to the influence of Moody or to the spiritual movement which took place in Inverkip at that time (Gammie, 1933, pp. 34-9).

18. *TB*, 14/05/1874; 02/07/1874, quoted in Sprange, pp. 317-18.

19. In 1877 Shaw and others formed a Brethren Assembly in the town. Shaw went on to become a prominent Brethren member, founding and editing two further magazines (Hugh Douglas, *Roderick Lawson of Maybole: A Remarkable Victorian Minister*, Ayrshire, 1978).

one hundred and twenty people. Further south in Ayrshire, the area around Girvan was stirred, especially when a great conference was held in Littleton barn near the village, where Patrick Riddel, a Borders wrestler-turned-evangelist, spoke.

John Ritchie was converted in 1871 in Inverurie, Aberdeenshire, at the age of eleven under the ministry of Brethren evangelist, Donald Ross. 'His avidity for the Word of God, his wonderfully retentive memory, his fluent and flaming appeals to the consciences of his hearers, his indomitable zeal in the service of his Master', all combined to mark him out as a worthy evangelist and soon he gave himself entirely to the Lord's work. The year 1874 found him in Dalmellington, Ayrshire, where he engaged in house-to-house visitation and open-air campaigns as well as regular indoor meetings. Soon he was 'in the midst of a gracious work of God'. After Ritchie got married in Kirriemuir in 1877, the newly-weds set up their first home in this Ayrshire village, where 'over sixty young believers required his care'.[20]

Newmilns and Galston

Several weaving communities in North Ayrshire were touched by revival breezes at this time, all of them having been severely affected by a hand-loom weavers' strike some months previously. From Newmilns, weaver and local United Presbyterian Church elder, Hugh Morton, wrote: 'We have had a shower of revival influence here for the last few weeks, and I am glad to say that a good many give evidence of a change of heart and life. Since I remember, we have never had such an outpouring of the Spirit of God.'[21] The human instruments responsible for the movement were evangelists Murray and Cameron, who came to Newmilns for two weeks but ended up staying more than twice that long, before one transferred to Darvel and the other to Galston, located just a mile west of Newmilns, in each of which location a promising work also commenced.

Galston in fact enjoyed 'a large spiritual blessing' from the spring of 1874, which, almost a year later, had still not abated. An earnest worker in the movement provided the details: 'Our Wednesday work consists of cottage prayer-meetings, fourteen of which are carried on

---

20. Pickering, pp. 307-10; *TB*, 13/08/1874.

21. Robert Gilchrist, *The Life-Story of Hugh Morton, Newmilns*, Ardrossan, 1895, p. 151.

in the town, besides others in surrounding villages, the attendance in the aggregate being over 300.' At one small colliery hamlet great earnestness was apparent. The people had been in general careless, many of them 'improvident and dissipated'. But many of these were now regular attendants at the daily worship, a few had publicly professed to 'belong to Christ' and in several of the houses prayer meetings were regularly held. Ninety, young and old, were present at one of these. Latterly a 'remarkable feature of the movement' was the 'great work amongst the children'. Three hundred met regularly, not a few of whom were able to give 'good reason for their faith in the lamb slain'.[22]

Dumfriesshire

Lockerbie was another town not visited by Moody where a decided movement of spiritual quickening occurred, as it did also in Moffat, to the north. The Scottish Evangelistic Society reported that in Biggar (situated on the border of South Lanarkshire), 'a great work of God' took place during 1874. The movement here continued into the following year, when in February united meetings led by John Colville and D. Cameron were 'greatly blessed'.[23] Meanwhile, in Ecclefechan, just south of Lockerbie, the United Presbyterian congregation also witnessed awakening at this time.[24]

In the Dumfries neighbourhood, 'much prayer, labour and expectation on the part of the Lord's people' was carried on after hearing of the marked revival blessing in Edinburgh and Glasgow under Moody and Sankey. When evangelists John M. Scroggie and W. D. Dunn came to hold open-air services in the early autumn of 1874, many who had been working for years in Dumfries could say, 'Seldom have our hearts been more filled with thankfulness to God than they have been at these street gatherings. ... A large number of young men and women, and little children too, are taking their stand on the Lord's side', and it was believed that 'hundreds are being savingly converted to God'.[25]

The Rev. Kenneth Moody Stuart – son of Alexander Moody Stuart, and author of his biography as well as that of Brownlow North –

---

22. *TB*, 24/12/1874, p. 589; 18/02/1875, p. 717.

23. *TB*, 14/01/1875, p. 633; Colville, p. 205.

24. Proceedings of the UPC Synod Appendix, 1874, pp. 198-9; 1875, pp. 814-15.

25. *TB*, 30/04/1874, p. 38; 24/09/1874, p. 374.

claimed that 'in most of the small towns in Annandale there has been an awakening, now in one locality, now in another' during the first seven months of 1874. Nevertheless, he also admitted that he could not report 'that the community as a whole has in this district been moved as in some other places, or even that the Lord's people have been generally stirred up to prayer and effort'.[26]

The Border Counties

In the summer of 1874, 'religious services' were held on a grassy holm at the confluence of the rivers Whiteadder and Blackadder, near Chirnside. The place was historical as well as beautiful, being near the spot called East Nisbet, where, almost exactly two hundred years previously (1677), the Covenanters observed one of their largest Communions.[27] The evening was very fine, and the attendance numerous – there being about one thousand persons present. In Chirnside, itself, considerable interest developed, while the weekly union prayer meeting in the neighbouring village of Allanton increased to three times the former average attendance.

A blind evangelist by the name of Turnbull held a series of meetings in Hawick in the autumn of 1874. He was said to have been 'utterly devoid of all clap-trap and sensationalism', his forte evidently being his clarity in enunciating the truths of Christ, and pointing out the way of salvation. Sometimes as many as four or five hundred remained to the anxious meetings, of whom about one-half were either enquiring further as to the way of life, or had already come to 'a knowledge of the truth' through the former services.[28]

Fife

It is recorded that a decided spiritual movement occurred among a number of congregations in Fife during 1873–74.[29] Ministers and laymen came from Edinburgh, Dundee and elsewhere to Kirkcaldy's west end; visitors 'who, coming from the bosom of the work in those

---

26. ibid., 20/08/1874, p. 295.

27. For more on East Nisbet, and the widespread spiritual movement across Scotland during these momentous times, see my *Land of Many Revivals*, pp. 63-89.

28. *TB*, 03/12/1874, p. 542.

29. Findlay, pp. 155-6.

places, brought with them a heavenly aroma, most refreshing to the people'.[30] Much apparent fruit resulted, not least when the Earl of Cavan came to speak, numbers being converted through his instrumentality. A special work of grace was done among the young. So many were the anxious that sometimes they could only be spoken to in groups. In a young women's Bible class, at least seventy were awakened and many of these were soon after brought to Christ. Similar meetings were held in the east end of town; these were similarly blessed, and through a variety of means, many souls were led into new life.

Considerable attention was awakened in the Fife coastal village of Elie, on hearing of two young men from that locality who had gone to reside in Edinburgh, where they had come under influence of the gospel during Moody and Sankey's visit. Both men were converted shortly after the Americans left the city for Glasgow. 'But the blessing came at last in an unexpected way', when the Grand Lodge of the Freemasons in Elie decreed that the week beginning 8 March was to be 'a week of prayer for the advancement of the objects which they have in view'. The Elie and Earlsferry Lodge decided that the best way to make men sober was to make them Christians, so resolved that the meetings should be wholly evangelistic. The management of them fell into the hands of the chaplain – and he happened to be the minister of the Free Church! The meetings went on for four weeks, after which, with many being in deep anxiety for the salvation of their souls, the workers endeavoured 'to carry home the sheaves'.[31]

Cellardyke

In Cellardyke believers commenced a prayer meeting during the last week of 1873. The first converts were all female so they prayed fervently for the young men of the district, and in a short time, over fifty – nearly all fishermen – had confessed Christ. Special prayer was next made for mothers, then fathers, and then the elderly, each with remarkable results. Prayer meetings were also held on the boats at sea, while onshore every house in the district was visited.[32] Meetings continued nightly for over five months, often with an attendance of from three hundred to four hundred.

---

30. *TB*, 21/05/1874, p. 83.

31. ibid., 18/04/1874, pp. 13-14.

32. John MacPherson, *Revival and Revival Work: A Record of the Labours of D. L. Moody & Ira D. Sankey, and Other Evangelists*, London, 1876, pp. 105-8; FCSRSRM, 1876, p. 5.

Latterly, boats were at sea for the first three or four days of the week, but it could be said that on weekend evenings, when everyone was on shore, the meetings were as large as ever. On Saturday nights, following devotional exercises, the meetings were thrown open to the simple and modest testimony of the young fisherman, five minutes only being allowed to each speaker, with hymns sung at intervals. A further striking feature of the work was noted as being the gathering of from twenty to forty young children for religious instruction every night for nearly six months, this meeting being conducted by two of the Sabbath-school teachers.

Perthshire

Perth

In conjunction with Moody and Sankey's week-long mission in Perth at the start of June 1874, Professor Martin arrived and began a good work among the youth of the town. As a result, Mrs Stewart Sandeman (wife of the late missionary/evangelist, David Sandeman) had cause to believe that 'a great blessing' had descended among the young. At her own meetings several 'new bright faces – big boys, fourteen to sixteen or so – appeared'. One pupil from Sharpe's School was converted in Glasgow. On her return home she was believed to have been the means of leading thirty other girls to Christ.[33]

Crieff and Comrie

A deputation from the Edinburgh Young Men's Committee went to Crieff, where it was deemed advantageous to hold separate meetings for young men and young women. In each case, 'a number that surprised all present' came forward as professing Christ and were spoken to as a company. Said the Rev. Henderson, 'It is only possible to rejoice with trembling.' From here, 'bands of willing workers' moved out to neighbouring villages such as Muthill, Monzie and Trinity-Gask, and in each place jewels were 'won for the Master's crown'. The work in Comrie seemed initially confined almost entirely to young women. Accordingly, a special effort was made to reach the opposite sex by holding a men's meeting. Here, 'the Holy Spirit's presence seemed manifested in a most overpowering measure, there being a rapt stillness over the audience, and not a few being melted to tears'. Further south,

---

33. M. Barbour, pp. 222-3.

it was said of Callander that 'although the blessing has not visited us like a shower, we have had a continual dropping'.[34]

Strathtay

Alexander MacRae opined that generally, the movement of 1874–75 'touched Perthshire but lightly', though he gives evidence of widespread influence in the locality of Strathtay, following the 'long lonely cry for that place' from God's faithful.[35] A correspondent for the *Times of Blessing* recorded: 'During the past seven months a mighty movement of grace has been experienced throughout the valley of Strathtay.' Remarkably, it was granted that evangelistic meetings be held in the chapel of Grandtully Castle, 'until recently a place of Popish worship. ... This object was long and anxiously prayed for, and when seemingly insurmountable difficulties appeared, the Lord in His own way removed them all.' At the second service held there, about an hour before the time of meeting, the chapel was filled, and crowds of earnest worshippers were gathering towards it from every point. A relocation became necessary, and choir and congregation marched as a body to a nearby church. Said one who witnessed the thrilling scenes, 'It was a grand sight, on a lovely Sabbath evening, to see such a body of people intent upon the things of eternity, and to hear the hill-side re-echo to the lively strains of "Hold the Fort", as the great congregation moved to the place of adjournment.' A deep spirit of solemnity prevailed, and not a few, in whose memories the days of Robert Findlater, John McDonald and William Chalmers Burns were still fragrant, were heard to say, 'We never saw such a day in Grandtully.'[36]

Auchterarder

The awakening in Auchterarder, in south Perthshire, was closely con-nected with the Week of Prayer – meetings in which all three churches in town participated. But several converts told their minister, the Rev. Milne, that they had been awakened the previous autumn (before Moody and

---

34. *TB*, 18/04/1874, pp. 14-15; 04/06/1874, p. 119; 07/05/1874, p. 55.

35. MacRae, 1906, p. 122; M. Barbour, p. 223.

36. *TB*, 20/08/1874, p. 302. Given the outstanding blessing attending the minis-tries of each of these three men of God, this seems an astonishing statement. Another record has it that 'several of the older people made the remark that there had never been such a meeting at Grandtully since the days of William Burns, whose labours, 35 years ago, were greatly blessed in that locality' (ibid.).

Sankey's arrival in Scotland). It was at this earlier date also that attempts were made to hold a series of meetings, but neither preachers nor suitable accommodation could be got. Milne opined that God was 'secretly preparing a blessing while he seemed to be shutting the door ... when His time had come, we not only got the use of the Aytoun Hall for the meetings, but ministers and honoured Christian laymen came to our help in ways altogether unexpected. The mountains, before which in autumn we had turned back discouraged, now bowed at the presence of the Lord.' Among the many souls hopefully converted was a young woman awakened in 1867, during a season of spiritual quickening, who now suddenly found peace after words quoted to her in connection with some lines of a Sankey hymn. The work was almost entirely confined to churchgoing people, and to those who had been instructed in Sabbath school and Bible classes. Concluded Milne, 'the people say a fire has been kindled in the parish which will burn to generations following'.[37]

Logierait and Blair Atholl

Whole households were among those that passed from darkness into light in Logierait. Further north, the Rev. D. Shaw of Kingussie reported: 'There is most manifestly a gracious work of God at present at Blair Atholl, as well as at Pitlochry and other places around', following the visit of two evangelists. When Shaw requested to speak to the young Christians after a service in the former village, 'almost the whole of the awakened remained. They were in five or six groups here and there through the church ... their minds seemed opened to the truth, and the eyes of some of the dear lads and girls were beaming with joy at having found Christ as a Saviour from sin and wrath'.[38]

Clackmannanshire

At Clackmannan, the United Presbyterian minister was amazed that for nearly thirty nights in succession, in a small country town previously most indifferent to spiritual things, there should be 'many deeply impressed, and in tears; some who would not go away till they saw their way to a joyful resting in the Lord'.[39]

---

37. ibid., 7/05/1874, pp. 61-2.
38. ibid., 28/05/1874, p. 102.
39. Proceedings of the UPC Synod Appendix, 1874, pp. 198-9; 1875, pp. 814-15.

In Dollar, a parish whose total population was less than 2,500, an average of eight hundred people, and on weekends over 1,200, attended the nightly meetings held in a large hall. Said the Rev. G. H. Knight, 'There never was such a time of blessing in Dollar before. ... The movement took a deep hold of the boys and girls attending the academy; and at a closing meeting for those alone who professed to have accepted Christ and His salvation during the three weeks of our meetings, more than 180 gathered together confessing their Saviour.' Because of such numbers, there was considerably less scoffing from school-peers than might otherwise have been the case. The children commenced their own prayer meetings, and Knight, who dropped in on one, 'felt it exceedingly interesting to hear their simple, artless prayers for their companions still unsaved, and for themselves that they might be all kept steadfast and grow Christ-like.' But the blessing was not confined to the young, and 'in some households nearly every member ... professed a saving change'.[40]

Aberdeenshire

Natural Progression

A correspondent for the *Times of Blessing* (a weekly journal begun in early 1874, to provide detailed accounts of the progression of the religious movement ongoing in the country), thoroughly cognisant of the geography of Banffshire and Aberdeenshire, noted how revival spread through these counties along the routes of its natural waterways. 'Commencing at Portsoy, on the Moray Firth, not far from the mouth of the Deveron, and moving inland, nearly along its source', he stated, one arrives at, in turn, Portsoy, Cornhill, Marnoch, and Rothiemay.[41] (Another writer noted, however, that the revival began in inland parishes, appearing first in Marnoch, then at Drumblade, then at Rothiemay, then at Cornhill, from where it spread north towards the Banffshire coast, 'the interest deepening all along'.[42])

Following then, the course of the river Bogie upwards from its entrance into the Deveron, you come to Rothiemay, Drumblade, Gartly and eastward to Culsalmond (near the source of the Ury).

---

40. *TB*, 18/04/1874, p. 14.

41. ibid., 09/07/1874, p. 199.

42. ibid., 07/05/1874, p. 54.

Then following from Gartly southward (along the source of the Bogie), you reach Kennethmont, Premnay, Oyne, Garioch, Oldmeldrum and Inverurie. By this point one is on the banks of the Don, just fifteen miles from Aberdeen. This, the correspondent suggested, was a similar course to that which the revival in inland Aberdeenshire took. 'And thus in thirteen contiguous parishes, which, following the course indicated above, extend at least fifty miles in length by many in breadth along the banks of these rivers, the God of our salvation has been graciously sending streams of blessing from that river of life the streams whereof make glad the city of our God.'[43]

The movement in this region seems to have had its beginnings well prior to Moody and Sankey's visit to Scotland. Rev. James Murker of Banff could testify that during 1873, 'The Lord has enabled me to preach and conduct meetings in upwards of fifty parishes in the counties of Aberdeen and Banff, and in connection with them I have conversed personally with about 4,000, all in the hard struggle of seeking salvation.'[44]

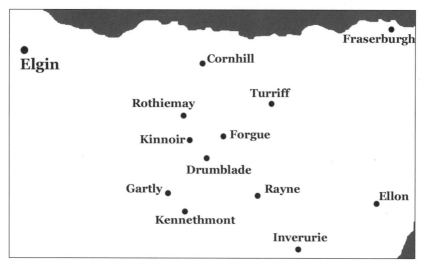

Drumblade and Kinnoir

In Drumblade parish, newly instated prayer meetings at first attracted only seven or eight. Those present at the noonday meetings in Edinburgh during Moody's campaign there often, by request, bore Drumblade on their hearts in prayer. In addition, the Free Church

43. ibid., 09/07/1874, p. 199.

44. Stark, p. 94.

minister invited the young folk in the congregation to tea at his house; some fifty responded and that night saw the first convert. 'The sight of one or two other friends weeping and seeking the Saviour' made a deep impression on the others, and a fortnight later, when an all-day meeting was held on the Sabbath, the church was thronged. The preaching of the minister had also become 'peculiarly solemn and urgent'. By now the blessing had come in showers. 'Anxious ones, by forties and fifties, would remain night after night. For four weeks the church was crowded by eager and solemnised audiences; and many were ready to stand up in the meeting to request that they might be prayed for, and many also, equally publicly, to give thanks for peace found in believing.'[45]

After a few weeks as many as four hundred were gathering together for prayer. With only a few exceptions, all the young men and women of the congregation were among those who professed to have obtained mercy. One night, prayer was offered for four unbelieving young men, well known in the congregation for their utter indifference to the interests of the soul. Within three days all four were seen standing up and bearing joyful testimony to the grace of God. Meanwhile, a different group of 'four young men were found at midnight on the highway wrestling with God in prayer for one another, all of them in the lowest depths of soul-trouble. ... A passer-by, hearing the sounds of an agony, which, happily, he can understand, stops his horse. They request him to come and pray with them, for their distress is great, almost past endurance. Cheerfully complying with their request he steps down from his gig to offer the prayer of faith with them and for them ... in due course of the divine mercy and purpose, as it would seem, the four young men passed from the bondage of sin into the glorious liberty of the sons of God.'[46]

Over forty children's conversions were recorded. It was often through these that their parents also surrendered to Christ. 'Oh, father, just trust Him!' said a little believing boy of twelve to his father, who had returned from a meeting in a state of such anxiety that he could not conceal it from his family. Curiously enough, what all the teachings, counsels and prayers of ministers and others in the inquiry room had

---

45. *TB*, 25/04/1874, p. 26.
46. Macpherson, 1876, p. 114-15.

failed to accomplish, was effected by the words of the child. The father was enabled to put his trust in Christ, and soon he and his family were rejoicing in the Lord. Some two hundred people in total professed faith as a result of the revival in Drumblade. Of these, twenty had been members of the church, five of whom were deacons. After eighteen months nearly all professions were said to be still holding fast.

Kinnoir, an outlying part of the parish of Huntly, is bounded on two sides by Drumblade and Rothiemay, both of which were richly blessed in the spring of 1874. This led to much prayer and expectation by the faithful in Kinnoir, and special meetings were commenced in the wooden church erected in the days of the Duchess of Gordon. These went on week after week for four weeks, being abandoned mainly because of the approach of the harvest. It was said, 'There has not been a night since the Tuesday of the first week in which we have not had as much work as we could overtake among the anxious.' As a result believers were said to have been 'very much refreshed and the whole district has been stirred'.[47] Also close to Huntly, the Rev. Wishart of Forgue told of a great movement among the people of his congregation and district. A large church, seating seven hundred or eight hundred, was filled night after night for weeks, people coming as far as six or seven miles to be present.

Cornhill

The Rev. George Macdonald was only inducted to the Banffshire parish of Ordiquhill and Ord at the start of 1874 but, thanks to the wave of blessing spreading over the country during this period, was honoured to see, remarkably, about one hundred people gathered in, by their own profession, in the first three and a half months of his ministry. By this time the ordinary congregational prayer meeting was attracting near to three hundred, which in a country district was in Macdonald's eyes clear evidence of 'widespread and lively interest in divine things'.[48]

One tiny village within the parish was particularly blessed. The rural hamlet of Cornhill was the scene of a 'remarkable work of grace', which 'threw its hallowed influence' over portions of seven or eight surrounding parishes. The awakening was almost entirely confined to the Free Church. Seating five hundred people, the church sanctuary was soon filled on

---

47. *TB*, 17/09/1874, p. 359.
48. *TB*, 25/04/1874, p. 26.

weeknights. On some occasions as many as seventy or eighty, in deep distress of spirit, remained for conversation. One night the session-house, a room capable of accommodating sixty, was filled with inquirers twice over. 'It was touching to see', noted Macdonald, 'so many on their knees, prostrate at the mercy-seat, sending up piercing cries for salvation. ... Over two hundred in anxiety were conversed with.'[49]

The work of grace was most notable among the better-educated and in 'godly families', especially those of elders and deacons. A 'remarkable blessing' fell on the young men, some forty of whom instituted a prayer meeting for themselves, almost the entire band taking a judicious and edifying part in the exercises.[50] In some cases the blessing enjoyed by the children produced the deepest anxiety in their parents. One young convert passed away shortly after, his consistent life and triumphant death leaving a fragrant memory and making a deep impression.

To the north-west of Cornhill parish, 'anxious that they should not be passed over when showers of mercy were falling so plenteously' over surrounding districts, believers of Fordyce waited on God, and in time they too, received blessing.[51]

Rothiemay and Turriff

The Rev. Dr MacPhail said that following the visit of Moody to the region, Rothiemay, was 'greatly blessed with aftermaths of grace, and very many were added to the Lord'.[52]

Meanwhile, it was repeatedly remarked of Turriff, to the east of Marnoch, that the place was 'proof against such innovations as revivals', especially when no great result had been obtained from the hard-wrought efforts of Duncan Matheson and other zealous evangelists in days past. However, by the autumn of 1874 blessing had descended. In particular, there was reported 'a decided movement among the young' and at special meetings for them, the interest manifested by the children was described as 'something remarkable'.[53]

---

49. ibid., pp. 109-11.

50. ibid., pp. 110-12.

51. ibid., 12/11/1874, p. 490; Matthews, p. 14.

52. ibid.

53. *TB*, 19/11/1874, p. 504.

Gartly and Kennethmont

The Rev. Hugh McIntosh of Gartly reported in the summer of 1874: 'By the blessing of the Lord upon the labours of a succession of able and devoted men of God, a deep religious spirit had for long dwelt among these quiet glens. Besides, about eighteen months ago, there was a real and deep but quiet work among us, which every week for three or four months brought inquirers to the manse, and which added about thirty members to the church.' Special meetings were commenced with news of revival blessing in the south of Scotland.

> The way in which they remained was remarkable. After the first meeting, all left the church, except three or four. Having spoken to them for about fifteen minutes, we looked round and saw the door open, and a number of anxious faces looking in. Thinking that they were perhaps more curious than anxious, I went hurriedly to the door, and in an abrupt, stern tone, said, 'If you wish to come, you had better do it at once; if not, I am to shut the door.' Scarcely were the words spoken when about thirty of them, mostly young people from twelve to 25 years, poured into the church and such a scene of weeping followed as I have seldom or never witnessed – it was indeed a Bochim. The work was now begun in earnest. The tidings quickly spread.

Many notable incidents followed, including that of seven girls from the female school nearby taking advantage of the short interval between school hours to come to the manse to get a word about their souls and to request that thanks be given to God in the meeting of that evening, for having given them to Christ, as their own Saviour.[54]

In less than a month, 250 anxious enquirers were brought to light, which McIntosh considered to be around a third of the population of the parish, (which totalled 970) excluding the sick and infants. Of these 250, around 180 had made a profession of faith, the majority of whom were men. Indeed, at the meetings, the proportion of men to women had been about seven to one. Being a widely scattered parish, most meetings, except on Sabbaths, were held in barns and granaries throughout the district. 'And in these', recalled one worker, 'with audiences varying from 80 to 150, we had some of our most precious and productive meetings.' There was said to have been not a single farm

---

54. ibid., 09/07/1874, p. 198.

for six miles along in which there were not some who had professed, and among them, many entire families. There were just seven farms in the whole parish of fourteen miles in which there had been no one that professed. In some instances men would walk, after a hard day's labour, some four or six miles to the meeting. Testimony was also born to the quietness of the work, which the minister could not explain other than by saying that it was 'God's work'.[55]

McIntosh considered that perhaps the best proof of the genuineness of the work was afforded on the evening of the Huntly feeing market, when many were wont to go to great excesses. On that evening, the meeting, which was held in a small corner of the parish far up among the hills, was as crowded as usual with about eighty to one hundred people, made up mainly of young men and women who had left the market several hours sooner than usual in order to be present at the meeting.

The Rev. John Coutts of Kennethmont Free Church reported 'a sudden, remarkable and greatly increased readiness to hear the word and to assemble for prayer among themselves' on the part of the people of his district. In one place, the attendance at a meeting held on Sabbath evenings rose almost at a bound from fifty to 150 or two hundred. Rejoiced Coutts, 'A class of forty or fifty young people meets weekly with the minister for Bible reading, and almost all of them profess to know the Lord.'[56]

Rayne, Garioch and Inverurie

During the six months that William Robertson Nicoll spent as assistant minister at Rayne in 1874, he found 'spiritual interest strangely quickened all through the countryside. The scattered population gathered eagerly to special evangelistic services, while enduring results were produced in numbers of human lives.' The Rev. George Bain of Chapel of Garioch, close to Rayne, who had witnessed dramatic revival in his parish fourteen years previously (see Chapter 11), referred to 'meetings which had been held in his district, and to the fact of many anxious ones having been conversed with'.[57] In Inverurie also, 'A season of special blessing' took place. In particular, 'signs of spiritual quickening' appeared among the

---

55. ibid., 07/05/1874, p. 54.

56. ibid., 25/04/1874, pp. 26-7.

57. Darlow, p. 27-8.

Free Church congregation around this time, manifesting themselves 'in larger attendance at public worship and in greater liberality'.[58]

Coastal Aberdeenshire

Aberdeen

In the city of Aberdeen the moving of the Holy Spirit preceded the arrival of Moody and Sankey (14 June) by several months. A week of children's meetings in February attracted eight hundred nightly, while meetings led by Mr Daniels of the Scottish Evangelistic Society drew as many as 1,500 on some occasions. Altogether, they had dealt personally with two thousand anxious souls. Meanwhile, at the end of March came news of a 'remarkable work of grace that has broken out in one of our large industrial schools here. About a fortnight ago, after an address on Sabbath afternoon, out of about 270 boys, 170 held up their hands as wishing to give themselves to Christ, and among about sixty girls, twenty were under deep concern, and these among the worst behaved in the school. Many have professed since, and the testimony of the teachers is that there has been a corresponding change in their conduct.' Major Ross of the Free Church reported that 'he had been greatly moved when one of his own children, of a very violent temper, was brought to Christ' at meetings for the young held every Saturday afternoon in Aberdeen. 'The change in the child's disposition was now most marked', he said.[59]

Moody's visit to the city attracted immense interest, with an estimated 21,000 attending an open-air meeting on the Links one fine June evening. Dozens of ministers from in and around Aberdeen were among the multitude who went to hear the American preacher.[60] Although the campaign brought great spiritual renewal to Aberdeen churches, it also created challenges for many ministers in the town.[61]

---

58. *TB*, 04/06/1874, p. 116; Crichton, p. 15.

59. *The Christian*, 05/03/1874, quoted in Sprange, p. 248; *TB*, 14/01/1875, p. 632; 04/06/1874, p. 125.

60. Clark, pp. 144-5. One of these was Clarence Chambers, pastor of Crown Terrace Baptist Church and father-to-be of renowned inspirational author, Oswald Chambers, who was born just a month after Moody's departure from the city.

61. Stirred with a collective desire for change, the Crown Terrace congregation began to criticise the style of its church services, and, in November 1876, called for

Footdee and Torry

Dr Alexander Spence, minister of St Clements Free Church in Footdee since the Disruption of 1843, mentioned, on the testimony of Mr Mackay, superintendent of the North-East Coast Mission, and of his own knowledge, that 'a remarkable movement' had been going on for some weeks at Footdee. No fewer than one hundred of the fishing population there had made a hopeful profession of faith in Christ within a few weeks, the majority being young men and women. Most, too, were the sons and daughters of praying parents. Interestingly, Spence also remarked on the fact that 'It is now five years since the last work of grace in Footdee' (i.e., 1869 – see pp. 453-4), as if that was a lamentable fact.[62]

The Rev. Innes of Torry, then a small fishing village across the River Dee from Aberdeen, reported that a band of praying people in his congregation had, ever since the last gracious work among them (1869), continued pleading for a fresh revival. When blessing attending Moody's efforts in southern Scotland became known to the people of Torry, they were stirred to more fervent waiting on God. The minister also introduced among the young the use of Sankey's hymns, expounding the gospel to them from the hymn-lyrics. 'The fruits of the movement', Innes noted, were to be seen in 'eighty who profess to have come to the Saviour', thirty of whom, he was hopeful, would partake of Communion the following Sabbath, half of these being heads of families.[63]

Gardenstown

In 1874 Jacob Primmer came to Gardenstown – a village of 'about seven hundred – nearly all fishermen and coopers' – to assist the parish minister, the Rev. James Cruden. At this time there was no Church of Scotland in the village; the congregation of Gardenstown and Crovie met for worship in a granary. Primmer encouraged the people to build a church, and with the help of the fishermen, a building to seat four hundred was completed within a year. On a Sunday evening this was

---

Chambers to resign his charge. He did so some months later (David MacCasland, *Oswald Chambers: Abandoned to God*, Nashville, 1993, pp. 21-4).

62. *TB*, 25/04/1874, p. 26.

63. ibid.

often filled to capacity. Further west, of the picturesque port of Portsoy, it was recorded, 'a good work is at present being done'.[64]

On becoming aware of the success of Moody and Sankey's mission in central Scotland, Primmer felt it would be beneficial to hold similar meetings in his own locality. He contacted the Rev. John Gilmour, Minister of the United Presbyterian Church, and found that he too was keen on such an effort. Thus it was that, despite some preliminary and concluding friction, meetings were conducted alternately in the meeting houses of the two churches. This resulted in 'a revival for more than a twelvemonth, during which time a large number decided to give their hearts to Christ, and become real Christians. There was also a remarkable revival amongst the children.' Said Primmer, 'It was a blessed work of grace, and I enjoyed it heartily.'[65]

The Rev. Gardner of New Deer told of what he had seen of the Lord's gracious work further east along the coast, in the townships of St Combs, Cairnbulg and Peterhead, mentioning that, one day sixteen people travelled from St Combs to Rathen, a distance of three miles, to converse with the minister there about their souls' salvation. A day or two afterwards, seven or eight people felt constrained, through spiritual distress, to seek similar counsel and prayer.[66]

Coastal Moray

Awakening along the Moray coast during this period was extensive. Occurring at the season when the Banff and Moray fishermen are all at home, the work of grace in Edinburgh roused a spirit of expectation among these sea-borne communities, which led to continued earnest prayer, until at last, 'The Lord Himself came in power to quicken His people, and to bring the unsaved into His kingdom.' As on former occasions with few exceptions – notably the commencement of the 1860 awakening – the absence of human instrumentality in the form of a visiting evangelist was noted. Indeed, older believers remarked that in 1874 the Lord came with 'greater power than at any of these former

---

64. ibid., 09/07/1874, p. 199.

65. Jacob Primmer, *Life of Jacob Primmer, Minister of the Church of Scotland*, Edinburgh, 1916, pp. 26-7.

66. *TB*, 25/04/1874, p. 27.

times of visitation (1860, 1862, 1864, 1871).'[67] The work was greatest in Buckie,[68] although on either side, at Portessie and Portgordon, the work of revival had begun and was apparently completed before any spiritual movement could be discerned in this more populous centre.

Buckie

Initially the meetings in Buckie were what could at best be described as 'successful. But the power from above was still wanting. These meetings had ceased, when the spirit of grace and supplication was poured out upon believers, and then the fire came down from heaven.' One Christian man, not a native of Buckie, who had known the town well for thirty years, and had spent his best days in it, said he had been praying for a movement like this for twenty years, and that the actual reality had far exceeded his highest expectations. Many of those who had determinedly opposed the work of grace in former years were now 'entirely subdued under the mighty power of God', and were the first to acknowledge their former spiritual blindness, 'and to tell what the Lord had done for them'.[69] As soon as the meetings became overcrowded, the different churches were opened, and the Free, Established and United Presbyterian churches were in succession occupied on different evenings. These meetings continued almost daily until the men left for the Lewis fishing grounds. All agreed in saying that, with exception of a very few occasions, when excitable human accompaniments of a work of the Spirit were attempted to be introduced, chiefly by strangers, the meetings were characterised by great solemnity and deep feeling.

---

67. The actual dates recorded in this study when revival spread through north-east fishing communities are 1860, 1863, 1866–67 and 1871.

68. *TB*, 21/05/1874, pp. 83-4. One wonders if this could possibly be the place referred to by Colonel Davidson of the Scottish Evangelistic Society, who records 'a very dead place in Banffshire, where, after a fortnight of meetings, a work of grace was effected, as large, in proportion, as the work in Edinburgh' (*TB*, 14/01/1875, p. 633).

69. *TB*, 21/05/1874, pp. 83-4. Rev. Ker of Deskford spoke of 'a partial movement' taking place in 1874 in 'the largest and most central village of the group' of villages along this coastline, presumably referring to Buckie. However, Ker believed, as he did of other revival movements that occurred in these locations after 1860 and up to this date, that 'the human elements were the most marked' and that emotionalism played a prominent role (*The Christian*, 17/06/1880, p. 7).

Revival also broke out among the Baptists of Lossiemouth sometime during the short ministry there of the Rev. G. Whittet between 1873 and 1876, when, according to George Yullie, 'the Church greatly increased in numbers'. This appears to have been the result of a campaign by an evangelist following Moody's visit to the north.[70]

Portgordon

It was in the autumn of 1874 that the people of Portgordon deemed as appropriate a great demonstration in the form of a march from the village to the Highland home of the Duke of Richmond at Gordon Castle, as a means of thanksgiving for his provision of free education to their children as well as for providing funds for a magnificent new harbour, recently completed. Early in the morning they set off, men and women at equal pace, and shoulder to shoulder, almost all waving flags over their heads. The mottos of most flags were of a religious nature – 'Rejoice in the Lord'; 'God is my Father'; 'Be Sober and Watch unto Prayer'; 'Temperance, Love and Unity'; 'Washed in the Blood of Christ'; 'Abstain From the Appearance of Evil'; 'Praise and Salvation'; etc. – revealing the depth to which Portgordon had immersed itself in pure evangelical spirituality over the past twenty years. The *Elgin Courant* made clear that their religious faith did not sour the people of Portgordon, 'which religion was never intended to do, for they enjoyed themselves to the full under the fluttering bunting that displayed their veneration and love of sacred things, but to inspire them with the feeling by no means common in villages of its class – that it is a shame for a fisherman to be seen going into a public house, and that a man's highest duty is to act well his part in his life, and to be fully prepared for what follows'.[71]

Inland Moray

But it wasn't only fishing communities that were affected by revival influences. The Rev. James Morrison of Urquhart, a parish to the east of Elgin, had the privilege of seeing for himself 'the marvellous work of grace' ongoing at Chryston, North Lanarkshire, as well as, during the same week, hearing Moody and Sankey minister in Glasgow.

---

70. Yuille, p. 98; Bebbington, 1988, p. 268.

71. *Elgin Courant*, quoted in McHardie, pp. 250-1.

'Impressions were made' on his own Moray congregation following his return north. Nightly meetings were held for several weeks, and 'so suddenly had the shower of blessing descended, and with such power was God's Spirit working, that often the first notice we had of persons being awakened was seeing them rise and follow those who professed faith in Christ. ... Our half-yearly communion followed so close upon the late time of blessing that we did not look for a large increase in our new communicants; yet we had 22.'[72] This, however, was well under a third of the actual total number who had recently professed faith.

Further south, a significant work of grace commenced in the Speyside village of Craigellachie, near Aberlour, in 1873, shortly after Brethren assemblies were formed there (see pp. 455-6). Wrote one of their number: 'The Lord has saved a few fine young men, and He is begun in the school. A few of the scholars, from ten years old to fourteen have got Jesus, and the school is in an uproar. It is only yet being made known round about.' Confirming this testimony a week later, a colleague wrote: 'Several young men are now praising God for the salvation of their precious souls; also a good many young boys and girls. It is really fine to hear them singing the hymns; how heartily they praise God; the most are very fine cases.'[73]

The Highlands

Twenty-one-year-old George Gordon Macleod, son of the Rev. Adam Gordon Macleod, Free Church minister of the Inverness-shire parish of Croy, was a student at New College, Edinburgh, at the time of Moody's celebrated visit to Scotland. Like a great many students of his time, he felt the influence of the evangelist's meetings. When he travelled north in the summer of 1874 he carried this influence with him. He instituted a series of evangelistic services which became the means of considerable good in the district. Before returning to Edinburgh in the autumn, many people had expressed their appreciation for his labours of love among them, a significant number testifying to a saving change in their characters through his instrumentality.[74]

---

72. *TB*, 04/06/1874, p. 116.

73. The Northern Assemblies, 01/06/1873, quoted in Sprange, pp. 332-3.

74. Rev. James Halliday, *Memoir of the Rev. George Gordon Macleod*, Edinburgh, 1886, p. 7.

A number of Christian men at Fort William, who had been quickened by reports of the work of the Spirit through Moody in the south, commenced cottage meetings, which grew over time. During some special meetings held in the Free Church, 'a goodly number' of young men and women professed faith in Christ. Meanwhile, in Lochaber, a Sabbath school was formed in a district in Morven where there had been none before. It was stated also that 'Evangelistic services are held in five places about this neighbourhood'.[75]

The tireless Rev. MacGreggor, long-standing Free Church minister in the Caithness parish of Canisbay, delighted to hear of the success of Moody and Sankey's efforts throughout Scotland, and was even more pleased to find that Moody was venturing as far north as Caithness. Ever diligent for gospel service, it was said that when MacGreggor 'ceased not to warn every one day and night with tears (in the most literal sense), the usual results followed'. A very encouraging thirty-five names were added to the Free Church roll in 1874 as a result of awakening in the parish following Moody's visit to Wick and Thurso. Interestingly, this was in fact the same number as was added to the congregation following the 1859–61 revival (see p. 41).[76]

---

75. Proceedings of the UPC Synod Appendix, 10/09/1874, p. 350.

76. FCSRSRM, 1884, p. 18; Baikie, pp. 57-8, 62. Such results were seen as all the more noteworthy given that Canisbay was one of the few northern districts scarcely affected by the Disruption. Few in the parish left the Established church – the minister being highly popular with his congregation. A still more notable revival than either the 1859-61 or the 1874 seasons of blessing was one that showered on Canisbay in 1886 (Lennie, 2009, pp. 50-3). One Caithness woman known for her remarkable piety in these days was Mrs William Ronaldson. So highly did she regard communal prayer that even on a particular night of terrific storm she made her way to the Noreland Farm prayer meeting, where, though alone, she said she enjoyed 'the best (meeting) I had for many a day'. Her biographer, Rev. Angus Mackay, tells the same or a similar story in regard to a prayer meeting held in a country school, which had begun to dwindle in numbers to such an extent that one night just one woman appeared, finding her way by means of a lantern. A few days later, a man who used to attend asked her who had turned up that night. 'God the Father was there, God the Son was there, God the Holy Spirit was there, and we had God's Word there too, and we had a great meeting'! This story passed round the community and people became ashamed of their non-attendance. They began coming again to the prayer meetings, and, notes Mackay, 'a true revival followed' (*Memoirs of a Caithness Worthy, Mrs. William Ronaldson, 1828-1919*, Inverness, 1920, pp. 38-9).

Of the general effects of the spiritual awakening that spread through parts of the Highlands at this time, one reporter wrote: 'Mr Moody's addresses melted the hearts of thousands while Mr Sankey's hymns have become as great favourites in the Highlands as they are in the south of Scotland. In the remote Highland glen you may hear the sound of hymn-singing; shepherds on the steep hill-sides sing Sankey's hymns while tending their sheep, errand boys whistle the tunes as they walk along the streets of the Highland towns, while in not a few of the lordly castles of the north the same hymns are often sung.' In one (unnamed) part of the Highlands the work was so great that the ministers and other workers were quite exhausted by their labours. Night after night the inquiry rooms were crowded, and by day a great many could be seen going to the manses to speak to the ministers about 'the one thing needful. All fear of man was laid aside. Even in shops and other public places the salvation of the soul was the principal topic of conversation.'[77]

A parish minister in an unspecified district in the north of Scotland wrote of the work of the Spirit in his locality: 'We have had many union prayer and evangelistic meetings; but the fruit of them was not seen in any after meetings, but has been discovered, so far as my own congregation is concerned, by personal visitation. What I find is, that many who perhaps before had some experience of saving truth have come under the power of a much more vital and gladdening faith; that the few who previously worked with me, do so much more zealously now; and that within my congregation some seven or eight seem to have got a new heart and a new hope, and are rejoicing in an accepted Christ.'[78]

In many towns, villages and rural districts, during the time of the Communion season held in Presbyterian churches towards the close of 1874, it was claimed, 'The number of applicants for admission to the Lord's Table was very large – one Free Church minister had sixty new communicants.' Additionally was it stated, 'In several northern towns daily noon prayer-meetings are held. … Young Men's Christian Associations, cottage meetings, Bible readings, prayer-meetings, evangelistic meetings, are being carried on with great vigour and success.'[79]

77. *TB*, 10/09/1874, p. 350.

78. ibid., 07/05/1874, p. 58.

79. ibid., 14/01/1875, p. 634.

Western Isles and Argyll

Lewis

Alexander MacRae records that 'In 1874, when Mr Moody's work was so greatly blessed on the mainland, the isles, especially Tiree and Lewis, were experiencing a gracious awakening.'[80] The Lewis reference apparently relates to Ness. From this parish a local source provides a more cautious estimate:

> Little or nothing is generally known (in Lewis) of the present movement (in mainland Scotland); and what is more, the vague idea which some have of it makes not a very favourable impression, or rather it makes an unfavourable impression, on the people.[81] Nevertheless, it seems to us that clouds fraught with blessing – a cloud it is true, not bigger than a man's hand – hover about the country. ... The people of God in this quarter, even in the face of very unfavourable circumstances, seem to be experiencing a reviving. The means of grace seem to be more than usually a source of refreshing to them.[82]

In regard to believers of north Lewis, the report continues:

> Their tone and conduct seem more charitable towards those with whom they had been at variance; they breathe a forgiving spirit towards their enemies, and a spirit of brotherly love towards one another. Their sympathies are extended to those that are without, while there is a manifest yearning over Christless friends and dear ones yet unsaved. Their hearts seem greatly enlarged in their intercessory prayers. The means of grace are multiplied; and not a few of the young as well as the aged seem to be interested in the proceedings. At the meetings there is a good attention given both by old and young, and an air of solemnity seems to pervade the whole assembly. Even in

---

80. MacRae, 1906, p. 14. This remark is also quoted by Couper (Roberts, 1995, p. 330). Couper adds that 'the only point of contact' between the movements in Tiree and Lewis and those on the mainland was 'that they were going on at the same time'. With regard to Tiree, at least, this isn't altogether accurate, as the revival here was almost certainly influenced by Moody's work on the Scottish mainland (see below).

81. Yet, clearly not all believers in Lewis were opposed to the Moody campaign. Mr A. Morison, an elder from Stornoway, was one of 2,500 people who attended a service conducted by Moody on the Links in Dornoch in August 1874 (*TB*, 03/09/1874, p. 332).

82. A Lewis correspondent to *Times of Blessing*, 04/02/1875, p. 683.

meetings where it was not customary to see any young people, a few slip in among their more aged friends, these being evidently anxious to hear what the Lord has to say. We hail these signs as so many raindrops, harbingers of a shower of blessing.[83]

Tiree

In Tiree, a work of grace commenced in the Baptist Chapel in Balemartin in August 1874, when Duncan Macfarlane spoke of what he had seen and heard at Moody's campaigns in both Glasgow and Elgin. During those visits, Macfarlane had requested that Moody come to Tiree to hold meetings. While Moody could not oblige, he challenged Macfarlane to preach God's love for sinners in a similar manner to his own. Macfarlane, it seems, readily accepted the challenge.

Meetings were held in Balemartin every night for three weeks, and, noted Alexander McNeil, a Free Church missionary and native of Tiree, 'The Lord poured out such a blessing on our labours that it might truly be said there was no room to receive it.' Macfarlane, astonished at developments, wrote to a colleague:

How very much I wish you were with us in Tyree these blessed days! The like of this awakening was never seen in Tyree. I thought I would never see anything like Moody's meetings, but the meetings here are fully equal to them in proportion to the number of the people. Fancy, on a busy harvest evening, Balemartin Chapel is filled at 5 o'clock, the hour of service being 7. In the meetings of inquirers there are from sixty to eighty who remain each night, anxious to be spoken to about their souls. Never home before 12. From 500 to 600 attend meetings every night. The doors and windows are left open, to let the people outside hear. The whole island is moved.[84]

---

83. ibid.; apart from this article, I have been unable to uncover any evidence of a general awakening on Lewis at this time. A comprehensive report compiled by two evangelistic deputies of the Free Church following an extensive tour of the island in 1873–74 made no mention of a revival. On the contrary, it concluded: 'There is nothing like general concern among the congregations at present, and although most of the ministers speak with hopefulness of individual cases coming occasionally under their notice, and some believe that a quickening influence has been for some time at work, there are frequent complaints of prevailing deadness' (Appendix to FCSRSRM, 1874, p. 13).

84. *TB*, 07/01/1875, p. 621; 01/10/1874, p. 389.

All denominations heartily participated in the work. Alexander Farquharson, pastor of the Congregational Church, 'enthusiastically played his part in seeking to win folk for Christ'.[85] At meetings held by Free Church ministers in the independent church at Cavlis, one man quipped, 'The church, as an Irishman would say, was filled outside and in'! In time, however, suspicion and dissension arose against the Baptists. Alexander McNeil of the Free Church wrote: 'The Baptist minister has rather taken up a denominational position of late by baptising some of the converts, and in consequence the other ministers do not now work with him. I think it is a great pity that he should have broken up the unanimity which prevailed so long and with such marked success.' [86] It is likely that the other denominations also felt uneasy with the pattern of meetings being conducted in Balemartin Chapel, the original centre of the movement.

Exceptionally strong gales towards the close of September failed to dampen interest, and wrote one island resident: 'It was most cheering to see groups wending their way from all quarters towards the church … the younger folks were helping the older ones to face the gale', as they came from a distance of up to five miles. Repeatedly, 'every corner of the (Gott) church, which is seated for 750, was crammed. And when it is remembered that there were two other crowded meetings in the West on each of these evenings, one will come to see how thoroughly the whole island has been moved.'[87]

A meeting in October 'for conference and prayer' drew representatives from Arran, Islay, Mull, Coll, Skye, as well as many from Tiree itself. At its close, candidates found 'a congregation of five hundred waiting for us in the open air for a parting meeting', which was conducted at the sheltered 'McLean's Hillock'. A local missionary claimed that 'not less than three hundred persons professed to have found the Lord during the last few weeks', and that 'the island will henceforth occupy a very different position in the Christian world than it has done in the past'.[88]

---

85. Donald McKinnon, a fruit of the awakening, later emigrated to Manilla, Ontario, where converts of the 1840s revival in Tiree had previously been the means of much blessing and became pastor of the Congregational church there in 1878.

86. *TB*, 17/01/1875, p. 621.

87. ibid.

88. ibid. In particular the awakening was seen as something of a landmark in the Baptist Church, to which all subsequent revivals on the island were compared. It

The revival continued for two months and 116, sixty and thirty to forty new members were added to the Baptist, Established and Congregational Churches respectively, with a smaller number joining the Free Church.

Mull

Believers in Mull were at least in part influenced by the movement that had begun in Tiree in August 1874. In the granite quarries of Torosay, near Craignure in the north-east of the island, one person testified gladly, 'The men meet every dinner-hour to read the Bible. … One of the chief men is testifying for Christ.' Meanwhile on the Ross of Mull, in the far south-west of the island, there were 'signs of blessing' among 'the lighthouse community' on the island of Erraid (about forty people). On this same promontory, in the township of Bunessan and Kinrra, as well as across the Sound, on the Celtic island of Iona, meetings were said to have been held 'continuously'.[89] However welcome these glad tidings, an even more powerful season of revival came to Mull just over a year after the falling of these drops of blessing (see p. 593).

Argyll

In a great many places visited by revival at this time, no outside evangelist was employed, while in places like Campbeltown, which Moody visited in September 1874 (see p. 535), a gracious and powerful revival had already moved the town six months previously. In this, the two Established Churches (English and Gaelic), the two Free Churches and the United Presbyterian Church, all worked together.[90] The work had gone on for some time before evangelists D. M. Cameron and John Colville, a native of the town, came to assist. Overwhelmed at the sight of 'so many seeking the Saviour', and in being 'engaged till a late hour in pointing weeping souls to Jesus', Colville exulted, 'Brother, the cream is coming to the top!' He had especial joy in speaking to these young people, a number of whose parents had been personal friends of

---

also set the course of future ordained ministries; Duncan Macfarlane succeeded his brother John, and he in turn was succeeded by Donald MacArthur, one of the first converts of the revival.

89. *TB*, 10/09/1874, p. 350.

90. Proceedings of the Synod of the UPC, 1874, pp. 192-5; Robert White, *Semi-Jubilee of Rev. John S. Bowie: Sketch of his Life and Work*, Edinburgh, 1900, pp. 18-19. See also Pollock, pp. 146-7.

his own. Colville's biographer said of him: 'His joy in connection with this spiritual harvest in his native town has been infinitely more than the joy of those whose corn and wine abound.'[91]

Following the impetus given from Moody's visit to Campbeltown in late August, the town was divided into twenty districts, where it was claimed, 'About one hundred visitors are willingly labouring; weekly meetings are being held in the houses of the poor, in schoolrooms or elsewhere.' Among those who worked arduously here after Moody's departure was Miss Cotton from England, who addressed large meetings of both men and women, but also met with the 'poorest and most degraded' of the population.[92]

Meanwhile, in the Free Church Presbytery of Dunoon, on the Cowal peninsula, as a result of a spiritual movement in 1874, a correspondent in an unnamed village recorded with a number of years hindsight: 'About 45 professed to have received blessing, thirty to have undergone a saving change, eighteen were admitted at next communion, five became office bearers, and about the same number Sabbath school teachers. That revival rendered vital religion a reality in the village.' In Dunoon itself, there were around a hundred professed converts, who were, years later, 'standing well, having come out clearly on the Lord's side from the first', though many of the young men had previously been notorious characters for drinking and other sins. Most of them were now abstainers, acknowledging drink to be 'the curse of Dunoon as it is of Britain'. A Y.M.C.A. was formed in November 1874, the membership of which quickly grew to sixty.[93]

---

91. Colville, pp. 201-5.

92. *TB*, 11/02/1875, p. 698; 24/09/1874, p. 377; 11/02/1875, p. 698. Campbeltown turned out to be a favourite destination of Moody's, for it was the only place outside the main cities that he visited on all three of his evangelistic visits, i.e., in 1874, 1882 and 1891.

93. FCSRSRM, 1889, p. 22; *TB*, 25/02/1875, p. 731.

Dr James Julius Wood

Caricature of Moody & Sankey, 1874

Dugald Christie, Missionary
to Manchuria

Keir Hardie

Duncan Main, Missionary
to Hangzhou

'The Ninety & Nine'
– a little-known
poem set to music by
Sankey during the
Scotland campaign

CHAPTER 22

'Moody Revival' – Appraisal

Reasons for the Americans' Success

With the advantage of hindsight, religious commentators have suggested a number of factors pertaining to the ecclesiological situation in Scotland in the early 1870s that were conducive to a fresh outbreak of revival. According to Callum Brown, evangelicals regarded the two biggest threats to the progress of the Church as being ongoing dissension with Roman Catholicism, and the more recent problem of secularist influences (intellectual and social developments resulting from Darwinism, liberal biblical criticism and new leisure activities). 'The revival was seen by the evangelicals as an opportunity to scourge the middle classes of secularist influences', noted Brown, their readiness to take up the cause being an indication of the sense of insecurity which these forces had created. All this produced a unique situation for a religious revival to develop amongst the middle classes in the early 1870s.[1]

In a more immediate sense, many people were attracted to the change in theological emphasis in revival preaching occasioned by Moody. Previous revivals had stressed sin and the need for repentance; Moody stressed the assurance of salvation through faith and the certainty and joyousness of heaven as a result. 'It seems to have been the optimistic tone of Moody's preaching which formed the basis for broad appeal', observed Brown, along with the similar emphasis on praise and optimism in Sankey's singing and harmonium-playing. Such emphasis on religious opportunity through salvation being hopeful and not despairing helped make revivalism acceptable to the

---

1. Brown, 1981, pp. 445-6.

middle classes.[2] According to Scottish historian T. M. Devine, the reaction to Moody and Sankey 'demonstrated that puritanism was indeed faltering and that there was not the same appetite for hell-fire preaching'.[3]

The strict control of revival meetings was another factor leading to appeal among middle-class Scots. The meetings were highly organised and efficiently run, operating in a well-controlled manner. Said Adam Smith, 'Moody suffered no fools, and every symptom of the hysteria which often breaks out in such movements was promptly suppressed.' *The Times*, too, noted that expressions of overt emotion, so common during the 1859–60 revival, were absent from Moody's meetings.[4]

In his fine analysis of Moody's campaign in Britain, John Coffey concludes: 'Religion was a powerful political force in Victorian Britain. A more secular future lay ahead, of course, and evangelical Christianity was soon to enter into decline. At this stage, however, evangelicals were not yet retreating into their sub-cultural ghetto. Moody and Sankey's campaign marked a high point of evangelical self-confidence and influence on British social and political life. One might even speak of the mid-1870s as "The evangelical moment".'[5]

A significant part of Moody's success lay in the fact that he brought a degree of unity, albeit temporary, to the Protestant Church in Scotland amidst ongoing ecclesiastical disputes and the confusion and insecurities caused by a plethora of complex issues relating to forces such as industrialisation and urbanisation that were affecting Europe in the mid-to-late 1800s. Findlay ably sums up the results of Moody and Sankey's Scottish mission: 'For thousands of Scottish churchmen in 1874 there was no doubt about the effectiveness of the fascinating preacher from America. Forced to struggle with a bewildering array of complex issues … sweeping over the western world in the nineteenth century, facing tensions within the churches created by longstanding

2. ibid., pp. 439-40.

3. Devine, p. 37.

4. Smith, 1899, p. 57; *The Times*, 01/12/1874, quoted in Scotland, p. 151.

5. John Coffey, 'Moody and Sankey's Mission to Britain, 1873-1875', in Biagini, *Citizenship and Community: Liberals, Radicals and Collective Identities in the British Isles, 1865-1931*, Cambridge, 1996, p. 119.

ecclesiastical and theological disputes, Moody's simple message and call for unity among churchmen seemed irresistible.'[6]

Objections to Moody and Sankey

Moody's Methods

Many of the things that attracted so many people to Moody and Sankey's meetings were the very same things that others were strongly opposed to. Some of these objections have already been referred to. Moody's periodic use of anecdotes, personal testimonies and the like, many church leaders found too conversational and informal. More controversial still was Moody's use of the inquiry room, and his call for immediate conversion. These were regarded as Arminian in the extreme, and utterly unbiblical. As already noted, John Kennedy of Dingwall charged Moody with preaching 'another gospel'.

Some cautioned that Moody gave 'a decided impetus to the spread of Arminian teaching in Scotland'. According to Stewart and Cameron, he helped to give the doctrine of a universal Atonement an 'almost unchallenged place in its theology'. He lowered the conception of conversion until it came to be well-nigh emptied of spiritual significance. And he did 'much to eliminate the element of healthy, godly fear from modern religion, giving currency in its place to a certain jauntiness of assurance which too often reared its head from a very slender basis of experience'.[7]

Some of the strongest objections came from Free Church minister, the Rev. Salmond, who claimed that Moody was anti-intellectual in orientation, he confused the practical with the spiritual, and his 'Arminian narrowness' left to mainstream Scottish evangelicalism 'a middle-class spirituality or even a sentimentality which alienated both the thoughtful and the poor alike'.[8] Of even greater significance, according to Salmond, it was largely because of Moody that Calvinism

---

6. Findlay, p. 163.

7. Rev. Alexander Stewart and Rev. J. Kennedy Cameron, *The Free Church of Scotland 1843–1910*, Edinburgh, 1910, p. 52. Iain D. Campbell quipped that 'the reader would not guess from [Stewart and Cameron's] account that the reason for their visit lay with the Free Church itself' (Iain D. Campbell, *Fixing the Indemnity: The Life and Work of Sir George Adam Smith (1856–1942)*, Carlisle, 2004, p. 21).

8. Stewart and Cameron, p. 38.

in Scotland ceased to be a real force and was superseded by what Salmond calls 'a new kind of Arminian evangelical fundamentalism'.[9] True evangelicalism in Scotland never recovered from this blow, he lamented. More negatively still, John Kent claimed that Moody's mission marked the withdrawal of evangelicals from involvement in society and was, 'anti-modernist, anti-materialist, anti-democratic and often anti-intellectual'.[10]

Middle-Class Appeal

All classes were attracted to Moody's meetings in Scotland. Callum Brown, however, claims that 'the urban middle classes' were the prime target of the revivalists in 1873–5. Thus, it was that the University of Edinburgh, Merchant Company schools, the teacher-training School at Moray House, and the Free Church divinity hall (New College), were all especially affected by visits from Moody and Sankey. In Glasgow, many of the revival meetings were held 'in the middle-class west end'.[11] In his biography of Moody, J. F. Findlay further noted that in Scotland the soberest assessments prepared by officials of churches generally sympathetic with Moody's work spelled out his 'clear failure to reach the unchurched'.[12]

Dr Julius Wood of the Free Church of Scotland, too, a strong supporter of Moody's mission, was led to concede that the movement did not reach much beyond the 'outwardly decent and orderly and church-going part of the community', and therefore little effect was produced on the 'masses among whom ignorance and open wickedness

---

9. ibid., p. 46. Salmond believed that 'Scottish evangelicalism (traditional Calvinism) could have weathered the later nineteenth-century crisis of faith were it not for the adverse effect brought to bear on the Scottish Church by D. L. Moody and his new-style evangelism' (ibid., p. 4).

10. Kent also claimed that 'in the Scottish Lowlands, where relations between the State and Free Presbyterian Churches had been embittered for a generation', a 'neutral revivalist' such as Moody profited from the mood of nostalgia for great days similar to those prior to the schism of 1843 (Kent, *Holding the Fort*, p. 137). J. S. Salmond is of the same opinion, believing that Moody brought a false sense of security into a situation which bordered on 'a melting pot of socio-theological ferment' (Rev. Dr J. S. Salmond, *Moody Blues: D. L. Moody's Affect on the Scottish Church*, London, 1992, p. 50).

11. Brown, 1981, pp. 446-7.

12. J. F. Findlay, quoted in Scotland, p. 148.

abound and abide'. According to a recent and highly unsympathetic work on the effect of Moody's campaigns in Scotland by the Rev. Dr J. S. Salmond, Moody's first mission to Britain 'barely touched the plight of the lower orders'.[13] Moody himself was keenly aware of this inability to draw the masses, so he used a different approach to revivalism in his later visits to Scotland. During his 1881–82 mission, Salmond concedes, Moody spent much more time in the poorer districts of the cities; while he also held more meetings for particular groups, e.g., one for reformed drunkards, another for carters, etc. Additionally, he began to use an elaborate ticket scheme, whereby tickets were issued by the minister of each parish to ensure an attendance of non-church people and also to prevent existing believers from going to meeting after meeting. Yet according to Salmond, even this new approach failed to work because Moody persistently failed to question existing structures of society and, like most middle-class Church leaders of the time, was inclined to look for the remedy in terms of changing the individual.

John Kent likewise claimed that Moody and Sankey failed to reach the working classes, and that their popularity was really confined to 'the evangelical sub-culture', whose members attended the meetings again and again.[14] Kent's work has been regarded by some other academics, however, as negative and unsupported.[15] John Coffey shows that in the 1870s in particular, Moody was far from being a reactionary pietist, and he provided much inspiration for organisations working among the poor and deprived. George Adam Smith also declared that during this period, 'there was no preacher more civic or more practical among us.' Coffey also provides evidence to show that Moody and Sankey did indeed reach Britain's working classes in 1873–75, and that their appeal transcended barriers of gender, age and class.[16] Nigel Scotland confirms Coffey's stance, showing that when Moody held meetings in areas where the poor lived in large numbers, his work was clearly effective.[17]

13. Salmond, p. 35.

14. Kent, 1978, p. 137.

15. e.g., see J. Holmes, pp. 55, 91, 168.

16. Coffey, pp. 95-8.

17. Scotland, pp. 148-9.

Of great significance here is the irrefutable evidence that the revival caused an increase in mission work amongst Glasgow's working classes. Many new mission stations and churches were founded in the years immediately following Moody's visit, particularly occasioned by the reform in worship that resulted from the influence of Ira Sankey. In addition, religious voluntary organisations grew substantially in the 1870s. Sunday schools, Bands of Hope, young men's and women's institutes, and unaffiliated bodies all increased in number as a direct consequence of the revival.

Sankey's Hymns

In regard to Sankey, while the singing of hymns in public worship was still very much a contentious issue in Scotland, Sankey's music came in for particular criticism from certain quarters. His very simple tunes, with their rousing and repetitive choruses, were considered to be more like music hall entertainment than sacred music. Meanwhile his lyrics, being deeply sentimental, were criticised for promoting a cheap emotionalism. However, as Secession minister in Greenock, the Rev. James Kerr, commented regarding many of Sankey's songs as songs – 'cold must the heart be that is not refreshed by "Jesus of Nazareth passeth by"'. But while as religious poetry they were often excellent, Kerr felt they were not suitable as worship to God, for in many there was no direct address to God whatsoever. He mentions numerous Sankey titles as evidence – 'The Bee Saved from the Spider', 'Praise of a Dead Body', 'To a Spirit Deceased', etc. While acknowledging that Sankey did not regard all his music as songs of praise, but rather as 'singing the gospel' (along the same lines that Moody 'preached the gospel'), he nonetheless felt this was not the way God should be served by anyone with a high sense of the majesty and glory of God.[18]

---

18. A. Holmes, pp. 47-9. J. Holmes, p. 71. Regarding opposition to Sankey's use of his portable organ, similar criticisms had in fact been levelled at another American musician who visited Glasgow just two years previously, in 1872. In that year, objection was made to Philip Phillips using an organ during a charity concert. A compromise was eventually reached, and Phillips later claimed that his confrontation had prepared the way for Sankey, who after initial criticisms, found his efforts generally well received. For an academic discussion on the influence of Sankey's music on the Scottish Church see Elizabeth P. Thomson, 'The Impetus Given to the Use of Instrumental Music in Scottish Churches by the Visit of Moody and Sankey to Scotland in 1873-74', in *RSCHS* vol. 36, 2006, pp. 175-94.

Objection to the use of 'human hymns' in public worship was especially strong among several leaders within Scotland's Presbyterian churches. The Rev. James Begg of the Free Church, for example, wrote a number of pamphlets against the reforms in worship.

Moody in fact considered Presbyterian worship as a whole to be most unappealing to the non-church-going and hoped that ministers would make their services more popular by shortening their sermons and increasing praise, thus, overall, making church services shorter. Indeed, time proved that Presbyterian acceptance of instrumental music in worship was the most tangible product of the Moody-Sankey revival of 1873–75. Organs and hymns had been used by a number of evangelists during the revival of 1859–61 – though not in Presbyterian churches. It is true that there had been a push within both the Established and Free Church to introduce hymns prior to Sankey's visit to Scotland, resulting in these denominations producing their own hymn-books, in 1870 and 1872 respectively. Ultimately, however, it was felt to be the popularity of Sankey's hymns that had a special share in superseding the sole use of the Psalms in public worship.

Then, in 1876 the Established Church gave its formal sanction to the use of the organ in congregational services, and by 1880 organs were being installed in most Presbyterian churches in Scotland. As a result of the shortening of sermons and the introduction of hymns and organs, the tone of public worship changed from what some considered to be 'dour puritanism' to a more joyful thanksgiving. The increased role of the laity was seen as a further result. It became customary for the congregation to stand singing and to sit for prayer, a reversal of the standard practice in Scotland. The outstanding success of the new style of hymnody in British churches can be gleaned from the fact that the hymn book, *Sacred Songs and Solos* compiled by Sankey, and containing many of his tunes, had sold ninety million copies by 1940 in Britain alone.

Results of the Movement

Moody's visit to Scotland shot him to fame, not just throughout the United Kingdom, but also in his native America ('Moody was introduced to America by Great Britain' as Couper put it). In the States he was hitherto little-known, but was soon to become one of the country's most prominent figures, tirelessly evangelising and campaigning for social causes, until his death in 1899.[19]

A spiritual harvest was recorded by all of Scotland's major denominations. For the Baptists, about 780 new members were received in 1874, fairly evenly distributed amongst the Scottish churches.[20] For example, in Charlotte Chapel, which benefited significantly from the movement,[21] and in Edinburgh's Dublin Street, there were thirty-two and forty-six baptisms respectively, while in Glasgow, thirty-five were baptised into the Govan fellowship, giving an increase of almost 50 per cent. In Forfar forty-seven additions were made to the Baptist Church roll and twenty-eight in Arbroath, doubling the membership there. A new church that was formed in Dundee with about forty people increased to seventy during 1874.[22] Twenty-five accessions were made to the Baptist Church in the Orkney isle of Burray, while around forty professions of faith were recorded in only a few months in the more northerly isle of Eday. Places as far apart as Wishaw and Lossiemouth also saw considerable expansion. Scarcely a Baptist congregation was untouched by this movement.[23]

Brethren numbers were also boosted by the Moody mission, which acted as an impulse to many within this group.[24] Alexander Marshall

---

19. Roberts, 1995, p. 323. During his 1873–75 visit to the UK, Moody also had remarkable success in the largest cities in Ireland and England, though apparently without the accompanying general awakening that arose in Scotland.

20. This was in addition to those who started attending their local Baptist congregation as a result of the revival and who may have been considered savingly changed, but who, as yet, hadn't requested to be added as members through baptism. In some parts of Scotland, notably Edinburgh, some Episcopalian ministers heartily co-operated with the evangelists. This work was carried on largely by Episcopalian clergy in the wake of Moody's visit; e.g., successful missions were conducted in Edinburgh by Rev. Pigott, vicar of Doncaster and by Father Benson.

21. Noel Gibbard, *Fire on the Altar: A History and Evaluation of the 1904-05 Welsh Revival*, Bridgend, 2005, p. 109.

22. Sixth Annual Report of the Baptist Union of Scotland, 1874, pp. 14-15.

23. Derek Murray, *The First 100 Years: The Baptist Union of Scotland*, Glasgow, n.d., p. 60.

24. In Glasgow's east end, the Camlachie Carters Mission was founded in 1873 in the immediate aftermath of Moody's campaign; this formed itself into a Brethren assembly in the early 1890s.

got involved as a worker in the Glasgow meetings, later becoming a prominent leader of the Scottish Brethren movement. Some Brethren, however, felt it improper to attend Moody's non-denominational meetings on the grounds that it would be compromising with the 'evils' of other denominations from which they had fled. Others criticised the style of the American evangelists, and 'the excessive use of anecdotes, pathetic and sentimental, which work on the natural emotions'. While the use of the organ in public worship also came in for considerable criticism, one Brethren man, Robert F. Beveridge, received the urge to use his voice in solo singing after hearing Sankey in Glasgow, and soon became known as *'Scotland's Sankey'*, also composing his own evangelistic hymns.[25]

A year after the evangelists had left Glasgow, Andrew Bonar remarked on the permanence of the work then carried on and invited any who wished to come and see for themselves how extensive and sincere the work had been. Personally, he could say – noting that many of his ministerial colleagues could say likewise: 'The fruit of last year has been as satisfactory in every way as at any period in my ministry, while it has also had some new features of special interest.'[26]

South-African-born revivalist, Andrew Murray (who studied in Aberdeen and whose father was a native of Scotland), paid a visit to Edinburgh in 1877, a few years after Moody's campaign. He sought to evaluate the condition of the Church in the nation and made a point of speaking with several 'grey-haired ministers' who had acknowledged how much they had learned from the American evangelists. As a result of his enquiries and observations, Murray attributed to the influence of Moody the fact that even in Scotland there was much more readiness now to speak out about one's religion and much more warmth of spirit. 'I noticed that the whole religious tone of Scotland has been lifted up and brightened most remarkably', he remarked. 'I do praise God for it.'[27]

A fascinating survey of the many churches in the city of Glasgow and neighbourhood, including immediately adjacent districts,

---

25. Dickson, 2002, p. 160, 140.

26. Moody, pp. 182-3.

27. Leona Choy, *Andrew & Emma Murray: An Intimate Portrait of their Marriage and Ministry*, Winchester, 2000, pp. 123, 126.

covering the period from the start of 1874 to the time of Moody's departure from Glasgow in mid-May of that year, revealed 316 congregations with the total number of professing converts being 3,133 (1,670 males, 1,463 females). These came in the following proportions: 66 Free Church congregations, 1,048 converts; 62 United Presbyterian churches, 856 converts; 60 Established churches, 495 converts; 15 Congregational churches, 132 converts; 8 Baptist churches, 91 converts; 8 Reformed Presbyterian churches, 58 converts; 9 Episcopalian churches, 47 converts; 6 Evangelical Union churches, 36 converts; 10 Methodist churches, 30 converts; 6 Brethren Assemblies, 21 converts; 2 Original Secession churches, 7 converts; Seamen's Chapel, 4 converts; 2 Society of Friends churches, 4 converts; 1 Catholic Apostolic Church, 1 convert; 1 Christ's Church, 1 convert; Dr P. Hately Waddell's church, 1 convert; 52 country churches, 118 converts; no church given, 65 converts; no congregation given, 9 converts; unascertained, 64 converts.[28]

And while it is true that the Highlands and Islands weren't nearly as deeply affected by Moody's visit as other parts of Scotland, as we have seen, meetings that the two evangelists held in a number of specific towns and villages they travelled to were indeed very successful, while various other Highland communities were also spiritually blessed around this time. In addition, it is a little-known fact that during the years immediately following Moody's UK campaign, some of his sermons were translated into Gaelic. Eight thousand copies were sold, and by 1884 another printing was being called for.

Acceptance as a Genuine Revival
It has been generally accepted, even by those who have opposed his methods, that Moody's ministry in Scotland in 1873–74 – as distinct from the vast majority of his later crusades, both in Scotland and elsewhere in the world – was accompanied by at least a degree of genuine spiritual revival. While highly favourable assessments of his

---

28. The highest number within a congregation came from Andrew Bonar's Finnieston Free Church, which reported 92 professed converts; this was followed by Augustine Free Church (Rev. Riddell), 70 converts; Kelvinside Free Church (Rev. W. R. Taylor), 64 converts; East Campbell Street United Presbyterian Church (Dr Wallace), 49 converts; Anderston Free Church (Rev. Somerville), 48, and so on.

work abound in contemporary and later accounts,[29] the views of more conservative commentators are well-worth noting. A report in 1874 from the Free Church, the views of whose ministers varied considerably in regard to Moody and Sankey and their mission, nevertheless enthused wholeheartedly that, 'The religious movement of this year has been very extensive … a great many places all over Scotland … have shared in it.' Indeed, the Rev. Dr Julius Wood went so far as to describe the movement as 'an outpouring of the Holy Spirit more extensive and remarkable than has taken place since Apostolic times'.[30]

Though in no way applauding Moody's ministry as a whole, and insisting that his later crusades were 'more the work of good men in evangelism than the extraordinary work of God in revival', Presbyterian revival historian Richard Owen Roberts nevertheless accepts that 'genuine revival did accompany Moody's ministry in Great Britain in the 1870s'.[31] Writing almost a century after this visit, James Findlay, the most cautious biographer of the American evangelist, wrote regarding his first Scottish visit: 'Moody undoubtedly came closer than at any time in his career to igniting a revival in the classic sense in which Christians had viewed that phenomenon up to the nineteenth century.'[32] In like vein, Reformed historian, Iain H. Murray, while thoroughly dismissive of Moody's revival 'methods', admits that Glasgow and Edinburgh 'were deeply stirred', and almost reluctantly concedes that 'perhaps what happened in Scotland contained elements of true revival'.[33] One

---

29. e.g., Cairns, p. 159; Davies, p. 171; Clark, pp. 47-163; various biographies of Moody, e.g., by W. R. Moody, Wilbur Chapman, J. J. Ellis, etc.

30. FCSRSRM, 1874, p. 2; J. R. Fleming, *A History of the Church in Scotland*, Edinburgh, 1927–33, pp. 236-7. One Scottish history book incorrectly states that Moody inaugurated a 'ten-year religious revival campaign throughout the country' (David Ross, *Chronology of Scottish History*, Lanark, 2002, p. 104).

31. Richard Owen Roberts, *An Annotated Bibliography of Revival Literature*, Wheaton, 1987, p. 301.

32. Findlay, p. 157. As evidence of the unique intensity of response that Moody provoked in Scotland, Findlay mentions the dozens of letters – favourable and critical – printed in major Glasgow and Edinburgh newspapers both during and after the revival, commenting on aspects of the work. 'At no other time in Moody's career did his efforts evoke a comparable public response', says Findlay (p. 156).

33. Iain H. Murray, *Revival and Revivalism: The Making and Marring of American Evangelicalism 1750-1858*, Edinburgh, 1994, pp. 402-3.

must remember, in any case, that the spiritual impact on Scotland of events of 1873–4 weren't defined by the evangelistic campaign of Moody and Sankey, but rather a spiritual movement spread across a great many parts of Scotland quite apart from any personal visit from the Americans.

Lasting Impact

Notwithstanding the positive features of the Moody mission, some, especially with considerable hindsight, voiced their criticisms of its lasting effects. Writing more than twenty years after Moody and Sankey's visit, Adam Smith could see how 'so vast and rapid a movement was bound to suffer the defects of its qualities'. Among these he notes that many of the converts lapsed into worldliness (especially drunkenness); many also regarded the excitement and enthusiasm of the meetings to be normative (of these Smith says, 'their excitement and the habits which it has formed have not been beneficial to Christianity') and the idealism of the whole Mission movement, Smith felt, 'conspired with the general excitement to destroy in a certain class of minds all sense for facts'.[34]

Adding to these concerns, Callum Brown noted that revivalism (especially that of 1873–74) seemed to 'redirect evangelical concern away from collectivist social action'. The emphasis was on the individual and his or her activity to achieve salvation through mass revivalism. Brown felt this led to serious consequences for evangelicalism and for organised religion as a whole after 1880. 'Evangelicalism as a framework for social action now placed emphasis on emotion and not education as the basis for social improvement. One significant result was the decline in evangelical interest in certain types of state intervention in social reform. Whilst evangelical support for state regulation of morality and individual concern grew (in the field of temperance legislation in particular), evangelical support for schemes like municipal slum-clearance dissipated.'[35]

On a more positive note, the verdict of P. Carnegie Simpson on Moody's impact on Scottish Church life highlights the 'new spirit'

---

34. Quoted in I. D. Campbell, p. 24.

35. Brown, 1981, pp. 450-1. Brown also suggests that liberal evangelicals were the most prominent group of clergy on revival platforms in 1873–4. 'Some of them were to lead the churches towards a new social theology after 1880' (ibid., p. 457).

of evangelicalism he felt Moody helped to disseminate; 'Moody's preaching of a "free Gospel" to all sinners did more to relieve Scotland generally ... of the old hyper-Calvinism doctrine of election and of what theologians call "a limited atonement" and to bring home the sense of the love and grace of God towards all men, than did even the teaching of John Macleod Campbell', he wrote.[36]

Another enduring legacy of the movement was that men of promise fresh out of college entered with enthusiasm into the work of evangelism (one example being James Stalker, ordained in Kirkcaldy in 1874). A further lasting result was an increased concern by the Church regarding the social needs of the urban poor. For example, in Scotland's largest city, the Glasgow United Evangelistic Association was formed, which offered free breakfasts on Sundays and opened an orphan home in Saltcoats, accommodating forty. In addition, an industrial feeding school was established for 'ill-fed or ill-clad children', and a boarding house was opened in Glasgow for young women. Missions were also made 'to the criminal classes and the relief of the friendless'.[37] One University Professor made the remarkable statement in 1883 that more than three quarters of the whole number of students of the classes in the Faculties of Arts and taking a full undergraduate curriculum were preparing for the ministry of the three Presbyterian Churches of Scotland. This course of events, he claimed, was chiefly due to the aftermath of the 'Moody revival'. J. R. Fleming opined that 'the revival of 1874 made such a mark on Scottish life that its traces were manifest for at least half a century later'.[38]

---

36. Patrick Carnegie Simpson, *Life of Principal Rainy*, 1909. vol. 1, p. 408, quoted in *DSCHT*, p. 606.

37. Smith 1899, p. 61.

38. Fleming, pp. 216, 237.

John Ritchie   *W. D. Dunn*

Alexander Marshall   *William Robertson*   *Roderick Lawson*

Glen More, Mull

CHAPTER 23

Post-Moody Awakenings 1875–79

Introduction

In the years immediately following Moody and Sankey's visit to
Scotland, a plethora of other evangelists rose up to reap a rich harvest
across the land. The labours of John M. Scroggie and W. D. Dunn, who
had begun to make a name for themselves as formidable evangelists
in southern Scotland several months before the arrival in Edinburgh
of the Americans, were in even greater demand after their departure.
Invitations poured in on them, and their evangelistic services were
rendered in places such as Coatbridge, Wishaw, Motherwell, Carluke,
Edinburgh, Leith, Glasgow, Stockton, Darlington and other populous
communities. As a result of their success, their names became more
renowned in some parts of Scotland than ever those of Moody and
Sankey did. In the mid-to-late 1870s, many hundreds were brought
to the 'matchless love of Christ' through Scroggie and Dunn's labours,
particularly in numerous towns of Dumfriesshire (in 1874–75, not least
Dumfries itself – see p. 548), and in Dalkeith in 1879, where 'tokens of a
mighty shower of blessing and a great gathering of souls was manifested'.[1]

Outbreaks of localised revival were witnessed during these few
years in different parts of the country, from the most northerly island

---

1. *The Christian*, 21/01/1875, 13/02/1879; *TB*, 24/09/1874. The two men continued
to labour together successfully for fifteen years, until the impossibility of fulfilling all the invitations that reached them necessitated that they begin to undertake
missions separately. Scroggie passed away in 1895. By this time Dunn was based in
Anniesland, a few miles north of Glasgow, from where he translated to Cambuslang
in 1898. He was still to be found conducting campaigns as late as 1920 (Lennie,
2009, p. 166).

in Shetland to southern Ayrshire; from the easternmost parts of
Forfarshire to the Western Isles. We will look at these movements in
an approximately chronological order, noting that only two of them
– those which arose in Maybole and Kilmarnock – had any seeming
connection – direct or otherwise – with Moody and Sankey's Scotland
mission of a few years previously.

Maybole

Following the dramatic revival that took place in Maybole in 1874, in
great part through the enterprising labours of parish minister/evangelist,
Roderick Lawson, a group of believers from the village, mainly young
men, made visits to nearby communities. A deep awakening commenced
in the fishing village of Dunure in 1875, continuing for many months.
Soon it was reported that 'a good number of those wild and careless
men are giving evidence of conversion to God'.[2]

Ferryden

According to a Free Church Report, there was a spiritual movement
in Ferryden in 1874, which yet again, remarkably, exhibited 'all the
features of a general, deep and overwhelmingly earnest awakening' the
following year, subsequent to the visit of two agents of the Edinburgh
Evangelistic Society in November 1875. What ensued was 'literally a
pressing into the Kingdom'. The village was said to have been 'pervaded
from east to west and it may be questioned if there is a family without
a member awakened or saved'. Around sixty communicants were
admitted to the Free Church roll for the first time.[3]

Croy and Lybster

Meanwhile, a century after the saintly James Calder witnessed
revival in the Inverness-shire parish of Croy, there occurred in the
district, about the year 1875, 'a great revival' among the Free Church
congregation, then pastored by the Rev. Adam Gordon Macleod. Sixty

---

2. FCSRSRM, 1876. p. 3.

3. ibid.,1889, p. 7; *The Christian*, 18/11/1875, p. 17. Another east coast congregation greatly blessed in the immediate post-Moody period was Fraserburgh United
Presbyterian Church, which, following the arrival of Rev. John Smith in October
1875, multiplied fourfold within two years (Anonymous, *Thirty Years of Broughton
Place Church*, Edinburgh, 1914, p. 39).

people subsequently joined the church.[4] Further north, 'an interesting movement' took place in the fishing village of Lybster along the south Caithness coast in early 1876 under the regular ministry. Besides crowded attendances on Sabbath, there were held 'large meetings on weekdays', and many were said to have been 'inquiring after the way of salvation'.[5]

Shetland

A period of revivalist activity occurred in some of the country districts of Shetland during the 1870s, as a result of William Gibson Sloan's itinerant preaching during repeated visits to and from his labours in the Faroe Islands (see also p. 419). Between March and December 1875, and aided by one or another visiting Brethren evangelist, around forty people professed to trust Jesus or 'appeared to see the Truth' as Sloan often put it.[6] These took place in the west-side communities of Whiteness, Tresta, Selivoe, Skeld and Walls. As a result, a new assembly arose at Selivoe at this time, while intensive evangelism led to another new group forming further south in Sandwick.

Meanwhile, as a result of Sloan visiting at least one outlying Shetland isle it was found that crowds could be drawn quickly and easily to hear the gospel preached, even during the busy harvest season in most favourable weather conditions. This location was Unst, the most northerly island in Britain.[7] This intrepid 'Fisherman of Faroe' was not the only reaper of such northerly harvest, however. Another, unnamed evangelist at work in this 'isle of the Northern Sea' wrote enthusiastically of the ongoing work to Bella Darling, a member of Edinburgh's Broughton Place United Presbyterian Church (see p. 529). In a letter dated

---

4. Andrew Gordon MacLeod, *Biography of the Rev. Adam Gordon MacLeod, Minister of the Free Church, Croy*, Inverness, 1898, p. 32. Remarkably, all seven of Macleod's surviving sons passed through Edinburgh University and became clergymen, many of them transferring south of the border to take up ministerial charges. One of them, George Gordon, is referred to elsewhere in this section (see p. 594).

5. FCSRSRM, 1876, p. 3.

6. Kelling, p. 95.

7. Dickson, 2002, p. 101. Dickson suggested it might have been Papa Stour which, despite having only two houses, had twelve members in the assembly which existed in 1884. Revivalist activity continued in various parts of the Shetland mainland during the 1880s.

3 August 1875, he wrote: 'We still have meetings every evening in the week and the good Lord still condescends to use us as His instruments, or messengers of good. Oh, how glorious is His grace!' As to the depth of the movement, he related: 'The revival wave has passed over the entire island, from east to west, and from south to north; and week by week the work is deepening and many souls are being saved. … Even one soul saved – what a work – work for eternity. … What a blessing and joy to be owned of God as a co-worker with Him! What has the world for its votaries in comparison with that!'[8]

The proposal was made that Ms Darling, accompanied by her godly father, should journey to Unst to further reap the spiritual harvest – given that they had 'few equals' both in singing the gospel and counselling anxious souls. But the voyage was considered too long. Instead, 'as the revival wave spread and hundreds were being awakened', Bella prayed constantly for her evangelist friend, who later testified that the results of his labours in Unst were largely owing to her prayers of faith and the prophetic biblical texts which she was accustomed to send him.[9]

Kilmarnock

In 1876, a decade after his conversion at the age of twenty, Alexander Marshall, a native of Stranraer, entered into full-time gospel ministry. Even before this date his evangelistic labours had shown signs of divine blessing. During Moody's visit to Glasgow, the young believer had served, with commendation from the likes of Andrew Bonar, as a helper in the after-meetings, pointing scores of anxious souls 'to the Saviour'. In Kilmarnock an awakening began in 1876 when the young evangelist, aided by Rice T. Hopkins, with whose Brethren theology Marshall fully accorded, held a campaign in the town.[10] Such was the ingathering of souls that in 1879 – the same year that Marshall went to work among settlers in the Canadian provinces – John Ritchie moved with his family to make their home in this Ayrshire town; it being felt that his labours would be invaluable to the recent converts.[11]

---

8. S. MacNaughton, pp. 120-1.

9. Sadly, Bella shortly after took ill, and died aged nineteen, in November 1875.

10. John Hawthorn, *Alexander Marshall: Evangelist, Author and Pioneer*, Glasgow, 1929 (reprinted 1988), p. 61.

11. Pickering, pp. 308-9.

Mull

Beginning in autumn 1875 and continuing into 1876, a dramatic awakening occurred among the Baptists in Mull, who, it seems, were not especially affected by the spirit of awakening that came to some groups the previous year (see p. 572). Charles Macquarie (Jnr) of Bunessan, a leader in the Ross Baptist Church, had crossed over to Tiree to preach during the revival that had sprung up on that island in 1874, and he brought back revival impulses to Mull. In Tobermory Baptist Church, Duncan MacFarlane baptised twenty-five candidates between December 1875 and March 1876. In Ross itself, the revival helped augment Baptist membership from a despairing low of sixteen in 1869 to sixty-eight in 1876. During the period of frosts in the winter of 1875–76, the ice was frequently broken on convenient lochs for the immersion of converts. The success of this denomination had the effect of firing others to increased exertion, and the Free Church was soon organising successful evangelical operations.[12] This, and reports of revival from Stornoway a few years later, had the effect of inaugurating a further season of revival blessing in Mull in 1881.[13]

Duns

A regular united evangelistic meeting had been set up in the Berwickshire county town of Duns in the spring of 1874, during which the youth of the neighbourhood in particular had been stirred to anxious enquiry. In the mid to late 1870s William Robertson of Carrubbers Close Mission was asked to assist at meetings in the town. During the prayer meeting, Robertson 'rather feared that the choir were not all Christians' so he arranged to speak to them privately. 'A very blessed time' followed and soon 'the choir was running over with joy and gladness of heart and gratitude to God for His most wonderful goodness'.[14] The meetings were continued by several preachers for some weeks, and the work seemed to spread like wildfire. The people came to the meetings from three or four miles around, and at a large farmsteading where there were a number of houses, it was said that there was not one single house in which there

---

12. See *The Oban Times*, 19/02/1876, quoted in Meek, 1991, p. 13.

13. Lennie, 2009, pp. 38-9.

14. R. M. Robertson, pp. 65-7.

was not blessing. As in Mull, a further shower of spiritual favour was poured on this town just a few years later, in 1883–4.[15]

Carnwarth

George Gordon Macleod, one of the seven sons of Adam Gordon Macleod of Croy, each of whom became a minister in his own right, was one of many divinity students touched by Moody's visit to Edinburgh in 1873–4. Three years later Macleod was inducted as Free Church minister of Carnwath in south-east Lanarkshire. The young minister threw himself into the work and quickly became widely known for his striking sermon delivery and uncommon fearlessness. In great demand at Y.M.C.A. and Temperance Society meetings, on occasions no hall was sufficient to contain those who flocked to hear him. But Macleod was not seeking popularity. He longed for a reviving of the dry bones in his district. He became an indefatigable visitor, showing great concern for the spiritual needs of all with whom he came into contact. Alarmed at the seeming indifference of his people to true spiritual values, he wrote at the start of 1877: 'If God does not visit us with showers of blessing, ere spring we shall be as dry as desert sand.'[16]

His prayers were heard, and in the spring the long-sought showers came. Meetings were held every night of the week, always being crowded. Many waited in anxiety to be spoken to privately, and Macleod would write in his journal lists of their names, as well as the names of many who professed to have undergone a saving change. To these names were added interesting notes, showing the intimate degree to which the pastor sought to know individual cases. In particular, Sunday, 26 March was noted as being 'a day of marvellous power'. Macleod's popularity increased – as too did scathing criticism from some – and again and again the minister prayed to be saved from all self-seeking and self-glorification, 'especially that kind of pride that boasts of humility'.[17]

Coll

A time of spiritual quickening began in the spring of 1879 in one of the 'Ladies' schools' on the island of Coll, and in connection with meetings

---

15. Lennie, 2009, pp. 43-4.

16. Halliday, p. 27.

17. ibid.

for prayer commenced by the young local teacher. After a time a deep interest in divine things began to pervade the whole island. The Rev. Fraser of the Free Church threw himself heartily into the movement, and soon received assistance from four mainland ministers. From all five men the most gratifying accounts were received. Meetings on week and Sabbath days were crowded, and on one occasion Fraser admitted more communicants than in the previous twenty years of his ministry.[18] By 1880 the meetings were still being largely attended, and the minister, along with others who visited the place at this time, reported that 'the good work is deepening in those who were then (in 1879) its subjects, though its visible extension among others may not be now so marked'.[19]

18. PGAFCS, 1880, p. 205.

19. FCSRSRM, 1880, p. 20.

BIBLIOGRAPHY

Primary Books Consulted

Scottish History

Anson, P. F., *Fishing Boats and Fisherfolk on the East Coast*, London, 1930.

Calder, Walter, *Strathy: An Account of the Parish*, Wick, 1897.

Devine, T. M., *The Scottish Nation*, London, 1999.

Fraser, Alexander, *Tarbat, Easter Ross: A Historical Sketch*, Evanton Ross & Cromarty Heritage Society, 1988.

Fyall, Aitken, *St Monans: History, Customs and Superstitions*, Edinburgh, 1999.

Green, George Garden, *Gordonhaven: Scenes and Sketches of Fisher Life in the North, by an Old Fisherman*, Edinburgh, 1887.

Gunn, Adam, *Sutherland and Reay Country*, Glasgow, 1897.

Hossack, B. H., *Kirkwall in the Orkneys*, Kirkwall, 1900.

Hutchison, James, *Miners, Weavers and the Open Book: A History of Kilsyth*, Cumbernauld, 1986.

Lynch, Michael, *Scotland: A New History*, London, 1991.

McDowall, William, *History of the Burgh of Dumfries*, Dumfries, 2006.

Maclean, Charles, *Island on the Edge of the World*, Edinburgh, 1972.

Macrae, Alexander, *Kinlochbervie: Being the Story and Traditions of a Remote Highland Parish and its People*, Tongue, 1932.

Magnusson, Magnus, *Scotland: The Story of a Nation*, London, 2000.

Miller, Hugh, *Sutherland and the Sutherlanders; Their Religious and Social Condition*, Edinburgh, 1844.

Miller, Hugh, *Scenes and Legends of the North of Scotland; or, The Traditional History of Cromarty*, Edinburgh, 1869.

Morgan, Diane, *The Villages of Aberdeen: Footdee and her Shipyards*, Aberdeen, 1993.

Patrick, Belle, *Recollections of East Fife Fisher Folk*, Edinburgh, 2003.

Sands, J., *Out of the World; or, Life in St Kilda*, Edinburgh, 1876.

Steel, Tom, *The Life and Death of St Kilda*, Glasgow, 1975.

Tinch, David M. N., *Shoal and Sheaf: Orkney's Pictorial Heritage*, Kirkwall, 1988.

Watson, Harry D., *Kilrenny and Cellardyke*, Edinburgh, 1986.

Biographies, Memoirs and Diaries

Adam, Hector M., *James Jolly, Minister of Dr Chalmers' Territorial Church, Edinburgh: Memorials of an Earnest Life and Faithful Ministry*, Edinburgh, 1888.

Adamson, William, *The Life of the Rev. Fergus Ferguson, M.A., D.D., Minister of Montrose Street Evangelical Union Church*, London, 1900.

Alexander, W. Lindsay, *Memoir of the Rev. John Watson, Late Pastor of the Congregational Church in Musselburgh, and Secretary of the Congregational Union for Scotland*, Edinburgh, 1845.

Allan, James B., *Rev. John Duncan, D.D., Trinity Congregational Church, Aberdeen. A Memoir and a Tribute*, London, 1909.

Anderson, James, *Evangelist: An Outline of my Life, or Selections from a Fifty Years Religious Experience*, Whitburn, 1912.

Anonymous, *Horatius Bonar D.D.: A Memorial*, Edinburgh, 1890.

Appasamy, A. J., *Write the Vision: A Biography of J. Edwin Orr*, London, 1964.

Auld, Alexander, *Life of John Kennedy*, London, 1887.

Barbour, G. F., *The Life of Alexander Whyte*, London, 1923.

Barbour, Margaret F., *Memoir of Mrs. Stewart Sandeman of Bonskeid and Springland*, London, 1883.

Beaton, Rev. Donald, *Memoir and Sermons of the Rev. Alexander Macleod*, Wick, 1925.

Beggs, R. J., *Rev. Thomas Toye: God's Instrument in the 1859 Revival*, Belfast, 2009.

Blaikie, W. G., *David Brown: Professor and Principal of the Free Church College*, London, 1898.

Blair, Rev. James, *The Scottish Evangelist. The Life and Labours of the Rev. James Blair, of the Bridge of Allan*, Glasgow, 1860.

Bonar, Andrew A., *Memoir and Remains of the Rev. Robert Murray McCheyne*, Edinburgh, 1844 (reprinted 1886).

Bonar, Andrew A., *Memoir of the Life and Brief Ministry of the Rev. David Sandeman, Missionary to China*, London, 1861.

Bonar, Andrew A., *James Scott: A Labourer for God*, London, 1885.

Bonar, Horatius, *Life of the Rev. John Milne of Perth*, London, 1869.

Bonar, Marjory (Ed.), *Diary & Life of Andrew Bonar*, Edinburgh, 1894.

Bowes, H. R. (Ed.), *Samuel Dunn's Shetland and Orkney Journal 1822–1825*, Sheffield, 1976.

Bowes, John, *The Autobiography or History of the Life of John Bowes*, Glasgow, 1872.

Brown, David, *The Life of Rabbi Duncan*, Glasgow, 1986.

Brown, James, *Life of W. B. Robertson of Irvine*, Glasgow, 1889.

Burns, Islay, *The Pastor of Kilsyth, or, Memorials of the Life and Times of the Rev. W. H. Burns, D.D.*, London, 1860.

Burns, Islay, *Memoir of the Rev. Wm. C. Burns, Missionary to China from the English Presbyterian Church*, London, 1870.

Burns, Islay, *Select Remains of Islay Burns*, London, 1874.

Campbell, Iain D., *Fixing the Indemnity: The Life and Work of Sir George Adam Smith (1856–1942)*, Carlisle, 2004.

Campbell, Norman, *One of Heaven's Jewels: Rev. Archibald Cook of Daviot and the (Free) North Church, Inverness*, Stornoway, 2009.

Clare, W. H., *Pioneer Preaching or Work Well Done*, London, n.d.

Coley, Samuel, *The Life of Rev. Thomas Collins*, London, 1876.

Collins, G. N. M., *Principal John Macleod D.D.*, Edinburgh, 1951.

Collins, G. N. M., *Big MacRae: The Rev. John MacRae, (1794–1876): Memorials of a Notable Ministry*, Edinburgh, 1976.

Collins, G. N. M., *Gleanings from the Diary & Ministry of James Morrison*, Edinburgh, 1984.

Colville, Mrs, *John Colville of Burnside, Campbeltown: Evangelist: A Memoir of his Life and Work*, Edinburgh, 1888.

Dallimore, Arnold, *The Life of Edward Irving: the Fore-runner of the Charismatic Movement*, Edinburgh, 1983.

Darlow, Thomas H., *William Robertson Nicoll: Life and Letters*, Edinburgh, 1925.

Douglas, Hugh, *Roderick Lawson of Maybole: A Remarkable Victorian Minister*, Ayrshire, 1978.

Drake, Rev. John, *The Wallacestone Reformer; or, A Sketch of the Life and Labours of Mr Alexander Patrick, Wesleyan Local Preacher*, Kirkintilloch, 1848.

Drummond, A.L., *Edward Irving and His Circle*, Cambridge, 1934.

Dyer, George, *Christhood: As Seen in the Life Work of Mary Dyer*, London, 1889.

Findlay, James F., *Dwight L. Moody, American Evangelist, 1837–1899*, Chicago, 1969.

Fitchett, W. H., *Wesley and his Century: A Study in Spiritual Forces*, London, 1906.

G, H. I., *Jessie McFarlane, a Tribute of Affection*, London, 1872.

Gammie, Alexander, *Rev. John McNeill: His Life and Work*, London, 1933.

Gillies, Donald, *The Life and Work of the Very Rev. Roderick MacLeod of Snizort*, Skeabost Bridge, 1969.

Gordon, Mrs, *Hay MacDowall Grant of Arndilly: His Life, Labours and Teachings*, London, 1876.

Guthrie, Arthur, *Robertson of Irvine: Poet-Preacher*, Ardrossan, 1889.

Guthrie, C. J. G., *Life of Thomas Guthrie*, Glasgow, 1897.

Halliday, Rev. James, *Memoir of the Rev. George Gordon Macleod*, Edinburgh, 1886.

Harding, William Henry, *James Turner*, London, 1912.

Hawthorn, John, *Alexander Marshall: Evangelist, Author and Pioneer*, Glasgow, 1929 (reprinted1988).

Headley, Rev. P. C., *The Reaper and the Harvest: Or Scenes and Incidents in Connection with the Work of the Holy Spirit in the Life and Labours of Rev. Edward Hammond*, New York, 1884.

Keddie, John, *George Smeaton: Learned Theologian and Biblical Scholar*, Darlington, 2007.

Kelling, Fred, *Fisherman of Faroe*, Gota, 1993.

Kennedy, Howard A., *Old Highland Days: The Reminiscences of Dr John Kennedy*, London, 1901.

Kennedy, Rev. John, *The Apostle of the North*, London, 1866 (reprinted Glasgow, 1979).

Kirk, H., *Memoirs of Rev. John Kirk D.D.*, Edinburgh, 1888.

Leask, W. Keith, *Dr Thomas McLauchlan*, Edinburgh, 1905.

M. H. M., *James Robertson of Newington: A Memorial of his Life and Work*, Edinburgh, 1887.

Macaulay, Rev. Murdo, *Hector Cameron of Lochs and Back*, Edinburgh, 1982.

McCrie, Thomas, *Life of Thomas McCrie, D.D.*, Edinburgh, 1840.

McCrie, Thomas (Ed.), *The Life of Mr Robert Blair*, Edinburgh, 1848.

McDowell, Ian, *Rice Thomas Hopkins 1842–1916: An Open Brother*, unpublished paper, n.d.

Macfarlane, Rev. D., *Memoir and Remains of Rev. D. Macdonald, Shieldaig*, Glasgow, 1903.

Macgregor, Duncan, *Campbell of Kiltearn*, Edinburgh, 1874.

McHardie, Elizabeth, *James Turner: or, How to Reach the Masses*, Aberdeen, 1875.

McIver, 'Story of a Lewis Catechist: The Life of Angus McIver', serialised in *The Stornoway Gazette*, 22/1/1972.

Mackay, Alexander, *Life and Times of Rev. George Davidson*, Latheron: Edinburgh, 1875.

Mackay, Rev. Angus, *Memoirs of a Caithness Worthy, Mrs. William Ronaldson, 1828–1919*, Inverness, 1920.

McKendrick, James, *What We Have Seen & Heard During 25 Years of Evangelistic Labours*, Arbroath, 1914.

Mackenzie, Rev. Alexander, *The Rev. John Mackay, M.A., Student, Pastor, General Assembly's Highland Evangelist*, Paisley, 1921.

Mackenzie, Neil, *Episode in the Life of the Rev. Neil Mackenzie at St Kilda*, (privately published) Aberfeldy, 1911.

MacLeod, Rev. Donald, *Memoirs of Norman Macleod*, vol. 2, London, 1876.

MacLeod, Andrew Gordon, *Biography of the Rev. Adam Gordon MacLeod, minister of the Free Church, Croy*, Inverness, 1898.

Macleod, Principal J., *Donald Munro of Ferintosh and Rogart, with sketch of Rev. John Graham*, Inverness, 1939.

MacNaughton, Samuel, *Joy in Jesus: Brief Memorials of Bella Darling*, Edinburgh, 1876.

McNaughton, William D., *Journal of William McKillican*, Glasgow, 1994.

Macpherson, John, *The Christian Hero: A Sketch of the Life of Robert Annan*, London, 1867.

Macpherson, John, *The Life and Labours of Duncan Matheson: The Scottish Evangelist*, London, 1871.

Macrae, Alexander, *The Life of Gustavus Aird, A.M., D.D., Creich, Moderator of the Free Church, 1888*, Stirling, 1908.

Macrae, David, *George Gilfillan: Anecdotes and Reminiscences*, Glasgow, 1891.

Moody, W. R., *The Life of Dwight L. Moody*, London, n.d.

Nicolson, Nicol, *Reverend John Macrae ('Mac-Rath Mor' – Big Macrae) of Knockbain, Greenock and Lewis: A Short Account of his Life and Fragments of his Preaching*, 1924.

Nixon, William, *Autobiographical Notes*, Perth, 1929.

Oliphant, Mrs, *The Life of Edward Irving*, London, 1862.

Paterson, Rev. J., *Richard Weaver's Life Story*, London, 1897.

Paterson, Rev. John, *Memoir of Robert Paterson, D.D.*, Kirkwall: Edinburgh, 1874.

Pollock, John, *Moody Without Sankey*, London, 1963 (reprinted 1995).

Primmer, Jacob, *Life of Jacob Primmer, Minister of the Church of Scotland*, Edinburgh, 1916.

Radcliffe, Mrs, *Recollections of Reginald Radcliffe*, London, n.d.

Robbie, W., *The Life and Labours of the Late James Turner of Peterhead*, Aberdeen, 1863.

Robertson, R. M., *William Robertson of Carrubbers Close Mission*, Edinburgh, 1914.

Robinson, J. Campbell, *The Rev. Alexander McIntyre*, Phahran: Australia, 1929.

Rosell, Garth M. and Dupuis, Richard A. G. (Eds), *The Memoirs of Charles G. Finney*, Grand Rapids, 1989.

Ross, Charles W. (Ed), *Donald Ross: Pioneer Evangelist*, Kilmarnock, 1890 (reprinted 1987).

Ross, James, *Donald McQueen: Catechist in Bracadale*, London, 1893.

Row, W., *The Life of Mr Robert Blair*, Edinburgh, 1848.

Sankey, Ira D., *My Life and Sacred Songs*, London, 1906.

Scroggie, Jeannie, *A Life in the Love of God*, London, 1908.

Shaw, Ian J., *The Greatest Is Charity: The Life of Andrew Reed, Preacher and Philanthropist*, Darlington, 2005.

Simpson, P. Carnegie, *The Life of Principal Rainy*, London, 1909.

Simpson, William, *A Famous Lady Preacher: A Forgotten Episode in Highland Church History*, Inverness, 1926.

Smith, George Adam, *The Life of Henry Drummond*, London, 1899.

Smith, George, *Stephen Hislop, Pioneer Missionary & Naturalist in Central India from 1844 to 1863*, London, 1888.

Smith, Rev. J. A., *Sinclair Thomson: The Shetland Apostle*, Lerwick, 1969.

Smith, John, *Memorials of the Rev. John Smith*, Edinburgh, 1888.

Stark, James, *John Murker of Banff; A Picture of Religious Life and Character in the North*, London, 1887.

Story, Robert H., *Memoir of the Life of the Rev. Robert Story, Late Minister of Rosneath, Dunbartonshire*, Cambridge, 1862.

Stuart, A. Moody, *Life of John Duncan*, Edinburgh, 1991.

Stuart, Rev. A. Moody, *Life and Letters of Elizabeth, Last Duchess of Gordon*, London, 1865.

Stuart, K. Moody, *Brownlow North: The Story of his Life and Work*, London, 1878.

Stuart, K. Moody, *Alexander Moody Stuart*, London, 1899.

Taylor, William (Ed.), *Diary of James Calder*, Stirling, 1875.

Toye, Jane, *Brief Memorials of the Late Rev. Thomas Toye, Belfast*, Belfast, 1873.

Valen, L. J. van, *Constrained By His Love: A New Biography on Robert Murray McCheyne*, Fearn, 2002.

Various Contributors, *Memories of Dr Horatius Bonar, by Relatives and Public Men*, Edinburgh, 1909.

Wells, James, *The Life of James Hood Wilson D.D. of the Barclay Church, Edinburgh*, London, 1904.

White, Charles Edward, *The Beauty of Holiness: Phoebe Palmer as Theologian, Revivalist, Feminist and Humanitarian*, Grand Rapids, 1986.

White, Robert, *Semi-Jubilee of Rev. John S. Bowie: Sketch of his Life and Work*, Edinburgh, 1900.

Wodrow, Robert, *Life of James Wodrow*, Edinburgh, 1828.

Woods, C. E., *Memoirs and Letters of Canon Hay Aitken*, London, 1928.

Young, Rev. James, *Life of John Welsh, Minister of Ayr*, Edinburgh, 1865.

Biography – Collective

Anonymous, *Sidelights on Two Notable Ministries*, Inverness, 1970.

Beaton, Rev. Donald, *Scottish Heroines of the Faith: being brief sketches of noble women of the Reformation and Covenant Times*, 1909.

Beaton, Rev. Donald, *Some Noted Ministers of the Northern Highlands*, Inverness, 1929 (reprinted 1985).

Bruce, W. S., *Reminiscences of Men and Manners During the Past Seventy Years*, Aberdeen, 1929.

Carruthers, R., *Biographies of Highland Clergymen*, Inverness, 1889.

Carswell, Donald, *Brother Scots*, London, 1927.

Collins, G. N. M., *Men of the Burning Heart*, Edinburgh, 1983.

Dodds, James, *Personal Reminiscences and Biographical Sketches*, Edinburgh, 1888.

Goodfellow, Rev. Alexander, *Two Old Worthies of Orkney, or the Sayings and Doings of John Gerard and Matthew Armour*, Stromness, 1925.

Greig, J. (Ed.), *Disruption Worthies of the Highlands & Islands – Another Memorial of 1843*, Edinburgh, 1877.

Haldane, Alexander, *The Lives of Robert & James Haldane*, London, 1852 (reprinted 1990).

Howie, John, *The Scots Worthies*, 1870 (reprinted 1995).

Hudson, J. H., Jarvie, T. W. and Stein, J., *Let the Fire Burn*, Dundee, 1978.

Ker, John and Watson, Jean L., *Lives of Ebenezer and Ralph Erskine*, Edinburgh, 1890.

MacCowan, Roderick, *The Men of Skye*, Glasgow, 1902.

Macfarlane, Rev. Norman C., *The "Men" of the Lews*, Stornoway, 1924.

Macfarlane, Rev. Norman C., *Apostles of the North: Sketches of Some Highland Ministers*, Stornoway, 1989.

MacKinnon, Donald, *Clerical Men of Skye*, Dingwall, 1930.

Morrison, Annie, *Christian Women*, Lewis, n.d.

Nicoll, W. Robertson, *Princes of the Church*, London, 1921.

Pickering, Henry, *Chief men Among the Brethren*, London, 1931 (reprinted 1996).

Shenton, Tim, *Forgotten Heroes of Revival*, Leominster, 2004.

Thomson, A. B., *Sketches of Some Baptist Pioneers in Scotland*, Glasgow, 1903.

Tweedie, Rev. W. K. (Ed.), *Select Biographies*, Edinburgh, 1847.

Various Contributors, *A Memorial of Disruption Worthies*, Dalkeith, 1886.

Various Contributors, *Our Church Fathers: Being Biographical Sketches of Disruption Fathers in and Around the Presbytery of Elgin*, Elgin, 1899.

Wiesebe, Warren W., *Living with the Giants: The Lives of Great Men of the Faith*, Grand Rapids, 1998.

Wylie, Rev. James, *Disruption Worthies – A Memorial of 1843*, Edinburgh, 1881.

Revival Books and Pamphlets

Anonymous, *Narrative of the Revival in Perth in 1860*, Perth, 1885.

Bailie, W. D., *The Six Mile Water Revival of 1625*, Belfast, 1976.

Baikie, J. M., *Revivals in the Far North*, Wick, n.d.

Cairns, E. E., *An Endless Line of Splendor*, Wheaton, 1986.

Carson, John T., *God's River in Spate: The Story of the Religious Awakening of Ulster in 1859*, Belfast, 1958.

Carwardine, Richard J., *Transatlantic Revivalism: Popular Evangelicalism in Britain and America, 1790–1865*, Westport: Conn., 1978.

Church of Scotland Presbytery of Aberdeen, *Evidence on the Subject of Revivals Taken Before the Presbytery of Aberdeen*, Aberdeen, 1841.

Clark, Rufus W., *The Work of God in Great Britain under Messrs. Moody & Sankey, 1873 to 1875*, London, 1875.

Couper, W. J., *Scottish Revivals*, Dundee, 1918.

Davies, R. E., *I Will Pour Out My Spirit: A History and Theology of Revivals and Evangelical Awakenings*, Tunbridge Wells, 1992.

Duncan, Mary Lundie, *History of Revivals of Religion in the British Isles, Especially Scotland*, Edinburgh, 1836.

Edwards, Brian H., *Revival: A People Saturated with God*, Darlington, 1990.

Evans, Eifion, *The Welsh Revival of 1904*, London, 1969.

Fawcett, Arthur, *The Cambuslang Revival: The Scottish Evangelical Revival of the Eighteenth Century*, Edinburgh, 1971.

Ferguson, John, *When God Came Down: An Account of the North Uist Revival 1957–58*, Inverness, 2000.

Gibbard, Noel, *Fire on the Altar: A History and Evaluation of the 1904-05 Welsh Revival*, Bridgend, 2005.

Gibson, William, *The Year of Grace: A History of the Ulster Revival of 1859*, Belfast, 1860.

Gillies, John, *Historical Collections of Accounts of Revival*, Kelso, 1845 (reprinted 1981).

Gregory, Rev. Alexander, *A Brief Account of the Religious Awakening in Cellardyke*, Edinburgh, 1860.

Holland, H. W., *The Kilsyth Revival (Scotland)*, London, 1867.

Holmes, Janice, *Religious Revivals in Britain and Ireland, 1859–1905*, Dublin, 2000.

Jeffrey, Kenneth S., *When the Lord Walked the Land: The 1858–62 Revival in the North East of Scotland*, Carlisle, 2002.

Johnson, Henry, *Stories of Great Revivals*, London, 1906.

Jones, D. Geraint, *Favoured with Frequent Revivals: Revivals in Wales 1762–1862*, Cardiff, 2001.

Kent, John, *Holding the Fort: Studies in Victorian Revivalism*, London, 1978.

Long, Teresa, *The Revival of 1857–58: Interpreting an American Awakening*, New York, 1998.

McDow, Malcolm and Reid, Alvin L., *Firefall: How God has Shaped History through Revivals*, Nashville, 1997.

Macfarlan, Duncan, *The Revivals of the Eighteenth Century, Particularly at Cambuslang*, Edinburgh, 1847.

McGill, H., *On the Present Revival of Religion in Scotland: A paper read at the Annual Conference of the Evangelical Alliance in October 1860 at Nottingham*, London, 1860.

MacGillvary, Angus, *Sketches of Religion and Revivals of Religion in the North Highlands During the Last Century*, Edinburgh, 1859.

McLoughlin, William G., *Revivals, Awakenings and Reform: An Essay on Religion and Social Change in America, 1607–1977*, Chicago, 1978.

McKinnon, L. M., *The Skye Revivals*, printed privately, 1995.

MacMillan, D. (Ed), *Restoration in the Church: Reports of Revivals 1625–1839*, 1839 (reprinted 1989).

Macpherson, John, *Revival and Revival work: A Record of the Labours of D. L. Moody & Ira D. Sankey, and Other Evangelists*, London, 1875.

Macrae, Alexander, *Revivals in the Highlands & Islands in the 19th Century*, Stirling, 1906 (reprinted 1998).

Matthews, T. T. (Ed.), *Reminiscences of the Revival of Fifty-Nine and the Sixties*, Aberdeen, 1910.

Moore, Rev. Samuel J., *The Great Revival in Ireland 1859*, reprinted Lisburn, n.d.

Murray, Iain H., *Revival and Revivalism: The Making and Marring of American Evangelicalism 1750–1858*, Edinburgh, 1994.

Murray, Iain H., *Pentecost Today? The Biblical Basis for Understanding Revival*, Edinburgh, 1998.

Nixon, William, *An Account of the Work of God at Ferryden*, London, 1860.

Orr, J. Edwin, *The Second Evangelical Awakening*, London, 1949.

Orr, J. Edwin, *The Fervent Prayer: The Worldwide Impact of the Great Awakening of 1858*, Chicago, 1974.

Orr, J. Edwin, *The Eager Feet: Evangelical Awakenings 1790–1830*, Chicago, 1975.

Orr, J. Edwin, *The Event of the Century: The 1857–1858 Awakening*, Wheaton, 1989.

Osborn, H. H., *Revival; God's Spotlight: The Significance of Revivals and Why They Cease*, Godalming, 1996.

Paisley, Ian R., *The '59 Revival: An Authentic History of the Great Ulster Awakening of 1859*, Belfast, 1958.

Peckham, Colin and Mary, *Sounds from Heaven: The Revival on the Isle of Lewis, 1949–1952*, Fearn, 2004.

Piggin, Stuart, *Firestorm of the Lord*, Carlisle, 2000.

Poole Connor, B. J., *Visitations of Grace*, 1960.

Reid, William, *Authentic Records of Revival*, London, 1860 (reprinted 1980).

Ritchie, Jackie, *Floods Upon the Dry Ground: God Working Among Fisherfolk*, Peterhead.

Roberts, Richard Owen, *An Annotated Bibliography of Revival Literature*, Wheaton, 1987.

Roberts, Richard Owen, *Revival*, Wheaton, 1991.

Roberts, Richard Owen, *Scotland Saw His Glory*, Wheaton, 1995.

Salmond, Rev. Dr J. S., *Moody Blues*, London, 1992.

Schmidt, Leigh Eric, *Holy Fairs: Scotland and the Making of American Revivalism*, Princeton, NJ, 1989. Scotland, Nigel, *Apostles of the Spirit and Fire: American Revivalists and Victorian Britain*, Carlisle, 2009.

Scott, Alfred Russell, *The Ulster Revival of 1859*, Ballymena, 1994.

Shearer, John, *Old Time Revivals: How the Fire of God Spread in Days Now Past and Gone*, Glasgow, 1930.

Sibbett, R. M., *The Revival in Ulster, or The Story of a Worker*, Belfast, 1909.

Sprange, Harry, *Kingdom Kids: Children in Revival*, Fearn, 1993.

Various Contributors, *The Revival of Religion': Addresses by Scottish Evangelical Leaders delivered in Glasgow in 1840*, Edinburgh, 1840.

Walker, A and Aune, Kristin (Eds), *On Revival: A Critical Examination*, Carlisle, 2003.

Wallis, Arthur, *In the Day of Thy Power*, Alresford, 1956.

Walters, David, *Children Aflame*, South Carolina, 1995.

Watt, D. (Ed.), *A Narrative of the Great Religious Revival in Annan in 1861*, Annan, 1898.

Westerkamp, Marilyn, *Triumph of the Laity Scots-Irish Piety and the Great Awakening, 1625–1760*, Oxford, 1988.

Whyte, Rev. William, *Revival in Rose Street: A History of Charlotte Baptist Chapel, Edinburgh*, Edinburgh, n.d.

Local Church History

Adamson, Thomas, *Free Anderston Church, Glasgow*, Glasgow, 1900.

Ansdell, Douglas, *People of the Great Faith: The Highland Church 1690–1900*, Stornoway, 1998.

Anonymous, *Annual Report of the West Coast Mission*, Oban, 1863.

Anonymous, *Memorial Sketch: Free North Church, Greenock, and its First Minister, David Boyd*, Greenock, 1900.

Anonymous, *Thirty Years of Broughton Place Church*, Edinburgh, 1914.

Baird, William, *Sixty Years of Church Life in Ayr. The History of Ayr Free Church from 1836 to 1896*, Ayr, 1896.

Bardgett, Frank, *North Coast Parish: Strathy and Halladale: A Historical Guide To A Post-Clearance Parish And Its Church*, Strathy, 1990.

Bardgett, Frank D., *Two Millennia of Church and Community in Orkney*, Edinburgh, 2000.

Binnie, Thomas, *Sketch of the History of the First Reformed Presbyterian Congregation, now the Great Hamilton Street Free Church, Glasgow*, Paisley, 1888.

Cameron, John K., *The Church in Arran*, Edinburgh, 1912.

Campbell, Murdoch, *Gleanings of Highland Harvest*, Stornoway, 1953 (reprinted Fearn, 1989).

Cordiner, James, *Fragments From the Past: An Account of People and Events in the Assemblies of Northern Scotland*, London, 1961.

Couper, W. J., *Kilbirnie West: A History of Kilbirnie West United Free 1824–1924*, Kilbirnie, 1923.

Gall, James, *Report of Carrubbers' Close Mission*, Edinburgh, 1861.

Gall, James, *The Revival of Pentecostal Christianity. The History of Carubbers Close Mission*, London, 1882.

General Assembly of the Free Church of Scotland, *The Present Work of Grace: Being Notes of a Conference on Thursday 27th May 1869*.

Grieve, William, *A Short History of Shotts Parish Church*, Shotts, 1928.

Harcus, Henry, *The History of the Orkney Baptist Churches*, Ayr, 1898.

Hughes, Edward Duncan, *What God Hath Wrought: The Story of the YMCA, Inverness*, Inverness, n.d.

Inglis, Rev. Andrew, *Notes of the History of Dudhope Free Church, Lochee Road, Dundee*, Dundee, 1890.

Kennedy, John, *Days of the Fathers in Ross-shire*, Edinburgh, 1861 (reprinted 1979).

Kilpatrick, Daniel R., *The Religious History of Cowcaddens*, Glasgow, 1867.

Laurie, John, *Chronicles of the Evangelical Union Church of Leith*, Edinburgh, 1871.

Lawson, Bill, *St Kilda and its Church*, Northton, 1993.

Lyall, Francis and Still, William, *History of Gilcomston South Church, Aberdeen, 1868–1968*, Aberdeen, 1968.

Macaulay, Rev. Murdo, *Aspects of the Religious History of Lewis Up to the Disruption of 1843*, Inverness, n.d.

MacColl, Dugald, *Among the Masses: or, Work in the Wynds*, Glasgow, 1867.

Macdonald, Angus, *An Enduring Testimony: Inverness East Church*, Inverness, 1998.

Macdonald, Ian R., *Glasgow's Gaelic Churches: Highland Religion in an Urban Setting 1690–1995*, Edinburgh, 1995.

MacInnes, Rev. David, *Kilmuir Church, North Uist 1894–1994*, Kilmuir, 1994.

McInnes, John, *The Evangelical Movement in the Highlands of Scotland 1688–1800*, Aberdeen, 1951.

Mackay, John, *The Church in the Highlands or The Progress of Evangelical Religion in Gaelic Scotland 563–1843*, London, 1914.

Macleod, Rev. Calum I. (Ed.), *Pronnagan: Gospel Advent in Barvas Parish*, Barvas, 2008.

Macleod, J., *By-paths of Highland Church History*, Edinburgh, 1965.

Macleod, John, *Memories of the Far North*, Caithness, 1919.

MacLeod, John, *Banner In The West: A Spiritual History of Lewis and Harris*, Edinburgh, 2008.

Macleod, J. M., *A Brief Record of the Church in Uig (Lewis) Up To the Union of 1929*, Stornoway, 1994.

McNaughton, William D., *Orkney Congregationalism*, Kirkcaldy, n.d.

McNaughton, William D., *Helensburgh and Alexandria: A Tale of Two Congregational Churches*, Glasgow, 1996.

McNaughton, William D., *Early Congregational Independency in Shetland*, Lerwick, 2005.

Martin, John R., *The Church Chronicles of Nigg*, Nigg, 1967.

Meek, Donald E., *Island Harvest : A History of Tiree Baptist Church 1838–1988*, Tiree, 1988.

Meek, Donald E., *Sunshine and Shadow: The Story of the Baptists of Mull*, Edinburgh, 1991.

Munro, Rev. Donald, *Records of Grace in Sutherland*, Edinburgh, 1953.

Murray, John J., *The Church on the Hill Oban Free High Church a History and Guide*, Oban, 1984.

Noble, John, *Religious Life In Ross*, Inverness, 1909.

Ogilvy, David, *Historical Sketch of the Free Church of Scotland in the Parish of Dalziel from the Disruption in 1843 to the Union in 1900*, Glasgow, 1900.

Reed, Laurance, *The Soay of our Forefathers'* Edinburgh, 2002.

Robson, Michael, *St Kilda: Church, Visitors and "Natives"*, Port of Ness, 2005.

Sage, Donald, *Memorabilia Domestica*, 1889 (reprinted 1975).

Sinclair, Dugald, *Journal of Itinerating Exertions in Some of the More Destitute Parts of Scotland*, Edinburgh, 1814–17.

Stuart, Rev. Atholl, *Blair Atholl as it Was and Is*, Edinburgh, 1857.

Talbot, Brian R. *Standing on the Rock: A History of Stirling Baptist Church, 1805–2005*, Stirling, 2005.

Taylor, Steve, *The Skye Revivals*, Chichester, 2003.

Thomson, D. P., *Tales of the Far North West: A Sutherlandshire Miscellany*, Inverness, 1955.

Various, *A Collace Miscellany*, Collace, 1993.

Wemyss, Robert, *The Church in the Square: A Brief History of the West United Free Church, Helensburgh*, Helensburgh, 1925.

Scottish Church History – General

Beattie, David, *Brethren: The Story of a Great Recovery*, Kilmarnock, 1940.

Bebbington, D.W., *The Baptists in Scotland*, Glasgow, 1988.

Bebbington, D.W., *Evangelicalism in Modern Britain: A History From the 1730's To the 1980s*, London, 1989.

Bebbington, D. W., *The Dominance of Evangelicalism: The Age of Spurgeon and Moody*, Leicester, 2005.

Brown, Callum G., *The Social History of Religion in Scotland since 1730*, London, 1987.

Brown, Callum G., *The Death of Christian Britain*, London, 2001.

Brown, Stewart J. and Fry, Michael (Eds), *Scotland in the Age of the Disruption*, Edinburgh, 1993.

Brown, Thomas, *Annals of the Disruption*, Edinburgh, 1893.

Bulloch, James and Andrew Drummond, *The Church in Victorian Scotland 1843–1874*, Edinburgh, 1975.

Burgess, Stanley (Ed.), *The New International Dictionary of Pentecostal and Charismatic Movements*, Grand Rapids, 2002.

Burleigh, J. S. H., *A Church History of Scotland*, London, 1960.

Collins, G. N. M., *The Heritage of Our Fathers: The Free Church of Scotland: her Origin and Testimony*, Edinburgh, 1976.

Dickson, Neil T. R., *Brethren in Scotland 1838–2000: A Social Study of an Evangelical Movement*, Carlisle, 2002.

Drummond, Andrew L. and Bulloch, James, *The Church in Victorian Scotland 1843–74*, Edinburgh, 1975.

Escott, H., *A History of Scottish Congregationalism*, Glasgow, 1960.

Ferguson, Fergus, *History of the Evangelical Union*, Glasgow, 1886.

Fleming, J. R., *A History of the Church in Scotland 1843–1874*, Edinburgh, 1927–33.

Henderson, G. D., *The Church of Scotland: A Short History*, Edinburgh, 1939.

Henderson, G. D., *Heritage: A Study of the Disruption*, Edinburgh, 1943.

Henderson, Henry, *The Religious Controversies of Scotland*, Edinburgh, 1905.

Hetherington, W. M., *History of the Church of Scotland*, Edinburgh, 1848.

Knox, John, *The Reformation in Scotland*, Edinburgh (1982 edition).

Lindsay, T. M., *The Reformation in Scotland*, Edinburgh, 1882 (reprinted 2006).

McCrie, Thomas, *The Story of the Scottish Church*, 1874 (reprinted 1988).

McNaughton, William D., *A Few Historical Notes on Early Congregational Independency in Scotland*, Kirkcaldy, 2000.

McNaughton, William D., *Early Congregational Independency in the Highlands and Islands and the North-East of Scotland*, Glasgow, 2003.

McNaughton, William D., *Early Congregational Independency in Lowland Scotland*, Vol 1, Glasgow, 2005.

McNaughton, William D., *Early Congregational Independency in Lowland Scotland*, Vol 2, Glasgow, 2007.

Macpherson, John, *A History of the Church in Scotland From the Earliest Times Down to the Present Day*, Paisley, 1901.

Murray, Derek, *The First 100 Years: The Baptist Union of Scotland*, Glasgow, n.d.

Murray, Iain H., *A Scottish Christian Heritage*, Edinburgh, 2006.

Renwick, A. M., and Harman, A. M., *The Story of the Church*, 1958.

Ross, David, *Chronology of Scottish History*, Lanark, 2002.

Small, Robert, *History of the Congregations of the United Presbyterian Church*, Edinburgh, 1904.

Smellie, Alexander, *Men of the Covenant: The Story of the Scottish Church in the Years of the Persecution*, London, 1903.

Stevenson, David, *The Covenanters: The National Covenant and Scotland*, Edinburgh, 1988.

Stewart, Rev. Alexander and Cameron, Rev. J. Kennedy, *The Free Church of Scotland, 1843–1910*, Edinburgh, 1910.

Struthers, Gavin, *History of the Rise, Progress and Principles of the Relief Church*, Glasgow, 1843.

Swift, Wesley F., *Methodism in Scotland: The First Hundred Years*, London, 1947.

Talbot, Brian, *The Search for a Common Identity: the Origins of the Baptist Union of Scotland 1800–1870*, Carlisle, 2003.

Vos, Johannes G., *The Scottish Covenanters: Their Origins, History and Distinctive Doctrines*, Edinburgh, 1998.

Walker, N., *Chapters from the History of the Free Church of Scotland*, Edinburgh, 1895.

Watters, A. C., *History of the British Churches of Christ*, Birmingham, 1947.

Yuille, Rev. George, *History of the Baptists in Scotland*, Glasgow, 1926.

Miscellaneous

Campbell, Duncan, *God's Answer*, Edinburgh, 1960.

Duncan, David, *Discourses by the Late Rev. David Duncan, Minister of the United Presbyterian Church*, Edinburgh, 1867.

Duncan, John, *In the Pulpit and at the Communion Table*, Edinburgh, 1874.

Guinness, Henry Grattan, *Preaching for the Million*, London, 1859.

Hempton, David and Hill, Myrtle, *Evangelical Protestantism in Ulster Society, 1740–1890*, London, 1992.

Isaac, Peter, *A History of Evangelical Christianity in Cornwall*, Gerrard's Cross, 2000.

Jones, R Tudur, *Faith and Crisis of a Nation: Wales, 1890–1914*, Cardiff, 2004.

Kennedy, John and Bonar, Horatius, *Evangelism: A Reformed Debate*, Portdinorwic, 1997.

Kent, John, *Wesley and the Wesleyans: Religion in Eighteenth-Century Britain*, Cambridge, 2002.

MacGregor, Rev. Malcom, *Prefatory Memoir'* in Rev. William Forbes, *Communion and Other Sermons'* (partly edited by the late Rev. John Kennedy), London, 1867.

McIntosh, John, *Church and Theology in Enlightenment Scotland: The Popular Party 1740–1800*, East Linton, 1998.

McPhail, John S., *Memorial Sermons of The Rev. W. S. McDougall, with a Sketch of His Life*, Edinburgh, 1897.

Morris, R. J., *Cholera, 1832 The Social Response to an Epidemic*, London, 1976.

Murray, Iain H., *The Puritan Hope*, Edinburgh, 1971 (reprinted 1991).

Murray, John, *Collected Writings of John Murray*, Edinburgh, 1982.

Presbytery of Aberdeen – Report, *Evidence on the Subject of Revivals*

Robertson, Rev. A., *A Vindication of the Religion of the Land from Misrepresentation and an Exposure of the Absurd Pretensions of the Gareloch Enthusiasts, in a Letter to Thomas Erskine, Esq., Advocate*, Edinburgh, 1830.

Robertson, John D. M., *Kirkwall Ba': Between the Water and the Wall*, Edinburgh, 2005.

Somerville, W. F. (Ed.), *Precious Seed Sown in Many Lands*, London, 1890.

Stewart, Andrew (Ed.), *The "Albatross" Yacht Mission: A Story of Joyous Christian Adventure*, Edinburgh, n.d.

Strachan, Gordon, *The Pentecostal Theology of Edward Irvine*, London, 1973.

Taylor, Steve, *Skye Revival*, CD ROM, 2003.

Thomson, D. P., *Personal Encounters*, Crieff, 1967.

Thomson, E. P., *The Making of the English Working Class*, London, 1963.

Unpublished Theses

Brown, Callum Graham, *Religion and the Development of an Urban Society: Glasgow 1780–1914*, vol. 1, Unpublished Ph.D. thesis, University of Glasgow, 1981.

Buchanan, Andrew D., *Brethren Revivals 1859–70*, Unpublished Paper, B.A., University of Stirling, 1990.

Bussey, Oscar, *The Religious Awakening of 1858–60 in Great Britain and Ireland*, Unpublished Ph.D. thesis, University of Edinburgh, 1947.

Macleod, Roderick, *The Progress of Evangelicalism in the Western Isles, 1800–1850*, Unpublished Ph.D. thesis, University of Edinburgh, 1977.

McNaughton, Arthur W., *A Study of the Phenomena of Prostration Arising From Conviction of Sin*, Unpublished Ph.D. thesis, University of Edinburgh, 1937.

Marrs, Clifford James, *The 1859 Religious Revival in Scotland: A Review and Critique of the Movement with Particular Reference to the City of Glasgow*, Unpublished Ph.D. thesis, University of Glasgow, 1995.

Robertson, George Booth. *Spiritual Awakening in the North-East of Scotland and the Description of the Church in 1843*, Unpublished Ph.D. thesis, University of Aberdeen, 1970.

Journals and Articles

Andsell, Douglas, 'The 1843 Disruption of the Church of Scotland in the Isle of Lewis' in *RSCHS*, vol. 24 (1990–2).

Berg, Professor Johannes Van Den, 'The Evangelical Revival in Scotland and the Nineteenth –century "Reveil" in the Netherlands', in *RSCHS*, vol. 25 (1995).

Coffey, John, 'Moody and Sankey's Mission to Britain, 1873–1875', quoted in Biagini, *Citizenship and Community: Liberals, Radicals and Collective Identities in the British Isles, 1865–1931*, Cambridge, 1996.

Dallimore, Arnold, 'Whitefield and the Evangelical Revival in Scotland', *BoT*, vol. 79.

Dickson, Neil T. R., *Revivalism and the Limits of Co-operation: Brethren Orkney Origins in the 1860s*, private paper.

Duthie, John L., 'Philanthropy and Evangelism' in *The Scottish Historical Review*, 1984.

Edinburgh Christian Instructor, April, May 1838.

Jones, G. Penrhyn, 'Cholera in Wales' in *National Library of Wales Journal*, vol. 10/3, Summer 1958.

Landsman, Ned, 'Evangelists and their Hearers: Popular Interpretation of Revivalist Preaching in Eighteenth-Century Scotland' in *Journal of British Studies*, vol. 28, 1989.

Luker, David, 'Revivalism in Theory and Practice: The Case of Cornish Methodism' in *The Journal of Ecclesiastical History*, 37, no. 4 (October 1986).

MacInnes, Allan I., 'Evangelical Protestantism' in Graham Walker and Tom Gallacher, *Sermons and Battle Hymns: Protestant Popular Culture in Modern Scotland*, Edinburgh, 1990.

Mackay, W. R., 'Early Evangelical Religion in the Far North: a Kulturkampf' in *RSCHS*, vol. 26.

Macleod, Rev. William, 'The Beginning of Evangelical Religion in Skye', *BoT*, vols 383–384, Aug./Sept. 1995.

McNaughton, William D., 'Revival and Reality: Congregationalists and Religious Revival in Nineteenth-Century Scotland' in *RSCHS* 33, 2003.

Mechie, S., 'The Psychology of the Cambuslang Revival' in *RSCHS*, vol. 10, 1948–50.

Medley, A. W., 'Horatius Bonar D.D. A Brief Sketch to Commemorate the Centenary of his Death' in *The Evangelical Library Bulletin*, Spring 1989, no. 82.

Meek, D. E., 'Evangelical Missionaries in the Early Nineteenth Century Highlands' quoted in *Transactions of the Gaelic Society of Inverness*, vol. 56, 1989.

Meek, D. E., 'Dugald Sinclair. The Life and Work of a Highland Itinerant Missionary: Dugald Sinclair' in *Scottish Studies*, vol. 30, 1991.

Meek, D. E. 'The Preacher, the Press-gang and the Landlord: the Impressment and Vindication of the Rev. Donald MacArthur', in *RSCHS*, vol. 25, 1995.

Meek, D. E., 'Falling Down as if Dead: Attitudes to unusual phenomena in the Skye revival of 1841-1842' in *Scottish Bulletin of Evangelical Theology*, vol. 13/4, Autumn 1995.

Meek, D. E., 'Gaelic Bible, Revival and Mission: The Spiritual Rebirth of the Nineteenth-Century Highlands' in James Kirk (Ed.), The Church in the Highlands, Edinburgh, 1998.

Meek, D. E., 'Religious Life in the Highlands Since the Reformation' in Michael Lynch (Ed.), *The Oxford Companion to Scottish History*, Oxford, 2001.

Miller, R. Strang, 'Greatheart of China: A Brief Life of William Chalmers Burns, MA, Scottish Evangelist and Revival Leader, and Early Missionary to China' in Various, *Five Pioneer Missionaries*, Edinburgh, 1965.

Muir, Alex, 'Revival in Scotland: A personal perspective' in *Prophecy Today*, vol. 1, no. 4, 1985.

Muirhead, Andrew T. N. 'A Secession Congregation in its Community: the Stirling congregation of the Rev. Ebenezer Erskine 1731-1754' in *SCHCR*, vol. 20, 1986.

Muirhead, Ian A., 'The Revival as a Dimension of Scottish Church History' in *RSCHS*, vol. 20, 1980.

Murray, Iain H., 'The Puritans and Revival Christianity', *BoT*, Sept. 1969.

Nicholls, John, 'The Revival of 1859 in Scotland' in *BoT*, vol. 259, Apr 1985.

Reeves, Dudley, 'Charles Simeon in Scotland' in *BoT*, vol. 112, Jan. 1973.

Reeves, Dudley, 'Rowland Hill in Scotland' in *BoT*, vols 118–119, July/Aug. 1973.

Rendall, Jocelyn, 'The Orkney Revivals' in *The Orkney View*, 1994.

Robb, George, 'Popular Religion and the Christianization of the Scottish Highlands' in *Journal of Religious History*, vol. 16, 1990.

Roberts, Maurice J., 'John Welsh of Ayr' in *BoT*, vol. 174, March 1978.

Roberts, Maurice, 'Remembering the 1859 Revival in Scotland' in *BoT*, vols 352, 354, Jan–March 1993.

Roxburgh, Kenneth B. E., 'Revival, An Aspect of Scottish Religious Identity' in Robert Pope (Ed.), *Religion and National Identity: Wales and Scotland c.1700–2000*, Cardiff, 2001.

Talbot, Brian, 'Reserved from Erroneous Views? The Contribution of Francis Johnston as a Baptist Voice in the Scottish Evangelical Debate, in the Mid-Nineteenth Century, on the Work of the Holy Spirit' in Dyfed Wyn Roberts (Ed.), *Revival Renewal and the Holy Spirit*, Carlisle, 2009.

Taylor, William, 'The Diary of James Calder' in *BoT*, vol. 130, July/Aug. 1974.

Thomson, Elizabeth P., 'The Impetus Given to the Use of Instrumental Music in Scottish Churches by the Visit of Moody and Sankey to Scotland in 1873-74' in *RSCHS*, vol. 36, 2006.

Timms, Stephen MP, 'Christianity and Politics' quoted in *The Bible in Transmission*, Autumn 2001.

Walker, R. B., 'The Growth of Wesleyan Methodism in Victorian England and Wales' in *Journal of Ecclesiastical History*, vol. 24, 1973.

PEOPLE INDEX

PLACES INDEX

Christian Focus Publications

Our mission statement –

STAYING FAITHFUL

In dependence upon God we seek to impact the world through literature faithful to His infallible Word, the Bible. Our aim is to ensure that the Lord Jesus Christ is presented as the only hope to obtain forgiveness of sin, live a useful life and look forward to heaven with Him.

Our books are published in four imprints:

CHRISTIAN FOCUS

Popular works including biographies, commentaries, basic doctrine and Christian living.

CHRISTIAN HERITAGE

Books representing some of the best material from the rich heritage of the church.

MENTOR

Books written at a level suitable for Bible College and seminary students, pastors, and other serious readers. The imprint includes commentaries, doctrinal studies, examination of current issues and church history.

CF4•K

Children's books for quality Bible teaching and for all age groups: Sunday school curriculum, puzzle and activity books; personal and family devotional titles, biographies and inspirational stories – because you are never too young to know Jesus!

Christian Focus Publications Ltd,
Geanies House, Fearn, Ross-shire,
IV20 1TW, Scotland, United Kingdom.
www.christianfocus.com
blog.christianfocus.com